WORKER WELL-BEING AND PUBLIC POLICY

RESEARCH IN LABOR ECONOMICS

Series Editor: Solomon W. Polachek

RESEARCH IN LABOR ECONOMICS VOLUME 22

WORKER WELL-BEING AND PUBLIC POLICY

EDITED BY

SOLOMON W. POLACHEK

Department of Economics, State University of New York at Binghamton, USA and Industrial Relations Section, Economics Department, Princeton University, USA

2003

JAI
An imprint of Elsevier Science

Amsterdam – Boston – London – New York – Oxford – Paris
San Diego – San Francisco – Singapore – Sydney – Tokyo

ELSEVIER SCIENCE Ltd
The Boulevard, Langford Lane
Kidlington, Oxford OX5 1GB, UK

© 2003 Elsevier Science Ltd. All rights reserved.

This work is protected under copyright by Elsevier Science, and the following terms and conditions apply to its use:

Photocopying
Single photocopies of single chapters may be made for personal use as allowed by national copyright laws. Permission of the Publisher and payment of a fee is required for all other photocopying, including multiple or systematic copying, copying for advertising or promotional purposes, resale, and all forms of document delivery. Special rates are available for educational institutions that wish to make photocopies for non-profit educational classroom use.

Permissions may be sought directly from Elsevier Science Global Rights Department, PO Box 800, Oxford OX5 1DX, UK; phone: (+44) 1865 843830, fax: (+44) 1865 853333, e-mail: permissions@elsevier.co.uk. You may also contact Global Rights directly through Elsevier's home page (http://www.elsevier.com), by selecting 'Obtaining Permissions'.

In the USA, users may clear permissions and make payments through the Copyright Clearance Center, Inc., 222 Rosewood Drive, Danvers, MA 01923, USA; phone: (+1) (978) 7508400, fax: (+1) (978) 7504744, and in the UK through the Copyright Licensing Agency Rapid Clearance Service (CLARCS), 90 Tottenham Court Road, London W1P 0LP, UK; phone: (+44) 207 631 5555; fax: (+44) 207 631 5500. Other countries may have a local reprographic rights agency for payments.

Derivative Works
Tables of contents may be reproduced for internal circulation, but permission of Elsevier Science is required for external resale or distribution of such material.
Permission of the Publisher is required for all other derivative works, including compilations and translations.

Electronic Storage or Usage
Permission of the Publisher is required to store or use electronically any material contained in this work, including any chapter or part of a chapter.

Except as outlined above, no part of this work may be reproduced, stored in a retrieval system or transmitted in any form or by any means, electronic, mechanical, photocopying, recording or otherwise, without prior written permission of the Publisher.
Address permissions requests to: Elsevier Science Global Rights Department, at the mail, fax and e-mail addresses noted above.

Notice
No responsibility is assumed by the Publisher for any injury and/or damage to persons or property as a matter of products liability, negligence or otherwise, or from any use or operation of any methods, products, instructions or ideas contained in the material herein. Because of rapid advances in the medical sciences, in particular, independent verification of diagnoses and drug dosages should be made.

First edition 2003

Library of Congress Cataloging in Publication Data
A catalogue record from the British Library has been applied for.

ISBN: 0-7623-1026-X
ISSN: 0147-9121 (Series)

⊗ The paper used in this publication meets the requirements of ANSI/NISO Z39.48-1992 (Permanence of Paper).
Printed in The Netherlands.

CONTENTS

LIST OF CONTRIBUTORS ... ix

PREFACE
    Solomon W. Polachek ... xiii

ACCOUNTING FOR INCOME INEQUALITY AND ITS CHANGE: A NEW METHOD, WITH APPLICATION TO THE DISTRIBUTION OF EARNINGS IN THE UNITED STATES
    Gary S. Fields ... 1

THE RELATIONSHIP BETWEEN THE ECONOMY AND THE WELFARE CASELOAD: A DYNAMIC APPROACH
    Steven Haider, Jacob Klerman and Elizabeth Roth ... 39

NEW JERSEY'S FAMILY CAP AND FAMILY SIZE DECISIONS: FINDINGS FROM A FIVE-YEAR EVALUATION
    Michael J. Camasso, Radha Jagannathan, Mark Killingsworth and Carol Harvey ... 71

TRACKING THE HOUSEHOLD INCOME OF SSDI AND SSI APPLICANTS
    John Bound, Richard V. Burkhauser and Austin Nichols ... 113

MINIMUM WAGES AND ON-THE-JOB TRAINING
    Daron Acemoglu and Jörn-Steffen Pischke ... 159

RACIAL AND ETHNIC DIFFERENCES IN PENSION WEALTH
    William E. Even and David A. Macpherson ... 203

COUNTY-LEVEL ESTIMATES OF THE EMPLOYMENT
PROSPECTS OF LOW-SKILL WORKERS
David C. Ribar — *227*

DETERMINANTS OF IMMIGRANT SELECTIVITY AND
SKILLS
Madeline Zavodny — *269*

IMMIGRATION AND THE LABOR FORCE PARTICIPATION
OF LOW-SKILL NATIVE WORKERS
Hannes Johannsson, Stephan Weiler and Steven Shulman — *291*

CHILDREN, NON-DISCRIMINATORY PROVISION OF
FRINGE BENEFITS, AND HOUSEHOLD LABOR
MARKET DECISIONS
*Mark C. Berger, Dan A. Black, Amitabh Chandra
and Frank A. Scott* — *309*

WAGE GAINS FROM BETTER HEALTH AND
EMPLOYMENT-BASED HEALTH INSURANCE
*Paul Fronstin, Alphonse G. Holtmann and
Kerry Anne McGeary* — *351*

THE FAMILY GAP IN PAY: EVIDENCE FROM SEVEN
INDUSTRIALIZED COUNTRIES
Susan Harkness and Jane Waldfogel — *369*

WHY CHOOSE WOMEN'S WORK IF IT PAYS LESS? A
STRUCTURAL MODEL OF OCCUPATIONAL CHOICE
M. Melinda Pitts — *415*

NEW EVIDENCE ON CULTURE AND THE GENDER WAGE
GAP: A COMPARISON ACROSS ETHNIC ORIGIN GROUPS
Heather Antecol — *447*

GENDER DIFFERENCES IN REASONS FOR JOB MOBILITY
INTENTIONS IN HIGHER EDUCATION
   Jennifer VanGilder, John Robst and Solomon Polachek   *465*

LIST OF CONTRIBUTORS

Daron Acemoglu	Department of Economics, Massachusetts Institute of Technology, USA
Heather Anectol	Department of Economics, Claremont McKenna College, USA
Mark C. Berger	Department of Economics, University of Kentucky, USA
Dan A. Black	Center for Policy Research, Syracuse University, USA
John Bound	Department of Economics, University of Michigan, USA, and NBER
Richard V. Burkhauser	Department of Policy Analysis and Management, Cornell University, USA
Michael J. Camasso	Center for Urban Policy Research, Rutgers University, USA
Amitabh Chandra	Department of Economics, Dartmouth College, USA
William E. Even	Department of Economics, Miami University, USA
Gary S. Fields	School of Industrial Relations, Cornell University, USA
Paul Fronstin	Employee Benefit Research Institute, Washington, DC, USA
Steven J. Haider	RAND Corporation, USA
Susan Harkness	University of Sussex, UK

Carol Harvey	Center for State Health Policy, Rutgers University, USA
Alphonse G. Holtmann	Department of Economics, University of Miami, USA
Radha Jagannathan	Bloustein School of Planning and Public Policy, Rutgers University, USA
Hannes Johannsson	Department of Economics, University of Nebraska – Kearney, USA
Mark Killingsworth	Department of Economics, Rutgers University, USA
Jacob Alex Klerman	RAND Corporation, USA
David A. Macpherson	Department of Economics, Florida State University, USA
Kerry Anne McGeary	Department of Economics, University of Miami, USA
Austin Nichols	Department of Economics, University of Michigan, USA
Jörn-Steffen Pischke	Department of Economics and Centre for Economic Performance, London School of Economics, UK
M. Melinda Pitts	Research Department, Federal Reserve Bank of Atlanta, USA
Solomon W. Polachek	Department of Economics, State University of New York at Binghamton, USA and Industrial Relations Section, Princeton University, USA
David C. Ribar	Department of Economics, The George Washington University, USA
John Robst	Centers for Medicare & Medicaid Services, USA
Elizabeth Roth	RAND Corporation, USA

Frank A. Scott	Department of Economics, University of Kentucky, USA
Steven Shulman	Department of Economics, Colorado State University, USA
Jennifer VanGuilder	Department of Economics, California State University – Bakersfield, USA
Jane Waldfogel	School of Social Work, Columbia University, USA and Centre for Analysis of Exclusion, London School of Economics, UK
Stephan Weiler	Department of Economics, Colorado State University, USA
Madeline Zavodny	Department of Economics, Occidental College, USA

PREFACE

This volume is devoted to a number of multifaceted issues regarding worker well-being. Of the 15 chapters, the first two are the most general, dealing with overall earnings distribution and overall changes in welfare policy. The remaining chapters examine specific aspects of human welfare. They cover fertility, disability, minimum wage, pension wealth, human capital investment, migration, health, and earnings. The book culminates with four chapters relating to gender and the family. Ultimately, determining who works, how much is earned, and how these earnings get distributed define the components of individual and social welfare. The topics covered in this volume shed light on these questions.

Perhaps no question is more pertinent to worker well-being than explaining changes in overall income inequality. Given that income distribution has widened at least over the last two decades, the topic is now crucially important. Thus, this volume begins with a chapter on income inequality. In this first chapter, Gary Fields devises procedures capable of addressing two questions. First, he examines the *level* of inequality, and second he examines *differences* in inequality. In both, he looks at causal factors. With respect to the latter question, he evaluates how particular economic factors explain differences in income inequality between one time period and another. He applies the technique to analyze the changes in U.S. labor earnings inequality between 1979 and 1999. The approach is quite general. Without making stringent assumptions, Fields derives a decomposition approach that yields the same power, independent of a number of inequality measures. These include the Gini coefficient, the Atkinson index, generalized entropy as well as various centile measures. Thus, the approach is potentially useful, should one want to consider the earnings determinants analyzed in each of the remaining chapters.

At the same time that the earnings distribution widened, the proportion of U.S. families on welfare got smaller. In the second chapter, Steven Haider, Jacob Klerman, and Elizabeth Roth examine why between 1994 and 2000 welfare levels declined by more than 50%, a decline, to my knowledge, not seen before in the U.S. To do this, Haider et al. adopt a stock flow model that describes the probability that a person on aid will remain on aid. They use California data to apply the model. A simple version attributes over 50% of the dramatic decline in national welfare case loads to the improved economy. A more complex model incorporating employment and earnings, particularly in the retail trade sector, explains over 90% of the decline.

Evaluating government programs is essential to understanding human well-being. As an example, the next chapter examines how welfare policies affect fertility. Of late a significant number of states introduced a family cap to limit welfare benefits for families having additional children. In 1992, New Jersey was the first state to adopt a family cap. One unique feature about New Jersey is that it is the only state to provide experimental evidence of the family cap's impact both on abortions and contraception, in addition to the standard information on births. In the third chapter, Michael J. Camasso, Radha Jagannathan, Mark Killingsworth, and Carol Harvey make use of these data to look at how family caps affect fertility. They find that births decline and that abortions increase as a result of New Jersey's welfare limitations for additional children born.

In the next chapter, John Bound, Richard Burkhauser, and Austin Nichols examine another aspect of welfare, namely disability. They concentrate on the two separate U.S. federal disability programs – Social Security Disability Insurance (SSDI) and Supplemental Security Income (SSI). The SSDI is primarily an insurance program for substantially employed workers forced to exit the labor market because of a disability. The SSI is a means-tested welfare program aimed at the aged, blind, and otherwise disabled. Bound et al. seek to measure changes in the sources and amount of household income for working-age men and women who apply for SSDI and SSI benefits. They use unique data obtained by merging Survey of Income and Program Participation (SIPP) and Social Security Administration (SSA) Disability data in the 38 month period prior and 39 month period following application for disability. While they find that earnings decline 12–24 months prior to applying for disability, the decline six months prior to applying predominates. During the period immediately before and after application, earnings decline relatively little. In percentage terms, those with higher initial earnings lose more than lower income individuals. Clearly the lower replacement rate established in the SSDI program and the low absolute level of protection provided to all SSI applicants had an impact.

Next, the volume considers minimum wage as a welfare policy geared towards low-income workers. One effect of raising the minimum wage is on training. Common wisdom indicates that firms provide employees less training in response to minimum wage increases. If the government increases the minimum wage, then a firm will be unable to lower wages sufficiently in order to finance training. As a result, training will be reduced. Indeed a number of studies support this hypothesis. However Daron Acemoglu and Jörn-Steffen Pischke introduce a possibility that differs. They argue that minimum wages lead firms to lay off the least productive workers, but to use the rents generated by other more productive low skill workers to pay for training. Based on this line of reasoning, they develop a "hybrid" empirical model to show that both layoffs and training can occur.

Retirement income is also important to human welfare. Especially significant is why pension accumulation differs by race. In the next chapter, William Even and David Macpherson compare black and white pension wealth accumulation. Contrary to popular belief, they find small race differences, once one adjusts for worker pension coverage and worker characteristics. They conclude that getting a job with pension benefits is crucial to accumulating the funds needed for a pension.

Well-being also depends on geography. In the next chapter, David Ribar makes three contributions relating geography to economic well-being. First, he constructs gender-specific annual employment and wage estimates for small geographic areas. Second, he examines the sensitivity of employment and earnings to changes in local labor market conditions. Third, he sheds light on what constitutes a local labor market. He finds that throughout the 1990s, employment conditions weakened for the less educated, despite steady growth, rising productivity, and diminishing unemployment for the overall economy. Changes in local employment conditions change employment and earnings only modestly. However, increases in minimum wage seem to induce more of the low skilled to work.

Region plays another important role. For migrants, country of origin influences the labor market skills they bring with them. In the next chapter, Madeline Zavodny addresses the question: how do source country characteristics alter the skills that migrants bring to their destination countries? The innovation is to compare migrant occupations to home country occupations, rather than simply using earnings as done in past studies. While the paper finds that the proportion of immigrants in skilled occupations is related to the proportion in source countries, it also observes that the proportion of skilled is not necessarily related to the return to skills in one's country of origin. In many ways this latter result – that the returns to skill (actually income inequality) in the country of origin are not related to the percentage in skilled occupations – is the most interesting. Migrant selectivity has been important to the migration literature despite mixed empirical evidence. In part, the lack of consistent empirical evidence may be due to the complexity of the migration decision across different skill levels, cultures, human networks and national economies. The results in this paper provide support for more empirical testing.

Determining who immigrates is important, but so is the impact these migrants have on destination labor markets. Hannes Johannsson, Stephan Weiler, and Steven Shulman show that low-skilled natives exit local labor markets to respond to immigrant inflows. The higher an area's immigrant density, the stronger the exodus. This exodus leads to selection biases that push wages of the remaining workers up, making the impact of immigration on wages difficult to discern.

However, once accounting for this bias, the chapter finds that appropriately measured native wages fall most when immigrant density is high. In contrast, a sparse immigrant density mitigates the decline in native wages. By taking into account the decreased participation of native workers, the authors find in-migration to effect the labor market more greatly than previously measured.

Especially because of high costs, the availability of health insurance is also paramount to well-being. As with pensions, health insurance is a common fringe benefit in better jobs, most likely because the after-tax price falls as employee earnings rise. Thus, firms with disproportionate numbers of high-wage workers should offer superior health insurance. Within families, this means that the high wage spouse more likely obtains the health insurance as an on-the-job fringe benefit. In the next chapter, Mark Berger, Dan Black, Amitabh Chandra, and Frank Scott apply implications relating to the division of labor within the family to predict that specialization becomes stronger as the number of children increase so that the spouse specializing in childcare will have lower hours worked, lower wages and fewer fringes. Then, using data from the April 1993 Current Population Survey, they go on to show that families are less likely to obtain health insurance from the spouse that specializes in child care.

Given health status, how does having health insurance affect one's earnings? Paul Fronstin, Al Holtmann, and Kerry McGeary develop a three-equation simultaneous equations model to answer the question. One equation models insurance, another health status, and a third earnings. As expected, they first find that having a higher paid job increases the likelihood of employer-supplied health insurance. Second, they find that higher earnings resulted in worse health for women, but had no effect on men's health. Third, they find health insurance increases women's health but not men's. Finally, they find that health insurance increased earnings for both men and women. In sum, the results indicate that the effects of health insurance transcend the basic purpose of health insurance as simply a conduit for obtaining health care. At least indirectly, according to the authors, insurance increases earnings, and this increases human well-being.

Perhaps one of the most significant labor market trends affecting family welfare is women's continually increasing labor force participation. Of course, related to women's work activities are women's earning. My own early research dealt with how earnings are related to marital status, number of children, and lifetime work. Whereas I examined this relationship for the United States, Susan Harkness and Jane Waldfogel use micro-data from seven industrial countries to compare family wage and employment gaps, which they define to be earnings and work differences between women with and without children. They find large differences in the family gap in pay, with the United Kingdom displaying the biggest wage penalties of the seven countries they study. They also find the gender and family pay gaps to be related to gender and family employment gaps. Countries where there is a large negative effect of children on women's pay tend to have a large gender gap in pay as well, and countries where mothers have lower employment rates have lower employment rates of women overall. Clearly the human capital approach is consistent with their findings. Where children do not deter women's work, women accumulate greater amounts of human capital. Acquiring more human capital raises wages and decreases the gender wage gap.

Despite the human capital model's power in explaining gender wage differences, not all adhere to human capital. As an alternative, some advocate a "crowding" model. According to the crowding model, discriminatory corporate behavior segregates women into relatively more menial jobs. The oversupply of women crowded into these jobs exacerbates their low pay. The point of the next chapter, by Melinda Pitts, is to develop a model of why women choose "female" occupations. Pitts's model adopts a hedonic approach, which entails computing a woman's probability of choosing a female occupation, based on relative wage gains associated with characteristics of female relative to male occupations as well as each individual's personal attributes. The chapter finds that women choose female occupations because female occupations pay these women more. As such, women and their jobs are efficiently matched. Thus, the paper casts doubt on the crowding model since women optimally choose their occupations.

The gender wage gap is not uniform. Male-female wage differences vary by ethnicity. In the penultimate chapter, Heather Antecol finds gender wage gaps to be positively correlated with gender wage gaps back in each ethnicity group's country of origin. From this she surmises that culture is important in explaining the male-female wage differential. Antecol's further analysis reveals that this correlation is mitigated when one controls for ethnic group differences in female labor force participation. From this, she surmises that cultural effects manifest themselves through differing home country labor force participation rates. Women immigrants from countries with less female labor force participation work less in the U.S. after emigrating. Working less implies acquiring less human capital and having lower wages. Consequently, Antecol's results are consistent with the human capital approach.

Another reason for the gender wage gap is women's relative inability to move from job to job, when compared to men. Yet job change is an important avenue for gaining higher wages. Higher wages through mobility is especially true in the academic labor market. This volume's final chapter examines gender differences in job mobility intentions in the academic labor market. Using the data from the 1993 National Study on Post-Secondary Faculty, Jennifer Van Gilder, John Robst and I find that women are twice as eager as men to move from one university to another, but that this difference diminishes dramatically with length of employment. Indeed, gender differences in mobility intentions become minor once one controls for tenure. For both men and women, monetary incentives as well as considerations regarding spousal employment are important motivating factors.

As with past volumes, I aimed to maintain the highest levels of scholarship and to focus on important issues. I encourage readers who have prepared manuscripts that meet these stringent standards to submit them to me for possible inclusion in future volumes. For insightful editorial advice in preparing this volume, I thank Randy Filer, Judith Hellerstein, Soo Hwang, John Jackson, Christian Keith, Arlene Leibowitz, Audrey Light, Karen Lumbard, Brian Main, Robert Margo, Anne Polivka, Mark Regets, Cordelia Reimers, Edward Schumacher, David Smith, Paula Stephan, Insan Tunali, Jennifer van Guilder, Jennifer Ward-Batts, Bruce Weinberg, Anne Winkler, Steve Woodbury, Linda Wong, and Junsen Zhang. I am especially indebted to the Industrial Relations Section at Princeton University for hosting me during the final editing stages of this volume, while on my 2002–2003 sabbatical year.

Solomon W. Polachek
Editor

ACCOUNTING FOR INCOME INEQUALITY AND ITS CHANGE: A NEW METHOD, WITH APPLICATION TO THE DISTRIBUTION OF EARNINGS IN THE UNITED STATES

Gary S. Fields

ABSTRACT

This paper devises a new method for using the information contained in income-generating equations to "account for" or "decompose" the level of income inequality in a country and its change over time. In the levels decomposition, the shares attributed to each explanatory factor are independent of the particular inequality measure used. In the change decomposition, methods are presented to break down the contribution of each explanatory factor into a coefficients effect, a correlation effect, and a standard deviation effect. In an application to rising earnings inequality in the United States, it is found that schooling is the single most explanatory variable, only one other variable (occupation) has any appreciable role to play, and all of schooling's effect was a coefficients effect.

1. INTRODUCTION

For decades, economists and other social scientists have sought to understand the inequality of income (or earnings or wages) using regression models.[1] Typically, the logarithm of the income of individual i in country/group/time t is regressed on a number of explanatory variables. Assuming that these have been chosen carefully in light of theory and past empirical findings, the question then is how to use the information contained in such income-generating equations to "account for" or "decompose" income inequality.[2,3]

This paper proposes a new methodology for answering two questions.[4] First, given an income-generating function estimated by a standard semi-log regression, how much income inequality is accounted for by each explanatory factor? This shall be termed the "levels question," the answer to which is of the form "$x\%$ of the inequality of income is attributable to education, $y\%$ to region, $z\%$ to gender, etc." Second, denoting the two countries, groups, or dates by 1 and 2 respectively, given estimates of comparable income-generating functions

$$\ln(Y_{i1}) = \alpha_1 + \sum_j \beta_{j1} x_{ij1} + \varepsilon_{i1} \qquad (1)$$

and

$$\ln(Y_{i2}) = \alpha_2 + \sum_j \beta_{j2} x_{ij2} + \varepsilon_{i2} \qquad (2)$$

how much of the difference in income inequality between one country and another, between one group and another within a country, or between one date and another is accounted for by education, by potential experience, and by the other explanatory factors? This shall be called the "differences question."[5]

Past literature, reviewed in Sections 2.4 and 3.4, provides approximate regression-based answers to these two questions, but until now, no exact decomposition has been available. This paper shows that such a decomposition can be gotten and further that under a quite acceptable set of assumptions, the percentage contribution of a given explanatory factor x_j at time t is *independent* of which inequality measure is chosen. The new procedure for the levels question is presented in Section 2 and for the difference question in Section 3.

Section 4 applies these methodologies to quantify the role of different explanatory factors in accounting for levels of earnings inequality at a point in time and the change in earnings inequality over the last twenty years in the United States. Section 5 sums up.

Before proceeding, it should be noted that the methods developed in this paper are quite general. Although the motivating questions and the methods derived are presented in terms of inequality of *income*, the same techniques are applicable to answering the levels question and the difference question for *any* continuous variable.

2. ACCOUNTING FOR INCOME INEQUALITY AT A POINT IN TIME

In this section, a method is proposed to account for the inequality of income in a single survey. Start with an income-generating function, based on human capital theory or some other underlying theoretical model, in which income is a function of a certain number of "variables" or "factors." The decomposition is based on the income-generating function (1), which can be rewritten as

$$\ln Y_{it} = a'_t Z_{it} \tag{3a}$$

where

$$a_t = [\alpha_t \beta_{1t}, \beta_{2t}, \ldots, \beta_{Jt}, 1] \tag{3b}$$

and

$$Z_{it} = [1, x_{i1t}, x_{i2t}, \ldots, x_{iJt}, \varepsilon_{it}]. \tag{3c}$$

On the assumption that "good" estimates have been gotten for the coefficients on the variables, the strategy for deriving a useful decomposition equation is first to decompose the log-variance of income and then to show that the same decomposition applies to other inequality measures as well.[6]

2.1. Decomposing the Log-variance

Starting with the income-generating functions Eqs (3a)–(3c), take the variance of both sides. On the left-hand side is a simple measure of inequality, the log-variance. The variance of the right-hand side can be manipulated using the following:

Theorem (Mood, Graybill & Boes). Let $A_1, \ldots, A_P$ and $B_1, \ldots, B_Q$ be two sets of random variables, and let $a_1, \ldots, a_P$ and $b_1, \ldots, b_Q$ be two sets of constants. Then

$$\text{cov}\left[\sum_{p=1}^{P} a_p A_p, \sum_{q=1}^{Q} b_q B_q\right] = \sum_{p=1}^{P}\sum_{q=1}^{Q} a_p b_q \text{cov}[A_p, B_q]. \tag{4}$$

Applying this theorem in the context of a single random variable $\ln Y$ such that

$$\ln Y = \sum_{j=1}^{J+2} a_j Z_j,$$

we have

$$\text{cov}\left[\sum_{j=1}^{J+2} a_j Z_j, \ln Y\right] = \sum_{j=1}^{J+2} \text{cov}[a_j Z_j, \ln Y]. \tag{5}$$

But because the left-hand side of Eq. (5) is the covariance between $\ln Y$ and itself, it is simply the variance of $\ln Y$. Thus,

$$\sigma^2(\ln Y) = \sum_{j=1}^{J+2} \text{cov}[a_j Z_j, \ln Y], \tag{6a}$$

or, upon dividing through by $\sigma^2(\ln Y)$,

$$100\% = \frac{\sum_{j=1}^{J+2} \text{cov}[a_j Z_j, \ln Y]}{\sigma^2(\ln Y)} \equiv \sum_{j=1}^{J+2} s_j(\ln Y), \tag{6b}$$

where each $s_j(\ln Y)$ is a so-called "relative factor inequality weight" given by[7]

$$s_j(\ln Y) = \frac{\text{cov}[a_j Z_j, \ln Y]}{\sigma^2(\ln Y)}. \tag{6c}$$

It may be noted that when the last element of Z is excluded, the remaining relative factor inequality weights

$$\frac{\sum_{j=1}^{J+1} \text{cov}[a_j Z_j, \ln Y]}{\sigma^2(\ln Y)}$$

sum exactly to $R^2(\ln Y)$.

One more bit of algebra proves useful. The ordinary correlation coefficient is related to the covariance by

$$\text{cor}[a_j Z_j, \ln Y] = \frac{\text{cov}[a_j Z_j, \ln Y]}{\sigma(a_j Z_j)\sigma(\ln Y)}. \tag{7}$$

Combining Eqs (6a)–(6c) and Eq. (7), we then have:

Result 1. Given the income-generating function Eqs (3a)–(3c), let $s_j(\ln Y)$ denote the share of the log-variance of income that is attributable to the j'th explanatory factor and let $R^2(\ln Y)$ be the fraction of the log-variance that is explained by all of the Zs taken together. Then, the log-variance of income can be decomposed as

$$s_j(\ln Y) = \frac{\text{cov}[a_j Z_j, \ln Y]}{\sigma^2(\ln Y)} = \frac{a_j \sigma(Z_j)\text{cor}[Z_j, \ln Y]}{\sigma(\ln Y)} \qquad (8a)$$

where

$$\sum_{j=1}^{J+2} s_j(\ln Y) = 100\% \qquad (8b)$$

and

$$\sum_{j=1}^{J+1} s_j(\ln Y) = R^2(\ln Y). \qquad (8c)$$

The fraction that is explained by the j'th explanatory factor, $p_j(\ln Y)$, is then

$$p_j(\ln Y) \equiv \frac{s_j(\ln Y)}{R^2(\ln Y)}. \qquad (8d)$$

Equations (8a)–(8d) provide a full and exact decomposition of the log-variance. However, because of problems with the log-variance (Foster & Ok, 1999; Sen, 1973), it would be nice to be able to decompose other inequality measures besides the log-variance. This proves to be quite possible.

2.2. Extension to Other Inequality Measures

Result 1 can be extended to other inequality measures by borrowing from a literature which at first would appear to have nothing to do with the problem at hand, namely, the literature on decomposition of inequality by additive factor components. In this literature, the i'th recipient unit's total income Y_i is expressed as the sum of its income from each of several factor components, e.g. labor income, capital income, transfer income, etc.:

$$Y_i = \sum_k Y_{ik}. \qquad (9)$$

Let N denote the total number of income recipients, $Y \equiv (Y_1 \ldots Y_N)$, and $Y_k \equiv (Y_{1k} \ldots Y_{Nk})$. The question asked in this literature is, what fraction of total income inequality, gauged by an inequality measure $I(Y)$ is accounted for by labor income, by capital income, by transfer income, etc.?

Define a "relative factor inequality weight" s_k to be the percentage of income inequality that is accounted for by the k'th factor – for instance, how much of the inequality of total income is accounted for by the inequality of labor income. An important theorem on decomposition by additive factor components is due to Shorrocks (1982), who shows:

Theorem (Shorrocks, 1982). Under the six assumptions enumerated in the Appendix, the relative factor inequality weights s_k are given by

$$s_k = \frac{\text{cov}(Y_k, Y)}{\sigma^2(Y)} \tag{10a}$$

such that

$$\sum_k s_k = 1 \tag{10b}$$

for *any* inequality index $I(Y)$ which is continuous and symmetric and for which $I(\mu, \mu, \ldots, \mu) = 0$.[8]

Virtually all inequality indices satisfy these conditions, including the Gini coefficient, the Atkinson index, the generalized entropy family, the coefficient of variation, and various centile measures.

Shorrocks's theorem is directly applicable to the question dealt with here, namely, using income-generating functions to account for income inequality. The standard income-generating function written in the form

$$\ln Y_{it} = a_t' Z_{it} \tag{3a}$$

has the same additive form as the equation expressing total income as the sum of the income from each component

$$Y_i = \sum_k Y_{ik}. \tag{9}$$

Note too that when the inequality of Eq. (9) is decomposed, Shorrocks obtains $s_k = \text{cov}(Y_k, Y)/\sigma^2(Y)$ such that $\sum_k s_k = 1$, which has the same form as Eq. (8) with Y_k replacing $a_j Z_j$ and Y replacing $\ln Y$. Now, taking advantage of this homeomorphism and applying Shorrocks's theorem, we get the following key result:

Result 2. Given the income-generating function Eqs (3a)–(3c), let an inequality index $I(\ln Y)$ be defined on the vector of log-incomes $\ln Y \equiv (\ln Y_1, \ldots, \ln Y_N)$. Under the six axioms enumerated in the Appendix, the decomposition of income inequality given by

$$s_j(\ln Y) = \frac{\text{cov}[a_j Z_j, \ln Y]}{\sigma^2(\ln Y)} = \frac{a_j \sigma(Z_j) \text{cor}[Z_j, \ln Y]}{\sigma(\ln Y)} \tag{8a}$$

where

$$\sum_{j=1}^{J+2} s_j(\ln Y) = 100\%, \qquad (8b)$$

$$\sum_{j=1}^{J+1} s_j(\ln Y) = R^2(\ln Y), \qquad (8c)$$

and

$$p_j(\ln Y) \equiv \frac{s_j(\ln Y)}{R^2(\ln Y)} \qquad (8d)$$

holds for *any* inequality index $I(\ln Y_1, \ldots, \ln Y_N)$ which is continuous and symmetric and for which $I(\mu, \mu, \ldots, \mu) = 0$.

These conditions can be shown to hold for a broad class of inequality measures by the following argument.[9] The standard inequality measures defined on the vector of incomes $Y = (Y_1, \ldots, Y_N)$ are continuous and symmetric functions that equal zero when all income recipients receive the mean income. In such a function, substitute the identity $e^{\ln Y_i} = Y_i$ wherever Y_i occurs. The resultant inequality measure $I(\ln Y_1, \ldots, \ln Y_N)$ defined on the vector of log-incomes is also continuous and symmetric and satisfies the property $I(\mu, \mu, \ldots, \mu) = 0$, and therefore the factor inequality weights from Result 2 can be applied to these standard measures.

Result 2 is quite powerful. It says that as long as we agree on the log-linear model (3) and on the decomposition rules, we do not need to agree on which particular inequality measure to decompose, because we get the *same* percentage effect for the *j*'th explanatory factor for a broad class of inequality measures applied to the logarithms of income. Included in this class are the Gini coefficient, the Atkinson index, the generalized entropy family, and various centile measures.

2.3. Different Kinds of Explanatory Variables in Practice

We have just seen that the percentage contribution of the *j*'th variable to total income inequality is given by Eq. (8). For explanatory factors that enter the income-generating function as simple variables (e.g. years of education or a dummy variable for union membership), each of the components on the right hand side of Eq. (8a) has a straightforward interpretation. However, not all explanatory variables enter the earnings function in this way. There are three types of such variables: (1) A categorical variable entered as a string of dummy explanatory variables;[10] (2) An explanatory variable which has a non-linear (say, quadratic) effect;[11] and (3) Two or more explanatory variables which enter interactively.[12]

To deal with the first two of these issues in the levels decomposition, the solution is the same. Define the generic factor "industry" as the composite of the industry dummy variables IND_1, IND_2, ... and the generic factor "experience" as the composite of EXP and EXP^2 (and higher-order terms if included). Sum the s_j's for IND_1, IND_2, ... to get a good measure of the overall importance of "industry," and likewise for EXP and EXP^2 for a measure of the importance of "experience."

Interactions pose more of a problem. Thus far, the J variables determining log-income have been assumed to enter the income-generating function additively. As long as this assumption is maintained, the model gives a factor inequality weight s_j for each factor, these factor inequality weights are identical for a broad class of inequality measures, and the sum of these factor inequality weights is R^2. Thus, for example, to account for inequality among a sample of working men and women using a Mincer-type human capital specification, one might run an income-generating function of the form

$$\log y = a + b_1 \text{EDUC} + b_2 \text{EXP} + b_3 \text{EXPSQ} + b_4 \text{GENDER} + e_i \quad (11)$$

and, using the results above, derive s_j's for education, experience, and gender.

One might object to the specification in Eq. (11) on the grounds that it assumes that education and experience have the same effect on income regardless of gender, whereas ample empirical research shows that this is not the case (e.g. Blau, Ferber & Winkler, 1998). Suppose that the analyst wished to include these variables interactively, thereby allowing for the possibility that education and experience affect income differently for men and for women. One way of doing this would be to interact gender with the other variables in a single equation

$$\log y = a + b_1 \text{EDUC} + b_2 \text{EXP} + b_3 \text{EXPSQ} + b_4 \text{GENDER} + b_5 \text{GENDER}$$
$$\times \text{EDUC} + b_6 \text{GENDER} \times \text{EXP} + b_7 \text{GENDER} \times \text{EXPSQ} + e_{ii} \quad (12)$$

The problem with this is that the seven resulting s_j's would no longer decompose neatly into education, experience, and gender components.

Another way of allowing for interactions would be to run separate income-generating functions for men and for women

$$\log y^m = a^m + b_1^m \text{EDUC} + b_2^m \text{EXP} + b_3^m \text{EXPSQ} + e_i^m \quad (13a)$$

$$\log y^f = a^f + b_1^f \text{EDUC} + b_2^f \text{EXP} + b_3^f \text{EXPSQ} + e_i^f \quad (13b)$$

and to regard inequality in the full sample as consisting of inequality among men, inequality among women, and inequality between men and women. The problems

Accounting for Income Inequality and its Change

with this way of allowing for interactions are that the class of axiomatically-justified ways of cardinalizing such a decomposition remains quite broad, and further, the results are not identical for different inequality measures that might be chosen.[13] Thus, under this option, the agreement of results independently of the inequality measure chosen is lost.

It is up to the individual analyst to decide which is the best choice for him or her. The empirical work below adopts the first of these, i.e. Eq. (11).

2.4. Comparison with Other Level Decompositions

Decompositions in the human capital tradition have a long history dating back to the pioneering work of Mincer (1958, 1970, 1974), Becker (1964, 1967), and others. One such decomposition was suggested by Chiswick and Mincer (1972), who showed that when earnings depend on schooling (S), experience (EXP), and weeks worked (WEEKS) in the following way

$$\ln(w_i) = a + b_1 S_i + b_2(A_i - S_i - 5) + b_3 \ln(\text{WEEKS}_i) + \varepsilon, \quad (14)$$

then income inequality as measured by the log-variance can be decomposed as

$$\sigma^2(\ln(w_i)) = (b_1 - b_2)\sigma^2(S) + b_2^2 \sigma^2(A) + b_3^2 \sigma^2(\ln \text{WEEKS}) + [2b_2(b_1 - b_2)]$$
$$\times R_{a,s}\sigma(A)\sigma(S) + [2b_3(b_1 - b_2)]R_{\ln \text{weeks},s}\sigma(\ln \text{WEEKS})\sigma(S)$$
$$+ [2b_2 b_3]R_{a,\ln \text{weeks}}\sigma(\ln \text{WEEKS}) + \sigma^2(\varepsilon). \quad (15)$$

The first three terms on the right hand side of Eq. (15) are the variances of schooling, age and log-weeks weighted by the regression coefficients; the next three are interactions among the regressors; and the last is the variance of the error term. The strength of this method is that it decomposes the percentage of inequality explained by the regressors (64.8% in Chiswick and Mincer's empirical application for the United States) into components associated with schooling, experience, and weeks worked.[14] On the other hand, the Chiswick–Mincer method does not give "pure" effects of the regressors, it cannot handle a quadratic in experience or in other variables, and it quickly becomes unwieldy as further explanatory variables are added.

More recently, Mincer (1997) has decomposed the log-variance into four components:

- I: the variance due to schooling wage differentials,
- II: the residual variance at overtaking, reflecting differentials within schooling groups,

- III: the variance component due to differences in returns to post-school investments,
- IV: the contribution of between-experience-group wage differentials, which reflects the steepness of the age income-generating profile.

This decomposition shares the same features as those raised at the end of the preceding paragraph.

Other variance-based decompositions have been proposed. Given two sources 1 and 2 such that $Y = X_1 + X_2$, we know that

$$\text{Var}(Y) = \underbrace{\mu_2^2 \text{var}(X_1)}_{A} + \underbrace{\mu_1^2 \text{var}(X_2)}_{B} + \underbrace{2\mu_1\mu_2\text{cov}(X_1, X_2)}_{C}.$$

Goldberger (1970) reports Burt and Finley's (1968) suggestion to allocate $A + B + C$ into $A + C/2$ as the share of X_1 and $B + C/2$ as the share of X_2. Given $Y = \Sigma_k Y_k$, the variance can be decomposed so that half the value of all the interaction terms involving factor k is assigned to that factor (Shorrocks, 1982, 1999). Because the decomposition rule given in Result 2 is equivalent to the "natural" decomposition of the log-variance, that same fifty-fifty assignment of the covariance holds for the present method as well.

A number of other decompositions have appeared in the literature based on linear income-generating functions. Both the standard ANOVA model and the regression-based alternative proposed by Behrman, Knight and Sabot (1983) give the proportion of the log-variance of earnings explained by each independent variable. However, in neither method are the shares due to each factor derived axiomatically, as Shorrocks's s_j's are.

Another regression-based framework is that of Morduch and Sicular (1998). Income (rather than its logarithm) is regressed on a number of explanatory variables. The main empirical conclusion from Morduch and Sicular's work is that the results vary enormously.[15] This is why a robust decomposition rule, derived axiomatically, may be preferable.

A different strand in the literature abandons the regression framework entirely and examines between-group and within-group inequality. For example, Cowell and Jenkins (1995) partition the population into a set of mutually exclusive and jointly exhaustive subgroups – in their empirical application to the United States, forty-eight sex-race-age-employment status cells are used. The authors then calculate how much inequality is between sex cells, between sex-race cells, and so on and find that "not very much" of U.S. inequality is explained by population characteristics. More important for present purposes is the fact that unlike the method devised in Sections 2.1 and 2.2, the relative contributions of these various characteristics (sex, race, age, and employment status) depend critically on the order in which they are introduced into the analysis. Alternatively, one might introduce the various characteristics one by one, but then the effects are gross ones not controlling for the effect of any other variable.[16]

Other authors have considered the role of one or a small number of explanatory variables. For example, Almeida dos Reis and Paes de Barros (1991) determined how much education contributes to the overall inequality of wages by calculating the amount by which inequality (measured by Theil's L-index) would fall if proportional transfers were made from better-educated groups to less-educated groups so that the group means were equalized. They estimate that such transfers would cut wage inequality in Brazil in half. However, because they include only a single explanatory variable, there is no way to tell whether education contributes more to inequality in this sense than do other factors. Lam and Levison (1991) adopted a similar procedure. Lam (1999) included three explanatory variables (schooling, age, and race) and found that schooling plays a very large role in explaining earnings inequality in both Korea and South Africa and in the latter case race plays a large role.

A quite different type of decomposition comes from the factor components literature. Fei, Ranis and Kuo (1978) and Pyatt, Chen and Fei (1980) decomposed total inequality into terms attributable to each factor component (e.g. labor income, capital income, land income). Fei, Ranis and Kuo showed that the Gini coefficient of total income can be decomposed into a weighted sum of "pseudo-Ginis," the weights being given by the corresponding factor shares:

$$G(Y) = \sum_k \phi_k(Y_k), \tag{16a}$$

where $Y =$ total income, $Y_k =$ income from the k'th factor component, $\phi_k \equiv \sum_i Y_{ik} / \sum_k \sum_i Y_{ik}$ is the share of income from factor k in total income, and (Y_k) is the "pseudo-Gini coefficient" of income from factor k.[17]

Pyatt, Chen and Fei then showed that the pseudo-Gini coefficient (which they call the "concentration ratio") is in turn the product of the ordinary factor Gini $G(Y_k)$ and a "rank correlation ratio"

$$R_k = \frac{\text{cov}(Y_k, \rho)}{\text{cov}(Y_k, \rho_k)}$$

$$= \frac{\text{covariance between factor income amount and total income rank}}{\text{covariance between factor income amount and factor income rank}} \tag{16b}$$

and therefore:

$$G(Y) = \sum_k \phi_k G(Y_k) R_k. \tag{16c}$$

Dividing (16c) by $G(Y)$, one obtains

$$100\% = \frac{\sum_k \phi_k G(Y_k) R_k}{G(Y)} \equiv \sum_k s_k, \quad (16d)$$

the sum of the Fei–Ranis–Kuo–Pyatt–Chen relative factor inequality weights. Thus, both the Fei–Ranis–Kuo–Pyatt–Chen decomposition and the Shorrocks decomposition provide an additive decomposition of total inequality into the contribution of each income source. It should be noted that the relative factor inequality weights given by the two decompositions (the s_k in Eq. (16d) and the s_j in Eq. (10a) are not the same, the difference being due to the different decomposition rules used by the different authors.

3. ACCOUNTING FOR DIFFERENCES IN INCOME INEQUALITY

Section 2 established a methodology to account for the *level* of income inequality in a particular country at a particular time. In this section, a method is proposed to account for *differences* in income inequality between one country, group, or time and another.[18] Specifically, we ask: How much of the difference in inequality between one country/group/time and another is attributable to each income determinant? Which is relatively more important in accounting for these differences: differences in education, in experience, in gender, etc.?

3.1. The Relative Importance of Different Income Determinants in Explaining Inequality Differences

Result 2 established that the j'th factor's percentage contribution to the *level* of inequality is the same for a broad class of inequality measures. This leads one to ask, are the percentage contributions to the *changes* in inequality similarly independent of how inequality is measured? The answer is readily seen to be "no": the amount by which inequality rose or fell – and perhaps even *whether* inequality rose or fell – depends on how inequality is measured. Clearly, the answer to the changes question must be index-specific.

For any given inequality measure $I(\cdot)$, we may write the change in inequality in terms of each period's factor inequality weight and each period's inequality level as

$$I(\cdot)_2 - I(\cdot)_1 = \sum_j [s_{j,2}I(\cdot)_2 - s_{j,1}I(\cdot)_1]. \tag{17a}$$

Define the contribution of factor j to the change in inequality for an arbitrary inequality measure $I(\cdot)$ as

$$\Pi_j(I(\cdot)) \equiv \frac{s_{j,2}I(\cdot)_2 - s_{j,1}I(\cdot)_1}{I(\cdot)_2 - I(\cdot)_1}. \tag{17b}$$

From this, we may derive

$$100\% = \frac{\sum_j [s_{j,2}I(\cdot)_2 - s_{j,1}I(\cdot)_1]}{I(\cdot)_2 - I(\cdot)_1} = \sum_j \Pi_j(I(\cdot)), \tag{17c}$$

the $\Pi_j(I(\cdot))$'s denoting the contribution of the j'th explanatory factor to the change in inequality measured by inequality index $I(\cdot)$. Thus:

Result 3. The contribution of the j'th factor to the change in a particular inequality measure between country/group/time 1 and country/group/time 2 is given by

$$\Pi_j(I(\cdot)) \equiv \frac{s_{j,2}I(\cdot)_2 - s_{j,1}I(\cdot)_1}{I(\cdot)_2 - I(\cdot)_1}. \tag{17b}$$

Writing P_j as a function of $I(\cdot)$ makes explicit that the explanatory contribution of the j'th factor depends on the inequality measure used. It is an empirical question whether the choice of inequality measure makes a large difference or a small one in any particular context.

3.2. Decomposing Differences in the s_j's

Next, let us consider how to account for the sources of changing contributions of the various factors explaining income inequality. If the same income-generating functions have been run for two samples at different dates and the s_j's given by Eq. (8a) are found to differ, one may ask, "why"? To what extent is the change in any given s_j due to differences between the regression coefficients in the two years? To differences in the inequality of the explanatory variable? To differences in the covariance or the correlation between the explanatory variable and income?

For infinitesimal changes, an exact decomposition of the difference in any given s_j can be obtained by logarithmically differentiating Eq. (8a). This produces:

$$\widehat{s_j(\ln Y)} = \widehat{a_j} + \widehat{\sigma(Z_j)} + \widehat{\text{cor}[Z_j, \ln Y]} - \widehat{\sigma(\ln Y)}, \tag{18}$$

the ^ over the variable indicating a percentage rate of growth. This equation proves to be directly useful in this form. In real-world applications, the changes in each component are non-infinitesimal. Dividing through by pctchng($s_j(\ln Y)$), the change in s_j may then be approximated by[19]

$$1 \approx \frac{\text{pctchng}(a_j)}{\text{pctchng}(s_j(\ln Y))} + \frac{\text{pctchng}[\sigma(Z_j)]}{\text{pctchng}(s_j(\ln Y))} + \frac{\text{pctchng}[\text{cor}[Z_j, \ln Y]]}{\text{pctchng}(s_j(\ln Y))} - \frac{\text{pctchng}[\sigma(\ln Y)]}{\text{pctchng}(s_j(\ln Y))}. \tag{19}$$

An objection can be raised to the right-most decomposition of levels in Eq. (8a) and the consequent decomposition of changes in Eq. (19), which is that a_j and cor[Z_j, ln Y] are both functions of cov[Z_j, ln Y], so that one cannot be varied without the other.[20] This objection can be overcome by making a further approximation. If the j'th income-determining factor were orthogonal to the other income-determining factors, that determinant's factor inequality weight would equal

$$s_j(\ln Y) = \frac{a_j^2 \sigma^2(Z_j)}{\sigma^2(\ln Y)}. \tag{20}$$

The changes over time would then decompose approximately as

$$1 \approx \frac{2\text{pctchng}(a_j)}{\text{pctchng}(s_j(\ln Y))} + \frac{2\text{pctchng}[\sigma(Z_j)]}{\text{pctchng}(s_j(\ln Y))} - \frac{2\text{pctchng}[\sigma(\ln Y)]}{\text{pctchng}(s_j(\ln Y))}. \tag{21}$$

("Approximately" for two reasons: (i) real-world changes are not infinitesimal; and (ii) the j'th regressor is typically not orthogonal to the other regressors.) On the other hand, the advantage of the decomposition in Eq. (21) over that in Eq. (19) is that it says that the j'th regressor in the income-generating function contributes more to explaining an observed increase in inequality: (a) the larger is the increase in the regression coefficient of that variable; and (b) the larger is the increase in the inequality of that variable as measured by the standard deviation – both intuitively appealing results. In the case of falling inequality, Eq. (21) says that the j'th regressor contributes more to the decrease in inequality: (a) the larger is the decrease in the regression coefficient on that factor; and (b) the larger is the decrease in the standard deviation of that factor.

Using these alternative decompositions, we then have:

Result 4. The change in the j'th explanatory factor's relative factor inequality weight can be expressed as

$$1 \approx \frac{\text{pctchng}(a_j)}{\text{pctchng}(s_j(\ln Y))} + \frac{\text{pctchng}[\sigma(Z_j)]}{\text{pctchng}(s_j(\ln Y))} + \frac{\text{pctchng}[\text{cor}[Z_j, \ln Y]]}{\text{pctchng}(s_j(\ln Y))}$$
$$- \frac{\text{pctchng}[\sigma(\ln Y)]}{\text{pctchng}(s_j(\ln Y))} \quad (19)$$

or as

$$1 \approx \frac{2\text{pctchng}(a_j)}{\text{pctchng}(s_j(\ln Y))} + \frac{2\text{pctchng}[\sigma(Z_j)]}{\text{pctchng}(s_j(\ln Y))} - \frac{2\text{pctchng}[\sigma(\ln Y)]}{\text{pctchng}(s_j(\ln Y))}. \quad (21)$$

3.3. Decomposing Total Inequality Into Price Effects and Quantity Effects

Another decomposition is possible if one is willing to choose the log-variance (i.e. the variance of the logarithms of income) as the measure of income inequality; this decomposition is due to Yun (2002). In the work of Juhn, Murphy and Pierce (described below), the price effect of a variable in accounting for the change in inequality between a base income distribution "1" and a comparison income distribution "2" is defined as the difference between the inequality of distribution 2 and the inequality of an auxiliary distribution which uses the prices of distribution 1 and the quantities and residuals of distribution 2. For the i'th individual, income in the auxiliary distribution is given by

$$\ln Y_{i,\text{aux}} = \sum_j a_{j1} Z_{ij2}. \quad (22)$$

From Eq. (8), the variance of $\ln Y_{\text{aux}}$ can be composed as

$$\sigma^2(\ln Y_{\text{aux}}) = \sum_j a_{j1} \sigma(Z_{j2}) \text{cor}(Z_{j2}, \ln Y_{\text{aux}}) \sigma(\ln Y_{\text{aux}}). \quad (23)$$

Using the auxiliary distribution, we have that the difference in inequality between distributions 1 and 2 can be expressed as

$$I_2 - I_1 = (I_2 - I_{\text{aux}}) + (I_{\text{aux}} - I_1),$$

which, for the log-variance, decomposes as

$$\sigma^2(\ln Y_2) - \sigma^2(\ln Y_1) = \sum_j a_{j2}\sigma(Z_{j2})\text{cor}(Z_{j2}, \ln Y_2)\sigma(\ln Y_2)$$

$$- \sum_j a_{j1}\sigma(Z_{j2})\text{cor}(Z_{j2}, \ln Y_{\text{aux}})\sigma(\ln Y_{\text{aux}})$$

$$+ \sum_j a_{j1}\sigma(Z_{j2})\text{cor}(Z_{j2}, \ln Y_{\text{aux}})\sigma(\ln Y_{\text{aux}})$$

$$- \sum_j a_{j1}\sigma(Z_{j1})\text{cor}(Z_{j1}, \ln Y_1)\sigma(\ln Y_1). \qquad (24)$$

Upon regrouping, we obtain

Result 5. The change in inequality between two distributions 1 and 2 can be decomposed as

$$\sigma^2(\ln Y_2) - \sigma^2(\ln Y_1) = \sum_j [a_{j2}\sigma(Z_{j2})\text{cor}(Z_{j2}, \ln Y_2)\sigma(\ln Y_2)$$

$$- a_{j1}\sigma(Z_{j2})\text{cor}(Z_{j2}, \ln Y_{\text{aux}})\sigma(\ln Y_{\text{aux}})]$$

$$+ \sum_j [a_{j1}\sigma(Z_{j2})\text{cor}(Z_{j2}, \ln Y_{\text{aux}})\sigma(\ln Y_{\text{aux}})$$

$$- a_{j1}\sigma(Z_{j1})\text{cor}(Z_{j1}, \ln Y_1)\sigma(\ln Y_1)]. \qquad (25)$$

The variables in Eq. (25) have a clear interpretation: in Juhn, Murphy and Pierce's terminology, each term in the first summation is the price effect of the j'th variable, while each term in the second summation is the quantity effect of the j'th variable.

Finally, in parallel with the decompositions in Eqs (19) and (21), we may want to know what fraction of the j'th variable's factor inequality weight is attributable to the price effect of the j'th variable and what fraction to its quantity effect. Taking the terms for the j'th variable and dividing by the change in that variable's factor inequality weight, we obtain:

Result 6. The change in the j'th explanatory factor's relative factor inequality weight can be expressed as

$$1 = \frac{[a_{j2}\sigma(Z_{j2})\text{cor}(Z_{j2}, \ln Y_2)\sigma(\ln Y_2) - a_{j1}\sigma(Z_{j2})\text{cor}(Z_{j2}, \ln Y_{\text{aux}})\sigma(\ln Y_{\text{aux}})]}{s_j(\ln Y_2) - s_j(\ln Y_1)}$$

$$+ \frac{[a_{j1}\sigma(Z_{j2})\text{cor}(Z_{j2}, \ln Y_{\text{aux}})\sigma(\ln Y_{\text{aux}}) - a_{j1}\sigma(Z_{j1})\text{cor}(Z_{j1}, \ln Y_1)\sigma(\ln Y_1)]}{s_j(\ln Y_2) - s_j(\ln Y_1)},$$

$$(26)$$

where the first term is the percentage contribution of the price effect and the second is the percentage contribution of the quantity effect.

This completes the presentation of the decompositions for analyzing differences in the income distributions between one year/group/place and another. Before turning to empirical applications of these three methods, let us now compare the decompositions given by Eqs (19), (21), and (26) with other decompositions that have been carried out by others.

3.4. Comparison with Other Difference Decompositions

Decomposing differences in income inequality in the way described in Results 3, 4, and 6 offers several advantages compared with other decompositions of inequality differences that have been suggested in the literature.

Using an income-generating function framework, Juhn, Murphy and Pierce (1991, 1993) and followers (e.g. Blau & Kahn, 1997; Robbins & Gindling, 1999) have decomposed the change over time in quantile differentials (90-50, 90-10, and 50-10) into components due to changes in observed quantities, components due to changes in observed prices, and a residual (termed "unobserved prices and quantities"). One advantage of the decomposition proposed here is that it uses a more comprehensive measure of inequality than the 90-50, 90-10, or 50-10 differentials, and in fact much of the decomposition analysis can be done entirely non-parametrically. Another advantage is that the factor inequality weights derived here (the s_j's) measure the relative importance of each particular explanatory factor rather than the changes in prices or the changes in quantities taken as a group.

Another literature has decomposed the difference in wage inequality between unionized and non-unionized workers. Freeman (1980) showed that given two income-generating functions

$$\ln(Y_{i1}) = a_1 + \sum_{j=1}^{J} b_{j1} x_{ij1} + \varepsilon_{i1} \qquad (2a)$$

and

$$\ln(Y_{i2}) = a_2 + \sum_{j=1}^{J} b_{j2} x_{ij2} + \varepsilon_{i2}, \qquad (2b)$$

the extent to which var(ln(Y_{i1})) differs from var(ln(Y_{i2})) as a result of differences in the characteristics in the samples can be gauged by

$$\sum_{j=1}^{J}(b_j)^2[\sigma^2(x_{j1}) - \sigma^2(x_{j2})] + \sum_{j=1}^{J}\sum_{j'=1}^{J} b_j b'_j[(x_{j1}x_{j'1}) - (x_{j2}x_{j'2})] \quad (27)$$

where $\sigma^2(x_{j1})$ is the variance in characteristic j in group 1, $\sigma(x_{j1}x_{j'1})$ is the covariance in characteristics j and j' among members of group 1, and $\sigma^2(x_{j2})$ and $(x_{j2}x_{j'2})$ are the corresponding terms in group 2. But as Freeman notes, Eq. (27) is only an "approximate standardization for differences in characteristics," because all second- and higher-order covariance terms are omitted. The decomposition using Eq. (8) gives an exact standardization.

A more recent follow-up literature has estimated the effect of declining unionization rates in the United States on the log-variance of wages (Card, 1996; Freeman, 1993). Both these studies estimate the effect of the change in unionization rates on the log-variance of wages assuming that the union-non-union wage gap and the within-sector effect of unions on the log-variance of wages are unchanged. If these factors do change, then the Freeman and Card methodologies do not give an answer. By contrast, the method presented above is multivariate and applies in such situations.

Another regression-based approach is to be found in two papers by Bourguignon and co-authors (Bourguignon & Martinez, 1997; Bourguignon, Fournier & Gurgand, 1998). The essence of their procedure is to run two regressions for a base year 1 and a final year 2 and then to decompose the changes into price, quantity, and residual effects. Given the basic wage equations

$$\ln w_{1i} = x_{1i} b_1 + u_{1i} \quad (28)$$

and

$$\ln w_{2j} = x_{2j} b_2 + u_{2j}$$

for the two years, the decomposition equations are

$$W_2 - W_1 = \Delta_b + \Delta X + \Delta_\sigma, \quad (29)$$

where

$$\Delta_b = X_1(b_2 - b_1); \quad \Delta X = b_1(X_2 - X_1); \quad \Delta_\sigma = U_2 - U_1. \quad (30)$$

(The capital letters in Eqs (29) and (30) signify vectors.) With adjustment for participation or not and employed or not, the model becomes

$$\ln w_{ki} = P_{ki}(x_{ki}, y_{ki}) E_{ki}(x_{ki}, y_{ki})(x_{ki} b_k + u_{ki}) \quad (31)$$

with

$$P_{ki}(x_{ki}, y_{ki}) = 1 \text{ or } 0 \quad \text{as} \quad x_{ki}a_k + y_{ki}c_k + v_{ki} \gtreqqless 0$$

and

$$E_{ki}(x_{ki}, y_{ki}) = 1 \text{ or } 0 \quad \text{as} \quad x_{ki}d_k + y_{ki}f_k + t_{ki} \gtreqqless 0$$

and an analogous decomposition is performed.

The Bourguignon method gives a thorough accounting of the routes by which a change in an explanatory factor affects income inequality. However, implementing that method requires heavy econometrics. By contrast, the method derived above is easier to apply, but it produces only an incomplete decomposition. What is interesting empirically is that both methods have been used to understand changing income inequality in Taiwan, and they both produced the conclusion that the major factors affecting income inequality there were an increased coefficient on education, which raised income inequality, and a reduction in the inequality of years of education, which lowered income inequality (Bourguignon, Fournier & Gurgand, 1998; Fields & Mitchell, 1999).

Then, there is the recent and comprehensive method of DiNardo, Fortin and Lemieux (1996). These authors gauge the effect of various labor market changes on the density function of wages in the United States between 1979 and 1988. Once they estimate the effect of a given change on the entire density function, they then calculate the implied effect on various inequality measures including the Gini coefficient, the Theil index, and various percentile differentials (e.g. 90-10).

Their method is most easily understood if we adopt the following notation:[21]

A = actual wage distribution in 1988
B = 1988 wage distribution adjusted for 1979 minimum wage
C = 1988 wage distribution adjusted for 1979 minimum wage and 1979 unionization
D = 1988 wage distribution adjusted for 1979 minimum wage, 1979 unionization, and 1979 other attributes (which include experience, schooling, race, full-time/part-time, and dummy variables for SMSA, occupation, and industry)
E = 1988 wage distribution adjusted for 1979 minimum wage, 1979 unionization, 1979 other attributes, and 1979 supply and demand
F = 1988 wage distribution adjusted for everything including a residual, which is then the actual wage distribution in 1979.

Their key equation takes the form

$$A - F = [A - B] + [B - C] + [C - D] + [D - E] + [E - F], \quad (32)$$

where $A - B = 1988$ wage distribution adjusted for 1979 minimum wage $=$ "effect" of minimum wage;[22] $B - C = B$ adjusted for change in unionization rate $=$ "effect" of unionization; $C - D = C$ adjusted for changes in other attributes $=$ "effect" of other attributes; $D - E = D$ adjusted for supply and demand $=$ "effect" of supply and demand; $E - F = E$ adjusted for residual $=$ "effect" of residual.

The principal advantages of the DiNardo–Fortin–Lemieux method compared with the decomposition procedure described in Results 3 and 4 are that it estimates the effect of a given income determinant on the entire wage distribution and it does not rely on a particular functional form. However, the main disadvantage of their method is that each "effect" depends on the order in which the adjustment is done.

On the other hand, the method derived here has advantages of its own. Because it relies on a regression framework, it expresses inequality levels and inequality changes as functions of the very income determinants that economists are accustomed to using. Also, in explaining income levels, it assigns the same weights to each income determinant regardless of the inequality measure used. And as a practical matter, the required calculations in the present method are easier to make. It is left to the reader to weigh the two methods' respective pros and cons.

Finally, mention should be made of two other decompositions with quite different purposes. Moffitt and Gottschalk (1995) decompose changes in inequality over time into two components, one representing the variance in the permanent component of income and the other the variance in the transitory component. Layard and Zabalza (1979) decompose the inequality of family income into the variances and covariances of incomes of family members. Neither of these is directly relevant to the problem considered here.

4. EMPIRICAL APPLICATION: ANALYZING THE SOURCES OF RISING EARNINGS INEQUALITY IN THE UNITED STATES

Official publications and academic studies have shown a substantial increase in income inequality in the United States over the last twenty years (Economic Report of the President, 1999; Forster & Pellizzari, 2000; Katz & Autor, 1999; Levy, 1999). In this section, the methods developed in Sections 2 and 3 are used to quantify the contributions of various factors in accounting for the amount of labor earnings inequality at a point in time (the "levels" question) and also the increase in inequality of labor earnings (the "differences" question).

Data for this analysis come from the Annual Demographic Surveys (March supplements) to the 1980 and 2000 U.S. Current Population Surveys. The March supplements contain respondents' reports on labor earnings in the preceding year. The 1980 CPS was chosen as the starting point, because it has been the base year for a number of important empirical studies (Bound & Johnson, 1992; DiNardo, Fortin & Lemieux, 1996; Katz & Murphy, 1992) and because earnings inequality had not yet started rising in the United States at that time. The 2000 CPS was chosen as comparison year so as to be able to speak about changes in inequality over a twenty year period.

Following Katz and Murphy (1992), Juhn, Murphy and Pierce (1993), Blau, Ferber and Winkler (1998), and Katz and Autor (1999), the sample and variables were defined as follows. The sample consists of men and women who were full-year, full-time wage and salaried employees, 18–64 years of age. The dependent variable used in the analysis is weekly earnings, measured in logs. The explanatory variables are gender (two categories), race (two categories), education (four categories, also entered continuously – see below), potential experience and its square, occupation (three categories), industry (three categories), and geographic region (four categories). Descriptive statistics on these variables are presented in Table 1.

In this data set, the distribution of labor earnings became unambiguously more unequal. Figure 1 displays the Lorenz curves, showing a clear Lorenz-worsening and therefore an increase in inequality for a broad range of inequality measures. The most commonly-used summary statistic of inequality, the Gini coefficient, rose from 0.274 in 1979 to 0.338 in 1999 among this sample of workers. Another commonly-used inequality measure, the variance of the logarithms of income, increased too, from 0.262 to 0.380. Increases in inequality of this magnitude are large, both by the standards of changes that typically take place within countries and by the standards of international differences in inequality at a point in time (Atkinson, 1997; Forster & Pellizzari, 2000).

The first step in the decomposition analysis is to run the earnings functions (1) and (2). Log-earnings is a linear function of gender, race, potential experience and its square, four schooling categories, three occupational categories, three industry categories, and four region categories. The empirical results are given in Table 2. We see that in both years, all variables included in the regression are statistically significant at conventional levels, and together they explain 41.5% of the variance of log-earnings in 1979 and 38.3% of the variance in 1999.

The levels question is: Of these statistically significant variables, which are how important in accounting for the levels of inequality in 1979 and 1999? The answer is given in columns (1) and (2) of Table 3. In 1999, after the residual, schooling was the most important variable, with a factor inequality weight of 16.1%. Other

Table 1. United States: Descriptive Statistics.

Variable Group	Independent Variable	1979		1999	
		Mean	Std. Dev.	Mean	Std. Dev.
Gender	Male	0.62	0.48	0.56	0.50
	Female	0.38	0.48	0.44	0.50
Race	White	0.89	0.32	0.83	0.37
	Nonwhite	0.11	0.32	0.17	0.37
Experience	Potential experience	16.64	12.71	19.03	10.97
	Potential experience squared	438.48	524.31	482.59	461.27
Schooling	Less than complete high school	0.17	0.38	0.09	0.29
	High school grad	0.41	0.49	0.32	0.47
	Some college	0.21	0.41	0.29	0.46
	College grad and beyond	0.21	0.41	0.30	0.46
Occupation	Executive, professional, and technical	0.29	0.46	0.36	0.48
	Sales & admin. support	0.24	0.42	0.25	0.43
	All other	0.47	0.50	0.39	0.49
Industry	Public administration, professional, & related services	0.28	0.45	0.31	0.46
	All other services, finance, trade, transport	0.35	0.48	0.42	0.49
	Manufacturing, construction, mining, agriculture	0.38	0.48	0.27	0.45
Region	Northeast	0.22	0.42	0.17	0.38
	North Central	0.27	0.44	0.24	0.43
	South	0.22	0.42	0.25	0.43
	West	0.28	0.45	0.34	0.47

variables with sizeable shares were occupation (9.1%), experience (6.6%), and gender (5.7%). Three other variables had shares that were effectively zero – region (0.5%), race (0.4%), and industry (0.0%). What we see, then, is that although all of these explanatory factors were statistically significant determinants of earnings levels, their importance differs enormously: schooling was about twice as important as each of the next three closest variables and orders of magnitude higher than the three least important variables. These differences in relative importance could not have been seen from standard regression output alone.[23]

Turning our attention now to the question of how much of the increase in earnings inequality was due to each of these factors ("the differences question"), columns (3) and (4) of Table 3 give the answer using Eq. (17b) in Result 3. The decompositions

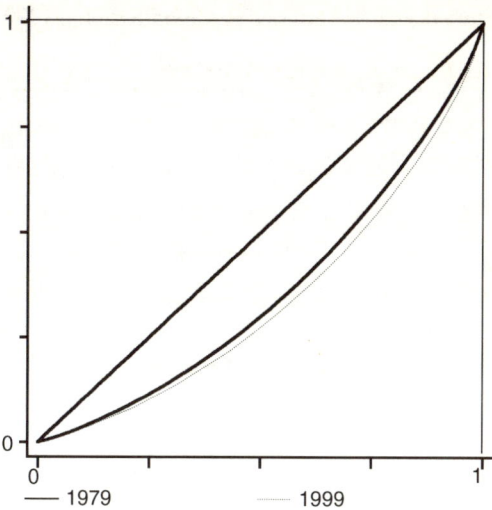

Fig. 1. Lorenz Curves for the Distribution of Earnings in the United States, 1979 and 1999.

of both inequality measures show that the largest share of the increase in earnings inequality was accounted for by an increase in residual inequality. Previously, it was known that earnings inequality had increased within education/experience/... cells (Juhn, Murphy & Pierce, 1993; Katz & Murphy, 1992; Murphy & Welch, 1992; Welch, 1999) but the relative weight of this factor vis-à-vis other factors was not known. Looking at "real" variables, we find here too that the differences in their explanatory contributions are enormous. Schooling is the largest such variable, accounting for 56% of the increase in the Gini coefficient and 34% of the increase in the log-variance. Occupation was half as important as schooling, accounting for 28% of the increase in the Gini coefficient and 18% of the increase in the log-variance. Four other variables – race, experience, industry, and region – contributed essentially nothing. Finally, gender had a sizeable effect but it does not contribute to the explanation; because gender changes were in the equalizing direction but inequality increased, gender's weight is strongly negative. In sum, some of the variables that were found in columns (1) and (2) to be statistically significant determinants of earnings *levels* are economically insignificant in accounting for *changes* in earnings inequality.

Looking more deeply into the role of the single most important variable, schooling, we may ask to what extent schooling's contribution to rising earnings inequality was due to increased dispersion of earnings between workers with

Table 2. United States: Earnings Equation Results, 1979 and 1999.

Variable Group	Independent Variable	1979	1999
Gender	Male	0.432	0.316
		(98.08)	(55.79)
Race	White	0.097	0.066
		(15.83)	(9.50)
Experience	Potential experience	0.033	0.040
		(62.24)	(48.50)
	Potential experience squared	−0.001	−0.001
		(−46.86)	(−34.01)
Schooling (Less than complete high school omitted)	High school grad	0.191	0.272
		(32.43)	(27.33)
	Some college	0.289	0.417
		(41.11)	(40.09)
	College grad and beyond	0.447	0.729
		(55.73)	(63.62)
Occupation (Executive, prof, and technical omitted)	Sales & admin support	−0.171	−0.233
		(−28.56)	(−30.98)
	All other	−0.226	−0.341
		(−39.03)	(−45.34)
Industry (Public administration, professional & related services omitted)	All other services, finance, trade, transport	0.038	0.067
		(7.34)	(10.14)
	Manufacturing, construction, mining, agriculture	0.149	0.172
		(27.64)	(23.02)
Region (Northeast omitted)	North Central	0.042	−0.054
		(7.78)	(−6.63)
	South	−0.080	−0.106
		(−13.91)	(−13.07)
	West	0.012	−0.085
		(2.28)	(−11.14)
Constant		5.540	5.439
		(482.59)	(330.59)
Adjusted R^2		0.4146	0.3833
F-statistic		2128.02	1578.61
N		42,045	35,579

Notes: Dependent Variable: Logarithm of Labor Earnings. Schooling Measured in Categories (t-statistics in parentheses).

Table 3. United States: The Contribution of Each Explanatory Factor to Earnings Inequality and to the Change in Inequality, 1979–1999 (Schooling Measured in Categories).

	Factor Inequality Weight of that Factor in that Year		Contribution of that Factor to the Change in Inequality as Measured by:	
	$s_j(\ln Y)$, 1979	$s_j(\ln Y)$, 1999	π_j(Gini), 1979–1999	π_j(log-variance), 1979–1999
	(1)	(2)	(3)	(4)
Gender	0.180	0.057	−0.55	−0.22
Race	0.008	0.004	−0.02	−0.01
Experience	0.072	0.066	0.04	0.05
Schooling in categories	0.080	0.161	0.56	0.34
Occupation	0.053	0.091	0.28	0.18
Industry	0.012	0.000	−0.06	−0.03
Region	0.010	0.005	−0.02	0.00
Residual	0.585	0.617	0.77	0.69

Notes: For definition of $s_j(\ln Y)$, see Eq. (8a). For definition of $\pi_j(\cdot)$, see Eq. (17b).

different educational attainments, to what extent to increased inequality of years of schooling, and to what extent to other factors. So that the inequality of years of schooling could be calculated in answering this question, schooling in categories was replaced by a continuous schooling variable, entered linearly. The regression results appear in Table A1 in the Appendix and the first decomposition results in Table A2 in the Appendix. These results show a rise in the coefficient on schooling (sometimes called a "rate of return"), which has been found in many, many prior studies. They also show reduced inequality in years of schooling, which as well has been found in past work. Based on these findings, we can further decompose the effect of schooling to understand why it contributed what it did, using Eqs (19), (21), and (26) in Results 4 and 6. The results, presented in Table 4, show that using all three alternative methods, schooling contributed to rising inequality entirely because of a rising coefficients effect and not at all because of an increase in inequality of years of schooling.

The final step in the U.S. analysis is to disaggregate by gender. This is done because the gender variable makes a negative contribution to explaining rising inequality, and so we want to know whether the same factors that are important or unimportant for the two genders taken together are similarly important or unimportant when the two are considered separately. The results are shown in Table 5.

Table 4. United States: Decomposing the Contribution of Years of Education to Changing Inequality of Labor Earnings, 1979 and 1999.

	Components of Education's Factor Inequality Weight		Percentage of Change in Education's Factor Inequality Weight Explained by:		
	1979	1999	(19)	(21)	(26)
Education's factor inequality weight	0.089	0.161			
Coefficient on years of education	0.054	0.088	0.84	1.69	1.05
Standard deviation of years of education	2.812	2.570	−0.15	−0.31	−0.05
Correlation between labor earnings and years of education	0.301	0.438	0.64	n.a.	n.a.
Standard deviation of labor earnings	0.512	0.617	−0.32	−0.64	n.a.
Total			1.01	0.74	1.00

The top part of the table shows that earnings inequality increased for both women and men. To understand why, earnings equations were run within gender (using schooling in years) and factor inequality weights and the contributions of each factor to changes in inequality were calculated.

For women, after the residual, the big variables accounting for earnings inequality in each year are schooling and occupation. These are also the biggest variables explaining the increase in earnings inequality, with schooling exhibiting about twice as large an effect as occupation. Lastly, for women, schooling contributed to rising inequality entirely because of increased differences in earnings across schooling levels and not at all because of inequality of years of schooling; in fact, years of schooling became distributed slightly more equally for women during that twenty year period.

For men, schooling was also a leading factor accounting for rising earnings inequality in both years. Unlike women, for men, experience was as important a factor in 1979 as schooling was, but by 1999, its relative contribution had fallen in half. Occupation's role increased from 1979 to 1999 and came to equal the role of experience in the latter year. As with women, in explaining the increase in earnings inequality for men, schooling had the largest effect, followed by occupation; experience and other variables explained virtually nothing. Finally, for men as for women, schooling's contribution to rising inequality is seen to be a coefficients effect and not an inequality-of-schooling effect.

Table 5. Analyzing Rising Earnings Inequality for Women and Men Separately.

Part A. United States: Rising Earnings Inequality for Women, 1979–1999

Inequality Index	1979	1999
Gini coefficient	0.236	0.317
Log-variance	0.175	0.330

United States: The Contribution of Each Explanatory Factor to Earnings Inequality and to the Change in Inequality for Women, 1979–1999

	$s_j(\ln Y)$, 1979	$s_j(\ln Y)$, 1999	π_j(Gini), 1979–1999	π_j(log-variance), 1979–1999
	(1)	(2)	(3)	(4)
Race	0.000	0.000	0.00	0.00
Experience	0.028	0.041	0.08	0.06
Schooling in years	0.112	0.183	0.39	0.26
Occupation	0.131	0.137	0.15	0.14
Industry	0.000	−0.008	−0.03	−0.02
Region	0.009	0.006	0.00	0.00
Residual	0.720	0.641	0.41	0.55

United States: Decomposing the Contribution of Years of Education to Changing Inequality of Labor Earnings for Women, 1979 and 1999

	Components of Education's Factor Inequality Weight		Share of Change in Education's Factor Inequality Weight Explained by:		
	1979	1999	(19)	(21)	(26)
Education's factor inequality weight	0.112	0.183			
Coefficient on years of schooling	0.048	0.090	1.27	2.54	0.97
Standard deviation of years of schooling	2.536	2.427	−0.09	−0.018	0.03
Corr. between earnings and schooling	0.386	0.482	0.46	n.a.	n.a.
Standard deviation of labor earnings	0.419	0.575	−0.65	−1.31	n.a.
Total			0.98	1.05	1.000

Table 5. (Continued)

Part B. United States: Rising Earnings Inequality for Men, 1979–1999

Inequality Index	1979	1999
Gini coefficient	0.256	0.336
Log-variance	0.233	0.385

United States: The Contribution of Each Explanatory Factor to Earnings Inequality and to the Change in Inequality for Men, 1979–1999

	$s_j(\ln Y)$, 1979	$s_j(\ln Y)$, 1999	$\pi_j(\text{Gini})$, 1979–1999	$\pi_j(\text{log-variance})$, 1979–1999
	(1)	(2)	(3)	(4)
Race	0.018	0.007	−0.03	−0.01
Experience	0.125	0.093	−0.01	0.04
Schooling in years	0.115	0.166	0.33	0.24
Occupation	0.047	0.093	0.24	0.16
Industry	−0.001	−0.007	−0.03	−0.02
Region	0.013	0.005	−0.02	−0.01
Residual	0.683	0.642	0.51	0.58

United States: Decomposing the Contribution of Years of Education to Changing Inequality of Labor Earnings for Men, 1979 and 1999

	Components of Education's Factor Inequality Weight		Share of Change in Education's Factor Inequality Weight Explained by:		
	1979	1999	(19)	(21)	(26)
Education's factor inequality weight	0.115	0.166			
Coefficient on years of schooling	0.057	0.086	1.10	2.20	1.05
Standard deviation of years of schooling	2.966	2.671	−0.29	−0.57	−0.05
Corr. between earnings and schooling	0.326	0.448	0.87	n.a.	n.a.
Standard deviation of labor earnings	0.483	0.621	−0.68	−1.37	n.a.
Total			0.99	0.25	1.00

Notes: For definition of $s_j(\ln Y)$, see Eq. (8a). For definition of $\pi_j(\cdot)$, see Eq. (17b).

In sum, for the empirical study of the United States, we have learned that earnings inequality increased overall and for women and men separately; that seven variables were statistically significant determinants of earnings (gender, race, potential experience, schooling, occupation, industry, and region); that despite all being statistically significant, their contribution to rising inequality differed enormously, with schooling being far and away the most important variable and many other variables (race, experience, gender, industry, and region) having no role to play at all; and that schooling's effect was entirely a coefficients effect and not at all due to rising inequality of schooling.

5. CONCLUSION

This paper has presented a methodology to account for (a) income inequality *levels* in a given country, group, or time period and (b) *differences* in income inequality between one country and other, between one group and another, or between one time period and another. To sum up what should be done:

- For a log-income-based levels calculation, run a standard semi-logarithmic income-generating function (3) for a particular country, group, or date. Using Eqs (8a)–(8d) in Result 2, calculate the relative factor inequality weights $s_j(\ln Y)$ and the corresponding percentage contributions $p_j(\ln Y)$ for each explanatory factor. If you accept the decomposition rules in the Appendix, you get the same $s_j(\ln Y)$'s and $p_j(\ln Y)$'s for virtually any inequality measure calculated on the vector of log-incomes.
- To account for the role of a given income determinant in explaining the change in inequality based on a particular inequality measure $I(\cdot)$, you can use Eq. (17b) in Result 3 to gauge the proportion of the rise or fall in inequality according to that measure that is accounted for by each explanatory factor.
- Finally, to explain why each explanatory factor contributed to an increase or decrease in income inequality between one country/group/date and another, you can use Eqs (19), (21), and (26) in Results 4 and 6 to get a decomposition into a coefficients effect, a standard deviation effect, and a correlation effect.

As an application of this approach, these methods were then used to analyze labor earnings inequality in the United States in 1979 and 1999 and the increase in labor earnings inequality between those two years. Explanatory variables included gender, race, potential experience, schooling, occupation, industry, and region. Although all variables were found to be statistically significant determinants of earnings in both years, the decomposition analysis revealed enormous differences in their explanatory power. In explaining the *levels* of inequality, schooling exhibited the largest explanatory power, followed by occupation, experience, and gender; the three remaining variables – region, race, and industry – had no appreciable effect at all. Then, in explaining the *increase* in inequality, schooling was again the single most important variable, but only one other variable (occupation) has any appreciable role to play; gender worked in the equalizing direction and all other variables contributed essentially zero explanatory power. All of schooling's effect was a coefficients effect and none an inequality-of-schooling effect. All of these results hold when women and men are analyzed separately.

Before ending, one final point bears repetition. Although this entire paper has been cast in terms of *income* inequality, this methodology can be used to apply regression analysis to the decomposition of *anything*. The usefulness of the method is limited only by the meaningfulness of the regression to which it is applied.

NOTES

1. The literature uses several different income concepts: "income" denotes the recipient unit's income from all sources, "earnings" denotes income from employment or self-employment, and "wages" denotes earnings per hour. It also uses several different recipient units including families, households, and individuals. To avoid having to refer repeatedly to income/earnings/wages among households/families/individuals/workers, the following discussion is cast in terms of "incomes" among "individuals" except for those empirical studies that specifically used something else.
2. The terminology "income-generating function" is used in place of "earnings function" or "wage equation," because the method is general enough to allow for non-labor income to be included along with labor income in the regression if the analyst so chooses.
3. What follows is a "decomposition" in the sense that the overall inequality in a population is broken down into a number of components such that the whole is equal to the sum of its parts. The term "decomposition" has been used in this sense in many types of income distribution studies including the literature on inequality decomposition by factor components (e.g. Fei, Ranis & Kuo, 1978; Pyatt, Chen & Fei, 1980; Shorrocks, 1982) and the literature decomposing differences in mean incomes between groups (Blinder, 1973; Oaxaca, 1973; Oaxaca & Ransom, 1994). However, the term "decomposition" has also been used in a more restrictive sense by Bourguignon (1979), who defines an income inequality measure to be decomposable when the total inequality of a population can be broken down into a weighted average of: (i) the inequality existing within subgroups of the population using that same inequality measure; and (ii) the inequality existing between the subgroups. In what follows, the term "decomposition" is used in the less restrictive sense, whereby the total inequality in a population is expressed as the sum of a number of terms, each corresponding to an explanatory variable in the income-generating equation.
4. Since this paper has been circulated in working paper form, the decompositions derived here have been used in a number of studies including works by Arcos (1996), Fields et al. (1998), Sánchez–Torres and Nuñez (1998), Fields and Mitchell (1999), Ravallion and

Chen (1999), Fields and Yoo (2000), Contreras (2000), Andersen (2000), Redmund and Kattuman (2001), Gindling and Trejos (2001), Heltberg (2001), and Yun (2002).

5. Note that the latter question is why one income distribution is more *equal* than another, not why one has a higher *mean* than another. The latter is the question addressed in the Blinder-Oaxaca types of decompositions.

6. Throughout this paper, a single regressor in the income-generating equation is called a "variable." Sometimes, there are natural groupings of "variables" into "factors." So for example, EXP is a variable, EXPSQ is another variable, and the two together constitute the factor "experience."

7. After this paper had been circulating in working paper form for some time, Arthur Goldberger brought to my attention a passage in his 1964 book (pp. 197–200) in which he stated without proof or axiomatic justification that in the standard linear model $Y = X\beta + \varepsilon$, the total residual sum of squares could be decomposed as TSSR $= b_1 m_{1y} + \cdots + b_K m_{Ky}$, where $m_{jy} = T\sum(x_j - \bar{x}_j)(y - \bar{y})$. This produces the so-called "separate determination coefficient" $d_{yj}^2 = b_j(m_{jy}/m_{yy})$ which, after appropriate substitutions, can be shown to equal $b_j \left(\sum(x - \bar{x})(y - \bar{y})/\sum(y - \bar{y})^2\right) = b_j(\text{cov}(x, y)/\text{var}(y))$. This is precisely Eq. (6c) with income as the dependent variable in place of log-income. Goldberger notes that d_{yj}^2 is "not widely used." I myself have never seen it used in the income inequality literature.

8. μ is the mean of total income.

9. I thank an anonymous referee for this insight.

10. This may arise for a variable which is inherently categorical (e.g. industry, occupation) or for a continuous variable which is censored (e.g. years of education, where all that is known is the highest level attended or completed but not the number of years).

11. Experience and experience squared are commonly included in earnings functions.

12. Earnings functions often contain a unionization variable interacted with years of education or experience.

13. See Cowell and Jenkins (1995) for a comprehensive discussion of the issues involved.

14. An even higher R-squared was found by Plotnick (1982) when log-earnings was used as the dependent variable in place of log-income and when the percentage of male workers in unions was added to the equation.

15. They find that in Zouping Country (China) in 1993, the decompositions of different inequality measures produce an education effect ranging from +174% to −30% and village effects ranging from +125% to −467%.

16. See also Ahuja et al.'s (1997) applications of the Cowell–Jenkins method to China and Thailand.

17. The pseudo-Gini coefficient of a factor component is the Gini coefficient that is obtained if income recipients are arrayed in increasing order of total income rather than in increasing order of income from that factor.

18. Though the presentation in the text is in terms of changes in income inequality over time, the same methodology can be used to account for inequality differences between one country and another or between one group and another within a country. The reader is reminded that the question here is what accounts for differences in *inequality* between one time/country/group and another, *not* what accounts for differences in *means*.

19. This expression has the following feature. Suppose that, holding the distribution of all the Z_js constant, all incomes were to change by the same non-zero scalar multiple. Then all terms on the right hand side of Eq. (19) would be zero, thereby satisfying the

intuitively appealing adding-up constraint that the share of inequality accounted for by the j'th explanatory factor is unchanged in such a case.

20. In the case of a single regressor, $a_j = \text{cov}(X, \ln Y)/\sigma^2(X)$ and $\text{cor}[X, \ln Y] = \text{cov}[X, \ln Y]/\sigma_X \sigma_{\ln Y}$. In the multiple regression case, the corresponding expressions are more complicated but the functional dependence remains.

21. All wage and minimum wage figures below are expressed in 1979 dollars.

22. In this case, the adjustment is achieved by asking, "How would the 1988 distribution of wages have been different if the minimum wage had been raised to its (real) 1979 level rather than being at its actual (real) 1988 level?" Other adjustments are made by asking similar counterfactuals, i.e. "How would the 1988 distribution of wages have been different if the variable in question had been distributed as it was in 1979 rather than as it actually was in 1988?"

23. In 1979, the most important variable was gender, followed by schooling and experience with approximately equal importance. The same point holds: the relative contributions of different statistically significant variables could not have been seen from the regression equation alone.

ACKNOWLEDGMENTS

This work was financed in part by a grant from the Organisation for Economic Co-Operation and Development. Thanks are gratefully extended to Jesse Leary and Paola Valenti for invaluable programming assistance, to Bob Hutchens, George Jakubson, and Larry Kahn for many helpful discussions during the preparation of this paper, and to François Bourguignon, Leonard Cheng, Arthur Goldberger, Larry Katz, Jacob Mincer, Jonathan Morduch, Efe Ok, Solomon Polachek, and Grace Tsiang for useful comments and suggestions. Earlier versions of this paper were presented at Cornell, Yale, Harvard, Columbia, the City University of New York, Les Facultés Universitaires Notre-Dame de la Paix, and the American Economic Association annual meetings.

REFERENCES

Ahuja, V., Bidawi, B., Ferreira, F., & Walton, M. (1997). *Everyone's miracle?* Washington: World Bank.

Almeida dos Reis, J. G., & de Barros, R. E. (1991). Wage inequality and the distribution of education. *Journal of Development Economics, 36*(1), 117–143.

Andersen, L. E. (2000). Social mobility in Latin America. Unpublished Working Paper, Universidad Católica Boliviana.

Arcos, X. R. (1996). *Descomposición de la desigualdad del consumo en Ecuador.* Masters Thesis, Cornell University, Ithaca, New York.

Atkinson, A. B. (1997). Bringing income distribution in from the cold. *Economic Journal, 107,* 297–321.

Becker, G. S. (1964). *Human capital*. New York: National Bureau of Economic Research.
Becker, G. S. (1967). *Human capital and the personal distribution of income: An analytical approach*. W. S. Woytinski Lecture, University of Michigan.
Behrman, J. R., Knight, J. B., & Sabot, R. H. (1983). A simulation alternative to the comparative R^2 approach to decomposing inequality. *Oxford Bulletin of Economics and Statistics, 45*, 307–312.
Blau, F. D., Ferber, M. A., & Winkler, A. (1998). *The economics of women, men, and work* (3rd ed.). Englewood Cliffs, NJ: Prentice-Hall.
Blau, F. D., & Kahn, L. M. (1997). Swimming upstream: Trends in the gender wage differential in the 1980s. *Journal of Labor Economics, 15*(1), 1–42.
Blinder, A. S. (1973). Wage discrimination: Reduced form and structural estimates. *Journal of Human Resources, 8*, 436–455.
Bound, J., & Johnson, G. (1992). Changes in the structure of wages in the 1980s: An evaluation of alternative explanations. *American Economic Review, 82*, 371–392.
Bourguignon, F., Fournier, M., & Gurgand, M. (1998). *Distribution, development and education: Taiwan, 1979–1992*. DELTA, processed.
Bourguignon, F., & Martinez, M. (1997). *Decomposition of the change in the distribution of primary family incomes: A microsimulation approach applied to France, 1979–1989*. DELTA, processed.
Burt, O. R., & Finley, R. M. (1968). Statistical analysis of identities in random variables. *American Journal of Agricultural Economics, 50*, 734–744.
Card, D. (1996). The effect of unions on the structure of wages: A longitudinal analysis. *Econometrica, 64*(4), 957–979.
Chiswick, B. R., & Mincer, J. (1972). Time-series changes in personal income inequality in the United States from 1939, with projections to 1985. *Journal of Political Economy, 80*(3) (May/June, Part II), S34–S66.
Contreras, D. (2000). *Explaining wage inequality in Chile: Does education really matter?* Department of Economics, Universidad de Chile, Chile.
Cowell, F. A., & Jenkins, S. P. (1995). How much inequality can we explain? A methodology and an application to the United States. *The Economic Journal, 105*(429), 421–430.
DiNardo, J., Fortin, N. M., & Lemieux, T. (1996). Labor market institutions and the distribution of wages, 1973–1992: A semiparametric approach. *Econometrica, 64*(5), 1001–1044.
Economic Report of the President 1999 (1999). Washington: U.S. Government Printing Office.
Fei, J. C. H., Ranis, G., & Kuo, S. W. Y. (1978). Growth and the family distribution of income by factor components. *Quarterly Journal of Economics, 92*(1), 17–53.
Fields, G. S., Leary, J., López Calva, L., & Pérez de Rada, E. (1998). *Education's crucial role in explaining labor income inequality in Urban Bolivia*. Cornell University, processed.
Fields, G. S., & Mitchell, J. (1999). Changing income inequality in Taiwan: A decomposition analysis. In: T. N. Srinivasan & G. Saxonhouse (Eds), *Development, Duality, and the International Regime: Essays in Honor of Gustav Ranis*. Ann Arbor: University of Michigan Press.
Fields, G. S., & Yoo, G. (2000). Falling labor income inequality in Korea's economic growth: Patterns and underlying causes. *Review of Income and Wealth, 46*(2), 139–159.
Forster, M. F., & Pellizzari, M. (2000). *Trends and driving factors in income distribution and poverty in the OECD area*. OECD Labour Market and Social Policy Occasional Paper No. 42.
Foster, J. E., & Ok, E. A. (1999). Lorenz dominance and the variance of logarithms. *Econometrica, 67*(4), 901–907.
Freeman, R. (1980). Union wage practices and the dispersion of wages. *Industrial and Labor Relations Review, 36*(1), 3–21.

Freeman, R. (1993). How much has de-unionization contributed to the rise in male earnings inequality? In: S. Danziger & P. Gottschalk (Eds), *Uneven Tides: Rising Inequality in America*. New York: Russell Sage Foundation.

Gindling, T. H., & Trejos, J. D. (2001). *Cambios en la desigualdad del ingreso laboral en Costa Rica, 1976–1999: Medidas y causas*. Universidad de Costa Rica, Costa Rica.

Goldberger, A. (1964). *Econometric theory*. New York: Wiley.

Goldberger, A. (1970). On the statistical analysis of identities: Comment. *American Journal of Agricultural Economics, 52*(1), 154–155.

Heltberg, R. (2001). Analyzing inequality using income regressions: Vietnam, 1992–1997. Unpublished Working Paper, University of Copenhagen, Denmark.

Juhn, C., Murphy, K. M., & Pierce, B. (1991). Accounting for the slowdown in black-white wage convergence. In: M. Kosters (Ed.), *Workers and Their Wages*. Washington, DC: American Enterprise Institute Press.

Juhn, C., Murphy, K. M., & Pierce, B. (1993). Wage inequality and the rise in returns to skill. *Journal of Political Economy, 101*(3), 410–442.

Katz, L. F., & Autor, D. H. (1999). Changes in the wage structure and earnings inequality. In: O. Ashenfelter & D. Card (Eds), *Handbook of Labor Economics*. Amsterdam: North-Holland.

Katz, L. F., & Murphy, K. M. (1992). Changes in relative wages, 1963–1987: Supply and demand factors. *Quarterly Journal of Economics, 107*(1), 35–78.

Lam, D. (1999). *Generating extreme inequality: Schooling, earnings, and intergenerational transmission of human capital in South Africa and Brazil*. University of Michigan, processed.

Lam, D., & Levison, D. (1991). Declining inequality in schooling in Brazil and its effects on inequality in earnings. *Journal of Development Economics, 37*, 199–225.

Layard, R., & Zabalza, A. (1979). Family income distribution: Explanation and policy evaluation. *Journal of Political Economy, 87*(5), S133–S161.

Levy, F. (1999). *The new dollars and dreams*. New York: Russell Sage Foundation.

Mincer, J. (1958). Investment in human capital and personal income distribution. *Journal of Political Economy, 66*, 281–302.

Mincer, J. (1970). The distribution of labor incomes: A survey with special reference to the human capital approach. *Journal of Economic Literature, 8*(1), 1–26.

Mincer, J. (1974). *Schooling, experience, and earnings*. New York: National Bureau of Economic Research.

Mincer, J. (1997). Changes in wage inequality, 1970–1990. In: S. W. Polachek (Ed.), *Research in Labor Economics* (Vol. 16). Greenwich, CT: JAI Press.

Moffitt, R. A., & Gottschalk, P. (1995). *Trends in the autocovariance structure of earnings in the U.S.: 1969–1987*. Brown University and Boston College.

Mood, A. M., Graybill, F. A., & Boes, D. C. (1974). *Introduction to the theory of statistics* (3rd ed.). New York: McGraw-Hill.

Morduch, J., & Sicular, T. (1998). Rethinking inequality decomposition, with evidence from rural China. Harvard Institute for International Development Working Paper No. 636.

Murphy, K. M., & Welch, F. (1992). The structure of wages. *Quarterly Journal of Economics, 107*(1), 285–326.

Oaxaca, R. L. (1973). Male-female wage differentials in urban labor markets. *International Economic Review, 14*(3), 693–709.

Oaxaca, R. L., & Ransom, M. R. (1994). On discrimination and the decomposition of wage differentials. *Journal of Econometrics, 61*(1), 5–21.

Plotnick, R. D. (1982). Trends in male earnings inequality. *Southern Economic Journal, 48*(3), 724–732.
Pyatt, G., Chen, C., & Fei, J. (1980). The distribution of income by factor components. *Quarterly Journal of Economics, 95*(3), 451–473.
Ravallion, M., & Chen, S. (1999). When economic reform is faster than statistical reform: Measuring and explaining income inequality in rural China. *Oxford Bulletin of Economics and Statistics, 61*(1), 33–56.
Redmund, G., & Kattuman, P. (2001). *Employment polarisation and inequality in the U.K. and Hungary.* University of New South Wales and Cambridge University, U.K.
Robbins, D., & Gindling, T. H. (1999). Trade liberalization and the relative wages for more-skilled workers in Costa Rica. *Review of Development Economics, 3*(2), 140–154.
Sánchez-Torres, F., & Nuñez, J. N. (1998). Descomposición de la desigualdad del ingreso laboral urbano: 1976–1997. In: F. Sánchez-Torres (Ed.), *La Distribución del Ingreso en Colombia.* Bogotá: Departamento Nacional de Planeación.
Sen, A. (1973). *On economic inequality.* Oxford: Oxford University Press.
Shorrocks, A. F. (1982). Inequality decomposition by factor components. *Econometrica, 50*(1), 193–211.
Shorrocks, A. F. (1999). *Decomposition procedures for distributional analysis: A unified framework based on the shapely value.* University of Essex, processed.
Welch, F. (1999). In defense of inequality. *American Economic Review, 89*(2), 1–17.
Yun, M. (2002). *Earnings inequality in USA, 1961–1999: Comparing inequality using earnings equations.* University of Western Ontario, processed.

APPENDIX

Conditions on the Decomposition

In the text, Shorrocks's theorem makes reference to six conditions on the decomposition itself. Let Y^{ik} denote the income of the i'th income recipient from factor k, $Y^k = (Y^{i1}, \ldots, Y^{iK})$ be the vector of incomes from the k'th factor, $Y^i = \sum_k Y^{ik}$ be the i'th recipient's total income, N be the total number of income recipients, and K be the total number of factor income components. Let $I(Y)$ be an inequality measure defined on the space of total incomes $Y = (Y^1, Y^2, \ldots, Y^N)$ and let $S_k = S_k(Y^1, \ldots, Y^K; K)$ be the amount of inequality accounted for by each of the K components. Using this notation, Shorrocks's six conditions may be expressed thus:

Condition 1 (Number of Components). The inequality measure $I(Y)$ is to be divided into K components, one for each income factor, denoted $S_k(Y^1, \ldots, Y^K; K)$.

Condition 2. (a) (Continuity). Each S_k is continuous in Y^k. (b) (Symmetric Treatment of Factors). If $\pi_1, \ldots, \pi_k$ is any permutation of $1, \ldots, K$, $S_k(Y^1, \ldots, Y^K; K) = S_{\pi k}(Y^{\pi 1}, \ldots, Y^{\pi k}; K)$.

Condition 3 (Independence of the Level of Disaggregation). The amount of inequality accounted for by any one factor S_k does not depend on how the other factors are grouped.

Condition 4 (Consistent Decomposition). The contributions S_k sum to the overall amount of inequality, viz., $\sum_k S_k(Y^1, \ldots, Y^K; K) = I(Y)$.

Condition 5. (a) (Population Symmetry) If P is any $n \times n$ permutation matrix, $S(Y^k P, YP) = S(Y^k, Y)$; (b) (Normalization for Equal Factor Distribution) If all income recipients have the same value for the k'th factor, then the share of inequality accounted for by that factor $S(m_k e, Y) = 0$ for all μ_k.

Condition 6 (Two Factor Symmetry). Suppose the distribution of factor 2 incomes Y^2 is simply a permutation of that for factor 1, Y^1. Then if those were the only two sources of income, Y^1 and Y^2 should receive the same value in the decomposition. Thus, for all permutation matrices P, $S(Y^1, Y^1 + Y^1 P) = S(Y^1 P, Y^1 + Y^1 P)$.

These six conditions generate the factor inequality weights s_k given in the text by

$$s_k = \frac{\text{cov}(Y_k, Y)}{\sigma^2(Y)} \tag{10a}$$

such that

$$\sum_k s_k = 1. \tag{10b}$$

Table A1. United States: Earnings Equation Results, 1979 and 1999.

Variable Group	Independent Variable	1979	1999
Gender	Male	0.432	0.316
		(98.96)	(55.9)
Race	White	0.098	0.071
		(15.94)	(10.13)
Experience	Potential experience	0.032	0.039
		(60.84)	(47.14)
	Potential experience squared	−0.001	−0.001
		(−44.89)	(−32.75)
Schooling	High school grad	0.054	0.088
		(60.23)	(70.65)
Occupation (Executive, prof, and technical omitted)	Sales & admin support	−0.164	−0.236
		(−28.14)	(−31.92)
	All other	−0.222	−0.353
		(−39.46)	(−47.72)
Industry (Public administration, professional & related services omitted)	All other services, finance, trade, transport	0.046	0.079
		(8.82)	(11.80)
	Manufacturing, construction, mining, agriculture	0.157	0.185
		(29.19)	(24.70)
Region (Northeast omitted)	North Central	0.043	−0.055
		(7.83)	(−6.78)
	South	−0.077	−0.108
		(−13.44)	(−13.37)
	West	0.021	−0.074
		(3.81)	(−9.65)
Constant		5.080	4.678
		(304.02)	(199.50)
Adjusted R^2		0.4200	0.3842
F-statistic		2538.46	1850.63
N		42,045	35,579

Notes: Dependent Variable: Logarithm of Labor Earnings. Schooling Measured in Categories (t-statistics in parentheses).

Table A2. United States: The Contribution of Each Explanatory Factor to Earnings Inequality and to the Change in Inequality, 1979–1999 (Schooling Measured in Years).

	Factor Inequality Weight of that Factor in that Year		Contribution of that Factor to the Change in Inequality as Measured by:	
	$s_j(\ln Y)$, 1979	$s_j(\ln Y)$, 1999	$\pi_j(\text{Gini})$, 1979–1999	$\pi_j(\text{log-variance})$, 1979–1999
	(1)	(2)	(3)	(4)
Gender	0.180	0.057	−0.55	−0.22
Race	0.008	0.004	−0.02	−0.01
Experience	0.070	0.064	0.03	0.05
Schooling in categories	0.089	0.161	0.52	0.32
Occupation	0.051	0.094	0.30	0.19
Industry	0.012	0.000	−0.06	−0.03
Region	0.010	0.005	−0.02	0.00
Residual	0.580	0.616	0.79	0.70

Notes: For definition of $s_j(\ln Y)$, see Eq. (8a). For definition of $\pi_j(\cdot)$, see Eq. (17b).

THE RELATIONSHIP BETWEEN THE ECONOMY AND THE WELFARE CASELOAD: A DYNAMIC APPROACH

Steven J. Haider, Jacob Alex Klerman and Elizabeth Roth

ABSTRACT

Nationally, the welfare caseload declined by more than 50% between 1994 and 2000. Considerable research has been devoted to understanding what caused this decline. Much of the literature examining these changes has modeled the total caseload (the stock) directly. Klerman and Haider (forthcoming) model the underlying flows and show analytically and empirically that previous methods are likely to be biased because they ignore important dynamics. However, due to their focus on the bias of the stock models, they present only limited results concerning the robustness of their findings and utilize only a single measure of economic conditions, the unemployment rate. This paper examines the robustness of the basic stock-flow model developed in Klerman and Haider (forthcoming), considering both richer dynamic specifications and richer measures of economic condition. We find that more complex dynamic specifications do not change the substantive conclusions, but richer measures of the economy do. While a model that only includes the unemployment rate attributes about half of the California caseload decline between 1995 and 1998 to the economy, models that incorporate richer measures of the economy attribute more than 90% of the decline to the economy.

1. INTRODUCTION

Nationally, the welfare caseload declined by more than 50% between 1994 and 2000. The causes of this large decline are the subject of considerable debate. The decline occurred simultaneously with a robust economic expansion, a series of major welfare reforms, and major changes in several other public policies such as the federal Earned Income Tax Credit (EITC) and the minimum wage. Understanding the separate roles of each of these possible causes is important for evaluating the effectiveness of welfare reform and planning for future budgetary outlays.

Many studies have considered why the caseload declined. Most of the studies model the change in the caseload directly, reaching widely varying conclusions (e.g. CEA, 1997, 1999; Levine & Whitmore, 1998; Ziliak et al., 2000). Klerman and Haider (forthcoming) argue that much of the variation in conclusions across these studies can be explained with an explicit model of the underlying caseload dynamics. Specifically, they develop a model that views today's caseload as the result of previous flows on and off of welfare. They demonstrate that the conventional methods that model the caseload stock are likely to be biased. Furthermore, they develop an alternative strategy based on estimating the flow relationships and then simulated the changes on the caseload level (the "stock"). They implement this stock-flow approach on California data and find that approximately half of California's caseload decline from its peak in 1995 to the end of their data in 1998 can be attributed to the improving economy. Because that paper focused on the biases associated with modeling the stocks directly, they only present limited results on the robustness of their findings.

In this paper, we examine in greater detail the specification of a stock-flow model and the measurement of economic conditions. First, we examine the sensitivity of the results to richer specifications of the underlying dynamics, including allowing the process of re-entry to differ from initial entry and allowing the effect of the economy to vary with duration. Second, much of the previous literature assessing the change in the caseload uses only the unemployment rate to measure economic conditions. Two recent studies suggest that a richer set of measures of the economy substantially improves the fit of the model and perhaps increases the share of observed changes due to the economy (see Bartik & Eberts, 1999; Hoynes, 2000). We also estimate dynamic models with additional measures of the economy.

Our results suggest two main conclusions. First, we demonstrate that the simple dynamic structure estimated in Klerman and Haider (forthcoming) is sufficient to capture empirically the underlying dynamic process of how the economy affects the welfare caseload. Second, including measures of earnings in the retail trade sector substantially increases the estimated role for the economy in explaining the caseload decline: our preferred model suggests that approximately 90% of the caseload decline in California is due to the improving economy, broadly defined. We interpret this finding to imply that the conventional unemployment rate is an imperfect proxy for economic conditions for the welfare population. Taken together, these findings provide further support for the conclusion that conventional stock models underestimate the role of the improving economy for the caseload decline. It is worth noting, however, that welfare reform occurred later and was less drastic in California than in most other states. Thus, because the role of policy might have been larger in other states, it is possible that the role of the economy would be smaller if a similar approach could be applied.

The balance of this paper is organized as follows. We begin, in Section 2, with a brief review of the literature. Section 3 discusses our data. Section 4 describes the baseline model and findings. Section 5 explores the sensitivity of these findings to altering the dynamic structure of the model. Section 6 considers the sensitivity of the model to using additional measures of economic conditions. We conclude in Section 7 with a summary and discussion of the findings.

2. A REVIEW OF THE LITERATURE

Most previous studies have directly modeled the aggregate welfare caseload to assess its various determinants. In particular, previous studies have estimated models of the form,

$$\ln n_{jt} = \alpha + \beta Y_{jt} + \lambda W_{jt} + \pi X_{jt} + \gamma_t + \delta_j + \phi_j t + \varepsilon_{jt} \quad (1)$$

where, for state j and year t, n_{jt} is the per capita welfare caseload, Y_{jt} is the unemployment rate, W_{jt} is measures of the welfare policy, and X_{jt} is a vector of other regressors. Some papers have augmented this model to include lagged values of the unemployment rate, lagged values of the dependent variable, and other control variables (see CEA, 1997, 1999; Figlio & Ziliak, 1999; Levine & Whitmore, 1998; Ziliak et al., 2000).[1]

These studies have come to widely varying conclusions. CEA (1997) attributes 44% of the decline in the caseload from 1993 to 1996 to economic conditions and 31% of the decline to welfare waivers. Ziliak et al. (2000), examining the same question, attributes nearly two-thirds of the decline to economic conditions and nothing to welfare waivers. Figlio and Ziliak (1999) attempt to reconcile these results and conclude that the primary reason for different results rests with differences in modeling the "dynamics," where dynamics refers to whether lagged dependent variables are included and whether the models are estimated in levels or differences. CEA (1999) updates the CEA (1997) and also notes that their results are highly sensitive; in particular, CEA (1999) reports that the estimated role of the economy is reduced by one half when the regression model includes two annual lags of the unemployment rate versus a regression model with only one annual lag of the unemployment rate.

This literature has developed nearly independently of a body of research that directly examines flows onto and off of welfare (e.g. Bane & Ellwood, 1986; Hoynes, 2000; Hutchens, 1981).[2] Those studies provide strong empirical evidence that welfare receipt in a particular period is dependent on previous welfare receipt and length of welfare receipt, even conditional on covariates.

Klerman and Haider (forthcoming) reconsider the caseload literature by specifying a model that is directly based on the underlying flows onto and off of welfare and then simulating the impact on the caseload levels. They refer to this model as a stock-flow model. Relying on such a model, they demonstrate analytically that the conventional models are likely to be misspecified whenever welfare receipt in a particular period depends on welfare receipt in previous periods. They then demonstrate that this misspecification can explain several empirical anomalies in the earlier national caseload literature.

Klerman and Haider (forthcoming) also report new estimates of the role of the economy that are based directly on this stock-flow model. The model is a direct application of Markov chain models that have been used in many other contexts (e.g. Heckman & Walker, 1990; Moffitt & Rendall, 1995). To implement the model, they first estimate the relationship between the flows onto and off of welfare and the unemployment rate. Given the parameter estimates and the initial distribution of the population on and off aid, they then simulate the implied path of the caseload for an arbitrary path of the explanatory variables. Klerman and Haider (forthcoming) conclude that about half of the California caseload decline can be attributed to changing economic conditions, as measured by the unemployment rate.

3. THE DATA

Our primary data set is based on micro-level, administrative data from the California Medi-Cal Eligibility Determination System (MEDS). We also rely on various publicly available data sets for population characteristics and measures of economic conditions.

3.1. The Medi-Cal Eligibility Data System (MEDS)

Directly estimating the stock-flow model requires panel data on individuals, with sufficiently varying explanatory variables (e.g. economic conditions), for a sufficiently long time period, and for a sufficiently large sample. Although national data would be preferable, suitable data unfortunately do not appear to exist. There is no individual-level administrative data at the national level and the available panel surveys have samples too small to allow estimation of the transitions that are the focus of this study (e.g. the Panel Study of Income Dynamics or the Survey of Income and Program Participation).[3]

California is a large state with more than 20% of the U.S. welfare caseload and more than 10% of the U.S. population. Thus, caseload trends in California comprise a significant share of the caseload trends in the U.S. Moreover, there is significant diversity in economic conditions across California's counties. This diversity allows us to use an identification strategy that is similar to that used in the national literature. Whereas the national literature relies on cross-state variation (controlling for time fixed effects) to identify the role of the economy, we rely on cross-county variation (controlling for time fixed effects) to identify the role of the economy.

Using California administrative data has one major disadvantage: we do not have a plausible identification strategy to separate policy effects from more general statewide time effects.[4] Thus, while we can directly estimate the effect of the economy, we cannot directly estimate the effect of welfare reform or other statewide (or national) policy changes. We show below, however, that our methods substantially increase the estimated effect of the economy, and thus decrease the possible effect of welfare reform.

The MEDS provides a monthly roster of all Medi-Cal (Medicaid in California) participants in California from January 1987 to December 1998. The source of eligibility for Medi-Cal is also indicated, and because all welfare participants are eligible for Medi-Cal, the MEDS effectively serves as a roster of all welfare recipients in California.[5] Individual identifiers make it possible to follow individuals over time. In addition, the MEDS contains basic information about age, gender, type of aid, and race for each person on welfare. Because the MEDS data are recorded as part of an ongoing administrative process, biases associated with self-reports are absent.

We construct an analysis file by drawing a stratified random sample of approximately 3% of the individuals on the full MEDS file. Consistent with our focus on the effect of county level variation in the economy, the stratified sample is chosen to yield approximately equal number of observations in each of California's counties.[6] This scheme results in an analysis file that contains a sample of 282,381 people who received cash assistance, comprising 487,641 spells and 10,966,420 person-months, during the years 1989 to 1998 (our eventual sample period). We consider a person as the unit of analysis rather than a case because persons are well-defined longitudinally, even if case membership changes.

We modify this basic extract along two dimensions to obtain our analysis file. First, to avoid some problems related to small samples, we aggregate California's five smallest counties into a single "county" for analysis purposes. The five smallest counties are Alpine, Colusa, Modoc, Mono, and Sierra; combined, their welfare population represents well under 1% of the state's welfare population. We perform all of our analyses on these 53 counties and one county group; hereafter, we will simply refer to our analysis considering 54 counties. Second, previous research indicates that there is considerable "churning" on and off welfare in the MEDS data. This churning is likely due to underlying administrative procedures rather than "real" entrances and exits (see Hoynes, 2000). To mitigate such concerns, we recode one-month spells on and off of aid as not having occurred, following Hoynes (2000).

3.2. Other Data Sources

We also use data from several other sources. First, we present tabulations from California's official caseload filings with the California Department of Social Services, the so-called CA237 data. These data are used to verify the quality of the caseload information available in the MEDS. The CA237 data are described in detail in Haider et al. (1999).

We use population estimates for each county in California from the Demographic Research Unit of the California Department of Finance.[7] These data are designated as the single official source of demographic data for State planning and budgeting. The data are only available annually, so we use simple linear interpolation to obtain monthly county data. Throughout, we consider the population at risk of going on aid to be all individuals aged 0 to 49.[8]

Our models are designed to explore the effects of the aggregate state of the economy on the aggregate welfare caseload. As one measure of the aggregate state of the economy, we use county-level unemployment estimates produced by the U.S. Department of Labor as part of their Local Area Unemployment Statistics program. These estimates are produced through a cooperative effort by federal and state agencies and are based on the Current Population Survey data, Current Employment Statistics data, and state unemployment insurance data.

To derive employment rates, we use the civilian employment estimates produced by the California Employment Development Department. We calculate the employment rates by dividing by the county population aged 15–64. The underlying data for these estimates come from the unemployment insurance filings (the so-called ES202 data).

Finally, we use county-level retail trade earnings data prepared by the U.S. Department of Commerce, Bureau of Economic Analysis and archived at University of Virginia Geospatial and Statistical Data Center.[9] We convert all earnings measures to January 1998 dollars using BLS's consumer price index for urban consumers. The data are also only available by year, so we use simple linear interpolation to obtain monthly county data.[10]

3.3. Descriptive Results

Figure 1 plots the aggregate monthly caseload estimated from our MEDS-based analysis file, the official state caseload counts (based on county-level CA237 reports), and the unemployment rate. The figure shows that the MEDS tracks the official CA237 caseload very well.

Figure 1 also demonstrates that the paths of the caseload and the unemployment rate suggest a role for the economy in explaining the caseload decline. In

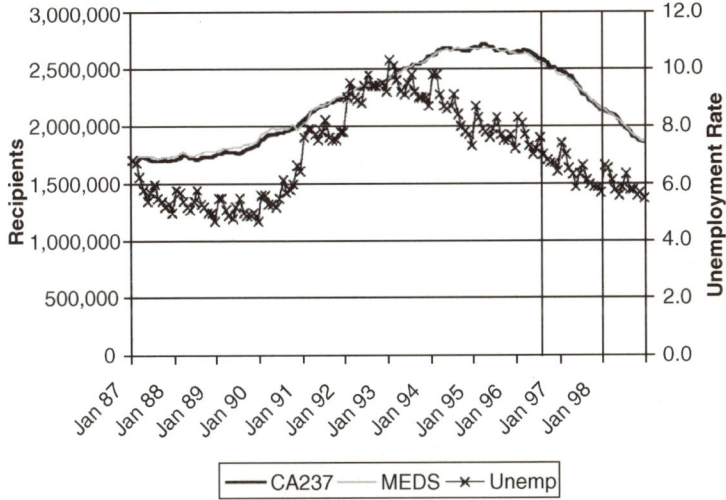

Fig. 1
Welfare Recipients and Unemployment Rate in California. *Note:* Authors' computations from the MEDS, CA237, and the California unemployment rate. The CA237 is the official California welfare caseload. The MEDS represents an estimate of the caseload based on the 3% sample we analyze in this paper. The first vertical line represents in the passage of the federal welfare reform legislation (PRWORA, August 1996) and the second vertical line represents the implementation of the California welfare reform (CalWORKs, January 1998).

Table 1. Short Term Spell Durations, 1989–1997.

Spell Start Period	Spells	Average Monthly Entry Rate	Average Monthly Continuation Rate for Spells that Lasted			
			2–5 Months	6–11 Months	12–17 Months	18 + Months
1/89–12/90	70,721	0.0032	0.938	0.943	0.964	0.979
1/91–12/92	79,620	0.0037	0.942	0.950	0.968	0.982
1/93–12/94	80,863	0.0037	0.946	0.951	0.968	0.982
1/95–12/96	72,234	0.0031	0.942	0.949	0.962	0.977
1/97–12/97	29,862	0.0024	0.933	0.942	X	X

Note: An "X" indicates that the probability could not be calculated because of right-censoring.
Source: Authors' tabulations from the MEDS.

particular, the caseload increased during the early 1990s and then declined during the late 1990s, similar to the trend for the United States as a whole. At the peak of the welfare caseload in March 1995, there were approximately 2.7 million people receiving AFDC/TANF in California. In the last month of our sample period, December 1998, there are only 1.9 million people on aid, representing a decline from the peak of 31%. Because the population increased during the same time frame, the per capita caseload declined slightly more, about 33%. Turning to the unemployment rate, the figure shows that the unemployment rate increased then decreased, following a similar pattern to that of the caseload. In particular, the unemployment rate declined from 10% at its peak to 6% at the end of our sample period.

The basis of the stock-flow model is that entry onto and exit from welfare vary with economic conditions. Table 1 presents the average monthly entry rate and the average monthly continuation rate (i.e. one minus the exit rate) for two-year intervals between 1989 and 1997. These tabulations reveal several important characteristics of the data. First, the levels of the entry and continuation rates in Table 1 are quite different, suggesting that dynamics could be important. The average monthly entry rate for those who were not on welfare in 1989–1990 was 0.0032 and average monthly continuation rate for those who were on welfare for two to five months was 0.938. Second, both the entry and continuation rates are counter-cyclical. The entry rate increased during the recession of the early 1990s (from 0.0032 to 0.0037) and then declined during the recovery (back to 0.0024). Similarly, for all durations, the continuation rate increased then decreased. Both the entry and continuation rate patterns would cause the aggregate caseload size to vary counter-cyclically with economic conditions. Finally, the continuation rate is higher for individuals who have been on aid longer (i.e. there is duration dependence).

4. AN EMPIRICALLY TRACTABLE STOCK-FLOW MODEL

In this section, we first describe the basic stock-flow model that was examined in Klerman and Haider (forthcoming), which will be denoted as our baseline model. Second, we develop the methods for estimating the underlying flow relationships. Third, we present the results for the baseline model.

4.1. The Baseline Stock-Flow Model

The stock-flow representation is a straightforward application of a Markov Chain process. Specifically, consider a standard Markov Chain,

$$\underset{(Q \times 1)}{S_t} = M\left(\underset{(Q \times Q)}{X_t}, \theta\right) \underset{(Q \times 1)}{S_{t-1}}, \tag{2}$$

where S_t is a vector that contains the number of individuals in each of Q states, M is the transition matrix between the states (that depends on regressors X_t and a parameter vector θ), and t indexes time. A simple specification would allow for only two states, where an individual is either on welfare or off welfare. A richer specification, consistent with the finding of duration dependence, would disaggregate the on-welfare state by length of the current spell. The effect of potential explanatory variables X_t is captured in the transition matrix M.

More specifically, let $e(Y_t)$ denote the probability that an individual enters aid (unconditional on duration) and $c^k(Y_t)$ denote the probability that a person who has been on aid for k periods remains on aid, with both flow rates being a function of economic conditions, Y_t. Then, aid receipt can be represented with the equation,

$$\begin{bmatrix} S_{r,1,t} \\ S_{r,2,t} \\ S_{r,3,t} \\ \vdots \\ S_{r,\bar{k}-1,t} \\ S_{r,\bar{k},t} \\ S_{n,t} \end{bmatrix} = \begin{bmatrix} 0 & 0 & \cdots & 0 & 0 & e(Y_t) \\ c^1(Y_t) & 0 & \cdots & 0 & 0 & 0 \\ 0 & c^2(Y_t) & \cdots & 0 & 0 & 0 \\ \vdots & \vdots & \ddots & \vdots & \vdots & \vdots \\ 0 & 0 & \cdots & 0 & 0 & 0 \\ 0 & 0 & \cdots & c^{\bar{k}-1}(Y_t) & c^{\bar{k}}(Y_t) & 0 \\ 1-c^1(Y_t) & 1-c^2(Y_t) & \cdots & 1-c^{\bar{k}-1}(Y_t) & 1-c^{\bar{k}}(Y_t) & 1-e(Y_t) \end{bmatrix} \begin{bmatrix} S_{r,1,t-1} \\ S_{r,2,t-1} \\ S_{r,3,t-1} \\ \vdots \\ S_{r,\bar{k}-1,t-1} \\ S_{r,\bar{k},t-1} \\ S_{n,t-1} \end{bmatrix}, \tag{3}$$

where S_{rkt} is the number of individuals who are receiving aid for the kth consecutive period at time t and S_{nt} is the number of individuals not on aid. To handle an initial conditions problem, this formulation assumes that the continuation rate varies through period $\bar{k}$ and is constant thereafter; we discuss this assumption in further detail below.

This equation can be used to simulate the impact of economic conditions on the caseload stock implied by the underlying flow relationships. We first estimate models for the flows (i.e. the entry rate and the continuation rate) to obtain estimates of the parameter vector θ. Then, for any arbitrary specification for economic conditions $\tilde{Y}_t$, we calculate the implied transition matrix M and simulate the caseload for the following period. Thus, given an initial stock S_t and any arbitrary path for economic conditions, $\{\tilde{Y}_{t+h}\}_{h=1}^{H}$, we can simulate the future stock in period $t + h$ as,

$$S_{t+h} = \left(\prod_{p=1}^{h} M[\tilde{Y}_{t+p}, \theta]\right) S_t. \qquad (4)$$

To explore the effect of the economy on the welfare caseload, we simulate the model for the observed path of the economy and for an explicitly specified counterfactual path. The difference between the two paths of the total caseload is the implied effect of the economy.

We specify caseload simulations that are intended to provide an answer to the question that is usually posed in the literature: "How much of the caseload decline (from its peak) is due to economic conditions?" To answer this question, we compare the results from a simulation based on the actual path of the economy and other factors (proxied for by the time fixed effects) to the results from a simulation where we instead specify that the unemployment rate path follows its actual path until its peak in January 1993 and then remains constant. The difference between the two paths is our estimate of the caseload decline that can be attributed to the improvement in the economy.

4.2. Specifying the Flow Relationships

The basis for the simulation model is the empirical relationship between the flows (the entry and continuation rates) and the economic conditions. Following much of the literature, we estimate the entry rate with a logit specification (e.g. Bane & Ellwood, 1986; Blank & Ruggles, 1996; Hoynes, 2000). For the continuation rate, we employ a linear probability model for computational ease, given that our micro data set includes approximately 10 million person-months. Both empirical models are traditional hazard models that examine the probability that someone changes states (either on to or off of welfare) conditional on being at risk of changing states.

Because the MEDS data include information only for those on welfare, we estimate our model for the entry rate's dependence on the unemployment rate using a grouped-data logit model (Maddala, 1983). We calculate the entry rate for county j in month t, e_{jt}, as the ratio of the number of entrants observed in the MEDS relative to the number of people at risk of going on aid (i.e. the total population less those already on welfare). We then estimate a grouped-data logit model at the county-month level that includes the unemployment rate and fixed effects for time and county,

$$\ln\frac{e_{jt}}{1-e_{jt}} = \alpha_e + \beta_e Y_{jt} + \gamma_t + \delta_j + \varepsilon_{jt}. \tag{5}$$

Rather than including a full set of dummy variables for each calendar month, we include a discontinuous piecewise linear annual spline to capture general time trends. In other words, we include year dummy variables and the appropriate interactions to allow for different linear time trends by year, and we do not restrict the linear trends to be continuous between years (i.e. between December of one year and January of the next year). This discontinuity is allowed to more closely mimic the annual time effects that are conventionally used in the national literature. We also include calendar month dummies (i.e. a dummy for January, February, etc.) to capture seasonal variation.

We estimate the continuation rate at duration k, $c^k(Y_t)$, using individual-level data. The continuation rate is simply one minus the conventional hazard rate for exiting welfare, and thus the estimation problems are equivalent. Let C_{ijt} be an indicator variable equal to one when individual i in county j continues on aid in month t. Consider the model,

$$\Pr[C_{ijt}=1|k] = f(\alpha_c + \beta_c Y_{jt} + \gamma_t + \delta_j + g_c(k_{ijt})), \tag{6}$$

where k_{ijt} is a specification for duration and $g_c(k_{ijt})$ is a flexible specification for the dependence of the continuation probability on k_{ijt}. Again, we choose f to be a linear function due to the size of our data set. Finally, we modify the basic specification by adopting the same specification for the time effects as was adopted for the entry rate model (i.e. a discontinuous piece-wise annual spline and calendar month dummies).

One complication is that we only have data on current welfare receipt status, so we do not know the length of welfare receipt for individuals who are on aid in the first month of our data. To address this form of left censoring, we assume that the probability of continuation becomes constant after $\bar{k}$ periods on aid and then discard the first $\bar{k}$ periods of the data. Therefore, any person continuously on aid from the start of our data to period $\bar{k}+1$ is in the constant part of the hazard, making the left censoring irrelevant. For everyone else, we

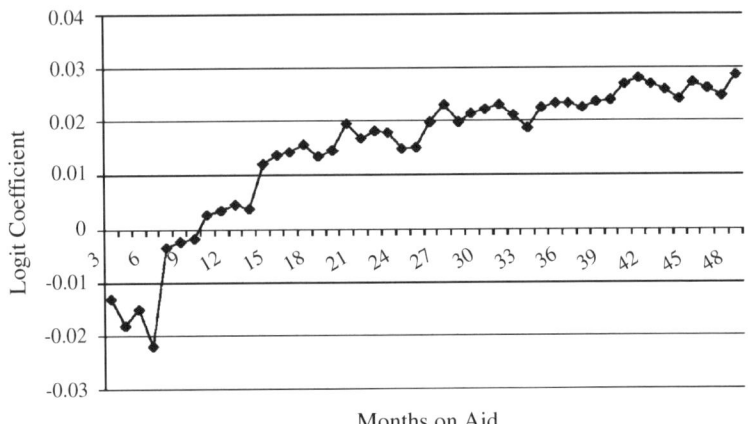

Fig. 2

The Variation in Continuation by Duration on Aid. *Note:* Authors' computations from the MEDS. This figure graphs the logit coefficients for 47 dummy variables for time on aid from the continuation regression; $\bar{k}$ is set to 48. The model contains county fixed effects and a flexible spline in time. See the text for further details. Standard errors are in parentheses.

know the exact duration. The form of the transition matrix in Eq. (3) includes this assumption.

To motivate our choice for the functional form of $g_c(k_{ijt})$, we present estimates of Eq. (6) in which we include twelve lags of the unemployment rate, set $\bar{k} = 48$, and specify $g_c(k_{ijt})$ to be 48 monthly dummies. We graph the regression coefficients of these monthly dummies in Fig. 2. It is clear that there is a systematic relationship between the probability of continuing on welfare and duration on welfare. After an initial decline in the probability of continuing, the probability increases relatively smoothly. Given these results, we specify that $g_c(k_{ijt})$ includes dummy variables for the first six months to capture the initial decline and then a quartic in k_{ijt} to capture the subsequent increase. We also initially set $\bar{k}$ to be 24 months and drop the first 24 months of data.

4.3. Baseline Results

Table 2 presents the baseline estimates of the effect of economic conditions on entry and continuation (i.e. one minus exit). Our baseline specification sets $\bar{k} = 24$ and includes the current unemployment rate and no lags (columns 1 and 5).

As expected, the entry rate and the continuation rate are counter-cyclical. A higher unemployment rate causes more people to enter welfare and fewer to leave.

Table 2. Probability of Entry and Continuation Regressions.

Regressors	Probability of Entry (Grouped Logit)				Probability of Continuation (OLS: coeffs & s.e. × 100)			
	1	2	3	4	5	6	7	8
Unemp. Rate	0.034	0.029	0.035	0.022	0.111	0.126	0.120	0.111
	(0.003)	(0.006)	(0.006)	(0.007)	(0.005)	(0.009)	(0.010)	(0.011)
UR-1st lag		0.019	0.024	0.030		−0.024	−0.040	−0.046
		(0.008)	(0.008)	(0.009)		(0.013)	(0.013)	(0.014)
UR-2nd lag		−0.019	−0.038	−0.038		0.007	0.074	0.089
		(0.006)	(0.009)	(0.009)		(0.009)	(0.014)	(0.014)
UR-3rd lag			0.010	0.013			−0.100	−0.095
			(0.009)	(0.009)			(0.014)	(0.014)
UR-4th lag			0.005	0.016			0.075	0.067
			(0.008)	(0.009)			(0.013)	(0.013)
UR-5th lag			0.006	−0.013			−0.036	−0.018
			(0.006)	(0.009)			(0.009)	(0.014)
UR-6th lag				0.014				−0.026
				(0.009)				(0.014)
UR-7th lag				0.001				−0.029
				(0.009)				(0.014)
UR-8th lag				−0.007				0.063
				(0.009)				(0.014)
UR-9th lag				0.008				−0.012
				(0.008)				(0.014)
UR-10th lag				0.012				−0.005
				(0.008)				(0.013)
UR-11th lag				0.003				0.0009
				(0.007)				(0.0101)
Sum of coeffs.	0.034	0.029	0.042	0.061	0.111	0.109	0.092	0.100
R-squared	0.8220	0.8223	0.8228	0.8238	0.0096	0.0096	0.0096	0.0096
Observations	6,480	6,480	6,480	6,480	9,080,952	9,070,952	9,070,952	9,070,952

Note: We use monthly data for the period January 1989 to December 1998 for each set of models, with the lags referring to monthly lags; $\bar{k}$ is set to 24 for the continuation models. All models contain county fixed effects and a flexible spline in time. See the text for further details. Standard errors are in parentheses.

Source: Authors' computations from the MEDS.

The contemporaneous effects are clearly statistically significant (*t*-statistics greater than 4). Furthermore, unlike the common finding for models of the stocks (i.e. the aggregate caseload), there is little evidence of dependence of the transitions on lagged measures of the unemployment rate (models 2 and 6). For the entry rate models, the first and second lags offset each other (the first is positive, the second negative). For the continuation rate, one of the lags is negative (the "wrong sign") and they are both much smaller than the contemporaneous effect (less than a fifth).

We compute the implied effect of the economy on the stock by simulation. Figure 3 presents the results graphically. The heavy line is the path of the actual per capita caseload and the medium line is the path of the simulated caseload based on the actual values of the unemployment rate. As expected, the lines are quite close. The light line gives the path of the caseload implied by the model

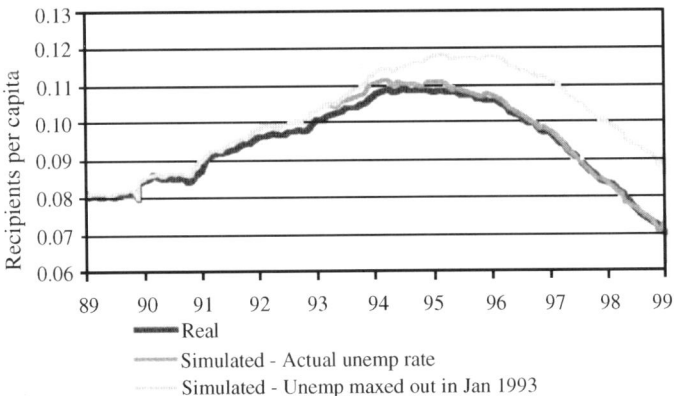

Fig. 3

The Simulated Welfare Caseload in California – Holding the Unemployment Rate Constant in January 1993. *Note:* Authors' computations from the MEDS. The three lines correspond to the real number of recipients per capita over time, and simulations based on the actual unemployment rate (mean of 0–2 lags in the unemployment rate) and based on holding the unemployment rate held constant after January 1993 (mean of 0–2 lags in the unemployment rate).

if the unemployment rate had stayed permanently at its peak of January 1993. In both simulations, the time fixed effects, which capture non-economic factors such as welfare policy, follow their estimated values. By the end of the simulation period, these fixed effects pull down both of the simulated paths, including the one in which the unemployment rate is held at its peak level. Clearly, non-economic factors have an important role to play in explaining the caseload decline.

Nevertheless, the economy clearly also plays a major role. The implied effect of the economy is given by the difference between the two paths. If the unemployment rate had remained at its peak, the caseload would have continued to rise for approximately another two years before the fixed effects would have pulled it down. Instead, the simulated caseload based on the actual unemployment rate rises only about 5% before peaking in early 1995 and then begins to fall, first slowly and then rapidly.

Table 3 summarizes the effect of the economy on the caseload using our baseline model. The first column of the top panel presents our baseline model ($\bar{k} = 24$ with no lags of the unemployment rate). For the actual unemployment rate, the caseload peaks in March of 1995 at 11.1% of the population. It then falls to 7.3% at the end of our data (December 1998), a total decline of 34.3%. The counterfactual simulation (holding the unemployment rate at its maximum of January 1993)

Table 3. Basic Stock-Flow Simulations of the Role of the Economy, $\bar{k} = 24$.

Simulations	0 Lag Model	2 Lag Model	5 Lag Model	11 Lag Model
(1) Actual unemployment rate				
Simulated March 1995 level	0.111	0.111	0.111	0.111
Simulated December 1998 level	0.073	0.073	0.073	0.073
Simulated percent decline	−34.3%	−34.3%	−34.3%	−34.2%
(2) Unemp. rate remains constant after 1/93				
Simulated December 1998 level	0.091	0.090	0.090	0.091
Simulated percent decline	−18.3%	−19.0%	−18.5%	−18.4%
(3) Decline attributable to economic conditions	46.7%	44.7%	45.9%	46.4%

Note: Simulations are based on the stock-flow model. Calculations are based on monthly data for the period January 1989 to December 1998. See the text further details.
Source: Authors' computations from the MEDS.

implies that over the same period (January 1993 to December 1998) the caseload would have declined to 9.1% of the population, representing only an 18.3% decline in the caseload. We interpret these results as implying that almost half (46.7%) of the caseload decline is due to the economy; i.e. $(34.3 − 18.3)/34.3 = 46.7$.

5. EXTENSIONS OF THE BASIC STOCK-FLOW MODEL

In this section, we consider various extensions to the basic stock-flow model to examine its sensitivity to specification changes. We consider the sensitivity of the results to including different numbers of unemployment rate lags, changing the treatment of initial conditions, allowing the probability of re-entry to differ from the probability of new entry, and allowing the impact of economic conditions to vary by length of time on aid.

5.1. Specifying the Number of Unemployment Rate Lags

Klerman and Haider (forthcoming) demonstrate that models of the aggregate caseload are highly sensitive to the number of lags that were included in the empirical model and provide evidence that this sensitivity arises from the aggregate caseload literature ignoring the underlying stock-flow process. In this section, we present results that include different numbers of unemployment rate lags to examine the sensitivity of the stock-flow model to different numbers of lags.

Table 2 reports regression coefficients for entry (columns 2 to 4) and continuation (columns 6 to 8) models with two, five, and eleven lags. In almost all cases, the contemporaneous effect is the largest and has the expected sign. We note that coefficients across lag lengths vary considerably in magnitude, sign, and significance. This pattern is likely due to a combination of measurement error and high serial correlation in the monthly unemployment rate, rather than representing any real economic phenomenon. Using the sum of the coefficients as a proxy for the long-run effect of a permanent change in the unemployment rate, we find that the effects increase as additional lags are added in the entry regressions but decline slightly as additional lags are added in the continuation regressions (see the second to last row of Table 2).

Our primary interest, however, is the implication of these estimates for the aggregate caseload, obtained through simulations. The simulated changes in the caseload suggest that the estimated effect of the economy changes very little when different numbers of unemployment rate lags are included. The results displayed in Table 3 imply that 46.7%, 44.7%, 45.9%, and 46.4% of the caseload decline is due to economic conditions using the 0, 2, 5, and 11 lag models, respectively. Thus, the empirical evidence suggests that very few monthly unemployment rate lags are needed to capture the underlying correlations in the data.

5.2. The Treatment of Initial Conditions

As described above, we assume that the hazard of leaving welfare is constant after a particular length of time (called $\bar{k}$) to solve an initial conditions problem. The choice of $\bar{k}$ involves balancing two considerations: the larger our choice of $\bar{k}$, the better the model corresponds to the actual pattern in the data (see Fig. 2); however, the smaller our choice of $\bar{k}$, the less data we will need to drop to solve the initial conditions problem. The baseline specification sets $\bar{k} = 24$. Figure 2 suggests that the true value of $\bar{k}$ is higher than 24 months. The duration hazard coefficients are still increasing at 24 months; however, the coefficients are largely constant after 36 months.

To examine the sensitivity of the simulated effect of the economy to the 24-month assumption in our baseline model, we present simulations in Table 4 for models that are the same as the baseline specification except for setting $\bar{k}$ to be 36 months. Such a specification change requires us to drop an additional twelve months of data as compared to the baseline specification to handle the initial conditions problem. As is clear from the results, the role of the economy becomes slightly more important with just over 50% of the decline being attributable to the economy for the $\bar{k} = 36$ model. However, these estimates are sufficiently similar

Table 4. Basic Stock-Flow Simulations of the Role of the Economy, $\bar{k} = 36$.

Simulations	0 Lag Model	2 Lag Model	5 Lag Model	11 Lag Model
(1) Actual unemployment rate				
Simulated March 1995 level	0.114	0.114	0.114	0.114
Simulated December 1998 level	0.075	0.075	0.075	0.075
Simulated percent decline	−34.1%	−34.1%	−34.1%	−34.0%
(2) Unemp. rate remains constant after 1/93				
Simulated December 1998 level	0.095	0.095	0.096	0.098
Simulated percent decline	−16.7%	−17.0%	−15.3%	−14.1%
(3) Decline attributable to economic conditions	51.1%	50.2%	55.0%	58.5%

Note: Simulations are based on the stock-flow model. Calculations are based on monthly data for the period January 1990 to December 1998. See the text further details.
Source: Authors' computations from the MEDS.

that we conclude our baseline assumption of $\bar{k} = 24$ is reasonable and that the inclusion of additional lags does not appreciably matter.

5.3. Distinguishing New Entry from Re-entry

The basic model implicitly assumes that once a recipient leaves welfare, his or her probability of re-entering welfare is the same as the probability of entry for someone who has never been on welfare. This assumption seems overly restrictive and is different from the specification used by other researchers (e.g. Gittleman, 2001). In this sub-section, we allow the probability of re-entry to differ from the probability of new entry and to vary with length of time since last on aid.

A similar initial conditions problem is faced when modeling re-entry as was faced when modeling continuation. In particular, we only observe current welfare status for the period 1987–1998. When someone first enters welfare during our sample period, we do not know if they had received welfare prior to 1987. We address this initial conditions problem in a manner analogous to our approach in the continuation regression. Specifically, we assume that the probability of re-entry varies through a specific period, called $\bar{l}$, and thereafter to be identical. By then discarding the first $\bar{l}$ periods of data, all entrants can appropriately be classified as a new entrant (not being on welfare in the last $\bar{l}$ periods) or a re-entry (having been on welfare in the last $\bar{l}$ periods).

We incorporate these extensions by expanding the state-space implicit in Eq. (3). Specifically, define S_{olt} to be the number of people who have been off aid for l

consecutive periods at time t. We allow the re-entry rate (b) to vary with time off aid through $\bar{l}$; after $\bar{l}$, those have been on aid are assumed to be identical to those who have never been on aid. Thus, we re-define Eq. (5) to be the hazard of entry for individuals who have not been on aid for the past $\bar{l}$ months and specify a re-entry hazard, similar to Eq. (6), for all individuals who have been off aid for 1 to $\bar{l}$ months. For the case where $\bar{k} = \bar{l} = 4$, the implied Markov structure can be represented by,

$$\begin{bmatrix} S(r,1,t) \\ S(r,2,t) \\ S(r,3,t) \\ S(r,4,t) \\ S(o,1,t) \\ S(o,2,t) \\ S(o,3,t) \\ S(o,4,t) \\ S(n,t) \end{bmatrix} = \begin{bmatrix} 0 & 0 & 0 & 0 & b^1 & b^2 & b^3 & b^4 & e \\ c^1 & 0 & 0 & 0 & 0 & 0 & 0 & 0 & 0 \\ 0 & c^2 & 0 & 0 & 0 & 0 & 0 & 0 & 0 \\ 0 & 0 & c^3 & c^4 & 0 & 0 & 0 & 0 & 0 \\ 1-c^1 & 1-c^2 & 1-c^3 & 1-c^4 & 0 & 0 & 0 & 0 & 0 \\ 0 & 0 & 0 & 0 & 1-b^1 & 0 & 0 & 0 & 0 \\ 0 & 0 & 0 & 0 & 0 & 1-b^2 & 0 & 0 & 0 \\ 0 & 0 & 0 & 0 & 0 & 0 & 1-b^3 & 0 & 0 \\ 0 & 0 & 0 & 0 & 0 & 0 & 0 & 1-b^4 & 1-e \end{bmatrix} \begin{bmatrix} S(r,1,t-1) \\ S(r,2,t-1) \\ S(r,3,t-1) \\ S(r,4,t-1) \\ S(o,1,t-1) \\ S(o,2,t-1) \\ S(o,3,t-1) \\ S(o,4,t-1) \\ S(n,t-1) \end{bmatrix}.$$

(7)

We estimate the re-entry probability analogously to our approach to estimating continuation. Let R_{ijt} be an indicator variable equal to one for whether individual i in county j re-enters aid month t. Consider the model

$$\Pr[R_{ijt} = 1 | l] = f(\alpha_r + \beta_r Y_{ijt} + \gamma_t + \delta_j + g_r(l_{ijt})), \qquad (8)$$

where $g_r(l_{ijt})$ is a flexible functional form for duration dependence. To empirically implement the model, we specify the time effects and duration effects as in the continuation rate regressions. Furthermore, we set $\bar{l} = \bar{k} = 24$ and drop the first 24 months of data.

Table 5 presents the entry and re-entry regression results (corresponding to the left panel of Table 2), reclassifying all entries as either being new entries or re-entries. The new entry regressions look qualitatively similar to the baseline entry regressions. The current unemployment rate effect is about the same. The one and two lag effects are again largely offsetting. The results in columns 4 through 6 show that re-entry is also affected by the unemployment rate.

Our primary interest is the implied overall change in the role of the economy. Table 6 gives the results of the simulation of the stock when separating new entry from re-entry, similar to the results in Table 3 where new entry and re-entry were not treated separately. As is readily apparent, the results are very similar. For example, the results in Tables 3 and 6 imply similar roles for the economy across all four models (42.2–47.5% in the models that account for re-entry, versus 44.7–46.7%

Table 5. Probability of New Entry versus Re-Entry.

Regressors	Probability of New Entry (Grouped Logit)				Probability of Re-Entry (OLS: coeffs & s.e. × 100)			
	1	2	3	4	5	6	7	8
Unemp. Rate	0.036	0.037	0.048	0.025	0.026	0.088	0.008	−0.045
	(0.004)	(0.007)	(0.007)	(0.008)	(0.005)	(0.009)	(0.010)	(0.011)
UR-1st lag		−0.005	−0.001	0.006		−0.074	−0.090	0.103
		(0.010)	(0.010)	(0.010)		(0.013)	(0.014)	(0.014)
UR-2nd lag		0.007	−0.005	−0.002		−0.008	0.041	−0.033
		(0.007)	(0.010)	(0.010)		(0.009)	(0.014)	(0.014)
UR-3rd lag			−0.004	0.001			0.044	−0.031
			(0.010)	(0.010)			(0.014)	(0.014)
UR-4th lag			−0.002	0.009			−0.157	0.140
			(0.010)	(0.010)			(0.013)	(0.014)
UR-5th lag			0.029	0.009			0.063	−0.073
			(0.007)	(0.010)			(0.009)	(0.014)
UR-6th lag				0.018				−0.030
				(0.011)				(0.014)
UR-7th lag				−0.008				0.033
				(0.010)				(0.014)
UR-8th lag				−0.005				0.058
				(0.010)				(0.014)
UR-9th lag				0.025				−0.070
				(0.010)				(0.014)
UR-10th lag				−0.010				0.093
				(0.010)				(0.013)
UR-11th lag				0.023				−0.112
				(0.008)				(0.010)
Sum of coeffs.	0.036	0.038	0.066	0.090	0.026	0.006	−0.024	0.034
R-squared	0.7799	0.7800	0.7814	0.7831	0.0228	0.0228	0.0228	0.0228
Observations	6,480	6,480	6,480	6,480	6,275,041	6,275,041	6,275,041	6,275,041

Note: We use monthly data for the period January 1989 to December 1998 for each set of models, with $\bar{k}$ set to 24 for the re-entry models. All models contain county fixed effects and a flexible spline in time. See the text for further details. Standard errors are in parentheses.
Source: Authors' computations from the MEDS.

in the models that do not), although the exact ranking across the models has changed. Thus, our results suggest that the processes of entry and re-entry are different but separating the two is not empirically important from the perspective of understanding the impact of economic conditions on the welfare caseload.

5.4. Allowing Differential Impacts of the Unemployment Rate by Duration

The baseline model implicitly assumes that the impact of the economy is invariant with respect to how long individuals have been on aid, i.e. that there is no interaction between duration and the economy. Given the strong duration dependence found in Fig. 2, it is plausible that the effect of the economy (as proxied by the unemployment

Table 6. Simulations that Distinguish between New Entry and Re-entry.

Simulations	0 Lag Model	2 Lag Model	5 Lag Model	11 Lag Model
(1) Actual unemployment rate				
Simulated March 1995 level	0.112	0.112	0.112	0.112
Simulated December 1998 level	0.074	0.074	0.075	0.075
Simulated percent decline	−33.3%	−33.3%	−33.3%	−33.2%
(2) Unemp. rate remains constant after 1/93				
Simulated December 1998 level	0.090	0.091	0.092	0.092
Simulated percent decline	−19.3%	−18.1%	−17.5%	−17.8%
(3) Decline attributable to economic conditions	42.2%	45.7%	47.5%	46.3%

Note: We use monthly data for the period January 1989 to December 1998 for each set of models, with $\bar{k}$ set to 24 for the continuation and re-entry models. The calculations are based on the flow results in Tables 2 and 5.

Source: Authors' computations from the MEDS.

rate) also varies with duration. For example, long-term welfare users might be less able to find employment during economic expansions because of human capital depreciation from being out of the labor market or due to stigma associated with being on welfare. We explore this possibility in this sub-section.

Based on the results in the previous sub-section, we define our base model to include only the contemporaneous unemployment rate. We then allow the impact of the unemployment rate to vary by duration with two different specifications. In the first specification, we include interactions with three duration dummies (on aid for 0–11 months, 12–23 months, and 24+ months). In the second specification, we include an interaction of the unemployment rate with a continuous measure of time on aid (called k).

In the specification with dummy variables (column 2 of Table 7), the coefficients in the continuation models are essentially identical, with coefficients of 0.114, 0.103, and 0.112 for the 0–11 month, 12–23 month, and 24+ month interactions, respectively (each with standard errors of approximately 0.006). The second specification (in column 2) in which the effect of the economy is allowed to vary linearly with duration gives equivalent results. The point estimate on the interaction term is zero to three decimal places.

We simulate the implications for these flow relationships to changes in the caseload stock and present the results in Table 8. Given the flow regressions, it is not surprising that the implied effects of the economy do not change much as compared to the baseline results in Table 3. In particular, the role for the economy is still

Table 7. Continuation Regressions Interacting Unemployment with Duration.

Regressors	Probability of Contiuation (OLS: coeffs & s.e. × 100)	
	1	2
Unemp0		0.117
		(0.006)
Unemp0 × dur0–11	0.114	
	(0.006)	
Unemp0 × dur11–23	0.103	
	(0.006)	
Unemp0 × dur24+	0.112	
	(0.005)	
Unemp0 × t		-3×10^{-4}
		(2×10^{-4})
R-squared	0.0096	0.0096
Observations	9,070,952	9,070,952

Note: We use monthly data for the period January 1989 to December 1998 for each set of models; $\bar{k}$ is set to 24 for the continuation models. All models contain county fixed effects and a flexible spline in time. See the text for further details. Standard errors are in parentheses.
Source: Authors' computations from the MEDS.

approximately 40% (see Table 8). Therefore, these results suggest that the base-case assumption that the relationship between continuation and the unemployment rate is additive and invariant across durations is consistent with the empirical evidence.

Table 8. Simulations that Allow for Duration Interactions.

Simulations	Baseline	1	2
(1) Actual unemployment rate			
Simulated March 1995 level	0.111	0.111	0.111
Simulated December 1998 level	0.073	0.073	0.073
Simulated percent decline	−34.3%	−34.3%	−34.3%
(2) Unemp. rate remains constant after 1/93			
Simulated December 1998 level	0.091	0.088	0.088
Simulated percent decline	−18.3%	−20.4%	−20.5%
(3) Decline attributable to economic conditions	46.7%	40.5%	40.3%

Note: We use monthly data for the period January 1989 to December 1998 for each set of models, with $\bar{k}$ set to 24 for the continuation models. The calculations are based on the flow results in Tables 2 and 7.
Source: Authors' computations from the MEDS.

6. ALTERNATIVE MEASURES OF ECONOMIC CONDITIONS

Following the previous literature, our baseline model uses the unemployment rate as its proxy for economic conditions. However, there are at least three reasons why the unemployment rate might be an incomplete proxy. First, the unemployment rate is likely to be measured with error, particularly given that we use monthly county-level estimates. The county-level measures that we use are produced as part of the joint federal-state Local Area Unemployment Statistics program, administered by the Bureau of Labor Statistics. These unemployment rates are constructed through a synthetic estimation process that relies on state-level estimates derived from the Current Population Survey and is then extended to smaller areas using Current Employment Statistics and state unemployment insurance data. It seems likely that this process yields estimates with considerable measurement error.[11] To the extent that the measurement error is serially uncorrelated, the coefficient on the unemployment rate will tend to suffer from attenuation bias, i.e. point estimates that are too small in absolute value. Including multiple lags of the unemployment rate (as we did above) will partially correct our simulations for such attenuation bias.

Second, even if perfectly measured, the unemployment rate might be the wrong measure of economic opportunity for the welfare population. As is well known, the Bureau of Labor Statistics definition of unemployed requires that an individual be actively seeking employment. If individuals who go on welfare do not seek employment, then counties with high welfare rolls might have a low unemployment rate even though individuals initially go onto welfare because of the lack of economic opportunity.

Third, and more generally, it seems likely that the economy is not a one-dimensional concept. For example, the labor market opportunities might change differentially for a low-skilled person versus a high-skilled person, and a uni-dimensional measure such as the unemployment rate could not capture differential movements. Moreover, it is not just the probability of working that is important, but also the wages that would be received when working. The idea of treating the economy as a multi-dimensional concept and using multiple proxies is consistent with other work in the regional economics literature (Bartik, 1991, 1996; Blanchard & Katz, 1992) and in labor economics (Davis & Haltiwanger, 1992; Katz & Murphy, 1992).

The argument for a multi-dimensional conceptualization of the economy seems particularly strong for the population most at risk of entering welfare. The high-risk population tends to be young, single women with little experience and few skills. For such individuals, labor market outcomes at the bottom of the skill distribution seem most relevant, and tightness or slack at the top or even middle of the labor market is likely to be less important. Of course, we expect that outcomes for the bottom of the labor market will be positively correlated with outcomes for the labor market as a whole. It is, however, far from clear how strong that correlation will be. The literature on increasing earnings inequality (e.g. Juhn, 1992; Juhn, Murphy & Pierce, 1993; Katz & Murphy, 1992) suggests that labor market outcomes have diverged widely at the top and bottom of the distribution. Consistent with this perspective, some of the papers in the regional economics literature find differential effects of various proxies across segments of the labor market (e.g. Bartik, 1991, 1996; Blanchard & Katz, 1992). Thus, we would like to have a proxy for the economy that is more targeted at the bottom of the labor market.

Three other papers of which we are aware have made similar arguments and explore an expanded set of proxies for economic conditions. Each of them finds an important role for additional measures of the economy. Bartik and Eberts (1999) estimate models similar to the conventional caseload literature (using national data and including state and year fixed effects) and find strong effects of the employment growth rate, even when the unemployment rate is also included. They find some evidence to support the inclusion of current or lagged values of the employment rate for high school graduates, the wage premium implied by a state's industry composition, and the employment rate implied by a state's industry composition. Ribar (2000) constructs a county-level index of labor market opportunity for low-skilled individuals and finds that the index predicts caseload transitions significantly better than the local area unemployment rate.

Most relevant to our work is Hoynes (2000), who also uses California MEDS data. She explores the effect of economic conditions on exit from and re-entry onto welfare. She does not examine the impact of economic conditions on entry, and thus cannot explore the effect of the economy on the total caseload. Hoynes (2000) finds that average earnings overall, in services, and in retail trade have a significant effect on continuation and re-entry, over and above the unemployment rate. In fact, when she includes county and time fixed effects (as we do), inclusion of the earnings measures make the effect of the unemployment rate much smaller, statistically indistinguishable from zero. She also considers models with employment (total and by sector) and the employment-to-population ratio (total and by sector). Overall she concludes "models that control for labor market conditions using employment-based measures perform better than unemployment rates."

6.1. Four Measures of Economic Conditions

To explore the sensitivity of our results, we consider four additional measures: the employment rate, the employment growth rate, earnings per worker in the retail trade sector, and the growth rate of earnings per worker in the retail trade sector.

These additional measures are intended to remedy some of the problems with the unemployment rate previously discussed. The employment rate is similar to the unemployment rate in that it is intended to measure the broad, economic activity in the county; however, the employment rate should be measured with less error because it is based on administrative data compiled as part of the unemployment insurance system. Moreover, it is not sensitive to a discouraged worker effect. The employment growth rate is intended to be a measure of the slack in the labor market, rather than a measure of the general economic activity (see Bartik & Eberts, 1999).

The measures of earnings in the retail trade are intended to provide additional information about the opportunities in the labor market for welfare recipients. Earnings per worker in the retail trade sector are intended to provide a more specific measure of the opportunities available to this group. We also include the growth rate in earnings as another measure of slack in the labor market.

Table 9 presents a correlation matrix for the various economic condition measures. Given that many of the underlying concepts are conceptually closely related, the actual correlations are small. The largest correlation (in absolute value) is between the earnings per worker and the growth rate in earnings per worker (−0.74), followed by the correlation between the unemployment rate and the growth rate in earnings per worker (0.51). Notably, the correlation between the unemployment rate and the employment growth rate is very small (−0.05). Thus, the simple correlations suggest that the various measures are somewhat distinct.

Table 9. Correlations Among Various Measures of Economic Conditions.

	Unemployment Rate	Employment Rate	Employment Growth Rate	Per Worker Earnings	Per Worker Earnings Growth
Unemployment rate	1				
Employment rate	−0.397	1			
	<0.0001				
Employment rate growth rate	−0.052	0.044	1		
	<0.0001	0.0004			
Per worker earnings (retail)	−0.251	0.114	0.033	1	
	<0.0001	<0.0001	0.008		
Per worker earnings (retail) growth rate	0.050	−0.265	−0.009	−0.741	1
	<0.0001	<0.0001	0.478	<0.0001	
Observations	6480	6480	6480	6480	6480

Note: We use monthly data for the period January 1989 to December 1998. The calculations are weighted by county population.
Source: Authors' computations from the unemployment rate.

Table 10. Entry Regressions Using Other Measures of Economic Conditions.

Regressors	Probability of Entry (Grouped Logit)			
	1	2	3	4
Unemployment rate	0.018	0.030	0.031	0.015
	(0.003)	(0.003)	(0.003)	(0.004)
Employment rate	−0.018			−0.016
	(0.002)			(0.002)
Employment growth rate	0.005		0.002	0.005
	(0.002)		(0.002)	(0.002)
Per worker earnings (retail)		−2.649	−1.220	−1.608
		(0.715)	(0.150)	(0.719)
Per worker earnings (retail) growth rate		−0.144		−0.049
		(0.070)		(0.070)
R-squared	0.8249	0.8239	0.8238	0.8264
Observations	6480	6480	6480	6480

Note: We use monthly data for the period January 1989 to December 1998. All models contain county fixed effects and a flexible spline in time. See the text for further details. Standard errors are in parentheses.
Source: Authors' computations from the MEDS.

6.2. Results with Alternative Measures

Turning to the effects on the transition rates, Table 10 presents results for entry rate regressions and Table 11 presents results for continuation rate regressions. For both sets of regressions, each of the additional measures of economic conditions enters with the expected sign and is statistically significant. The only exception to this pattern is that the growth rate in earnings per worker is not significant in the model when all measures are included simultaneously in the entry regressions (column 4 in Table 10).

Again, our main interest is in the total impact of the economy on the per capita caseload. In Table 12, we present simulations based on the flow estimates of Tables 10 and 11. Unlike our other sensitivity analyses, Table 12 suggests that the simulated effect of the economy is very sensitive to changes in how the economy is measured. In the baseline specification, the economy explains 46.7% (0 lag model and $\bar{k} = 24$ from Table 3). Including the employment rate and the employment growth rate has little effect on the total estimate, with the estimated role for the economy changing marginally to 46.2%. Strikingly, including per worker earnings in retail trade causes a sharp increase in the effect of the economy. For example, in the model that includes earnings and the earnings growth rate, we compute that fraction attributable to the economy

Table 11. Continuation Regressions Using Alternative Measures of Economic Conditions.

Regressors	(OLS: both coeffs & s.e. × 100)			
	1	2	3	4
Unemployment rate	0.116	0.104	0.098	0.115
	(0.006)	(0.005)	(0.005)	(0.006)
Employment rate	0.009			0.015
	(0.003)			(0.003)
Employment growth rate	−0.018		−0.017	−0.019
	(0.004)		(0.004)	(0.004)
Per worker earnings (retail)		−15.291	−3.530	−16.025
		(1.430)	(0.308)	(1.444)
Per worker earnings (retail) growth rate		−1.155		−1.218
		(0.137)		(0.138)
R-squared	0.0096	0.0096	0.0096	0.0096
Observations	9,070,952	9,070,952	9,070,952	9,070,952

Note: We use monthly data for the period January 1989 to December 1998 for each set of models; $\bar{k}$ is set to 24 for the continuation models. All models contain county fixed effects and a flexible spline in time. See the text for further details. Standard errors are in parentheses.
Source: Authors' computations from the MEDS.

Table 12. Simulations with Alternative Measures of Economic Conditions.

Simulations	Baseline	1	2	3	4
(1) Actual unemployment rate					
Simulated March 1995 level	0.111	0.111	0.111	0.111	0.111
Simulated December 1998 level	0.073	0.073	0.073	0.073	0.073
Simulated percent decline	−34.3%	−34.1%	−34.0%	−34.1%	−33.8%
(2) Unemp. rate remains constant after unemployment rate peak (1/93)					
Simulated December 1998 level	0.091	0.090	0.108	0.108	0.108
Simulated percent decline	−18.3%	−18.4%	−2.1%	−3.0%	−2.1%
(3) Decline attributable to economic conditions	46.7%	46.2%	93.7%	91.3%	93.7%

Note: We use monthly data for the period January 1989 to December 1998 for each set of models, with $\bar{k}$ set to 24 for the continuation models. The baseline model corresponds to the results from the 0 lag model in Table 3. Models 1 through 4 correspond to the flow models 1 through 4 in Tables 10 and 11, respectively.
Source: Authors' computations from the MEDS.

approximately doubles to 93.7% (see model 2). The results remain at a similar level with various other combinations of economic conditions, including all of the measures (model 4). Therefore, we conclude that approximately 90% of the caseload decline in California from 1995 to 1998 is due to economic conditions.

Substantively, two aspects of these results deserve comment. First, these results suggest that the wage level provides important additional information about economic conditions not captured by the unemployment rate. Second, welfare reform was not passed in California until 1998 and then was only slowly implemented over the year; thus, it is unlikely that these changes in the unemployment rate or earnings could have been caused by policy changes. Moreover, it is likely that the role for the economy in other states would be smaller because California adopted its policy changes relatively late and the changes were less dramatic than those in other states.

7. DISCUSSION AND CONCLUSION

Klerman and Haider (forthcoming) propose a stock-flow model of the welfare caseload and then estimate the model using California data. This paper has explored the sensitivity of the stock-flow approach to two sets of specification choices. First, the paper explored the sensitivity of the empirical model to several structural changes, including the treatment of initial conditions, distinguishing entry from re-entry, and allowing economic effects on continuation to vary with duration. None of the substantive conclusions of the basic model change. In particular, regardless of the specification changes, the economy explains approximately half of California's 31% caseload decline from its peak in March 1995 to the end of our data in December 1998.

In contrast to this null result, varying the measure of economic conditions has a large effect on the substantive results. Following the majority of previous research, our baseline model uses the conventional unemployment rate as a proxy for economic conditions. Consistent with other studies that have also augmented the measure of economic conditions, we find that the unemployment rate alone is not sufficient to capture the effect of economic conditions on the welfare caseload. Furthermore, including per worker earnings as a measure of economic conditions doubles the estimated role for the economy. In the models that include earnings in retail trade, the economy explains more than 90% of the caseload decline. We conclude that a dynamic model with a rich parameterization for economic conditions can explain the overwhelming share of the caseload decline in California over this period. Furthermore, this estimated effect is much larger than that obtained either from aggregate regressions or from our stock-flow approach when only the unemployment rate is used as a proxy for economic conditions.

Combined with the comparison between conventional stock models and the stock-flow models reported in Klerman and Haider (forthcoming), our results have important implications for understanding the causes of the decline in the U.S. welfare caseload in the late-1990s. Klerman and Haider (forthcoming) find that, when using the unemployment rate alone, the stock-flow approach yields estimated effects of the economy larger than those implied by the conventional stock models (e.g. CEA, 1997). The results presented here suggest that the basic stock-flow analysis is robust to many different changes in the structure of the model, but expanding the measures for the economy substantially increases the estimated role of the economy in the caseload decline.

These results suggest several broader conclusions. First, because we find an even larger role for the economy, it is more likely that there will be substantial increases in the caseload with the next recession. Second, even though we do not examine the impact of policy directly, our results have important implications for understanding the potential role for policy. As the estimated role of the economy expands, the potential role for welfare reform contracts. We note, however, that the specific percentage estimates of the decline due to the economy presented here should not necessarily be applied directly to other states. In particular, the process of welfare reform began later and was less drastic in California than in the rest of the United States and our data only cover the period through the end of 1998, so it is possible that policy changes had a greater impact in other states and in California for a later period.

Finally, our results suggest that it is possible and useful to model the underlying dynamics directly and to derive the implications for the stock by simulation. Arguments similar to those made here also apply to the impact of policy on the welfare caseload. Moreover, it is likely that similar dynamics are relevant to many other government assistance programs, such as Food Stamps and Medicaid (Schoeni, 2001). Finally, many other processes that are inherently persistent should be expected to evolve similarly, such as occupational structures and prison populations.

NOTES

1. Other studies have used similar models to examine the impact of welfare reform on other outcomes (Currie & Grogger, 2001; Moffitt, 1999; Schoeni & Blank, 2001).
2. Hutchens (1981) examines separately entry onto and exit off of welfare. Bane and Ellwood (1986) and Blank (1989) examine the determinants of welfare spell lengths. Moffitt (1992) provides a useful review of the earlier studies. Hoynes and MaCurdy (1994) examine

how changes in program generosity affect spell length. Gittleman (2001) and Hoynes (2000) are more recent studies of welfare dynamics.

3. Hoynes (2000) argues that the small sample sizes usually available in survey data have caused researchers to conclude that economic conditions are unimportant. The paper relies on a different extract from the same database for its analysis.

4. The national stock literature uses time fixed effects in their specifications, and we adopt a similar specification for our flow models. This allows us to isolate the impact of moving to a stock-flow model as compared to the conventional models in the literature. However, the major policy changes that happened in California during our time period mainly took place at the state level.

5. Throughout this paper, we use the term "welfare" to refer to the Aid For Families with Dependent Children (AFDC) program that was changed to the Temporary Assistance for Needy Families (TANF) program. The programs provide financial assistance to needy families (usually headed by a single mother) with children. Program participation can be identified with the MEDS data because welfare recipients are categorically eligible for Medi-Cal (the California implementation of Medicaid), and such eligibility is designated in the database.

6. Specifically, we draw a monthly random sample of individuals who are entering aid for the first time in our sample period. We then follow each of these individuals to the end of our sample period. This strategy effectively provides a sample that contains an initial cross-section of everyone on aid, and then refreshes this initial cross-section with a sample of new entrants.

7. We obtained these data from their website (http://www.dof.ca.gov/html/demograp/data.htm) in December 2000.

8. We include men and women because our analysis includes children and the smaller AFDC-Unemployed Parent program (AFDC-UP), which provides welfare benefits to two parent families in which the husband has recently lost a job.

9. We obtained these data from their website (http://fisher.lib.virginia.edu/reis) in January 2001.

10. As noted, some of our underlying data are at the monthly level (welfare recipients, unemployment, and employment) and some of our data are at the annual level (population and earnings). We choose to perform our empirical analysis at the monthly level, and thus interpolate the annual data to the monthly level. Another empirical strategy would be to aggregate the monthly data to the annual level for analysis purposes. We believe our strategy to be more appropriate because welfare receipt is a discrete time process that occurs at the monthly level. Moreover, given that we will include flexible time splines in all of our analysis, the mechanical time correlation implied by the interpolation should not affect our estimates.

11. It should be noted that the state level unemployment estimates are also presumably estimated with measurement error, particularly for the states with a small population. The state unemployment estimates are largely based on the Current Population Survey (CPS), and the CPS sample is small for the small states.

ACKNOWLEDGMENTS

This work is funded by U.S. Department of Health and Human Services (#99ASPE34A). The opinions and conclusions expressed herein are solely those of the authors and should not be construed as representing the opinions or policy of any of the sponsors or related agencies. Some of the analyses use California administrative data that cannot be released to other researchers without the permission of the State of California. We gratefully acknowledge the expert programming assistance of Janet Hanley and Laurie McDonald.

REFERENCES

Bane, M. J., & Ellwood, D. (1986). Slipping into and out of poverty: The dynamics of spells. *Journal of Human Resources, 21*(1), 1–23.

Bartik, T. J. (1991). *Who benefits from state and local economic development policies?* Kalamazoo, MI: W. E. Upjohn Institute for Employment Research.

Bartik, T. J. (1996). The distributional effects of local labor demand and industrial mix: Estimates using individual panel data. *Journal of Urban Economics, 40*, 150–178.

Bartik, T. J., & Eberts, R. W. (November, 1999). *Examining the effect of industry trends and structure on welfare caseloads*. Mimeograph, W. E. Upjohn Institute for Employment Research, Kalamazoo, MI.

Blanchard, O. J., & Katz, L. F. (1992). Regional evolutions. *Brookings Papers on Economic Activities, 1*, 1–75.

Blank, R. (1989). Analyzing the duration of welfare spells. *Journal of Public Economics, 39*(3), 245–273.

Blank, R., & Ruggles, P. (1996). When do women use AFDC and food stamps? The dynamics of eligibility vs. participation. *Journal of Human Resources, 31*(1), 57–89.

Council of Economic Advisers (May, 1997). *Technical report: Explaining the decline in welfare receipt, 1993–1996*. A Report by the Council of Economic Advisors, Washington, DC.

Council of Economic Advisers (August, 1999). *Technical report: The effects of welfare policy and the economic expansion on welfare caseloads: An update*. A Report by the Council of Economic Advisors, Washington, DC.

Currie, J., & Grogger, J. (2001). Explaining recent declines in the food stamp program participation. In: W. G. Gale & J. Rothenberg Pack (Eds), *Brookings and Wharton Papers on Urban Affairs*. Washington, DC: Brooking Institution Press.

Davis, S. J., & Haltiwanger, J. C. (1992). Gross job creation, gross job destruction, and employment reallocation. *Quarterly Journal of Economics, 107*, 819–863.

Figlio, D., & Ziliak, J. (1999). Welfare reform, the business cycle, and the decline in AFDC caseloads. In: S. Danziger (Ed.), *Economic Conditions and Welfare Reform*. Kalamazoo, MI: W. E. Upjohn Institute for Employment Research.

Gittleman, M. (2001). Declining caseloads: What do the dynamics of welfare participation reveal? *Industrial Relations, 40*(4), 537–570.

Haider, S., Klerman, J. A., Hanley, J., McDonald, L., Roth, E., Hiatt, L., & Suttorp, M. (May, 1999). *Welfare reform in california: design of the impact analysis, preliminary investigations of caseload data*. Draft of DRR(L)–2077/1-CDSS, RAND, Santa Monica, CA.

Heckman, J., & Walker, J. (1990). The relationship between wages and income and the timing and spacing of births: Evidence from Swedish longitudinal data. *Econometrica, 58*(6), 1411–1441.

Hoynes, H. W. (2000). Local labor markets and welfare spells: Do demand conditions matter? *Review of Economics and Statistics, 82*(3), 351–368.

Hoynes, H. W., & MaCurdy, T. (1994). Has the decline in benefits shortened welfare spells? *American Economic Review, 84*(2), 43–48.

Hutchens, R. (1981). Entry and exit transitions in a government transfer program: The case of aid to families with dependent children. *Journal of Human Resources, 16*(2).

Juhn, C. (1992). Decline of male labor market participation: The role of declining market opportunities. *Quarterly Journal of Economics, 107*(1), 79–121.

Juhn, C., Murphy, K. M., & Pierce, B. (1993). Wage inequality and the rise in returns to skill. *The Journal of Political Economy, 101*(3), 410–442.

Katz, L. F., & Murphy, K. M. (1992). Changes in relative wages, 1963–1987: Supply and demand factors. *Quarterly Journal of Economics, 107*(1), 35–78.

Klerman, J. A., & Haider, S. J. (forthcoming). A stock-flow analysis of the welfare caseload. *Journal of Human Resources* (forthcoming 2004).

Levine, P., & Whitmore, D. (1998). The impact of welfare reform on the AFDC caseload. *National Tax Association Proceedings* (pp. 24–33). Washington, DC: National Tax Association.

Maddala, G. (1983). *Limited-dependent and qualitative variables in econometrics*. Cambridge: Cambridge University Press.

Moffitt, R. (1992). Incentive effects of the U.S. welfare system: A review. *Journal of Economic Literature, 30*, 1–61.

Moffitt, R. (May, 1999). The effect of pre-PRWORA waivers on AFDC caseloads and female earnings, income, and labor force behavior. In: S. Danziger (Ed.), *Economic Conditions and Welfare Reform*. Kalamazoo, MI: W. E. Upjohn Institute for Employment Research.

Moffitt, R., & Rendall, M. (1995). Cohort trends in the lifetime distribution of female family headship in the United States, 1968–1985. *Demography, 32*(3), 407–424.

Ribar, D. (March, 2000). *Transitions from welfare and the employment prospects of low-skill workers*. Manuscript.

Schoeni, R. F. (2001). Comment on: Currie and Grogger, explaining recent declines in food stamp program participation. In: W. G. Gale & J. R. Pack (Eds), *Brookings and Wharton Papers on Urban Affairs*. Washington, DC: Brookings Institution Press.

Schoeni, R., & Blank, R. (September, 2001). *What has welfare reform accomplished? Impacts on welfare participation, employment, income, poverty, and family structure*. Manuscript, University of Michigan, Ann Arbor.

Ziliak, J., Figlio, D., Davis, E., & Connolly, L. (2000). Accounting for the decline in AFDC caseloads: Welfare reform or economic growth? *Journal of Human Resources, 35*(3), 570–586.

NEW JERSEY'S FAMILY CAP AND FAMILY SIZE DECISIONS: FINDINGS FROM A FIVE-YEAR EVALUATION

Michael J. Camasso, Radha Jagannathan,
Mark Killingsworth and Carol Harvey

INTRODUCTION

The causal relationship between the size of welfare benefits and the birth decisions of women on welfare has been explored in a number of studies using a variety of analytical approaches applied to vital statistics data, data from the Current Population Survey, the Panel Study of Income Dynamics, or similar survey data. These studies typically use non-experimental methods to relate differences in birth rates or birth decisions across states to differences in welfare benefits levels. Analyses of this type have been criticized on several grounds. Benefits across states may be correlated with unobserved interstate differences that may also be related to birth decisions. Very often, these studies measure the key independent variable, welfare benefits level, as the cash benefit guarantee under the Aid to Families with Dependent Children (AFDC) program for a household of fixed size, varying this amount by state of residence. Actual benefits paid will vary with household size, number of AFDC-eligible household members, other sources of income, and other factors.

The introduction of family cap welfare policies by a number of states has spurred new interest in the relationship between birth decisions and welfare benefits. These policies withhold increases in welfare cash grants for children conceived and/or born while the mother is on welfare. New Jersey was the first state to introduce a family cap policy in 1992 as part of its Family Development Program welfare reform. By August 1996, when Congress passed the Personal Responsibility and Work Opportunity Reconciliation Act (PRWORA) of 1996, a total of nineteen states had introduced some type of family cap measure within a Section 1115-waivered welfare program or demonstration. When AFDC was replaced by a block grant program, Temporary Assistance for Needy Families (TANF), individual states were free to implement or terminate a family cap without federal approval. Currently, twenty-three states, including New Jersey, have introduced or retained some sort of family cap rule in their TANF programs.[1]

Federally-mandated evaluations of Section 1115-waivered family cap provisions offer new opportunities to model fertility responses of women on welfare to specific changes in benefits levels. The five-year evaluation of New Jersey's Family Development Program is unique among the eighty-one waivered experiments approved during the Bush (I) and Clinton administrations. While several evaluations have examined the impact of incremental benefit changes on births (Fein, 1999; Fein, Beecroft, Hamilton & Lee, 1998; Fein & Karweit, 1997; Mills, Kornfeld, Peck, Porcari & Others, 1999), the New Jersey evaluation is the only study that provides experimental evidence of Section 1115-waivered family cap provision impacts on abortions and contraception use, as well as on births (see Harvey, Camasso & Jagannathan, 2000). Data on abortions is especially difficult to obtain at the individual level for welfare recipients. New Jersey's Medicaid policy, which pays for any abortion requested by women receiving AFDC, coupled with an administrative database structure that links payments, births, and abortions and the State's willingness to explore a possible birth rate-abortion rate connection, greatly facilitated this investigation.

This evaluation employed an experimental design with the random selection of over eight thousand AFDC cases into experimental and control groups. Since the evaluation data arise from a controlled experiment within a single state, observed outcomes are closely linked to the actual or potential lost benefits associated with an additional child born to each AFDC household in the experiment. This experimental design offers a distinct advantage over family cap studies based on cross-sectional data over all states, in that the findings are not confounded by cross-state differences in demographics, economic conditions, administrative or programmatic attributes of the various state welfare systems (including differences in benefits levels or structure), or differences in actual family cap policy rules and their implementation.

NEW JERSEY'S FAMILY CAP AND THE FAMILY DEVELOPMENT PROGRAM

In July 1992, the State of New Jersey implemented a Section 1115-waivered welfare reform measure that became known as the "family cap." Under this welfare provision, children who were conceived while the mother was receiving AFDC benefits would not be included among eligible household members for the purposes of calculating the size of the AFDC cash grant. Put another way, the household would not receive any additional cash assistance for that child, although the child would be eligible for other benefits, including Medicaid and food stamps.

The loss in cash benefits varies with AFDC-eligible household size. For example, in the absence of the family cap, a woman on welfare with one eligible child would receive $322 per month in cash assistance in New Jersey; this amount would increase by $102 per month for one additional child, and by $64 per month for the next additional child. Food stamp benefits will also increase, but by less than the maximum allowable increase due to the incremental income from AFDC benefits.[2] Once the family cap is effective, the household does not receive any additional cash assistance when another child is born. However, the incremental food stamp benefit would be somewhat higher for this household, since there is no offset due to additional income from AFDC.[3]

The family cap was part of a more comprehensive set of welfare reforms implemented in New Jersey, termed the Family Development Program (FDP). The stated objectives of this welfare reform were three-fold: To break the cycle of poverty by providing expanded training and educational opportunities to AFDC clients; to enhance individual responsibility; and to strengthen and reunite families. Other programmatic elements included an enhanced earnings disregard for households with capped grants,[4] a two-year extension of Medicaid benefits for those cases that exited AFDC for employment,[5] a reduction or elimination of the "marriage penalty" (that is, the loss of cash benefits for children once the mother (re)marries), a requirement that women with children age two or older participate in education or training programs (JOBS) designed to improve their labor market opportunities, and changes in sanctions for failure to participate in the JOBS program.[6] Certain FDP provisions, including the family cap, the enhanced earnings disregard, and the elimination of the marriage penalty, went into effect statewide on October 1, 1992. The remaining provisions, including the two-year Medicaid extension and changes in JOBS-related rules, were phased in on a county-by-county basis. FDP became fully effective throughout New Jersey on January 1, 1995.

Permission from the Administration for Children and Families, U.S. Department of Health and Human Services (ACF-USDHHS) to implement the Family Development Program was tied to a federal requirement to assess its impacts, costs, and benefits. In addition to the usual welfare reform impacts on welfare dependency, employment, and earnings, the federally mandated evaluation of the Family Development Program included an assessment of programmatic impacts on the childbearing decisions of women on welfare.

PRIOR STUDIES ON THE RELATIONSHIP BETWEEN WELFARE BENEFITS AND FERTILITY

Economic theory suggests that increasing the subsidy that women on welfare receive when the household size increases due to the birth of another child will increase the propensity of women on welfare to give birth. However, evidence from prior empirical work on the relationship between welfare benefits and births is far from conclusive. Most of these prior studies utilize either cross-state comparisons of birth rates and welfare benefits levels or micro-data on welfare recipients from large-scale population surveys. The birth outcomes analyzed vary from study to study, and do not necessarily center on the behavior of the AFDC population. Instead of births among women on AFDC, many of these studies look at a wider range of outcomes, including out-of-wedlock births to all women (see Bernstam, 1988; Ellwood & Bane, 1985) and to specific subgroups (such as teens or members of minority groups, as in Duncan & Hoffman, 1990; or Plotnick, 1990), as well as all births (in and out of wedlock), regardless of the welfare status of the mother (see Schultz, 1994, 1995). Studies that focus on the relationship between welfare receipt and births also vary in how they measure welfare benefits. Some utilize maximum state-wide benefits for a model household configuration (Lundberg & Plotnick, 1995), while others use the incremental benefit received with the birth of an additional child (see Robins & Fronstin, 1996; or Argys, Averett & Rees, 2000). Most recently, a number of studies (Brinig & Buckley, 1999; Clarke & Strauss, 1998; Hoffman & Foster, 2000; Horvath & Peters, 2002; Mach, 2001; Rosenzweig, 1999) find a relatively large and statistically significant positive relationship between AFDC benefit generosity and non-marital childbearing among young women. Recent work by Grogger and Bronars (2001) and Fairlie and London (1997), however, find no evidence of a relationship between marginal benefits paid at the birth of an additional child and fertility. All of these studies used non-experimental methods to explore the relationship between welfare benefit levels and fertility.

Significant differences among study results abound in the research on AFDC and fertility. Some variation in the literature is likely due to nuances in the measurement of the policy variable (levels or changes of welfare benefits) and in the dependent variable (rates, ratios, likelihoods, and so on, measured for teenagers, all AFDC recipients, current AFDC recipients, and other specific groups).

More recent evidence on family cap impacts is available from Section 1115 evaluations in a few other states, all of which utilized an experimental design. Turturro, Benda and Turney (1997) conclude from their evaluation of the Arkansas Section 1115 waiver demonstration that there was no statistically significant difference between control and experimental groups in the number of births that occurred after the waiver start date. These researchers also conclude (from sub-sample data) that the Arkansas Section 1115 waiver did not influence participation in family planning services or the use of birth control methods.[7] Turturro et al. did not differentiate between the behavior of new applicants and longer-term welfare cases in their analyses, potentially confounding program effects with time spent on welfare. Preliminary results from the Arizona experiment (Mills et al., 1999) indicate a reduction in births among unwed minors in welfare households (but not among female household heads) in response to a family cap. There is some survey evidence from Delaware's experiment that a family cap policy may influence the child-bearing decisions of women on welfare (Fein, 1999). Fein reports that women with intermediate welfare spell lengths experienced a fertility rate that was six percent lower than that for control group members. He also notes that evaluation subjects who were subject to the family cap expressed less enthusiasm for having more children.

There has been much less empirical research to discern a link between AFDC benefit levels (or changes in benefit levels) and abortions.[8] An early study by Moore and Caldwell (1977) of teenagers found that benefit size is negatively related to the likelihood that a teenager will obtain an abortion. Matthews, Ribar and Wilhelm (1997) related the levels and changes in the levels of AFDC benefits to abortion and birth rates across all fifty states. Abortion rates were positively related to grant levels, but were not related to changes in grant levels. Once again, these studies utilized non-experimental methods.

Blank, George and London (1994) utilize Alan Guttmacher Institute data from 1974–1988 to determine if changes in AFDC grant levels influence abortion rates, abortion rates for state residents and non-residents, and abortion rates by age and race. Overall, these analyses yield no significant AFDC effect, although the authors note that this may be explained by a lack of variation in their benefit measures over time; state-level variations in benefits may have been captured by state fixed effects in their models. To our knowledge, the evaluation of New Jersey's family cap is the only Section 1115 waivered evaluation to examine the impact of family cap policies on abortion rates.

DATA SOURCES

Data on births and abortions among women of childbearing age in the welfare population in New Jersey are obtained from administrative records maintained by the state welfare and medical assistance agencies. Administrative welfare records maintained by the New Jersey Department of Human Services-Division of Family Development (NJDHS-DFD) identify births reported for all women receiving AFDC cash assistance during a given quarter. We focus on the impact of FDP and the family cap only on "own" births where we can link the child to his/her birth mother within our administrative data sources, because we have the most accurate information on the birth mother characteristics for these births.[9] Between the fourth quarter of 1992 and the fourth quarter of 1996, we can identify the birth mothers for between 80 and 90% of all AFDC births each quarter.[10]

Abortion data come from Medicaid claims files. New Jersey is one of very few states extending Medicaid coverage to abortions. These claims files provide the most complete accounting of abortions performed for the AFDC population.[11]

Before proceeding with a formal analysis of the impact of New Jersey's Family Development Program on childbearing decisions of women on welfare, we compared quarterly trend data on births and abortions over time for this population to similar data for New Jersey's population of all women of child-bearing age (ages fifteen through forty-five) from 1991 through 1996.[12] While fertility rates for both women on AFDC and the entire population of women of childbearing age in New Jersey declined over our observation period, fertility rates among women on AFDC declined more rapidly than those observed in the population at large. In the first quarter of 1991 (and for some time thereafter), fertility rates among AFDC women were almost three times as high as those reported for the general population. By the end of our observation period, the fertility rate among women on AFDC was just double that of the general population. At least some of the divergence in trended fertility rates between the general and AFDC population may be explained by changes over time (among women in either group) in personal or other characteristics that can influence childbearing decisions. However, adjusting these descriptive data for age and racial differences between the two populations does not change our general observation that birth rates among AFDC women have declined relative to birth rates among the general population.

Abortion rates among females on AFDC were much higher than those observed over New Jersey's entire population of women of childbearing age between 1991 and 1996. At the beginning of 1991, abortion rates among women on AFDC were about six times higher than those observed over the general population. By the end of 1996, AFDC abortion rates averaged close to eight times higher than those reported for the general population. Abortion rates among women on AFDC were always higher than those reported for the general population, even after adjusting for age and race.

These trends in births and abortions over time among women on AFDC have been accompanied by significant changes in the AFDC caseload size and composition. Specifically:

- Active AFDC caseload size in New Jersey, that is, the number of AFDC cases that are presumptive eligible, active grants, suspended or Medicaid only, peaked during 1993–1994 and declined thereafter. As of the end of 1996, the total active AFDC caseload stood at 103,084 cases, a 5.6% decline since the beginning of our six-year observation period.
- The AFDC population is an aging population. A portion of this aging is due to the increase in the number of non-needy adult payees who are caring for children on AFDC. These "non-needy parent persons" average about forty-one years of age. Adult payees are also getting older. The average age of the female payee on AFDC has risen from 31.6 years in 1991 to about 33 years by 1996.
- The percentage of never married AFDC mothers rose from 61 to 66% in the six-year period studied.
- The percentage of two-adult households on AFDC increased slightly during the year 1992 from 3.4 to 5.4%, remained around 5% during 1994–1995 and declined in 1996.
- The educational attainment of females on AFDC rose between 1991 and 1996. More AFDC women completed high school. The percentage of AFDC women who went on to attend college increased from 8% to almost 11%.

The experimental design methodology described below should adequately control for all observable and unobservable changes in the AFDC population over our evaluation period. However, as a precaution, we also use multivariate estimation methods to examine the impact of the Family Development Program and its family cap on the birth and abortion decisions of women on welfare.

METHODOLOGY: EXPERIMENTAL DESIGN AND STATISTICAL ANALYSIS

Classic experimental design with randomization of subjects into experimental and control groups was designated by ACF-USDHHS as the methodology of choice for the evaluation of Section 1115 waivers issued during the Bush (I) and Clinton administrations. Randomized field trials had been employed in a number of national evaluations of employment and training programs including the

National Supported Work Demonstration (Hollister, Kemper & Maynard, 1984), the welfare-to-work experiments (Gueron & Pauly, 1991), and the National Job Training Partnership Act (JTPA) evaluation (Bloom, Orr & Cave et al., 1993).

Experiences from a number of Section 1115 waiver evaluations, however, have raised questions about the wisdom of using social experimentation. Some researchers concluded that experimental design was inappropriate for the evaluation of Wisconsin Works (Kaplan, 1997). This assessment stems from two serious flaws uncovered in the Wisconsin Works design: the difficulty in isolating a within-state control group from the incentives of a new policy that seeks to change the culture of public support expectations in a state; and the requirement that the state permit some recipients (control group members) to continue to rely on the pre-reform system, mandating program administrators to work with these clients under old rules (Haveman, 1997). Turturro, Benda and Turney (1997) note that the potential for contamination of the controls is especially high when a politically controversial and highly publicized waiver like the family cap is part of the experimental package. In the Arkansas Welfare Waiver and Demonstration Project, these researchers found no evidence for the effectiveness of a family cap on birth decisions or on other indicators of self sufficiency; they conjecture that impacts might have been blurred by the "bleeding of the (waiver) interventions to the control group via the social environment" (Turturro, Benda & Turney, 1997, p. 1). Many evaluators of Section 1115 welfare waivers, however, caution against the exaggeration of contamination effects in social experiments, especially if suspicions about contamination arise from client responses to survey questions (Bloom, Farrell, Kemple & Verma, 1999; Fein, Beecroft, Hamilton & Lee, 1998; Mills et al., 1999). The consensus, moreover, in this literature is that experimental contamination works to reduce statistical power, increasing the probability that a true policy or programmatic impact will go undetected and/or understating the treatment impact (Lipsey, 1990; Mohr, 1995). Cook and Campbell (1979) maintain that if there is reason to believe that the average amount of exposure to the treatment is less for controls than for experimental group members, data should be analyzed as if they come from a pure random experiment. Our analysis of treatment and environmental contamination in the FDP evaluation indicated that experimental group members had more exposure to both the message that they were subject to the family cap and to the actual experience of the family cap than did members of the control group (Camasso, Jagannathan, Harvey & Killingsworth, 2003).

A number of policy analysts (see Burtless, 1995; Burtless & Orr, 1986; Fraker & Maynard, 1987; Lalonde, 1986) argue persuasively that social experimentation, despite its costs, provides more valid estimates of treatment effects than a variety of non-experimental approaches. Lalonde, for example, shows how constructed controls in the Current Population Survey do not replicate experimentally-determined results from the National Supported Work Demonstration. More recently, Friedlander and Robins (1995) show that designs employing:

(a) controls from another state;
(b) statistically matched controls;
(c) within state-matched controls; and
(d) pre-post comparisons of cases within a particular area resulted in estimates of treatment effects that were usually quite different from experimental estimates derived from the same data.

The FDP Experiment

Experimental design was meant to provide a controlled test of New Jersey's Family Development Program (FDP). AFDC cases were selected at random from New Jersey's welfare rolls into experimental and control groups. Since cases are placed randomly into either a group receiving the FDP intervention (experimental) or a group not receiving the intervention (control), the experiences of the control group serve as a counterfactual, that is, as the outcome that would have been expected if FDP had not been implemented. Evaluation samples were drawn from two distinct groups within the welfare population:

- Families who were active on AFDC when the family cap provision of FDP was implemented on October 1, 1992 (ongoing cases); and
- Families who were certified for AFDC receipt between October 1, 1992 and December 1994 (new applicants).

New applicants, lacking a substantial period of experience with AFDC rules, could be expected to respond differently to FDP and its family cap, compared to ongoing cases. Cases selected into the evaluation sample were informed of their evaluation status when they applied or, for ongoing cases, when they visited the welfare office for re-certification.

Since cases were assigned randomly to either an experimental group subject to FDP waivers or a control group operating under preexistent AFDC rules in New Jersey, any post-assignment differences in births or abortions could, in principle, be interpreted as the effect of the FDP. The accuracy of the interpretation of program effect would, of course, depend on the continued integrity of the experiment: control group members must not have received FDP treatments and experimental group members must not have received rewards or punishments specified outside the FDP waivers.

We did encounter some evidence of actual treatment delivery contamination and of control group exposure to the experimental message. In November 1994 and again in January 1995, we discovered that the family cap was inappropriately applied to twenty-one cases in the control group. A majority of these cases were assigned to a single field office in one county, and tighter administrative controls were instituted immediately to prevent future incidents of this kind. Efforts to limit contamination through agency treatment delivery proved to be successful and we do not view contamination in treatment delivery as a major threat to the internal validity of our evaluation of birth and abortion impacts.

We were more concerned about the likelihood that control cases were contaminated through environmental exposure to the highly publicized family cap and its message that parents need to assume at least some financial responsibility for their children. The possibility of contamination of controls through environmental exposure was uncovered in a recipient survey undertaken in July 1995 (Camasso, Jagannathan & Harvey, 1996). A sample of 1,236 recipients (with a 41% response rate) were asked the following question, "Have you been told that you are included in a control group of welfare recipients who receive welfare benefits under the old welfare rules called REACH/JOBS?" While 65% of experimental group members identified themselves as experimental group cases, only about 40% of the control group members believed themselves to be in a control group. An analysis of birth and abortion behavior by actual experimental-control group assignment and their perceived group membership revealed that only actual (and not perceived) group assignment was related to child-bearing behavior.[13] We concluded that the survey respondents simply did not understand the survey question (Camasso, Jagannathan, Harvey & Killingsworth, 2003). It is also possible that bias could have entered into the experiment as a result of participant perceptions that the experiment was a temporary condition. We believe this is unlikely since the controls were asked to continue with the traditional AFDC program and the experimental cases were informed that they were subject to the program rules that New Jersey had adopted statewide as its new public assistance program.

The Research Sample

The original sampling plan outlined by the NJDHS-DFD called for the random assignment of 9,000 cases into equal groupings of ongoing recipients and newly certified entrants. Both ongoing cases (active as of October 1, 1992) and new cases (certified since October 1, 1992) were to be randomly assigned to experimental or control status on the basis of the last four digits of the case head's social security number. Experimental groups were to be populated with 3,000 cases and control

Table 1. Sampling Design for the Collection of Administrative Data on Experimental and Control Cases.

Sample Group	Case Type	Number of Cases
FDP experimentals	New	2,233
	Ongoing	3,268
Controls	New	1,285
	Ongoing	1,607

groups with 1,500 cases. Sample cases were to be drawn from the ten counties where the Family Development Program was to be implemented first, that is, Essex, Camden, Hudson, Atlantic, Cumberland, Mercer, Middlesex, Monmouth, Passaic and Union Counties.[14] These counties accounted for over 85% of the AFDC cases in New Jersey.

Sample selection for new applicants was planned to last for one year, ending on September 30, 1993. However, a shortfall in the expected number of new applicants led to an extension of sample selection until the end of December 1994. The final sample contained 8,393 evaluation subjects distributed by sample subgroup as depicted in Table 1.

Potentially, we had seventeen quarterly observations (from the fourth quarter of 1992 through the fourth quarter of 1996) for each ongoing case, with somewhat fewer observations for new cases selected into the sample after the fourth quarter of 1992. While we intended to pool these observations for analysis, our analytical approach had to account for the impact of attrition from the sample on our ability to obtain reliable data on births and abortions. Over the evaluation period, many evaluation subjects left AFDC for varying periods of time. Some cases left permanently, while others cycled back onto the welfare rolls. An examination of the duration of welfare spells and reasons for leaving welfare did not reveal any significant differences between experimental and control cases. Following the policy objectives of FDP, we excluded any quarterly observations in which the case was not enrolled on AFDC, since births, abortions or other fertility behaviors occurring in such quarters were not subject to the family cap provision. It is also important to note that "off-quarter" births and abortions are not easily tracked in New Jersey, with the reliability of abortion data being especially questionable.[15]

In Tables 2 and 3, we show the sample characteristics of ongoing and new applicant cases. Characteristics are measured in December 1994, December 1995 and December 1996. These tables show that new applicants tend to be younger than ongoing cases, to have fewer children on AFDC and are more likely to have completed high school and to have attended college. New applicants are also less

Table 2. Sample Characteristics of Ongoing Cases by Experimental and Control Group Status.

	Experimental Cases			Control Cases		
	Dec. 1994	Dec. 1995	Dec. 1996	Dec. 1994	Dec. 1995	Dec. 1996
Characteristic						
Mean						
Female head age	30.6	31.5	32.2	30.7	31.5	32.2
Eligible children[a]	2.0	2.0	2.0	2.1	2.2	2.2
Household size[a]	4.1	4.1	4.1	4.1	4.2	4.2
Percentage						
White	13.0	12.1	11.3	13.0	13.1	10.8
Black	54.7	56.3	56.6	56.6	56.7	59.1
Hispanic	31.4	30.8	31.4	29.6	29.4	29.6
Percentage						
High school dropout	43.4	44.1	44.1	43.8	46.2	46.8
High school graduate	37.7	38.3	38.1	38.5	36.7	35.5
College	7.8	7.1	6.9	8.2	7.1	8.2
Unknown education	0.7	0.5	0.6	0.5	0.6	0.2
Never married (%)	71.9	72.4	72.3	74.7	74.8	76.9
Number of cases[b]	1812	1523	1273	857	725	602

[a] Counts of children or household members used in the calculation of cash grant.
[b] Numbers may differ from those presented in Table 1 due both to attrition from the sample and, more rarely, due to cases with missing values on the administrative database.

likely to have never married, and were also slightly less likely to be either African-American or Hispanic.

Descriptive Results: Births and Abortions

Since evaluation cases were assigned at random into experimental and control groups, these two groups can be viewed as statistically equivalent, at least at the time of assignment. Hence, in principle, any post-assignment differences in average outcomes between the two groups, as documented above, can be interpreted as resulting from the Family Development Program and its family cap. Following this strategy, we compute simple birth and abortion rates after pooling seventeen quarters of data, and compare experimental and control group rates.[16] These rates are provided in Table 4 for all cases combined, for ongoing cases, and for new applicants.

Table 3. Sample Characteristics of New Cases by Experimental and Control Group Status.

	Experimental Cases			Control Cases		
	Dec. 1994	Dec. 1995	Dec. 1996	Dec. 1994	Dec. 1995	Dec. 1996
Characteristic						
Mean						
Female head age	28.2	28.5	29.4	28.6	29.0	29.5
Eligible children[a]	1.6	1.6	1.6	1.7	1.9	1.9
Household size[a]	4.0	4.0	4.1	4.1	4.1	4.3
Percentage						
White	16.9	14.7	13.2	18.1	17.0	18.3
Black	49.2	52.3	53.4	50.4	50.4	51.0
Hispanic	31.8	30.7	30.7	29.6	30.5	29.6
Percentage						
High school dropout	34.1	36.3	40.3	32.2	31.8	35.4
High school graduate	45.8	44.6	42.6	42.8	44.6	41.4
College	10.8	10.1	8.9	15.9	14.2	14.2
Unknown education	0.4	0.5	0.3	0.8	0.9	1.1
Never married (%)	66.2	69.5	69.3	65.1	67.3	69.6
Number of cases[b]	1139	837	612	619	452	355

[a] Counts of children or household members used in the calculation of cash grant.
[b] Numbers may differ from those presented in Table 1 due both to attrition from the sample and, more rarely, due to cases with missing values on the administrative database.

Birth rates were lower among experimental subjects over the study period, compared with control group users (see Panel A). This decline is especially pronounced among new applicant cases. Overall, we observe a 7% decline in births that is statistically significant for all cases (ongoing cases and new applicants combined) in our evaluation sample.

Likewise, overall abortion rates are 11% higher among experimental subjects, compared with control group subjects (see Panel B). The difference is statistically significant for all cases combined; this difference is, in large measure, concentrated among new applicants.

Regression Models and Estimation Methods

We follow our simple descriptive comparisons with more elaborate regression models that improve the precision of the impact estimates by controlling for the

Table 4. Comparison of Experimental Birth and Abortion Outcomes.

	All Cases		Ongoing Cases		New Applicant	
	Experimental	Control	Experimental	Control	Experimental	Control
Panel A: Births						
Number of births	1124	607	664	323	460	284
Person quarters	44828	22313	31349	14853	13479	7460
Birth rate	0.025	0.027	0.021	0.022	0.034	0.038
Percent difference (Experimental − Control)/Control	−0.074*		−0.045		−0.105	
Panel B: Abortions						
Number of abortions	1399	617	958	436	441	181
Person quarters	44828	22313	31349	14853	13479	7460
Abortion rate	0.031	0.028	0.031	0.029	0.033	0.024
Percent difference (Experimental − Control)/Control	0.107**		0.069		0.375**	

Note: Starred differences are significant at the 90% (*) or 95% (**) confidence levels.

passage of time and for other relevant factors that might influence birth and abortion outcomes. Specifically, we estimate three separate probit models as follows:

$$P(\text{OUTCOME})_{it} = \beta_0 + \beta_1 \text{TIME}_t + \beta_2 \text{STATUS}_i + \beta_3 (\text{STATUS}_i \times \text{TIME}_t) + \beta_4 \text{QUARTER} + e_{it} \quad (1)$$

$$P(\text{OUTCOME})_{it} = \beta_0 + \beta_1 \text{TIME}_t + \beta_2 \text{STATUS}_i + \beta_3 (\text{STATUS}_i \times \text{TIME}_t) + \beta_4 \text{QUARTER} + \lambda_1 \text{PERSON}_i + \lambda_2 \text{KIDS}_i + \lambda_3 \text{CONTEXT}_t + e_{it} \quad (2)$$

$$P(\text{OUTCOME})_{it} = \beta_0 + \beta_1 \text{TIME}_t + \beta_4 \text{QUARTER} + \gamma_1 \text{MIDDLE} + \gamma_2 (\text{TIME}_t \times \text{MIDDLE}) + \gamma_3 \text{AFTER} + \gamma_4 (\text{TIME}_t \times \text{AFTER}) + \lambda_1 \text{PERSON}_i + \lambda_2 \text{KIDS}_i + \lambda_3 \text{CONTEXT}_t + e_{it} \quad (3)$$

where the subscripts *it* indicate individual AFDC female case head (age fifteen through forty-five) i in quarter t. (OUTCOME) refers to either births recorded on a case where the birth mother heads the case (own births) or abortion(s) obtained by the AFDC case head. P(OUTCOME) refers to the probability that the outcome in question will occur. Models were estimated separately for new applicant and ongoing cases.

The first model is our baseline model and focuses on the simple impact of the family cap on observed outcomes (either births or abortions). TIME_t measures the effects of otherwise unmeasured factors that change smoothly over time. Time trend influence was modeled using both linear and quadratic terms; our results were invariant to this specification of the time trend. Seasonal indicator variables (QUARTER) were also included to capture seasonal patterns in both births and abortions.

The program effect of FDP and the family cap is measured as a dichotomous variable ($STATUS_i$) with experimental group cases (those subject to FDP and its family cap) receiving a value of one and control cases (those subject to the former welfare program) coded as zero, for each quarter since the time of random assignment. In addition, we include an interaction term ($STATUS_i \times TIME_t$) to measure changes in treatment impact over time. While this coding poses no problem when we analyze abortion outcomes, it could underestimate birth effects, since only those births conceived while on welfare are subject to the family cap. To ensure that our program effect measures applied only to births potentially subject to the family cap, our dependent variable only included those births that occurred ten or more months after the case was assigned to the sample.

The second model (2) adds variables denoting personal and socioeconomic influences. The individual factors $PERSON_i$ measure characteristics of the AFDC female case head, including recipient race, age, education, and marital status. Variables such as recipient age are exogenous, that is, they change over time for reasons that have nothing to do with FDP. However, other variables (like education or marital status) may be endogenous, since the Family Development Program could exert some influence over these behaviors. We fix age, marital status and educational attainment for each case at its initial value at entry into the sample to limit the possibility of endogeneity among our independent variables. Data on all individual characteristics is obtained from administrative welfare records.

We also include an array of variables to capture characteristics of the children in the household ($KIDS_i$). Specifically, we adjust for the total number of AFDC-eligible children in the household, the ages of both the female's own children and other children (related or unrelated to the female) and the presence of children receiving SSI in the household. Adjustments for the number and ages of the welfare recipient's own (biological and adopted) children are commonplace in the literature (see, for example, Argys, Averett & Rees, 2000; Fairlie & London, 1997; Hill & O'Neill, 1993; Rank, 1989). Our inclusion of all children in the household, both related and unrelated to the recipient, reflects our acknowledgement of the important role that blended families can have on birth decisions (Case, Lin & McLanahan, 1999; Winkler, 1993). The inclusion of children in the household by the type of financial support each receives allows us to focus on the role played by AFDC cash assistance payments on birth decisions. Once again, these variables are fixed at their initial values, that is, their values at time of entry into the sample.

A series of economic and contextual variables ($CONTEXT_t$) are included to capture location-specific criteria such as local economic conditions and county-specific program implementation variables, as well as other possible time-invariant but unobservable influences operating at the county level. These covariates include a series of nine dummy variables to represent the counties in the sample, with Union County, New Jersey serving as a reference category. We also include county unemployment rates from December 1992 through December 1996 to control for changes in local labor market conditions over the study period. Finally, county-level JOBS/FDP program participation rates provide some indication of the extent to which educational and training options were available to welfare recipients in each county under the Family Development Program. County participation rates vary over time within each county, with large variations across counties.

In our final specification, we allow the impact of the family cap on birth decisions to vary over time by dividing the evaluation period into two periods: an initial implementation period (MIDDLE) lasting four quarters (from the fourth quarter of 1992 through the third quarter of 1993) and a fully-operational period from December 1993 through December 1996 (AFTER). Both MIDDLE and AFTER take a value of one for experimental group subjects, and zero for control group subjects during the time period referenced. Interactions with our TIME variable are also included.

Finally, e_{it} indicates the error term in all three specifications.

We estimate our probit models using robust regression to adjust standard errors of estimates for repeated observations in a panel. Huber-weighted standard errors produced by these regressions are reported.[17] In addition to reporting the direction of the treatment effect we undertake a series of simulations to provide a range for the magnitude of the effect. The simulations are constructed in this way: we set individual characteristics at their initial values and, using the estimated regression coefficients from Eq. (2), compute a predicted probability of a birth (abortion) for each welfare recipient. We then average these probabilities across all individuals in each quarter for both experimental and control groups. These averaged probabilities are then multiplied by the appropriate number of cases at risk of experiencing a birth (abortion). The average percent difference between the experimental and control group births represents the percent change in overall births (abortions) that is attributed to the family cap. It should be noted that while the simulations are provided to graphically describe the time-path of the family cap impact, they do not constitute an estimate in a formal statistical sense, since the simulations use the coefficients from the estimated models without regard to their standard errors.

REGRESSION RESULTS

Separate birth models are estimated for ongoing cases and new applicants. Complete regression results for the entire model are provided in Tables A1 and A2 in the Appendix; here we report only estimated regression coefficients for the time and experimental status variables.

Table 5 presents coefficient estimates for ongoing cases; coefficient estimates for births among new applicants are found in Table 6. Births decline over time for both ongoing cases and new applicants. However, these subgroups differ in their response to the introduction of a family cap rule. There is little response to this rule among our sample of ongoing cases; estimated coefficients on the experimental status indicator are not statistically significant. New applicant cases,

Table 5. Estimated Models: Births among Ongoing Cases.

	MODEL 1 Coefficient (Std. Error)	MODEL 2 Coefficient (Std. Error)	MODEL 3 Coefficient (Std. Error)
Constant	−1.903	0.760	0.630
	(0.047)	(1.410)	(1.419)
Time	−0.009**	−0.016**	−0.015**
	(0.004)	(0.007)	(0.007)
Status (Experimental = 1)	0.040	0.025	
	(0.050)	(0.051)	
Time × Status	−0.007	−0.007	
	(0.005)	(0.006)	
Middle (Dec. 1992–Sept. 1993)			0.052
			(0.089)
Middle × Time			−0.028
			(0.031)
After (Dec. 1993–Dec. 1996)			0.101
			(0.075)
After × Time			−0.013*
			(0.007)
June	−0.071*	−0.072*	−0.062
	(0.039)	(0.042)	(0.043)
September	−0.059	−0.080*	−0.057
	(0.040)	(0.046)	(0.048)
December	−0.063*	−0.081**	−0.078*
	(0.036)	(0.040)	(0.043)

Note: Huber-adjusted standard errors in parentheses. Starred coefficients are significant at the 90% (*) or 95% (**) confidence level.

Table 6. Estimated Models: Births among New Applicants.

	MODEL 1 Coefficient (Std. Error)	MODEL 2 Coefficient (Std. Error)	MODEL 3 Coefficient (Std. Error)
Constant	−1.560 (0.056)	−0.101 (1.212)	0.248 (1.221)
Time	−0.053** (0.008)	−0.042** (0.010)	−0.046** (0.010)
Status (Experimental = 1)	−0.117** (0.058)	−0.128** (0.055)	
Time × Status	0.013 (0.010)	0.018* (0.011)	
Middle (Dec. 1992–Sept. 1993)			0.156 (0.120)
Middle × Time			−0.090 (0.063)
After (Dec. 1993–Dec. 1996)			−0.205** (0.063)
After × Time			0.027** (0.011)
June	0.077 (0.050)	0.085 (0.053)	0.076 (0.054)
September	0.130** (0.050)	0.196** (0.060)	0.166** (0.062)
December	0.084* (0.050)	0.157** (0.060)	0.132** (0.061)

Note: Huber-adjusted standard errors in parentheses. Starred coefficients are significant at the 90% (*) or 95% (**) confidence level.

a group that is younger and with less welfare experience, are more responsive to the introduction of a family cap. The estimated coefficient on the experimental status variable is negative and significant in both Model 1 (baseline model) and Model 2 (full covariate model). Because the models also include an interaction term between time and experimental status, we present a graphical summary of the birth impact for new cases in Fig. 1, generated from simulations using coefficients from Model 2. Figure 1 shows that the birth impact varies over time; the vertical distance between the two curves is narrow at the beginning of the experiment, widens in mid-1993 and tapers again for the remainder of the study period.

The introduction of a family cap late in 1992 did not immediately affect birth rates. Since the regulation applied only to children who were conceived while their mothers were receiving AFDC, we could not expect to observe any birth effects

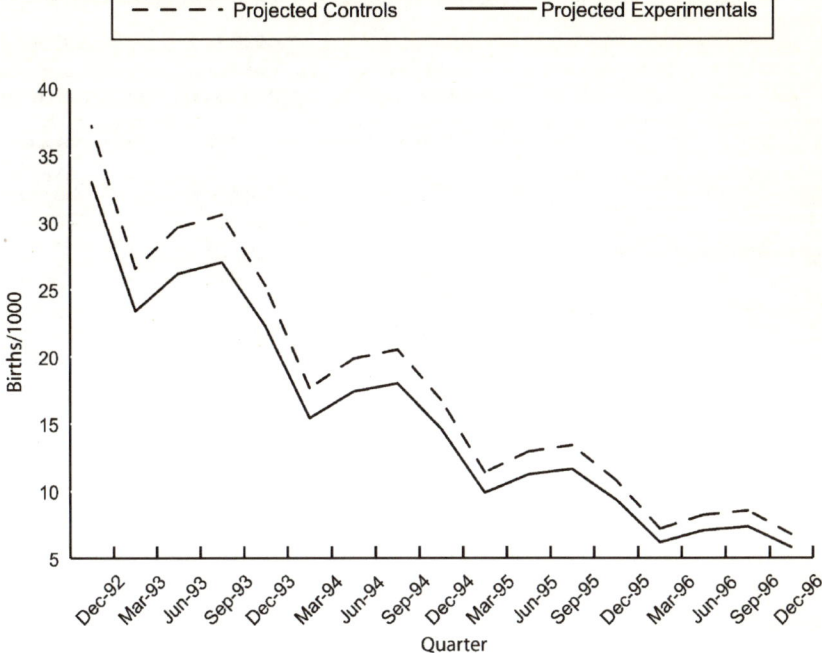

Fig. 1. Births per 1000 Projected from Probit Model for New Cases by Quarter.

until at least ten months after the family cap took effect. This is indeed what we find when we examine the estimated coefficients in Model 3, where significant birth impacts are observed among experimental groups subjects beginning in the fourth quarter of 1993 (a full year after the implementation of the family cap). While we find a statistically-significant decline in birth rates among new applicants during the period beginning in the fourth quarter of 1993 (as evidenced by the negative and statistically-significant coefficient on AFTER), this impact becomes weaker over time; note the positive and statistically-significant coefficient on the interaction between AFTER and TIME.[18]

Tables 7 and 8 provide model estimates for abortions among ongoing cases and new applicants, respectively. Complete regression results are provided in Tables A3 and A4 in the Appendix. The Family Development Program and its family cap had no statistically significant impact on abortions among our sample of ongoing AFDC cases. However, we observe a statistically-significant increase in abortions among new applicants in our evaluation sample who were subject to the family cap, compared with otherwise similar control group cases. The

Table 7. Estimated Models: Abortions among Ongoing Cases.

	MODEL 1 Coefficient (Std. Error)	MODEL 2 Coefficient (Std. Error)	MODEL 3 Coefficient (Std. Error)
Constant	−1.760 (0.048)	−2.354 (1.412)	−2.434 (1.428)
Time	−0.013** (0.005)	−0.025** (0.007)	−0.024** (0.008)
Status (Experimental = 1)	−0.017 (0.054)	−0.020 (0.056)	
Time × Status	0.005 (0.006)	0.006 (0.006)	
Middle (Dec. 1992–Sept. 1993)			−0.081 (0.090)
Middle × Time			0.031 (0.028)
After (Dec. 1993–Dec. 1996)			−0.017 (0.075)
After × Time			0.005 (0.007)
June	−0.014 (0.031)	−0.021 (0.033)	−0.025 (0.034)
September	−0.018 (0.033)	−0.024 (0.038)	−0.031 (0.040)
December	0.075** (0.032)	−0.099** (0.037)	−0.089** (0.039)

Note: Huber-adjusted standard errors in parentheses. Starred coefficients are significant at the 90% (*) or 95% (**) confidence level.

tendency to respond to the family cap by aborting pregnancies declined over time from the end of 1993 onward, as evidenced by the negative (but statistically insignificant) coefficient on the interaction between AFTER and time. Another way to see this declining difference between experimental and controls is the time-path for the abortion effect presented in Fig. 2.[19]

Sensitivity Analysis

To examine the robustness of these impact estimates, we tested a series of alternative model specifications and estimation procedures. Alternative estimation procedures (including linear probability models, logistic regression, and Poisson

Table 8. Estimated Models: Abortions among New Applicants.

	MODEL 1 Coefficient (Std. Error)	MODEL 2 Coefficient (Std. Error)	MODEL 3 Coefficient (Std. Error)
Constant	−1.972 (0.066)	−1.537 (1.527)	−1.773 (1.534)
Time	0.011 (0.007)	−0.002 (0.009)	<0.001 (0.009)
Status (Experimental = 1)	0.171** (0.072)	0.189** (0.075)	
Time × Status	−0.006 (0.009)	−0.011 (0.009)	
Middle (Dec. 1992–Sept. 1993)			−0.143 (0.166)
Middle × Time			0.120* (0.066)
After (Dec. 1993–Dec. 1996)			0.230** (0.080)
After × Time			−0.016 (0.010)
June	−0.069 (0.048)	−0.069 (0.051)	−0.067 (0.051)
September	−0.094** (0.046)	−0.129** (0.053)	−0.115** (0.055)
December	−0.129** (0.048)	−0.184** (0.055)	−0.167** (0.057)

Note: Huber-adjusted standard errors in parentheses. Starred coefficients are significant at the 90% (*) or 95% (**) confidence level.

regression) yield the same substantive conclusions as our probit models. Likewise, altering the methodology in other ways does not alter the results. While we use regression methods to control for differences in baseline characteristics when estimating FDP impacts on births and abortions, case level observations on births may not be independent, and conventional regression analyses could lead to incorrect standard errors and statistical tests of significance. For example, a woman who gives birth in one quarter will not be able to give birth again within the next three quarters. To address the possibility of lack of independence on observations, we removed quarterly observations where a birth will not be observed for biological reasons, that is, because of a birth within three quarters prior to that quarter. None of our risk-pool adjustments yielded impact estimates that differed greatly from the estimates presented here.

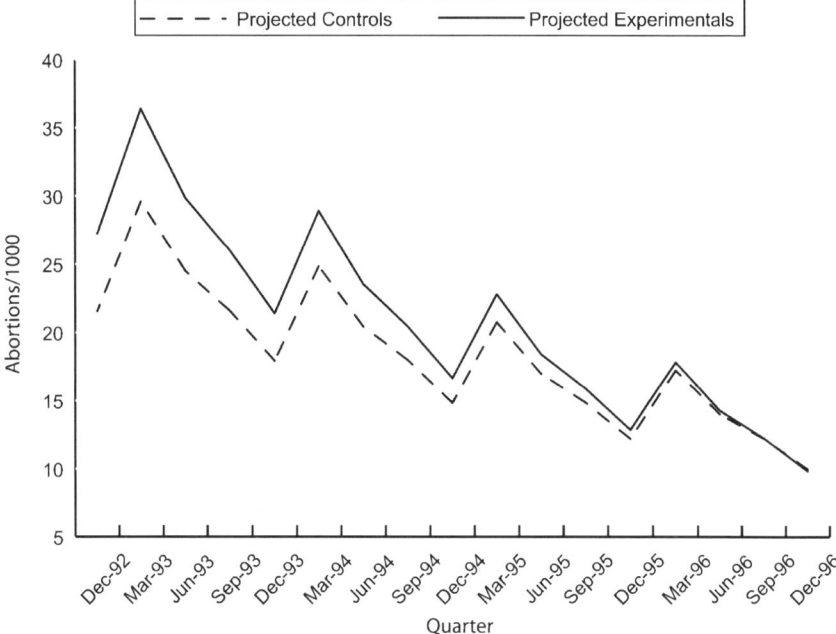

Fig. 2. Abortions Projected from Probit Model for New Cases by Quarter.

SUMMARY AND DISCUSSION

Our analysis finds a link between the implementation of a family cap policy in New Jersey and the birth decisions of women on welfare. Births to women on welfare who were affected by this policy declined, even after accounting for personal characteristics and other factors that influence birth decisions. Data on other FDP impacts showed no significant programmatic impacts on employment or earnings (Camasso, Harvey, Jagannathan & Killingsworth, 1998b), thus, differences in labor market participation (unmeasured in our models) would not explain these differences in birth (or abortion) outcomes. Moreover, this response was, by and large, limited to women with shorter welfare histories; birth rates among women who have been on welfare longer were not appreciably responsive to the introduction of the family cap.

At least some of this reduction in births was associated with an increased incidence of abortion among these same women in our data. This reaction to the family cap was, again, exhibited by that subgroup within the welfare population who were younger, more well-educated, and who had spent, cumulatively, less time on welfare. These findings appear to be robust with respect to model specification.

The timing of these birth and abortion reactions is also noteworthy. The reduction in births declines as time passes between the implementation of the family cap and the end of 1996. Birth and abortion impacts were more likely to be observed beginning in the fourth quarter of 1993, when the first children conceived after the implementation of the family cap would have been born. Both birth and abortion impacts decline over time. However, the birth effect persists through the end of the observation period (see Fig. 1), while the abortion impact diminishes much more rapidly (see Fig. 2). This implies that women of childbearing age on AFDC became more successful in avoiding pregnancy as time went on. We have reason from other analyses to believe that this is, in fact, the case (Jagannathan & Camasso, 2003). Similar analyses of the impact of FDP and the family cap on the use of family planning services and contraception by women on AFDC indicate a marked increase in the use of both by these women after the onset of the family cap policy in New Jersey (see Camasso, Harvey, Jagannathan & Killingsworth, 1998a, b, for more details).

As indicated earlier, it may be difficult to insulate the control group in experimental designs used to evaluate highly publicized social policy ventures, from widespread contamination. While we have reason to believe that such contamination likely occurred in the Family Development Program evaluation, it clearly did not seriously compromise the experiment. We still found statistically significant differences between experimentals and controls in key outcomes. To the extent that the experiment was contaminated, our results likely understate the true impacts on births and abortions (Camasso, Jagannathan, Harvey & Killingsworth, 2003).

We emphasize that our analysis is limited to the family formation decisions of these women while they are on AFDC. We cannot say anything about the longer-term impacts of a family cap policy on these decisions after these women left the welfare rolls. Nor can we shed any light on the impact of family cap policies on family formation decisions by young women, particularly teens, who are potential welfare candidates. Whether family cap policies will significantly reduce out-of-wedlock birth rates remains an open question.

We also note that the family cap was but one provision in a package of welfare reforms that constituted the Family Development Program. Is it possible that the birth and abortion impacts that we documented arose, at least in part, as a response to any other FDP provisions? The experiment itself was not designed to disentangle the separate effects of each programmatic element on measured outcomes, and we are unable, at this juncture, to do so analytically. However, it is difficult to argue that such provisions as a two-year Medicaid extension, a reduction in the "marriage penalty," or stricter JOBS program participation requirements could have nearly as much influence on child-bearing decisions as a family cap provision, since the family cap is the only component of the New Jersey waiver package that directly targets birth decisions.

The family cap, viewed by some as a punitive measure, was intended by New Jersey's policy makers as a positive step towards encouraging individual responsibility. By removing the additional cash benefit paid for those children conceived by women on AFDC, the State of New Jersey sent a clear message: women on AFDC, like all other women in the state, will take their financial ability to support another child into consideration before conceiving and bearing another child. We have shown that women on welfare responded to that message. The Family Development Program and its family cap had a definite if limited impact on the family formation decisions of women on AFDC in New Jersey.

Can our results be used to predict the impact of a family cap on AFDC/TANF births and abortions elsewhere? That is a difficult question to answer. The age, race, and ethnic composition of caseloads in other states, along with local labor market conditions, the exact size of the benefits loss, and the availability of family planning and abortion services will all play a role in determining the outcome. The latter point is particularly important, as New Jersey is one of only fifteen states that provide Medicaid funding for abortion services. Family cap impacts in most other states, where abortion services may not be as easily accessible to women on AFDC, may be quite different. Based on our findings, however, it is quite reasonable to hypothesize that the implementation of a family cap may very well increase abortions in states like New Jersey that provide public funding for this procedure.[20] It is also reasonable to examine the effectiveness of the PRWORA provision that offers cash rewards to these states for decreases in birth rates if these reductions are not linked to increases in abortion rates (Dye & Presser, 1999; Rivers, 2001). Our research will hopefully stimulate investigation into this area of intersecting and possibly conflicting policy initiatives.

NOTES

1. This according to U.S. General Accounting Office (2001). Since our analysis utilizes data from the pre-TANF period, we use the prior welfare program terminology, AFDC, when referring to the welfare program that was eventually replaced by TANF.

2. Food stamp recipients are required to use 30% of any income for food. Thus, the maximum food stamp allotment is reduced by an amount equal to 30% of other income. For example, an increase in AFDC benefits of $102 attributable to the birth of a second child will reduce the maximum food stamp allotment for a family of three by $127.20, or 30% of $424 in income from AFDC.

3. Under the family cap, this same household (mother and one child) would not receive an additional $102 per month in cash benefits with the birth of a second child; the monthly cash benefit would remain at $322. However, the maximum food stamp benefit per month (for a family of three), would only be reduced by $96.60, or 30% of $322.

4. Under this enhanced earnings disregard, women with children affected by the family cap were able to keep a higher percentage of their earned income without losing benefits. Specifically, these women could keep earnings amounting to 50% of their cash benefits with no loss of benefits for the first four months of employment, compared with 30% of cash benefits for other AFDC recipients who found employment.

5. Under federal regulations, New Jersey was only required to offer a one-year Medicaid extension.

6. Federal regulations required that women with children age six or older participate in these JOBS activities; under the prior welfare program in New Jersey, the JOBS participation requirement was extended to women with children age three or older.

7. The contraception results are drawn from a small subsample of experimental and control group cases, however, and gaps in the data and other difficulties with Arkansas administrative data could have influenced the analysis of birth and family planning outcomes (Turturro et al., 1997).

8. However, other studies examine the impact on abortions of other public policy measures, such as changes in public funding for abortions, parental consent regulations, and similar measures. See Blank, George and London (1994).

9. Each AFDC case record includes a series of child records, one for each child in the household. Within each child record is a field that identifies the relationship between the child on that record and the female AFDC payee. When that indicator shows that the female payee is that child's mother, then we have identified an "own" birth to the payee. There may well be other newborn children (with mothers also on welfare) who are listed on, for example, their grandmother's AFDC grant. Administrative data sources do not allow us to reliably identify the mothers of these children, even if these mothers reside in the same household.

10. Medicaid claims files maintained by the NJDHS-Division of Medical Assistance and Health Services (DMAHS) provide another possible source of data on AFDC births. When we compare the number of all births reported to Medicaid with all AFDC births known to the welfare authorities, we find that these counts track each other closely prior to the beginning of 1995, although Medicaid births were historically higher. Beginning in 1995, births recorded in the welfare records exceed those reported to Medicaid, and the difference between the two widens over time. During this same period, New Jersey mandated managed care enrollment within Medicaid for AFDC recipients. At the beginning of 1996, 36.6% of all AFDC cases were enrolled in a Medicaid managed care plan; this percentage rose to 82.6% by the end of 1996. We believe that delays in reporting claims by managed care providers under contract with Medicaid accounts for a portion of the decline in Medicaid births since June 1995. We conclude that birth data from Medicaid claims files become less reliable as AFDC cases shifted over to managed care.

11. The introduction of mandatory managed care enrollment for Medicaid recipients does not affect reported abortions in the Medicaid claims files, as abortions are provided on a fee-for-service basis and are not covered by Medicaid managed care plans.

12. Data on births among the general population in New Jersey are available through Vital Statistics records maintained by the New Jersey Department of Health and Senior

Services (NJDHSS). Information on the number of abortions per quarter among all women of childbearing age in New Jersey were provided by the State of New Jersey Department of Health and Senior Services, through the NJDHSS Hospital/Abortion Facility Induced Pregnancy Termination reporting system. Abortions to New Jersey residents performed by both in-state and out-of-state facilities are included in this reporting system. For purposes of comparison with state-wide trend data, fertility and abortion rates among women on welfare are calculated for all births reported to welfare authorities. In our subsequent analysis of family cap impacts, however, we count only those outcomes (births or abortions) for which we can identify the birth mother. These data are provided in Camasso, Harvey, Jagannathan and Killingsworth (1998a).

13. When survey respondents were asked explicitly if the "family cap" had influenced specific behaviors, experimental cases were significantly more likely than control cases to state that they decided putting off having more children; advised a friend to have an abortion; began to use contraception methods more consistently; began the use of different contraception methods; got a check-up for health problems resulting from the use of a birth control method; got advice from family planning counselors about an unwanted pregnancy; received counseling about birth control; received counseling about whether or not to have a abortion; and tried harder to get off welfare (Camasso et al., 1996).

14. FDP became fully effective in Essex, Camden and Hudson Counties on October 1, 1992. Atlantic, Cumberland, Mercer, Passaic and Union Counties were brought into the Family Development Program on October 1, 1993. FDP implementation in Middlesex and Monmouth Counties was delayed until January 1, 1995, when FDP became fully effective throughout the State.

15. Not all of the cases that leave the AFDC rolls will retain eligibility for Medicaid in New Jersey. Births for these cases cannot be tracked through vital statistics records, as birth certificate information in New Jersey did not, over the study period, include the mother's social security number. Survey data on pregnancy outcomes is not always reliable, particularly when dealing with the issue of abortion. A comparison of administrative data on pregnancy outcomes with information on pregnancies, births, and abortions obtained through an interim survey of evaluation subjects indicated significant disparities between these two sources of information (Jagannathan, 2001).

16. These rates are computed by dividing the number of events (births or abortions) by the number of observations that are at risk of experiencing the event. The number of observations is expressed as person-quarters. We treat multiple births as exogenous, and children from these births are counted as a single event. It should be noted that multiple births are a relatively rare event in the experiment and are proportional to the sample sizes of experimental and control cases. The number of twin events reported in the ongoing cases sample was nine for experimentals and four for controls. In the new case sample, it was five for experimentals and three for controls. One set of triplets was recorded for ongoing experimental cases.

17. See Huber (1964, 1981) for an exposition of these robust regression methods.

18. Estimated coefficients for personal, household, and economic/contextual covariates generally behave as expected. Birth probabilities among blacks are higher, and in the case of ongoing sub-sample, statistically significant. As women's education increases, their birth probability declines; for ongoing cases, this education effect is statistically significant. The likelihood of a birth decreases with increasing age. The number of eligible children has the expected negative association with the probability of a birth; this probability declines in a

nearly linear fashion. When we examine the effect of the number of previous biological children the mother has had, we see that the younger the child(ren), the higher the probability of an additional birth. This, however, is not the case for non-biological children (Other children). Finally, we see that having biological children who receive disability benefits under the Supplemental Security Income (SSI) program lowers the probability of birth for both new and ongoing cases. One important influence on childbirth decisions, the mother's ability to get a job and/or previous work history, could not be included in these models due to data limitations.

19. Women who were never married, who are more educated, or who are black have an increased probability of an abortion during our observation period. We do not find any systematic relationship between number of AFDC-eligible children or biological children and the probability of abortion. There is a negative relationship between the number of biological children receiving SSI and the probability of abortion. Overall, the relationships between the covariates and abortion are what we would expect to find from the available literature on the correlates on abortion behavior.

20. The other states are Alaska, California, Connecticut, Hawaii, Idaho, Illinois, Massachusetts, Minnesota, Montana, New York, Oregon, Vermont, Washington, and West Virginia (NARAL, 1998).

ACKNOWLEDGMENTS

Funding for this research was provided by USDHHS, Administration for Children and Families, and the New Jersey Department of Human Services. Earlier drafts of this paper were presented at the NBER Universities Research Conference on the Impact of Recent Federal and State Reforms in Public Assistance and Social Insurance Programs (May 14–15, 1999), the annual meetings of the American Economic Association in January, 2000, and at seminars at Rutgers University, Syracuse University, and Princeton University. The authors gratefully acknowledge helpful comments and suggestions received from Stacy Dickert-Conlin, Phillip Levine, and Douglas Holtz-Eakin, and other seminar attendees, as well as from an anonymous referee. We take full responsibility for any remaining errors of commission or omission.

REFERENCES

Argys, L. M., Averett, S., & Rees, D. I. (2000). Welfare generosity, pregnancies and abortions among unmarried AFDC recipients. *Journal of Population Economics, 13*, 569–594.

Bernstam, M. S. (1988). Malthus and the evaluation of the welfare state: An essay on the second invisible hand. Working paper E-88–41, 43. Hoover Institute.

Blank, R., George, C. C., & London, R. A. (1994). State abortion rates: The impact of policies, providers, politics, demographics and economic environment. Working paper No. 4853. National Bureau of Economic Research.

Bloom, D., Farrell, M., Kemple, J. J., & Verma, N. (1999). *The family transition program: Implementation and three-year impacts of Florida's initial time-limited welfare program.* New York: Manpower Demonstration Research Corporation.

Bloom, H. S., Orr, L. L., Cave, G., Bell, S. H., & Doolittle, F. (1993). *The national JTPA study: Title IIA impacts on earnings and employment at 18 months.* Bethesda, MD: Abt Associates, Inc.

Brinig, M. F., & Buckley, F. (1999). The price of virtue. *Public Choice, 98,* 111–129.

Burtless, G. (1995). The case for randomized field trials on economic and policy research. *Journal of Economic Perspectives, 9,* 63–84.

Burtless, G., & Orr, L. L. (1986). Are classic experiments needed for manpower policy? *Journal of Human Resources, 21,* 606–639.

Camasso, M. J., Harvey, C., Jagannathan, R., & Killingsworth, M. (1998a). *A final report on the impact of New Jersey's Family Development Program: Results from a pre-post analysis of AFDC case heads from 1990–1996.* Research report submitted to the New Jersey Department of Human Services.

Camasso, M. J., Harvey, C., Jagannathan, R., & Killingsworth, M. (1998b). *A final report on the impact of New Jersey's Family Development Program, experimental-control group analysis.* Research report submitted to the New Jersey Department of Human Services.

Camasso, M. J., Jagannathan, R., & Harvey, C. (1996). The recipient's perspective: Welfare mothers assess New Jersey's Family Development Program and the family cap. Unpublished manuscript: School of Social Work, Rutgers University.

Camasso, M. J., Jagannathan, R., Harvey, C., & Killingsworth, M. (2003). The use of client surveys to gauge the level of contamination in social experiments. Unpublished manuscript. Center for Urban Policy Research, Rutgers University.

Case, A., Lin, I. F., & McLanahan, S. (1999). How hungry is the selfish gene? Working paper No. 7401. National Bureau of Economic Research.

Clarke, G. R. G., & Strauss, R. P. (1998). Children as income-producing assets: The case of teen illegitimacy and government transfers. *Southern Economic Journal, 64,* 827–856.

Cook, T. D., & Campbell, D. T. (1979). *Quasi-experimentation: Design and analysis issues for field settings.* Chicago: Rand McNally.

Duncan, G. J., & Hoffman, S. D. (1990). Welfare benefits, economic opportunities and out-of-wedlock births among black teenage girls. *Demography, 27,* 519–535.

Dye, J. L., & Presser, H. B. (1999). The state bonus to reduce a decrease in illegitimacy: Flawed methods and questionable effects. *Family Planning Perspectives, 31,* 142–147.

Ellwood, D., & Bane, M. J. (1985). The impact of AFDC on family structure and living arrangements. In: R. Ehrenberg (Ed.), *Research in Labor Economics.* Greenwich, CT: JAI Press.

Fairlie, R. W., & London, R. A. (1997). The effects of incremental benefits levels on births to AFDC recipients. *Journal of Policy Analysis and Management, 16,* 575–597.

Fein, D. (1999). Will welfare reform influence marriage and fertility? Early evidence from the ABC demonstration. Unpublished manuscript. Abt Associates.

Fein, D., Beecroft, E., Hamilton, W., & Lee, W. S. (1998). *The Indiana welfare reform evaluation: Program implementation and economic impacts after two years.* Cambridge, MA: Abt Associates.

Fein, D., & Karweit, J. (1997). *The ABC evaluation: The early economic impacts of Deleware's a better chance welfare reform program.* Cambridge, MA: Abt Associates, Inc.

Fraker, T., & Maynard, R. (1987). The adequacy of comparison group designs for evaluations of employment-related programs. *The Journal of Human Resources, 22,* 194–227.

Friedlander, D., & Robins, P. K. (1995). Evaluating program evaluations: New evidence in commonly used non-experimental methods. *American Economic Review, 85,* 923–937.

Grogger, J., & Bronars, S. G. (2001). The effect of welfare payments on the marriage and fertility behavior of unwed mothers: Results from a twins experiment. *Journal of Political Economy, 109*, 529–545.

Gueron, J. M., & Pauly, E. (1991). *From welfare to work*. New York: Russell Sage Foundation.

Harvey, C., Camasso, M. J., & Jagannathan, R. (2000). Evaluating welfare reform waivers under Section 1115. *Journal of Economic Perspectives, 14*, 165–188.

Haveman, R. (1997). A pre-post design for state-based evaluation of national welfare reform. *Focus, 18*, 11–17.

Hill, M. A., & O'Neill, J. (1993). Underclass behaviors in the United States: Measurement and analysis of determinants. Unpublished manuscript. Center for the Study of Business and Government, Baruch College, City University of New York.

Hoffman, S. D., & Foster, E. M. (2000). AFDC benefits and non-marital births to young women. *Journal of Human Resources, 35*, 376–391.

Hollister, R. G., Kemper, P., & Maynard, R. A. (1984). *The national supported work demonstration*. Madison and London: University of Wisconsin Press.

Horvath, R. A., & Peters, H. E. (2002). Welfare waivers and non-marital childbearing. In: G. Duncan & P. L. Chase-Lansdale (Eds), *For Better and for Worse: Welfare Reform and the Well-Being of Children and Families*. New York: Russell Sage.

Huber, P. J. (1964). Robust estimates of a location parameter. *Annals of Mathematical Statistics, 35*, 73–101.

Huber, P. J. (1981). *Robust statistics*. New York: Wiley and Sons.

Jagannathan, R., & Camasso, M. J. (2003). Family cap and nonmarital fertility: The racial conditioning of policy effects. *Journal of Marriage and the Family, 65*, 52–71.

Jagannathan, R. (2001). Relying on surveys to understand abortions. Some cautionary evidence. *American Journal of Public Health, 91*, 1825–1831.

Kaplan, T. (1997). Evaluating comprehensive state welfare reforms: An overview. *Focus, 18*, 1–4.

Lalonde, R. J. (1986). Evaluating the econometric evaluations of training programs with experimental data. *American Economic Review, 76*, 604–620.

Lipsey, M. W. (1990). *Design sensitivity: Statistical power for experimental research*. Newbury Park, CA: Sage.

Lundberg, S., & Plotnick, R. D. (1995). Adolescent premarital childbearing: Do economic incentives matter? *Journal of Labor Economics, 13*, 177–201.

Mach, T. L. (2001). Measuring the impact of family caps on childbearing decisions. Unpublished manuscript. University of Albany, Department of Economics.

Matthews, S., Ribar, D., & Wilhelm, M. (1997). The effects of economic conditions and access to reproductive health services on state abortion rates and birthrates. *Family Planning Perspectives, 29*, 52–60.

Mills, G., Kornfeld, R., Peck, L., Porcari, D., Straubinger, J., Johnson, Z., & Cabral, C. (1999). *Evaluation of Arizona EMPOWER welfare reform demonstration. Impact study interim report*. Cambridge, MA: Abt Associates, Inc.

Mohr, L. B. (1995). *Impact analysis for program evaluation*. Thousand Oaks, CA: Sage.

Moore, K. A., & Caldwell, S. (1977). The effect of government policies on out-of-wedlock sex and pregnancy. *Family Planning Perspectives, 9*, 164–169.

NARAL (1998). *A state-by-state review of abortion and reproductive rights* (Special ed.). Washington, DC: National Abortion and Reproductive Rights Action League.

Plotnick, R. (1990). Welfare and out-of-wedlock childbearing: Evidence from the 1980s. *Journal of Marriage and the Family, 52*, 735–746.

Rank, M. R. (1989). Fertility among women on welfare: Incidence and determinants. *American Sociological Review, 54*, 296–304.

Rivers, K. (2001). Has welfare reform reduced nonmarital births? Population Reference Bureau. http://www.prb.org/pt/2001/febmar2001/welfare.html.

Robins, P. K., & Fronstin, P. (1996). Welfare benefits and birth decisions of never-married women. *Population Research and Policy Review, 15*, 21–43.

Rosenzweig, M. (1999). Welfare, marital prospects, and non-marital childbearing. *Journal of Political Economy, 107*, S3–S32.

Schultz, T. P. (1994). Marital status and fertility in the United States. *Journal of Human Resources, 29*, 637–669.

Schultz, T. P. (1995). Eroding the economic foundations of marriage and fertility in the United States. Unpublished manuscript. Yale University.

Turturro, C., Benda, B., & Turney, H. (1997). *Arkansas welfare waiver demonstration project*. Little Rock, AR: University of Arkansas.

U.S. General Accounting Office (2001). *Welfare reform: More research needed on TANF family caps and other policies for reducing out-of-wedlock births*. (GA)-01-924. Washington, DC: GAO.

Winkler, A. (1993). The living arrangements of single mothers with dependent children: An added perspective. *American Journal of Economics and Sociology, 52*, 1–18.

APPENDIX

Table A1. Estimated Models: Births among Ongoing Cases.

	MODEL 1 Coefficient (Std. Error)	MODEL 2 Coefficient (Std. Error)	MODEL 3 Coefficient (Std. Error)
Constant	−1.903	0.760	0.630
	(0.047)	(1.410)	(1.419)
Time	−0.009**	−0.016**	−0.015**
	(0.004)	(0.007)	(0.007)
Status (Experimental = 1)	0.040	0.025	
	(0.050)	(0.051)	
Time × Status	−0.007	−0.007	
	(0.005)	(0.006)	
Middle (Dec. 1992–Sept. 1993)			0.052
			(0.089)
Middle × Time			−0.028
			(0.031)
After (Dec. 1993–Dec. 1996)			0.101
			(0.075)
After × Time			−0.013*
			(0.007)
June	−0.071*	−0.072*	−0.062
	(0.039)	(0.042)	(0.043)

Table A1. *(Continued)*

	MODEL 1 Coefficient (Std. Error)	MODEL 2 Coefficient (Std. Error)	MODEL 3 Coefficient (Std. Error)
September	−0.059 (0.040)	−0.080* (0.046)	−0.057 (0.048)
December	−0.063* (0.036)	−0.081** (0.040)	−0.078* (0.043)
Personal characteristics			
Black		0.103** (0.047)	0.103** (0.047)
Hispanic		0.040 (0.049)	0.040 (0.049)
No high school degree		−0.039 (0.053)	−0.039 (0.053)
High school diploma/GED only		−0.101* (0.056)	−0.101* (0.056)
Some college/college degree		−0.221** (0.086)	−0.221** (0.087)
Marital status (Single = 1)		−0.039 (0.039)	−0.039 (0.039)
Age		−0.215 (0.151)	−0.214 (0.151)
Age^2		0.008 (0.005)	0.008 (0.005)
Age^3		<0.001* (<0.001)	<0.001* (<0.001)
Household composition			
One AFDC-eligible child		−0.514** (0.084)	−0.514** (0.084)
Two AFDC-eligible children		−0.739** (0.088)	−0.739** (0.088)
Three AFDC-eligible children		−0.945** (0.105)	−0.944** (0.105)
Four or more AFDC-eligible children		−1.067** (0.132)	−1.067** (0.132)
Own child(ren) age 2 or younger		0.288** (0.032)	0.288** (0.032)
Own child(ren) age 2 to 4 years		0.206** (0.031)	0.207** (0.031)
Own child(ren) age 5 to 10 years		0.126** (0.025)	0.126** (0.025)
Own child(ren) age 11 to 13 years		0.062 (0.041)	0.061 (0.041)

Table A1. (*Continued*)

	MODEL 1 Coefficient (Std. Error)	MODEL 2 Coefficient (Std. Error)	MODEL 3 Coefficient (Std. Error)
Own child(ren) age 13 to 18 years		0.055 (0.040)	0.055 (0.040)
Other child(ren) age 2 or younger		0.088 (0.132)	0.087 (0.132)
Other child(ren) age 2 to 4 years		0.105 (0.087)	0.105 (0.087)
Other child(ren) age 4 to 10 years		0.004 (0.055)	0.004 (0.055)
Other child(ren) age 11 to 13 years		−0.039 (0.080)	−0.039 (0.080)
Other child(ren) age 13 to 18 years		−0.025 (0.069)	−0.025 (0.069)
One or more own children receive SSI		−0.187** (0.083)	−0.188** (0.083)
One or more other children receive SSI		−0.316 (0.326)	−0.316 (0.326)
Economic/Contextual factors			
Live in Atlantic County		0.123 (0.108)	0.096 (0.115)
Live in Camden County		0.084 (0.077)	0.094 (0.079)
Live in Cumberland County		0.089 (0.149)	0.037 (0.169)
Live in Essex County		0.012 (0.094)	0.006 (0.095)
Live in Hudson County		0.009 (0.104)	−0.016 (0.111)
Live in Mercer County		0.064 (0.089)	0.084 (0.094)
Live in Middlesex County		0.042 (0.086)	0.051 (0.087)
Live in Monmouth County		0.086 (0.084)	0.090 (0.084)
Live in Passaic County		0.101 (0.097)	0.075 (0.105)
Local unemployment rate		−0.019 (0.030)	−0.007 (0.035)
County FDP/JOBS participation rate		0.001 (0.003)	0.002 (0.003)

Note: Huber-adjusted standard errors in parentheses. Starred coefficients are significant at the 90% (*) or 95% (**) confidence level.

Table A2. Estimated Models: Births among New Applicants.

	MODEL 1 Coefficient (Std. Error)	MODEL 2 Coefficient (Std. Error)	MODEL 3 Coefficient (Std. Error)
Constant	−1.560 (0.056)	−0.101 (1.212)	0.248 (1.221)
Time	−0.053** (0.008)	−0.042** (0.010)	−0.046** (0.010)
Status (Experimental = 1)	−0.117** (0.058)	−0.128** (0.055)	
Time × Status	0.013 (0.010)	0.018* (0.011)	
Middle (Dec. 1992–Sept. 1993)			0.156 (0.120)
Middle × Time			−0.090 (0.063)
After (Dec. 1993–Dec. 1996)			−0.205** (0.063)
After × Time			0.027** (0.011)
June	0.077 (0.050)	0.085 (0.053)	0.076 (0.054)
September	0.130** (0.050)	0.196** (0.060)	0.166** (0.062)
December	0.084* (0.050)	0.157** (0.060)	0.132** (0.061)
Personal characteristics			
Black		0.063 (0.050)	0.065 (0.050)
Hispanic		0.010 (0.054)	0.014 (0.054)
No high school degree		−0.010 (0.065)	−0.009 (0.065)
High school diploma/GED only		−0.093 (0.065)	−0.094 (0.065)
Some college/college degree		−0.092 (0.078)	−0.092 (0.078)
Marital status (Single = 1)		−0.011 (0.043)	−0.011 (0.043)
Age		−0.209 (0.131)	−0.209 (0.131)
Age^2		0.008* (0.005)	0.008* (0.005)
Age^3		<0.001* (<0.001)	<0.001* (<0.001)

Table A2. (*Continued*)

	MODEL 1 Coefficient (Std. Error)	MODEL 2 Coefficient (Std. Error)	MODEL 3 Coefficient (Std. Error)
Household composition			
One AFDC-eligible child		−0.770**	−0.768**
		(0.116)	(0.116)
Two AFDC-eligible children		−1.302**	−1.297**
		(0.181)	(0.181)
Three AFDC-eligible children		−2.209**	−2.191**
		(0.418)	(0.420)
Four or more AFDC-eligible children		−0.509	−0.521
		(0.472)	(0.474)
Own child(ren) age 2 or younger		0.213**	0.217**
		(0.086)	(0.088)
Own child(ren) age 2 to 4 years		0.119	0.123
		(0.088)	(0.089)
Own child(ren) age 4 to 10 years		0.069*	0.066
		(0.040)	(0.040)
Own child(ren) age 11 to 13 years		−0.110	−0.103
		(0.234)	(0.235)
Own child(ren) age 13 to 18 years		−0.132	−0.134
		(0.134)	(0.134)
Other child(ren) age 2 or younger		−0.071	−0.071
		(0.127)	(0.127)
Other child(ren) age 2 to 4 Years		−0.576	−0.577
		(0.368)	(0.367)
Other child(ren) age 4 to 10 Years		0.084	0.084
		(0.110)	(0.110)
Other child(ren) age 11 to 13 years		−0.180	−0.191
		(0.240)	(0.243)
Other child(ren) age 13 to 18 years		−0.058	−0.063
		(0.086)	(0.087)
One eligible own child age 2 or younger		0.076	0.072
		(0.113)	(0.114)
One eligible own child age 2 to 4 years		0.186	0.179
		(0.119)	(0.119)
One eligible own child age 4 to 10 years		0.183**	0.185**
		(0.077)	(0.077)
One eligible own child age 10 to 13 years		−0.146	−0.153
		(0.291)	(0.291)
Two eligible own children ages 2 or younger		0.214*	0.209*
		(0.122)	(0.123)
Two eligible own children ages 2 to 4 years		0.350**	0.341**
		(0.128)	(0.129)

Table A2. (*Continued*)

	MODEL 1 Coefficient (Std. Error)	MODEL 2 Coefficient (Std. Error)	MODEL 3 Coefficient (Std. Error)
Two eligible own children ages 4 to 10 years		0.197**	0.195**
		(0.090)	(0.090)
Two eligible own children ages 10 to 13 years		0.337	0.329
		(0.259)	(0.261)
Two eligible own children ages 13 to 18 years		0.116	0.116
		(0.158)	(0.158)
Three eligible own children ages 2 or younger		0.484**	0.476**
		(0.174)	(0.175)
Three eligible own children ages 2 to 4 years		0.466**	0.455**
		(0.186)	(0.187)
Three eligible own children ages 4 to 10 years		0.332**	0.328**
		(0.143)	(0.144)
Three eligible own children ages 10 to 13 years		0.388	0.377
		(0.262)	(0.263)
Three eligible own children ages 13 to 18 years		0.729**	0.727**
		(0.194)	(0.196)
Four or more eligible own children ages 2 or younger		−0.449**	−0.451**
		(0.204)	(0.205)
Four or more eligible own children ages 2 to 4 years		0.060	0.056
		(0.159)	(0.161)
Four or more eligible own children ages 4 to 10 years		−0.271*	−0.264*
		(0.145)	(0.146)
Four or more eligible own children ages 10 to 13 years		−0.017	−0.023
		(0.279)	(0.281)
Four or more eligible own children ages 13 to 18 years		0.115	0.122
		(0.217)	(0.218)
One or more own children receive SSI		−0.548**	−0.542**
		(0.181)	(0.180)
One or more other children receive SSI		−0.196	−0.188
		(0.204)	(0.204)
Economic/Contextual factors			
Live in Atlantic County		−0.033	0.047
		(0.128)	(0.132)
Live in Camden County		0.061	0.041
		(0.085)	(0.084)
Live in Cumberland County		−0.211	−0.064
		(0.212)	(0.217)
Live in Essex County		−0.302**	−0.254**
		(0.094)	(0.097)
Live in Hudson County		−0.349**	−0.245**
		(0.100)	(0.112)

Table A2. (*Continued*)

	MODEL 1 Coefficient (Std. Error)	MODEL 2 Coefficient (Std. Error)	MODEL 3 Coefficient (Std. Error)
Live in Mercer County		0.273**	0.206**
		(0.093)	(0.097)
Live in Middlesex County		0.022	0.005
		(0.085)	(0.085)
Live in Monmouth County		0.045	0.030
		(0.080)	(0.080)
Live in Passaic County		−0.238**	−0.145
		(0.115)	(0.123)
Local unemployment rate		0.120**	0.077*
		(0.036)	(0.040)
County FDP/JOBS participation rate		−0.004	−0.004
		(0.005)	(0.004)

Note: Huber-adjusted standard errors in parentheses. Starred coefficients are significant at the 90% (*) or 95% (**) confidence level.

Table A3. Estimated Models: Abortions among Ongoing Cases.

	MODEL 1 Coefficient (Std. Error)	MODEL 2 Coefficient (Std. Error)	MODEL 3 Coefficient (Std. Error)
Constant	−1.760	−2.354	−2.434
	(0.048)	(1.412)	(1.428)
Time	−0.013**	−0.025**	−0.024**
	(0.005)	(0.007)	(0.008)
Status (Experimental = 1)	−0.017	−0.020	
	(0.054)	(0.056)	
Time × Status	0.005	0.006	
	(0.006)	(0.006)	
Middle (Dec. 1992–Sept. 1993)			−0.081
			(0.090)
Middle × Time			0.031
			(0.028)
After (Dec. 1993–Dec. 1996)			−0.017
			(0.075)
After × Time			0.005
			(0.007)
June	−0.014	−0.021	−0.025
	(0.031)	(0.033)	(0.034)
September	−0.018	−0.024	−0.031
	(0.033)	(0.038)	(0.040)

Table A3. *(Continued)*

	MODEL 1 Coefficient (Std. Error)	MODEL 2 Coefficient (Std. Error)	MODEL 3 Coefficient (Std. Error)
December	−0.075** (0.032)	−0.099** (0.037)	−0.089** (0.039)
Personal characteristics			
Black		0.289** (0.065)	0.289** (0.065)
Hispanic		0.109 (0.067)	0.109 (0.067)
No high school degree		0.097 (0.065)	0.097 (0.065)
High school diploma/GED only		0.102 (0.067)	0.102 (0.067)
Some college/college degree		0.214** (0.087)	0.214** (0.087)
Marital status (Single = 1)		0.140** (0.047)	0.140** (0.047)
Age		0.185 (0.148)	0.186 (0.148)
Age^2		−0.008 (0.005)	−0.008 (0.005)
Age^3		<0.001* (<0.001)	<0.001* (<0.001)
Household composition			
One AFDC-eligible child		−0.194 (0.127)	−0.194 (0.127)
Two AFDC-eligible children		−0.168 (0.132)	−0.168 (0.132)
Three AFDC-eligible children		−0.201 (0.145)	−0.201 (0.145)
Four or more AFDC-eligible children		−0.128 (0.168)	−0.128 (0.168)
Own child(ren) age 2 or younger		0.048 (0.036)	0.049 (0.036)
Own child(ren) age 2 to 4 years		−0.016 (0.037)	−0.016 (0.037)
Own child(ren) age 4 to 10 years		−0.013 (0.030)	−0.013 (0.030)
Own child(ren) age 11 to 13 years		0.006 (0.044)	0.006 (0.044)
Own child(ren) age 13 to 18 years		0.148** (0.037)	0.147** (0.037)

Table A3. (*Continued*)

	MODEL 1 Coefficient (Std. Error)	MODEL 2 Coefficient (Std. Error)	MODEL 3 Coefficient (Std. Error)
Other child(ren) age 2 or younger		0.066	0.066
		(0.091)	(0.091)
Other child(ren) age 2 to 4 years		0.217**	0.217**
		(0.077)	(0.077)
Other child(ren) age 4 to 10 years		−0.011	−0.011
		(0.055)	(0.055)
Other child(ren) age 11 to 13 years		−0.038	−0.038
		(0.074)	(0.074)
Other child(ren) age 13 to 18 years		0.010	0.010
		(0.052)	(0.052)
One or more own children receive SSI		−0.075	−0.075
		(0.085)	(0.085)
One or more other children receive SSI		0.251	0.251
		(0.159)	(0.159)
Economic/Contextual factors			
Live in Atlantic County		−0.209*	−0.228*
		(0.117)	(0.122)
Live in Camden County		−0.207**	−0.201**
		(0.084)	(0.085)
Live in Cumberland County		−0.552**	−0.587**
		(0.195)	(0.208)
Live in Essex County		0.094	0.088
		(0.099)	(0.100)
Live in Hudson County		0.069	0.050
		(0.102)	(0.108)
Live in Mercer County		−0.319**	−0.305**
		(0.107)	(0.111)
Live in Middlesex County		−0.184*	−0.179*
		(0.107)	(0.108)
Live in Monmouth County		−0.029	−0.026
		(0.090)	(0.090)
Live in Passaic County		0.137	0.119
		(0.106)	(0.114)
Local unemployment rate		−0.052*	−0.043
		(0.029)	(0.034)
County FDP/JOBS participation rate		0.002	0.002
		(0.004)	(0.004)

Note: Huber-adjusted standard errors in parentheses. Starred coefficients are significant at the 90% (*) or 95% (**) confidence level.

Table A4. Estimated Models: Abortions among New Applicants.

	MODEL 1 Coefficient (Std. Error)	MODEL 2 Coefficient (Std. Error)	MODEL 3 Coefficient (Std. Error)
Constant	−1.972 (0.066)	−1.537 (1.527)	−1.773 (1.534)
Time	0.011 (0.007)	−0.002 (0.009)	<0.001 (0.009)
Status (Experimental = 1)	0.171** (0.072)	0.189** (0.075)	
Time × Status	−0.006 (0.009)	−0.011 (0.009)	
Middle (Dec. 1992–Sept. 1993)			−0.143 (0.166)
Middle × Time			0.120* (0.066)
After (Dec. 1993–Dec. 1996)			0.230** (0.080)
After × Time			−0.016 (0.010)
June	−0.069 (0.048)	−0.069 (0.051)	−0.067 (0.051)
September	−0.094** (0.046)	−0.129** (0.053)	−0.115** (0.055)
December	−0.129** (0.048)	−0.184** (0.055)	−0.167** (0.057)
Personal characteristics			
Black		0.114* (0.068)	0.111 (0.068)
Hispanic		−0.028 (0.076)	−0.030 (0.076)
No high school degree		0.197** (0.099)	0.196** (0.099)
High school diploma/GED only		0.235** (0.102)	0.234** (0.102)
Some college/college degree		0.190 (0.121)	0.190 (0.121)
Marital status (Single = 1)		0.181** (0.063)	0.181** (0.063)
Age		0.041 (0.162)	0.040 (0.162)
Age^2		−0.003 (0.006)	−0.003 (0.006)
Age^3		<0.001 (<0.001)	<0.001 (<0.001)

Table A4. (*Continued*)

	MODEL 1 Coefficient (Std. Error)	MODEL 2 Coefficient (Std. Error)	MODEL 3 Coefficient (Std. Error)
Household composition			
One AFDC-eligible child		−0.271 (0.186)	−0.266 (0.186)
Two AFDC-eligible children		−0.159 (0.242)	−0.158 (0.242)
Three AFDC-eligible children		−0.195 (0.640)	−0.187 (0.640)
Four or more AFDC-eligible children		−0.744 (0.469)	−0.739 (0.470)
Own child(ren) age 2 or younger		−0.259 (0.171)	−0.258 (0.171)
Own child(ren) age 2 to 4 years		−0.093 (0.195)	−0.095 (0.195)
Own child(ren) age 4 to 10 years		0.119 (0.101)	0.120 (0.101)
Own child(ren) age 11 to 13 years		0.033 (0.221)	0.040 (0.222)
Own child(ren) age 13 to 18 years		−0.082 (0.179)	−0.084 (0.179)
Other child(ren) age 2 or younger		0.049 (0.170)	0.048 (0.171)
Other child(ren) age 2 to 4 years		0.163 (0.198)	0.168 (0.197)
Other child(ren) age 4 to 10 years		−0.286* (0.171)	−0.288* (0.172)
Other child(ren) age 11 to 13 years		−0.305 (0.442)	−0.312 (0.443)
Other child(ren) age 13 to 18 years		−0.063 (0.132)	−0.062 (0.132)
One eligible own child age 2 or younger		0.200 (0.190)	0.199 (0.190)
One eligible own child age 2 to 4 years		0.121 (0.214)	0.123 (0.214)
One eligible own child age 4 to 10 years		−0.228* (0.136)	−0.230* (0.136)
One eligible own child age 10 to 13 years		−0.059 (0.277)	−0.065 (0.278)
Two eligible own children ages 2 or younger		0.203 (0.199)	0.204 (0.199)
Two eligible own children ages 2 to 4 years		0.027 (0.229)	0.032 (0.229)

Table A4. (Continued)

	MODEL 1 Coefficient (Std. Error)	MODEL 2 Coefficient (Std. Error)	MODEL 3 Coefficient (Std. Error)
Two eligible own children ages 4 to 10 years		−0.234* (0.131)	−0.233* (0.131)
Two eligible own children ages 10 to 13 years		−0.193 (0.249)	−0.200 (0.250)
Two eligible own children ages 13 to 18 years		0.034 (0.201)	0.037 (0.201)
Three eligible own children ages 2 or younger		0.348 (0.284)	0.347 (0.285)
Three eligible own children ages 2 to 4 years		0.038 (0.302)	0.039 (0.302)
Three eligible own children ages 4 to 10 years		−0.076 (0.231)	−0.078 (0.231)
Three eligible own children ages 10 to 13 years		−0.352 (0.304)	−0.363 (0.306)
Three eligible own children ages 13 to 18 years		0.294 (0.285)	0.294 (0.285)
Four or more eligible own children ages 2 or younger		0.568** (0.203)	0.568** (0.203)
Four or more eligible own children ages 2 to 4 years		0.245 (0.261)	0.249 (0.261)
Four or more eligible own children ages 4 to 10 years		−0.161 (0.175)	−0.165 (0.175)
Four or more eligible own children ages 10 to 13 years		−0.244 (0.319)	−0.253 (0.320)
Four or more eligible own children ages 13 to 18 years		0.261 (0.210)	0.262 (0.210)
One or more own children receive SSI		−0.256* (0.148)	−0.257* (0.148)
One or more other children receive SSI		−0.195 (0.405)	−0.197 (0.406)
Economic/Contextual factors			
Live in Atlantic County		−0.116 (0.160)	−0.185 (0.164)
Live in Camden County		−0.188 (0.117)	−0.171 (0.118)
Live in Cumberland County		−0.575** (0.237)	−0.699** (0.247)
Live in Essex County		0.276** (0.108)	0.245** (0.111)
Live in Hudson County		0.134 (0.138)	0.056 (0.147)

Table A4. (*Continued*)

	MODEL 1 Coefficient (Std. Error)	MODEL 2 Coefficient (Std. Error)	MODEL 3 Coefficient (Std. Error)
Live in Mercer County		−0.261**	−0.215
		(0.130)	(0.134)
Live in Middlesex County		0.039	0.050
		(0.106)	(0.107)
Live in Monmouth County		0.107	0.115
		(0.104)	(0.105)
Live in Passaic County		0.167	0.094
		(0.131)	(0.137)
Local unemployment rate		−0.057	−0.025
		(0.042)	(0.046)
County FDP/JOBS participation rate		0.008*	0.008*
		(0.004)	(0.004)

Note: Huber-adjusted standard errors in parentheses. Starred coefficients are significant at the 90% (*) or 95% (**) confidence level.

TRACKING THE HOUSEHOLD INCOME OF SSDI AND SSI APPLICANTS

John Bound, Richard V. Burkhauser and Austin Nichols

ABSTRACT

Using panel data from the Survey of Income and Program Participation linked to Social Security Administration disability determination records we trace the pattern of household income and the sources of that income from 38 months prior to 39 months following application for Social Security Disability Insurance (SSDI) and Supplemental Security Insurance (SSI). We find that the average applicant's labor earnings declines dramatically beginning six months before application but the average applicant's household income drops much less dramatically both in the months just before or just after application and over the next three years, and does so even for those denied benefits. However, we also found substantial heterogeneity in household income outcomes in both the SSDI and SSI applicant population. Our quantile regressions suggest that higher income households experience greater percentage declines in their post-application income. Such results are consistent with the lower replacement rate for higher earners established in the SSDI program and the low absolute level of protection provided to all SSI applicants regardless of income prior to application.

INTRODUCTION

The onset of disability can pose a significant threat to work and economic well-being. To mitigate the consequences of such an event on both employment and household income, a network of public and private programs has been established. The two most important federal transfer programs targeted on working-age men and women who experience the onset of a severe work-limiting health condition are Social Security Disability Insurance (SSDI) and Supplemental Security Income (SSI).

SSDI is a social insurance program for regularly employed workers that provides benefits based on a worker's past earnings. (For a more complete discussion of SSDI, see Bound & Burkhauser, 1999; Burkhauser & Daly, 2002.) SSI is a mean-tested categorical welfare program that provides a federal minimum cash benefit, which can be supplemental by state funds. (For a more complete discussion of SSI, see Daly & Burkhauser, forthcoming.) Both programs use the same strict definition of eligibility: "the inability to engage in substantial gainful activity, by reason of a medically determinable physical or mental impairment that is expected to result in death or last at least 12 months" (United States Social Security Administration, 2001). Applicants must be unable to do any work that exists in the national economy for which they are qualified by virtue of age, education, and work experience. In addition, for SSDI there is a five-month waiting period before permanent benefits are paid.

The strictness of the SSDI and SSI eligibility rules together with the imposition of a waiting period for SSDI are consistent with a public policy that seeks to limit disability benefits to those who are permanently and totally unable to work. However, the lack of a universal short-term disability transfer program suggests that the onset of a severe disability could result in a substantial decline in household income before SSDI or SSI benefits become available.

In this paper we make use of a nationally representative public use household panel linked to restricted Social Security Administration administrative records to measure changes in the sources and amount of household income of working-age men and women who apply for SSDI and SSI benefits. We show that while applicants experience substantial declines in their labor earnings in the months around their application and subsequent admission onto the rolls, on average these declines lead to more modest declines in their household income. However, there is considerable heterogeneity of outcomes within the population, and a significant minority of applicants experience substantial declines in their household incomes.

BACKGROUND

There are two separate federal disability programs in the U.S. – Social Security Disability Insurance (SSDI) and Supplemental Security Income (SSI). SSDI is part of the Old-Age, Survivor, and Disability Insurance (OASDI) program. The goal of this social insurance program is to provide "earnings replacement insurance" for those who exit the labor market because of disability or retirement. Benefits for this program are based on past labor earnings and financed through a tax on those earnings. Participation in the retirement and disability programs requires a substantial record of employment. While OASDI has a redistribution as well as an insurance goal and, hence, provides lower earners with higher replacement rates, the presumption is that other sources of household income – e.g. the labor earnings of other workers in the household, returns from savings and investments, private pensions or disability insurance, etc. – will provide substantial income to a beneficiary's household following his or her exit from work.[1]

In contrast, Supplemental Security Income is a means-tested cash transfer program aimed at aged, blind, and disabled adults and disabled children. It is funded by general revenues. Past taxes paid do not affect the amount of benefits received. The SSI adult disability program target population is working-age men and women whose disabilities are as severe as those necessary for eligibility for SSDI, but who either did not participate in the labor market sufficiently to receive SSDI benefits or whose SSDI benefits and other sources of household income are below the maximum allowable level to receive SSI benefits. In 2000, the maximum monthly federal SSI benefit was $512 ($769 for a jointly eligible couple).[2] While SSDI and SSI are both administered by SSA and share common disability criteria for eligibility, they are meant to protect two quite different populations.

To be eligible for SSDI benefits an individual must have had a significant recent attachment to the workforce, while to be eligible for SSI an individual's income and assets must be below a legislated maximum. In addition, to receive benefits from either program the individual must be determined to be disabled through a complex process, outlined below.[3]

As the first step in establishing eligibility, the SSA field office screens out applicants who are currently gainfully employed.[4] The field office also verifies insured status or, in the case of SSI, does a preliminary check for financial eligibility based on income and assets. If the applicant is not ruled ineligible at this stage, the application is sent to one of the 54 Disability Determination Service (DDS) centers, usually in the state where the claimant resides. A DDS officer then makes a medical determination of disability based on federal regulations (Lahari, Vaughan & Wixon, 1995). Applicants denied benefits at this point can appeal, first to the same DDS center that made the original determination, then to an Administrative Law Judge (ALJ), and then to the central Appeals Board in Washington. Those denied benefits at this level can appeal to a federal court, although only a tiny fraction of those who initially apply for SSDI or SSI benefits ever do so.[5] As a result of this appeal process the application for SSDI or SSI benefits can potentially take years. However, the vast majority of cases are decided reasonably quickly. In our data, roughly 80% of applicants have a decision within six months and over 95% within 12 months of applying for benefits (see Table A1). It is also the case that, applicants who are denied benefits at any or all levels of their initial application process can and do reapply for SSDI benefits. (See United States Social Security Administration, 2001 for a fuller discussion of this entire process.)

DATA

The Survey of Income and Program Participation (SIPP) is a series of United States Census Bureau panel surveys of representative populations of the United States. New panels were fielded in 1990, 1991, 1992, and 1993.[6] For each of four months beginning in February 1990, the Census Bureau interviewed a new rotation group that was itself a random sample of the United States population for the 1990 SIPP panel. These four rotation groups were interviewed eight times at four-month intervals. Each interview contains monthly information for the preceding four months. Hence, monthly panel information is available for up to 32 months on each individual in the 1990 SIPP panel over a 35-month period from October 1989 through August 1992. In 1991, a new SIPP panel was fielded using the same panel design, and in 1992 and 1993 a similar design using an additional ninth wave of interviews was used to provide a total of 36 months of data. Among other things, the SIPP panel data contain detailed information on the sources and amount of income of respondents and their households over a 32- to 36-month period. Hence, it is a useful data set for measuring changes in short term economic well-being.

The data used in this project are the 1990–1993 panels of the SIPP matched to the disability determination records from DDS and ALJ stages of the determination process of those who applied for SSDI or SSI and whose applications were acted upon between 1986 and 1994, for the 1990 and 1991 panels, and between 1977 and 1997, for the 1992 and 1993 panels.[7] This matching procedure produced a total of 9,691 SIPP respondents who are identified as having applied for SSDI or SSI, with the bulk of the applications occurring during the late 1980s and 1990s.

Because we are interested in separately following those who were awarded and those who were denied benefits, we only include applicants in our sample who had reached at least the stage of being awarded or denied benefits at the DDS level.[8] Hence, from these 9,691 SIPP respondents, we construct a sample of 7,637 applicants whose matched administrative records contain valid information on their date of birth, filing date, decision date, and decision outcome to at least the DDS level. Our sample respondents may have filed more than once in the years covered by the administrative data, and may had several actions taken in their file over various stages of the disability determination process recorded in their administrative record. We focus on the first application we observe in the data and the last action we observe on that application. Hence, some applicants who were denied benefits at the last stage we observe may not have completed all the appeals and may eventually be accepted. Likewise, some may reapply and eventually be accepted.

We focus on the first application date we can observe in the administrative records data to set the timing of employment and household income in the SIPP data to before and after application for either SSDI and SSI benefits. Since we are interested in comparing different patterns between those who are accepted onto the SSDI or SSI rolls and those who are denied benefits, it is necessary to define our measure of this outcome variable. Ideally, we would like to have full information on the ultimate outcome of the application process for SSDI or SSI benefits. But, as we have discussed above, for some applicants who are denied benefits the process to final appeal can be long, and in some cases we will only have outcome information on the medical determination at the DDS level or that information plus outcomes at one or more of the four possible appeal stages.

We define applicants as accepted or denied based on the most advanced level of the first application process we observe in our data. The vast majority of cases in our sample contain complete information on the first application process we observe. However, some of these cases are incomplete. Hence, it is possible that applicants we classify as denied are accepted at a higher level of appeal that we do not observe. Nevertheless, since the applicants awarded benefits in our data are similar to the overall fraction of social security beneficiaries awarded during this time period, it seems unlikely that we have misclassified many cases.[9] Finally, some individuals whom we currently classify as denied benefits on their first application will subsequently reapply and be accepted.

ANALYTIC STRATEGY

In our analysis we merge our four SIPP panels but do not do so along a calendar time dimension. Instead, we focus on an event – the initial application month and year for SSDI or SSI benefits that we observe in the data – and array our data by individual from the months prior to application $(t - i)$ through the months following applications $(t + i)$ where t is the month of application. For those who applied for benefits prior to, or in the early waves of, our SIPP data, we have information on their household income following application. For those who applied for benefits in a middle wave of our SIPP data, we have information on their household income in the months just prior to application and just following application. For those who applied for benefits in the later waves of our SIPP data or just afterwards, we have information on their household income in the months prior to application. Using this approach, we are able to obtain snapshots of respondents' average household income in the months and years prior to and following their application for SSDI or SSI benefits that extend beyond the maximum of 36 months that any one respondent is followed in a given SIPP panel.

A balanced panel, containing many years of household income prior to application and many years of household income following application for every respondent, would be ideal for tracking the consequences of the onset of a work limitation sufficient to induce an application for SSDI or SSI benefits on the applicant's household income. In this case, we could simply follow cohorts of applications from several years prior to several years after the application. However, the fact that we observed households for at most 36 months precludes us from doing this.

To better understand what we can and cannot do with our data, it is useful to consider a simplified version of our SIPP-administrative records data (see Table 1). Imagine that we were working with a survey that interviewed individuals in March 1991 and then again in March 1993. Respondents were asked about household income for the calendar month preceding each interview (i.e. February 1991 and February 1993). The sample is limited to those who applied for disability benefits in January of 1989, 1991, 1993 or 1995. We are following the household income of the applicant from two years prior to two years after the application. We can think of the data as composed of four distinct samples. As can be seen in row 1, for those who apply in 1989, we can observe their household income two years after application. For those who apply in 1991, we can observe (row 2) their household income immediately after and two years after application. For those who apply in 1993, we can observe (row 3) their household income both two years prior to and immediately after the application. For those who apply in 1995, we can observe (row 4) their household income two years prior to the application.

Combining the 1993 and 1995 applicant samples yields a snapshot of household income two years prior to the application. In a similar fashion, combining 1991 and 1993 applicant samples yields snapshots of household income immediately

Table 1. The Number of Years Between the Year Income is Observed and the Application Year.

Application Month and Year	Month and Year Income Data is Observed	
	February 1991	February 1993
January 1989	+2	–
January 1991	0	+2
January 1993	–2	0
January 1995	–	–2

after application, and combining 1989 and 1991 samples yields snapshots two years after application. Furthermore, a comparison of these snapshots provides a measure of how mean household income changes from two years prior to two years after an application. These partially matched samples provide a valid way to infer what the mean change in an applicant cohort's household income was over the application period, so long as the cohorts of applicants can be thought of as coming from a random sample of the same population.

However, if different applicant cohorts represent different populations (imagine, for example, that the more recent cohorts tend to have higher baseline household income), then the comparison of the mean household income of the different populations will overstate the mean change in household income over the application event.

An alternative approach would be to use the 1993 applicant cohort to make inferences about the mean change in household income from two years prior to application to just after application, and use the 1991 applicant cohort to make inferences about the mean change in household income from just after application to two years after the application. Since these are within-cohort comparisons, differences across cohorts will not bias our estimates. Furthermore, by splicing these two comparisons together we can get an estimate of the mean change in household income from two years prior to two years after the application.[10]

Splicing together cohorts allows us to obtain within-cohort estimates of the mean change in household income from before to after the application. However, we cannot use the same kind of analysis to examine the distribution of income changes. We can use the 1993 cohort to look at the distribution of household income changes from two years before to just after application. In the same way, we can use the 1991 applicant cohort to examine the distribution of changes from the date of application to two years later. However, there is no way to examine the distribution of household income changes from two years before to two years after the application. To do so requires a longer panel.

Returning to our actual data, we first compare three discrete time periods – 36–38 months prior to application, 1–3 months after application, and 37–39 months after application – to obtain a first glimpse of how average household income and its sources change across the months prior to and after benefits application. We do so by comparing our cross-sectional snapshots of people at various times around application. The first period is roughly prior to the onset of a disability (our baseline period). The second period is just following application for benefits, when it is unlikely that a decision with respect to eligibility and payment has been made.[11] The third is long enough after the application process began to roughly capture its outcome on average household income.

While these cross-sectional snapshots will give us a measure of the employment and household income of individuals at various moments around the time they are applying for SSDI or SSI benefits, they do not follow the same individuals across time and, therefore, do not give us a direct measure of the extent to which those applying for SSDI or SSI have been able to avoid significant drops in household incomes. To answer this question, we need to follow individuals over time and compare their incomes prior to applying for SSDI or SSI benefits to their incomes after doing so. Given the shortness of the SIPP panel data, we cannot cover the entire period by simply following a single cohort of individuals through the application process. Instead we track the household income of overlapping sets of individuals. To do this efficiently, we estimate fixed-effect regression models where the dependent variable is total household income and explanatory variables include individual fixed effects and calendar month fixed effects together with dummy variables indicating the duration since application.

Finally, we use a balanced panel design to capture the heterogeneity of changes in household income that individuals experience between 12 and 15 months prior to application and one to three months following application. Because we require income information on each individual in our sample for both periods, the time between the two periods we are considering is shorter and our sample sizes are smaller than in our other analyses.

RESULTS

Socio-Economic Characteristics of SSDI and SSI Applicants Before Application

Table 2 shows the dramatic difference between the average SSDI and SSI applicant prior to application for these programs. Column 1 reports the average socio-economic characteristics of men and women aged 18–61 in the first wave of any of the four SIPP panels used in our analysis, who did not apply for SSDI or SSI benefits over the period covered by our SSA record data.[12] Column 2 contains the mean socio-economic characteristics of the first-wave SIPP respondents who only applied for SSDI benefits over the period covered in our SSA record data. Column 3 does the same for those who only applied for SSI benefits and Column 4 does so for those who applied for both SSDI and SSI benefits.

On average, SSDI and SSI applicants have dramatically different socio-economic characteristics. The average SSDI applicant is more likely to be older, male, white, non-Hispanic, married, have at least a high school degree, live in a smaller household, and have more financial wealth than the average SSI applicant.[13] The average applicant for both SSDI and SSI falls somewhere between these two averages.

Table 2. Socio-Economic Characteristics of SSDI and SSI Applicants.

Socio-Economic Characteristic	Non-Applicants[a]	Social Security Disability Insurance[b]	Supplemental Security Income[b]	Both[c]
Mean Age	37	47	40	41
Gender				
Percentage Male	49.1	58.5	31.7	56.5
Race or Ethnicity				
Percentage White, Non-Hispanic	77.3	78.5	53.2	61.5
Percentage Black, Non-Hispanic	10.0	11.7	26.5	25.1
Percentage Hispanic	8.8	7.4	14.0	11.2
Percentage Other	3.9	2.4	6.3	2.2
Education				
Percentage Less than 12 Years of Education	12.6	24.7	46.9	36.6
Percentage 12 Years or More of Education	87.4	75.3	53.1	63.4
Marital Status				
Percentage Married, Spouse Present	58.6	64.5	33.2	38.3
Percentage Widowed	1.7	4.0	6.1	4.6
Percentage Divorced or Separated	12.1	17.3	27.8	30.2
Percentage Never Married	26.7	13.6	31.9	25.6
Household Size[d]				
Mean Number of People	2.9	2.2	2.5	2.2
Financial Wealth[e]				
25th Percentile	90	159	0	0
50th Percentile	1,670	1,622	0	29
75th Percentile	11,051	11,039	572	954
Economic Well-Being				
Mean Household Income[e]	3,727	3,458	1,530	2,023
Mean Income/Needs[e]	4.2	4.1	1.6	2.3
Number of Individuals in Sample	108,004	1228	662	1052
Number of Individuals in Subsample[e]	–	527	253	425

Source: 1990–1993 SIPP data merged to Social Security Administration disability determination records.

[a] Non-applicants include all adults aged 18 through 61 who appear in any first wave of SIPP data who are not found to apply for SSDI or SSI over the period of our Social Security Administrative records.
[b] Applicants based on Social Security Administrative records.
[c] SSI applicants who also applied for SSDI based on Social Security Administration records.
[d] Household size statistics are calculated counting each household once (i.e. not at the individual level, unlike the rest of the analysis).
[e] Included in subsamples are those applicants with wealth or first wave household income observed at least 12 months prior to application. Wealth and income are reported in January 1990 dollars.

Because application for SSDI and SSI benefits is coincident with low labor earnings, in our last comparison in Table 2 we look at the subsample of respondents on whom we have household income information at least 12 months prior to their application in the first wave of one of our four SIPP panels. Not surprisingly, given the social insurance nature of SSDI versus the means-tested nature of SSI, the pre-application household income of SSDI applicants is more than twice that of SSI applicants and is very close to that of non-applicants. When we divide household income by the official United States Census poverty line for an appropriate size household, the resulting pre-application income-to-needs ratio of SSDI applicants is more than twice that of SSI applicants and is almost exactly that of non-applicants. SSDI and SSI are meant to provide protection to quite different populations. Table 2 demonstrates that this is what they do. In all subsequent analyses we will separately consider these two distinct populations.[14]

Changes in Earnings and Employment Before and After SSDI or SSI Application

The onset of a disability that is severe enough to induce a worker to apply for SSDI or SSI benefits, given these programs' strict eligibility standards, is likely to have a dramatic effect on the worker's labor earnings and household income. The effect on household income is likely to be even greater if the worker is denied benefits.

In Table 3 we look at mean monthly labor earnings and the employment rates of our sample of SSDI or SSI applicants disaggregated by whether or not they were awarded or denied benefits.[15] We look across three distinct periods. The first is between 36 and 38 months before application. We use this baseline period to approximate the average labor earnings and employment of applicants before the onset of a disability began to affect these outcomes.[16] The second period is one to three months following application. This is roughly coincident with the waiting period for SSDI applicants, during which employment is likely to be near its lowest level and, for most SSDI and SSI applicants, the period before an initial disability determination has been made and benefits have begun.[17]

The third period is 37–39 months after application. We use this period to approximate employment and earnings levels after the full application process has been completed and either benefits have begun (either after the first disability determination or after subsequent appeals) or the respondent has learned that benefits will not be awarded and has had the opportunity to try to return to work.[18]

Table 3 shows that prior to application for SSDI benefits, those awarded benefits are more likely to be employed and to have higher average monthly labor earnings

Table 3. Average Monthly Labor Earnings and Employment Rates and How They Changed Before and After Application for SSDI and SSI.[a]

Population	Before Application[b]		Application[c]			After Application[d]		
	Monthly Labor Earnings[e]	Employment Rate[f]	Monthly Labor Earnings[e]	Employment Rate[f]	Percent of Before Earnings[g]	Monthly Labor Earnings[e]	Employment Rate[f]	Percent of Before Earnings[h]
Social Security Disability Insurance								
Awarded SSDI	1,575	87	248	16	16	87	11	6
Denied SSDI	1,248	81	154	17	12	434	31	35
Supplemental Security Income								
Awarded SSI	144	25	17	6	12	63	12	44
Denied SSI	260	28	89	15	34	105	19	40

Source: 1990–1993 SIPP data merged to Social Security Administration disability determination records.
[a] January 1990 dollars.
[b] 36–38 months prior to application.
[c] 1–3 months after application.
[d] 37–39 months after application.
[e] Average includes zeros.
[f] Positive labor earnings in at least one month over the period.
[g] Average monthly labor earnings during application period divided by average monthly labor earnings before application.
[h] Average monthly labor earnings after application divided by average monthly labor earnings before application.

than those denied benefits. But both groups experience a dramatic drop in both their average monthly labor earnings and their employment during the period just after application. The average monthly labor earnings of those awarded SSDI benefits in the months just after application are only 16% of their previous average monthly labor earnings, and those of applicants denied SSDI benefits are only 12% of their previous level. In our final period of observation, 37–39 months after application, those awarded SSDI benefits have even lower average employment and labor earnings than they do just after application. Those denied SSDI benefits increase their employment and average labor earnings above their low levels just after application but still have average labor earnings and employment rates substantially below their pre-application levels.

SSI applicants are dramatically different from SSDI applicants in their employment and labor earnings patterns. First and most importantly, the vast majority of SSI applicants are not employed 36–38 months before application for SSI benefits. This in large part explains why they are not applying for SSDI benefits. It is unlikely that they are eligible. Only 25 (28%) of those awarded SSI (those denied) were working before their application and their average monthly labor earnings were only $144 ($260). Both their employment and average monthly labor earnings are a small fraction of the employment and average monthly labor earnings of SSDI applicants over this same period. While the percentage fall in their average monthly labor earnings is about as great as that of SSDI applicants, the absolute drop in their average monthly labor earnings is far smaller since their baseline level of earnings was so much lower. The average SSI awardee's labor earnings in the period 37–39 months after application remains very low, although it is somewhat higher than just after application. Those SSI applicants denied benefits also have small increases in their average monthly labor earnings from their low levels just after application, but their average monthly labor earnings are still only 40% of their pre-SSI-application levels.

Table 3 shows that both SSDI and SSI applicants experience dramatic drops in their average labor earnings across the period three years before to three years after application. But the absolute amount of household income that must be replaced by other sources because of this drop is much greater for SSDI applicants because their employment and labor earnings are much more important prior to application.

Changes in Household Income and Its Sources
Before and After SSDI and SSI Application

In Table 4, we look at the average monthly household income of SSDI and SSI applicants across these same three periods. Once again we see dramatic

Table 4. Average Monthly Household Income and How It Changed Before and After Application.[a]

Population	Before Application[b]	Application[c]		After Application[d]	
	Monthly Household Income	Monthly Household Income	Replacement Rate[e]	Monthly Household Income	Replacement Rate[f]
Social Security Disability Insurance					
Awarded SSDI	3,254	2,455	75	2,420	74
Denied SSDI	3,001	2,105	70	2,540	85
Supplemental Security Income					
Awarded SSI	1,405	1,553	111	1,639	117
Denied SSI	1,701	1,406	83	1,437	84

Source: 1990–1993 SIPP panels merged to Social Security Administration disability determination records.
[a] January 1990 dollars.
[b] 36–38 months prior to application.
[c] 1–3 months after application.
[d] 37–39 months after application.
[e] Household income during the application period divided by household income before application.
[f] Household income after application period divided by household income before application.

differences between our SSDI and SSI applicant populations. Prior to application, those awarded SSDI benefits have higher average monthly household income than those denied benefits. But in contrast to the dramatic declines in their average monthly labor earnings shown in Table 3, they both experience only modest declines in their average household income just after application, even in the absence, for the most part, of SSDI benefits. Those awarded benefits still have 75% of their pre-application household income. Those denied benefits still have 70% of their pre-application household income. Surprisingly, three years later the average household income of SSDI awardees remains at approximately the same level as it was just after application, while the average household income of those denied benefits rises to 85% of its pre-application level despite their not receiving SSDI benefits.

Table 5 provides a possible explanation for the relatively small changes in SSDI income levels across the three time periods, despite the dramatic and persistent decline in labor earnings report in Table 3. In Table 5, we disaggregate mean monthly household income into its components.[19] The dramatic decline in the labor earnings of SSDI applicants (both those awarded and denied) is offset during the application period by increases in private pensions and veterans' benefits, which are likely to be disability related, as well as temporary disability and workers' compensation benefits. Unemployment insurance benefits also increase.[20] Finally, we report some increase in own Social Security benefits, which may either be misreported, or based on a swift decision in which the waiting period was judged to occur prior to application.

These results are important because they suggest that, while the United States has no universal temporary or short-term disability transfer system, on average, SSDI applicants are sufficiently covered by some combination of employer-based disability programs, workers' compensation, or other public disability or general transfer programs to offset dramatic drops in their labor earnings in the months before SSDI benefits become available. Somewhat surprisingly, the earnings of a spouse declined between the two periods and hence were not a source of additional household income, although the earnings of other household members did increase over the period. On net, however, additional labor earnings by other household members do not appear to be a source of alternative household income during the months immediately after application for SSDI benefits.

The mean monthly household income of SSDI applicants who were awarded benefits remained at about the same level 37–39 months after application as it was during the period one to three months after application, but the sources of that income substantially changed. Over the two periods, SSDI benefits rose dramatically, but this increase was more than offset by declines in applicants' earnings, the earnings of other household members, temporary disability benefits,

Table 5. Average Monthly Household Income by Sources and How They Changed Before and After Application.[a]

Household Income	Before Application[b]				Application[c]				After Application[d]			
	SSDI		SSI		SSDI		SSI		SSDI		SSI	
	Awarded	Denied	Awarded	Denied	Awarded	Denied	Awarded	Denied	Awarded	Denied	Awarded	Denied
All	3,254	3,001	1,405	1,701	2,455	2,105	1,553	1,406	2,420	2,540	1,639	1,437
Labor Earnings	2,804	2,584	840	1,047	1,457	1,291	926	726	1,164	1,639	846	725
Own	1,575	1,248	144	260	248	154	17	89	87	434	63	105
Spouse	858	971	296	276	703	705	189	126	608	827	60	131
Others	371	366	400	512	507	432	719	511	469	378	723	489
Property	113	87	19	6	105	93	40	16	68	94	28	49
Pensions	105	72	33	49	267	185	36	32	296	256	55	100
Veterans Benefits	10	14	10	28	24	24	17	41	42	15	21	13
Private Transfers	26	27	42	12	15	8	9	56	7	30	17	13
Temporary Disability	14	2	4	2	50	78	0	1	22	7	0	0
Workers' Compensation	36	67	16	18	147	173	5	13	43	59	3	4
Unemployment Income	31	32	23	33	52	57	42	34	6	25	13	10
Social Security	81	54	105	144	244	96	129	108	655	317	166	149
Own	10	8	12	11	116	1	30	2	539	210	59	40
SSI	6	6	56	58	20	13	98	61	60	27	331	136
Own	1	2	1	29	14	0	51	16	49	15	257	93
Other Transfers Except SSI	14	27	236	274	17	31	240	278	29	43	154	223
AFDC	6	14	111	160	7	8	113	116	11	16	57	78
Noncash Transfers	7	8	96	106	5	14	95	130	11	16	56	103
All Other Income												

Source: 1990–1993 SIPP panels merged to Social Security Administration disability determination records.
[a] January 1990 dollars.
[b] 36–38 months prior to application.
[c] 1–3 months after application.
[d] 37–39 months after application.

unemployment insurance, and workers' compensation. This further suggests that on average the current patchwork of short-term public and private programs provide sufficient benefits to smooth the transition from full labor force participation to permanent movement onto the SSDI rolls.

For those who were denied SSDI benefits, household income rises substantially between the period just after application and 37–39 months after application. In part, this is because their Social Security income rises, although to a much lower level than for those who are awarded benefits. It is likely that most of these increases are from subsequent awards of SSDI benefits based on reapplication after the original application process yielded a denial.[21] The increase in average household income in the period just after application for those who are denied benefits come from increases in their own earnings and those of their spouse, as well as from increases in employer pension income. Those increases more than offset declines in temporary disability and workers' compensation payments.

Table 4 reveals a different pattern of household income changes for SSI applicants than for SSDI applicants. Those denied SSI benefits actually have higher average household income before application than do those awarded SSI benefits, although both groups have much lower average monthly household income than do SSDI applicants. As Table 3 revealed, while the average labor earnings of SSI applicants fell dramatically in percentage terms thereafter, in absolute terms the decline was modest since their average labor earnings were already quite low. Hence, it is not so surprising that the average household income of those denied SSI benefits was still 83% of its pre-application level in the month just after application. Somewhat more surprising, SSI awardees actually experienced an increase in average household income in the months just after their initial application. The average household income of both groups grew slightly between the months just after application and in the period 37–39 months after application.

Once again, Table 5 provides some insight into the pattern. For SSI awardees, the small absolute decline in their own average labor earnings and that of their spouse was more than offset by an increase in the labor earnings of other household members. How or why this relatively large rise in the average labor earnings of other household members occurs is beyond the scope of this study. It could be an increase in the average labor earnings of household members in the house in the period before application or it could also be that some SSI applicants move into a household with higher labor earners in order to share their resources and to receive care.[22]

The average household income of SSI initial awardees increases slightly between the months just after application and 37–39 months after application, but the sources of this increase change substantially between the two periods.

Average SSI income more than triples to $331 per month but this increase is mostly offset by declines in Aid to Family with Dependent Children (AFDC) and other welfare transfers and in spouses' labor earnings. For those denied SSI benefits, the decline in own earnings and in a spouse's earnings are only slightly offset by increases in veterans' benefits and private transfers. The small increase in average household income between the months just after application and 37–39 months after application is primarily driven by relatively small increases in pension income, Social Security benefits, SSI benefits, and own earnings.

Estimating Month-to-Month Changes Using Fixed-Effect Regressions

In the previous sections, we used our unbalanced panel data to describe how household income varied across points approximately three years before, immediately after, and three years after application for SSDI and SSI benefits. In this section we describe average changes each month in key sources of household income and in total household income for our sample of SSDI and SSI applicants from 36–38 months prior to application to 39 months after application.

Since we are still restricted by our data, we are not able to follow the same population across all time periods. We can, however, approximate what we would find if we had a longer panel by using these data to estimate a series of fixed-effect regressions that include dummy variables for the months prior to and subsequent to application. Since the time period in the constant term represents the period 36–38 months prior to application, the regression coefficients can be interpreted as the changes in household income relative to this pre-application baseline. The inclusion of fixed-effects in our model allows us to interpret the observed patterns as reflecting what happens on average, to applicants' household income during the time before and after application for SSDI or SSI benefits.[23]

Labor Earnings and Employment Trends

Figure 1A is based on our estimates of the average monthly labor earnings of SSDI applicants, as reported in Table 3, and Fig. 1B is based on our estimate of their employment. The average monthly labor earnings of SSDI applicants awarded benefits begin to decline as early as 24 months prior to application but do so more dramatically beginning about 12 months prior to application. Average labor earnings level off about three months after application and remain at that low level thereafter. Monthly employment rates show a similar pattern.

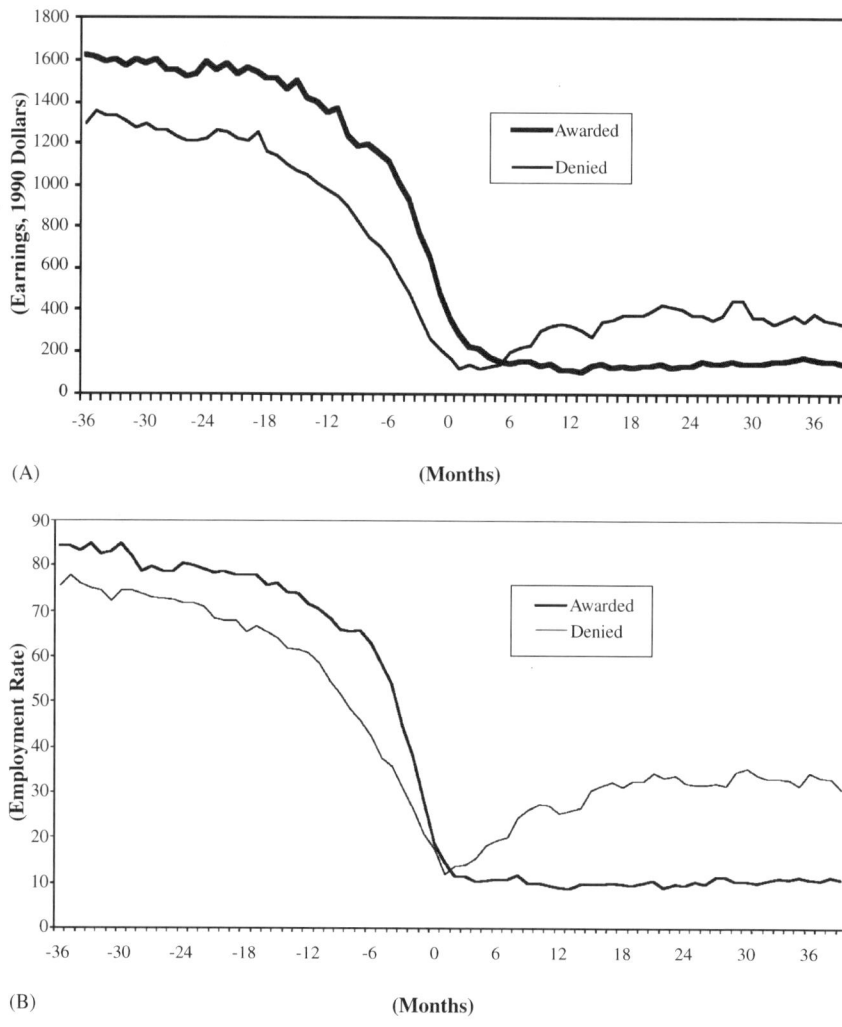

Fig. 1

Monthly (A) Labor Earnings and (B) Employment Rates of SSDI Applicants Awarded and Denied Benefits, Before and After Application. *Notes:* All monthly earnings are in 1990 dollars; zero is the month of SSDI application; any persons who report positive labor earnings in a given month are considered to be employed in that month. *Source:* Matched Survey of Income and Program Participation and SSA administrative records.

The average monthly labor earnings of SSDI applicants who were denied benefits are uniformly below those of SSDI applicants awarded benefits prior to application, but they cross over a few months after application and continue to be above them throughout the rest of the period of our study. Note however that the average labor earnings of both groups are at much lower absolute levels following their application for SSDI benefits then before. The monthly employment rates of these SSDI applicants show a similar pattern.

Figures 2A and B illustrate our results for SSI applicants reported in Table 3. The employment rates and average monthly labor earnings of SSI applicants awarded benefits are dramatically below those of SSDI applicants in the month prior to application. On average they experience only a small decline from their low baseline average monthly labor earnings beginning about six months prior to application. Employment is also low but stable until about six months prior to application. It then falls below 10% and remains at approximately this level over the rest of the period.

The month-to-month pattern for those denied SSI benefits is closer to that of those denied SSDI benefits, but at a dramatically lower level. Average monthly labor earnings and employment decline modestly until about three months before application. They then both drop faster until about three months after application. Thereafter they increase slightly. The employment of those denied SSI benefits is approximately the same as those awarded SSI benefits until just before application (two to three months), but their employment rates are consistently above those of initial SSI awardees thereafter.

Household Income Trends

Figures 3–6 illustrate the results we report in Table 4. In Fig. 3 we trace the percentage change in average monthly household income of SSDI awardees from baseline (36–38 months prior to application). The thick solid line is based on our fixed-effect regression. Average household income starts to decline two years before application but does so more dramatically six months to a year before application. Just after application, the trend reverses for about one year, after which average household income is relatively stable, approximately 25% below average household income at baseline.

As we saw in Table 3 and in Fig. 1A, the average monthly labor earnings of SSDI awardees decline dramatically over the same period. To show the importance of changes in all other sources of household income in ameliorating drops in household income caused by lost labor earnings, we simulate how much average household income would have fallen had no other income sources changed from

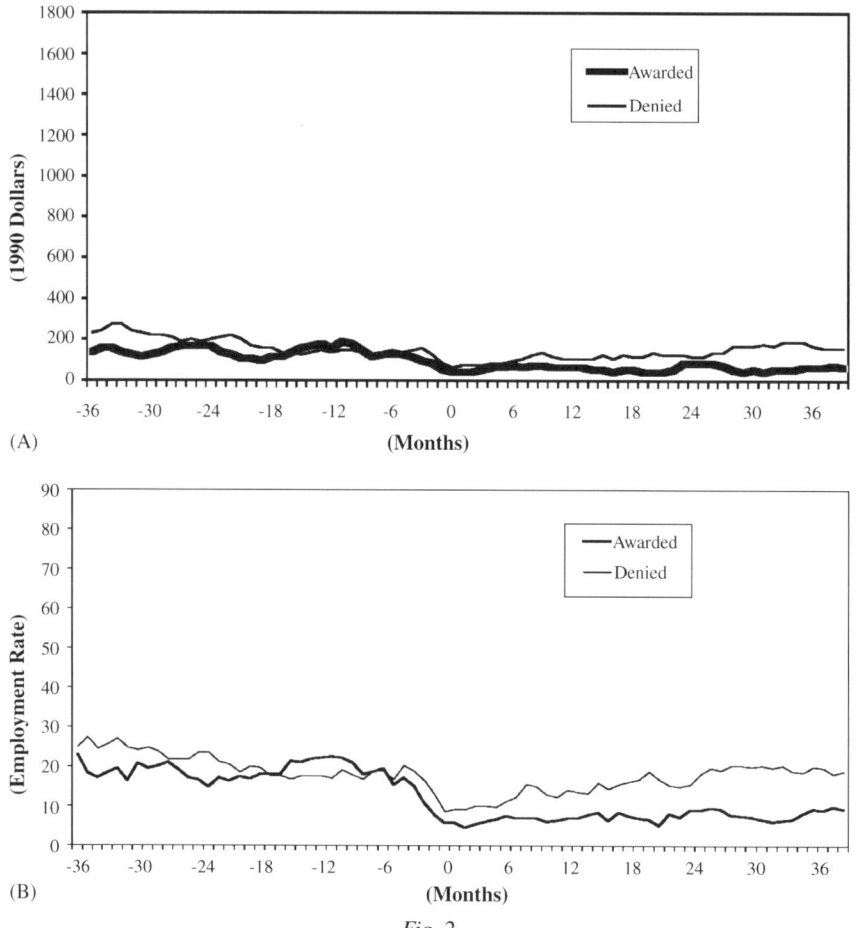

Fig. 2

Monthly (A) Labor Earnings and (B) Employment of SSI Applicants Awarded and Denied Benefits, Before and After Application. *Notes:* All monthly earnings are in 1990 dollars; zero is the month of SSI application. *Source:* Matched Survey of Income and Program Participation and SSA administrative records.

their baseline levels except the labor earnings of the SSDI awardees.[24] The thin solid line in Fig. 3 represents the simulated change in average household income caused solely by the actual decline in average labor earnings, holding all other sources of household income constant at their baseline levels. The difference between this line and the zero percentage line shows the importance of applicants' lost labor earnings as a share of average household income at baseline. The time

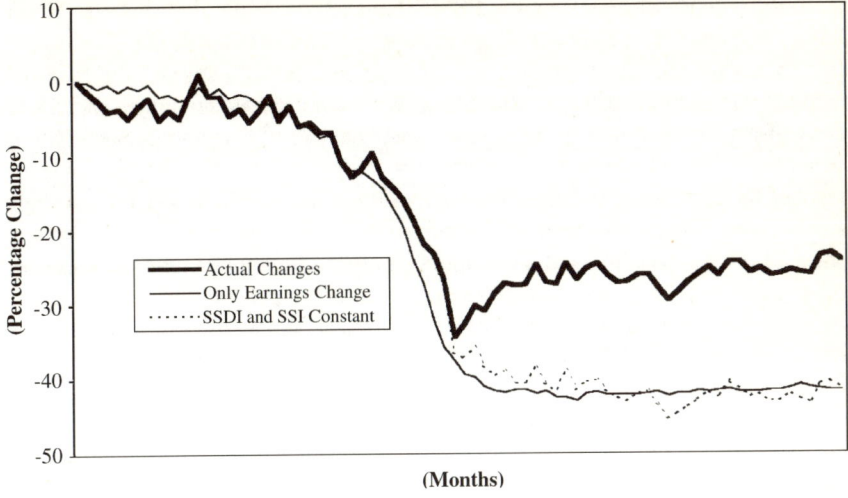

Fig. 3

Actual and Simulated Percentage Change in Monthly Household Income from Baseline of SSDI Applicants Awarded Benefits, Before and After Application. *Notes:* Zero is the month of SSDI application; actual percentage change in household income from baseline at 36–38 months before application; simulated percentage change in household income from baseline of 36–38 months before application allowing only applicants labor earnings to change from baseline; simulated percentage change in household income from baseline at 36–38 months before application allowing all other sources of income to change but holding SSDI and SSI at their baseline levels. *Source:* Matched Survey of Income and Program Participation and SSA administrative records.

pattern in Fig. 3 with respect to the average applicant's lost labor earnings on household income parallels Fig. 1A. The simulated decline in average household income begins slowly but rapidly increases about 12 months before application, levels off in the months immediately after application, and remains at that reduced level thereafter, on average about 45% below average household income at baseline. As can be seen by comparing the thin solid line to the actual outcomes represented by the thick solid line, increases in other sources of household income offset the decrease in labor earnings so that six months after initial application, household income is only 25% below baseline. Hence, for SSDI applicants who are awarded benefits the drop in their average household income is not as serious in percentage terms as the drop in their labor earnings both because labor earnings only provided about 50% of household income (see Table 5) and because household income from other sources grew after application for SSDI awardees.

To get a sense of how important SSDI benefits are in the replacement of lost labor earnings, we report the findings of a second simulation in Fig. 3. The dashed line represents the simulated change in average household income from baseline caused by the actual change in all other sources of household income except SSDI and SSI payments, which are held at their baseline level.[25] The importance of SSDI benefits begins to be seen a few months after application, when they account for most of the increase in income from sources other than applicants' labor earnings as represented by the gap between the thin solid line and the dotted line. As Table 5 shows, between baseline and the month just after initial application, increases in other sources of income – unemployment insurance, pension income, veterans' benefits, temporary disability income, and workers' compensation – offset some of the decline in lost labor earnings. But a few months after application, declines in these benefits as well as in other household labor earnings leave SSDI as the single most important alternative source of household income.

In Fig. 4 we trace the actual percentage changes in average monthly household income from baseline (thick solid line) and repeat our two simulations (thin solid

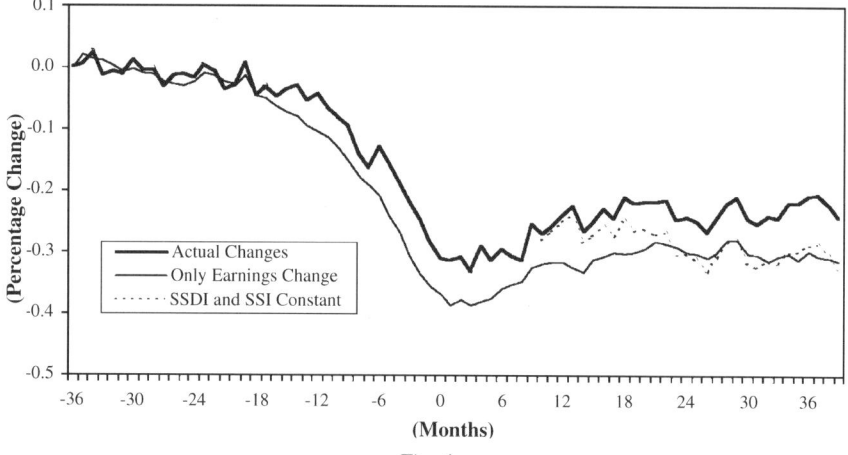

Fig. 4

Actual and Simulated Percentage Change in Monthly Household Income from Baseline of SSDI Applicants Denied Benefits, Before and After Application. *Notes:* Zero is the month of SSDI application; actual percentage change in household income from baseline at 36–38 months before application; simulated percentage change in household income from baseline at 36–38 months before application, allowing only applicants' labor earnings to change from baseline; simulated percentage change in household income from baseline at 36–38 months before application, allowing all other sources of income to change but holding SSDI and SSI at their baseline levels. *Source:* Matched Survey of Income and Program Participation and SSA administrative records.

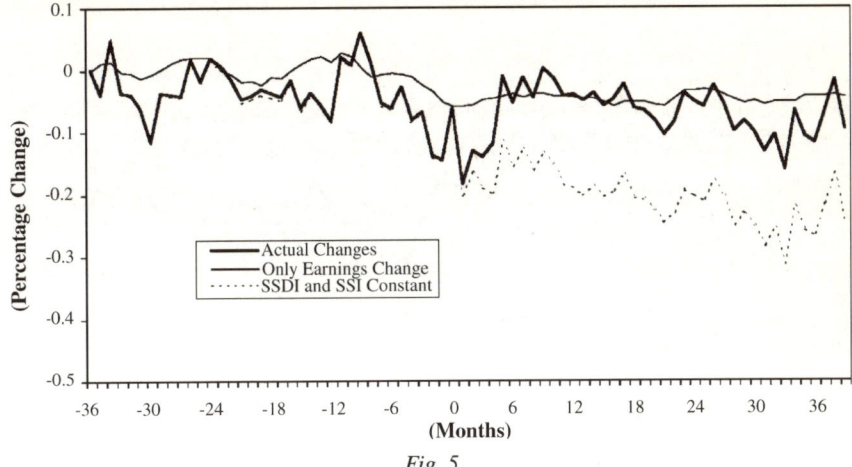

Fig. 5

Actual and Simulated Percentage Change in Monthly Household Income from Baseline of SSI Applicants Awarded Benefits, Before and After Application. *Notes:* Zero is the month of SSDI application; actual percentage change in household income from baseline at 36–38 months before application; simulated percentage change in household income from baseline at 36–38 months before application, allowing only applicants' labor earnings to change from baseline; simulated percentage change in household income from baseline at 36–38 months before application, allowing all other sources of income to change but holding SSDI and SSI at their baseline levels. *Source:* Matched Survey of Income and Program Participation and SSA administrative records.

and dash lines) for SSDI applicants who are denied benefits. As in Fig. 3, the thick solid line tracking actual changes in household income from baseline shows a steady decline starting two years before application increasing dramatically six months to a year before application. Just after application, household income rises until about one year after application and then remains approximately level about 20% below baseline. The thin solid line representing declines in household income caused by labor earnings alone, holding all other sources of income at their baseline levels, moves increasingly below the thick solid line over time but hits a valley at about 40% below baseline just after application and then rises as employment increases (see Fig. 1). This is quite different from the pattern discussed in Fig. 3 and shows that applicants' average lost earnings are much less of a problem for those denied benefits than for those receiving SSDI benefits.

Likewise, the dashed line representing simulated declines in income, holding SSDI and SSI at their baseline levels and allowing all other sources of income to vary, is now much closer to the thick solid line. Hence, SSDI and SSI income is much less important for denied SSDI applicants than for accepted applicants in

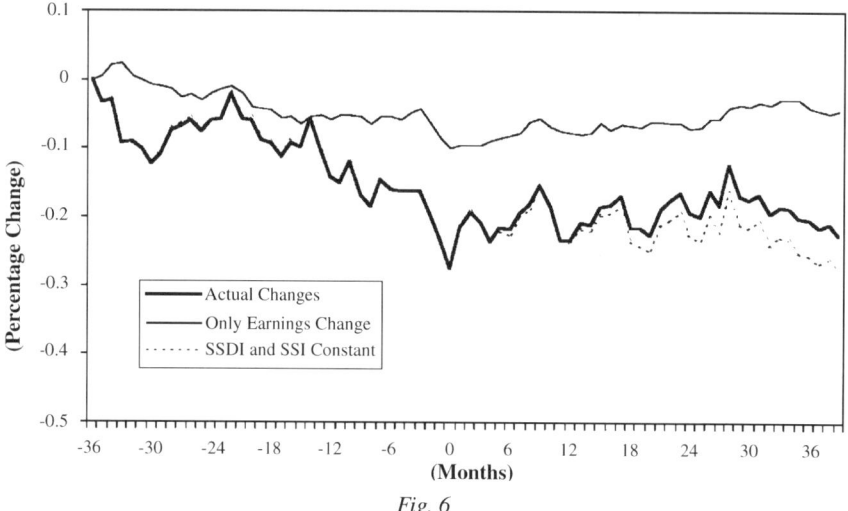

Fig. 6

Actual and Simulated Percentage Change in Monthly Household Income form Baseline of SSI Applicants Denied Benefits, Before and After Application. *Notes:* Zero is the month of SSDI application; actual percentage change in household income from baseline at 36–38 months before application; simulated percentage change in household income from baseline at 36–38 months before application, allowing only applicants' labor earnings to change from baseline; simulated percentage change in household income from baseline at 36–38 months before application, allowing all other sources of income to change but holding SSDI and SSI at their baseline levels. *Source:* Matched Survey of Income and Program Participation and SSA administrative records.

Fig. 3. Increases in household income (thick solid line) following application are primarily due to increases in applicants' labor earnings in the months following application. The declining dashed line, however, shows increases in average SSDI and SSI benefits begin to be an important source of household income about 18 months after application, suggesting that some of the applicants who were denied benefits at the point we observed them eventually went into these programs.

Figure 5 reports actual changes in average monthly household income and repeats our two simulations for SSI applicants who are awarded benefits. The thin solid line representing declines in household income caused by labor earnings alone, holding other sources of income constant, is now mostly above the thick solid line representing actual changes in income. Furthermore, the thin solid line only slightly varies from baseline. These results are expected. As we saw in Fig. 2A, the average labor earnings of SSI applicants who are awarded benefits do not begin to decline until just a few months before application. Even then, as we saw in Table 5, applicants' average labor earnings only contributed a small share to their average household income. Hence, dramatic percentage declines in applicants' average labor earnings translate into very modest declines in average household income from baseline even 39 months after a successful application for SSI benefits. In contrast, as the dashed line shows, the simulated loss of average SSDI and SSI benefits, allowing other sources of income to vary from baseline, would have had a major impact on household income after SSI application. This last point reinforces our finding in Table 5 that much of the increase in average SSI benefits in the months after application was offset by declines in income sources other than applicants' labor earnings, such as spouses' earnings, AFDC, and other welfare transfers.

Figure 6 illustrates actual changes in average monthly household income and repeats our two simulations for SSI applicants who are denied benefits. The thin solid line representing declines in household income caused by labor earnings alone, holding other sources of income constant, drops almost continuously until application, but even at its lowest levels, right around the time of SSI benefit application, it never falls below 10% of baseline earnings and represents less than a 5% decline from baseline by the 39th month. Declines in other sources of income are far more important in explaining the decline in the average household income of this population.

These figures together suggest that dramatic declines in average monthly labor earnings from baseline for SSDI and SSI applicants translate into a much more modest decline in monthly household income. This is especially true for SSI applicants, because their labor earnings are a relatively unimportant source of household income. It is also true of SSDI applicants, because their SSDI benefits quickly offset a substantial share of their lost labor earnings.

Figures 7 through 13 illustrate the results we report in Table 5. Each figure reports the average value of a specific source of household income for each of the four groups of applicants. Figure 7 shows that average own Social Security benefits begin to rise in the months around application for those awarded SSDI benefits but dramatically rise three to four months after application and continue to rise until about 15 months after application. Thereafter, they are relatively stable. Some of those denied SSDI benefits begin to receive their own Social Security benefits around nine months after application and experience modest but steady increases thereafter.[26] However, 39 months after application, their own average Social Security benefits are still less than one-half those of applicants who were awarded SSDI benefits. SSI applicants experience very small increases in their own Social Security benefits after application for SSI benefits.

Figure 8 shows that both those who are awarded and those who are denied SSDI benefits have about $100 in average monthly employer pension income 36

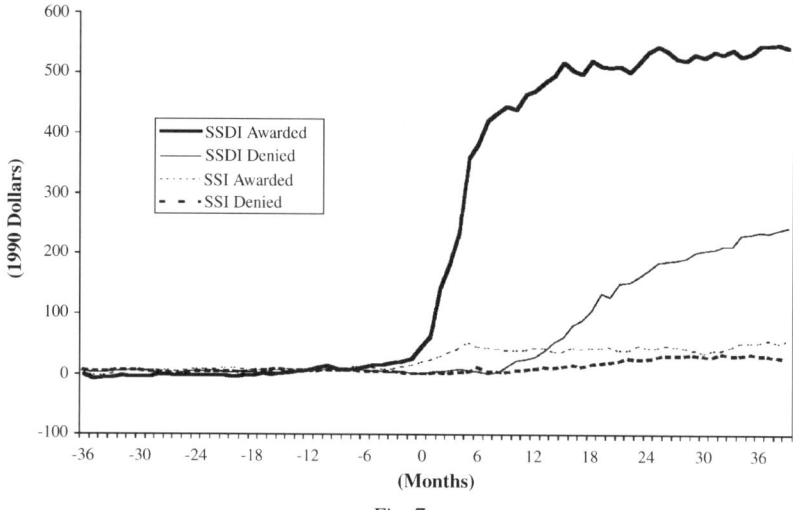

Fig. 7

Average Monthly Social Security Benefits of Applicants Before and After SSDI or SSI Application. *Notes:* All monthly social security benefits are in 1990 dollars; zero is the month of SSDI or SSI application. *Source:* Matched Survey of Income and Program Participation and SSA administrative records.

months prior to their application for SSDI benefits. For those who are accepted, these benefits steadily rise over the subsequent six years with substantial increases occurring in the month following application for SSDI benefits. Average benefit levels reach $400 per month three years after application. Those denied SSDI benefits have more modest increases in their employer pension income over the same period and reach average benefit levels of about $200 per month at 39 months after application. Those who apply for SSI benefits have much more modest employer pension benefits over the entire period of our analysis, but they do experience small increases in the months following SSI application.

Figure 9 shows that both those who are awarded and those who are denied SSDI benefits experience substantial increases in temporary insurance benefits, including workers' compensation, unemployment insurance, and temporary private insurance benefits, in the months immediately preceding and following their SSDI application. Interestingly, the benefits of those denied SSDI benefits are on average higher during this period. Those applying for SSI benefits experience no such rise in temporary benefits over the period. Instead, they experience a slow decline from a low baseline level over the entire period.

Figure 10 shows the average monthly labor earnings of the spouses of applicants for SSDI or SSI benefits. The average labor earnings of the spouses of those who

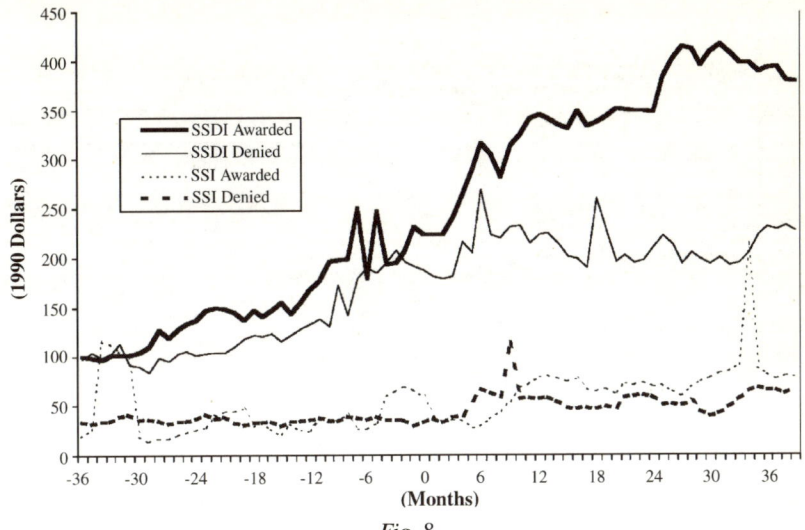

Fig. 8

Average Monthly Employer Pension Benefits of Applicants Before and After SSDI or SSI Application. *Notes:* All monthly employer pension benefits are in 1990 dollars; zero is the month of SSDI or SSI application. *Source:* Matched Survey of Income and Program Participation and SSA administrative records.

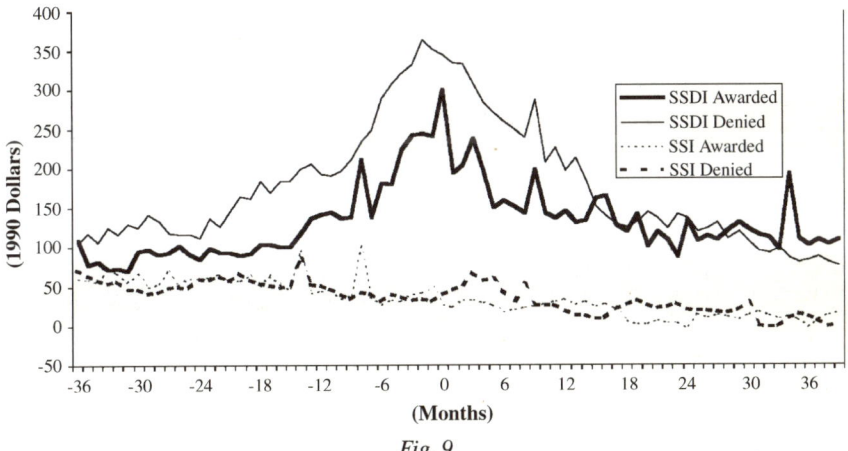

Fig. 9

Average Monthly Temporary Insurance Benefits Before and After SSDI or SSI Application. *Notes:* All monthly temporary insurance benefits are in 1990 dollars; zero is the month of SSDI or SSI benefit; temporary Benefits include Workers' Compensation, Unemployment Insurance, and temporary private insurance benefits. *Source:* Matched Survey of Income and Program Participation and SSA administrative records.

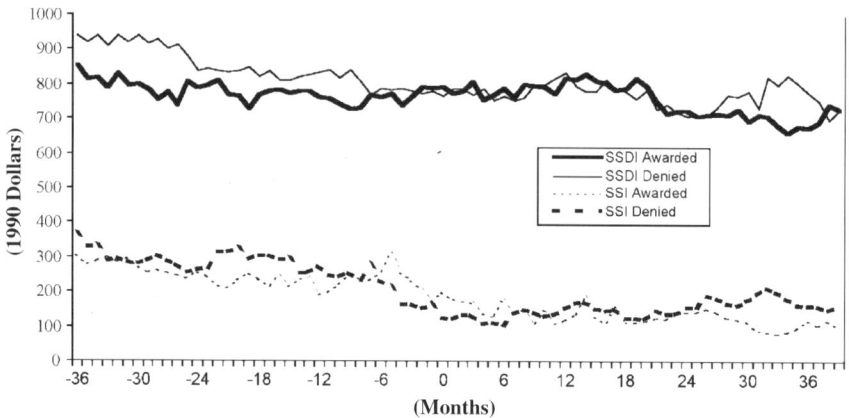

Fig. 10

Average Monthly Labor Earnings of Applicant's Spouse Before and After SSDI or SSI Application. *Notes:* All monthly spouse's labor earnings are in 1990 dollars; zero is the month of SSDI or SSI application. *Source:* Matched Survey of Income and Program Participation and SSA administrative records.

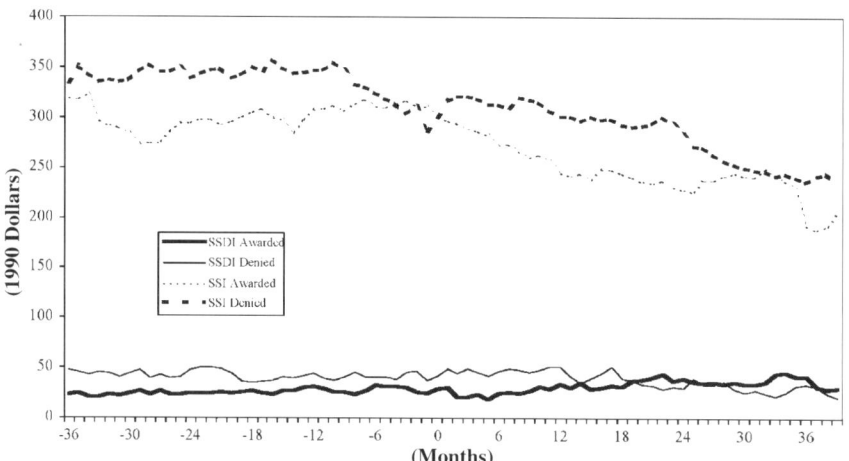

Fig. 11

Average Monthly Government Welfare Transfers Except SSI Before and After SSDI or SSI Application. *Notes:* All monthly transfer except SSI amounts are in 1990 dollars; zero is the month of benefit. *Source:* Matched Survey of Income and Program Participation and SSA administrative records.

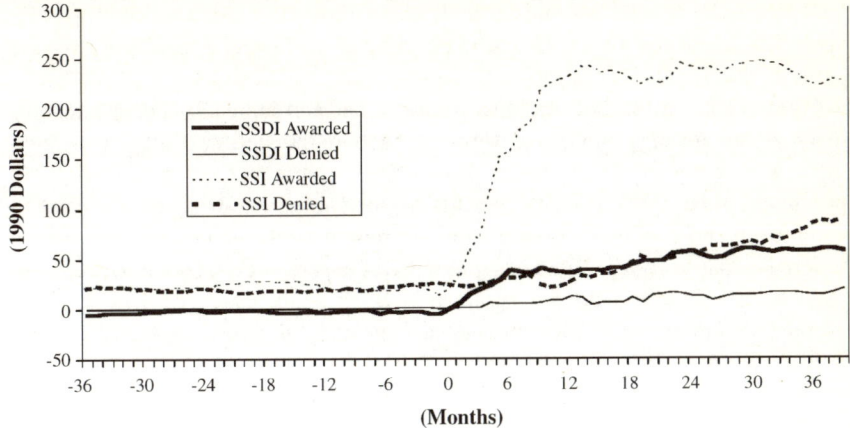

Fig. 12
Average Monthly SSI Benefits of Applicants Before and After SSDI or SSI Application. *Notes:* All monthly SSI benefits amounts are in 1990 dollars; zero is the month of SSDI or SSI application. *Source:* Matched Survey of Income and Program Participation and SSA administrative records.

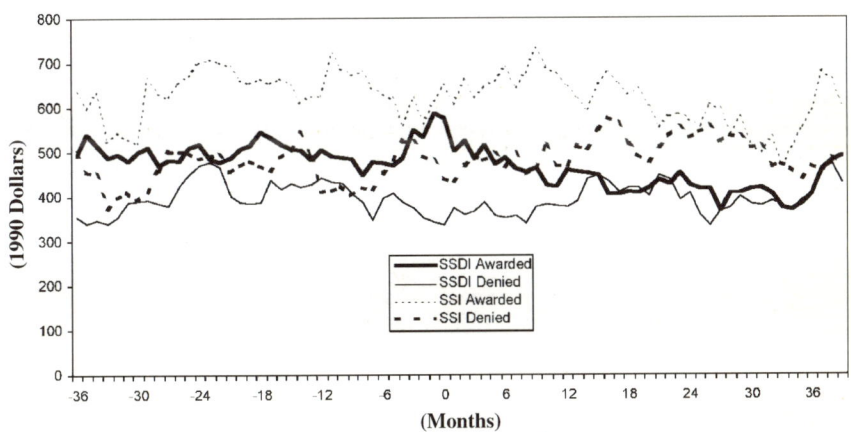

Fig. 13
Average Monthly Labor Earnings of Household Members Other Than Applicant and Applicant's Spouse Before and After SSDI or SSI Application. *Notes:* All monthly earnings are in 1990 dollars; zero is the month of SSDI or SSI application. *Source:* Matched Survey of Income and Program Participation and SSA administrative records.

apply for SSDI benefits are substantially above those of the spouses of those who apply for SSI benefits over the entire period, but they decline modestly over the entire period for all four groups.

Figure 11 shows that both those who are awarded and denied SSI benefits receive much greater average monthly government welfare transfers (except SSI) than do those who apply for SSDI. Those denied SSI benefits receive on average $350 per month at baseline, but their benefits begin to fall around six months prior to application and decline to around $250 per month by the end of the time period covered by our analyses. Those accepted for SSI experience a substantial decline in their welfare benefits following application. SSDI applicants receive a very small average amount of welfare transfers at baseline and this amount remains constant over the entire period of our analyses.

Figure 12 shows that SSI awardees experience a rapid rise in their own SSI benefits over the first year following application, after which they remain at about $225 per month. Those denied SSI benefits experience a much smaller increase in their own SSI benefits, beginning around one year after initial application, which is still at a relatively low level ($75 per month) 39 months after application. Those awarded SSDI report a small amount of their own SSI payments following application for SSDI.[27]

Figure 13 shows that the labor earnings of household members other than applicants' and the applicants' spouses are important. While the amounts do not differ dramatically across our four groups, they do as share of total household income (Table 5). For SSI applicants especially, they are very important source of income. But as was the case with spouses' labor earnings, we find no clear change in the size of these earnings around the time of application.[28]

Appendix Figs A1 through A7 report how the monthly prevalence rates of the seven sources of household income discussed above vary over the relevant time period for our four groups of initial applicants. The trends follow closely those in Figs 7 through 13.

Heterogeneity Within the SSDI and SSI Applicant Population

Thus far, we have tracked the average monthly employment and labor earnings of SSDI and SSI applicants as well as their average monthly household income and its sources in the three years before and after application. We have shown that there are considerable differences in average outcomes between SSDI and SSI applicants and some differences between applicants who are awarded and denied benefits within these programs. We now focus on the much greater heterogeneity of outcomes obscured by these averages.

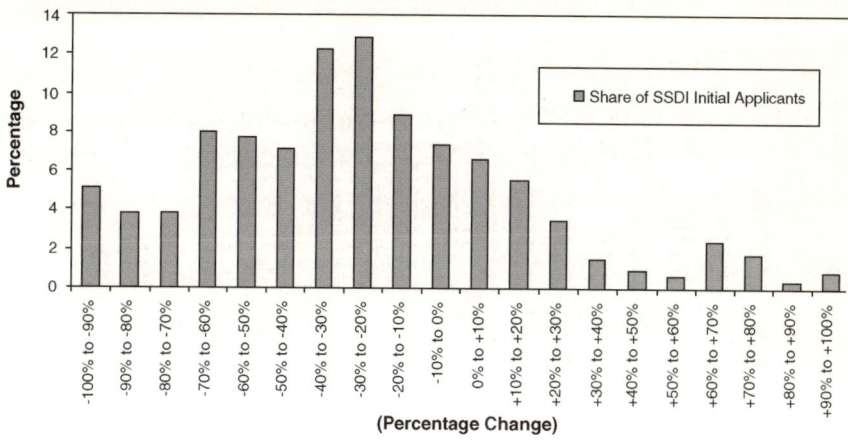

Fig. 14

Distribution of Percentage Change in Household Income of Applicants Before and After Application for SSDI Benefits. *Note:* A percent change between 13–15 months prior to SSDI application and 1–3 months after initial SSDI application. *Source:* Matched Survey of Income and Program Participation and SSA administrative records.

To examine how the applicants' average household income changes around the time of application for SSDI or SSI benefits, it is sufficient to compare the average household income of one set of applicants several years before they apply for benefits to the household income of another set of applicants several years after they apply. As long as these two sets of applicants represent random samples from the same population, the comparison is valid and should give an unbiased estimate of the change in mean household income. However, to study the distribution in the change of their household income around the period of time individuals apply for SSDI or SSI, we need to follow the same set of applicants across time. In order to do this, with our SIPP-administrative data, we need to substantially shorten our time horizon, since we must have information on the same individual over the entire horizon we choose.

In Fig. 14 we plot the distribution of percentage changes in household income between 12–14 months prior to SSDI application and 1–3 months after SSDI application. The median drop in household income is 27%, but there is considerable heterogeneity around this average. While about 40% of SSDI applicants experience a decline in their household income of no more than 20%, about 30% experience declines of between 20 and 50%, and about 30% experience declines of 50% or more.

In Fig. 15 we report the results over the same time period around application for those who apply for SSI benefits. The median decline for SSI applicants is only

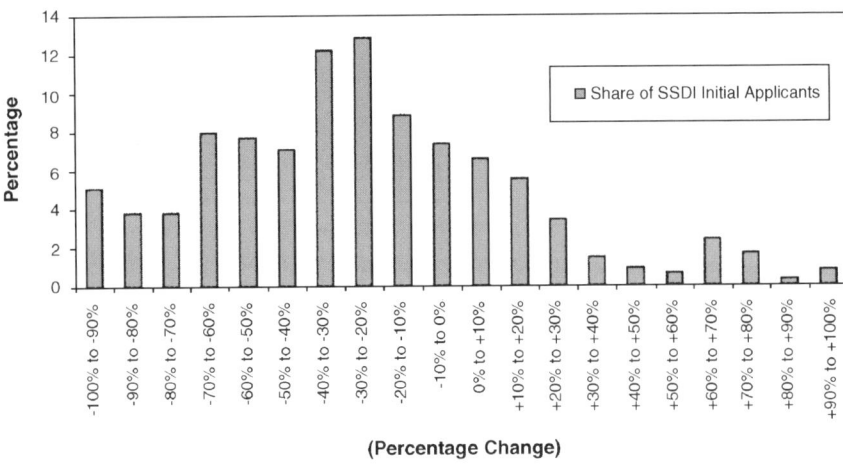

Fig. 15

Distribution of Percentage Change in Household Income of Applicants Before and After Application for SSI Benefits. Rich: shouldn't legend read SSI Initial Applicants? *Note:* A percent change between 13–15 months prior to SSDI SSI? application and 1–3 months after initial SSI application. *Source:* Matched Survey of Income and Program Participation and SSA administrative records.

6%, but there is also heterogeneity around this average. While about 30% of SSI applicants experience gains and about 30% experience declines of no more than 20%, about 20% experience declines of 20–50%, and 20% experience decline of more than 50%.

To further explore the heterogeneity of outcomes in our population of SSDI and SSI applicants, we estimate a series of quantile regressions. We do this because we suspect that applicants' position in the monthly household income distribution prior to application will be related to their percentage decline in monthly household income that we observed in Figs 14 and 15. Results from our quantile regressions are reported in Table 6. The first three columns represent estimates for the 25th percentile, the 50th percentile, and the 75th percentile of SSDI applicants. The last three columns do the same for SSI applicants.

To illustrate how to interpret the reported estimates, we focus on the first row of estimates. The estimate of -0.19 in the first row, second column, indicates that a 10% increase in household income at baseline (i.e. a 0.1 ln point increase) is associated with a 0.019 percentage point decline for the person in the median income household. The negative numbers in the first row indicate that for both SSDI and SSI applicants, the higher their initial level of monthly household income at baseline, 12–14 months prior to application, the larger is their percentage decline

Table 6. Percentage Change in SSDI and SSI Applicants' Mean Household Income.

	SSDI Percentile			SSI Percentile		
	25	50	75	25	50	75
Log of Income at Baseline	−0.12*	−0.19*	−0.37*	−0.18*	−0.18*	−0.30*
	(0.03)	(0.03)	(0.05)	(0.06)	(0.05)	(0.08)
Share of Own Labor	−0.33*	−0.33*	−0.34*	−0.53*	−0.62*	−0.64*
Earnings at Baseline	(0.07)	(0.077)	(0.11)	(0.15)	(0.17)	(0.23)
Age at Baseline (×100)	−0.24	−0.24	−0.03	−0.34	−0.29	−0.67
	(0.21)	(0.23)	(0.37)	(0.35)	(0.35)	(0.46)
Awarded Benefits	0.04	0.05	0.16*	0.05	0.09	0.19
	(0.04)	(0.05)	(0.08)	(0.09)	(0.09)	(0.11)
Female	0.01	−0.03	−0.01	−0.03	−0.05	−0.17
	(0.04)	(0.05)	(0.07)	(0.11)	(0.10)	(0.12)
Married at Baseline	0.30*	0.20*	0.21*	−0.11	−0.01	0.01
	(0.05)	(0.05)	(0.08)	(0.09)	(0.09)	(0.11)
Constant	0.51	1.28	2.86	1.17	1.34	2.61
	(0.26)	(0.27)	(0.46)	(0.46)	(0.42)	(0.62)
N	394	394	394	228	228	228
Sample Quartiles	−0.58	−0.27	0.01	−0.39	−0.06	0.17

Note: The dependent variable is the difference between household income one to three months after application and 12–14 months before application in January 1990 dollars.
Source: 1990–1993 SIPP data merged to Social Security Administration disability determination records.
*Significant at the 95% level.

in monthly household income over the period. The fact that baseline household income is associated with a bigger change at the 75th percentile than at the 50th percentile indicates that applicants who live in relatively higher income households at baseline are more likely to experience larger percentage drops in their household income than are applicants who live in lower income households at baseline. This is not surprising, since they have further to drop before they reach the social safety net related to exit from the labor market for disabilities at either the minimum absolute household income level, in the case of SSI, or at a disproportionately lower household income level, in the case of SSDI.

Looking at the other coefficients in the quantile regression, we see that the share of baseline household income that comes from the applicants' own labor earnings is also related to the size of the drop in household income. For example, holding the baseline level of household income constant, a 25% shift in the share of baseline household income coming from the applicants' own labor earnings is associated with close to a 10% larger drop in the median applicant's household income. The importance of own labor earnings found here is consistent with our findings in the previous sections. The only other variable that is significant, and then only for SSDI applicants, is marital status at baseline. For SSDI applicants, other things equal, being married at baseline is associated with an increased drop in household income of the person in the median income household of 20 percentage points relative to being single.

SUMMARY AND CONCLUSIONS

Using panel data from SIPP linked to SSA disability determination records we traced the pattern of household income and the sources of that income from 38 months prior to 39 months following application for SSDI or SSI benefits. Despite the fact that SSDI and SSI are run by a common agency – the Social Security Administration – and use common criteria for eligibility on medical and vocational grounds, SSDI and SSI provide protection to quite distinct populations. We found that the average SSDI applicant had more than twice the monthly household income of the average SSI applicant and his or her labor earnings comprised a much larger share of that income. This fact led us to separately evaluate the pattern of household income change for these two distinct groups and also to divide our samples into those who were awarded benefits and those who were denied benefits. In general we find that differences in outcomes between program populations are greater than differences in outcomes within populations.

In all cases, the applicants' average labor earnings declined dramatically beginning six months before application, although in most cases these declines were evident 12–24 months prior to application. Percentage declines in the average labor earnings of SSDI applicants were potentially more serious with respect to declines in their household income than for SSI applicants, because their labor earnings were a much more important component of their household income prior to application.

Unlike most European countries, the United States has no universal short-term disability program, and it imposes a five month waiting period before SSDI payments can be made. Nevertheless, we found that average household income dropped much less dramatically than labor earnings for SSDI and SSI applicants both in the months just before or just after application and over the next three years, and did so even for those denied benefits.

For SSI applicants the primary reason for this relative modest decline in household income was that on average their labor earnings did not play an important role in their household income even three years prior to application.

Hence, very large percentage declines in their own labor earnings translated into much smaller percentage declines in their household's income over the period. There were, however, some important changes in the composition of other sources of income. For SSI awardees, declines in AFDC and other welfare benefits as well as in spouses' labor earnings offset much of the gains from SSI in the months just after application for benefits.

SSDI applicants experienced a much greater potential decline in their household income associated with a decline in their labor earnings, since their labor earnings were on average a much greater component of their household income prior to application. In the early months following SSDI application, a patchwork of temporary disability benefits (e.g. workers' compensation, unemployment insurance, veterans' benefits, and employer pension benefits) offset declines in SSDI applicants' own labor earnings and their spouses' earnings. In the longer run, most of these temporary sources of income declined and were replaced by SSDI benefits. For those SSDI applicants who were denied benefits, the fall in their household income was somewhat greater immediately following application, but less so thereafter as their own labor earnings rose.

But while the average declines in household income from baseline for applicants are relatively modest, we found substantial heterogeneity in outcomes in both the SSDI and SSI applicant population. Almost 30 (20%) of SSDI (SSI) applicants experienced a 50% or greater decline in household income between baseline (12–14 months prior to initial application) and a period just after initial application (one to three months). Our quantile regressions suggest that it is higher income households that experience the greater percentage declines in their post-application income. Such results are consistent with the lower replacement rate established in the SSDI program and the low absolute level of protection provided to all SSI applicants regardless of income prior to application.

NOTES

1. See Bound and Burkhauser (1999) for a detailed discussion of the SSDI program, its goals and its effect on behavior and economic well-being.
2. See Daly and Burkhauser (forthcoming) for a detailed discussion of the SSI program, its goals, and its effects on behavior and economic well-being.
3. To be eligible for SSDI benefits, workers must be both disability-insured and fully insured. Workers aged 31 or older are disability-insured if they have worked in Social Security covered employment during 20 of the 40 quarters prior to their date of disablement. They are fully insured if they have worked in covered employment for, on average, one out every four quarters between the year they turned 21 and the year before the year in which they reached age 62 or became disabled.

4. Gainful employment is typically defined as earning more than a substantial gainful activity (SGA) amount. During most of the 1990s, the maximum SGA was $500 per month. In 1999, SGA was increased to $700 per month. It was raised to $740 per month in 2001.

5. In recent years, roughly 0.2% of those applying for SSDI benefits end up appealing to the Federal Counts (U.S. House of Representative, 1993).

6. SIPP panels were fielded in earlier and later years but are not currently matched to Social Security Administration administrative records.

7. These data were originally compiled for Lahari, Vaughan and Wixon (1995) and Hu, Lahari, Vaughan and Wixon (1997) for their study of the application for SSDI and SSI benefits.

8. We focus on the first application we observe in our administrative data. Since our data do not cover the entire lifetime of our applicants, it is possible that some applicants had previously applied and were denied benefits.

9. There is other evidence that we have not misclassified many cases. The administrative records we receive extend from about 17 to 41 months after the last data point we have in the SIPP, depending on the SIPP panel used. We have less information on those who apply close to the end of our administrative record information. To the extent that this is a problem, we would expect to observe systematic differences between the 1990 and 1991 SIPP-merged panels and between the 1992 and 1993 SIPP-merged panels (since both panels in each pair are matched to the same time window of administrative data, but contain earlier and later cohorts). When we separately calculated the tables produced here by panel year, we found no significant differences between cohorts from adjacent SIPP panels. Hence, we do not consider this to be a serious problem. There are, however, some differences between panels related to the growth of the SSDI and SSI populations over this time period. To the extent that we misclassify applicants, we will misclassify only those applying close to the end of the period on which we have administrative information. Hence, the income information we have on these individuals will cover the time before they apply for SSDI or SSI benefits.

10. If the household income changes are different for the 1991 and 1993 cohorts, then, while the estimates of the mean change of household income from two years prior to just after the application, and from just after to two years after are both valid, the estimate of the change of household income from two years prior to two years after the application will represent a composite of the corresponding changes for the two cohorts, and will not represent a valid estimate of the change for any one cohort.

11. For most SSDI applicants these months probably fall within the waiting period. In addition, neither SSDI nor SSI applicants are likely to be receiving benefits yet, simply because of ordinary delays in the disability determination decision process and in the processing of payments.

12. Here and in all subsequent analyses we restrict our sample to respondents who are aged 18 through 61. Because we are looking at the individual and not the household as our unit of analysis, some individuals in column 1 can live in the households of those who have applied for SSDI or SSI benefits.

13. In this table and in all subsequent tables and figures all dollar values have been adjusted to January 1990 values using the CPI All Urban Consumer Index.

14. All the analyses done on these two populations were also carried out on the population that applied for both programs. These results are available from the authors.

15. As discussed above, some of those we observe as being denied benefits eventually receive them at a more advanced level of the appeal process or based on a subsequent reapplication.

16. Ideally we would like to follow our samples from the point just before their disability began to affect their labor earnings. To do so we would need greater information on their lifetime earnings profile. Burkhauser, Butler and Weathers (2002) report that about 55% of men and women in their sample of SSDI applicants from the Health and Retirement Study experienced a health condition that began to interfere with their work longer than three years before application and 36% had such an experience more than ten years before application. This suggests that tracing applicants' household income back 36–38 months before applications is not sufficient to observe all of them before their disability has had some effect on the sources and amount of their household income.

17. This may not prove to be the case for two reasons. First, the waiting period for SSDI applicants is officially defined as the first five months following the time the disability first led to earnings below SGA. Workers who have disability-related earnings below SGA prior to application and who obtain a quick positive disability determination may already be receiving benefits during this period. Second, and perhaps more important, the income data in the SIPP is self-reported and the timing of income flows may not be precise. The SIPP re-surveys households every four months. There is evidence that individuals do not accurately remember the time of income receipt during the four-month window preceding an interview. Thus, income changes that occur between windows are more accurately reported than are changes that occur within windows. In our case, applications do not line up with the four-month windows, but occur randomly within them. For this reason, we expect a smearing across time of income flows. Still we expect the general patterns we find to reflect the pattern of household income during the period around the application for SSDI or SSI benefits. The finding of more transitions at the "seam" than at other points in a retrospective history pieced together from a series of interviews has been documented repeatedly (Burkhead & Coder, 1985; Hill, 1987; Moore & Kasprzyk, 1984).

18. The actual amount of labor earnings and program income in this period is also subject to error. While SIPP does a better job of capturing transfer income than other national data sets, our SSA matched data suggest that SSDI benefits are underreported. We find that only 90% of those whom we know from the SSA administrative record data were awarded SSDI benefits report positive amounts of Social Security income even 12 months after their award. It is also possible that respondents misreport the sources of their income.

19. Later in the text we provide fixed-effect estimates of average monthly labor earnings and household income and its sources for our four populations.

20. The SIPP does not clearly identify employer-provided disability insurance income. Bureau of Labor Statistic surveys show that more than 50% of the workforce is eligible for paid sick leave. In addition, roughly 30% are covered by some kind of sickness or accident insurance that continues to cover workers after they have exhausted their sick leave, for typically between six and twelve months, while 25% are covered by some kind of long-term disability plan, often as part of their pension (Kerns, 1994). Despite the fact that the SIPP does not ask explicitly about employer-provided disability insurance, it is possible that respondents may report this income. Thus, for example, a person on sick leave or receiving sickness or accident insurance benefits might report this income as part of their labor earnings. On the other hand, long-term disability insurance income may show up as pension income. It is also possible that such income is simply not reported.

21. It is also possible that some of their Social Security benefits are from other components of OASDI. Because we stop observing people at the point they reach age 62, it is unlikely that these are retirement benefits, but they could come from widow's benefits.

22. We follow applicants in our analysis. Because the composition of their households may change over time, we do not know how the lives of other household members are affected by the disability of the applicants.

23. The actual regressions used to estimate all our fixed-effect results as well as a discussion of the methods used in our analysis may be found in the technical appendix. The results we report in the figures in the text came from unweighted regressions. The weighted regressions yielded similar results. These results are available from the authors.

24. We estimate separate fixed-effect regressions for applicants' labor earnings and applicants' household income. We then graph the coefficients from these regressions, divided by average household income 36–38 months prior to application within the regression sample. Our fixed-effect regressions are presented in the technical appendix.

25. We estimate separate fixed-effect regressions for applicants' own Social Security income and for household income. We then graph the coefficients from the household income regression and the difference of the household income and their own Social Security income regressions, divided by average household income 36–38 months prior to application within the regression sample. These fixed-effect regressions are described in the technical appendix.

26. For the most part these own Social Security benefits are based on a re-application for SSDI after an initial denial, although in some cases they could be awarded based on appeals after the last stage of the first application process we observe or from other Social Security programs or simply misreports.

27. While we attempt to remove those who simultaneously apply for SSDI and SSI, it is possible that errors in the data cause this result.

28. On average, approximately 36% of other household members are applicants' adult children, 10% are applicants' parents, 17% are applicants' other relatives, and the rest are adults who are unrelated to the applicant by blood or marriage.

ACKNOWLEDGMENTS

This study was funded by a grant from the United States Social Security Administration (SSA) to the Michigan Retirement Research Center. We thank William G. Johnson, J. S. Butler, Howard Iams, and Mary Daly for useful comments on this paper. We thank Martha Bonney for editing and Flo Allen for word-processing various versions of this paper. The opinions and conclusions are solely those of the authors and should not be construed as representing the opinions or policy of SSA or any agency of the Federal Government. Austin Nichols was also funded from a training grant from the National Institute on Aging through the Population Studies Center at the University of Michigan.

REFERENCES

Bound, J., & Burkhauser, R. V. (1999). Economic analysis of transfer programs targeted on people with disabilities. In: O. C. Ashenfelter & D. Card (Eds), *Handbook of Labor Economics* (Vol. 3C, pp. 3417–3528). Amsterdam: Elsevier Science.

Burkhauser, R. V., & Daly, M. C. (2002). U.S. disability policy in a changing environment. *Journal of Economic Perspectives*, *16*(1), 213–224.

Burkhauser, R. V., Butler, J. S., & Weathers, R. R., II (2002). How policy variables influence the timing of social security disability insurance applications. *Social Security Bulletin*, *64*(1), 1–32.

Burkhead, D., & Coder, J. (1985). Gross changes in income recipiency from the survey of income and program participation. Proceedings of the Section on Social Statistics, American Statistical Association (pp. 351–356).

Daly, M. C., & Burkhauser, R. V. (forthcoming). The supplemental security income program. In: R. Moffitt (Ed.), *Means Tested Transfer Programs in the United States*. Chicago, IL: University of Chicago Press for the NBER.

Hill, D. H. (1987). Response errors around the seam: Analysis of change in a panel with overlapping reference periods. Proceedings of the Section on Survey Research Methods, American Statistical Association (pp. 210–215).

Hu, J., Lahari, K., Vaughan, D. R., & Wixon, B. (1997). Structural model of social security's disability determination process. Social Security Administration, Office of Research, Evaluation and Statistics, Working Paper No. 72.

Kerns, W. L. (1994). Protection against income loss during the first six months of illness or injury. *Social Security Bulletin*, *57*, 88–92.

Lahari, K., Vaughan, D. R., & Wixon, B. (1995). Modeling social security's sequential disability determination using matched SIPP data. *Social Security Bulletin*, *58*, 3–42.

Moore, J. C., & Kasprzyk, D. (1984). Month-to-month recipiency turnover in the ISDP. Proceedings of the Section on Survey Research Methods, American Statistical Association (pp. 726–731).

United States Congress, House of Representatives, Committee on Ways and Means (1993). *Background material on data and programs within the jurisdiction of the committee of ways and means*. Washington, DC: Government Printing Office.

United States, Social Security Administration (2001). *Annual statistical supplement to the social security bulletin*. Washington, DC: Government Printing Office.

APPENDIX

Fixed-Effect Regressions

Figures A1, A2 and 6 through 13 are constructed using estimated coefficients from regressions with the format in Eq. (A1) below. Fixed effects are included for each individual applicant, i, and for each calendar month, t, in the sample period. A set of indicator variables for months relative to application month is also included. These variables (month zero, for example, representing the month of application, or month twelve, to take another example, representing the month one year subsequent to application) are equal to one if observation of income data is

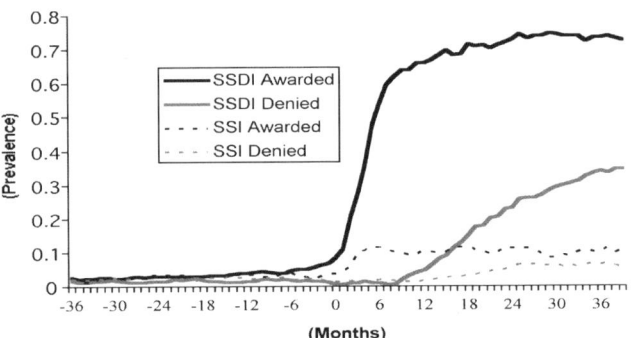

Fig. A1
Prevalence of Positive Social Security Benefits in the Monthly Household Income of Applicants Before and After Application for SSDI and SSI. *Note:* Zero is the month of initial SSDI or SSI application benefit. *Source:* Matched Survey of Income and Program Participation and SSA administrative records.

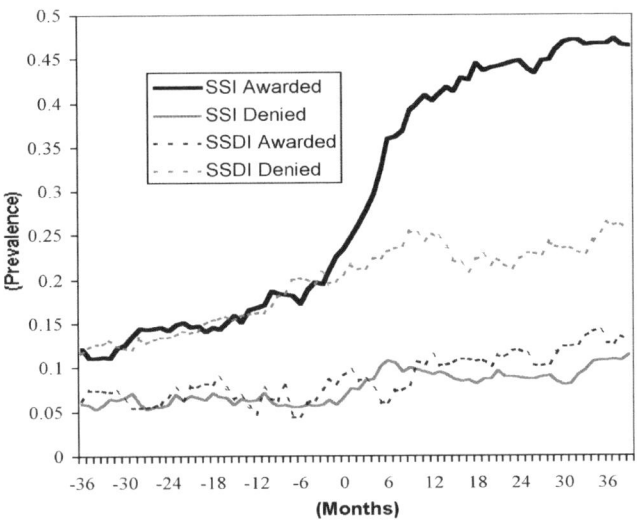

Fig. A2
Prevalence of Positive Employer Pension Benefits in the Monthly Household Income of Applicants Before and After Application for SSDI and SSI. *Note:* Zero is the month of initial SSDI or SSI application. *Source:* Matched Survey of Income and Program Participation and SSA administrative records.

taken from the month corresponding to the indicator variable, and zero otherwise. Thus the equations have the form:

$$y_{it} = \alpha_i + \gamma_t + \sum_j \beta_j m_{ij} + \varepsilon_{it} \tag{A1}$$

where y_{it} represents monthly income (in January 1990 dollars) for applicant i in time period t, the α's and the γ's represent applicant and calendar month fixed effects, and the m_{ij}'s represent the month relative to application month indicator variables. Months from 35 months before to 39 months after application each have one indicator variable corresponding to that month. Data from 39 or more months prior to application or 40 or more months subsequent to application are excluded from the regression sample, so that the coefficients (the β's in the equation) on application month indicator variables are interpreted as the average change from the level observed 36–38 months prior to application. The procedure for obtaining the values reported in Figs 1B, 2B and all the appendix figures is the same, except that the dependent variables are indicator variables that equal one if the income is positive in the given month.

For purposes of presentation, we report the β's relative to average baseline incomes (i.e. relative to the average α_i). Thus, the values in the figures can be interpreted as the average change in income from a particular source relative to baseline. Figures 3–6 are based on similar regressions. However, here the

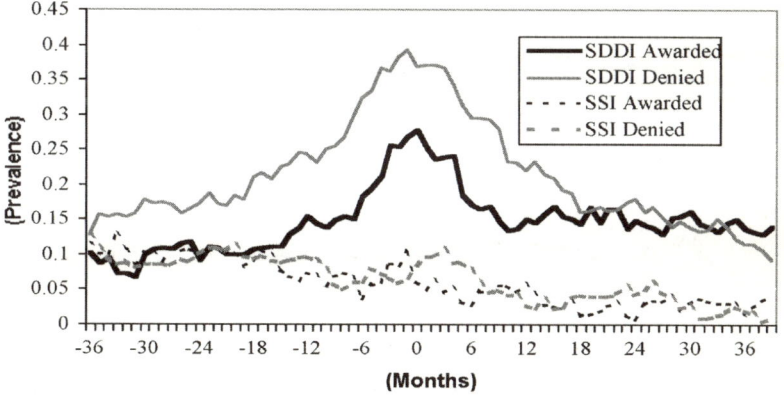

Fig. A3

Prevalence of Positive Temporary Insurance Benefits in the Monthly Household Income of Applicants Before and After Application for SSDI and SSI. *Note:* Zero is the month of initial SSDI or SSI application. *Source:* Matched Survey of Income and Program Participation and SSA administrative records.

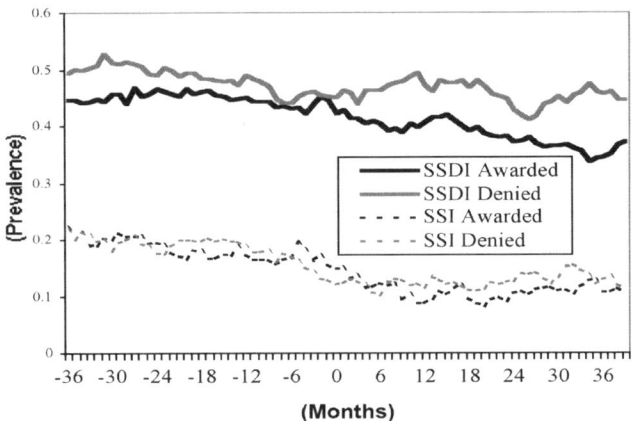

Fig. A4
Prevalence of Positive Spouse Labor Earnings in the Monthly Household Income of Applicants Before and After Application for SSDI and SSI. *Note:* Zero is the month of initial SSDI or SSI application. *Source:* Matched Survey of Income and Program Participation and SSA administrative records.

coefficients for changes in total household income are converted into percentage changes by dividing by baseline total household income 36–38 months prior to application. Thus, the bold solid line in each of these graphs represents the percentage change since baseline in average total household income. The simulated changes are constructed using coefficients from separate fixed-effect regressions with the same structure. The schedule marked "simulated percentage change in household

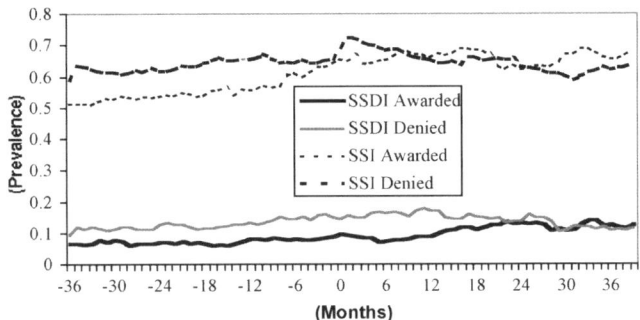

Fig. A5
Prevalence of Positive Government Welfare Transfers Except SSI Benefits in the Monthly Household Income of Applicant Before and After Application for SSDI and SSI. *Note:* Zero is the month of initial SSDI or SSI application. *Source:* Matched Survey of Income and Program Participation and SSA administrative records.

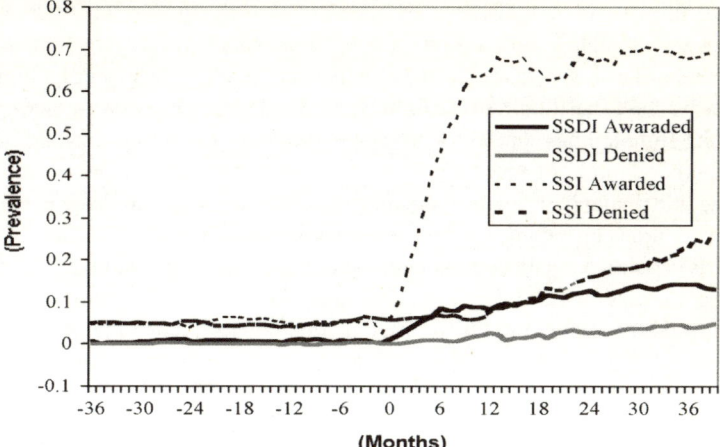

Fig. A6

Prevalence of Positive SSI Benefits in the Monthly Household Income of Applicants Before and After Application for SSDI and SSI. *Note:* Zero is the month of initial SSDI or SSI application. *Source:* Matched Survey of Income and Program Participation and SSA administrative records.

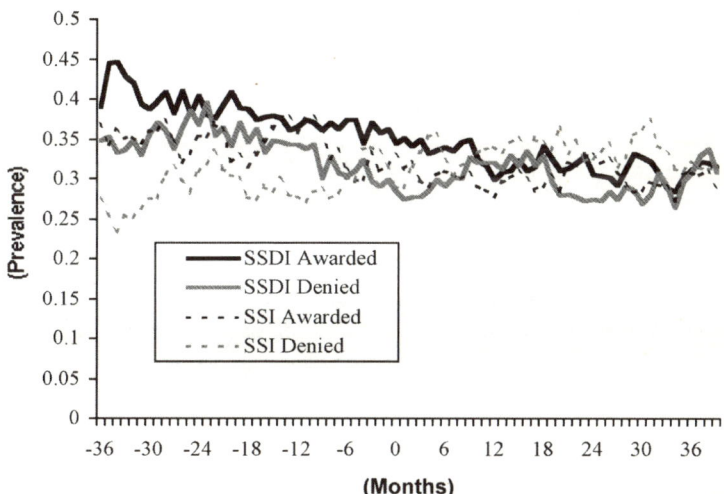

Fig. A7

Prevalence of Positive Earnings of Household Members Other Than Applicant or Applicant's Spouse in the Monthly Household Income of Applicants Before and After Application for SSDI and SSI. *Note:* Zero is the month of initial SSDI or SSI application. *Source:* Matched Survey of Income and Program Participation and SSA administrative records.

income, allowing only applicants' labor earnings to change" is constructed using coefficients estimated from a regression of applicants labor earnings on application months. The coefficients from the regression of applicants labor earnings are divided by baseline total household income 36–38 months prior to application. Thus, the simulations represent what would have happened to household income had all other sources of income stayed constant at their baseline level. Similarly, the schedule marked "simulated percentage change in household income, allowing all other sources of income to change but holding SSDI and SSI at their baseline levels" is constructed using coefficients estimated from a regression of total household income less own SSDI and SSI on application months. The coefficients from this regression are then divided by baseline total household income 36–38 months prior to application to covert into simulated percentage changes. Therefore, these simulations represent what would have happened to household income had there been no change in own SSDI and SSI benefits relative to baseline.

Tables

The average income levels and participation rates reported for three-month periods surrounding application for SSDI or SSI benefits in Tables 3–5 are calculated by averaging first across observed data for an individual, then across individuals weighted by the population weights for individuals as of their entry into the SIPP. The unweighted results are very similar to the reported weighted results. If only one or two months are observed for an individual, only those months are used in constructing individual averages; these individuals are not weighted less when averaging across individuals.

Participation rates are constructed using indicator variables for positive income in a given month. Since an individual may or may not have positive income in any month in the relevant three-month window, individuals enter the cross-individual averages with a value of zero, one-third, one-half, two-thirds, or one, indicating no months of positive income, one positive out of three observed, one positive out of two observed, two positive out of three observed, or all positive amounts of income in observed months.

Definitions
All the information on household income comes from the SIPP data. It has been disaggregated to provide a general sense of how the sources of household income change across the months leading up to and following application for either SSDI or SSI benefits. The definition for the income categories we use in Tables 5 and 6 are listed below.

Table 5

- *Labor Earnings* include wage and salary income, self-employment income, and incidental or casual earnings.
- *Property Income* includes all income from assets, including rent and dividends.
- *Pension Income* includes railroad retirement pension; company or union pension; federal civil service, or other federal civilian employee pensions; U.S. military retirement pay; state government pensions; local government pensions; income from paid-up life insurance policies, or annuities; other payment for retirement, disability, or survivor.
- *Veterans Benefits* include all veterans benefits.
- *Private Transfers* includes income assistance from a charitable group, money from relatives or friends, and lump sum payments.
- *Temporary Disability Income* includes payments from an employer or union temporary sickness policy or own sickness, accident, or disability insurance policy.

Table A1. Cumulative Percent of Waiting Time for the Last Decision Observed.

Months	SSDI			SSI		
	All	Awarded	Denied	All	Awarded	Denied
0	3.2	5.0	1.3	1.1	1.0	1.1
1	24.7	30.9	18.4	9.0	9.9	8.5
2	45.8	52.3	39.4	28.0	33.3	25.0
3	62.9	67.3	58.4	47.8	54.1	44.1
4	74.7	77.6	71.8	63.5	70.0	59.6
5	82.7	83.8	81.6	75.4	80.2	72.5
6	87.4	87.1	87.7	83.6	87.7	81.2
7	91.0	89.7	92.2	89.6	92.7	87.8
8	92.8	90.9	94.7	92.5	95.4	90.8
9	94.6	92.4	96.9	95.5	97.3	94.4
10	95.5	93.2	97.8	96.8	97.6	96.4
15	98.3	97.3	99.3	99.2	99.3	99.2
20	99.2	98.6	99.8	99.8	99.7	99.9
25	99.5	99.2	99.9	99.9	99.8	100.0
30	99.7	99.4	100.0	99.9	99.8	100.0
35	99.9	99.7	100.0	99.9	99.8	100.0
45	99.9	99.9	100.0	99.9	100.0	100.0
50	100.0	100.0	100.0	100.0	100.0	100.0

Note: Unweighted data.
Source: 1990–1993 SIPP data merged to Social Security Administration Disability determination records.

- *Workers' Compensation* includes Workers Compensation payments to any household member.
- *Unemployment Insurance* includes Unemployment Insurance payments to any household member.
- *Social Security Income* includes all household social security income, including SSDI and OASI payments to retired, disabled, or survivor household members.
- *SSI* includes federal SSI payments to all household members.
- *Other Transfers except SSI* includes all other government transfers, including AFDC, General Assistance, and Noncash transfers.
- *AFDC* includes AFDC payments to any household member.
- *Noncash Transfers* include Food Stamps and any other noncash means-tested benefits.

Table 6

These are quantile regressions. The *dependent variable* is mean household income over the period 1–3 months after application minus mean household income over the period 12–14 months before application in January 1990 dollars.

- *Log of Income at Baseline* is the natural logarithm of mean household income over the period 12–14 months before application.
- *Share of Own Labor Earnings at baseline* is the ratio of mean own labor earnings (over the period 12–14 months before application) to mean household income (over the period 12–4 months before application).
- *Age at Baseline ($\times 100$)* is the applicant's age 14 months before application. The estimated coefficient has been multiplied by 100 for ease of exposition.
- *Awarded Benefits* is the final disposition of the first application observed. This variable is one if the applicant was awarded benefits and zero otherwise.
- *Female* equals one if the applicant is female and zero otherwise.

MINIMUM WAGES AND ON-THE-JOB TRAINING

Daron Acemoglu and Jörn-Steffen Pischke

1. INTRODUCTION

Much of the recent debate on the minimum wage has focused on its employment implications. The theory of human capital suggests that minimum wages should also have important adverse effects on human capital accumulation. In the standard human capital theory, as developed by Becker (1964), Ben-Porath (1967), and Mincer (1974), a large part of human capital is accumulated on the job, and workers often finance these investments through lower wages. A binding minimum wage will therefore reduce workplace training, as it prevents low wage workers from accepting the necessary wage cuts (Rosen, 1972). The early empirical literature has confirmed this prediction. The negative impact on human capital formation has been an important argument against minimum wages in the minds of many economists and policy-makers, and an important piece of evidence in support of the standard theory of human capital.

In this paper, we revisit the impact of minimum wages on training. We build on our previous work, Acemoglu and Pischke (1999b), which showed that a compression in the structure of wages can induce firm-sponsored training. We show that in non-competitive labor markets, minimum wages can increase – rather than decrease – training investments because they compress the wage structure.

The intuition for this result is that minimum wages make it less profitable to employ unskilled workers. When there are no rents in the employment relationship, as in a competitive labor market, the firm has no option but to lay off workers who

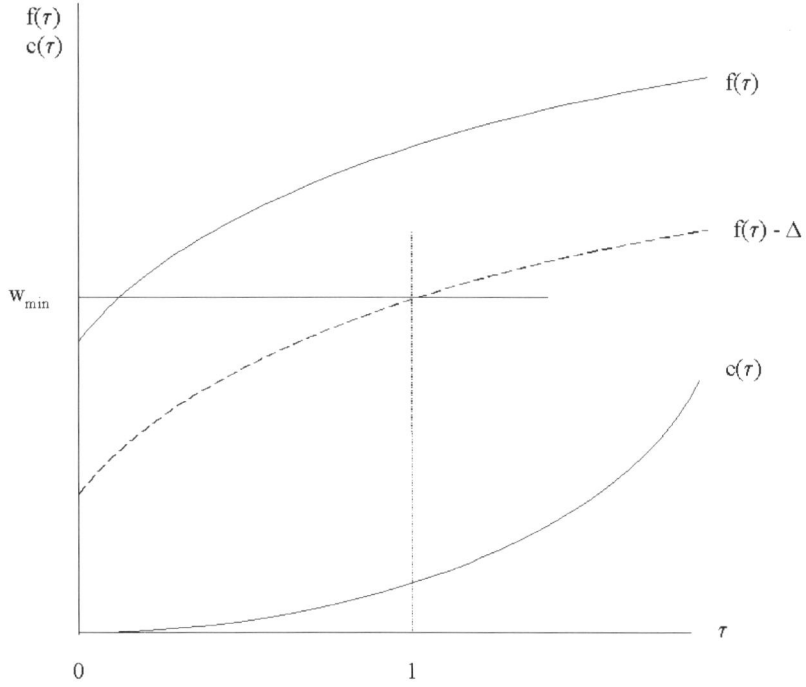

Fig. 1. Training with a Minimum Wage and Employment Rents.

were previously paid below the new minimum wage. In contrast, in the presence of labor market rents, it may be more profitable to increase the productivity of workers, who are already receiving high wages, rather than laying them off. Figure 1 illustrates this intuition diagrammatically. It draws the relation between worker skills, τ, productivity, $f(\tau)$, and wages $w(\tau)$. The gap between productivity and wages, Δ, is the rent that the firm obtains. A binding minimum wage, in the absence of such rents, forces the firm to lay off the worker. However, with Δ sufficiently high, the firm would like to retain the worker despite the higher wages dictated by the minimum wage. In this case, the firm would also like to increase the productivity of the worker. Without the minimum wage, the gap between $f(\tau)$ and $w(\tau)$ was constant, so there was no point in incurring costs of training. However, with a minimum wage, profits are less at $\tau = 0$ than at $\tau = 1$. So if the firm can increase its employee's skills to $\tau = 1$ at a moderate cost, it will prefer to do so. In essence, the minimum wage has made the firm the *de facto* residual claimant of the increase in the worker's productivity, whereas without the minimum wage, the worker was the residual claimant.

This reasoning suggests that a binding minimum wage may induce firms to invest more in the skills of their employees. Since this implication differs sharply from the prediction of the standard theory, empirical evidence on this point can shed light on whether non-competitive features affecting training decisions are important. Although existing evidence points to a negative effect of minimum wages on training, we argue that this evidence suffers from a number of problems. We therefore adopt a different approach and provide new empirical estimates that are quite different from those in the literature. We use the National Longitudinal Survey of Youth (NLSY) for the period 1987–1992. This period encompasses a number of state minimum wage increases as well as two federal increases in the minimum in 1990 and 1991. Our data therefore contain a large amount of within state variation in minimum wages. Furthermore, the NLSY is a panel of youths and oversamples those from disadvantaged backgrounds, so it contains a relatively high number of low wage workers directly affected by minimum wage increases.

Our empirical results show almost no evidence of a reduction in training in response to minimum wages. But, they also do not provide strong support for our alternative model. Overall, the evidence suggests that minimum wages appear to have little effect on training investments for low-wage workers. Although we cannot rule out modest positive or negative effects, our two standard error confidence bands exclude large negative effects of minimum wage increases on training – in fact, most of our most reliable estimates are positive.

An appealing way to explain the empirical findings is a hybrid model in which minimum wages increase training for some workers while reducing it for others. In this model, as in the standard theory, the wages of some workers are low because they are compensating their employers for investments in general skills. The minimum wage laws prevent this. This approach therefore suggests that minimum wages reduce the training of workers taking wage cuts to finance their training, while inducing further training for those who were constrained in their human capital investments. This hybrid model predicts that the impact of minimum wages should depend on the presence and size of labor market rents. We end the paper with some evidence pointing in this direction.

The rest of the paper is organized as follows. The following section discusses the previous empirical literature. Section 3 presents a simple theoretical setup where, contrary to the predictions of the standard theory, minimum wages increase training investments. In Section 4, we describe our data set, and discuss the empirical strategy to estimate the effects of minimum wages on training. Our results are presented in Section 5. Since the empirical evidence supports neither the standard Becker theory nor our model, in Section 6, we consider a hybrid model where minimum wages increase training for some workers, while reducing it for others.

In Section 7, we provide some additional empirical evidence on this hybrid model. Section 8 concludes.

2. A CRITIQUE OF THE PREVIOUS EMPIRICAL LITERATURE

There is a small empirical literature investigating the impact of minimum wages on training. Part of this literature focuses on whether minimum wage laws lead to slower observed wage growth in micro data. Both Leighton and Mincer (1981) and Hashimoto (1982) have found this to be the case and concluded that minimum wage laws lead to less training. But, since a minimum wage increases the wages of low paid workers, it can reduce wage growth without affecting training. Therefore, it is unsatisfactory to interpret the decline in age-earnings profiles as evidence of reduced investment in general training. Consistent with this view, Grossberg and Sicilian (1999) find no effect of minimum wages on training, but still find lower wage growth for minimum wage workers. Furthermore, Card and Krueger (1995) compared cross sectional wage profiles in California before and after the 1988 minimum wage increase with a number of comparison states. They also found flatter profiles in California after the minimum wage increase. However, they point out that the Californian profile also shifts up and does not cross the previous age-wage profile. This pattern contradicts the standard theory, but is consistent with the predictions of our model.

Given the difficulty of interpreting changes in the slope of wage profiles, we find it more compelling to look at the impact of minimum wages on training directly, but we are only aware of four previous studies doing this for the U.S. Leighton and Mincer (1981) use worker reported data on the receipt of training from the Panel Study of Income Dynamic (PSID) and the National Longitudinal Survey and find that workers in states with lower wages and therefore a more binding federal minimum wage receive significantly less training. Cross state comparisons may be confounded by the presence of other state effects, however. For example, industrial and occupational composition of employment varies substantially across states, and different industries and occupations have different skill requirements. These considerations suggest that across state comparisons are hard to interpret.

Schiller (1994) reports a similar finding using later data from the NLSY by comparing the training incidence of minimum wage workers with those earning higher wages. The evidence from this study is even harder to interpret because worker traits which lead to higher pay are typically also associated with more training. Grossberg and Sicilian (1999) use data from the Employment Opportunity Pilot Project (EOPP) and compare minimum wage workers both to workers earning slightly less and slightly more, ameliorating the problem of worker heterogeneity somewhat. They find insignificant negative effects on training for male minimum wage workers and insignificant positive effects for women. Leighton and Mincer only analyzed men, although women make up the majority of minimum wage workers.

Some o these problems are overcome in a more recent study by Neumark and Wascher (2001), who use Current Population Survey (CPS) supplements to compare the impact of minimum wages on training within states using comparisons of young workers in 1991 with older workers (who are less likely to be affected by the minimum wage) and with young workers in 1983. These comparisons assume that state differences in training levels are the same for younger and older workers and remain so over long time periods, which are stringent requirements. They also find negative effects of minimum wages on training, but these effects seem to be too large to be sensible.

To see why the effects implied Neumark and Washer's paper are implausibly large, note that their treatment group consists of all young workers. Not all of these workers are affected by the minimum wage, however. Let us assume, quite generously, that all workers earning less than 160% of the minimum are "affected" by the minimum wage. The 160% of the average federal minimum over the period they study is $5.60, and 40% of workers aged 20–24 are paid below this wage in 1991. Neumark and Washer's estimates imply that formal training among workers aged 20–24 in California (a high minimum wage state) was 3.2 percentage points lower than in states which were subject to the lower federal minimum. This point estimate, then, implies that among affected workers, training will be lower by approximately eight percentage points (i.e. 3.2 percentage points divided by 0.40). The average incidence of training among affected workers in low minimum wage states is 3.0% (much lower than among all workers aged 20–24 for whom the incidence is 10%). So this estimate implies that introducing California's minimum wage to low minimum wage states should have wiped out all training *two and a half times* among affected workers in these states! Clearly, an implausibly large effect.[1]

3. MINIMUM WAGES AND TRAINING IN NONCOMPETITIVE LABOR MARKETS

In this section, we use a two-period model to analyze the impact of minimum wages on training. The main result of this analysis is that plausible deviations from perfectly competitive labor markets, which introduce firm-specific rents and prevent workers from financing their own training, change the conclusions of

Becker's theory. Namely, we find that minimum wages can *increase* investments in general training.

3.1. Environment

The world lasts for two periods, 1 and 2. There is no discounting, and all agents are risk-neutral. There is a continuum of workers with mass 1, who supply labor inelastically. These workers differ by ability. More specifically, there is a distribution of abilities across workers denoted by $G(\eta)$ with support $[\underline{\eta}, \bar{\eta}]$. We introduce heterogeneity in abilities to capture the disemployment effects of the minimum wage. This feature will also be useful later in Section 6 when we discuss the possibility of workers paying for their own training.

We view period 1 as the early career of workers. A worker with ability η_i produces $\theta\eta_i$ in the first period, where $\theta < 1$. In the second period, he produces η_i. In addition, during the first period, he can be trained. To simplify the discussion we assume that training is indivisible, so only $\tau = 0$ (no training) and $\tau = 1$ (training) are possible. A worker who is trained produces $\eta_i + \phi$ in the second period where $\phi > 0$. Additive returns to training simplify the expressions, without affecting the results; moreover, they highlight that firm-sponsored training does not arise because of a complementarity between training and ability (a possibility demonstrated in Acemoglu & Pischke, 1999b).

We assume that training is general, so this increase in productivity applies equally in all firms. The cost of training, which is independent of ability, is incurred in terms of lower output in the first period and is equal to $c > 0$. In order to draw a stark contrast to the Becker model, we assume that all training investments have to be financed by the firm. This could be because training is non-contractible, so the firm can renege on its training promise even if the worker takes a wage cut to finance his training (see Acemoglu & Pischke, 1999a, for a discussion).

We assume:

Assumption 1. $\phi > c$,

which implies that training is productive.

There is free-entry at zero cost and all firms have access to the same technology. We also assume that the firm obtains an additional revenue δ, if the worker was employed in the first period with this firm. Therefore, δ is a firm-specific productivity increase, and it is the only deviation from competitive labor markets we introduce.

The presence of the term δ creates a match-specific surplus to be divided between the firm and the worker. We assume Bertrand competition among firms (or equivalently, firms make take it or leave it offers to workers). Since the second-best opportunity of workers does not include δ, initial employers capture the whole amount δ, only paying the "market wage," even though workers' productivity is higher than this. As will become apparent shortly, the presence of rents from the employment relationship is crucial, but the results would be unaffected if the worker captures a fraction $\beta < 1$ of this surplus. Observe also that this mobility cost implies that all workers will stay with their initial employer.[2]

3.2. Equilibrium Without Minimum Wages

Equilibrium can now be characterized by backward induction. In the second period, each firm is willing to pay up to η for an untrained worker of ability η employed by another firm, and is willing to pay $\eta + \phi$ for a trained worker. Bertrand competition then ensures that

$$w_2(\eta_i, NT) = \eta_i,$$
$$w_2(\eta_i, T) = \eta_i + \phi. \quad (1)$$

Using the fact that in equilibrium all workers stay with their first period employer,[3] the profits of a representative firm from a worker of ability η_i, as a function of its training strategy, NT or T, can be written as:

$$\Pi(\eta_i, NT) = (\theta\eta_i - w_1(\eta_i)) + (\eta_i + \delta - w_2(\eta_i, NT))$$
$$\Pi(\eta_i, T) = (\theta\eta_i - c - w_1(\eta_i)) + (\eta_i + \delta + \phi - w_2(\eta_i, T)), \quad (2)$$

where $w_1(\eta_i)$ is the first period wage of a worker with ability η_i. The first bracket in each expression therefore gives first period profits, while the second is profits in period 2. Substituting Eq. (1) into Eq. (2), we immediately see that $\Pi(\eta, T) - \Pi(\eta, NT) = -c$, irrespective of the value of η. That is, if it trains its employees, the firm simply loses the training cost. The reason is simple: a trained worker receives ϕ more in the second period, and this is exactly the increase in his contribution to the firm's output. So the worker is the full residual claimant of the increase in productivity due to training, and the second period profit of the firm is equal to δ, independent of whether the worker is trained. Since the training cost c has to be paid by the firm, it is not optimal for any firm to invest in its employee's skills. Although there are firm-specific rents, because they do not interact with training – in particular, they do not induce compression in the wage structure (see Acemoglu & Pischke, 1999b) – firms have no incentive to train, even though training is socially desirable.

To complete the characterization of the equilibrium, we have to determine first period wages. Firms have to make zero profits from all workers, and there is no training, so $\Pi(\eta_i, NT) = 0$ for all η_i. This gives:

$$w_1(\eta_i) = \theta\eta_i + \delta \tag{3}$$

A noteworthy feature is that compensation can be front-loaded or back-loaded. Front-loading arises because firms anticipate δ, the rent they will receive in the second period, and are willing to bid higher than the worker's current productivity.[4]

We can summarize this analysis (proof in the text):

Proposition 1. There is a unique equilibrium in which there is no training, all workers are employed, and receive the first period wage given by (3) and the second period wage $w_2(NT)$ given by (1).

So despite Assumption 1, which ensures that training is socially beneficial, there is no training in equilibrium. This is in line with Becker's standard theory; firms are unwilling to invest in the general skill of their employees as they do not receive any of the benefits of training, and here workers are assumed unable to "buy" training. However, there is full employment in this decentralized economy, in particular, the level of employment is equal to the labor force, 1.

3.3. The Impact of Minimum Wages on Training

Now consider the imposition of a minimum wage $w_M > \underline{\eta}$ that is binding for some (untrained) workers in the second period. We start by writing wages in the presence of minimum wage laws. With a similar reasoning to above, (1) changes to:

$$\begin{aligned} w_2(\eta_i, NT) &= \max\{w_M, \eta_i\}, \\ w_2(\eta_i T) &= \max\{w_M, \eta_i + \phi\}. \end{aligned} \tag{4}$$

These expressions feature the "max" operator because the minimum wage may be less than or greater than worker productivity. Profits with and without training are still:

$$\Pi(\eta_i, NT) = (\theta\eta_i - w_1(\eta_i)) + (\eta_i + \delta - w_2(\eta_i, NT))$$
$$\Pi(\eta_i, T) = (\theta\eta_i - c - w_1(\eta_i)) + (\eta_i + \delta + \phi - w_2(\eta_i, T))$$

where now $w_1(\eta_i) \geq w_M$.

First, consider a worker for whom

$$\eta_i \leq w_M - \phi. \tag{5}$$

In this case, the second period wage is equal to the minimum even if this worker is trained. Then,

$$\Pi(\eta_i, T) - \Pi_j(\eta_i, NT) = \phi - c. \tag{6}$$

Assumption 1 implies that Eq. (6) is strictly positive for all η_i. So in stark contrast to the economy without minimum wages, firms now prefer to train all their employees whose ability is low enough to satisfy Eq. (5). The firm has to pay the minimum wage irrespective of whether the worker is skilled or not, so the full return to training is captured by the employer – *the firm is now the full residual claimant.*

Next, consider a worker for whom Eq. (5) does not hold, so that the second period wage for this worker, if trained, exceeds the minimum. So he will be paid $w_2(\eta_i, T) = \eta_i + \phi$ if trained. Then,

$$\Pi_j(\eta_i, T) - \Pi_j(\eta_i, NT) = w_M - \eta_i - c, \qquad (7)$$

which can be positive or negative. If it is positive, i.e. if

$$\eta_i \leq w_M - c \qquad (8)$$

the firm makes higher profits from trained – rather than untrained – workers.

Because condition Eq. (8) is more restrictive than Eq. (5) (see Assumption 1), we will have $\Pi_j(\eta_i, T) \geq \Pi_j(\eta_i, NT)$ if and only if Eq. (8) is satisfied. Nevertheless, condition (8) is not sufficient for firm-sponsored training. Firms also need to make nonnegative profits; i.e.

$$\Pi_j(\eta_i, T) \geq 0. \qquad (9)$$

The minimum that a worker can be paid in the first period is w_M, although the first period wage may be higher than this. Hence, Eq. (9) requires

$$(1 + \theta)\eta_i + \delta + \phi - c - w_M - \max\{\eta_i + \phi, w_M\} \geq 0. \qquad (10)$$

All workers for whom Eqs (8) and (10) are satisfied will be trained.

We are now in a position to determine the equilibrium level of employment and training. First, consider workers with ability $\eta_i > w_M - c$. As indicated above, these workers will not obtain training, and will be employed as long as firms make zero profits. This requires

$$(1 + \theta)\eta_i + \delta - w_M - \max\{\eta_i, w_M\} \geq 0. \qquad (11)$$

Intuitively, in the second period, a worker with ability $\eta_i > w_M$ will receive the wage $w_2(\eta_i, NT) = \eta_i$. Therefore, the firm will employ this worker only if the loss that it makes in the first period, $\theta\eta_i - w_M$, is less than the profit it expects to make in the second period, δ. The calculation is somewhat different for a worker with $w_M - c < \eta_i < w_M$, since the minimum wage will be binding for this worker in the second period, and so the second period profit is $\eta_i + \delta - w_M$. Combining these conditions, the number of workers who will be employed, but not receive any training, is

$$N(w_M) = 1 - G\left(\max\left\{w_M - c; \frac{w_M - \delta}{\theta}, \frac{2w_M - \delta}{1 + \theta}\right\}\right), \quad (12)$$

where the "max" operator takes care of various cutoffs involved.

If, in contrast, $\eta_i \leq w_M - c$, then it is more profitable for a firm to train the worker rather than employ him as an untrained employee. Such a worker will be employed – and trained – as long as Eq. (10) holds. Therefore, the number of workers employed and trained is[5]

$$T(w_M) = \max\left\{\left[G(w_M - c) - G\left(\frac{w_M - \delta + c}{\theta}\right)\right]; 0\right\} \quad (13)$$

Here, the max operator takes care of the fact that the expression in the square bracket could be negative, in which case there would be no firm-sponsored training because the firm would not be able to make zero profits by training its employees. In fact, in this case, a necessary and sufficient condition for firm-sponsored training and for the introduction of a minimum wage to increase training is

$$\delta > \delta^* \equiv (1 - \theta)w_M + (1 + \theta)c. \quad (14)$$

This highlights the importance of firm-specific rents. If $\delta = 0$, then Eq. (14) cannot be satisfied and the firm will therefore not find it profitable to train. Therefore, the deviation from perfectly competitive labor markets is essential for minimum wages to increase training. It is only with sufficiently large rents – as implied by Eq. (14) – that there will also be any firm-sponsored training.

We can now state the main result of this section (proof in the text):

Proposition 2. Suppose that a minimum wage satisfying $w_M > \underline{\eta}$ is imposed. Then the level of employment is $N(w_M) + T(w_M)$ and $T(w_M)$ workers receive firm-sponsored trained where $N(w_M)$ is given by Eq. (12) and $T(w_M)$ is given by Eq. (13). $T(w_M)$ is strictly positive whenever Eq. (14) holds.

As in the standard neoclassical model, minimum wages reduce employment as now $N + T < 1$ (whenever the lower support of the ability distribution, $\underline{\eta}$, is less than $(w_M - \delta + c)/\theta$). But moderate minimum wages also induce firms to offer training to some of the affected workers. To see this, consider the introduction of a minimum wage w_M satisfying condition (14) above in an economy without minimum wage. Before the imposition of the minimum wage, there is no firm-sponsored training, and since workers are unable to "buy" training from their employers, there is no training at all. After the introduction of the minimum wage, training increases to $T(w_M)$. Therefore, minimum wages can increase training in this economy.

Intuitively, the firm has to pay minimum wages even for unskilled workers and a binding minimum wage reduces the rents the firm receives from the employment relationship. Training raises the worker's productivity, and therefore restores some of these rents. Firm-specific rents (labor market imperfections) are crucial for this result. As noted above, when $\delta = 0$, there will be no training, since in this case condition (14) can never be satisfied.

Figure 1 in the introduction gives the basic intuition. The minimum wage determines the wage both at $\tau = 0$ and $\tau = 1$, so all productivity increases from training accrue to the employer, as in the case when $\eta_i \leq w_M - \phi$. The most interesting case might be the one where $w_M - \phi < \eta_i \leq w_M - c$. If the minimum wage is low enough, it may induce the firm to sponsor training but the worker receives some of the proceeds from the training, because the productivity of the trained worker exceeds the minimum wage.[6]

Notice that the results continue to apply if w_M is a wage above the legal minimum that the firm has to pay to the worker, due to other imperfections such as bargaining. Therefore, if an increase in the minimum creates spillover effects to wages above the minimum, our analysis predicts that firms may also be induced to train the workers affected by these spillovers. In practice, minimum wages appear to create spillover effects (e.g. DiNardo, Fortin & Lemieux, 1996; Lee, 1999), so we expect them to also influence the training of low wage workers earning above the minimum.

Since the effect of minimum wages on training analyzed here differs sharply from the prediction of the standard Becker theory, empirical evidence on minimum wages and training can shed light on whether non-competitive features and restrictions on workers' ability to finance their own training are important. In the next part of the paper, we investigate whether minimum wages increase or reduce training investments for low-wage workers.

4. EMPIRICAL STRATEGY AND DATA

The federal minimum wage was unchanged between 1981 and 1990, but various states imposed their own minima above the federal level during the late 1980s. While minimum wages were rather uniform across states before 1987 and after 1991, there was substantial dispersion between these dates. We will exploit this variation. Table 1 displays the statutory minimum wages in the US states over this period.

We use two complementary approaches to identifying the impact of minimum wages on training. The first one, which we find most compelling, looks at the training of workers who are directly affected by an increase in the state or federal

Table 1. Minimum Wage and Relative Minimum by State and Year.

State	Statutory Minimum Wage						Minimum Wage/Avg. Median Wage Age 35–54					
	1987	1988	1989	1990	1991	1992	1987	1988	1989	1990	1991	1992
Alabama	3.35	3.35	3.35	3.80	4.25	4.25	0.308	0.306	0.305	0.344	0.383	0.381
Alaska	3.85	3.85	3.85	4.30	4.75	4.75	0.215	0.214	0.213	0.237	0.260	0.259
Arizona	3.35	3.35	3.35	3.80	4.25	4.25	0.262	0.261	0.260	0.293	0.326	0.325
Arkansas	3.35	3.35	3.35	3.80	4.25	4.25	0.342	0.341	0.339	0.382	0.426	0.424
California	3.35	3.35/4.25	4.25	4.25	4.25	4.25	0.234	0.279	0.294	0.292	0.291	0.290
Colorado	3.35	3.35	3.35	3.80	4.25	4.25	0.245	0.244	0.243	0.274	0.305	0.304
Connecticut	3.37/3.75	3.75/4.25	4.25	4.25	4.27	4.27	0.236	0.265	0.279	0.277	0.277	0.276
Delaware	3.35	3.35	3.35	3.80	4.25	4.25	0.242	0.241	0.240	0.270	0.301	0.300
Florida	3.35	3.35	3.35	3.80	4.25	4.25	0.304	0.303	0.302	0.340	0.378	0.377
Georgia	3.35	3.35	3.35	3.80	4.25	4.25	0.290	0.288	0.287	0.324	0.360	0.359
Hawaii	3.35/3.85	3.85	3.85	3.85	4.25	4.75/5.25	0.251	0.276	0.275	0.273	0.300	0.343
Idaho	3.35	3.35	3.35	3.80	4.25	4.25	0.296	0.294	0.293	0.330	0.368	0.366
Illinois	3.35	3.35	3.35	3.80	4.25	4.25	0.239	0.238	0.237	0.268	0.298	0.297
Indiana	3.35	3.35	3.35	3.80	4.25	4.25	0.281	0.280	0.279	0.314	0.350	0.348
Iowa	3.35	3.35	3.35/3.85	3.85/4.25	4.25/4.65	4.65	0.285	0.283	0.293	0.330	0.363	0.386
Kansas	3.35	3.35	3.35	3.80	4.25	4.25	0.270	0.269	0.267	0.301	0.335	0.334
Kentucky	3.35	3.35	3.35	3.80	4.25	4.25	0.291	0.290	0.288	0.325	0.362	0.361
Louisiana	3.35	3.35	3.35	3.80	4.25	4.25	0.289	0.288	0.286	0.323	0.359	0.358
Maryland	3.35	3.35	3.35	3.80	4.25	4.25	0.235	0.234	0.233	0.262	0.292	0.291
Massachusetts	3.55/3.65	3.65/3.75	3.75	3.80	4.25	4.25	0.250	0.256	0.256	0.258	0.287	0.286
Michigan	3.35	3.35	3.35	3.80	4.25	4.25	0.231	0.230	0.229	0.258	0.287	0.286
Minnesota	3.35/3.55	3.55/3.85	3.85/3.95	3.95/4.25ª	4.25	4.25	0.256	0.272	0.288	0.292	0.312	0.311
Mississippi	3.35	3.35	3.35	3.80	4.25	4.25	0.340	0.339	0.337	0.380	0.423	0.422
Missouri	3.35	3.35	3.35	3.80	4.25	4.25	0.279	0.278	0.277	0.312	0.348	0.346
Montana	3.35	3.35	3.35	3.80	4.25	4.25	0.292	0.290	0.289	0.326	0.363	0.361
Nebraska	3.35	3.35	3.35	3.80	4.25	4.25	0.303	0.302	0.300	0.338	0.377	0.375
Nevada	3.35	3.35	3.35	3.80	4.25	4.25	0.266	0.265	0.264	0.297	0.331	0.330
New Hampshire	3.45/3.55	3.55/3.65	3.65/3.75	3.75/3.85	4.25	4.25	0.257	0.263	0.269	0.277	0.308	0.307
New Jersey	3.35	3.35	3.35	3.80	4.25	5.05	0.216	0.216	0.214	0.242	0.269	0.319
New Mexico	3.35	3.35	3.35	3.80	4.25	4.25	0.284	0.283	0.281	0.317	0.353	0.352
New York	3.35	3.35	3.35	3.80	4.25	4.25	0.238	0.237	0.236	0.266	0.296	0.295

Minimum Wages and on-the-job Training

State										
North Carolina	3.35	3.35	3.80	4.25	4.25	0.315	0.313	0.312	0.352	0.391	0.390
North Dakota	3.35	3.35	3.80	4.25	4.25	0.291	0.290	0.288	0.325	0.361	0.360
Ohio	3.35	3.35	3.80	4.25	4.25	0.260	0.259	0.258	0.291	0.324	0.322
Oklahoma	3.35	3.35	3.80	4.25	4.25	0.282	0.281	0.279	0.315	0.350	0.349
Oregon	3.35	3.35/4.25[b]	4.25/4.75	4.75	4.75	0.262	0.261	0.287	0.336	0.364	0.363
Pennsylvania	3.35/3.70	3.70	3.80	4.25	4.25	0.269	0.273	0.294	0.300	0.334	0.333
Rhode Island	3.65/4.00	4.00/4.25	4.25	4.45	4.45	0.281	0.302	0.321	0.324	0.338	0.337
South Carolina	3.35	3.35	3.80	4.25	4.25	0.305	0.304	0.302	0.341	0.379	0.378
South Dakota	3.35	3.35	3.80	4.25	4.25	0.337	0.336	0.334	0.377	0.420	0.418
Tennessee	3.35	3.35	3.80	4.25	4.25	0.331	0.329	0.328	0.370	0.411	0.410
Texas	3.35	3.35	3.80	4.25	4.25	0.280	0.279	0.278	0.313	0.348	0.347
Utah	3.35	3.35	3.80	4.25	4.25	0.259	0.258	0.256	0.289	0.322	0.320
Vermont	3.45/3.55	3.55/3.65	3.65/3.75	4.25	4.25	0.306	0.313	0.320	0.324	0.361	0.360
Virginia	3.35	3.35	3.80	4.25	4.25	0.252	0.251	0.249	0.281	0.313	0.312
Washington	3.35	3.35/3.85	3.85/4.25	4.25	4.25	0.236	0.244	0.277	0.294	0.293	0.292
West Virginia	3.35	3.35	3.80	4.25	4.25	0.294	0.293	0.292	0.329	0.366	0.365
Wisconsin	3.35	3.35/3.65	3.80	4.25	4.25	0.270	0.269	0.286	0.302	0.336	0.335
Wyoming	3.35	3.35	3.80	4.25	4.25	0.263	0.262	0.261	0.294	0.327	0.326

Notes: Left-hand panel of the table shows the higher of the state or federal minimum wages in each state and year. Years begin in April of the year shown until March of the following year. Multiple minima are shown if the state minimum changed during the April to March period. The right-hand panel of the table shows the minimum wage divided by the median wage for male workers 35–54 years old in the state averaged for the 1987–1992 period.

[a]Minnesota: Only large employers covered by the new 1991 minimum wage.
[b]Oregon: Minimum wage changed from 3.35 to 3.85 and then 4.25 during the year.

minimum wage. The second approach looks at the relation between training and a measure of how binding the minimum wage is across regions. This latter approach is most closely related to the empirical work in the previous literature, and therefore serves as a check on the robustness of our results.

4.1. Empirical Specification

The most direct way to estimate the impact of the minimum wage on training outcomes is to look at workers who are actually affected by changes in the minimum wage. In order to illustrate the approach, consider the following regression equation

$$\tau_{irt} = \alpha m w_{irt} + \beta' x_{it} + d_t + v_r + \mu_i + \varepsilon_{irt} \qquad (15)$$

where τ_{irt} is a measure of training for individual i in region r at time t, d_t, v_r and μ_i are time, region, and individual effects, and x_{it} are other individual characteristics like education, age, gender, and information about the job an individual holds. mw_{irt} is a measure of whether the minimum wage binds for individual i in region r at time t. One measure for mw_{irt} would be whether the actual wage of an individual is close to the minimum wage for the region and time period. This has been the approach of Schiller (1994) and Grossberg and Sicilian (1999) using cross-sectional variation. But this strategy has the problem that other, possibly unobserved, person characteristics which are correlated with the individual's wage will also tend to be correlated with training receipt.

We therefore difference Eq. (15) to obtain

$$\Delta \tau_{irt} = \alpha \Delta m w_{irt} + \beta' \Delta x_{it} + \Delta d_t + \Delta \varepsilon_{irt}. \qquad (16)$$

Changes in training should now be related to changes in whether a worker is affected by the minimum wage. As a measure of $\Delta m w_{irt}$ we use a dummy variable which indicates that the minimum wage increased from one year to the next, and the worker earned below the new minimum wage in the base year. This measure captures workers who are directly affected by a change in the minimum wage, similar to Card's (1992) analysis of employment effects. The measure relies purely on the variation of the minimum wage and base period wages, but not changes in individual wages, which may be correlated with the timing of the training received by a worker. Our analysis will focus on individuals who do not move between states because moving would also confound $\Delta m w_{irt}$ with behavioral effects. Therefore, the region effect does not appear in Eq. (16).

Although we feel that this analysis of Eq. (16) exploits variation of the minimum wage most directly, hence gives the most reliable results, previous studies have relied on Eq. (15) to study the impact of the level of the minimum wage on training.

To make our results more comparable to these previous studies, we also undertake analysis of the levels equation. Rather than indicating affected workers directly, the variable mw_{irt} will in this case measure how binding the minimum wage is in a particular state or region. We start by using simply the actual minimum wage in region r at time t, w_{rt}^m. However, the same federal minimum affects more workers in low wage regions than in high wage regions, and this source of variation would not be captured by w_{rt}^m. Therefore, we prefer specifications in which a given level of the minimum wage is allowed to have different effects in different regions depending on their average wages. For this purpose, we consider relative minimum wage measures $w_{rt}^m/\overline{w}_r$, where $\overline{w}_r$ is a measure of the location of the wage distribution in region r (the median wage of older workers) over the whole sample period. This measure $\overline{w}_r$ should not be affected by the minimum wage itself, and therefore just parameterizes the wage distribution, and $w_{rt}^m/\overline{w}_r$ measures how high the minimum wage is relative to the region's wage distribution. Notice that we are not using $\overline{w}_{rt}$ which would move with the business cycle at the regional level, and might create a spurious correlation if training incidence were also cyclical.

An obvious choice for the regions are states, since minimum wages also vary at the state level. However, the wage distribution also varies within states, so that the relative minimum wage measure can be defined for smaller regions. Apart from states, we use two other measures. One partitions states into SMSAs and non-SMSA parts as our region definition. This lets us exploit the often substantial variation in wage levels between large SMSAs (like New York City) and rural areas in a state (like upstate New York) in the analysis. In total, we distinguish 136 regions. Details on the construction of these are available in Appendix A. When we use states or these smaller regions, our measure for $\overline{w}_r$ is the average of the median wages of male workers age 35–54 in each year between 1987 and 1992. The second "region" definition distinguishes between the male and female wage distribution within states, i.e. $\overline{w}_r$ uses the average of the median wages of male workers age 35–54 in the state if the respondent is male, and of the median wages of female workers age 35–54 if the respondent is female. This measure exploits the fact that women should be more affected by a given minimum wage than men because women tend to earn less than men.

In the right-hand panel of Table 1 we show the relative minimum wages using the male medians by state and year over the sample period. It is apparent that there is substantially more dispersion in this measure (which is still coarser than the other regional measures we use below) than in the minimum wage itself. For example, the federal minimum wage increases between 1989 and 1991 raised the relative minimum wage by only 0.055 in New Jersey but by 0.085 in Arkansas, both states without a state minimum wage above the federal level in 1989. This illustrates how the scaling of the minimum wage measure leverages the increase in the federal minimum wage across states with different wage distributions, even once we control for state effects.

There are a number of practical problems in implementing the estimation of Eqs (15) and (16). For example, training is not easily defined at a point in time. Because most training spells only last for a short period of time, we will define τ_{irt} as referring to all incidents of training within a single year. Thus, τ_{irt} will be 1 if the individual received any training during the year, and 0 otherwise. In the differenced Eq. (16), the dependent variable takes on the values -1, 0, and 1. We will estimate the models as linear probability models, facilitating differencing and the inclusion of fixed effects in the levels version.

Looking at a time period as long as a year has its drawbacks. The minimum wage may change within a year. In order to minimize the impact of this, we look at periods of 12 months starting in April and ending in March. Both federal minimum wage increases in 1990 and 1991 went into effect April 1. Some state minimum wage increases also took effect on April 1, but many did not. Whenever the minimum wage changed during the year, we use an employment weighted average of the minimum wage in effect during the year.

The covariance matrix of the error term in Eq. (16) will have a first order moving average structure at the individual level. We therefore estimate standard errors with the Huber estimator, which is robust to arbitrary cluster effects at the individual level. This covariance estimator is consistent in this case but not efficient. In Eq. (15), the key regressor, the minimum wage variable, only varies at the region and year level while we use individual level data. Conventional standard errors may therefore overstate the precision of the estimates (Moulton, 1986). Suppose the error term has the form $\varepsilon_{irt} = \lambda_i + \upsilon_{rt} + \xi_{irt}$, i.e. the error is composed of an individual level component λ_i, a region×time component υ_{rt}, and a component ξ_{irt}, which is uncorrelated across individuals, regions, and time periods. Notice that the error ε_{irt} will be heteroskedastic, since we are estimating a linear probability model. There is no straightforward way to calculate consistent standard errors for this error structure. We extend the standard Huber estimator to allow for both an individual level component and a region×time component in the error term. This estimator seems to perform well in practice in samples of our size. We report formulas and the results of some small Monte Carlo experiments in Appendix B.

4.2. The Data

Our data on training come from the National Longitudinal Survey of Youth (NLSY). The NLSY is a panel of youths aged 14–21 in 1979. This dataset is particularly suitable for this project because it samples young workers, and it oversamples those from disadvantaged backgrounds, who are more likely to work in jobs at or slightly above the minimum wage (see Card & Krueger, 1995). We will follow the cohorts interviewed in the NLSY from 1987 to 1992, years of significant changes in state and federal minimum wages. During the 1988–1992 surveys, the NLSY asked a consistent set of questions about on-the-job training during the previous year. The information about the training includes length and type of the program, site, and whether the explicit costs of the training were paid for by the employer or someone else. The first set of training questions in 1988 refer to a longer time frame than the questions in subsequent years, because no similar data were collected in 1987. In 1993, the module on training in the survey was expanded substantially and the survey switched from paper and pencil to computer assisted interviewing. We use some data from the 1993 survey to complement information on training during the April 1992 to March 1993 year. There were some other minor additions to the training questions before 1993 as well.

The sequence of questions on training begins with a lead-in stating

> I would now like to ask you about other types of schooling and training you may have had, excluding regular schooling we have already talked about. Some sources of occupational training programs include government training programs, business schools, apprenticeship programs, vocational or technical institutes, correspondence courses, company or military training, seminars, and adult education courses.

This suggests that respondents will mostly report relatively formal training programs and neglect other sources of informal on-the-job training, a suspicion which has been substantiated by Loewenstein and Spletzer (1999b) using the more detailed training data in the NLSY starting in 1993. While this may be a drawback, this limitation of the data is pervasive in this literature.

We are only interested in training programs which take place in firms, or are sponsored directly by the employer, not in courses taken by individuals outside work on their own initiative or government sponsored training programs. We therefore classify the following forms of training as "employer related training": any training for which the respondent gives as venue an apprenticeship program; formal company training; or seminars or training programs at work run by someone other than the employer; or if the respondent classifies the training as on-the-job training or work experience; or if the employer paid for the training (even though we do not interpret the answer to this question as the employer necessarily bearing the investment costs). We do not classify a training programs as employer related if the training was partly paid for by a government program.[7] For each training program we record the start date as reported on the 1988–1993 surveys. If this date falls within an April to March period between 1987 and 1993, we assign the training to this particular year. We treat observations with a missing start date as missing.[8]

We do not use any information on the job or employer in the estimation directly. However, training often takes place when individuals start new jobs, and minimum wage increases may affect turnover and hiring. Hence, it seems important to control for turnover in some fashion. We include a dummy variable for whether a respondent started any new job within a particular year from information in the work history module of the data.

We limit our sample to workers who have 12 years of education or less, a group most likely to be affected by the minimum wage. We use the oversamples of blacks, Hispanics and poor whites in the analysis, but we drop the military subsample. The results are weighted by the NLSY sampling weights throughout. Individuals living in the District of Columbia are excluded, because DC had a plethora of different minimum wage rules, making it hard to define a sensible overall measure of the minimum wage. Our basic sample includes all workers who report a wage at the interview for the current year and for the past year,[9] and who were employed for at least one month during the year according to the information in the work history module. We also restrict the sample to those with valid wage information. For the analysis using Eq. (16) we also exclude individuals who move between states.

In addition, we use the 1987–1993 outgoing rotation group files of the CPS. We calculate the median wage for workers age 35–54 from this data source to construct the relative minimum wage measure. The CPS outgoing rotation groups are large enough to do this even for smaller areas within states. For example, each region-year cell has at least 27 observations on older male workers, but few cells are that small, and the median number of observations is 274.

5. EMPIRICAL RESULTS

Table 2 reports means of some demographic indicators for the three samples from the NLSY. All samples include respondents with 12 years of schooling or less working in at least one month during the year. Since young adults still obtain additional schooling in this age range, the samples changes over time. The nonmover sample differs little from the unrestricted sample. About 20–25% of each sample report having started a new job during the calendar year. While this includes secondary and temporary jobs, the number matches relatively closely the fraction of low education workers in the same age group who report tenure of 12 month or less on their current job in the January 1991 CPS. This relatively high rate of job starts reflects the large turnover among young, low skilled workers.

The average nominal hourly wage in the basic sample rises from about $7.50 in 1987 to almost $10 in 1992. While a number of sample members earn the minimum wage or less, as shown in the last row, the majority of respondents earn far above

Table 2. Sample Means of Demographics (Standard Deviations in Parentheses).

Variable	Non-mover Sample		Unrestricted Sample		Low Wage Sample	
	1988	1992	1987	1992	1987	1992
Female	0.434	0.428	0.432	0.427	0.527	0.602
Black	0.134	0.132	0.128	0.133	0.169	0.204
Hispanic	0.067	0.067	0.064	0.067	0.061	0.073
Age	27.2	31.2	26.2	31.2	25.8	31.1
Less than high school	0.187	0.171	0.192	0.172	0.262	0.240
New job	0.273	0.216	0.268	0.220	0.338	0.323
Nominal hourly wage	8.16	9.71	7.58	9.70	5.13	5.91
	(5.36)	(6.54)	(5.51)	(6.51)	(2.57)	(2.82)
Real hourly wage (1982–1984$)	7.30	8.52	6.81	8.51	4.60	5.18
	(4.79)	(5.73)	(4.95)	(5.71)	(2.30)	(2.47)
Fraction earning minimum or less	0.042	0.058	0.068	0.059	0.155	0.162
Number of observations	3872	3094	3979	3143	1673	1049

Notes: Unbalanced panel from the NLSY. Unrestricted sample consists of individual-year observations that have high school education or less, work in at least one month of the year and in both the prior and current year have non-missing wage data. Non-mover sample excludes from the unrestricted sample individuals who have moved to a new state since the previous year. Low wage sample imposes on the unrestricted sample the restriction that the "CPS wage" in the previous year is less than or equal to 150% of the federal minimum wage. Year refers to April to March (of following calendar year). New job refers to the start of any new job during the year. Hourly wage is the "CPS wage" for workers employed at a "CPS job" only. NLSY data include black, Hispanic and poor white oversamples. The poor white oversamples were discontinued in the 1991 survey year, accounting for the lower number of observations in 1992. Statistics are weighted by the NLSY sampling weights.

the minimum wage. These samples therefore include many workers whose wage is not directly affected by the minimum. These higher wage workers effectively form our control group in the differenced analysis. When we look at the impact of the level of the minimum wage, on the other hand, most of the sample members are not directly affected by the minimum wage, a problem which has also affected previous studies. In order to address this issue we also use a low wage sample, defined as workers employed at a wage which is 150% of the federal minimum or less in the *previous* year. The last two columns give the basic descriptive statistics for this sample, which is about a third the size of the basic sample. These low wage workers include more women and blacks. The number of high school dropouts is only slightly higher. Average wages in this sample are much lower and do not grow substantially over the sample period, due to the sample selection. We think of this group as much more likely to be actually subject to the minimum wage or spillovers resulting from it. Since a larger fraction of these workers are directly affected by the minimum wage, the standard theory predicts that we should find larger negative effects in this sample.

Table 3 reports sample means for some of the key variables in our regressions. The first row of the table reports the incidence of training, which is around 10%. The only exception is 1987, where the measured incidence is much lower. This is presumably due to the fact that the training questions were first asked on the 1988 survey so that the questions referring to 1987 had a longer recall period than for later years. There is also a small drop in 1991, possibly due to the recession. If we exclude very short training spells of 1 day or less, the incidence drops to about 7–8%.

Our measure of the minimum wage in a region is the higher of the state and the federal minimum wage. In Table 3, we report the average minimum wage in a year across all regions. These averages are weighted by the residence of our sample population. In 1987, the average minimum wage was 3.36, when only Alaska, and the New England states had state minima above the federal minimum wage of 3.35. It rises to 3.44 in 1988, mainly reflecting the increase in the California state minimum, and increases further to 3.51 in 1989, due to new minimum wage laws in other states, among them Oregon, Washington, and Pennsylvania. The standard deviation across respondents reaches a high of 29 cents in this year, indicating a substantial amount of variation in state minimum wage levels. This variation drops substantially in 1990 and 1991, when the two federal increases raise the minima in those states which had not taken action before. The averages of 3.87 and 4.26 are now only slightly above the federal minimum wages of 3.80 and 4.25. In 1992, New Jersey raises its minimum wage to 5.05, increasing the spread again.

For our analysis of Eq. (16), we use four different measures for workers affected by the minimum wage. The first one includes all workers who earned less than the new minimum wage in a year prior to a minimum wage increase. This includes workers who report a wage below the initial minimum. The top panel of Table 3 shows that about 1.4% of the sample were affected by minimum wage increases in 1988, mostly due to the increase in the California minimum wage. The state increases in 1989 affect slightly more workers, but a large fraction of workers (7 and 9%, respectively) is only affected by the federal increases in 1990 and 1991. The second measure excludes workers below the minimum wage in the base year. It is not completely clear whether these workers should be considered affected or not. Minimum wage coverage was fairly universal during the time period we consider, so that these reports presumably reflect mostly measurement error.[10] Excluding workers with wages below the base period minimum cuts the fraction of affected workers about in half in each year.

Table 3. Sample Means of Key Variables (Standard Deviations in Parentheses).

Variable	1987	1988	1989	1990	1991	1992
Non-mover sample						
Training incidence		0.099	0.099	0.106	0.094	0.103
Nominal minimum wage		3.44	3.51	3.87	4.26	4.28
		(0.21)	(0.29)	(0.16)	(0.05)	(0.15)
Minimum wage increased and wage in prior year is below the current minimum wage		0.014	0.020	0.069	0.091	0.001
Minimum increased and wage in prior year is below the current minimum and above prior year minimum		0.007	0.008	0.034	0.050	0.000
Minimum wage increased and wage in prior year is below 150% of the current minimum wage		0.062	0.085	0.264	0.293	0.011
Minimum wage increased and wage in prior year is below 130% of the current minimum wage		0.041	0.058	0.166	0.204	0.007
Number of observations		3872	3793	3187	3128	3094
Unrestricted sample						
Training incidence	0.064	0.099	0.100	0.108	0.094	0.103
Nominal minimum wage	3.36	3.44	3.51	3.87	4.26	4.28
	(0.06)	(0.21)	(0.29)	(0.16)	(0.05)	(0.15)
Real minimum wage (1982–1984$)	3.02	3.08	3.12	3.42	3.75	3.76
	(0.05)	(0.19)	(0.26)	(0.14)	(0.05)	(0.13)
Minimum wage/median wage (men 35–54, states)	0.267	0.271	0.276	0.301	0.331	0.332
	(0.030)	(0.027)	(0.028)	(0.031)	(0.038)	(0.037)
Minimum wage/median wage (men 35–54, regions)	0.272	0.277	0.282	0.307	0.338	0.340
	(0.043)	(0.041)	(0.042)	(0.045)	(0.053)	(0.051)
Minimum wage/median wage (35–54, state and gender)	0.324	0.330	0.336	0.366	0.402	0.404
	(0.077)	(0.076)	(0.078)	(0.086)	(0.097)	(0.097)
Number of observations	3979	4046	3971	3303	3210	3143

Notes: See Table 2 for a description of the sample composition. Training incidence refers to employment related training. Minimum wage refers to the higher of the state or federal minimum applicable to an NLSY respondent. Median wage for 35–54-year-old workers are calculated from the CPS Outgoing Rotation Groups. The poor white oversamples were discontinued in the 1991 survey year, accounting for the lower number of observations in 1990–1992. Statistics are weighted by the NLSY sampling weights.

An increase in the minimum may also affect the wages of higher wage workers via spillover effects, and our model then predicts that their training should be affected. Lee (1999), for example, finds large spillover effects from the minimum wage changes during our sample period, and we report similar results below in Table 5. In order to investigate whether spillovers affect our results, we also report specifications that include workers who initially earned above the new minimum in the affected group. We choose alternatively 150 and 130% of the new minimum wage. This yields about two to four times as many affected workers as our original measure. The bottom panel of Table 3 reports the relative minimum wage measures, i.e. the minimum wage divided by the state, regional, or state/gender median for older workers. The changes in these measures over time reflect again the increases in various state minimum wages and the federal increases in 1990 and 1991.

5.1. Results Using Affected Workers

Regression results for the first differenced version of the model are displayed in Table 4. Apart from the minimum wage, the regressions include a constant (capturing any linear effects of age), a full set of time dummies and variables for the change in high school graduation status and for whether the worker took a new job. High school graduates are between 4 and 9 percentage points more likely to receive training. This effect is imprecisely estimated because there are few workers who acquire a high school degree or equivalent during the sample period. Workers starting a new job are 3–4 percentage points more likely to receive training and this effect is estimated quite precisely. These estimates are sensible and demonstrate that the training variable is able to pick up the expected variation in the data.

The coefficients on the variable for affected workers are directly interpretable as the effect of raising the minimum wage on the incidence of training. The table displays four different specifications corresponding to four different definitions of the "affected" variable and employs three different samples, and hence implicitly three different control groups. In column (1), we define all workers whose wage in the previous year is below the current minimum as affected. All other workers in the sample serve as the control group. The point estimate indicates that being affected by a minimum wage increase raises the probability of receiving training by 1 percentage point. The effect is not statistically significant, however.

The control group in column (1) comprises both higher workers in affected and unaffected states as well as low wage workers in states and periods which had no minimum changes. Even though our sample was chosen to represent a relatively homogeneous set of workers, there is a good deal of heterogeneity. It is therefore sensible to limit the control group to different subgroups. Column (2) uses the

Table 4. The Effect of Minimum Wage Increases on Affected Workers.

Comparison Group	All	Affected States	Low Wage Workers	All	Affected States	Low Wage Workers	All	All
Independent Variable	(1)	(2)	(3)	(4)	(5)	(6)	(7)	(8)
Minimum wage increased and wage in prior year is below the current minimum wage	0.009 (0.014)	0.011 (0.015)	0.003 (0.016)	—	—	—	—	—
Minimum increased and wage in prior year is below the current minimum and above prior year minimum	—	—	—	0.016 (0.019)	0.018 (0.020)	0.011 (0.021)	—	—
Minimum wage increased and wage in prior year is below 150% of the current minimum wage	—	—	—	—	—	—	0.005 (0.008)	—
Minimum wage increased and wage in prior year is below 130% of the current minimum wage	—	—	—	—	—	—	—	−0.003 (0.010)
Change in high school graduation status	0.070 (0.054)	0.091 (0.083)	0.040 (0.041)	0.070 (0.054)	0.090 (0.083)	0.040 (0.041)	0.070 (0.054)	0.071 (0.054)
Change in new job status	0.032 (0.008)	0.039 (0.012)	0.039 (0.011)	0.032 (0.008)	0.039 (0.012)	0.039 (0.011)	0.032 (0.008)	0.032 (0.008)
Number of observations	17074	7552	5873	17074	7552	5873	17074	17074

Notes: Non-mover sample, consisting of all workers with a high school education or less, who do not move between states from one year to the next. The low wage comparison sample consists of all workers with wages in the prior year below 150% of the current minimum wage. Dependent variable is the change in training incidence between two consecutive years. All regressions also include a constant and year dummies. Regressions are weighted by NSLY sampling weights. Standard errors are adjusted for the presence of individual effects in the error term, and therefore robust to the MA structure of the error.

same definition of the affected variable but limits the control group to higher wage workers in the states which were affected by minimum wage changes. The point estimate of the impact of minimum wages on training is almost the same. Column (3) performs the opposite exercise and limits the control group to other low workers rather than higher wage workers. We define this group as those workers whose wage in the previous period is less than 150% of the current minimum wage. Hence, it also includes workers in affected states and periods with wages slightly above those of affected workers. The effect of the minimum wage on training is again very similar but slightly lower now. Our conclusion is that the exact choice of control group plays very little role in the estimates.

The specifications in columns (1)–(3) counts workers who were reporting wages below the previous minimum in the base year as affected. It is possible that some of the wages below the initial minimum were due to measurement error, these workers really earn much higher wages and were not truly affected by the minimum. Therefore we exclude these workers from the affected group in the columns (4)–(6). The results are not very different. Changing the control group again makes little difference.

Neither of the previous specifications allows spillovers of the minimum wage on workers with slightly higher wages. In fact, these workers make up the bulk of the control group in columns (3) and (6). If we redefine instead the affected group as workers whose previous wage was within 150 or 130% of the new minimum wage in columns (7) and (8), we find basically zero effects of minimum wages on training. It is quite possible that the effects drop slightly because these specifications count too many workers as "affected".[11]

Overall, these results provide neither strong support for the standard theory nor for our model. Average training incidence for workers affected by a minimum wage increase is 5.2% for the measure of affected workers used in column (1). The 95% confidence interval is consistent with declines in training as large as 1.8 percentage points or increases up to 2.8 percentage points. This means we can reject that the minimum wage eliminates more than a third of the training in this group. Similar conclusions are obtained for the other specifications.

5.2. Results Using Minimum Wage Changes

While the results in Table 4 indicate no adverse effects of minimum wages on training, our methodology differs somewhat from the previous literature. In this section we present alternative results based on the regression Eq. (15). The sample we use in this section also includes workers who move from state to state between interviews, but this sample differs little from the non-mover sample.

Recall that this sample contains many workers not directly affected by the minimum wage, so it is natural to worry about whether minimum wages will have a significant effect on the earnings of workers in this sample, since in the absence of such a finding, we may expect no effect on training incidence either. Before turning to the impact of minimum wages on training, we therefore look at the effect of the minimum wage on actual wages. Table 5 displays quantile regression estimates of the real wage of workers in this sample on the real value of the minimum wage and a full set of year and state dummies. The first feature of the results is that low quantiles of the wage distribution are affected by changes in the minimum wage, which shows that minimum wages do have an effect on the wages of low paid workers. So according to the standard theory, there should be a negative effect on training.

A one dollar increase in the minimum wage raises wages of the 10th percentile worker in the NLSY by 37 cents, which may seem small. The second column in the table replicates these results with a comparable sample using the CPS outgoing rotation groups, with similar results, showing that these results are not particular to the NLSY. There are various reasons to expect why the coefficients even at the low quantiles should be less than one. There is certainly much measurement error in the wage reports of workers, biasing these coefficients down. Furthermore, Table 2 revealed that even workers at the 10th percentile will typically earn above the old minimum wage already, and therefore they may not receive the full increase when the minimum wage goes up. Nevertheless, the results in Table 5 show that workers as high as the 30th percentile of the wage distribution may be affected by minimum wage changes, and therefore their training may also be affected.

Table 5 also shows that there are many workers in this sample who are not affected by minimum wages. This means that our estimates of training effects will tend to be biased towards zero. This motivates our strategy to compare our basic results to those in the lower wage sample using only workers earning less than 150% of the federal minimum wage in the previous year, corresponding roughly to the workers up to the 30th percentile of the original sample. This sample more closely approximates the workers actually affected by the minimum wage or by spillovers resulting from the minimum. If the results in the larger sample are biased towards zero, then the more restrictive sample should lead to more extreme estimates.

Table 6 presents our regression results for the incidence of training on the minimum wage and relative minimum wage measures. We present four sets of regressions with and without time and region fixed effects, as well as one specification which includes individual instead of region fixed effects.[12] Other covariates in the regressions are dummies for blacks, Hispanics, females, high school graduates, and whether the individual started a new job during the year, and a linear variable for age.[13] The coefficients on the demographic covariates are again

Table 5. Quantile Regressions for Real Wage on Real Minimum Wage Unrestricted Sample.

Quantile	NLSY	CPS
0.10	0.376	0.247
	(0.087)	(0.024)
		[0.084]
0.20	0.156	0.137
	(0.105)	(0.011)
		[0.109]
0.30	0.146	0.052
	(0.163)	(0.016)
		[0.121]
0.40	0.049	0.032
	(0.158)	(0.045)
		[0.102]
0.50	0.137	0.000
	(0.178)	(0.025)
		[0.111]
0.60	0.029	0.130
	(0.173)	(0.053)
		[0.113]
0.70	−0.120	0.030
	(0.247)	(0.043)
		[0.135]
0.80	0.296	0.011
	(0.446)	(0.044)
		[0.198]
0.90	0.312	0.157
	(0.593)	(0.143)
		[0.282]
Year effects	Yes	Yes
State effects	Yes	Yes

Notes: Samples include respondents with a high school degree or less. Dependent variable is the real hourly wage. NLSY regressions are weighted by the NLSY sampling weights. Standard errors in parentheses are not adjusted for clusters in the error term. Bootstrapped standard errors using state × year blocks are in brackets (100 replications). Number of observations is 21,618 in the NLSY, and 119,464 in the CPS.

sensible. Blacks receive about 3 percentage points less training and Hispanics 1.5 percentage points less. Contrary to the typical finding in the literature, the effect for women is very small and insignificant in this low wage group. High school dropouts receive about 5 percentage points less training. Workers starting new jobs are slightly more likely to receive more training but the effect is only sizeable at 2 percentage points and significant once individual effects are controlled for.

Table 6. Panel Regressions for Training Incidence.

Sample	Independent Variable	(1)	(2)	(3)	(4)	(5)
Unrestricted	Real minimum wage	0.038	0.053	0.026	−0.007	−0.012
		(0.012)	(0.019)	(0.010)	(0.017)	(0.021)
Low wage	Real minimum wage	−0.002	−0.004	−0.001	−0.021	−0.034
		(0.015)	(0.031)	(0.013)	(0.032)	(0.054)
Unrestricted	Real minimum wage/avg. median wage (men 35–54, states)	−0.003 (0.081)	−0.186 (0.100)	0.305 (0.103)	−0.028 (0.211)	−0.099 (0.224)
Low wage	Real minimum wage/avg. median wage (men 35–54, states)	−0.020 (0.120)	−0.018 (0.142)	0.016 (0.153)	−0.169 (0.406)	0.198 (0.416)
Unrestricted	Real minimum wage/avg. median wage (men 35–54, regions)	−0.070 (0.060)	−0.177 (0.067)	0.307 (0.100)	0.038 (0.193)	0.050 (0.172)
Low wage	Real minimum wage/avg. median wage (men 35–54, regions)	−0.052 (0.079)	−0.063 (0.078)	0.050 (0.146)	0.117 (0.371)	0.270 (0.328)
Unrestricted	Real minimum wage/avg. median wage (35–54, state and gender)	−0.024 (0.063)	−0.169 (0.081)	0.237 (0.083)	0.047 (0.148)	−0.017 (0.167)
Low wage	Real minimum wage/avg. median wage (35–54, state and gender)	−0.037 (0.081)	−0.049 (0.096)	−0.013 (0.109)	−0.140 (0.248)	0.127 (0.313)
	Year effects	No	Yes	No	Yes	Yes
	State or region effects	No	No	Yes	Yes	No
	Individual effects	No	No	No	No	Yes

Notes: Sample includes respondents with a high school degree or less. Dependent variable is training incidence. All regressions also include a linear term in age, dummy variables for blacks, Hispanics, females, less than high school, whether the respondent started a new job within the year, and a constant where applicable. Regressions are weighted by the NLSY sampling weights. Standard errors in columns (1)–(4) are adjusted for the presence of state×time or region×time and individual effects in the error term (see Appendix B for details). Standard errors in columns (5) are adjusted for the presence of state×time effects in the error term. Number of observations is 21,652 in the unrestricted sample and 7,032 in the low wage sample.

If no region effects are included, as in columns (1) and (2), the effect of the minimum wage measure is positive and significant. This reflects that states with higher minimum wages tend to have more training. Because these states tend to have higher wages in general, this may simply mean that high and low wage states differ, for example in terms of their industrial and occupational structure. In fact, the positive result in column (2) vanishes when we look at the relative minimum wage measures below or when we control for state and time effects in column (4). This latter specification, which we prefer, suggests that higher minimum wages have a small negative effect on training. The federal minimum wage increased by 81 cents in real terms from 1989 to 1991. This increase led to about 0.6 percentage points less of training. We find similar results including individual fixed effects instead of state effects in column (5).[14]

The estimates are more negative if we look at the low wage sample in row 2. Unfortunately, these results are very imprecisely estimated and are consistent with both substantial negative and positive effects. One reason for this is that the minimum wage variable we are using in the first two rows does not exploit a relevant part of the information, which is that a given level of the minimum wage will have very different effects depending on how high wages are in a region. To exploit this information, we next turn to the relative minimum wage measures.

Rows 3 and 4 of the table report results where we divide the minimum wage by the median wage of older males in the state. The specification which exploits primarily the cross region variation in the minimum wage measure in column (2) now results in a moderate negative coefficient. In row 5 below, where we use more detailed regions and obtain more precise results, this coefficient is even significant. This specification compares most closely to the approach of Leighton and Mincer (1981). But the results in columns (4) or (5), which are much closer to zero, indicate again that the minimum wage measure was picking up across region differences in training incidence. We feel that the estimates including time and region or individual effects are most reliable. Some of the time variation of our training measure is likely due to the change in the survey questions and cyclical variations. Differences in training incidence across regions may reflect differences in industrial and occupational compositions. The negative effect of the minimum wage in column (2) is therefore likely to reflect the fact that higher wage regions tend to have more training. The results including time and region effects, which are the most reliable, do not indicate any negative effects of minimum wages on training.[15]

In order to interpret the magnitudes of the estimates and confidence intervals using this relative measure of the minimum wage, return to the bottom panel of Table 3. The relative minimum wages increased by about 5–6 percentage points from 1989 to 1991. To gauge the impact of the federal increases, it is more useful to calculate the means only for the states that were subject to the federal minimum in 1989. For these states, the federal increases raised the relative minimum wage measures by 0.07 using the male state or region medians, and by 0.08 using the state/gender medians. This means that a 95% confidence interval for the estimates in column (4) using state medians for the unrestricted sample excludes negative changes in training of 2.9 percentage points or larger in response to the federal increases. It is instructive to compare this result to the findings by Neumark and Wascher (2001), for example. Their point estimates imply that the California state minimum wage (which was similar in magnitude to the federal increase between 1989 and 1991) led to a decline in formal training of 3.2 percentage points among young workers age 20–24, a group with a similar average training incidence as our sample. We can reject a decrease of this size for our sample.

Looking at the low wage sample, we obtain a virtually identical point estimate when we include time and state effects. When we include individual instead of state effects, the point estimate is actually positive now. Thus, the results with the low wage sample do not indicate that the estimates for the basic sample were attenuated. These conclusions are unchanged when we look at the minimum wage measure scaled by alternative values of the median wage. In rows 5 and 6, we use the median wage for 136 regions smaller than the states. We find small positive point estimates for the basic sample, and slightly larger estimates in the low wage sample. To the degree that these results indicate attenuation in the basic sample, they suggest that the actual effect of minimum wages on training is positive, rather than negative. The within estimates using these smaller regions turn out not to be any more precise than the state results, however.

The last two rows in Table 6 present results scaling the minimum wage by the median wage for older workers in the same state and of the same gender as the respondent. The results for the basic sample are again rather similar to the previous measures. The results are now somewhat more precise, because there is more variation in the measure exploiting gender differences. For the low wage sample, the results are a bit different. Controlling for time and state effects, we now find a negative effect for minimum wages. However, this result is not replicated when we control for individual effects instead. In addition, if we tighten the low wage sample further to include only workers who earned less than 130% of the federal minimum wage in the previous year, we find a coefficient of 0.097 (with a standard error of 0.294). We conclude that the negative estimate for the low wage sample is much more likely an indication of the sampling variation of these estimates rather than evidence that the estimates for the basic sample are attenuated.

However, the results do not provide strong support for our model either. Although some of the estimates are positive, and our baseline estimate is consistent with a 3.8 percentage point increase in the training probability of affected workers, none of the positive effects are statistically significant.

5.3. Discussion of the Results

Overall, the results using either affected workers, which is our preferred methodology, or using minimum wage levels provide strong support neither for the standard theory nor for our alternative model based on labor market imperfections. In fact, most estimates show no – or little – effect of minimum wages on training. This may be due to a variety of reasons:

(1) Training incidence is relatively small in this sample of low wage workers, and with our sample size we may simply be unable to detect the effects of minimum

wages. Mismeasurement of training in the data, of which there undoubtedly will be some, will make this worse. However, we have demonstrated that we are able to detect numerically small but significant effects on other covariates. Our results also differ substantially from the previous literature and they are precise enough, for example, to reject the point estimates obtained by Neumark and Wascher (2001). Furthermore, our estimates are much more precise than theirs.

(2) Measurement error may bias our estimates towards zero. In particular, the regressions in Section 5.2 may include too many unaffected workers in the sample, therefore attenuating the effect. While not definite, we have probed this explanation by comparing the results from the base sample with a low wage sample. The pattern of results does not suggest a major role for attenuation bias.

(3) Our training measure does not distinguish general and specific training and most training in our sample may be specific. If this training is already being financed by firms, which could be likely for low wage workers, there is no reason to expect that minimum wages lead to a reduction in training. But the literature on this topic suggests that the bulk of reported training is very general. Loewenstein and Spletzer (1999a) find in later waves of the NLSY that 63% of all training is general, and in another 14% of training programs, most of the skills are reported to be general. They find similar results with other datasets as well.

(4) If most training is rather informal, the reduction in training may not show up in our data. While possible, we believe that it is unlikely that formal and informal training will behave very differently. Loewenstein and Spletzer (1999b) analyze questions on informal training in later waves of the NLSY, and find formal and informal training to be highly correlated. Furthermore, it would be inconsistent with Becker's theory or our alternative model if minimum wages had no effect on formal training.

(5) The implications of both Becker's or our theory can be seen most starkly if training is a zero-one choice. When training is a continuous choice, in Becker's theory, a higher minimum wage may eliminate some but not necessarily all training. This will happen because some workers earn low wages because they are financing their own training. A binding minimum wage will prevent them from financing all the previous training but it may still be consistent with some worker financed training. A similar argument could be made with respect to our model. Workers may have received firm financed training even in the absence of minimum wages (see Acemoglu & Pischke, 1999b). A minimum wage may have raised the intensity of training without a large effect on the number of trained workers. Given our results, we cannot rule these possibilities. For reasons stated above, we do not pursue the analysis of training durations.

(6) Finally, our finding of small overall effects on training could result from a combination of the effects in Becker's model and our theory, where minimum wages reduce training for some workers and induce training for others.

We do not believe that any single one of the statistical or theoretical arguments 1–5 above on its own is a sufficient explanation for our findings. Obviously, it is possible that a combination of these factors could account for our results. It is important to point out, however, that all of the points 1–4 also affect previous empirical studies on this topic, since they have analyzed similar data with analogous limitations. Since all the previous studies also have similar – and some other – problems, we find our results at least as reliable as other studies on the topic. We conclude that small effects of the minimum wage on training are therefore a distinct possibility. This makes the last explanation for the results appealing. In the next section, we develop a model which combines elements of Becker's theory with our model and derive some further empirical implications.

6. A HYBRID MODEL: THE EFFECT OF MINIMUM WAGES WHEN WORKERS CAN PAY FOR TRAINING

Our baseline model in Section 3 introduced two deviations from the standard Becker model. Labor markets were noncompetitive, and workers were unable to pay for training. Under these assumptions, we derived the opposite of the prediction of the standard Becker model: minimum wages were found to increase – rather than decrease – training. Since the empirical evidence seems to support neither the standard Becker model nor our model, we now generalize the model of Section 3 by allowing some of the workers to invest in their general training.

We maintain all the assumptions from Section 3, and in addition, assume that some of the workers can "buy" training from their employers, so the contractual problems discussed in Section 3 are absent, at least for a certain fraction of the workers. In particular, a fraction λ of the workers can pay for their training, as long as the minimum wages do not rule out wage cuts. The remaining $1 - \lambda$ fraction of the workers cannot. For example, these workers have a consumption commitment and cannot borrow to meet it if they take a wage cut to finance training.[16] For brevity, we will refer to this latter group of workers as "credit constrained."

6.1. Equilibrium Without Minimum Wages

Equilibrium wages without the minimum wage continue to be given by Eq. (1) in Section 3. Therefore, once again $\Pi_j(\eta_i, T) - \Pi_j(\eta_i, NT) = -c$, and firms have no incentive to invest in their employees' skills. But now, there can be worker-financed training. More specifically, Assumption 1 ensures that all workers who can afford it will prefer to get training by taking a wage cut. Therefore, a worker with access to credit will always receive training, whereas constrained workers will be unable to obtain training. All workers will be employed, and competition among firms will ensure that first-period wages are given by

$$w_1(\eta_i, T) = \theta\eta_i + \delta - c \qquad (17)$$

for workers financing their training, and

$$w_1(\eta_i, NT) = \theta\eta_i + \delta \qquad (18)$$

for workers not paying for their training.

In this competitive equilibrium, all training is therefore of the Becker-type, financed by workers taking a wage cut in the first period. The total number of workers obtaining training is simply

$$T^c = \lambda.$$

The only reason why the equilibrium is not first-best is because some of the workers are credit constrained and cannot invest in training even though doing so would increase total output.

6.2. The Impact of Minimum Wages on Training

Now consider a binding minimum wage, i.e. w_M such that $w_M > \underline{\eta}$. Similar reasoning to above immediately implies that second period wages are given by Eq. (4).

Let us first discuss the adverse effect of the minimum wage on investment in skills, which were absent in Section 3. Some of the workers previously financing their own training will now be unable to do so because paying for their own training would involve receiving a wage below the minimum in the first period. In particular, all workers with access to credit and productivity such that

$$\theta\eta_i + \delta - c < w_M. \qquad (19)$$

will be unable to take the necessary wage cut to finance training.[17] Therefore, the number workers obtaining training by taking a wage cut is now

$$\lambda\left[1 - G\left(\frac{w_M - \delta + c}{\theta}\right)\right], \qquad (20)$$

which is clearly a decreasing function of w_M. So a binding minimum wage reduces training for some workers. In a competitive labor market this is the only impact of the minimum wage on training. Since all training is general in this economy, the minimum wage eliminates all training among *affected* workers (i.e. those workers for whom Eq. (19) holds).

There is still the second mechanism at work which we described in Section 3 above. The introduction of a minimum wage induces firms to train some of their low skilled workers. Consider a worker who does not have access to credit, and hence could not afford to buy training when there was no minimum wage. From the results in Section 3, it is more profitable for a firm to pay for the training of some workers than to use them as unskilled employees. The analysis is identical to that in Section 3, except that the firm may finance the training of workers, who can pay for this training themselves, but are constrained by w_M. Equation (19) has to be satisfied for these workers, but this implies immediately that Eq. (10) has to be violated, i.e. it is not profitable for firms to sponsor training of these workers. Therefore, total training in equilibrium with a minimum wage is

$$T^{nc} = \lambda \left[1 - G\left(\frac{w_M - \delta + c}{\theta}\right) \right]$$
$$+ (1 - \lambda)\max\left\{ \left[G(w_M - c) - G\left(\frac{w_M - \delta + c}{\theta}\right) \right]; 0 \right\} \quad (21)$$

where the second term is the amount of firm-sponsored training given by $T(w_M)$ in Eq. (13) above.

Notice that if $\delta = 0$ – i.e. if there are no employment rents – then the term in the second line in Eq. (21) will be equal to zero as discussed in Section 3. In this case, $T^{nc} = \lambda[1 - G((w_M + c)/\theta)]$, and therefore, the implications of a minimum wage will be identical to the standard Becker model. In contrast, when $\delta > 0$, minimum wages can increase training.

Now consider the introduction of a minimum wage w_M, and compare two sectors with different values of δ, i.e. different amounts of rents. A prediction of the hybrid model here is that in sectors where $\delta < \delta^*$ given by Eq. (14) in Section 3, the introduction of the minimum wage reduces training, whereas in sectors with $\delta \geq \delta^*$, the minimum wage may increase training. This observation implies a useful empirical implication, which we will investigate empirically in the next section. In particular, we will look at the effect of minimum wages on sectors that differ by the extent of rents and competitiveness.

7. FURTHER EVIDENCE

In this section, we make a first attempt at providing some evidence that industry structure matters for the effects of minimum wages on training. We use the industry wage differential as a proxy for the rents present in an industry (see Katz & Summers, 1989). We estimated industry wage differentials for 47 two digit industries for all workers age 18–65 in the 1986 CPS Merged Outgoing Rotation Groups.[18] We then split these industries into two groups depending on the estimated wage differential, each group containing half of total employment in the CPS sample. The group with a lower industry wage differential is presumed to comprise more competitive industries, the group with higher industry wage differentials the less competitive ones. These groups are then assigned to each observation in the NLSY based on the industry affiliation in the previous year (since current industry affiliation may potentially be affected by the minimum wage).

In Table 7, we repeat the regressions for affected workers as in Table 4 using the whole sample, and add a dummy variable for less competitive industries and an interaction of this variable with the affected indicator. We also repeat the same regressions using the industry wage differential directly, rather than splitting industries into two distinct groups. In this case, we scaled the industry wage differential such that the industry with the lowest differential (private household services) is set to zero. The range of the industry wage differentials goes up to 0.85 (petroleum), the mean in the NLSY sample is 0.52, and the mean for affected workers is around 0.40. The model in the previous section predicts that the interaction term should have a positive coefficient – which would correspond to a more positive effect of minimum wages in less competitive industries.

The results in Table 7 are largely supportive of the model. When we use the interaction with the industry split we find zero or small negative coefficients on the variable for affected workers. This now captures the effect on workers in more competitive industries. The effects on the interaction with the indicator for a less competitive (higher industry wage differential) industry are throughout positive. The magnitude of the difference is quite substantial, though typically not statistically significant. In columns (2) and (3) the interaction term has a magnitude of about 0.03, indicating that training may go up by as much as 3 percentage points more for affected minimum wage workers in less competitive industries. The interaction effect is not very precisely estimated, however, because there are relatively few minimum wage workers in these high wage industries.

The results are similar when we use the industry wage differential directly, rather than a discrete industry split. The main effect on the indicator for affected workers is now to be interpreted as the effect on workers in the private household sector. This effect is large and negative. This is consistent with the notion that some workers in the sectors with the lowest industry wage differentials were financing some training themselves, and this training is being eliminated by the increase in the minimum wage. The interaction term with the industry wage differential is again positive and of the order of 0.1 in columns (6) and (7). This

Table 7. The Effect of Minimum Wage Increases on Affected Workers by Industry.

Independent Variable	(1)	(2)	(3)	(4)	(5)	(6)	(7)	(8)
Industry in prior year is less competitive	−0.007 (0.005)	−0.007 (0.005)	−0.010 (0.006)	−0.008 (0.006)	—	—	—	—
Industry wage differential in prior year	—	—	—	—	−0.024 (0.015)	−0.025 (0.015)	−0.038 (0.017)	−0.030 (0.016)
Minimum wage increased and wage in prior year is below the current minimum wage	0.005 (0.016)	—	—	—	−0.008 (0.027)	—	—	—
Minimum increased and wage in prior year is below the current minimum and above prior year minimum	—	0.008 (0.023)	—	—	—	−0.032 (0.039)	—	—
Minimum wage increased and wage in prior year is below 150% of the current minimum wage	—	—	−0.007 (0.011)	—	—	—	−0.044 (0.022)	—
Minimum wage increased and wage in prior year is below 130% of the current minimum wage	—	—	—	−0.006 (0.013)	—	—	—	−0.021 (0.035)
Minimum increased and wage in prior year is below the current minimum wage×less competitive industry	0.011 (0.039)	—	—	—	—	—	—	—
Minimum increased and prior wage is between current and prior minimum×less competitive industry	—	0.036 (0.039)	—	—	—	—	—	—

Table 7. (Continued)

Independent Variable	(1)	(2)	(3)	(4)	(5)	(6)	(7)	(8)
Minimum increased and prior wage is below 150% of the current minimum wage×less competitive industry	—	—	0.032 (0.020)	—	—	—	—	—
Minimum increased and prior wage is below 130% of the current minimum wage×less competitive industry	—	—	—	0.004 (0.024)	—	—	—	—
Minimum increased and wage in prior year is below the current minimum wage×industry wage differential	—	—	—	—	0.036 (0.073)	—	—	—
Minimum increased and wage is between current and prior minimum×industry wage differential	—	—	—	—	—	0.115 (0.095)	—	—
Minimum increased and prior wage is below 150% of the current minimum wage×industry wage differential	—	—	—	—	—	—	0.102 (0.045)	—
Minimum increased and prior wage is below 130% of the current minimum wage×industry wage differential	—	—	—	—	—	—	—	0.036 (0.052)

Notes: Non-mover sample, consisting of all workers with a high school education or less, who do not move between states from one year to the next. Dependent variable is the change in training incidence between two consecutive years. All regressions also include a constant, the change in high school graduation status and new job status, and year dummies. Regressions are weighted by NSLY sampling weights. Standard errors are adjusted for the presence of individual effects in the error term, and therefore robust to the MA structure of the error. Sample size is 17,052.

means that each 10 percentage point increase in the wage differential is associated with a 1 percentage point lower reduction in the amount of training due to the minimum wage. For example, the results in column (6) imply that the minimum wage has no effect on training in social services (with an industry wage differential of 0.32 above the private household sector), while raising training by 3 percentage points for a worker in the wholesale industry (with an industry wage differential of 0.56 above private household). When we allow for spillovers from the minimum wage, as in columns (7) and (8), the interaction term is significant. While these results are far from definite, they are encouraging for the hybrid model.

8. CONCLUDING REMARKS

This paper makes some theoretical as well as empirical contributions to the literature on minimum wages. The perceived wisdom is that minimum wages ought to lower training for affected workers. This conclusion is based on competitive labor markets and the ability of workers to "buy" training from firms. We show that it is possible to obtain the opposite theoretical prediction in a model where there are employment rents due to labor market fictions and workers cannot finance their own training.

In addition, we provide a new set of estimates based on minimum wage changes at the state and federal level during the late 1980s. This evidence indicates no or only small effects of minimum wages on training, a result which does not clearly support either model.

To reconcile these results, we integrate elements of the standard Becker model, where workers pay for general training, with a model in which firms pay for the training. The overall effect of minimum wages on training is ambiguous in this hybrid model, but the model also has some new predictions. The effect of minimum wages on training should depend on the labor market structure. When employment rents are more important, a positive effect of minimum wages on training is more likely. We provided evidence consistent with this implication using industry wage differentials as a measure of industry rents.

Future research should establish whether the relationship between the effect of minimum wages and the competitive conditions of the industry holds up in other dimensions as well. In addition, the model also implies that minimum wages should increase training more for workers who are more likely to be credit constrained. It would be interesting to investigate this issue. Unfortunately, the NLSY does not contain good measures of the extent of credit constraint for individuals, so this issue is also left for future research.

NOTES

1. In response to this criticism, Neumark and Washer now argue that workers earning above 160% of the minimum are also affected by the minimum wage.

2. Alternatively, we could have that a worker who changes jobs in the second period incurs a mobility cost δ, because he has to acquire some costly skills, specific to the new employer, before becoming productive. All our results continue to hold with this alternative interpretation. Also, in practice, workers earning close to the minimum wage have high mobility. Our results continue to hold if a fraction $s < 1$ of workers change jobs.

3. Even though workers do not receive any of the firm-specific rents, there is no labor mobility in equilibrium. Suppose this were not so, then the firm could offer ε more than the market wage and convince the worker to stay, so mobility cannot be part of an equilibrium.

4. In the case where the firm-specific rent δ is shared between the firm and the worker, there will be a further force towards an upward sloping wage profile. For example, if the worker receives a fraction β of this rent, the second period wage of an untrained worker will be $\eta_i + \beta\delta$, while his first period wage will be $\theta\eta_i + (1-\beta)\delta$. As β increases, the age-earnings profile becomes steeper.

5. The full expression for the number of workers who receive training is $\max\{[G(w_M - c) - G(\max\langle(w_M - \delta + c)/\theta, (2w_M - \delta - \phi + c)/(1+\theta)\rangle)], 0\}$. However, $w_M - c \geq (w_M - \delta + c)/\theta$ implies that $(w_M - \delta + c)/\theta \geq (2w_M - \delta - \phi + c)/(1+\theta)$ (since $\phi > c$ by Assumption 1).

6. This is special to the case where the firm has to choose a discrete level of training. If the firm could choose training continuously, it would never train the worker beyond the point where it has to pay above the minimum wage in the second period (see Fig. 1).

7. The most common government program, JTPA, involves wage subsidies up to 50% if trainees are placed with private sector employers. Hence, the incidence of training under this program is unlikely to be affected by minimum wage legislation.

8. The NLSY also provides information on the length of training. We do not use the duration of training directly, because of the frequency of missing values but we checked that our results are robust to excluding very short training spells.

9. The NLSY refers to this wage measure as the CPS wage because of the CPS style question. The CPS wage may refer to a prior job if the respondent is not working at the time of the interview.

10. It is also possible that respondents receiving tips do not include these in the wage measure.

11. The training question that we use includes very short training programs, and it is important to ensure that our results are not sensitive to eliminating these short spells. When we repeat these regressions excluding training spells lasting a single day or less, we obtain slightly smaller coefficients for affected workers, e.g. 0.004 for the measure in column (4) and -0.013 for the measure in column (8), while the standard errors are basically unchanged.

12. If training this year makes it less likely that the individual will be trained in the future, the individual effects model may be problematic. However, in our sample, training is positively correlated over time.

13. Curvature of the age profile is empirically unimportant for the small age range in the sample, therefore we do not include higher order terms.

14. In the specification with individual fixed effects, only the region×time clusters remain in the error term. The standard Huber estimator of the covariance matrix allowing for these clusters is consistent. Our standard errors in column (5) are therefore the most reliable. Interestingly, the standard errors on the minimum wage variable do not differ substantially from those in column (4).

15. Our theory predicts that minimum wages reduce employment, but our samples focus on employed workers. This might bias our estimates up. When we use a sample of respondents including non-workers, we actually find slightly more positive results, however.

16. For simplicity, we assume that the probability of being able to finance training is independent of the worker's ability. All the results go through in a more realistic model, where workers smooth consumption over the two periods and some workers are credit constrained.

17. This is without a training subminimum. In this model, as in the standard Becker model, introducing training subminima increases training.

18. The regression also includes years of schooling, a quartic in experience, dummies for female, married, a female-married interaction, black, Hispanic, SMSA, and three region dummies. The sample size is 169,921.

ACKNOWLEDGMENTS

We thank John Browning and especially Aimee Chin for excellent research assistance, and Joe Altonji, Richard Carson, Ken Chay, Jinyong Hahn, Lisa Lynch, Paul Oyer, Chris Taber, and Yoram Weiss for useful comments. The first draft of this paper was written while Pischke was a visiting scholar at the Northwestern University/University of Chicago Joint Center for Poverty Research. He is grateful for their hospitality and research support. Acemoglu is grateful for financial support under the National Science Foundation Grant SBR-9602116.

REFERENCES

Acemoglu, D., & Pischke, J.-S. (1999a). Beyond Becker: Training in imperfect labor markets. *Economic Journal Features, 109*, 112–142.

Acemoglu, D., & Pischke, J.-S. (1999b). The structure of wages and investment in general training. *Journal of Political Economy, 107*, 539–572.

Becker, G. (1964). *Human capital.* Chicago: University of Chicago Press.

Ben-Porath, Y. (1967). The production of human capital over the life cycle. *Journal of Political Economy, 75*, 352–365.

Card, D. (1992). Using regional variation in wages to measure the effect of the federal minimum wage. *Industrial and Labor Relations Review, 46*, 22–37.

Card, D., & Krueger, A. B. (1995). *Myth and measurement. The new economics of the minimum wage.* Princeton: Princeton University Press.

DiNardo, J., Fortin, N., & Lemieux, T. (1996). Labor market institutions, and the distribution of wages, 1973–1992: A semiparametric approach. *Econometrica, 64,* 1001–1044.

Grossberg, A. J., & Sicilian, P. (1999). Minimum wages, on-the-job-training, and wage growth. *Southern Economic Journal, 65,* 539–556.

Hashimoto, M. (1982). Minimum wage effects on training on the job. *American Economic Review, 72,* 1070–1087.

Katz, L., & Summers, L. (1989). Industry rents: Evidence and implications. *Brookings Papers on Economic Activity* (pp. 209–275). Washington, DC: Brookings Institution.

Lee, D. (1999). Wage inequality in the U.S. during the 1980s: Rising dispersion or falling minimum wage? *Quarterly Journal of Economics, 114,* 977–1023.

Leighton, L., & Mincer, J. (1981). The effects of the minimum wage on human capital formation. In: S. Rottenberg (Ed.), *The Economics of Legal Minimum Wages* (pp. 155–173). Washington: American Enterprise Institute for Public Policy Research.

Loewenstein, M. A., & Spletzer, J. R. (1999a). General and specific training: Evidence and implications. *Journal of Human Resources, 34,* 710–733.

Loewenstein, M. A., & Spletzer, J. R. (1999b). Formal and informal training: Evidence from the NLSY. *Research in Labor Economics, 18,* 403–438.

Mincer, J. (1974). *Schooling, experience, and earnings.* New York: Columbia University Press.

Moulton, B. R. (1986). Random group effects and the precision of regression estimates. *Journal of Econometrics, 32,* 385–397.

Neumark, D., & Wascher, W. (2001). Minimum wages and training revisited. *Journal of Labor Economics, 19,* 563–595.

Rosen, S. (1972). Learning and experience in the labor market. *Journal of Human Resources, 7,* 326–342.

Schiller, B. R. (1994). Moving up: The training and wage gains of minimum-wage entrants. *Social Science Quarterly, 75,* 622–636.

APPENDIX A
CONSTRUCTION OF REGIONS

Some of the minimum wage measures used in this paper scale the state minimum wage level by a regional reference wage. An NLSY respondent's reference wage is the median wage in his/her geographic region for 35–54-year-old male workers calculated from the CPS Outgoing Rotation Groups. This appendix explains how the regions were constructed.

To account for the fact that there is significant variation in average wages within many states, and to allow the minimum wage measure to have greater within-state variation, we used information on an NLSY respondent's CMSA/MSA of residence, ("msa_code"). Because of sample sizes, we used msa_code only for individuals residing in the large MSAs. For all other areas (i.e. smaller MSAs and non-MSAs), we used data on whether an individual resided in an MSA ("msa_status").

The following list contains the 35 MSAs we classified as large. We included the 20 CMSAs defined by the 1990 FIPS Guidelines (plus the St. Louis, MO CMSA, while we do not distinguish the Providence, RI CMSA from other metropolitan parts of RI) and added 15 MSAs with large populations.

Atlanta, GA
Baltimore, MD
Boston-Lawrence-Salem, MA-NH CMSA
Buffalo-Niagara Falls, NY CMSA
Chicago-Gary Lake County, IL-IN CMSA
Cincinnati-Hamilton, OH-KY CMSA
Cleveland-Akron-Lorraine, OH CMSA
Columbus, OH
Dallas-Fort Worth, TX CMSA
Denver-Boulder, CO CMSA
Detroit-Ann Arbor, MI CMSA
Hartford-New Britain-Middletown, CT CMSA
Houston, TX CMSA
Indianapolis, IN
Kansas City, KS
Los Angeles-Anaheim-Riverside, CA CMSA
Miami-Ft. Lauderdale, FL CMSA
Milwaukee-Racine, WI CMSA
Minneapolis-St. Paul, MN
New Orleans, LA
New York-New Jersey-Long Island, NY-NJ-CT CMSA
Norfolk-Virginia Beach-Newport News, VA
Orlando, FL
Philadelphia-Wilmington-Trenton, PA-DE-NJ CMSA
Phoenix, AZ
Pittsburgh-Beaver Valley, PA CMSA
Portland-Vancouver, OR CMSA
Sacramento, CA
St. Louis, MO CMSA
San Antonio, TX
San Diego, CA
San Francisco-Oakland-San Jose, CA CMSA
Seattle-Tacoma, WA CMSA
Tampa-St. Petersburg-Clearwater, FL
Washington, DC, DC-MD-VA

The full set of regions consists of state-msa_code level regions for the above 35 MSAs and state-msa_status level regions for all other areas. The example of an individual living in Massachusetts illustrates how the reference wage is chosen. If the individual lived in the Boston CMSA, the reference wage would be the median wage for 35–54-year-old male workers living in the Massachusetts part of the Boston CMSA (the "MSA median"). If the individual lived in a metropolitan area other than the Boston CMSA, the reference wage would be the median wage for 35–54-year-old male workers living in Massachusetts metropolitan areas other than the Boston CMSA. If the individual lived in a non-metropolitan area, the reference wage would be the median wage for 35–54-year-old male workers living in Massachusetts non-metropolitan areas ("non-MSA median").

For confidentiality reasons, both the NLSY and CPS sometimes suppress the specific MSA of residence for individuals in smaller MSAs and/or smaller states. In the CPS data, there were five states in which msa_status was sometimes suppressed: Maryland, Nevada, Rhode Island, Utah and Wyoming. We classified these suppressed observations as non-MSA, with the following rationale. In Maryland, the suppressed observations are from the Maryland part of the Philadelphia CMSA. In Nevada, they are from the non-central city part of the Reno MSA. In Rhode Island, they are from the Rhode Island part of the New London MSA. In Utah, they are from the Utah part of the Flagstaff MSA. Finally, no MSAs in Wyoming are identified. For all five states, an individual was either classified as living in an MSA or the information was suppressed, i.e. observations from fringes of MSAs were grouped with the non-MSA observations to ensure confidentiality. Thus, classifying all the individuals living in areas with suppressed codes as non-MSA seems the most sensible choice.

In addition, there are MSAs which straddle different states and sometimes part of an MSA in a particular state is not identified if the part is too small. This was the case for: the Indiana part of the Cincinnati MSA, the Maryland part of the Philadelphia CMSA, the North Carolina part of the Norfolk MSA and the Wisconsin part of the Chicago CMSA and Minneapolis MSA. The CPS groups these areas with other metropolitan areas, and thus it is appropriate to use the state-MSA median for these observations in the NLSY. Finally, in Maryland, the Cumberland, MD-WV MSA and the Hagerstown, MD MSA are not separately identified. Here we assign the non-MSA median since Maryland's non-MSA median is really a median excluding the Baltimore and Washington, D.C. MSAs.

In the NLSY data, there were two complications. First, as in the CPS, msa_status was suppressed for certain individuals. We dropped the suppressed observations (62 out of 21,680 observations from the Basic Sample). Second, the NLSY uses NECMAs for the New England states whereas the CPS uses CMSA/MSAs. The NLSY switched to NECMA codes in 1988; we constructed the NECMA codes for 1987 by using information on state and county of residence. We then mapped NECMA codes into MSA codes. Specifically, individuals living in the Boston NECMA or Hartford NECMA were classified as living in the Boston CMSA and Hartford CMSA, respectively. Also, individuals living in any NECMA were classified as living in an MSA.

All together, the unrestricted NLSY sample contains 21,618 observations from 136 regions and 753 region-year categories. Of the 136 regions, 44 correspond to state-msa_code level regions, 45 to state-MSA level regions and 47 to state-non-MSA regions. These regions form a partition of the country. The median number of observations in each region-year cell in the CPS is 274 and the range is 27 (for the Indiana part of the Chicago CMSA in 1991) to 2261 (the Los Angeles CMSA in 1990). Less than 10% of all cells have fewer than a 100 observations and less than 5% of the NLSY observations fall into those cells.

APPENDIX B
ESTIMATION OF THE STANDARD ERRORS

We assume that the error term has the form $\varepsilon_{ij} = \lambda_i + \upsilon_j + \xi_{ij}$ where i denotes individual and j denotes region×time. Let x_{ij} be a vector of right-hand side variables,

$$X_i = \begin{bmatrix} x'_{i1} \\ x'_{i2} \\ \vdots \\ x'_{iJ} \end{bmatrix}$$

the matrix of right-hand side variables for individual i, and X the stacked matrix of all the X_i's. To simultaneously adjust for individual and region×time effects, we use the covariance matrix

$$\hat{V} = (X'X)^{-1} X' \Omega X (X'X)^{-1}$$

where

$$X'\Omega X = \sum_i X'_i \hat{\varepsilon}_i \hat{\varepsilon}'_i X_i + \sum_{i \neq k} \sum_j \hat{\varepsilon}_{ij} \hat{\varepsilon}_{kj} x_{ij} x'_{kj}.$$

In order to get an idea how this covariance estimator performs in our sample, we conducted a small Monte Carlo experiment. For this experiment we generated samples with the same number of observations, individuals, regions, and time periods as in our unrestricted sample according to the design

$$y_{ij}^* = 0.4 + 0.1x_{1ij} + 0.1x_{2j} + 0.1x_{3i} + \lambda_i + \upsilon_j + \xi_{ij}$$

$$y_{ij} = \begin{cases} 1 & \text{if } p \leq y_{ij}^* \\ 0 & \text{if } p > y_{ij}^* \end{cases}$$

where p and each of the x's are drawn from a uniform (0,1) distribution and λ_i, υ_j, $\xi_{ij} \sim N(0, 0.1)$. In regression 1, we computed the OLS estimate of y on the three x's and constructed the covariance matrix above. In regression 2, we estimated the regression of y on the x's also including region and time fixed effects. We replicated each regression 10,000 times with the following results:

Regressor	Regression 1			Regression 2		
	x_{1ij}	x_{2j}	x_{3i}	x_{1ij}	x_{2j}	x_{3i}
Standard deviation of $\hat{\beta}$	0.0116	0.0320	0.0126	0.0116	0.0355	0.0124
Mean of estimated standard error	0.0116	0.0314	0.0124	0.0115	0.0304	0.0122
Year effects		No			Yes	
Region effects		No			Yes	

Regression 1 indicates that the covariance estimator does a good job in estimating the sampling variation for all regressors. However, in regression 2, the sampling variation for x_{2j}, which only varies at the region×time level, i.e. the analogue to our minimum wage measure, is understated by about 15%. Of course, these results are only suggestive. In our design, υ_j contributes a third to the total variance of the error term. The results would change as we change the relative variances of this error component.

RACIAL AND ETHNIC DIFFERENCES IN PENSION WEALTH

William E. Even and David A. Macpherson

ABSTRACT

It is well established that Black and Hispanic workers accumulate leszs wealth for retirement than white workers. This study provides evidence on whether racial and ethnic differences in private pension coverage and benefit levels contribute to the wealth differentials. Using data from the Current Population Survey, Survey of Consumer Finances and the Health and Retirement Survey, several consistent findings emerge. First, most of the racial and ethnic differences in pension benefit levels are accounted for by differences in worker charateristics. Second, among workers who are covered by a private pension, racial and ethnic differences in pension asset accumulation are quite small. Finally, exclusion of pension wealth has a small effect on the comparison of average levels of wealth across racial and ethnic groups, but has a substantial effect for comparisons at the bottom of the wealth distribution. Overall, the findings suggest that, holding worker characteristics constant, minority and majority workers accumulate very similar levels of wealth.

INTRODUCTION

Black and Hispanic Americans earn less and have less wealth than white Americans. Lower earnings in the black and Hispanic population are an obvious explanation for their lower wealth. However, several studies document that the gap in wealth is far larger than the gap in earnings. For example, Oliver and Shapiro (1995) report that among dual earner married couples, black households earn 77% as much as white households but have only 19% as much in net financial assets. Menchik and Jianakoplos (1997) find that black household income averages 63% of white household income, but black households average only 10–25% of the wealth held by whites.[1] While Hispanic households average 70% of white household income,[2] Smith (1995) reports that Hispanic households have only 30% of white household wealth. Moreover, Blau and Graham (1990) report that as much as three-quarters of the wealth gap between blacks and whites cannot be explained by differences in income and other demographic factors.

The reasons that blacks and Hispanics accumulate less wealth relative to income are not well understood. Some hypotheses that have been proposed include:

(1) differences in inheritances and/or the desire to leave a bequest;
(2) differences in life-expectancies;
(3) differences in labor market uncertainty that lead to different investment decisions and rates of return; and
(4) differential access to housing and loan markets that can affect the ability to build home equity.[3]

One issue that has received little attention in the literature is how the accumulation of pension wealth differs between blacks, Hispanics and whites. Given that blacks and Hispanics acquire less wealth than whites, it is interesting to ask whether they acquire less pension wealth. Unfortunately, most of the aforementioned studies ignore pension and Social Security wealth. One exception is Smith (1995), who argues that ignoring Social Security and private pension wealth has "an enormous impact on racial and ethnic disparities ... As the wealth concept is expanded these disparities narrow."[4] Adding Social Security and private pension wealth increases the black/white ratio of mean wealth from 0.27 to 0.46 and the Hispanic/white ratio from 0.35 to 0.43. If only pension wealth is added to net worth, the black/white ratio of mean wealth increases to 0.37 and the Hispanic/white ratio decreases to 0.32.

The purpose of this study is to determine the extent of racial and ethnic differences in pension wealth, investigate the reasons for these differences, and determine how pensions contribute to overall wealth differentials. Several findings emerge. First, during the mid-1990s, black and Hispanic retirees received substantially less income from pensions than white retirees. Second, most of the racial and ethnic differences in pension coverage and benefit accumulation can be accounted for by differences in labor market characteristics. Third, controlling for labor market characteristics, the proportion of wealth acccumulated in a pension is very similar across racial and ethnic groups.

PENSION INCOME AMONG THE ELDERLY

To provide some background on the extent of racial and ethnic differences in pension coverage and generosity among past generations of workers, we turn first to the September 1994 Current Population Survey (CPS). The September 1994 CPS data are used because of the supplemental questions asked regarding whether people were ever covered by an employer pension in the past, and the amount of pension income currently being received. The sample is restricted to people aged 55 and over who were previously employed but not in the labor force at the time of the survey. Summary statistics are provided in Table 1. The table reports the percentage of people that are currently receiving benefits from an employer pension. These statistics understate the fraction of people that were covered by a pension for at least two reasons: First, a worker may have received a pre-retirement lump sum distribution from a pension and not be currently receiving benefits. Second, a worker may have a balance in a defined contribution plan that was not annuitized. In the case of defined contribution plans, the CPS measures benefits only if the account balance was annuitized.

The results indicate that, among people over age 55 and out of the labor force, 33.5% of whites are receiving benefits, 26.1% of blacks, and 18.6% of Hispanics.[5] When the measure of pension coverage is broadened to include people that report coverage by a pension plan at any time in the past, coverage rates grow to 45.9% among whites, 37.1% among blacks, and 27.0% among Hispanics.

Since later sections of the paper discover that public sector employment contributes to racial and ethnic differences in pension coverage, Table 1 also provides statistics by public sector employment status.[6] Blacks are more likely and Hispanics less likely than whites to be employed in the public sector. Among those whose longest job was in the public sector, there is no statistically significant difference (at the 0.10 level) between whites and blacks, or whites and Hispanics in terms of their pension coverage. This result holds true whether coverage is measured by current receipt of pension income or coverage at any time in the past. The differences are, however, statistically significant in the private sector.

Table 2 lists the average annual benefit among people receiving a pension. These results indicate no statistically significant difference in annual benefits, though the small sample sizes for blacks and Hispanics generate rather imprecise estimates of the mean benefit level. When the analysis is done separately by public sector employment status, blacks are found to have significantly lower benefits than whites only among public sector employees. There is no statistically significant difference between Hispanic and white benefits in either the public or private sector.

Table 1. Pension Recipiency Rates for Persons 55 and Older who are not in the Labor Force.

Racial or Ethnic Group	Percent Whose Longest Job was in Private Sector	t-Statistic for Equality with White Population	Percent Receiving Pension Benefits	t-Statistic for Equality with White Population	Percent ever Covered by a Pension	t-Statistic for Equality with White Population	Sample Size
White	91.2	–	33.5	–	45.9	–	9,375
Black	85.1	−5.83	26.1	−4.35	37.1	−4.88	825
Hispanic	94.7	2.14	18.6	−5.57	27.0	−6.66	318
Public sector employees							
White	0	–	63.1	–	68.8	–	823
Black	0	–	55.3	−1.66	61.8	−1.55	123
Hispanic	0	–	58.8	−0.36	76.5	0.68	17
Private sector employees							
White	100	–	30.6	–	43.7	–	8,552
Black	100	–	20.9	−5.4	32.8	−5.64	702
Hispanic	100	–	16.3	−5.34	24.3	−6.72	301

Note: Data source is September 1994 Current Population Survey.

Table 2. Benefits on Main Pension Plan for Persons 55 and Older Receiving Pension Benefits.

Racial or Ethnic Group	Percent whose Longest Job was in Private Sector	t-Statistic for Equality with White Population	Average Pension Benefit	t-Statistic for Equality with White Population	Sample Size
White	83.5	–	$10,244	–	2,407
Black	68.4	–4.31	$9,293	–0.87	160
Hispanic	83.0	–0.54	$11,680	0.73	47
Public sector employees					
White	0	–	$18,591	–	390
Black	0	–	$12,278	–2.69	47
Hispanic	0	–	$17,084	–0.28	9
White	100	–	$8,629	–	2,017
Black	100	–	$8,052	–0.49	113
Hispanic	100	–	$10,401	0.89	38

Note: Data source is September 1994 Current Population Survey.

The above analysis reveals that, among elderly people with prior labor force experience that are currently out of the labor force, pension coverage is significantly lower among blacks and Hispanics than whites. However, given that a previously employed person is covered by a pension, differences in benefit levels across the racial and ethnic groupings are difficult to discern in the September 1994 CPS data. The small sample sizes for the minority groups, however, cast some doubt on the precision of the estimates.

COMPARISONS OF PENSION INCOME AT RETIREMENT

This section provides a comparison of expected pension benefits at retirement across racial and ethnic groups. The analysis relies on Wave I of the Health and Retirement Survey (HRS) and the 1992 Survey of Consumer Finances (SCF). Wave I of the HRS was started in 1992 and surveyed persons born between 1931 and 1941 about their health, retirement and economic status.[7] The survey included 12,652 people in 7,702 households. Our analysis restricts attention to "age-eligible" respondents (i.e. those born between 1931 and 1941) who worked more than 1000 hours in the past year, whose wage rate equals or exceeds the minimum wage of $4.25, are not self-employed, and who can be classified as either white, black, or Hispanic. This results in a sample of 4,458 individuals.

For the analysis on pension benefits, restricting the sample to those covered by a pension, currently or in the past and eliminating those with missing information on the necessary pension questions reduces the sample to 2,338 individuals.

The 1992 SCF provided detailed information on the financial status of U.S. households. The entire sample includes responses from 6,470 persons in 3,906 households, of which 1,450 households are an oversample of wealthier households. The SCF imputes values for missing data. To capture the underlying variance associated with the imputed values, each observation is repeated five times in the data set to reflect the underlying variance in imputed values.[8] Following the recommendation of Montalto and Sung (1996), all five observations are employed in our analysis. The resulting sample consists of 32,350 observations. Our analysis is restricted to individuals between the ages of 21 and 55 working more than 1000 hours per year, whose wage rate equals or exceeds the minimum wage of $4.25, are not self-employed, and who can be classified as either white, black, or Hispanic. This results in a sample of 9,863 observations.[9] For the analysis on pension benefits, restricting the sample to those covered by a pension, currently or in the past, and eliminating those with missing information on the necessary pension questions reduces the sample to 6,032 individuals.

Pension Coverage

Table 3 reports pension statistics from the HRS and SCF.[10] In comparison to the September 1994 CPS data examined earlier, coverage rates are higher for each racial and ethnic group in both the HRS and SCF. There are at least two plausible explanations for this. First, the HRS and SCF worker cohorts were born later than the CPS cohorts of people over age 55 who were out of the labor force. As a consequence, the CPS cohorts were in the labor market in earlier years when pension coverage was lower. Second, coverage by a defined contribution plan is missed in the CPS data unless it is converted into some form of annuity. In the HRS and SCF data, anyone with an account balance in a defined contribution plan is counted as covered.

The percentage of workers covered by a pension with their current employer is higher in the HRS than in the SCF for each racial and ethnic group. Part of the reason for this is that the HRS contains only workers in the 51–61 age group whereas the SCF contains workers between the ages of 21 and 55. Since pension coverage generally rises with worker age, the inclusion of younger workers in the SCF should result in a lower coverage rate.

Table 3 also presents statistics for a broader measure of pension coverage – whether a person is either currently covered by a pension or expects to receive

Table 3. Pension Coverage Rates from Current and Past Employers.

Race/Ethnic	Gender	% Covered by Pension with Current Employer		% Covered by Pension with either Current or Past Employer		Sample Size	
		1992 SCF	1992 HRS	1992 SCF	1992 HRS	1992 SCF	1992 HRS
White	–	60.7	71.9	65.2	81.7	8,349	3,430
Black	–	59.3	68.0	62.8	76.2	1,077	761
Hispanic	–	36.6	57.0	41.6	64.7	715	269
White	Male	62.6	77.0	67.2	88.1	5,926	1,580
Black	Male	58.6	71.6	60.4	80.4	656	438
Hispanic	Male	35.0	52.7	40.6	63.4	527	114
White	Female	57.4	66.0	61.6	74.2	2,300	1,850
Black	Female	60.8	65.2	67.2	72.9	410	323
Hispanic	Female	41.2	63.5	44.3	66.7	187	155

Note: The SCF sample is restricted to wage and salary workers aged 21–55 working at least 1,000 hours per year and earning at least the minimum wage. The HRS sample has the same restrictions except the age restriction is 51–62.

benefits from a past pension. While these coverage statistics are substantially higher than those based on current coverage alone, the pattern of differences in coverage across racial/ethnic groups is similar.

While the level of pension coverage differs across the HRS and SCF, several patterns persist and are worth noting. First, coverage rates are lowest among Hispanics and highest among whites. Second, as is true for the population as a whole, coverage is higher for men than women among whites. However, in the Hispanic population, women have higher pension coverage than men. In the black population, coverage is higher for men than women in the HRS, but the reverse is true in the SCF.

Pension Benefits

A comparison of pension saving across racial and ethnic groups requires a common measure across different types of pensions. To achieve this, we compute the annuity value of each pension type for a retirement at age 65. For defined benefit plans, this requires that the benefit formula be applied to a forecast of earnings and years of service at age 65. For defined contribution plans, account balances are projected for a retirement at age 65 and then an annuity factor is applied to convert the balance into a single life annuity. The methods employed are identical to those in Even and

Table 4. Projected Benefits at Age 65 from Pensions with Current and Past Employers.

Racial or Ethnic Group	Gender	All Workers			Workers Covered by a Current or Past Employer Pension		
		Average Pension Benefit	t-Statistic for Equality with White Population	Sample Size	Average Pension Benefit	t-Statistic for Equality with White Population	Sample Size
1992 HRS							
White	–	11,694	–	3,428	20,169	–	1,979
Black	–	7,185	–4.06	761	19,520	–0.3	274
Hispanic	–	4,306	–4.27	269	13,399	–1.88	85
Male	White	17,590	–	1,848	26,004	–	1,230
Male	Black	11,500	–2.94	323	25,150	–0.25	141
Male	Hispanic	4,720	–4.72	155	15,509	–1.93	48
Female	White	4,841	–	1,580	10,357	–	749
Female	Black	3,813	–1.41	438	12,778	1.41	133
Female	Hispanic	3,680	–0.86	114	10,605	0.09	37
1992 SCF							
White	–	16,967	–	8,181	26,259	–	5,173
Black	–	14,152	–3.18	1,009	23,458	–2.18	608
Hispanic	–	9,504	–6.97	673	24,953	–0.67	251
Male	White	19,350	–	5,807	28,987	–	3,817
Male	Black	14,475	–3.95	599	25,574	–1.89	331
Male	Hispanic	9,815	–7.23	507	25,720	–1.39	190
Female	White	11,310	–	2,251	18,590	–	1,310
Female	Black	14,156	2.56	399	21,350	1.71	272
Female	Hispanic	8,519	–1.67	165	22,663	1.26	60

Note: The SCF sample is restricted to wage and salary workers aged 21–55 working at least 1,000 hours per year and earning at least the minimum wage. The HRS sample has the same restrictions except the age restriction is 51–62.

Macpherson (1998). The data appendix provides a summary of the methodology and assumptions.

A list of mean benefit levels is presented in Table 4 by sex and race/ethnicity. Benefits from both past and present employers are summed and the results are presented for both the HRS and SCF. Without restricting the sample to workers expecting a pension from a current or past employer, blacks and Hispanics expect substantially less than whites in pension benefits. In the HRS data, whites expect an age 65 retirement benefit averaging $11,694; blacks expect $7,185; and Hispanics expect only $4,306. In the SCF data, the corresponding statistics are $16,967,

$14,152, and $9,504. In both data sets, the shortfall in black and Hispanic benefits relative to that of whites is statistically significant at the 0.05 level. However, when the analysis is done separately by sex, the shortfall for blacks and Hispanics is statistically significant at the 0.05 level only for men in both data sets. In fact, black females have expected benefits that are significantly higher than white women in the SCF data.

When the analysis is restricted to workers covered by a pension, a different picture emerges. Among men, blacks and Hispanics expect lower pension benefits than whites but the differences are not statistically significant at the 0.05 level. Among women, mean benefits are consistently lowest among whites in the two data sets but the differences are not statistically significant.

The major conclusions to be drawn from the above analysis are: (i) in the population as a whole, blacks and Hispanics expect lower levels of pension benefits; (ii) the shortfall in black and Hispanic pension benefits relative to whites is largely a male phenomenon; and (iii) given that a pension benefit is expected, blacks and Hispanics expect pension benefits that are comparable to those expected by whites. The fact that expected pension benefits among workers expecting a pension are similar across racial and ethnic groups is somewhat surprising given that blacks and Hispanics have lower earnings on average. This might suggest that blacks and Hispanics devote a larger share of their earnings to pension saving. To determine whether this is the case, we control for the effect of labor market experience and earnings history and pension accumulation.

To examine how pension accumulation compares across racial and ethnic groups, focus is placed on workers currently covered by a pension plan and the features of the plan. Pension coverage from past employers is not considered because too little is known about the provisions of past plans in the HRS and SCF data to calculate a pension saving rate. In Table 5, estimates of average pension benefits are presented for workers currently covered by a pension. Since these estimates exclude benefits from pensions with prior employers, the mean benefit levels are slightly lower than those presented in Table 4. Nevertheless, excluding benefits from past pensions has little effect on the patterns observed earlier. Mean pension benefits are highest among whites and lowest among Hispanics; racial and ethnic differences are more pronounced among men than women; and racial and ethnic differences in expected pension benefits are relatively modest among workers covered by a pension.

To provide some indication of the fraction of income replaced and the level of pension saving, two additional pension statistics are presented in Table 6. First, the replacement rate represents the age 65 pension annuity as a percentage of projected income at age 65. Second, the generosity rate represents the percentage of age 65 income replaced per year of service with the employer. The generosity

Table 5. Projected Benefits at Age 65 from Pensions with Current Employers.

Racial or Ethnic Group	Gender	All Workers			Workers Covered by a Current Employer Pension		
		Average Pension Benefit	t-Statistic for Equality with White Population	Sample Size	Average Pension Benefit	t-Statistic for Equality with White Population	Sample Size
1992 HRS							
White	–	9,367	–	3,430	19,495	–	1,639
Black	–	5,328	–4.18	761	17,225	–1.03	227
Hispanic	–	3,678	–3.75	269	12,669	–1.93	75
Male	White	13,689	–	1,850	24,440	–	1,015
Male	Black	7,754	–3.31	323	20,820	–1.05	112
Male	Hispanic	4,061	–4.02	155	14,679	–1.84	43
Female	White	4,339	–	1,580	11,173	–	625
Female	Black	3,432	–1.29	438	13,200	1.07	115
Female	Hispanic	3,099	–0.95	114	9,970	–0.38	32
1992 SCF							
White	–	16,200	–	8,181	26,940	–	4,802
Black	–	13,770	–2.78	1,009	24,362	–1.93	571
Hispanic	–	9,401	–6.44	673	27,993	0.5	223
Male	White	18,538	–	5,807	29,847	–	3,549
Male	Black	14,185	–3.57	599	25,981	–2.08	321
Male	Hispanic	9,680	–6.79	507	30,005	0.06	162
Female	White	10,615	–	2,251	18,780	–	1,207
Female	Black	13,626	2.78	399	22,813	2.38	245
Female	Hispanic	8,519	–1.29	165	22,663	1.2	60

Note: The SCF sample is restricted to wage and salary workers aged 21–55 working at least 1,000 hours per year and earning at least the minimum wage. The HRS sample has the same restrictions except the age restriction is 51–62.

rate is frequently included as part of a defined benefit formula. For defined contribution plans, the higher is the saving rate, the higher the implied generosity rate. A comparison of replacement rates removes the effect of salaries on pension benefits. That is, for example, if two workers are in identical defined benefit or defined contribution plans but one worker has twice the income of the other, her benefit will be twice as high but her replacement rate will be identical. A comparison of generosity rates helps control for the effect of both salaries and years of service on benefits.

The evidence on replacement rates in both the HRS and SCF indicates that, for both men and women, blacks have higher replacement rates than whites. The

Table 6. Generosity and Replacement Rates for Pension with Current Employer.

Racial or Ethnic Group	Gender	Generosity Rate[a]	t-Statistic for Equality with White Population	Replacement Rate[b]	t-Statistic for Equality with White Population	Sample Size
1992 HRS						
White	–	0.012	–	0.41	–	1,640
Black	–	0.014	2.13	0.48	2.16	227
Hispanic	–	0.011	−0.67	0.35	−1.29	75
White	Male	0.013	–	0.46	–	1,015
Black	Male	0.016	2.41	0.55	1.88	112
Hispanic	Male	0.011	−1.13	0.37	−1.32	43
White	Female	0.011	–	0.33	–	625
Black	Female	0.012	0.89	0.41	1.9	115
Hispanic	Female	0.012	0.44	0.32	−0.2	32
1992 SCF						
White	–	0.015	–	0.52	–	4,802
Black	–	0.018	6.22	0.63	6.31	571
Hispanic	–	0.021	7.5	0.74	8.09	223
White	Male	0.016	–	0.54	–	3,549
Black	Male	0.020	5.87	0.66	4.81	321
Hispanic	Male	0.021	5.17	0.77	7.05	162
White	Female	0.014	–	0.45	–	1,207
Black	Female	0.017	4.33	0.61	5.92	245
Hispanic	Female	0.023	6.01	0.67	4.14	60

Notes: The SCF sample is restricted to currently covered wage and salary workers aged 21–55 working at least 1,000 hours per year and earning at least the minimum wage. The HRS sample has the same restrictions except the age restriction is 51–62.

[a] The generosity rate is defined as the percentage of final salary received per year of service from the pension. For defined contribution plans, this is calculated by assuming that the retiree annuitizes the pension account at retirement. For defined benefit plans, it is calculated by dividing the annual benefit by the product of final salary and years of service.

[b] The replacement rate is defined as the percentage of final salary received from the pension after retirement.

evidence on Hispanics in the two data sets is mixed, however. In the HRS, there is no statistically significant difference in replacement rates between Hispanics and whites for either men or women. In the SCF, replacement rates are higher for Hispanics than whites for both men and women.

The range of replacement rates is generally higher in the SCF than the HRS. This could indicate that the pensions held by younger workers are more generous since the SCF represents a younger sample of people. Alternatively, it might indicate that the assumptions used to forecast benefits are too optimistic in terms of how the future will affect retirement benefits. For example, since the forecasts assume no employee turnover and no expenditure of pension savings prior to retirement, the forecast of benefits may be too high. The consequences of this will be greater in the SCF since it has younger workers.

Another possible explanation for differences in replacement rates could be differential time with the employer at the time of the survey. To control for the effect of years of service on the measure of pension saving, generosity rates (i.e. the replacement rate divided by years of service) are compared. In both the HRS and SCF, black men accumulate a larger fraction of salary per year of service than white men. Among Hispanic men, the results differ between the HRS and SCF. In the HRS, there is no significant difference between the generosity of white and Hispanic men. In the SCF, Hispanic men have significantly higher generosity rates. The HRS and SCF results on generosity rates also differ for women. In the HRS, black and Hispanic women have generosity rates that are not significantly different than that of white women. In the SCF, black and Hispanic women have significantly higher generosity rates. The different results across data sets could reflect the fact that the SCF sample is younger than the HRS sample.

Given that black men and women have higher pension generosity rates than their white counterparts, it is natural to ask why. In an attempt to provide an understanding of the source of the differential, a model of generosity rates was estimated to allow for a decomposition of the racial difference in generosity rates. Included in the list of explanatory variables for generosity rates were the worker's industry, occupation, firm and plant size, union status, income, experience, education age, and the type of plan (i.e. defined benefit, defined contribution, or both). The regression model for generosity rates had statistically significant explanatory power but could explain only a small fraction of the variation in generosity rates across workers.[11] Moreover, use of the regression coefficients for white men or women to perform a decomposition of racial and ethnic differences in generosity rates revealed that virtually none of the gap in generosity rates can be explained.

Since the explanatory variables available in the data sets cannot explain the higher pension generosity rates of blacks, it is worth speculating as to what excluded variables might be responsible. One obvious omission is whether the pension is a private or public pension plan. To a certain degree, this will be accounted for by the industry controls in the model but these are by no means perfect. Another possibility is that, in the pensions where workers are given control over the decision of how much to save, blacks may choose to save a larger fraction than whites. This is consistent with evidence found in other work (Even and Macpherson, 1998) where, ceteris paribus, black men are found to contribute more to 401(k) plans than white men.

PENSIONS AND RACIAL DIFFERENCES IN WEALTH

The evidence presented in the previous section suggests that, controlling for worker characteristics, blacks and Hispanics are as likely as whites to have a pension. Also, among workers with a pension, blacks save a larger fraction of their salaries. While pension income is an important source of retirement income, it is important to consider all the wealth that has been accumulated to measure differences in the standard of living beyond retirement.

In this section, we report on racial and ethnic differences in wealth using the SCF and HRS data. Wealth in both data sets is the sum of all financial assets (stocks, bonds, home equity, checking and saving accounts balances) less non-mortgage debt. We also generate an estimate of pension wealth at the worker's current age. For defined contribution plans, pension wealth includes the account balance for pensions with current and past employers. For defined benefit plans, pension wealth includes the present value of the annuity that is promised if the worker was to retire at age 65 but terminate employment today. For this calculation, we compute the present value of the defined benefit annuity based on years of service at the worker's current age but use the estimate of the workers' real earnings at retirement. Using estimates of real earnings at retirement (instead of current earnings) assumes that workers accumulate pension savings in a defined benefit plan according to an "implicit contract model" instead of a "legal liability" model. Among others, Ippolito (1985) provides evidence that the legal theory of pension accumulations in defined benefit plans is not consistent with the manner in which defined benefit plans affect earnings profiles.[12] Since it is difficult to divide financial assets between spouses in married households, all the net worth calculations for couples pool financial and pension assets of the partners.

Table 7 provides a summary of wealth with and without pensions by racial and ethnic groups. To provide some indication of the distribution of wealth, we also report "decile means" for non-pension wealth, pension wealth, and total wealth.[13] By construction, the decile means of the parts (non-pension wealth and pension wealth) sum to the whole (total wealth).

Several patterns stand out in the data. First, total wealth of blacks and Hispanics is substantially lower than that of whites in both the HRS and SCF. In the HRS, the mean of total wealth is $134,740 among blacks, $135,433 among Hispanics and $282,597 among whites. Thus, among workers approaching retirement (i.e. 51–61 year olds) whites have accumulated nearly twice as much in total wealth as blacks and Hispanics. The average levels of total wealth in the SCF among whites, blacks, and Hispanics are respectively $139,451; $84,296; and $62,101. As in the older HRS sample, total wealth of blacks and Hispanics is approximately one half

Table 7. Means and Distribution of Wealth.

	Average Wealth	10th Percentile	25th Percentile	50th Percentile	75th Percentile	90th Percentile
1992 HRS						
Non-pension wealth						
White	204,516	12,599	50,035	117,669	237,459	438,749
Black	92,500	−22	9,379	42,967	98,598	185,665
Hispanic	108,847	226	7,326	42,464	117,765	230,822
Pension wealth						
White	78,081	24,945	48,820	85,208	109,644	133,706
Black	42,240	13,339	20,503	46,421	68,945	94,752
Hispanic	26,586	10,969	4,785	12,063	37,215	64,224
Total wealth						
White	282,597	37,544	98,855	202,877	347,103	572,455
Black	134,740	13,317	29,882	89,388	167,543	280,417
Hispanic	135,433	11,195	12,112	54,526	154,979	295,046
Black Wealth/White Wealth						
Non-Pension Wealth	0.45	0.00	0.19	0.37	0.42	0.42
Pension Wealth	0.54	0.53	0.42	0.54	0.63	0.71
Total Wealth	0.48	0.35	0.30	0.44	0.48	0.49
Hispanic Wealth/White Wealth						
Non-Pension Wealth	0.53	0.02	0.15	0.36	0.50	0.53
Pension Wealth	0.34	0.44	0.10	0.14	0.34	0.48
Total Wealth	0.48	0.30	0.12	0.27	0.45	0.52
1992 SCF						
Non-pension wealth						
White	101,225	647	9,935	40,981	100,762	209,155
Black	49,769	−507	1,908	18,063	60,031	138,785
Hispanic	45,317	−4,176	580	11,242	47,308	117,979
Pension wealth						
White	38,226	6,733	10,733	21,473	49,772	93,903
Black	34,527	3,174	11,705	7,310	64,957	74,964
Hispanic	16,784	5,773	2,367	6,518	21,203	42,363
Total wealth						
White	139,451	7,380	20,667	62,454	150,534	303,058
Black	84,296	2,667	13,613	25,373	124,988	213,749
Hispanic	62,101	1,597	2,948	17,760	68,511	160,342
Black Wealth/White Wealth						
Non-Pension Wealth	0.49	−0.78	0.19	0.44	0.60	0.66
Pension Wealth	0.90	0.47	1.09	0.34	1.31	0.80
Total Wealth	0.60	0.36	0.66	0.41	0.83	0.71
Hispanic Wealth/White Wealth						
Non-Pension Wealth	0.45	−6.45	0.06	0.27	0.47	0.56
Pension Wealth	0.44	0.86	0.22	0.30	0.43	0.45
Total Wealth	0.45	0.22	0.14	0.28	0.46	0.53

Note: The SCF sample is restricted to wage and salary workers aged 21 to 55 working at least 1,000 hours per year and earning at least the minimum wage. The HRS sample has the same restrictions except the age restriction is 51 to 62.

of that for whites. Given that the SCF sample has younger workers than the HRS, the lower level of wealth in the SCF sample is not surprising.

The black-white wealth ratios we find in the HRS and SCF are substantially higher than those found in earlier studies. For example, Menchik and Jianakoplos (1997) reports that, in the 1989 Survey of Consumer Finances, the black-white ratio of non-pension household wealth is 0.23. Smith (1995) uses the 1992 HRS and finds a black-white ratio of non-pension household wealth of 0.27. Both of these estimates are substantially lower than reported here. The most significant difference between our study and these is that we restrict our analysis to people who work 1000 or more hours per year and earn a wage of at least $4.25 per hour. The aforementioned studies do not exclude households on the basis of employment status. Since the black population has a larger fraction of people that are unemployed or out of the labor force, our analysis excludes a larger fraction of people with low levels of income (and wealth) in the black population.[14] The reason we exclude the part-time and non-employed population is that we are interested primarily in the role of pensions on the wealth distribution.

To examine how pension saving affects the distribution of wealth, wealth ratios are computed with and without pension wealth included. When pension wealth is added to the wealth measure, the black-white ratio of mean wealth rises from 0.45 to 0.48 in the HRS and from 0.49 to 0.60 in the SCF. For the Hispanic-white comparison, adding pension wealth decreases the wealth ratio in the HRS from 0.53 to 0.48 but has no effect on the ratio in the SCF.

While the addition of pension wealth has relatively modest effects on the ratio of black and Hispanic wealth at the mean, the effects differ substantially across the wealth distribution. For all the racial and ethnic groups, pension wealth is a larger fraction of total wealth at the lower end of the wealth distribution. Moreover, at the lower end of the wealth distribution, black and Hispanic workers have a larger fraction of wealth in pension assets than whites. As a consequence, the addition of pension wealth has a greater effect on black and Hispanic wealth relative to whites at the lower end of the wealth distribution.

To examine why wealth accumulation among blacks and Hispanics is lower, a regression approach is followed. Table 8 presents the results of wealth regressions for blacks, whites, and Hispanics pooled. Dummy variables are included to indicate whether a person is black or Hispanic. The model is estimated with and without controls for characteristics that might influence wealth accumulation. The additional controls in the regression include earnings and its square, age and its square, an interaction between age and earnings, education, marital status, and union status. For workers with partners that have earnings, we also include spousal earnings and its square (set equal to zero for single workers and for spouses that are self-employed), a dummy variable indicating whether a person has a spouse

Table 8. Wealth Regressions.

	Non-Pension Wealth		Pension Wealth		Total Wealth	
1992 HRS						
Average value among whites	204,516		78,081		282,597	
Coefficient estimates[a]						
Black	−112,016	−38,859	−35,840	−7,839.42	−147,857	−46,698
	(5.88)	(2.17)	(4.43)	(1.06)	(6.82)	(2.39)
Hispanic	−95,669	−15,144	−51,494	−14,356	−147,163	−29,500
	(3.69)	(0.58)	(4.68)	(1.34)	(4.99)	(0.22)
Controls included?[a]	no	yes	no	yes	no	yes
Sample size	4,203	4,203	4,203	4,203	4,203	4,203
1992 SCF						
Average Value among whites	101,225		38,226		139,451	
Coefficient estimates[a]						
Black	−51,546	−9,477	−3,699	5,405	−55,155	−4,072
	(3.80)	(0.73)	(1.41)	(2.76)	(3.86)	(0.31)
Hispanic	−55,908	−4,648	−21,442	−1,287	−77,351	−5,936
	(3.38)	(0.28)	(6.70)	(0.52)	(4.43)	(0.36)
Controls included?	no	yes	no	yes	no	yes
Sample size	9,711	9,711	9,711	9,711	9,711	9,711

Notes: The SCF sample is restricted to wage and salary workers aged 21–55 working at least 1,000 hours per year and earning at least the minimum wage. The HRS sample has the same restrictions except the age restriction is 51–62.

Controls for personal characteristics include earnings, age, an interaction between age and earnings, education, marital status, and union status. For workers with partners that have earnings, we also include spousal characteristics. See text for more detail.

[a] t-statistics are given in parentheses.

that is self-employed, the spouse's years of education and its square, and the spouse's earnings interacted with age. For single workers, all the spousal variables are set equal to zero.

For each of the three wealth measures (non-pension, pension, and total wealth), we report the results of a regression of the wealth measures on a black and Hispanic dummy with and without controls for household characteristics. The results from the HRS regressions with only the black and Hispanic dummies match the results on average levels of wealth found in Table 7. The coefficients on racial and ethnic dummies indicate the size of the racial or ethnic gap relative to the white reference group. Including the control variables substantially reduces the size of the coefficients on the black and Hispanic dummies. For example, in the non-pension wealth equation, the coefficient on the black dummy variable drops from −112,016 to −38,859 when controls for household characteristics are included. The coefficient on the Hispanic dummy drops from −95,669 to −15,144. Consequently, approximately 65% of the shortfall in black non-pension wealth relative to whites can be accounted for by the controls included in the regression. For Hispanics, approximately 85% of shortfall can be explained.

When total (pension plus non-pension) wealth is considered, the results are quite similar. Approximately 70% of the black-white gap in total wealth is accounted for by differences in household characteristics; approximately 80% of the Hispanic-white gap can be explained.

After controlling for worker characteristics, pension wealth has relatively little effect on racial and ethnic differences in average wealth. Given the regression coefficients and assuming average characteristics, blacks are estimated to have 81% as much non-pension wealth as whites, and 83% as much total wealth; Hispanics are estimated to have 93% as much non-pension wealth as whites, and 90% as much total wealth. However, in the case of Hispanics, the shortfall in non-pension wealth and total wealth relative to whites is statistically insignificant after controlling for household characteristics.

In the SCF data, the absolute gap in wealth is much smaller than in the HRS data. This is expected given the younger ages of the workers and the smaller amounts of wealth accumulated. In the SCF, blacks and Hispanics have a statistically significant shortfall in non-pension and total wealth relative to whites. However, after controlling for household characteristics, there is no statistically significant shortfall for blacks or Hispanics. Thus, in the younger sample, while there are substantial racial and ethnic differences in wealth accumulation, the differences can be entirely accounted for by a small number of observed household characteristics.

SUMMARY AND CONCLUSIONS

Several studies establish that blacks and Hispanics have less wealth than whites. This study examined the extent to which pensions contribute to differential wealth accumulation. In our analysis of the September 1994 CPS, we demonstrated that, among people out of the labor force over age 55, blacks and Hispanics are substantially less likely to have pension coverage than whites. However, among those receiving a pension, expected benefits among black and Hispanic workers are quite similar to whites. The lack of information on prior labor market history in the CPS data, however, precludes an investigation of the source of these patterns.

Using data from the 1992 Survey of Consumer Finances (SCF) and the 1992 Health and Retirement Survey (HRS), we examine prospects for racial and ethnic differences in pension wealth among people working in 1992. The HRS and SCF are similar in that they both provide extensive information on pension plans and other financial assets. The major difference is that the HRS focuses on workers approaching retirement (aged 51–62). Our subsample of the SCF included workers between the ages of 21 and 55.

The analysis of the HRS and SCF revealed that blacks and Hispanics expect substantially less in pension benefits than whites in the male, but not the female, population. However, when the analysis is restricted to workers expecting a pension benefit, benefits among black and Hispanic workers are quite similar to those among white workers. This is similar to the result found in the September 1994 CPS for retired people. We also find some evidence that, when covered by a pension, black and Hispanic men and women accumulate a larger fraction of their salary in pensions, holding worker characteristics constant.

This study also examined the importance of including pension saving in calculating racial and ethnic differences in wealth. Comparing mean levels of wealth (including pension wealth), blacks and Hispanics have approximately one-half as much wealth as whites. The inclusion of pension wealth has little effect on the average wealth position of the minority groups relative to whites. However, examination of wealth differentials at different points of the wealth distribution reveals that pensions reduce the black-white and Hispanic-white wealth gap primarily at the bottom end of the wealth distribution. This reflects the fact that the fraction of wealth held in pensions is largest among low wealth households and this pattern is more pronounced in the black and Hispanic populations.

While Hispanics and blacks accumulate substantially less wealth than whites, our study finds that differences in earnings, education, spousal earnings, and other measures of household characteristics can account for virtually all of the racial and ethnic differences in wealth accumulation. Moreover, this result holds whether pension wealth is included or excluded from the measure of total wealth. Thus, the evidence suggests that differences in average wealth are neither amplified or dampened by racial or ethnic differences in pension saving.

What conclusions can be drawn from our study? First, while blacks and Hispanics accumulate substantially less wealth than whites, the majority of the differential can be accounted for by their lower earnings and other personal characteristics. One need not rely on racial or ethnic differences in attitudes about saving, life expectancy, or family structure to explain the majority of the difference in wealth accumulation. It should be emphasized, however, that our results apply to the working population only. To the extent that blacks and Hispanics are less likely to be employed and this reduces wealth accumulation, this conclusion might not apply.

A second conclusion is that pension saving does not appear to amplify or dampen mean differences in the accumulation of pension wealth. However, the impact of pension saving varies across the wealth distribution. In particular, since there are more black and Hispanic workers in the lower tail of the income distribution where wealth accumulation is very low, pension saving could have a substantial effect on the wealth positions of the minority groups. Our evidence suggests that 51–61 year old blacks and Hispanics at the tenth percentile of their group-specific wealth distribution had less than $300 of non-pension wealth. For whites, the tenth percentile had over $12,000 of non-pension wealth. The most meager pension plan would substantially improve the relative wealth position of blacks and Hispanics at the lower end of wealth distribution.

NOTES

1. Other studies that find that the earnings gap is less than the wealth gap include Blau and Graham (1990), Oliver and Shapiro (1995), and Snyder (1989).
2. This ratio was derived from the 1996 *Statistical Abstract of the United States*.
3. These hypotheses are mentioned by Blau and Graham (1990), Smith (1995), or Menchik and Jianakoplos (1997).
4. Smith (1995, p. S179).
5. The definition of Hispanic we employ includes only white Hispanics. Black Hispanics are defined as blacks. Asians and American Indians are excluded from the sample.
6. A person is classified as a public sector employee if his or her "longest job" was in the public sector.
7. The text describing the data and benefit calculations borrows heavily from our earlier study, Even and Macpherson (1998).
8. That is, for example, if income is imputed for an individual, the value of income will take on five different values for that person to reflect the variance in the estimate of income. If income is not imputed for an individual, it will take the same value for that person five times.
9. Notice that the sample size of 9,863 includes many individuals five times. However, since some of the variables that we delete on may be imputed (e.g. if the wage rate is less than $4.25), some individuals will not appear five times. The imputed value for a given variable may cause the observation to be excluded in some cases but not in others.
10. Since the HRS and SCF both over-sample some groups, all statistics and regressions rely upon the sample weights provided in the surveys.
11. The statistical significance of the regressions was based on an F-test of the null hypothesis that all coefficients in the regression, with the exception of that on the intercept, were equal to zero. For white men and women, the F-tests rejected the null at the 0.001 significance level. The conclusion that only a small fraction of the variation in generosity

rates can be accounted for by the explanatory variables is based on the fact that the adjusted R-squared in the regression equations ranged between 0.06 and 0.18.

12. The annuity factors and interest rates necessary for estimating the present value of the annuity are identical to those described in the data appendix.

13. To compute a "decile mean," we first rank people according to their total wealth. We then take all workers within 5% (plus or minus) of the relevant percentile of interest. The means of the variables of interest (non-pension wealth, pension wealth, and total wealth) are then computed for this sub-group. For example, to compute the decile mean at the 25th percentile, we take all workers that have total wealth that ranks them between the 20th and 30th percentile. For this sub-group, means are calculated for each of the wealth measures.

14. In 1996, the employment-population ratio for the population over age 16 was 64.1 among whites and 57.4 among blacks. The unemployment rates for the civilian non-institutionalized population were 4.7% among whites and 11.1% among blacks.

ACKNOWLEDGMENTS

The authors are grateful for valuable feedback from Steve Woodbury, the referee, participants at the Southern Economic Association meeting, Phyllis Fernandez, David McCarthy and Joe Piacentini.

REFERENCES

Blau, F. D., & Graham, J. W. (1990). Black-white differences in wealth and asset composition. *Quarterly Journal of Economics, 105*(May), 321–339.

Employee Benefit Research Institute (1997). *EBRI databook on employee benefits* (4th ed.). Washington, DC: Employee Benefit Research Institute.

Even, W. E., & Macpherson, D. A. (1998). The impact of rising 401(k) pension coverage on future pension income. Report submitted to Pension and Welfare Benefits Administration, U.S. Department of Labor.

Ippolito, R. A. (1985). The labor contract and true economic pension liabilities. *American Economic Review, 75*(December), 1031–1043.

Menchik, P. L., & Jianakoplos, N. A. (1997). Black-white wealth inequality: Is inheritance the reason? *Economic Inquiry, 35*(April), 428–442.

Montalto, C. P., & Sung, J. (1996). Multiple imputation in the 1992 survey of consumer finances. *Financial Counseling and Planning, 7*(1), 133–146.

Oliver, M. L., & Shapiro, T. M. (1995). *Black wealth/white wealth: A new perspective on racial inequality.* New York: Routledge.

Smith, J. P. (1995). Racial and ethnic differences in wealth in the health and retirement study. *Journal of Human Resources, 30*(Supplement), S158–S183.

Snyder, D. C. (1989). A data base with income and assets of new retirees by race and hispanic origin. *Review of Black Political Economy, 17*(Spring), 73–81.

Society of Actuaries Group Annuity Valuation Task Force (1996). 1994 group annuity mortality Tables and 1994 group reserving Table. *Transactions of the Society of Actuaries, 107*, 865–913.

APPENDIX

Estimation of Retirement Benefits in the HRS and SCF

In the Health and Retirement Survey (HRS) and the Survey of Consumer Finances (SCF), information is provided on pension coverage from current and past jobs. For current jobs, both data sets indicate the type of plan(s) that the worker has, the number of years in the plan, and other information that we use to forecast future retirement income at age 65.

In the case of DB plans, workers are asked when they expect to retire and the benefits they will receive at retirement. Benefits may be reported as either a percentage of final pay or as an absolute amount. To estimate what benefits are to be received at age 65, the following steps are taken. First, we project earnings at retirement by assuming a 1.1% annual growth rate in real wages. To translate this into a benefit at age 65, a "generosity factor" (the percentage of final pay replaced per year of service) is computed by dividing expected benefits at retirement by the product of years in plan and salary at retirement.[1] Benefits for an age 65 retirement are calculated as the product of the age 65 value of forecast earnings, number of years of service at 65, and the generosity factor.

For DC plans, information is provided on the current balance in the plan and the amount that the employer and employee contribute. To project the balance in the pension plan at age 65 in 1992 dollars, the current balance is compounded forward with real interest rates to age 65. The real interest rate is assumed to be equal to the yield on indexed Treasury bills in February 1998 (3.7%). Between 1992 and the year that the worker reaches age 65, it is assumed that both employer and employee contributions remain at the same percentage of pay and that real salary growth continues at 1.1%.

All workers are assumed to live to age 65 with certainty. Benefits from DC plans are converted into a single life annuity by applying annuity factors to the projected DC balance at age 65. In the case of benefits that a worker expects to receive from prior pension plans, both the HRS and SCF indicate the type of pension (i.e. DB or DC). However, when a lump sum was received or a person is currently receiving a benefit, only the HRS provides information on the type of pension. In both cases, it is possible to tell whether a person received a lump sum distribution at some point in the past, is currently receiving benefits, or expects to receive benefits in the future. In the HRS, workers receiving lump sums indicate whether they saved or spent it. Only those balances that were saved are counted as benefits from past pensions. Unfortunately, in the SCF, no such information is available. To adjust for this, estimates of the percentage of workers that save lump sum distributions by age of receipt, provided by EBRI (1997), are used to randomly assign workers into categories indicating whether they saved their lump sum distributions.[2] For those with a lump sum that was saved, an equivalent age 65 annuity is computed as follows: (1) the lump sum is compounded forward to 1992 assuming historical interest rates;[3] (2) the 1992 balance is compounded forward from 1992 to the year the person reaches age 65 using an assumed real interest rate of 3.7% (the rate on indexed Treasury bills); (3) the lump sum is converted into an annuity at age 65.[4] The annuity calculation assumes constant nominal payments and uses an assumed nominal interest rate beyond 1992 equal to that on 10 year Treasury bills in 1992 (7.0%) and the mortality table for group annuitants provided by the Society of Actuaries.[5] Using these assumptions, we estimate that a $100 payment at age 65 would buy a life annuity of $9.63 per year.[6]

Separate calculations are required for pension benefits that workers have already received or expect to receive from a past job. For workers that report they are currently receiving benefits, we calculate the age 65 equivalent annuity as follows: First, we compute the present value (in 1992 dollars) of benefits received between the starting age and 65. Second, we compute the lump sum cost of a life annuity starting at age 65 equal to the annual benefit paid by the pension. These two parts are added and then converted into an age 65 life annuity. When the benefits are indexed for inflation, appropriate adjustments are made to reflect the growth in nominal benefits over time.[7]

For workers that expect a future benefit, it may be either a lump sum or an annual benefit. For annual benefits that start before age 65, we estimate the expected present value of the annuity assuming the person lives with certainty to age 65 and has survivor probabilities given by the group annuitant mortality tables beyond age 65. For a person that expects to receive benefits starting after age 65, we estimate the expected present value of the annuity (again accounting for survival probabilities beyond age 65) and discount back to age 65. When cost-of-living adjustments are expected with future benefits, appropriate adjustments are made in evaluation of the annuity.

APPENDIX NOTES

1. Our methodology assumes that people report expected benefits in 1992 dollars.
2. Using Table 17.3 of EBRI (1997), we estimated the percentage of workers that used all of their lump sum for either: (i) tax qualified saving; (ii) non-tax qualified saving; or (iii) a mix of the two. This is a conservative estimate of the percentage of lump sums saved. The fraction of lump sums saved, by age group, are: 8.3% for 16–20 year olds; 21.7 for 21–30 year olds; 35 for 31–40

year olds; 40.2 for 41–50 year olds; 56.8 for 51–60 year olds; 57.6 for 61–64 year olds; and 21.4 for those 65 and over.
3. Interest rates prior to 1992 (the survey dates in HRS and SCF) are assumed equal to the rates observed on one-year U.S. Treasury bills plus 0.28%. We added 0.28% to the one year treasury rate to allow for the fact that returns on pension contributions will likely reflect interest rates on a longer term investment. The 0.28% per year is one-half of the average premium that five year bonds paid relative to one year bonds between 1953 and 1992.
4. When a worker receives cost-of-living adjustments, the real interest rate is used to compute the annuity rate. Otherwise, nominal rates are used.
5. The source of the mortality rates is Society of Actuaries Group Annuity Valuation Task Force (1996), Table 13. The group annuitant mortality tables provide gender specific mortality rates. We compute an average mortality rate by taking a weighted average of the gender specific mortality rates where the weights represent the predicted fraction of the population of a given gender based on their mortality experience assuming each sex is half of the population at age 65.
6. It is worth noting that we ignore differences between DB and DC plans in terms of survivor or disability benefits. In DC plans, the survivor has the right to the account balance. In DB plans, the survivor benefit is generally specified according to some formula tied to the worker's years of service and final salary.
7. Inflation prior to 1992 is measured by historical movements in the Consumer Price Index. Inflation beyond 1992 is assumed equal to 2.7% which equals the difference between the nominal yield on 10 year bonds and the real yield on indexed Treasury bills in 1998. When evaluating an annuity that is indexed for inflation, the real interest rate is used instead of the nominal rate.

COUNTY-LEVEL ESTIMATES OF THE EMPLOYMENT PROSPECTS OF LOW-SKILL WORKERS

David C. Ribar

INTRODUCTION

There can be no question that the aggregate economic performance of the United States over the 1990s was outstanding. Except for a brief recession in 1990–1991, the United States experienced steady growth, rising productivity, low and falling unemployment, and little inflation. Following sharp run-ups at the start of the decade, there were also declines in other social and economic indicators such as poverty, welfare caseloads, crime, and teenage birth rates. These trends suggest there were widespread increases in economic prosperity. In fact, however, we do not know exactly how the benefits of this performance were distributed.

There is plenty of evidence indicating that the benefits were uneven. For instance, while incomes for the wealthiest Americans increased, inflation-adjusted wages and earnings for the average worker were essentially unchanged by the end of the decade. At the bottom of the income distribution, poverty rates remained higher than levels recorded during the 1970s. The economy also generated very different outcomes for people in different parts of the country and with different levels of market skills.

To get some feel for the geographic differences in labor market conditions, consider a map (Fig. 1) that uses data from the 1990 Decennial Census to rank counties by the percentage of civilian, non-institutionalized working age adults

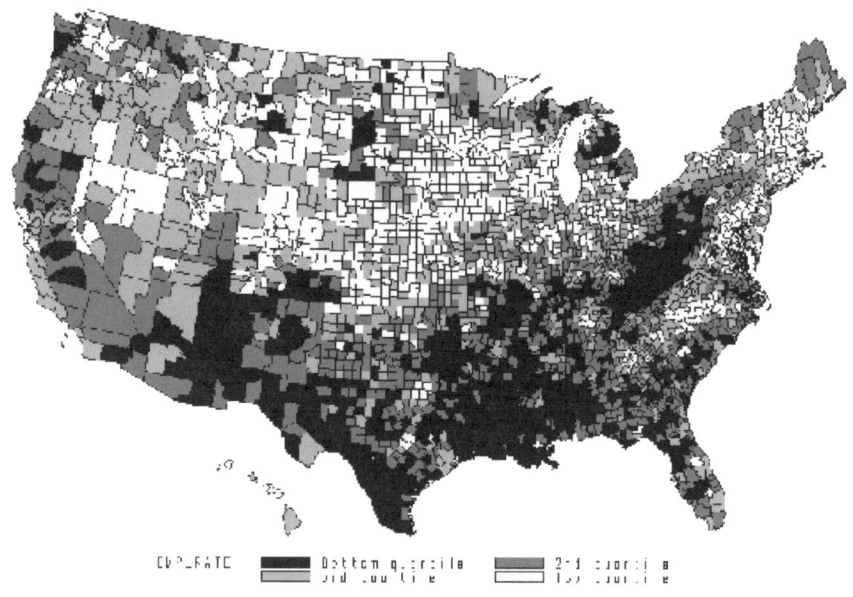

Fig. 1

Civilian Employment in U.S. Counties: 1989. *Note:* County estimates computed from the SEDF.

(ages 16–64) who worked at any time during 1989. In the map, counties are ranked into quartiles with progressively lighter shading used to identify quartiles with higher employment rates. The map reveals some pronounced differences across regions. Employment was relatively low in Appalachia and the South and relatively high in New England, the mid-Atlantic region, and the central plains. The existence of these types of regional differences is well known and has been documented in earlier analyses by Deming (1996) and Kasarda (1995).

What may be more surprising is the variability in employment rates within regions and even within narrower areas such as states and metropolitan statistical areas (MSAs). The map shows that employment rates differed greatly across counties. In fact, there were several places, such as Sonoma and Lake counties in California and Washtenaw and Wayne counties in Michigan, where adjacent counties within the same state or MSA were in the top and bottom quartiles of the employment distribution.

Employment rates and the spatial distribution of employment also vary with workers' demographic characteristics and skill levels. Nationally, employment rates are substantially higher for men than for women and for people with more

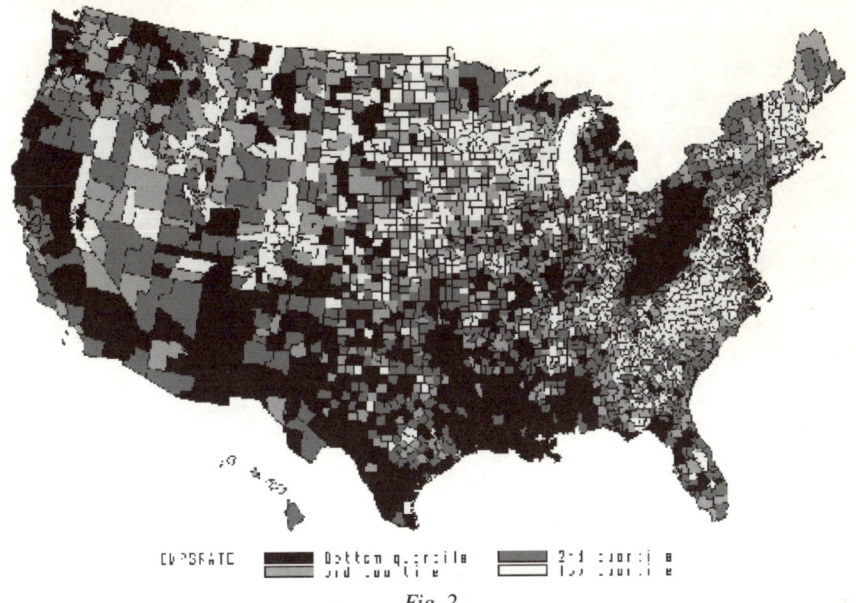

Fig. 2

Employment Among Female High School Graduates: 1989. *Note:* County estimates computed from the SEDF.

schooling than for people with less. Figure 2 shows the geographic pattern of employment in 1989 among women who were high school graduates but had not gone on to college. If we compare Figs 1 and 2, the pattern for female high school graduates was mostly similar to that of adults as a whole. However, there were some differences – e.g. employment among female high school graduates was relatively weaker in the western states and stronger in the south Atlantic states than for other adults.

The difference in the geographic pattern for more-educated women was even more striking. Figure 3 maps relative employment rates for women who were college graduates. As the figure indicates, there was much less of a general regional pattern and more within-region heterogeneity for more-educated women than for less-educated women.[1]

Figures 1–3 provide a snapshot of how labor market outcomes varied for people with different skill levels across the country in 1989. How has the picture changed since then? This study examines the local wage and employment opportunities for men and women with different levels of schooling over the period 1989–1997. Currently, reliable direct measures of wages and employment rates for different

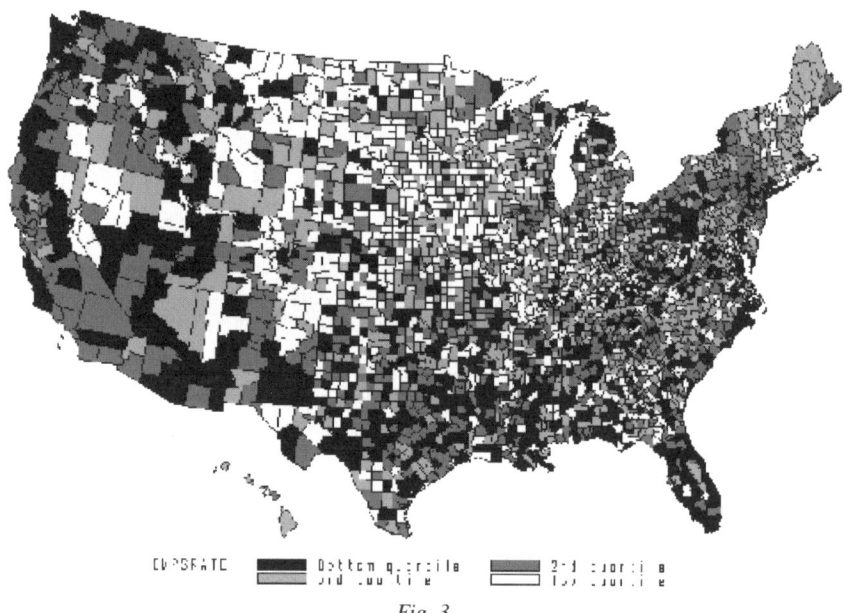

Fig. 3

Employment Among Female College Graduates: 1989. *Note:* County estimates computed from the SEDF.

demographic and skill groups are only available for large geographic areas such as regions and populous states or at infrequent intervals (e.g. from the Decennial Census) for some smaller areas.[2] This study constructs indirect annual county-level measures from 1989–1997 by combining skill-specific information on earnings and employment from the Sample Edited Detail File (SEDF) of the 1990 Decennial Census and the 1990–1998 Annual Demographic files of the Current Population Survey (CPS) with annual industry-specific information from the Regional Economic Information System (REIS). Special versions of the SEDF and CPS files that identify county of residence are used.

Specifically, the study regresses the low-skill wage and employment data from the SEDF and CPS files on a set of personal variables from the combined files and local employment measures derived from the REIS. The wage regressions are corrected for selectivity from the employment decision and account for area-specific effects as well as general time effects. Estimates from the regressions are then combined with the available employment data from the REIS to impute wage and employment rates for low-skill adults across counties.

The empirical analysis is straightforward but makes three important contributions. First, it constructs annual gender- and education-specific employment and wage estimates for small geographic areas – as mentioned, no such estimates existed before. These detailed estimates will be useful to policy makers. Characterizing labor market outcomes for people with different skills in different parts of the country has become especially critical in light of the changes in public assistance policies that have increased local autonomy and emphasized earnings as a route out of poverty. The best-known of these changes was The Personal Responsibility and Work Opportunity Reconciliation Act (PRWORA) of 1996, which increased the flexibility of states in providing cash assistance, training, and employment support to the poor and also incorporated tough work and work-readiness requirements for the beneficiaries of these programs. Other changes that preceded the PRWORA – such as the general decline in welfare benefits, the increase in the Earned Income Tax Credit, and the extension of Medicaid benefits to low-income, working families – also acted to shift the balance from welfare to work.

Second, the econometric models are used to examine the sensitivity of individual employment and earnings outcomes for different types of people to changes in the local employment rate and industrial composition of employment. This issue has been examined in other studies; however, those studies did not have access to broad-based, nationally representative data with the kind of geographic detail and controls considered here.

Third, because of the geographic detail, the analysis makes a methodological contribution by determining what constitutes a local labor market. Is the proper area a county, metropolitan area, state, or something else? Does the definition differ across workers with different skills? Previous researchers have been driven by reasons of data availability and convenience to adopt measures for relatively large geographic areas. This study finds that the use of narrower measures not only leads to better estimates but in some cases to substantively different results.

PREVIOUS RESEARCH

Numerous studies have examined the effects of local labor market conditions on wages, earnings and related outcomes. Additional research has investigated how employment rates vary across different types of workers. For brevity, this review focuses only on the subset of studies that have considered wage and employment outcomes for low-skill workers.

Much of the literature has considered specific groups of low-skill workers. For instance, Freeman (1991) and Freeman and Rodgers (1999) examined earnings among young men with low levels of schooling and found that their earnings were adversely affected by high general rates of metropolitan unemployment. Bartik and Eberts (1999), Card and Lemieux (1997), the Council of Economic Advisors (1997, 1999), Gittleman (2000), Figlio and Ziliak (1999), Fitzgerald (1995), and Harris (1993) examined the effects of labor market conditions on welfare receipt. With the exception of the study by Card and Lemieux, these studies found that tight labor markets reduced recipiency. Related studies by Bartik (1993) and Walters (1990) reported that high levels of labor demand reduced poverty.

The remaining studies have compared the effects of local labor conditions on the earnings of different types of workers. Topel (1986) found that employment growth and positive current employment shocks increased men's wages and that the effects were stronger for men with low levels of education. Hoynes (1999) similarly reported that low-skill workers' earnings, and especially low-skill women's earnings, responded more to labor market shocks than high-skill workers. Bartik (1999) found that the earnings of men who were not college graduates and women who were neither college graduates nor single heads of households were more sensitive to employment shocks than the earnings of more-educated men or women. However, he also found that the earnings of female non-graduates who were also single heads of households were less sensitive to shocks than those of other women.

Katz and Murphy (1992) found that shifts in demand were largely responsible for recent changes in the wage structure for skilled and unskilled workers. Juhn, Murphy and Pierce (1993) provided supporting evidence that increases in the returns to skills contributed to changes in the wage structure. In contrast, Bound and Holzer (1993) found that while industrial shifts (specifically, the decline in manufacturing employment) had a disproportionate negative effect on the employment of low-skill men, these shifts had little effect on their overall earnings.

While the existing research has been successful in identifying factors which determine low-skill employment opportunities, it provides only limited information regarding what the actual distribution of opportunities for men and women across local labor markets might look like. First, only a few of the studies (Bartik, 1999; Hoynes, 1999; Katz & Murphy, 1992) have explicitly considered low-skill women's earnings. Most of the studies have either focused on men's opportunities or obtained information on women's opportunities indirectly (for instance, by examining women's patterns of welfare receipt).

Second, almost all of the studies have considered labor market outcomes for relatively large areas such as major metropolitan areas (Bartik, 1993; Bound & Holzer, 1993; Freeman, 1982; Freeman & Rodgers, 1999; Hoynes, 1999), states (Bartik, 1999; C.E.A., 1997, 1999; Figlio & Ziliak, 1999; Topel, 1986), regions (Card & Lemieux, 1997), or the nation as a whole (Katz & Murphy, 1992). As we saw in the earlier figures, labor market opportunities within these broad areas may differ substantially.

Third, many of the studies have examined aggregate outcomes. The use of such data means that studies have been restricted in the types of controls they could include for both observed and unobserved differences across workers. Bils (1985) and Keane, Moffitt and Runkle (1988) have shown that failure to control for selectivity and heterogeneity in the unobserved determinants of wages results in biased estimates of the effects of economic conditions. Additionally, Blundell, Reed and Stoker (1999) have shown that the use of aggregate earnings and employment data to form wage measures introduces other biases.

DATA

The primary data for this analysis come from the Sample Edited Detail File of the 1990 Decennial Census and confidential versions of the 1990–1998 Annual Demographic (March) Supplements of the Current Population Survey. The information in the SEDF was coded from the "long forms" which were administered as part of the 1990 Decennial Census. Thus, it represents a very large (one-in-six) cross-section sample of the U.S. population. The March files of the CPS are smaller and sample roughly 60,000 households per year. Detailed geographic information is attached to both the SEDF and confidential versions of the CPS.[3]

Individual-Level Variables

The SEDF and March files of the CPS record comparable information on whether a person was employed during the previous year, the number of weeks the person worked, the number of hours worked in an average week, and the amount of money earned from different sources.[4] From these measures, I construct three variables: a dummy variable indicating employment during the previous year, weekly earnings during the previous year (total personal earnings divided by weeks worked), and hourly earnings during the previous year (total personal earnings divided by weeks and typical hours worked). Nominal amounts were re-expressed in constant 1998 dollars using the Consumer Price Index for Urban Consumers (CPI-U).

In addition to the economic variables, the SEDF and CPS also contain comparable information on the person's sex, age, ethnic origin, and schooling level. I use the sex and age information as recorded. From the ethnic origin data, I construct dummy indicators for people of African origin and people of other non-European origins (mostly native Americans, Asians, and Pacific Islanders); the omitted category is European origin. I also construct a separate dummy variable for Hispanic origin which may overlap with the other racial/ethnic categories. Using the schooling information, I distinguish between three types of people: those who did not complete high school, those who completed high school (or equivalent) but did not go on to college, and those who obtained more schooling (i.e. completed at least some college). Most of the empirical analysis focuses on people from the two lowest education groups.

From the combined data set, I select non-institutionalized, civilians who were 16 to 64 years of age. I then make a number of data exclusions. First, I exclude people below age 24 who were enrolled in school. Second, I drop observations for individuals whose earnings were in the top 1% of all earnings for each year or whose average weekly hours exceeded 98.[5] Third, I exclude observations if the calculation of real hourly or weekly earnings was unreasonable – below 75¢ or above $250 for hourly wages and below 75¢ or above $10,000 for weekly wages. Fourth, I drop observations with allocated economic or demographic data.[6] Even with these exclusions, the resulting data set still contains several million observations. To make the data more manageable, I randomly sample observations from the SEDF for counties with more than 100,000 residents (the sampling probability is 100,000/population) and re-weight the remaining observations accordingly. All of the statistical analyses incorporate sampling weights scaled to the annual sample sizes.

Means and standard deviations for the individual-level variables drawn from the SEDF and CPS files are reported in Appendix A. The appendix lists statistics separately for women and men in each of the three education categories.

Policy Variables

Two state-level policy variables relevant to the low-skill labor market have been merged into the analysis data set: the maximum AFDC benefits available to a family of three with no other income and the minimum wage in the state. The benefits measure is taken from various editions of the *Green Book* (U.S. House of Representatives, Committee on Ways and Means, various years) and is used to capture the income available if a family head does not work. The minimum wage measure is taken from papers by Neumark, Schweitzer and Wascher (1998) and Neumark (1999). Over the period of the study there were several increases in the federal minimum wage.[7] Additionally, a small number of states set minimum wages above the federal level and changed their wages at different times. The analysis adjusts the AFDC benefits and minimum wage measures for inflation using the CPI-U. Means and standard deviations for these variables also appear in Appendix A.

Measures of Local Labor Market Conditions

Using the geographic identifiers in the SEDF and CPS files, I can link the individual-level observations to some available measures of local labor market conditions. An important issue that must be addressed first, though, is the definition of the market itself – what are the geographic boundaries and what types of labor are involved?

There is little agreement in the existing empirical literature regarding what constitutes a "local" labor market. If we base our definition on the measures that have actually been employed in research, a fair definition of "local" would be any geographic area smaller than a Census region, with states and metropolitan areas being the most popular choices. While research by urban and regional economists and our earlier examination of county employment patterns each suggest that a narrower geographic definition should be adopted, labor market studies based on national samples have generally not considered smaller areas or incorporated information on commuting.[8]

Some data for smaller areas are available; however, these data have serious limitations. For instance, county-level employment, unemployment and labor force estimates are reported in the Geographic Profile of Employment and Unemployment from the Bureau of Labor Statistics. However, these data are not skill-specific. As we saw Figs 1–3, general aggregates may not reflect the opportunities for particular skill groups.

Another source of local economic data is the Regional Economic Information System from the Bureau of Economic Analysis, which reports annual total and industry-level earnings and employment within counties. The industry-specific data in the REIS are based primarily on administrative records (ES–202 forms) submitted by employers to state employment agencies. The limitation of these data is that they are specific to industries rather than skill groups and recorded on a place of work rather than a place of residence basis. Figure 4 illustrates the distortions that arise when place of work data are used. For each county in Fig. 4, employment rates are calculated by dividing the number of civilian jobs, as reported in the REIS, by the number of working age adults. Although some of the general regional patterns carry over from Fig. 1, others do not. In particular, relative employment rates in Texas look much better in Fig. 4 than in Fig. 1 while conditions in Maryland and Virginia look much worse. The place-of-work estimates also exhibit more variability within regions than do the place-of-residence estimates. A further shortcoming is that the rates based on place-of-work data take on values greater than one in locations like the District of Columbia with lots of in-commuting.

Measures of skill- and residence-specific opportunities can be estimated using data from the CPS and the SEDF. Both files contain information on worker

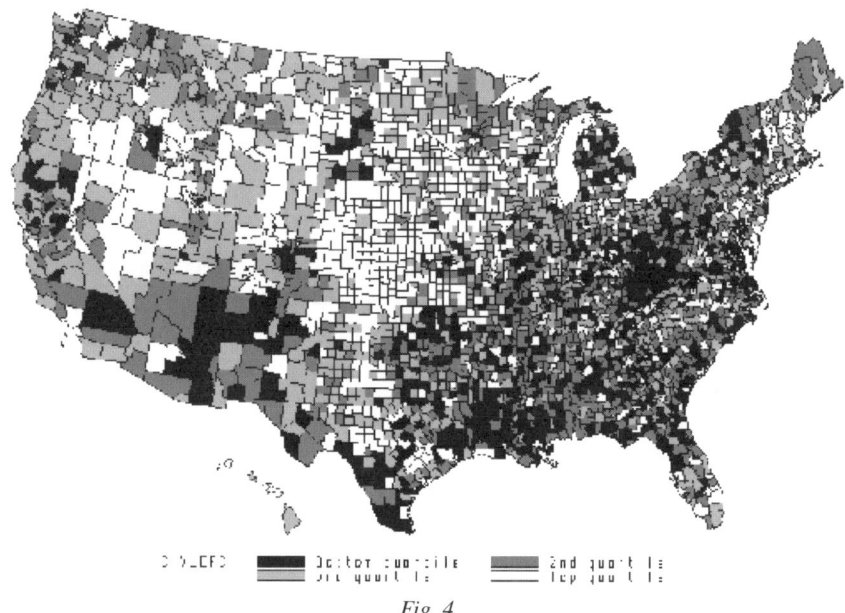

Fig. 4
Civilian Employment on a Place-of-Work Basis: 1989. *Note:* County employment data from the REIS.

characteristics including age and education that can be used to infer skill levels as well as data on labor market outcomes. However, once again there are limitations. The CPS can be used to construct statistics for the nation as a whole and for some large subnational areas; however, there are not enough observations to generate reliable estimates for small areas. The SEDF does include enough observations to produce reliable direct measures of skill- and residence-specific labor market outcomes for small areas but is only available at ten-year intervals.

To consider how the available labor market data for small areas might be adapted to reflect local, skill-specific job opportunities, I first use the SEDF to examine where and in which industries employees with different skill levels work. Table 1 reports summary statistics from the SEDF on the percentages of women and men with different education levels that (a) work and live in the same county and (b) work in various industries. As the figures indicate, commuting and industry patterns vary substantially across gender and skill groups.

On average, men are more likely than women to travel beyond their county of residence to get to work. Commuting across counties also increases with the level of schooling. Women with the least schooling have the lowest tendency to

Table 1. Percentages of Employees Working in County of Residence and in Different Industries by Gender and Education, 1989.

Working in	Women			Men		
	Less than High School	High School or GED	College	Less than High School	High School or GED	College
County of residence	85.4	81.1	78.1	78.0	72.3	71.3
Agriculture	1.8	1.2	0.8	6.6	3.8	1.9
Mining	0.1	0.2	0.2	1.2	1.3	0.8
Construction	1.0	1.5	1.2	14.0	12.5	6.1
Manufacturing	21.3	16.5	8.8	24.3	27.1	19.4
Trans. and utilities	1.9	4.1	4.0	6.4	9.2	6.9
Wholesale trade	2.7	3.5	2.8	5.0	6.2	5.7
Retail trade	32.9	23.0	13.0	21.8	15.9	12.6
Finance, ins., real estate	3.3	9.9	9.9	1.6	2.4	7.5
Services	27.2	27.2	37.0	12.8	11.6	21.9
Federal government	1.2	2.9	3.6	1.0	2.9	4.7
State/local government	6.7	10.0	18.7	5.3	7.1	12.5

Note: Data for non-institutionalized, civilian workers aged 16–64 from SEDF. Calculations use sample weights from SEDF.

commute; nevertheless, a substantial number still do commute. Nearly one-sixth of women with less than a high school diploma and one-fifth of women with a diploma (or equivalent) but no college commute across counties.

Table 1 also indicates that the employment of women with low levels of schooling is concentrated in three industries: manufacturing, retail trade, and services. More than four-fifths of women with less than a high school diploma are employed in these three industries with nearly a third working in the low-paid retail sector. Among women with a high school diploma but no college, two-thirds work in these three industries. While manufacturing, retail trade, and services account for more than half the employment among low-skilled men, a fourth industry – construction – is also important. The "big three" also account for just over half of the employment of more-educated men and women; however, the concentrations within specific industries differ substantially from those for less-educated workers, and other sectors such as public service account for a large share of employment.

The observed differences in industry employment and commuting patterns support the study's earlier findings that general population-wide aggregates and simple within-county measures may not accurately describe employment opportunities within gender and skill groups. In the subsequent empirical analyses, I therefore consider several alternative measures.

The easiest and most direct measure to implement is the number of civilian jobs in each county and year divided by the population of working age adults. We have already seen that this measure has a number of shortcomings. Nevertheless, because of its convenience, the measure has been used by other researchers and can be viewed as a kind of methodological baseline.

I also use measures of industry-specific employment in each county and year divided by the population of working age adults. To the extent that the use of skilled labor varies across industries, these measures may pick up differences in demand for specific skill groups. Two shortcomings with these measures, however, are that they do not account for commuting patterns and they make it difficult to analyze the effects of general labor market shocks.

As a first cut at addressing the commuting problem, I use the inter-county journey-to-work data available from the REIS to reweight the total civilian and industry-specific employment measures. The REIS journey-to-work matrices were constructed using data from the 1990 Decennial Census. The chief advantages of these adjustments is that they are publicly-available and specific to each county. The downside is that they do not account for the differences in commuting patterns across skill groups evidenced in Table 1.

For purposes of comparison with earlier studies, I also group the county-level data into state and labor-market-area aggregates. Several labor market area (LMA) definitions are available, I use the areas defined by Tolbert and Sizer (1996), who grouped counties on the basis of commuting ties reported in the 1990 Decennial Census.[9] The state and LMA definitions are easier to work with than the REIS journey-to-work matrices; however, they provide a less accurate description of commuting patterns for individual counties.

Lastly, I take a more formal approach and combine annual county-level place-of-work industry employment information from the REIS with employment weights derived from the confidential information in the SEDF to form county-of-residence measures of skill-specific opportunities. The approach is similar to that developed by Bowen and Finegan (1969) and adopted in numerous subsequent manpower studies to map industry employment data to demographic, skill or occupation groups; to my knowledge, though, the procedure has not been used in research studies to account for commuting patterns or define geographic labor markets.

In particular, I obtain total employment in one-digit S.I.C. industries for each county from 1989 through 1997.[10] Let $E_{REIS}(j, c, t)$ denote the total number of employees in industry j ($=1, J$) in county c ($=1, C$) in year t derived from the REIS. To re-weight these data, let $e_{SEDF}(s, r, j, c)$ denote the fraction of employees in industry j and county c with skills s (the six combinations of gender and schooling) who commute from county r as estimated from the SEDF. I construct a skill- and residence-specific employment index for year t using the weighting formula

$$\hat{M}(s, r, t) = \sum_{j=1}^{J} \left(\sum_{c=1}^{C} e_{SEDF}(s, r, j, c) E_{REIS}(j, c, t) \right). \quad (1)$$

In the empirical analysis, I re-express this figure as a proportion of working adults by dividing through by the total population aged 15–64 in the county of residence.

PROBIT AND REGRESSION ANALYSES

I use the combined individual-level data from the SEDF and CPS linked with the local labor market and policy variables to estimate skill-specific employment probits of the form

$$Y^*(i, s, r, t) = \Gamma'_{1s} L(s, r, t) + \Gamma'_{2s} L(s, r, t-1) + \Gamma'_{Xs} X(i, s, r, t) + \theta_{st}$$
$$+ \pi_{sk} + \eta(i, s, r, t). \tag{2a}$$

$$\text{If } Y^*(i, s, r, t) > 0 \begin{cases} 1(\text{employed}) & \text{if } Y(i, s, r, t) > 0 \\ 0(\text{not employed}) & \text{otherwise} \end{cases} \tag{2b}$$

and log wage regressions of the form

$$\ln W(i, s, r, t) = B'_{1s} L(s, r, t) + B'_{2s} L(s, r, t-1) + B'_{Xs} X(i, s, r, t)$$
$$+ \delta_{st} + \mu_{sk} + \lambda(i, s, r, t) + \varepsilon(i, s, r, t). \tag{3}$$

In the equations, $Y^*(i, s, r, t)$ is a continuous latent variable for employment; $Y(i, s, r, t)$ is the actual binary employment outcome, and $W(i, s, r, t)$ denotes hourly or weekly wages. The right hand sides of the equations include the current and lagged value of the local, possibly skill-specific, local labor market conditions, $L(s, r, t)$, and a vector of other observed variables, $X(i, s, r, t)$. Each equation also includes controls for year-specific fixed effects, θ_{st} and δ_{st}, and area-specific fixed effects, π_{sk} and μ_{sk}. The terms $\eta(i, s, r, t)$ and $\varepsilon(i, s, r, t)$ are individual-specific errors, and $\lambda(i, s, r, t)$ is the inverse mills ratio, which is used to correct the log wage equation for selectivity from the employment decision. Following Heckman (1979), a two-stage approach is used in which coefficient estimates from the employment probit are used to form estimates of $\lambda(i, s, r, t)$.

The employment and wage specifications were selected after some experimentation and consideration of trade-offs. One trade-off involves the definition of the area-specific effects. The preferred approach would be to account for as much geographic heterogeneity as possible by including controls for all 3,105 counties and county-equivalents in the data set. This approach, however, led to a number of problems. First, most of the counties in the United States have relatively few residents – the population size for the median county is roughly 25,000 people. When the sample selection criteria were applied and the analysis data set was stratified, cell sizes for many of the counties became too small to provide reliable estimates of county-specific effects. Second, small cell sizes also increased the possibility of inadvertent disclosure of personal information. USC Title 13 prohibits the Census Bureau from releasing data where the responses of particular individuals can be identified. Third, including controls for all counties was computationally unwieldy. Although the county fixed effects could be conditioned out of certain analyses, they could not be conditioned out in others, and estimates of these effects were required for the imputations.

In light of these considerations, the analysis includes separate controls for each of the counties that had 1990 populations in excess of 35,000 people (1,132 counties). While this identifies only about a third of all counties, the included counties account for nearly 90% of the total U.S. population. For the remaining counties, the analysis includes controls for LMAs (Tolbert & Sizer, 1996) within states. In the cases where LMAs extend across state boundaries, the controls distinguish between the portions of LMAs in different states.[11] Altogether, the analysis accounts for 1,578 different areas: 1,132 individual counties and 446 balance-of-LMA-within-state areas. The sizes of the resulting cells are relatively large; the median stratified area cell (area × gender × schooling level) contains over 600 employment observations and over 400 wage observations. More than 99% of the stratified area cells contain at least 100 employment observations, and 96.5% have at least 100 wage observations. The smallest cell contains 16 employment observations and 10 wage observations.

Comparison of Specifications

Table 2 lists results from nine specifications of the annual employment probit model (2) that incorporate alternative controls for local labor market conditions and area effects. Each specification is estimated separately for women and men in each of the three schooling categories. The results for women appear in the first three columns; the results for men appear in the next three columns. In addition to the local labor market variables and area fixed effects, all of the specifications include controls for a quadratic in age, indicators for African, Hispanic, and other non-European origins, dummy variables for general time effects, and an indicator for whether the observation came from the SEDF or CPS files. To assess the "fit" of each specification, Table 2 lists the log likelihood value from the probit model. To assess substantive differences across the models, Table 2 also reports a summary value indicating the simulated effect (based on the model coefficients) of a change in local employment equal to the total change experienced by the area from 1989–1997.[12] These summary values are used because it is difficult to

Table 2. Employment Probit Results Using Alternative Labor Market Measures and Alternative Area Controls.

	Women			Men		
	W/o HS	With HS	College	W/o HS	With HS	College
Civilian Employment						
Simulated effect of 1989–1997 local emp. changes	0.008	0.008	0.003	0.006	0.005	0.004
Log likelihood (1596)	−601408.4	−1082861.6	−903825.3	−471425.1	−463483.7	−374870.5
Civilian employment adjusted using REIS journey-to-work data						
Simulated effect of 1989–1997 local emp. changes	0.008	0.007	0.003	0.006	0.004	0.003
Log likelihood (1596)	−601413.2	−1082873.1	−903831.6	−471428.3	−463486.1	−374872.3
Industry-specific employment						
Simulated effect of 1989–1997 local emp. changes	0.005	0.006	0.001	0.004	0.002	0.003
Log likelihood (1610)	−601353.9	−1082794.9	−903802.5	−471360.3	−463457.3	−374856.2
Industry-specific employment adjusted using REIS journey-to-work data						
Simulated effect of 1989–1997 local emp. changes	0.013	0.013	0.005	0.010	0.007	0.005
Log likelihood (1610)	−601265.3	−1082652.3	−903756.9	−471336.8	−463398.1	−374823.6
Industry-specific state-level employment						
Simulated effect of 1989–1997 local emp. changes	−0.011	−0.027	−0.020	−0.033	−0.018	−0.019
Log likelihood (1610)	−601475.6	−1082869.8	−903771.4	−471440.6	−463508.0	−374869.5
Industry-specific LMA-level employment						
Simulated effect of 1989–1997 local emp. changes	0.023	0.024	0.015	−0.037	0.006	0.001
Log likelihood (1610)	−601472.6	−1082851.4	−903763.1	−471441.6	−463482.8	−374865.6
SEDF-weighted employment						
Simulated effect of 1989–1997 local emp. changes	0.008	0.010	0.007	0.002	0.001	0.003
Log likelihood (1596)	−601361.5	−1082787.8	−903796.1	−471437.5	−463484.3	−374855.4
Industry-specific employment adjusted using REIS journey-to-work data (no area fixed effects)						
Simulated effect of 1989–1997 local emp. changes	0.021	0.017	0.008	0.013	0.007	0.007
Log likelihood (33)	−608433.8	−1090090.5	−907702.3	−478206.3	−468352.7	−377884.4
Industry-specific employment adjusted using REIS journey-to-work data (state fixed effects)						
Simulated effect of 1989–1997 local emp. changes	0.020	0.015	0.004	0.013	0.007	0.006
Log likelihood (83)	−605606.1	−1087552.7	−906577.0	−476325.6	−467162.0	−377204.1

Note: Data from combined SEDF and CPS files. In addition to the listed variables, all models included controls for age, age squared, African origin, Hispanic origin, other non-European origin, state minimum wages, state welfare benefit levels, a CPS indicator, time dummy variables and county/LMA dummy variables unless otherwise noted. The number of explanatory variables in each model appear in parentheses.

compare raw coefficients across different specifications of the probit model and assess net impacts in the specifications with many economic variables.

The first row in Table 2 reports results from models that include the current and lagged values of total civilian employment scaled by the working age adult population in each person's county of residence. The coefficients for the local employment variables (not shown) are jointly significant for most groups and imply positive net effects for all groups. For all groups, the simulated effects on annual employment are modest. For women, a change in local employment conditions equivalent to the change experienced from 1989–1997 (the average county experienced about a 6% increase in the employment rate) is estimated to increase the probability of employment by between 0.3% and 0.8%; for men, the effects range from 0.4% to 0.6%. For both men and women, the effects diminish with the level of schooling. When the civilian employment measures are reweighted using the REIS journey-to-work data (second row), the likelihood values for the models decrease but the simulation results are nearly identical.

The third row reports results from employment models that include current and lagged measures of industry-specific employment per working age adult in the county of residence (see Appendix A for a breakdown of the industries). These specifications nest the specifications from the first row as special cases. For every gender and schooling subgroup, specification tests indicate that the separate industry measures are jointly significant; thus, we can reject the earlier models that only include total employment. The estimated effects of an employment change are weaker than in the first model but again show that the effects generally diminish with schooling.

The results in the fourth row come from models that use the REIS journey-to-work data to reweight the industry-specific employment figures for commuting. These models nest the models from the second row as special cases. Likelihood ratio tests indicate that these models outperform the models from the second row. In fact, the likelihood values for these models are the highest of any of the models considered. The simulations indicate that individual employment is more sensitive to local labor market changes than was the case in the previous specifications. However, the size of the effects is still modest. As before, the effects are larger for women than for men and for those with less schooling than for those with more.

The next two rows report results from models that include current and lagged industry-specific employment aggregated up to the state level (row 5) and the LMA level (row 6) as controls for labor demand conditions. Both specifications lead to much lower likelihood values as well as to substantially different estimated effects.

The seventh row reports results from models that use current and lagged measures of the skill- and residence-specific employment index (1) to account for local labor demand conditions. The specifications generate likelihood values that are lower than the models from row 4 that use separate, commuting-adjusted employment measures and in two cases lower than the models with just the civilian employment measures.

The final two rows list results from specifications which include separate, commuting-adjusted employment measures but drop all of the area effects (row 8) or control only for state effects (row 9). Comparisons of the likelihoods between these models and those in row 4 indicate that the county/LMA controls are jointly significant. Comparisons of the simulated effects across specifications indicate that omitting county/LMA controls (as most previous research as done) generally makes individual employment appear more sensitive to local labor market changes.[13]

Table 3 reports results for a similar exercise involving the log hourly earnings regressions. For alternative specifications, R^2 statistics and simulated effects of a local employment change equal to the change that occurred in each area over the period 1989–1997 are reported. The log hourly earnings models in Table 3 have the same explanatory variables as the employment probits except that the earnings models omit controls for state welfare benefits and (unless otherwise noted) include an inverse mills ratio to account for selectivity.

When we look at the results for the first seven specifications, we see that the goodness-of-fit measures are remarkably close. Within gender and schooling subgroups, none of the fit statistics differs by more than 0.001. Because of the enormous sample sizes, it is possible to reject some specifications; however, this would not be possible with smaller, commonly-used data sets. The specifications that lead to the best fit are those with industry-specific employment measures at either the county level or adjusted to reflect county-specific commuting (rows 3 and 4). Combining these results with those from Table 2, I adopt the probit and regression models with the adjustments for county-specific commuting as my preferred specifications.

The results for the models with commuting-adjusted, industry-specific employment measures indicate that an increase in local employment leads to a modest positive increase in hourly earnings. The predicted increases range from 1.1 to 3.5% for women and 0.2 to 1.7% for men. The results indicate that women's earnings are more sensitive than men's earnings to changes in local employment conditions and that the sensitivity generally increases with education. The finding that the responsiveness of earnings to changes in local demand conditions rises with schooling runs counter to the findings of previous local labor market studies such as Topel (1986) and Bartik (1999); however, the finding is consistent with the wage structure studies of Katz and Murphy (1992) and Juhn et al. (1993). Similar patterns appear in the results for the models which just use total

Table 3. Log Hourly Earnings Regression Results Using Alternative Labor Market Measures.

	Women			Men		
	W/o HS	With HS	College	W/o HS	With HS	College
Civilian employment						
Simulated effect of 1989–1997 local emp. changes	0.011	0.018	0.014	0.003	0.004	0.007
R^2 (1596)	0.0998	0.1343	0.1365	0.1859	0.2128	0.2001
Civilian employment adjusted using REIS journey-to-work data						
Simulated effect of 1989–1997 local emp. changes	0.010	0.017	0.013	0.003	0.004	0.007
R^2 (1596)	0.0998	0.1343	0.1365	0.1859	0.2128	0.2001
Industry-specific employment						
Simulated effect of 1989–1997 local emp. changes	−0.003	0.011	0.004	−0.013	−0.006	0.007
R^2 (1610)	0.0999	0.1345	0.1366	0.1864	0.2134	0.2005
Industry-specific employment adjusted using REIS journey-to-work data						
Simulated effect of 1989–1997 local emp. changes	0.011	0.035	0.026	0.002	0.009	0.017
R^2 (1610)	0.1000	0.1345	0.1366	0.1863	0.2133	0.2003
Industry-specific state-level employment						
Simulated effect of 1989–1997 local emp. changes	0.078	−0.042	−0.062	0.062	0.031	0.006
R^2 (1610)	0.0998	0.1344	0.1366	0.1860	0.2129	0.2001
Industry-specific LMA-level employment						
Simulated effect of 1989–1997 local emp. changes	0.014	0.086	0.064	0.031	0.058	0.032
R^2 (1610)	0.0999	0.1344	0.1366	0.1861	0.2130	0.2001
SEDF-weighted employment						
Simulated effect of 1989–1997 local emp. changes	0.009	0.023	0.036	−0.001	0.000	0.009
R^2 (1596)	0.0997	0.1343	0.1365	0.1859	0.2128	0.2002
Industry-specific employment adjusted using REIS journey-to-work data (no selectivity corr.)						
Simulated effect of 1989–1997 local emp. changes	0.000	0.010	0.009	−0.003	0.006	0.015
R^2 (1609)	0.0999	0.1334	0.1350	0.1860	0.2128	0.2000
Industry-specific employment adjusted using REIS journey-to-work data (no area fixed effects)						
Simulated effect of 1989–1997 local emp. changes	0.068	0.094	0.083	0.056	0.045	0.056
R^2 (33)	0.0820	0.1163	0.1181	0.1632	0.1897	0.1789
Industry-specific employment adjusted using REIS journey-to-work data (state fixed effects)						
Simulated effect of 1989–1997 local emp. changes	0.059	0.072	0.061	0.040	0.035	0.053
R^2 (83)	0.0882	0.1247	0.1290	0.1739	0.2012	0.1891

Note: Data from combined SEDF and CPS files. In addition to the listed variables, all models included controls for age, age squared, African origin, Hispanic origin, other non-European origin, state minimum wages, a CPS indicator, time dummy variables, county/LMA dummy variables, and selectivity unless otherwise noted. The number of explanatory variables in each model appear in parentheses.

civilian employment (rows 1 and 2) and the models which use the skill- and residence-weighted employment index (row 7).

As with the employment probits, the use of state- and LMA-level aggregates leads to poorer fits and substantively different results. For instance, the models with state aggregates (row 5) suggest that local employment changes had relatively large positive effects for people with the least amount of schooling and smaller or negative effects for people with more schooling. The fit statistics for the models are also worse, and the estimated impacts, larger when area fixed effects are omitted (row 9) and when state dummies are used in place of the county/LMA effects (row 10). When the selectivity adjustment is omitted (row 8), the estimated effect of the local employment conditions becomes weaker.

The specifications from Table 3 were re-estimated using weekly earnings, rather than hourly earnings, as the dependent variable. Weekly earnings capture more of an element of labor supply than do hourly earnings. They may also provide a better indication of the availability of full-time work. Despite these differences, the estimation results for the weekly earnings regressions were very similar to the results shown in Table 3.

Detailed Estimation Results

Table 4 lists coefficient estimates and standard errors from the preferred specifications of the employment probit model. The first eight rows contain the coefficients for the current, industry-specific, commuting-adjusted, local employment measures. The next eight rows contain the coefficients for the lagged values of these employment measures.

The results indicate that different industries contribute in different ways to the individual employment outcomes of men and women with different schooling levels. For women who did not complete high school, current manufacturing, finance, insurance and real estate employment and lagged government employment are estimated to have significant positive effects on the probability of working. For women who finished high school, current manufacturing and service and lagged retail employment are estimated to have significant positive effects while lagged mining and construction employment is estimated to have a significant negative effect. For women who completed at least some college, the coefficients on current government and lagged transportation, utility, wholesale trade, and retail trade employment are significantly positive. For men who did not finish high school, current mining, construction, manufacturing, transportation, utility, and wholesale trade and lagged retail trade and government employment have significant positive coefficients while lagged mining, construction, and

Table 4. Detailed Employment Probit Results.

	Women			Men		
	W/o HS	With HS	College	W/o HS	With HS	College
Current mining & constr. employment in area	−0.030 (0.425)	0.402 (0.325)	0.556 (0.410)	1.298*** (0.466)	−0.007 (0.466)	1.573** (0.635)
Current manufacturing employment in area	0.855** (0.355)	0.735*** (0.278)	0.042 (0.367)	1.747*** (0.386)	0.795** (0.394)	0.947* (0.553)
Current trans., util. & WT employment in area	0.945 (0.661)	0.671 (0.467)	−0.467 (0.529)	2.019*** (0.747)	0.845 (0.648)	−0.022 (0.800)
Current retail trade employment in area	0.257 (0.801)	0.200 (0.574)	−0.219 (0.676)	−1.400 (0.869)	0.262 (0.822)	0.259 (0.970)
Current F. I.&R. E. employment in area	2.567* (1.445)	1.447 (0.990)	1.640 (1.059)	2.364 (1.612)	4.507*** (1.391)	3.177** (1.550)
Current service employment in area	0.600 (0.557)	0.853** (0.378)	0.161 (0.421)	−0.338 (0.604)	0.928* (0.550)	−0.209 (0.453)
Current government employment in area	−1.272 (0.980)	0.553 (0.711)	1.905** (0.838)	−1.650 (1.046)	1.258 (0.981)	−1.130 (1.214)
Current agricultural employment in area	0.065 (0.486)	0.043 (0.369)	−0.479 (0.422)	−0.683 (0.535)	−0.218 (0.525)	−0.079 (0.619)
Lagged mining & constr. employment in area	−0.082 (0.438)	−0.567* (0.339)	−0.590 (0.428)	−1.264*** (0.480)	0.439 (0.473)	−1.248* (0.639)
Lagged manufacturing employment in area	0.304 (0.360)	0.334 (0.282)	0.553 (0.372)	−0.780** (0.392)	0.251 (0.401)	0.103 (0.560)
Lagged trans., util. & WT employment in area	−0.282 (0.698)	−0.299 (0.494)	0.960* (0.570)	−0.165 (0.780)	1.418** (0.688)	2.230*** (0.856)
Lagged retail trade employment in area	1.209 (0.835)	1.224** (0.599)	1.208* (0.707)	1.862** (0.909)	0.038 (0.857)	0.273 (1.018)
Lagged F. I.&R. E. employment in area	0.393 (1.428)	0.778 (0.987)	−0.344 (1.048)	−0.084 (1.595)	−3.045** (1.378)	−1.865 (1.520)

County-Level Estimates of the Employment Prospects of Low-Skill Workers

Lagged service employment in area	−0.061 (0.580)	−0.316 (0.397)	0.092 (0.442)	0.778 (0.629)	0.604 (0.497)
Lagged government employment in area	2.549** (1.001)	0.766 (0.730)	−0.895 (0.861)	2.309** (1.069)	2.457** (1.247)
Lagged agricultural employment in area	0.188 (0.494)	0.193 (0.376)	0.544 (0.429)	0.883 (0.545)	0.318 (0.628)
Log maximum AFDC benefits	−0.256*** (0.093)	0.033 (0.066)	0.028 (0.063)	−0.299*** (0.103)	−0.034 (0.088)
Log minimum wage	0.329*** (0.072)	0.277*** (0.054)	0.082* (0.049)	−0.141* (0.083)	−0.085 (0.068)
Age	0.078*** (0.001)	0.058*** (0.001)	0.039*** (0.001)	0.112*** (0.001)	0.155*** (0.001)
Age squared (/100)	−0.113*** (0.001)	−0.098*** (0.001)	−0.078*** (0.001)	−0.159*** (0.001)	−0.218*** (0.001)
African origin	−0.182*** (0.004)	−0.138*** (0.004)	0.078*** (0.004)	−0.528*** (0.005)	−0.467*** (0.006)
Hispanic origin	−0.140*** (0.005)	−0.085*** (0.005)	−0.075*** (0.005)	0.130*** (0.006)	0.016** (0.008)
Other non-white origin	−0.080*** (0.005)	−0.176*** (0.005)	−0.258*** (0.005)	−0.143*** (0.006)	−0.373*** (0.006)
Observation from CPS	0.076* (0.040)	0.102*** (0.026)	0.010 (0.035)	0.061 (0.044)	0.032 (0.052)
Year = 1990	−0.053 (0.042)	−0.033 (0.028)	−0.001 (0.037)	−0.010 (0.047)	−0.036 (0.054)
Year = 1991	−0.102** (0.044)	−0.057* (0.029)	0.009 (0.037)	−0.077 (0.048)	−0.114** (0.055)
Year = 1992	−0.146*** (0.044)	−0.057* (0.029)	0.011 (0.037)	−0.123** (0.049)	−0.165*** (0.055)
Year = 1993	−0.180*** (0.045)	−0.062** (0.030)	0.007 (0.038)	−0.263*** (0.050)	−0.255*** (0.055)

Table 4. (Continued)

	Women			Men		
	W/o HS	With HS	College	W/o HS	With HS	College
Year = 1994	−0.121***	−0.057*	0.025	−0.291***	−0.316***	−0.179***
	(0.046)	(0.030)	(0.038)	(0.050)	(0.044)	(0.056)
Year = 1995	−0.142***	−0.050	0.029	−0.286***	−0.323***	−0.226***
	(0.047)	(0.031)	(0.039)	(0.052)	(0.045)	(0.057)
Year = 1996	−0.154***	−0.035	0.021	−0.258***	−0.352***	−0.202***
	(0.049)	(0.033)	(0.040)	(0.054)	(0.047)	(0.058)
Year = 1997	−0.146***	−0.078**	0.015	−0.288***	−0.400***	−0.201***
	(0.052)	(0.035)	(0.041)	(0.057)	(0.050)	(0.060)
Log likelihood	−601265.3	−1082652.3	−903756.9	−471336.8	−463398.1	−374823.6
Observations	935122	1816643	1923289	888709	1506564	1799603

Note: Data from combined SEDF and CPS files. Local employment variables weighted to reflect commuting patterns using REIS journey-to-work data. All models also include county/LMA dummy variables. Standard errors appear in parentheses.

* Significant at 0.10 level.
** Significant at 0.05 level.
*** Significant at 0.01 level.

manufacturing employment have significant negative coefficients. For men who completed high school, current manufacturing, finance, insurance, real estate, and service and lagged transportation, utility, and wholesale trade employment have significant positive coefficients, and lagged finance, insurance, and real estate employment has a significant negative coefficient. For men with more schooling, the coefficients on current mining, construction, manufacturing, finance, insurance, and real estate and lagged transportation, utility, wholesale trade, and government employment are significantly positive, while the coefficient on lagged mining and construction is significantly negative. In most cases where there are positive and negative coefficients on current and lagged employment measures from the same industry, the net (long-term) effects are positive.

In the next row in Table 4, the estimated coefficient on the log of AFDC benefits is significantly negative for women (elasticity −0.23) and men who did not complete high school (elasticity −0.14) and for men who completed high school (elasticity −0.06) and close to zero for more-educated men and women. For less-educated women, the finding of negative effects is consistent with theory. For men, the negative results might reflect the effects of the AFDC-UP program or the effects of AFDC acting as a substitute for their own child support payments.

The next row lists coefficients from the log minimum wage variable. The coefficients are significantly positive for women in each schooling category (elasticities range from 0.30 to 0.03) as well as for men who completed high school (elasticity 0.10) but significantly negative for men who did not completed high school (elasticity −0.07). The positive coefficients are unexpected but not unprecedented (see, e.g. Card & Krueger, 1995). The results are, of course, consistent with the predicted effect of the minimum wage on labor supply. The lack of a strong labor demand response may reflect the study's use of an annual employment measure rather than a weekly measure; the demand effects might be more prominent if employment were examined along another margin.[14] The results also suggest that increases in the minimum wage lead to a substitution of female and higher-skilled male labor for low-skilled male labor.

The next five rows contain the coefficients for the age, race and ethnicity variables. The results for these variables are consistent with expectations and previous research. Employment increases initially with age then decreases. Employment is mostly lower for men and women of African and other non-European, non-Hispanic origins than for those of European origin. The coefficients for African men are particularly strong. The coefficients are also negative for Hispanic women as well as for Hispanic men who completed high school; however, the coefficient is positive for Hispanic men who did not complete high school.

The remaining rows list coefficients from a dummy variable indicating whether the observation came from the CPS rather than the SEDF and dummy variables for specific years of data. The CPS/SEDF sample dummy is included to capture systematic differences in reporting between the different surveys. The coefficient is identified because there are overlapping observations from the 1990 CPS and the SEDF. The estimates indicate that the CPS recorded slightly higher (1–4%) employment rates for people with a high school education or less than did the SEDF.

The coefficients on the time dummies indicate that, conditional on other economic and demographic changes, employment fell for less-educated women until about 1993, recovered slightly after that, then fell again. By 1997, the drop in conditional employment for women who did not finish high school was 6%, while the drop for those who completed high school was closer to 3%. For men, the declines over time in conditional employment were steeper. The coefficients indicate that conditional employment was 10% lower in 1997 than in 1989 for men who did not finish high school, 8% lower for men who only completed high school, and 3% lower for men with at least some college.

Table 5 reports coefficient estimates and heteroskedasticity-consistent standard errors for the preferred specifications of the log hourly earnings regressions. As with the previous table, the first eight rows list coefficients for the current, industry-specific, local employment measures, and the next eight rows list coefficients for the lagged local employment measures. The results indicate that there are numerous significant employment coefficients; thus, the local employment measures provide some explanatory power. Like the employment probit results, the size and direction of the effects varies across subgroups.

Hourly wages among less-educated workers are estimated to be more sensitive to changes in the minimum wage. The minimum wage coefficients are all significantly positive with elasticities that range from 0.08 to 0.36. Consistent with expectations, the estimated effects of the minimum wage decrease with skill level. When these coefficients are combined with the mostly positive estimates from the employment probits, the results indicate that increases in the minimum wage benefit women and high-school-educated men by both encouraging and rewarding work. For men who did not complete high school, the net effects still appear to be positive as the large positive earnings results outweigh the modest negative employment results.

Among the other variables in the hourly earnings regressions, age has a significantly positive coefficient, and age squared has a significantly negative coefficient for all six groups. The coefficients for the racial and ethnic minority indicators are all significantly negative and in many cases large. The estimated effects of African origin on men's wages are especially strong; the coefficients imply wage reductions of 24–29%.

The coefficients on the sample dummy indicate that the calculated wages for women and men who did not complete high school are 10–12% lower in the CPS

Table 5. Detailed Log Hourly Earnings Regression Results.

	Women			Men		
	W/o HS	With HS	College	W/o HS	With HS	College
Current mining & constr. employment in area	−0.099	0.234	0.324**	0.231	−0.188	0.097
	(0.254)	(0.159)	(0.157)	(0.211)	(0.142)	(0.150)
Current manufacturing employment in area	0.420*	0.251**	−0.413***	−0.260	−0.408***	−0.402***
	(0.223)	(0.121)	(0.133)	(0.173)	(0.113)	(0.124)
Current trans., util. & WT employment in area	0.613*	0.515***	−0.594***	0.651**	0.139	0.115
	(0.343)	(0.185)	(0.170)	(0.283)	(0.169)	(0.166)
Current retail trade employment in area	−0.756	−0.626**	−0.839***	0.453	−0.919***	0.048
	(0.489)	(0.259)	(0.270)	(0.402)	(0.241)	(0.260)
Current F. I.&R. E. employment in area	2.491***	1.423***	1.066***	0.573	0.175	0.791*
	(0.926)	(0.451)	(0.443)	(0.766)	(0.423)	(0.411)
Current service employment in area	−0.070	0.538***	0.373**	0.322	0.169	0.013
	(0.325)	(0.167)	(0.162)	(0.265)	(0.151)	(0.123)
Current government employment in area	−1.047*	0.180	0.932***	−1.433***	−0.306	−1.019***
	(0.598)	(0.326)	(0.338)	(0.478)	(0.309)	(0.319)
Current agricultural employment in area	1.255***	1.399***	0.315*	1.167***	1.390***	1.463***
	(0.309)	(0.175)	(0.187)	(0.254)	(0.169)	(0.178)
Lagged mining & constr. employment in area	0.128	−0.178	−0.242	0.220	0.747***	0.300*
	(0.267)	(0.169)	(0.167)	(0.217)	(0.146)	(0.155)
Lagged manufacturing employment in area	0.368*	0.728***	1.074***	0.677***	0.862***	0.796***
	(0.213)	(0.121)	(0.136)	(0.171)	(0.114)	(0.126)
Lagged trans., util. & WT employment in area	−0.413	−0.224	1.135***	0.265	0.771***	0.599***
	(0.360)	(0.199)	(0.192)	(0.301)	(0.185)	(0.184)
Lagged retail trade employment in area	1.492***	1.495***	1.440***	−0.320	0.878***	−0.067
	(0.520)	(0.272)	(0.283)	(0.418)	(0.251)	(0.272)
Lagged F. I.&R. E. employment in area	−0.194	1.316***	1.228***	0.580	0.352	−0.127
	(0.917)	(0.456)	(0.444)	(0.771)	(0.430)	(0.418)
Lagged service employment in area	0.153	−0.042	0.048	−0.318	−0.007	0.316**
	(0.341)	(0.174)	(0.172)	(0.277)	(0.159)	(0.135)
Lagged government employment in area	1.723***	1.017***	0.274	1.289***	0.276	1.458***
	(0.643)	(0.335)	(0.344)	(0.489)	(0.317)	(0.328)
Lagged agricultural employment in area	−1.187***	−1.290***	−0.266	−1.283***	−1.507***	−1.483***
	(0.314)	(0.178)	(0.190)	(0.258)	(0.172)	(0.181)
Log minimum wage	0.364***	0.298***	0.149***	0.332***	0.243***	0.077***
	(0.064)	(0.036)	(0.027)	(0.048)	(0.035)	(0.025)
Age	0.060***	0.088***	0.113***	0.082***	0.097***	0.107***
	(0.007)	(0.002)	(0.002)	(0.003)	(0.001)	(0.001)
Age squared (/100)	−0.071***	−0.118***	−0.156***	−0.089***	−0.107***	−0.113***
	(0.010)	(0.004)	(0.003)	(0.004)	(0.002)	(0.002)
African origin	−0.095***	−0.157***	−0.025***	−0.290***	−0.257***	−0.237***
	(0.018)	(0.006)	(0.004)	(0.015)	(0.008)	(0.005)
Hispanic origin	−0.155***	−0.117***	−0.171***	−0.134***	−0.077***	−0.105***
	(0.015)	(0.008)	(0.007)	(0.008)	(0.008)	(0.006)
Other non-white origin	−0.074***	−0.202***	−0.288***	−0.135***	−0.160***	−0.151***
	(0.012)	(0.010)	(0.010)	(0.008)	(0.008)	(0.006)
Observation from CPS	−0.099***	0.014**	−0.018***	−0.118***	−0.039***	−0.030***
	(0.013)	(0.006)	(0.006)	(0.009)	(0.006)	(0.005)
Year = 1990	−0.042***	−0.043***	−0.020**	−0.048***	−0.060***	−0.038***
	(0.016)	(0.008)	(0.008)	(0.013)	(0.008)	(0.007)
Year = 1991	−0.062***	−0.087***	−0.043***	−0.102***	−0.121***	−0.088***
	(0.018)	(0.009)	(0.008)	(0.014)	(0.009)	(0.008)
Year = 1992	−0.049**	−0.075***	−0.038***	−0.101***	−0.133***	−0.102***
	(0.020)	(0.009)	(0.008)	(0.014)	(0.009)	(0.008)
Year = 1993	−0.091***	−0.074***	−0.032***	−0.117***	−0.132***	−0.115***
	(0.021)	(0.009)	(0.008)	(0.015)	(0.009)	(0.008)

Table 5. (*Continued*)

	Women			Men		
	W/o HS	With HS	College	W/o HS	With HS	College
Year = 1994	−0.043***	−0.059***	−0.020**	−0.088***	−0.126***	−0.108***
	(0.019)	(0.009)	(0.008)	(0.015)	(0.009)	(0.008)
Year = 1995	−0.056***	−0.069***	−0.009	−0.099***	−0.132***	−0.112***
	(0.019)	(0.009)	(0.008)	(0.016)	(0.009)	(0.008)
Year = 1996	−0.062***	−0.065***	−0.018**	−0.137***	−0.145***	−0.112***
	(0.020)	(0.009)	(0.009)	(0.016)	(0.010)	(0.008)
Year = 1997	−0.088***	−0.070***	−0.010	−0.129***	−0.144***	−0.092***
	(0.020)	(0.011)	(0.009)	(0.016)	(0.010)	(0.009)
λ	0.491***	1.280***	2.004***	0.347***	0.368***	0.327***
	(0.139)	(0.066)	(0.075)	(0.053)	(0.033)	(0.033)
R^2	0.1000	0.1345	0.1366	0.1863	0.2133	0.2003
Observations	403318	1212107	1534728	634847	1348381	1679239

Note: Data from combined SEDF and CPS files. All models also include county/LMA dummy variables. Standard errors appear in parentheses.
*Significant at 0.10 level.
**Significant at 0.05 level.
***Significant at 0.01 level.

than in the SEDF. There are also statistically significant, though substantively smaller, differences between the samples for other groups of men and women. The results suggest that there are systematic differences in the ways that data are reported in the CPS and SEDF, especially for people with low levels of schooling. While I cannot be sure of the exact cause of the differences, a likely candidate is misreporting in the SEDF.

As with the employment probits, the time dummies in the wage regressions generate a downward trend. Conditional wages for all six groups fell through the early 1990s then began to recover. For less-educated men and women, conditional wages dropped again toward the middle of the 1990s. The results are consistent with previous findings of declining wages for less-educated men and women over this period.

One additional result that deserves some discussion is the relatively weak fit of the regressions, especially the three regressions for women. Although low R^2 statistics are common in regressions such as these with limited controls for skills and abilities, one might expect the inclusion of detailed area effects to lead to a better fit. Given that the combination of area effects, time effects, and local employment variables captures much of the possible market-level variation, the weak fit statistics suggest that short-term fluctuations in general market conditions play only a modest role in determining individual wage outcomes and that personal characteristics are more prominent.

EMPLOYMENT AND WAGE IMPUTATIONS

A key objective of this study is to generate estimates of employment and earnings outcomes in individual counties over time. As a first step in analyzing the properties of these estimates, the study uses the results from Tables 4 and 5 along with the county-level data from the REIS and the state-level policy variables to impute annual employment rates and hourly earnings over all counties from 1989–1997. To abstract from demographic differences across areas, it fixes the age and racial/ethnic background and imputes labor market outcomes for a representative person with given set of characteristics.

Figures 5 and 6 graph trends from 1989–1997 in the average imputed employment and wage rates for 30-year-old, non-Hispanic, whites. Separate trends are shown for women and men in each schooling category. To approximate national population estimates, the annual averages are weighted by the number of working-age adults in each county.

From Fig. 5, the imputed employment rates in each year were higher for men than for women and higher for people who completed high school than for those who did not. Employment probabilities among men declined over the period, with the least-educated men experiencing the sharpest declines. Among women who did not complete high school, employment probabilities dipped during the early 1990s and then rebounded to about their initial 1989 level. For women with more schooling, the trend in employment probabilities was flat.

The graphs in Fig. 6 depict the trends in imputed hourly wages based on the models from Table 5 that adjust for employment selectivity. The graphs show that predicted wages for women are very low, not just relative to men but also in absolute terms. For women who did not complete high school, the selectivity-corrected estimates are so low that the averages actually fall below the federal minimum wage in several years.

The low wage estimates for women give rise to the question – are the selectivity-corrected estimates reasonable? The selectivity adjustments are included to make the wage measures representative for the general population rather than just those who work. If people choose their employment status by comparing their available market wage with their reservation wage, we would expect the average market wage for all people to be lower than the average for workers. The observed controls in the regressions account for some of the differences in the wages available to workers and non-workers; the selectivity procedure adjusts for bias from the remaining, unobserved differences.

The magnitude of the underlying bias, and hence the impact of the correction, depends on the amount of selection and the strength of the relationship between the unobserved determinants of employment and wages. Several of the requirements

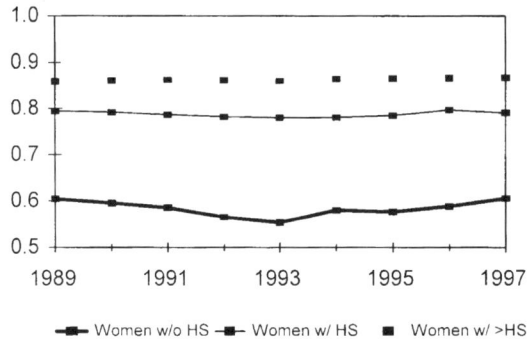

Predicted employment: 1989-97 Women

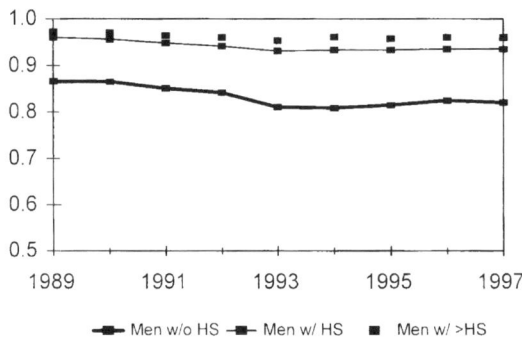

Predicted employment: 1989-97 Men

Fig. 5

Trends in Imputed Employment. *Note:* Figures based on population-weighted averages across counties using probit coefficients from Table 4 calculated for 30-year-old, non-Hispanic, whites.

for a large correction are present in the sample. First, there is a great deal of selection – wages are not observed for more than half of women who did not complete high school, a third of women who only finished high school, and a fifth of women who went on to college. Second, some research suggests that women's employment is more sensitive than men's to wage changes (Killingsworth & Heckman, 1986) and thus more sensitive to differences in unobserved wage characteristics.[15] Third, the unobserved determinants of wages among non-working women may be especially low due to a lack of work experience or interrupted job histories. Compensating differentials associated with jobs that accommodate household responsibilities such as child care might be another unmeasured factor.

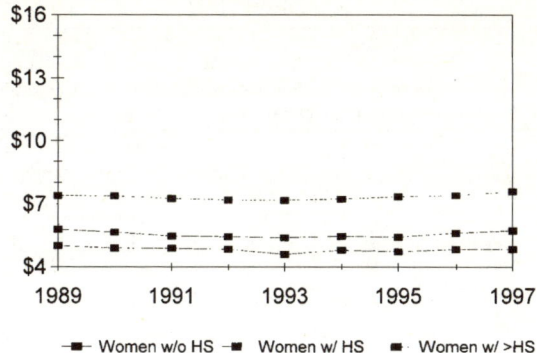

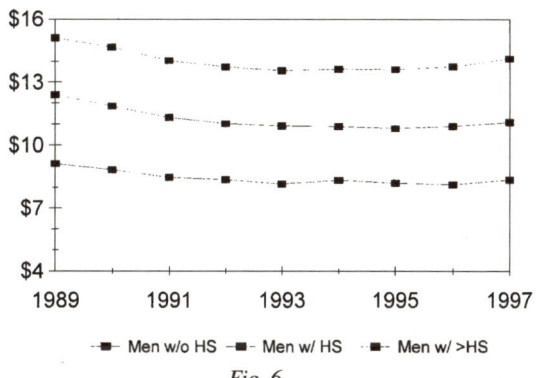

Fig. 6

Trends in Imputed Wage Measures. *Note:* Figures based on population-weighted averages across counties using regression coefficients from Table 5 calculated for 30-year-old, non-Hispanic, whites.

The graphs in Fig. 6 show that imputed hourly wages for men declined over the period 1989–1997 while hourly wages for women remained relatively flat. The difference between the 1989 and 1997 selectivity-adjusted wages was about 80¢ (8%) for men who did not complete high school, about $1.30 (10%) for men who completed high school, and about $1.00 (7%) for men with more schooling. For women who did not complete high school, selectivity-adjusted wages fell by 16¢, while for women with at least some college, selectivity-adjusted wages rose by 20¢.

We can also examine the cross-section variation in the data. Tables 6 and 7 show how the imputed employment and wage outcomes were distributed across counties.

Table 6. Distribution of Imputed Employment Outcomes Across Counties: 1997.

	Women			Men		
	Did not Complete HS	Completed High School	Completed Some College	Did not Complete HS	Completed High School	Completed Some College
Mean	0.60	0.79	0.87	0.82	0.94	0.96
95th percentile	0.75	0.88	0.92	0.92	0.98	0.98
90th percentile	0.72	0.86	0.91	0.90	0.97	0.98
75th percentile	0.67	0.84	0.89	0.87	0.96	0.97
50th percentile	0.62	0.80	0.87	0.83	0.95	0.96
25th percentile	0.55	0.76	0.84	0.78	0.93	0.95
10th percentile	0.47	0.71	0.82	0.72	0.90	0.93
5th percentile	0.41	0.67	0.80	0.68	0.88	0.92

Note: Figures calculated using probit coefficients from Table 4 calculated for 30-year-old, non-Hispanic, whites.

Table 6 lists predicted employment in 1997 for the average county and for different percentiles in the distribution of counties.[16] As in the previous figures, estimates are reported assuming a representative 30-year-old, non-Hispanic white. Table 7 reports a similar set of statistics for imputed, selectivity-adjusted hourly wages.

The results from Table 6 reveal that the geographic distribution of employment outcomes was wider for people who did not complete high school than for those who did. The distribution also varied more for women than for men. The employment rate for 30-year-old, non-Hispanic, white women who did not complete high school was 41% in the county at the 5th percentile, 62% in the median county, and 75% in the county at the 95th percentile. These figures compare to employment rates of 80% at the 5th percentile, 87% at the median, and 92% at the 95th percentile for 30-year-old, non-Hispanic, white women who went

Table 7. Distribution of Imputed Hourly Earnings Outcomes Across Counties: 1997.

	Women			Men		
	Did not Complete HS	Completed High School	Completed Some College	Did not Complete HS	Completed High School	Completed Some College
Mean	4.24	4.80	6.25	7.41	9.92	11.91
95th percentile	5.60	6.65	8.50	9.60	12.32	15.28
90th percentile	5.20	6.21	7.84	8.88	11.65	14.14
75th percentile	4.63	5.40	6.90	8.00	10.65	12.78
50th percentile	4.16	4.68	6.09	7.20	9.73	11.62
25th percentile	3.74	4.11	5.38	6.62	8.93	10.68
10th percentile	3.40	3.58	4.82	6.12	8.28	9.95
5th percentile	3.15	3.23	4.50	5.84	7.86	9.53

Note: Figures calculated using regression coefficients from Table 5 calculated for 30-year-old, non-Hispanic, whites.

on to college and employment rates of 92, 96, and 98% for men with at least some college.

Table 7 shows how wages varied across different groups and across counties. As with the employment results, there was a substantial amount of heterogeneity in the imputed wage outcomes. The estimates paint a bleak picture for less-educated workers and indicate that the average wage opportunities were very low. In 1997, the poverty threshold for a family of three (in constant 1998 dollars) was roughly $13,000. Ignoring taxes and transfers, a full-time, full-year job would have to pay about $6.50/hour to generate this much income. For women who did not complete high school, the computed wages were below the poverty level in 98% of the counties. Most counties (more than 90%) also offered below-poverty wages for women who completed high school. Among men who did not complete high school, average wages were computed to be below the poverty level in just under 25% of counties.

The low wage levels in Table 7 help to explain why employment and wages were found to be so sensitive to minimum wage changes in the econometric analyses. The estimates from Table 7 imply that state and federal minimum wages are higher than the wages that would otherwise be available to many low-skill people. The findings contrast with previous results which suggest that few people are directly or meaningfully affected by the minimum wage (see, e.g. Neumark et al., 1998). The difference in findings stems from the fact that most previous research has only compared the minimum wage to the wages of workers, not the wider population of workers and non-workers.[17]

The estimation results can also be used to examine how employment and earnings changed within counties over time. Table 8 lists the percentage of counties in which estimated employment probabilities for 30-year-old, non-Hispanic,

Table 8. Changes in Imputed Employment Outcomes Across Counties: 1989–1997.

	Women			Men		
	Did not Complete HS	Completed High School	Completed Some College	Did not Complete HS	Completed High School	Completed Some College
Fell over 5%	1.8	0.5	0.1	40.6	3.7	0.1
Fell 1–5%	19.2	17.4	1.1	56.7	85.4	55.5
Fell 0–1%	11.4	18.4	4.5	1.7	10.4	42.6
Grew 0–1%	16.1	25.6	28.3	0.6	0.4	1.6
Grew 1–5%	45.3	37.2	65.7	0.2	0.1	0.2
Grew over 5%	6.2	0.9	0.4	0.1	0.0	0.0

Note: Figures are percentages of counties in each category. The figures are calculated using probit coefficients from Table 4 calculated for 30-year-old, non-Hispanic, whites.

Table 9. Changes in Imputed Hourly Earnings Outcomes Across Counties: 1989–1997.

	Women			Men		
	Did not Complete HS	Completed High School	Completed Some College	Did not Complete HS	Completed High School	Completed Some College
Fell over 5%	11.0	7.9	1.9	60.5	86.5	49.4
Fell 1–5%	20.6	11.5	3.8	33.7	11.8	41.9
Fell 0–1%	9.4	5.3	2.7	2.1	0.7	3.6
Grew 0–1%	9.4	5.7	3.4	1.4	0.3	1.7
Grew 1–5%	33.5	29.7	24.2	1.7	0.5	2.5
Grew over 5%	16.1	39.9	64.0	0.5	0.3	0.9

Note: Figures are percentages of counties in each category. The figures are calculated using regression coefficients from Table 5 calculated for 30-year-old, non-Hispanic, whites.

whites increased or decreased over the period 1989–1997. The table distinguishes between large changes (over 5%), moderate changes (1 to 5%), and small changes (less than 1%) in each direction.

Table 8 shows that there was a lot of variation in employment growth patterns across counties, especially for women. For women who did not complete high school, employment probabilities increased in about two thirds of the counties and decreased in the remaining third.[18] The split between growing and declining counties was similar for women who completed high school, but more of the distribution was concentrated in counties that experienced small changes. For women with more education, employment rates increased in most counties. For men, employment decreased in most counties.

Table 9 reports similar statistics for wage changes. As with the employment results, the distribution of wage changes also varied across counties. For women, there were many counties where wages declined as well as many where wages grew. For men, wage opportunities declined in most counties. For both groups, wage growth was relatively worse on average for people with less schooling. Tables 8 and 9 clearly show that national time-series trends fail to capture the wide variation in growth patterns in local labor markets.

To get a sense of the detailed results for different local markets, I examine employment and wage outcomes for a handful of individual counties. Figure 7 shows how imputed employment rates for less-educated men and women changed across six selected counties over the period 1989–1997. The figure includes two large urban counties/areas, the District of Columbia (1990 population 604,000) and Los Angeles County (population 8,876,000), two counties with medium size cities, Linn County in Iowa (population 169,000, contains Cedar Rapids) and Ohio County in West Virginia (population 51,000, contains Wheeling), and two counties with medium population sizes but no major cities, Monroe

County in Pennsylvania (population 97,000, largest city East Stroudsburg) and Mississippi County in Arkansas (population 58,000, largest city Osceola). The counties were selected from different regions and indicate the types of counties that are uniquely identified in the analysis data set. As with the previous figures and tables, outcomes are imputed for 30-year-olds of non-Hispanic, European origin.

Figure 7 reconfirms that both the levels and trends in different types of employment varied greatly across and within counties and that strong employment

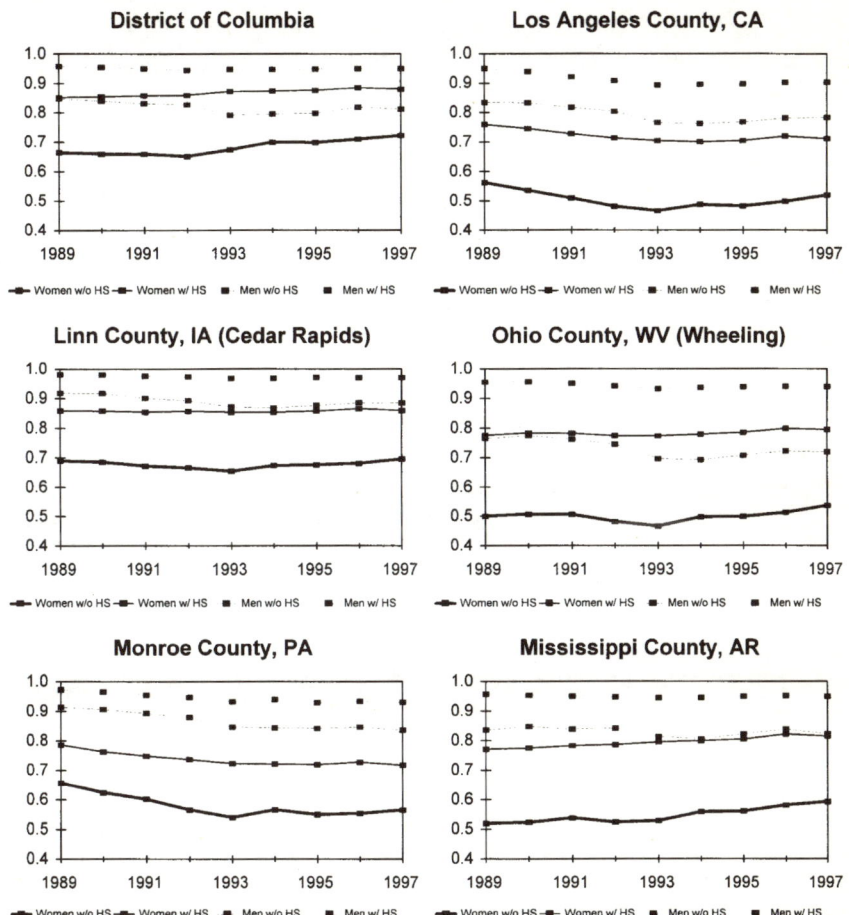

Fig. 7. Trends in Imputed Employment for Selected Counties.

conditions for one group in an area did not necessarily imply strong conditions for all groups. For instance, the levels and trends in low-skill men's employment in the District of Columbia were near the national averages; however, the levels of women's employment were higher than average, and women's employment in the District trended upward over time, rather than downward. In contrast, Los Angeles is an example of a county where employment for all groups was uniformly lower and dropped more sharply than the national average.

In Linn County, low-skill employment was higher than the national average and remained relatively constant over the period. In Ohio County, employment

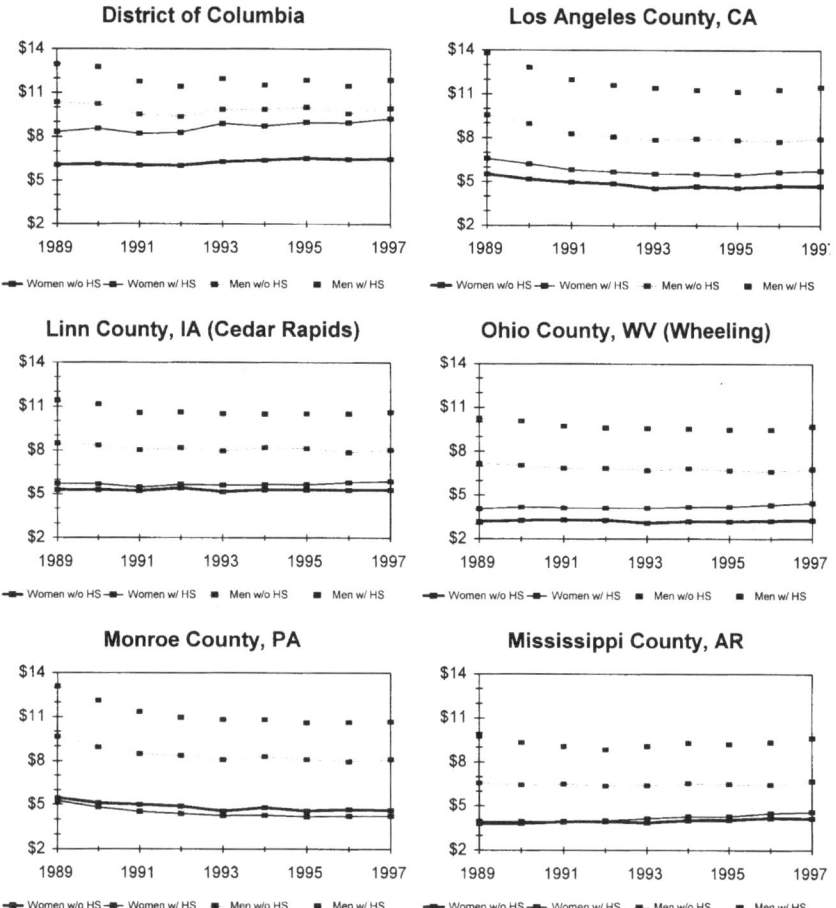

Fig. 8. Trends in Imputed Wages for Selected Counties.

among people who finished high school was slightly below average; however, employment among those who did not finish school was much lower than average. In Monroe County, low-skill employment rates were initially higher than the national rates in 1989 but converged toward the national rates over the next eight years by falling more sharply than the national average. Low-skill employment rates also converged toward the national average in Mississippi County but from different starting points – rates were lower in 1989 and grew more (or fell less) than the national average.

Figure 8 shows the trends in imputed, selectivity-adjusted hourly wages for the same groups and counties. Once again, the outcomes varied greatly across areas. In the District of Columbia, low-skill wages were higher than average in 1989. Wages for low-skill men fell, but not as much as the national average, and wages for low-skill women actually rose. In Los Angeles, low-skill wages were also initially higher than average but fell more sharply than the national trend.

In the other four counties, there were some differences from the national levels. Wages were slightly higher than average in Monroe County, slightly lower than average in Linn County, and much lower than average in Ohio County and Mississippi County. Nevertheless, the trends in low-skill wages in these four counties over time were very similar to the national trends.

CONCLUSION

This study employed a variety of data and methods to examine wage and employment opportunities for low-skill men and women over the period 1989–1997. Specifically, it combined individual-level data from the SEDF and different years of the CPS with the county-level employment measures and estimated econometric models of employment and wage outcomes for men and women with different levels of schooling. After comparing results from several alternative specifications, estimates from a set of preferred specifications were used to impute wage and employment rates for adults with different schooling levels across counties and over time. The analysis leads to several important substantive and methodological conclusions.

First, *the study shows that the proper geographic definition of a local labor market is approximately the county level.* Previous research has greatly strained the definition of "local" and relied on employment and wage data that are aggregated across large areas such as states and major metropolitan areas. The study's initial graphical analyses showed that employment and wage outcomes vary greatly from county to county, even within the same state or MSA. Other descriptive analyses demonstrated that most workers also live and work in the same county;

this is especially true of women and workers with low-levels of schooling. In the multivariate analyses, models with county-level economic measures performed better than models with state-level measures. Also, county/LMA fixed effects were more effective in accounting for unobserved heterogeneity than state fixed effects. Not only were the models that used narrower geographic definitions better, but they also led to substantively different estimates of the impact of local economic changes.

Second, *employment and wage trends within local markets differ according to skill level – accounting for gender and schooling differences matters*. Local markets that offer good opportunities to some types of workers do not necessarily offer good opportunities to other types. The analysis showed that there were counties where employment conditions for men were relatively strong while opportunities for women were relatively weak and vice versa. It also showed that there were areas where conditions were relatively strong for people who completed high school but weak for people who did not and vice versa. There were many areas where conditions for one skill group improved while conditions for other groups deteriorated. General employment statistics aggregated over different types of people do not capture this heterogeneity.

Third, *despite the aggregate growth in the economy, employment conditions remained very weak for less-educated workers in certain parts of the country*. Imputations based on the employment and wage models indicated that outcomes across different areas were very heterogenous. In the bottom tail of the distribution, employment and wage rates were extremely low. In many counties, the wages that less-educated men and women could expect to receive were well below the level needed to escape poverty.

Fourth, *the wages available to men and to women with low levels of schooling continued to decline over the 1990s*. Estimates from the study's models indicate that wages available to men declined noticeably over the period 1989–1997 in most parts of the country. Wages for women with low levels of schooling declined slightly on average and quite substantially in many counties.

Fifth, *changes in local employment conditions lead to only modest changes in less-educated men and women's employment and earnings*. Results from the preferred econometric models indicate that a one-year change in local employment conditions equivalent to the entire change experienced from 1989–1997 would increase less-educated men's employment by just under 1% and women's employment by just over 1%. A similar change in local employment conditions would increase less-educated men's hourly earnings by less than 1% and less-educated women's hourly earnings by about 1% to 3.5%. The estimation results indicate that the sensitivity of individual employment to local employment changes decreases with schooling while the sensitivity of hourly earnings increases with schooling.

Sixth, *increases in the minimum wage appear to be mostly beneficial*. Because the wages that low-skill individuals could command are so paltry in so many areas, there is a sizeable population that might not only see their available wages increase if the minimum were raised, but see wages increase by a great deal. Estimates from the study's models indicate that such an increase would encourage more low-skill people to work.

The primary goals of this study were to capture the detailed local labor market information available from the 1990 Decennial Census, to extrapolate from that baseline and approximate conditions in later years, and to analyze the resulting estimates. In the next few years, new micro-data will be directly available from the 2000 Decennial Census and thereafter from the American Community Survey. Once the ACS is on-line, it will be possible to examine annual local labor market conditions without extrapolating the data. There will still, however, be a need for inter-censal estimates for earlier years. Future work will consider how the 2000 Census and ACS can be combined with the existing data to improve the inter-censal estimates.

NOTES

1. Maps of relative employment among working-age men with different schooling levels (not shown) are very similar to those for women.

2. Starting in 2003, direct measures of these variables for small geographic areas will be available from the American Community Survey.

3. I obtained access to these files through a NSF/ASA/Census Bureau research fellowship.

4. Although several of the data concepts and questions in the surveys are similar, the collection methods are very different. The long forms of the Decennial Census are mostly self-administered, while the CPS is administered by trained interviewers. Several of the CPS questions involve both initial probes and follow ups. Because of these differences, responses to the two surveys are likely to differ (indeed, item non-response is much higher in the SEDF). See Patterson (1985) for a discussion of differences in responses to the 1980 Census and CPS.

5. Both the SEDF and the CPS mask (top-code) information for people with earnings above certain levels; however, the levels differ across data sets. The percentile cut-off trims the data more uniformly than dropping the top-coded observations would.

6. If a survey question in the SEDF or CPS was unanswered, the Census Bureau "allocated" a response using a hot deck procedure. Instead of using the allocated information, my study treats these data as missing and drops the corresponding observations. See Lillard et al. (1986) for a thorough discussion of allocation procedures and their potential effects on empirical labor analyses. Dropping observations with allocated data reduced the sample sizes in the SEDF by about a quarter and in the CPS files by about a tenth.

7. The federal minimum wage was $3.35 in 1989. It increased to $3.80 in 1990, $4.25 in 1991, and $4.75 in 1996.

8. Two exceptions are the public use Census data assembled by Tolbert and Killian (1987) and Tolbert and Sizer (1996) which use commuting data to group counties into labor market areas and the personal income measures assembled by the U.S. Bureau of Economic Analysis (1998) which account for inter-county commuting patterns. Hanushek (1981) also carefully considered the proper geographic dimensions of local labor markets but was forced to examine large and somewhat arbitrary groupings of counties because data for smaller areas were unavailable.

9. Alternative groupings of counties could be adopted. For instance, the Bureau of Labor Statistics defines its own set of labor market areas, and the Bureau of Economic Analysis groups counties into "economic areas." The analysis adopts the definitions from Tolbert and Sizer because the researchers impose fewer extraneous conditions on their county groupings and have made available a companion data set containing individual data from the 1990 Decennial Census.

10. For confidentiality purposes, the REIS suppresses information for counties with few employers. If data are suppressed, the analysis applies the state-level percentage of employment for the industry in that year to the reported total level of county employment. The imputed entries are then rescaled so that the industry data sum to the county's aggregate employment.

11. For instance, LMA 32 from Tolbert and Sizer (1996) contains Catahoula, Concordia, La Salle, Madison and Tensas parishes from Louisiana and Adams, Claiborne, Franklin, Jefferson and Warren counties from Mississippi. Of these parishes and counties, only two – Adams and Warren counties – have populations greater than 35,000. In my analysis, Adams and Warren counties are uniquely identified; Catahoula, Concordia, La Salle, Madison and Tensas parishes are grouped together, and Claiborne, Franklin and Jefferson counties are grouped together.

12. Specifically, the implied effects were obtained by: (1) taking observations from the 1998 CPS; (2) calculating the probability of employment for each observation at the 1996–1997 values of the local employment measures and at the reported values of the other personal and policy characteristics; (3) calculating the probability of employment for each observation at the 1988–1989 values of the local employment measures but at the reported values of the other personal and policy characteristics; and (4) taking the difference of the average of the two sets of probabilities.

13. The inclusion of fixed effects in the probit models leads to potentially inconsistent estimates because of the incidental parameters problem; however, because of the large numbers of observations for most areas, this is not a serious issue. Additional tests (not shown) also support the inclusion of general time effects and the choice of lag structure for the local employment variables.

14. There are a host of other specification issues such as including lags in the minimum wage measure, scaling the minimum wage measure by some local wage or coverage index, etc. that could also be considered (see Card & Krueger, 1995; Neumark, 1999; for discussions of the implications of alternative research designs). A complete investigation of these issues is beyond the scope of the present study.

15. Mroz (1987) found that econometric specification issues could account for much of married women's wage sensitivity.

16. The statistics in Tables 6, 7, 8 and 9 do not use population weights.

17. In making the case that the benefits of a minimum wage increase would be small, Neumark et al. (1998, Table 1) presented statistics on 16–24-year-old workers in 1995. They

reported that 4.3% of young workers earned less than the then existing minimum wage of $4.25 and that an additional 21.3% earned less than the prospective minimum wage of $5.15.

18. Recall that the tables do not use population weights. When weights are applied, the results are consistent with Fig. 5 and indicate that proportion of people in growing versus declining counties was almost evenly split.

ACKNOWLEDGMENTS

The research in this paper was conducted while the author was a research associate at the Center for Economic Studies, U.S. Bureau of the Census as part of an ASA/NSF/Census Bureau Research Fellowship. The author gratefully acknowledges each of these organizations for their financial and research support. He especially thanks the Center for Economic Studies for providing access to the data used in this study, Al Nucci for providing population estimates data, and Kim Bayard for helpful discussions regarding the SEDF data. A preliminary version of this paper was presented at the Winter 2000 Econometric Society Meetings in Boston, MA. The author thanks participants at that session and at American University, the Bureau of Labor Statistics, the Center for Economic Studies, the Institute for the Study of Labor, and Virginia Tech for useful comments. He also thanks Don Parsons and Tony Yezer for their suggestions. Research results and conclusions expressed are those of the author and are not necessarily shared by the Bureau of the Census or the Center for Economic Studies.

REFERENCES

Bartik, T. J. (1993). The effects of local labor demand on individual labor market outcomes for different demographic groups and the poor. Unpublished manuscript, W. E. Upjohn Institute for Employment Research.

Bartik, T. J. (1999). Aggregate effects in local labor markets of supply and demand shocks. Unpublished manuscript, W. E. Upjohn Institute for Employment Research.

Bartik, T. J., & Eberts, R. W. (1999). Examining the effect of industry trends and structure on welfare caseloads. Unpublished manuscript, W. E. Upjohn Institute for Employment Research.

Bils, M. J. (1985). Real wages over the business cycle: Evidence from panel data. *Journal of Political Economy, 93*(4), 666–689.

Blundell, R., Reed, H., & Stoker, T. (1999). Interpreting movements in aggregate wages: The role of labor market participation. Unpublished manuscript, University of California at Berkeley.

Bound, J., & Holzer, H. J. (1993). Industrial shifts, skills levels, and the labor market for white and black males. *Review of Economics and Statistics, 75*(3), 387–396.

Bowen, W. G., & Finegan, T. A. (1969). *The economics of labor force participation.* Princeton, NJ: Princeton University Press.

Card, D., & Krueger, A. B. (1995). *Myth and measurement: The new economics of the minimum wage.* Princeton, NJ: Princeton University Press.

Card, D., & Lemieux, T. (1997). Adapting to circumstances: The evolution of work, school, and living arrangements among North American youth. National Bureau of Economic Research working paper No. 6142.
Council of Economic Advisors (1997). Explaining the decline in welfare receipt, 1993–1996: Technical report. Unpublished manuscript, Executive Office of the President of the United States.
Council of Economic Advisors (1999). The effects of welfare policy and the economic expansion on welfare caseloads: An update. Unpublished manuscript, Executive Office of the President of the United States.
Deming, W. G. (1996). A decade of economic change and population shifts in U.S. regions. *Monthly Labor Review, 119*(11), 3–14.
Figlio, D. N., & Ziliak, J. P. (1999). Welfare reform, the business cycle, and the decline in AFDC caseloads. In: S. Danziger (Ed.), *Welfare Reform and the Economy: What Will Happen When a Recession Comes?* Kalamazoo, MI: Upjohn Institute for Employment Research.
Fitzgerald, J. M. (1995). Local labor markets and local area effects on welfare duration. *Journal of Policy Analysis and Management, 14*(1), 43–67.
Freeman, R. B. (1982). Economic determinants of geographic and individual variation in the labor market position of young persons. In: R. B. Freeman & D. A. Wise (Eds), *The Youth Labor Market Problem*. Chicago: University of Chicago Press.
Freeman, R. B. (1991). Employment and earnings of disadvantaged young men in a labor shortage economy. In: C. Jencks & P. E. Peterson (Eds), *The Urban Underclass*. Washington, DC: Brookings Institution.
Freeman, R. B., & Rodgers, W. M., III (1999). Area economic conditions and the labor market outcomes of young men in the 1990s expansion. National Bureau of Economic Research working paper No. 7037.
Gittleman, M. (2000). Declining caseloads: What do the dynamics of welfare participation reveal? Unpublished manuscript, Bureau of Labor Statistics.
Hanushek, E. A. (1981). Alternative models of earnings determination and labor market structures. *Journal of Human Resources, 16*(2), 238–259.
Harris, K. M. (1993). Work and welfare among single mothers in poverty. *American Journal of Sociology, 99*(2), 317–352.
Heckman, J. J. (1979). Sample selection bias as a specification error. *Econometrica, 47*(1), 153–162.
Hoynes, H. (1999). The employment, earnings and income of less skilled workers over the business cycle. National Bureau of Economic Research working paper No. 7188.
Juhn, C., Murphy, K., & Pierce, B. (1993). Wage inequality and the rise in the returns to skill. *Journal of Political Economy, 101*(3), 410–442.
Kasarda, J. D. (1995). Industrial restructuring and the changing location of jobs. In: R. Farley (Ed.), *State of the Union: America in the 1990s* (Vol. 1). New York: Russell Sage Foundation.
Katz, L., & Murphy, K. (1992). Changes in relative wages, 1963–1987: Supply and demand factors. *Quarterly Journal of Economics, 107*(1), 35–78.
Keane, M., Moffitt, R., & Runkle, D. (1988). Real wages over the business cycle: Estimating the impact of heterogeneity with micro data. *Journal of Political Economy, 96*(6), 1232–1266.
Killingsworth, M. R., & Heckman, J. J. (1986). Female labor supply: A survey. In: O. Ashenfelter & R. Layard (Eds), *Handbook of Labor Economics* (Vol. I). Amsterdam: North Holland.
Lillard, L., Smith, J. P., & Welch, F. (1986). What do we really know about wages? The importance of nonreporting and census imputation. *Journal of Political Economy, 94*(3, Part 1), 489–506.
Mroz, T. (1987). The sensitivity of an empirical model of married women's hours of work to economic and statistical assumptions. *Econometrica, 55*(4), 765–799.

Neumark, D. (1999). The employment effects of recent minimum wage increases: Evidence from a pre-specified research design. National Bureau of Economic Research working paper No. 7171.

Neumark, D., Schweitzer, M., & Wascher, W. (1998). The effects of minimum wages on the distribution of family incomes: A non-parametric analysis. National Bureau of Economic Research working paper No. 6536.

Patterson, G. (1985). Quality and comparability of personal income data from surveys and the decennial census. Unpublished manuscript, U.S. Bureau of the Census.

Tolbert, C. M., & Killian, M. S. (1987). *Labor market areas for the united states*. Washington, DC: U.S. Department of Agriculture.

Tolbert, C. M., & Sizer, M. (1996). *U.S. commuting zones and labor market areas: A 1990 update*. Washington, DC: U.S. Department of Agriculture.

Topel, R. H. (1986). Local labor markets. *Journal of Political Economy, 94*(3, Part 2), S111–S143.

U.S. Bureau of Economic Analysis (1998). *Regional economic information system: 1969–1996*. Washington, DC: U.S. Department of Commerce.

U.S. House of Representatives, Committee on Ways and Means (various years). *The green book: Background material and data on programs within the jurisdiction of the committee on ways and means*. Washington, DC: U.S. Government Printing Office.

Walters, S. J. K. (1990). Business climate and measured poverty: The evidence across states. *Atlantic Economic Journal, 18*(1), 20–26.

APPENDIX A
MEANS AND STANDARD DEVIATIONS
OF ANALYSIS VARIABLES

Variable	Women			Men		
	W/o HS	With HS	College	W/o HS	With HS	College
Hourly earnings[a]	9.28	10.86	15.42	13.28	15.63	21.04
	(9.81)	(9.13)	(11.59)	(11.60)	(11.27)	(14.15)
Weekly earnings[a]	322.04	386.35	570.63	538.09	658.53	907.45
	(330.96)	(311.13)	(417.63)	(435.93)	(440.74)	(577.17)
Employed last year?	0.43	0.67	0.80	0.72	0.88	0.93
	(0.50)	(0.47)	(0.40)	(0.45)	(0.32)	(0.25)
Total civilian employment per working age adult in county	0.80 (0.24)	0.81 (0.21)	0.85 (0.24)	0.80 (0.23)	0.80 (0.21)	0.85 (0.24)
Mining and construction emp. per working age adult in county	0.05 (0.03)	0.05 (0.02)	0.05 (0.02)	0.05 (0.03)	0.05 (0.03)	0.05 (0.02)
Manufacturing employment per working age adult in county	0.12 (0.07)	0.13 (0.07)	0.12 (0.07)	0.13 (0.07)	0.13 (0.07)	0.12 (0.07)

Appendix A. (*Continued*)

Variable	Women			Men		
	W/o HS	With HS	College	W/o HS	With HS	College
Trans., util., & whol. Trade emp. per working age adult in county	0.08 (0.04)	0.08 (0.04)	0.08 (0.04)	0.08 (0.04)	0.08 (0.04)	0.08 (0.04)
Retail trade employment per working age adult in county	0.13 (0.04)	0.14 (0.04)	0.14 (0.03)	0.13 (0.04)	0.14 (0.04)	0.14 (0.03)
Fin., ins. & real estate emp. per working age adult in county	0.06 (0.05)	0.06 (0.04)	0.07 (0.05)	0.06 (0.05)	0.06 (0.04)	0.07 (0.05)
Service employment per working age adult in county	0.22 (0.10)	0.22 (0.09)	0.24 (0.10)	0.22 (0.10)	0.22 (0.09)	0.24 (0.10)
Government employment per working age adult in county	0.11 (0.06)	0.11 (0.05)	0.11 (0.06)	0.11 (0.06)	0.10 (0.05)	0.11 (0.06)
Agricultural employment per working age adult in county	0.03 (0.04)	0.03 (0.04)	0.02 (0.04)	0.03 (0.04)	0.03 (0.04)	0.02 (0.04)
Estimated skill-specific emp. in county $\hat{M}(s,r,t)$	0.05 (0.02)	0.12 (0.03)	0.23 (0.06)	0.09 (0.03)	0.13 (0.04)	0.26 (0.06)
Maximum AFDC benefits for fam. of 3 w/no income in state	494.83 (216.00)	501.13 (193.02)	528.09 (204.69)	498.81 (214.54)	502.43 (192.79)	529.82 (204.86)
Minimum wage in state	4.65 (0.43)	4.62 (0.38)	4.68 (0.43)	4.65 (0.43)	4.62 (0.38)	4.68 (0.43)
Age	41.82 (14.38)	39.39 (13.07)	37.17 (11.02)	40.51 (14.53)	37.39 (12.69)	38.24 (11.08)
African origin	0.16 (0.37)	0.10 (0.30)	0.09 (0.29)	0.14 (0.35)	0.09 (0.29)	0.06 (0.25)
Hispanic origin	0.19 (0.40)	0.06 (0.23)	0.05 (0.21)	0.20 (0.40)	0.06 (0.24)	0.05 (0.21)
Other non-white origin	0.14 (0.35)	0.05 (0.21)	0.06 (0.23)	0.13 (0.34)	0.05 (0.22)	0.06 (0.24)
Observations	935,122	1,816,643	1,923,289	888,709	1,506,564	1,799,603

Note: Data from combined SEDF and CPS files. Standard deviations appear in parentheses. Estimates use files' sampling weights.

[a] Calculated only for workers.

DETERMINANTS OF IMMIGRANT SELECTIVITY AND SKILLS

Madeline Zavodny

ABSTRACT

Whether immigrants are positively or negatively self-selected is much disputed. Whereas most previous studies have addressed this question by comparing the earnings of immigrants to those of U.S. natives, this analysis uses occupation to examine the skill level of immigrants relative to their home country population. Data on the occupational distribution of individuals granted legal permanent residence in 1995 indicate that the proportion of immigrants in skilled occupations is related to the corresponding proportion in source countries but not necessarily to the return to skill and other economic factors in the country of origin.

1. INTRODUCTION

The debate about the costs and benefits of immigration to the United States centers on the issue of the skills of immigrants. However, it is not clear whether persons who choose to immigrate to the U.S. are more or less skilled, on average, than either the U.S. native-born population or than the pool of all potential immigrants. The factors that determine the average skill level among immigrants are also uncertain. This analysis adds to the literature an examination of the determinants of the average skill level of immigrants based on data on occupational distribution of immigrants.

Understanding the quality of immigrants and its determinants is important because of the large number of immigrants in the U.S. and because both their own economic outcomes and their effect on natives depends on relative skill levels. The foreign born composed slightly more than 10% of the U.S. population in 2000, representing an increase of over 11 million people since 1990 (U.S. Bureau of the Census, 2001). Higher immigration of unskilled individuals appears to depress the earnings of low-skilled immigrants already present in the U.S. as well as the earnings of low-skilled U.S. natives (e.g. Borjas, Freeman & Katz, 1997; Jaeger, 1996; Johnson, 1998).[1] Because low-skilled immigrants appear to be a complement to the labor of skilled workers, larger flows of unskilled immigrants boost the earnings of skilled U.S. natives and skilled immigrants (Jaeger, 1996; Johnson, 1998). Previous research suggests that higher levels of skilled migration have little effect on the earnings of U.S. natives (Borjas et al., 1997).

Comparing immigrants to U.S. natives is the primary method that has been used to examine whether immigrants are drawn from the top or bottom of the skill or income distribution. Borjas (1987, 1991) and Cobb-Clark (1993) estimated wage equations for immigrants and natives using data from decennial Censuses or the Current Population Survey (CPS) and examined the role of home-country political and economic conditions in country-level average relative wages. Barrett (1998) and Jasso, Rosenzweig and Smith (2000) used a similar method with administrative data from the Immigration and Naturalization Service (INS) on new legal permanent residents; because the INS data do not contain wages, they imputed wage data to immigrants on the basis of the wages of natives in the same occupation.[2]

Selection among immigrants has also been examined by comparing the skills of immigrants across source countries. Greenwood, McDowell and Waldman (1996) used administrative data to estimate the determinants of the fraction of new legal permanent residents from a country who are in skilled occupations. This method does not involve a comparison to the skills of U.S. natives or to the skills of the home country population but rather a comparison of immigrants' skill levels across countries of origin and within countries over time. However, Greenwood et al. did not directly examine the relationship between returns to skill and the average skill level of immigrants from a given country, which was a primary focus of the other papers.

The findings on immigrant selectivity are mixed. Barrett (1998), Borjas (1987, 1991) and Cobb-Clark (1993) conclude that immigrants are positively selected from countries with low rates of return to skill relative to the U.S. and negatively selected from countries with higher returns to skill, as measured by income inequality. Jasso et al. (2000), in contrast, find that lower skill prices in the country of origin, as measured by higher average schooling levels, are associated with lower immigrant quality. Greenwood et al. (1996) find a negative association between immigrants' skills and gross domestic product (GDP) per capita in the source country relative to the U.S., whereas Borjas and Barrett both report a positive relationship between source-country per capita GDP and the average wages of immigrants relative to U.S. natives.

This study uses INS data on the occupation of new legal permanent residents to examine the determinants of immigrant selection. The analysis makes several contributions to the literature. This study synthesizes the two previous methods used to examine immigrant selection by examining the relationship between differences across countries in the return to skill – the approach taken by Borjas and others – and the fraction of immigrants who are in skilled occupations, the measure of skill used by Greenwood et al. This study also investigates the relationship between the fraction of immigrants in skilled occupations and the comparable fraction in source countries, which has not been previously examined.

This analysis also establishes whether the fraction of immigrants who are in skilled occupations differs across admission categories and examines the applicability of the Roy selection model to immigrants admitted under different categories. Studies that use data on immigrants' relative earnings from the Census or the CPS are unable to examine the effect of admission category, which is available only in INS data.

The model presented in the next section predicts the relationship between the average skill level of immigrants from a given country and returns to skill, economic conditions, and the skill level of the home country population. These predictions are then tested using INS data on men who received legal permanent resident status in 1995. The results provide mixed support for the model, and the results vary somewhat across admission categories.

2. ANALYTICAL FRAMEWORK

Beginning with work by Sjaastad (1962), migration models posit that individuals live in the area where their utility is maximized. Such models hypothesize that individuals compare their utility in their current location to their expected utility in all other possible locations, including the disutility of moving to those locations, and choose the location with the highest utility. The literature on international migration has focused on the earnings component of utility, positing that individuals become immigrants when their expected earnings in the destination country, less migration costs, are higher than their earnings in the country of origin (Borjas, 1987, 1991; Chiswick, 1999; Taylor, 1987). Similar models have also been applied to domestic migration (e.g. Polachek & Horvath, 1977).

Borjas (2000) develops a model that predicts how relative returns to skill and other factors affect the average skill level of immigrants. The model, which is based on the Roy (1951) selection model, is briefly summarized here, and then its predictions are tested with data on the skill level of immigrants. In the model, immigrants' earnings in both the home country and the destination country depend on skill, which is denoted by S and is observed, and on unobservable factors denoted by ε. The distribution of earnings, w, in the home country and in the destination country, respectively, are given by

$$\ln w_0 = \mu_0 + \delta_0 S + \varepsilon_0 \tag{1}$$

and

$$\ln w_1 = \mu_1 + \delta_1 S + \varepsilon_1. \tag{2}$$

The coefficients δ_0 and δ_1 measure the return to skill in the home and destination countries, and μ_0 and μ_1 are mean (log) earnings. If δ_1 is larger than δ_0, the return to skill is higher in the destination country than in the country of origin. The random, unobserved components of earnings ε_0 and ε_1 are jointly normally distributed with mean zero, variances σ_0^2 and σ_1^2, and correlation coefficient ρ_{01}.

The distribution of skill in the home country is given by

$$S = \mu_s + \varepsilon_s, \tag{3}$$

where ε_s is assumed to be distributed normally with mean zero and variance σ_s^2 and to be uncorrelated with the difference in the random components of earnings between the destination country and the home country. Migration costs are assumed to be constant across individuals from a given country and equal to C.

Individuals live in the country in which their expected earnings are higher, given their skill level and migration costs. For an individual with skill level s, the decision to migrate can be represented by the index function I, where

$$I \approx \mu_1 - \mu_0 + (\delta_1 - \delta_0)s + \varepsilon_1 - \varepsilon_0 - \pi, \tag{4}$$

and $\pi = C/w_0$. Given skill level s, an individual migrates if $I > 0$.

As Borjas (2000) shows, the migration rate from the home country to the destination country is

$$P(z) = \Pr[\tau > -((\mu_1 - \mu_0) + (\delta_1 - \delta_0)\mu_s - \pi)] = 1 - \Phi(z), \tag{5}$$

where $\tau = (\varepsilon_1 - \varepsilon_0) + (\delta_1 - \delta_0)\varepsilon_s$ and $z = -((\mu_1 - \mu_0) + (\delta_1 - \delta_0)\mu_s - \pi)/\sigma_\tau$. The mean skill level of individuals who choose to migrate is

$$E(S|\mu_s, I > 0) = \mu_s + \frac{\sigma_s^2}{\sigma_\tau}(\delta_1 - \delta_0)\lambda \tag{6}$$

where $\lambda = \Phi(z)/(1 - \Phi(z))$.

Equation (6), which is the key equation in the model, predicts the effect of changes in average earnings in the source and destination countries on the average skill level of migrants. An increase in average earnings in the home country will raise (lower) the average skill level of migrants if the return to skill is higher (lower) in the destination than in the home country. Intuitively, an increase in average income in the home country reduces the incentive to migrate, and the effect is largest among persons at the margin for migrating. Because positive selection on skill occurs when the return to skill is higher in the destination than in the source country, the increase in average home country income reduces migration from the lower end of the skill distribution while not affecting migration from the upper end of the skill distribution, raising the average skill level of migrants. Similarly, if migrants are negatively selected – the case where the relative return to skill is lower in the destination – an increase in average income in the home country will lower the average skill of migrants by reducing migration from the upper end of the skill distribution without affecting migration at the lower end of the distribution.

An increase in average earnings in the destination country will raise the average skill level of immigrants if the return to skill is lower in the destination country than in the home country (the negative selection case). If immigrants are positively selected, however, an increase in average earnings in the destination will lower the average skill level among migrants because it will lead to more migration from the lower end of the skill distribution.

The relative return to skill also affects the average skill level among immigrants. When the return to skill is lower in the destination than in the home country, negative selection occurs. In this case, an increase in average earnings in the destination raises the skill threshold for migration, which boosts the average skill level of migrants. The opposite holds for the positive selection case. An increase in the return to skill in the country of origin will lower the average quality of migrants by reducing the incentive to migrate for individuals at the upper end of the skill distribution, whereas an increase in the return to skill in the destination country will raise the average quality of immigrants by increasing the incentive to migrate for more-skilled individuals.

Equation (6) also predicts the effect of changes in the average skill level in the source country and in migration costs on the average skill level of migrants. As Borjas (2000) shows, an increase in the average skill level in the source country raises the average skill level of migrants, but the effect is less than one-for-one. An increase in migration costs for all individuals will raise (lower) the average quality of migrants if the return to skill is higher (lower) in the destination country than in the home country. Intuitively, an increase in migration costs exacerbates the degree of positive or negative selection, which is determined by the relative return to skill across the two countries.

This model makes several simplifying assumptions. It does not include multiple destination countries, although individuals presumably choose between home and several potential destinations. Borjas, Bronars and Trejo (1992) show that, in a similar model with multiple destinations, individuals sort across areas based on relative returns to skill. Another assumption of the model here is that individuals make locational choices based solely on expected earnings. The majority of legal immigrants to the U.S. receive permanent resident status because they have relatives in the country, so desire to live near family members may influence migration decisions for many potential immigrants. The applicability of the model to immigrants admitted on the basis of family ties – instead of because of job skills or for other reasons – is examined below.

3. METHODS AND DATA

In the model developed above, the variables that determine the average skill level of immigrants are relative returns to skill, average earnings in the two countries, the average skill level in the home country, and migration costs. The empirical test of the model involves regressing a measure of immigrants' skill on proxies for these factors, which are described below after the basic regression framework is explained.

The theoretical model predicts that the effect of average earnings and migration costs on immigrants' skill depends on the relative return to skill. The regressions therefore include interactions of a measure indicating whether the return to skill in the home country is higher or lower than in the U.S. with variables measuring average income in source countries and migration costs, or

$$\% \text{ Skilled Migrants}_c = \alpha + \beta \% \text{ Skilled Home}_c + \delta \text{Gini}_c + \gamma_1 \text{Income}_c \\ \times \text{Low RR Skill}_c + \gamma_2 \text{Income}_c \times \text{High RR Skill}_c \\ + \phi_1 \text{Migration Costs}_c \times \text{Low RR Skill}_c \\ + \phi_2 \text{Migration Costs}_c \times \text{High RR Skill}_c + \varepsilon_c, \quad (7)$$

where c indexes countries. The *RR Skill* variables are dummy variables indicating whether a country's return to skill, as proxied by the Gini index, is lower or higher than in the U.S.; countries with a smaller Gini index than the U.S. are assumed to have a low relative return to skill, and vice versa. The theory predicts that immigrants' skills should be positively associated with the interaction terms for countries with relatively low returns to skill and negatively associated with the interaction terms for countries with relatively high returns to skill. The variables that are used to measure skill, income, and migration costs are explained next.

3.1. Immigrants' Skills

The measure of immigrants' skills used here is the fraction of immigrants who report being in a skilled occupation. The data on the skills and other characteristics of immigrants are from administrative data on men admitted as legal permanent residents to the U.S. The data, which are compiled by the INS, include the sex, age, class of admission, and country of origin of nearly all new "green card" recipients.[3] The data do not include any information about educational attainment or earnings, so occupation is the only available measure of skill. Data for fiscal year 1995, which is from October 1994 to September 1995, are used here. During this period, 720,461 individuals were admitted as legal permanent residents. Only men aged 16–64 (about 32% of all new legal permanent residents in 1995) are included in the sample used here.

The INS data include occupation for individuals aged 16 and older. For individuals admitted in employment-based admission classes, the occupation is the field they will perform in the U.S.[4] Immigrants admitted in other categories report their occupation in either the last country of residence or in the U.S.; immigrants who are already present in the U.S. and are adjusting their status presumably report their current occupation in the U.S., and immigrants newly arriving in the U.S. report their occupation in their country of last residence. Although some of these immigrants may not work in the same occupation in the U.S., occupation serves as proxy for human capital and skill level.

The INS data set has 25 occupational fields plus categories for students and children under age 16, homemakers, retired or unemployed individuals, and occupation not reported. Individuals who do not report an occupation or are students, homemakers, unemployed, or retired (about 40% of all new male immigrants aged 16–64) are not included in the main analysis here. Individuals are considered skilled if they report being in the "executive, administrative, and managerial" occupational field or in a professional or technical occupation.[5]

The INS data include over 200,000 men aged 16–64 from a total of 204 countries. As column 1 of Table 1 reports, about 21% of these immigrants report being in a skilled occupation. When the 40% of prime-aged men who do not report an occupation or are students, homemakers, unemployed or retired are not included, the number of countries of origin falls to 198. About 35% of these male immigrants are in skilled occupations (column 2).

Table 1. Comparison of Sample to All Immigrants in INS Data.

	All Immigrants	Occupation Reported	Sample
Percent in skilled occupations	21.1	35.1	36.6
Percent employment-based	14.5	19.0	20.0
Percent family reunification	56.6	55.0	62.7
Percent refugee or asylee	18.2	13.9	3.8
Percent adjusting status	53.7	49.8	44.8
Number of countries	204	198	51
Number of immigrants	229,657	138,153	65,918

Note: The data include men aged 16–64 admitted as legal permanent residents in fiscal year 1995, except for individuals legalized under the Immigration Reform and Control Act (IRCA).

This analysis focuses on a sample of immigrants from 51 countries for which occupational data on the source country labor force are also available. These 51 countries, which are listed in Table A1 in Appendix, account for 46% of male immigrants aged 16–64 and for 45% of all individuals admitted as legal permanent residents in 1995. As column 3 of Table 1 indicates, almost 37% of male immigrants from these countries who report an occupation are in skilled occupations. If individuals who do not report an occupation or are students, homemakers, unemployed, or retired were included, 23% would be in skilled occupations. The countries in the sample therefore appear to have slightly more skilled migrants than all immigrant-sending countries, but not substantially so.

3.2. Admission Categories

The INS data include immigrants' class of admission. There are three main reasons immigrants receive permanent resident status: they are related to a citizen or permanent resident (family reunification); they are admitted on the basis of job skills (employment-based); or they are a refugee or asylee adjusting to permanent resident status after at least one year in the U.S. Immigration law also allows some individuals to receive permanent resident status for other reasons, such as the diversity lottery program. Some of the regressions discussed below include variables measuring the fraction of immigrants in each of the three main admission classes in order to examine the relationship between the fraction of immigrants who are skilled and the distribution of immigrants across admission classes. In addition, the data are stratified by admission class in some specifications in order to examine the applicability of the selection model across admission classes.[6]

The distribution across admission categories of the immigrants from the 51 countries that are the focus of this analysis differs slightly from the distribution of all male immigrants aged 16–64. As Table 1 indicates, immigrants from the 51 countries are more likely to have been admitted under employment-based and family reunification preferences and less likely to have been admitted under refugee/asylee admission categories than immigrants as a whole. This is because the 51 countries do not include Cuba, Russia, and Vietnam, the primary countries of origin for refugees and asylees; occupational data for the home country population are not available for these countries.

More than one-half of new recipients of legal permanent residence are already present in the U.S. and are adjusting from another status. Individuals converting from H1-B visas (temporary visas for skilled workers) and refugees and asylees are examples of individuals converting status.[7] The fraction of immigrants from the 51 countries focused on here that are adjusting status is slightly lower than the corresponding fraction among all adult male immigrants, as Table 1 indicates. Some of the regressions discussed below control for the fraction of immigrants who are adjusting status because of concerns that occupational differences between new legal permanent residents already present in the U.S. and those coming from abroad may reflect differences in occupation structures across countries instead of differences in skill levels.

3.3. Economic Variables

The fraction of the population in the source country that is skilled is measured from the occupational distribution in that country. The International Labour Office (ILO) reports employment levels by occupation and sex for a large number of countries. The occupational classifications include executive/administrative/managerial and professional/technical, so a measure of skilled male workers in the home country analogous to the measure for immigrants is constructed using ILO data for 1995.[8] As the summary statistics in Table 2 indicate, about 22% of the home country male labor force, on average, works in skilled occupations.

As in previous research, a measure of income inequality is used here as the measure of the return to skill. The measure of income inequality used here is

Table 2. Summary Statistics.

Variable	Mean	Minimum	Maximum
Percent skilled, source country	22.3 (11.4)	4.0	49.1
Gini index	36.9 (10.3)	19.5	59.1
GDP per capita	11501 (11874)	280	42416
Distance	4343 (2164)	366	8783

Note: Standard deviations are in parentheses. The number of observations is 51.

the Gini index, which increases as income inequality increases. Assuming that countries with more compressed income distributions have lower rates of return to skill, the Gini index proxies for the return to skill. The index ranges from 19.5 (Slovakia) to over 59 (Paraguay) across the 51 countries, with a mean of about 37. The Gini index in the U.S. is 40.1.[9]

In the model, the direction of the effects of average income and migration costs depends on relative returns to skill. In the sample, 32 countries have greater income inequality than the U.S. and 19 have lower income inequality, as measured by the Gini coefficient. Countries with higher Gini indexes (higher returns to skill) than the U.S. tend to be Latin American and Asian nations, whereas countries with lower Gini indexes (lower returns to skill) tend to be European. The regressions estimated below include a linear variable measuring the Gini index in the country of origin as well as the interaction terms discussed above.

The income measure is the log of GDP per capita in 1995 in dollars.[10] Distance from the population center in the country of origin to New York, Miami, or Los Angeles (in thousands of miles) is used as the proxy for migration costs.[11] These variables are the standard measures of income and migration costs used in previous research.

The regressions reported below do not directly include variables measuring average income or the return to skill in the U.S., only in source countries. This analysis uses cross-sectional data, so all immigrants face the same return to skill and economic conditions in the U.S. in a given year; the constant in the regression captures these factors. If panel data were used, such variables would need to be included in the model. Using panel data would also offer the advantage of being able to include fixed country of origin effects. However, the covariates, particularly the measure of the return to skill, change only slowly over time and are not available on an annual basis for all countries. Distance, which proxies for migration costs, obviously does not change over time. Panel data methodologies therefore might not offer a substantial advantage over the cross-sectional approach used here.

The regressions are estimated using weighted least squares, where the weights are the number of immigrants from each country used to construct the sample. The weights are used to make the results reflective of the composition of legal immigrants. Controls for the distribution of immigrants across admission classes and for the fraction of immigrants adjusting status are included in some specifications. Dummy variables controlling for three of four continents are also included in some specifications to control for broad regions of origin.

The next section presents basic results and then stratifies the data by class of admission, followed by results for newly-arriving versus adjusting immigrants and principal versus "tied" immigrants.

4. RESULTS

The results provide mixed support for the theoretical model. Column 1 of Table 3 reports the results when variables measuring the average skill level of the home country, the Gini index in the home country, and the interactions with average income in the home country and migration costs are included in the regression. A 10 percentage point increase in the fraction of the home country

Table 3. Determinants of Fraction of Immigrants in Skilled Occupations.

Variable	(1)	(2)	(3)
Fraction skilled, source country	0.851	0.569	0.604
	(0.326)	(0.274)	(0.323)
Gini index	−0.011	−0.007	−0.004
	(0.011)	(0.009)	(0.009)
ln (GDP per capita) × low relative Gini index	0.004	0.011	−0.002
	(0.027)	(0.022)	(0.023)
ln (GDP per capita) × high relative Gini index	−0.029	−0.007	−0.001
	(0.030)	(0.026)	(0.030)
Distance × low relative Gini index	0.002	0.011	−0.003
	(0.013)	(0.011)	(0.017)
Distance × high relative Gini index	0.048	0.039	0.003
	(0.014)	(0.013)	(0.025)
Fraction employment-based immigrants		0.532	0.446
		(0.198)	(0.236)
Fraction family reunification immigrants		−0.151	−0.159
		(0.124)	(0.139)
Fraction refugees/asylees		−0.355	−0.418
		(0.272)	(0.288)
Fraction adjusting status		−0.095	0.008
		(0.203)	(0.223)
Europe			−0.060
			(0.140)
Asia			−0.002
			(0.132)
Latin America			−0.256
			(0.192)
Adjusted R^2	0.711	0.808	0.809

Note: The relative Gini index is the Gini index for the source country relative to the U.S. Each column is from a separate weighted least squares regression. The weights are the number of male immigrants aged 16–64 who reported an occupation. The regressions also include a constant. Fraction "other" is the omitted category for class of admission, and Oceania is the omitted geographic area. Standard errors are in parentheses.

labor force in skilled occupations is associated with an 8.5 percentage point rise in the fraction of immigrants from a country in skilled occupations; the model predicts that the relationship should be less than one-for-one, but the estimated coefficient is not significantly different from one. Skilled immigration is not significantly associated with income inequality, which proxies for the return to skill. GDP per capita is also not significantly associated with the fraction of immigrants who are skilled from countries with relatively low or high Gini indexes. Previous studies, in contrast, tended to find that average income is positively associated with immigrants' skill levels, but these studies did not interact average income with a measure of the relative return to skill.

Higher migration costs, as proxied by distance, are positively associated with the average skill level of immigrants from countries with higher income inequality than the U.S., whereas there is no association with the skills of immigrants from countries with relatively low income inequality. The result for countries with relatively high income inequality is not consistent with the model, which predicts that an increase in migration costs should increase the extent of negative selection from countries that have relatively high returns to skill (assuming that income inequality proxies for returns to skill). Jasso and Rosenzweig (1990) similarly find that greater distance is associated with positive selection of immigrants, although they do not distinguish between countries with high and low relative returns to skill.

Column 2 of Table 3 shows the results when controls for the distribution of immigrants across admission categories are included in the model. The fraction of immigrants admitted under employment-based preferences, relative to immigrants admitted in "other" categories, is significantly positively associated with the fraction of immigrants in skilled occupations. The fractions of immigrants admitted under family reunification admission categories, refugee/asylee categories, and adjusting status are not significantly related to the fraction of immigrants in skilled occupations.

Including controls for three of four regions slightly weakens the results, as column 3 indicates. The fraction of immigrants in skilled occupations is not significantly different across Europe, Asia, Latin America, and Oceania after controlling for other factors. The fraction of immigrants admitted in employment-based categories remains positively associated with the fraction of immigrants in skilled occupations but only at the 10% level. Similarly, the relationships between immigrants' skill levels and the skill level of the home country population and distance from countries with relatively high income inequality weaken when the regional controls are added to the regression.

4.1. Results by Admission Category

The above results suggest that the fraction of immigrants in skilled occupations may differ between immigrants admitted under employment-based preference categories and immigrants admitted under other categories.[12] The determinants of the fraction of immigrants in skilled occupations may also differ across preference categories. For example, employment-based immigrants might be more sensitive to relative returns to skill and other economic factors than family reunification immigrants, who may be moving primarily to be near relatives. Economic factors may not play a role in the migration decisions of refugees and asylees who are fleeing political persecution. Table 4 therefore shows the results when the data are stratified by major class of admission.

Table 4. Determinants of Fraction of Immigrants in Skilled Occupations, by Class of Admission.

Variable	Employment	Family	Refugee/Asylee	Other
Fraction skilled, source country	0.434	0.925	0.080	−0.079
	(0.364)	(0.306)	(0.268)	(0.297)
Gini index	0.002	−0.006	−0.003	−0.033
	(0.013)	(0.008)	(0.009)	(0.013)
ln (GDP per capita) × low relative Gini index	0.047	−0.025	−0.001	0.058
	(0.033)	(0.024)	(0.017)	(0.021)
ln (GDP per capita) × high relative Gini index	0.063	−0.028	−0.031	0.092
	(0.042)	(0.028)	(0.032)	(0.040)
Distance × low relative Gini index	−0.029	−0.003	−0.011	0.016
	(0.017)	(0.016)	(0.025)	(0.019)
Distance × high relative Gini index	−0.033	0.009	−0.003	−0.012
	(0.033)	(0.025)	(0.014)	(0.043)
Fraction adjusting status	1.396	0.164	–	−0.178
	(0.357)	(0.163)		(0.084)
Europe	−0.106	−0.025	0.073	−0.062
	(0.141)	(0.136)	(0.326)	(0.147)
Asia	0.005	0.089	0.244	−0.064
	(0.137)	(0.129)	(0.325)	(0.144)
Latin America	−0.518	−0.204	0.287	−0.100
	(0.222)	(0.190)	(0.338)	(0.218)
Number of countries	51	51	44	51
Adjusted R^2	0.724	0.768	0.288	0.488

Note: The relative Gini index is the Gini index for the source country relative to the U.S. Each column is from a separate weighted least squares regression. The weights are the number of male immigrants aged 16–64 who reported an occupation. Oceania is the omitted geographic area. Standard errors are in parentheses.

The results suggest that the determinants of the fraction of immigrants in skilled occupations differ somewhat across admission categories, but the results are not always as hypothesized. For example, the fraction of employment-based immigrants in skilled occupations appears to fall as distance increases among countries with lower income inequality than the U.S., the opposite result of that predicted by the model. Immigrants' skill levels are significantly associated with skill levels in the home country only among family reunification immigrants. Among immigrants admitted under miscellaneous admission categories, home country GDP is positively associated with skill levels for immigrants from countries with both relatively low and relatively high income inequality; the former result is consistent with the model, whereas the latter is not. The skill level of these "other" immigrants declines as income inequality increases, as predicted by the model. Although the Roy selection model seems best suited for explaining migration among employment-based immigrants, it does not better fit average skill levels among employment-based immigrants than among family reunification immigrants; the adjusted R-squared is slightly higher in the family reunification specification than in the employment-based regression.

Economic factors appear to play almost no role in the skills of refugees and asylees, as expected. The goodness of fit, as measured by the adjusted R-squared, is also substantially lower for refugees/asylees than for the other admission categories.[13] The results for refugees and asylees should be treated with caution, however, because the large refugee/asylee-sending countries are not included in the sample.

The coefficient on the variable that controls for the fraction of immigrants already present in the U.S. and adjusting status varies across preference categories. Recall that this variable is intended to control for differences between the occupational structure of the U.S. and other countries. The fraction of immigrants adjusting status is positively associated with the skills of employment-based immigrants even though members of this group should report the occupation they will hold in the U.S. regardless of their location at the time of admission. This may indicate that foreign-born persons already present in the U.S. are better able to find high-skilled jobs than individuals living overseas searching for an employer willing to sponsor them for employment-based admission. The fraction of immigrants adjusting status is negatively associated with the skills of immigrants admitted in "other" categories, in contrast. This suggests that immigrants admitted for miscellaneous reasons work in higher-skilled occupations in their home country than they do in the U.S., at least initially.

The previous results suggest that the percentage of immigrants in skilled occupations may depend on the percentage of immigrants adjusting status, although the direction of the relationship is unclear. Columns 1 and 2 of Table 5 therefore

Table 5. Determinants of Fraction of Newly-Arriving and Principal Immigrants in Skilled Occupations.

Variable	Newly-Arriving	Adjusting	Principal	Tied
Fraction skilled, source country	0.754	0.283	0.454	1.202
	(0.327)	(0.289)	(0.309)	(0.416)
Gini index	−0.008	−0.004	−0.003	−0.001
	(0.009)	(0.009)	(0.009)	(0.011)
ln (GDP per capita) × low relative Gini index	−0.023	0.018	0.002	−0.055
	(0.023)	(0.022)	(0.022)	(0.031)
ln (GDP per capita) × high relative Gini index	−0.023	0.028	0.006	−0.050
	(0.029)	(0.030)	(0.029)	(0.042)
Distance × low relative Gini index	−0.014	0.016	0.001	−0.012
	(0.017)	(0.015)	(0.016)	(0.019)
Distance × high relative Gini index	0.002	0.005	0.001	−0.013
	(0.026)	(0.023)	(0.024)	(0.031)
Fraction employment-based immigrants	0.355	0.907	0.723	−0.274
	(0.226)	(0.183)	(0.235)	(0.313)
Fraction family reunification immigrants	−0.257	0.420	−0.088	−0.167
	(0.092)	(0.190)	(0.133)	(0.193)
Fraction refugees/asylees	–	−0.096	−0.193	−0.931
		(0.168)	(0.267)	(0.455)
Fraction adjusting status	–	–	−0.208	0.520
			(0.209)	(0.366)
Europe	−0.151	0.070	−0.048	−0.219
	(0.147)	(0.125)	(0.131)	(0.188)
Asia	−0.025	−0.046	−0.041	0.043
	(0.137)	(0.113)	(0.123)	(0.177)
Latin America	−0.288	−0.249	−0.256	−0.391
	(0.207)	(0.166)	(0.180)	(0.249)
Number of countries	51	50	51	49
Adjusted R^2	0.767	0.879	0.833	0.727

Note: The relative Gini index is the Gini index for the source country relative to the U.S. Each column is from a separate weighted least squares regression. The weights are the number of male immigrants aged 16–64 who reported an occupation. Fraction "other" is the omitted category for class of admission, and Oceania is the omitted geographic area. Standard errors are in parentheses.

investigate whether the determinants of the fraction of newly-arriving immigrants in skilled occupations differ between newly-arriving immigrants and immigrants who are adjusting status. About 34% of newly-arriving immigrants are in skilled occupations, compared with 40% of all immigrants adjusting status; part of this difference may be because adjusting immigrants are already present in the U.S. and presumably report their U.S. occupation, whereas newly-arriving immigrants report their occupation in the home country, except for most immigrants admitted under employment-based categories.

The results indicate several differences between the determinants of the average skill levels of newly-arriving immigrants and adjusting immigrants. The fraction of newly-arriving immigrants in skilled occupations is significantly associated with the fraction of the home country labor force in skilled occupations, whereas the relationship is insignificant for immigrants adjusting status. The average skill level of adjusting immigrants increases as the fractions admitted under employment-based and family reunification preferences rise, whereas the average skill levels of newly-arriving immigrants falls as the fraction admitted under family reunification preferences rises. Relative income inequality and the other economic variables are not significantly related to the skill levels of either newly-arriving or already-present immigrants.

Columns 3 and 4 of Table 5 show the results if the sample is restricted to principal immigrants or "tied" immigrants, respectively. Tied immigrants receive legal permanent resident status because they are the spouse or minor child of a principal immigrant. Slightly less than 10% of immigrants in the main sample are tied immigrants. About 37% of principal immigrants are in skilled occupations, the same proportion as in the sample as a whole, compared with 34% of tied immigrants.

The results for principal immigrants are similar to those for all immigrants, which is not surprising since the vast majority of immigrants are principals. The percentage of tied immigrants in skilled occupations appears to decline as GDP per capita increases among countries with relatively low income inequality, the opposite result of that predicted by the model. Another difference is that the proportion of tied immigrants in skilled occupations declines as the fraction of refugees and asylees increases.

5. DISCUSSION

This study examined the determinants of the average skill level of immigrants using INS data on the occupation of new recipients of legal permanent resident status as a proxy for skill. Not surprisingly, immigrants admitted on the basis of job skills appear to have higher skill levels than individuals admitted because of family ties, refugees, asylees, and immigrants admitted for other reasons.

The results generally do not indicate that the income inequality – which is used to measure the return to skill – in the home country is significantly related to immigrants' average skill level, whereas the selection model predicts that skill levels should increase as the return to skill in the source country decreases relative to the U.S. Immigrants' skills appear to be related to average income in countries of origin and distances from the U.S. in some specifications, but the results are not always consistent with the predictions of the theoretical model. Although the selection model posits that the migration decision depends solely on economic factors, it does not better explain average skill levels among employment-based immigrants, who presumably are the group most likely to move to the U.S. for economic motives, than among family reunification immigrants. Previous research, in contrast, generally reported results consistent with selection models similar to the one developed here. These studies, however, used data that do not include class of admission or did not investigate the role of admission categories in the INS data.

There are several possible reasons why the results of this study are inconsistent with some of the predictions of the model. First, this analysis uses the Gini index as a proxy for the return to skill. Unreported results using the ratio of household income of the top 10% of households to the bottom 20% were similar to those shown here. Results using other measures that focus on inequality between the middle class and the upper and lower tails of the income distribution or on the relative size of the middle class might provide different results. In addition, relative income inequality may not capture relative returns to skill. Other factors, such as returns to schooling or work experience and institutional details like minimum wages, may be large components of the return to skill, particularly in a cross-country setting. Given the importance of relative returns to skill in the conventional selection model, research that critically examines measures of the returns to skill across countries would advance the literature.[14]

The use of immigrants' reported occupation as a measure of skill also may contribute to the failure of some of the results to match the theoretical predictions. Immigrants may work in different occupations in their home country than in the U.S., and skill transferability may differ across countries of origin, as noted by Duleep and Regets (1997, 1999). Occupation in the home country or initial occupation in the U.S. may therefore not be the best predictor of long run success.[15] Longitudinal or retrospective data on occupation held in both the country of origin and the destination over time are needed in order to determine whether immigrants are successful in the U.S.

NOTES

1. General equilibrium studies (Borjas et al., 1997; Jaeger, 1996; Johnson, 1998) report larger adverse wage effects than cross-area studies, such as Card (2001) and the papers surveyed in Borjas (1994) and Friedberg and Hunt (1995). The smaller effects in cross-area studies may be due to migration of labor or capital, endogenous locational

choice, or changes in output mix at the area level in response to immigrants' locational choices.

2. This imputation requires assuming that immigrants will work in these occupations in the U.S. and earn the same as natives, or at least that occupation at the time of receipt of legal permanent resident status is well-correlated with future earnings in the U.S., and that the transferability of occupation from the source country to the U.S. does not differ across countries.

3. The INS data do not include illegal aliens adjusting to legal permanent resident status under the Immigration Reform and Control Act (IRCA) of 1986. In 1995, only 4267 individuals were admitted under the IRCA provisions.

4. An exception is newly-arriving male immigrants accompanying a spouse who is the principal immigrant on an employment visa. These husbands presumably report the occupation they held in the country of last residence, and the principal spouse reports the occupation she will hold in the U.S. Less than 15% of male immigrants in employment-based admission classes are the accompanying spouse.

5. The skilled occupational categories correspond to codes 3-235 in the 1980 Census occupation codes. Greenwood et al. (1996) use the same categorization to classify immigrants as skilled.

6. It should be noted that immigrants may move across admission classes as the ease of entry changes across classes.

7. The main non-immigrant categories from which individuals in the sample converted to permanent resident status are temporary visitors for pleasure (25%), entry without inspection (23%), and H1 visas (13%).

8. Several limitations of the ILO data should be noted. The lower age limit for inclusion in the data and the categorization of members of the armed forces vary across countries. A few developing countries only include individuals in urban areas. Despite these limitations, the ILO is the only organization that reports occupational data for a large number of countries. Data from 1994 or 1996 are used for a few countries in order to increase the number of observations in the sample. The ILO occupational data for Ecuador and Paraguay are from 1994, and from 1996 for Honduras, Peru, Bangladesh, Croatia, and Australia. The data source is ILO (1996).

9. The income inequality data are from the World Bank (1997) and Tabatabai (1996) and for the closest year to 1995 available; the data are from the 1990s except for four countries with data from the 1980s (Austria, Hong Kong, Ireland and Singapore).

10. The GDP data are from the United Nations (1997) and the World Bank (1997). The GDP data are not adjusted for purchasing power parity.

11. The distance is air miles. The data are from the Distcalc program of the U.S. Department of Transportation, Bureau of Airline Statistics, which was graciously supplied by Jeff Gorham. The closest of the three U.S. cities to the home country is used, except Los Angeles is used instead of Miami as the gateway for Mexico.

12. The means indicate a similar pattern. The average fraction of immigrants in skilled occupations is 0.70 for employment-based immigrants, 0.26 for family reunification immigrants, 0.08 for refugees/asylees, and 0.42 for immigrants admitted in other categories.

13. All refugees and asylees are adjusting immigrant status, so the fraction adjusting variable is not included in the model.

14. Psacharopoulos (1994) provides a summary of the literature on international returns to education.

15. For example, Duleep and Dowhan (2000) find that average initial earnings of immigrants have declined over time, but the rate of earnings growth appears to have increased.

ACKNOWLEDGMENTS

The author thanks Solomon Polachek, Donna Ginther and Dan Waggoner for helpful comments. This paper was commenced when the author was at the Federal Reserve Bank of Atlanta. Any views expressed in this paper are those of the author and do not necessarily reflect those of the Federal Reserve Bank of Atlanta or the Federal Reserve System.

REFERENCES

Barrett, A. (1998). The effect of immigrant admission criteria on immigrant labor-market characteristics. *Population Research and Policy Review*, *17*(5), 436–456.
Borjas, G. J. (1987). Self-selection and the earnings of immigrants. *American Economic Review*, *77*(4), 531–553.
Borjas, G. J. (1991). Immigration and self-selection. In: J. M. Abowd & R. B. Freeman (Eds), *Immigration, Trade, and the Labor Market*. Chicago: University of Chicago Press.
Borjas, G. J. (1994). The economics of immigration. *Journal of Economic Literature*, *32*(4), 1667–1717.
Borjas, G. J. (2000). The economic analysis of immigration. In: O. Ashenfelter & D. Card (Eds), *Handbook of Labor Economics* (Vol. 3). Amsterdam: Elsevier.
Borjas, G. J., Bronars, S. G., & Trejo, S. J. (1992). Self-selection and internal migration in the United States. *Journal of Urban Economics*, *32*(2), 159–185.
Borjas, G. J., Freeman, R. B., & Katz, L. F. (1997). How much do immigration and trade affect labor market outcomes. *Brookings Papers on Economics Activity*, *1997*(1), 1–90.
Card, D. (2001). Immigrant inflows, native outflows, and the local labor market impacts of higher immigration. *Journal of Labor Economics*, *19*(1), 22–64.
Chiswick, B. R. (1999). Are immigrants favorably self-selected? *American Economic Review*, *89*(3), 181–185.
Cobb-Clark, D. A. (1993). Immigrant selectivity and wages: The evidence for women. *American Economic Review*, *83*(4), 986–993.
Duleep, H. O., & Dowhan, D. J. (2000). Has the labor market quality of U.S. immigrants fallen? Evidence from longitudinal data. Mimeo, Urban Institute.
Duleep, H. O., & Regets, M. C. (1997). Immigrant entry earnings and human capital growth: Evidence from the 1960–1980 censuses. In: S. W. Polachek (Ed.), *Research in Labor Economics* (Vol. 16). Greenwich, CT: JAI Press.
Duleep, H. O., & Regets, M. C. (1999). Immigrants and human capital investment. *American Economic Review*, *89*(2), 186–191.
Friedberg, R. M., & Hunt, J. (1995). The impact of immigrations on host country wages, employment, and growth. *Journal of Economic Perspectives*, *9*(1), 23–44.
Greenwood, M. J., McDowell, J. M., & Waldman, D. M. (1996). A model of the skill composition of U.S. immigration. *Applied Economics*, *28*(3), 299–308.

International Labor Office (1996). *Yearbook of labor statistics*. Geneva: International Labor Office.
Jaeger, D. A. (1996). Skill differences and the effect of immigrants on the wages of natives. U.S. Bureau of Labor Statistics Working Paper No. 273.
Jasso, G., & Rosenzweig, M. R. (1990). Self-selection and the earnings of immigrants: Comment. *American Economic Review*, *80*(2), 298–304.
Jasso, G., Rosenzweig, M. R., & Smith, J. P. (2000). The changing skill of new immigrants to the United States: Recent trends and their determinants. In: G. J. Borjas (Ed.), *Issues in the Economics of Immigration*. Chicago: University of Chicago Press.
Johnson, G. A. (1998). The impact of immigration on income distribution among minorities. In: D. S. Hamermesh & F. D. Bean (Eds), *Help or Hindrance? The Economic Implications of Immigration for African Americans*. New York: Russell Sage Foundation.
Polachek, S. W., & Horvath, F. W. (1977). A life cycle approach to migration: Analysis of the perspicacious peregrinator. In: R. Ehrenberg (Ed.), *Research in Labor Economics* (Vol. 1). Greenwich, CT: JAI Press.
Psacharopoulos, G. (1994). Returns to investment in education: A global update. *World Development*, *22*(9), 1325–1343.
Roy, A. D. (1951). Some thoughts on the distribution of earnings. *Oxford Economic Papers*, *3*, 135–146.
Sjaastad, L. (1962). The costs and returns of human migration. *Journal of Political Economy*, *70*(5,2), 80–93.
Tabatabai, H. (1996). *Statistics on poverty and income distribution: An ILO compendium of data*. Geneva: International Labour Office.
Taylor, J. E. (1987). Undocumented Mexico-U.S. migration and the returns to households in Mexico. *American Journal of Agricultural Economics*, *69*(3), 626–638.
United Nations (1997). *Statistical yearbook*. New York: United Nations.
U.S. Bureau of the Census (2001). The foreign-born population in the United States. *Current Population Reports* (P20–534).
World Bank (1997). *World development report*. Washington, DC: Oxford University Press.

APPENDIX

Table A1. Countries Included in the Sample.

Country	Percent Skilled	Number in Sample
Latin America		
Bolivia	28.0	264
Chile	35.1	302
Colombia	18.8	1915
Costa Rica	26.5	253
Ecuador	15.8	1321
El Salvador	4.3	2144
Honduras	14.0	864
Mexico	4.9	12400
Panama	32.9	234
Paraguay	28.6	63
Peru	24.5	1530

Table A1. (Continued)

Country	Percent Skilled	Number in Sample
Uruguay	32.3	96
Venezuela	59.2	588
Asia		
Bangladesh	39.1	1218
Hong Kong	54.4	2703
Israel	51.6	858
Japan	33.8	983
Korea	52.2	2143
Malaysia	51.0	359
Pakistan	44.7	2134
Philippines	42.5	7539
Singapore	72.2	115
Sri Lanka	60.6	231
Thailand	13.4	1026
Turkey	46.5	1243
Europe		
Austria	41.9	301
Belgium	69.3	179
Canada	68.4	4896
Croatia	18.4	456
Czech Republic	50.0	16
Denmark	64.9	154
Estonia	16.7	24
Finland	75.7	103
Germany	60.2	1552
Greece	25.9	642
Hungary	61.3	168
Ireland	45.9	1901
Italy	43.2	754
Latvia	47.9	71
Netherlands	69.1	414
Norway	62.1	140
Poland	31.3	3507
Portugal	12.4	715
Romania	48.9	1087
Slovakia	36.6	123
Slovenia	45.8	24
Spain	57.6	380
Switzerland	75.1	341
United Kingdom	66.0	4400
Oceania		
Australia	66.5	776
New Zealand	58.6	268

Note: Data are for the 1995 fiscal year and include only new recipients of legal permanent resident status (not including individuals legalized under the IRCA).

IMMIGRATION AND THE LABOR FORCE PARTICIPATION OF LOW-SKILL NATIVE WORKERS

Hannes Johannsson, Stephan Weiler and Steven Shulman

ABSTRACT

This paper analyzes the impact of immigration on low-skill native workers using pooled CPS data on cities in static and dynamic fixed effects models. Labor force participation is shown to be the dominant adjustment mechanism to immigrant inflows. Furthermore, native participation responses are stronger in immigrant-dense cities than in areas with sparser concentrations. These results hold after accounting for the potential endogeneity of immigrant locational decisions. The labor supply adjustments absorb most of the impact of immigration, and account for the weakness of the observed effects of immigration on wages and employment.

1. INTRODUCTION

Immigration has played a major role in shaping the evolution of the American labor force over the last century. Yet immigration's effects are still not completely understood. Studies using national data generally suggest that competing native labor suffers in response to immigrant inflows (see, for example, Borjas, Freeman & Katz, 1996). The negative impact of immigration on the economic prospects of native workers should be stronger in studies using more disaggregated data given the direct pressure concentrated immigrant inflows place on local labor markets. Low-skill natives who directly compete with the new low-skill arrivals should be particularly affected. Yet the existing estimates of the local impacts of immigration are surprisingly weak and inconsistent.

Past work has focused on immigration's long-term impact on wages and employment rather than its more immediate effects. As a result, these studies have tended to understate the impact of immigration, particularly on low-skill native workers. The short-term consequences of immigration eventually dissipate, but they nonetheless can impose real and enduring costs. This is particularly the case with respect to labor supply adjustments to immigration. Our evidence shows that labor supply adjustments are the dominant response to immigration. Immigration induced changes in the labor force participation rates of low-skill native workers represent a utility loss to them. Participation changes also serve to reduce the observed impact of immigration on their wages and employment.

Because previous studies have largely ignored this variable, they have understated the negative impact of immigration on low-skill native workers. The small estimates of the impact of immigration in these studies are implausible given the sheer size of immigrant inflows and their concentration in a few metropolitan areas. More recent work (Johannsson & Weiler, 2000) uses detailed panel data to analyze the short-term adjustment mechanisms of wages, unemployment, and labor force participation. The results show that labor force participation rate changes indeed play a crucial role in the adjustment process. When they are taken into account, immigration displays sizeable, negative impacts on low-skill native workers as has long been suspected.

The current study also shows that most of the impact of immigration is absorbed by participation rate adjustments among low-skill, native workers. Here, however, the emphasis is on the demographic context in which these adjustments take place. Cities with higher concentrations of immigrants are compared to cities with lower immigrant densities in order to analyze variations in the participation adjustment process. Exploiting annual data from the March Current Population Survey (CPS) in a pooled cross-sectional time series, both static and dynamic results demonstrate the surprisingly strong role of labor force participation in the adjustment process.

The principal finding is that native participation rates are most responsive to immigrant inflows in immigrant-dense areas. Low-skill workers in cities with high concentrations of immigrants are most likely to respond to further immigration by dropping out of the labor force. These workers are the ones in most direct competition with immigrants, suggesting that they comprise the lowest-skill portion of low-skill native workers. When they drop out of the labor force, sample selection bias pushes the wages and employment of the remaining workers up.

For this reason the negative impact of immigration on the wages of low-skill workers has been difficult to discern.

The next section reviews the simple theoretical premises of immigration research, previous findings, their limitations, and recent innovations. The ensuing empirical sections explicitly contrast cities with high- and low-immigrant densities to assess the differences in their adjustment processes. Chow tests are the principal tool used to distinguish the differing relationships between immigration and labor force participation. Using this approach, static short-term panel results are summarized in the third section. The fourth section explores the characteristics of immigrants' locational choices, which are then clarified through the dynamic adjustment process identified in the fifth section. A sixth section concludes.

2. A SIMPLE THEORY OF PARALLEL LABOR MARKETS

The following sketch summarizes the traditional local labor market model of immigration adjustment. Assume that similarly skilled natives and immigrants are substitutes in two parallel local labor markets. The net impact of immigration on the demand for native labor depends upon the balance between two opposing forces. On the one hand, increases in the supply of immigrant workers absorb some of the demand for substitute native workers. On the other hand, immigration adds to labor resources (as long as it exceeds any corresponding declines in native labor force participation) and so adds to economic growth. The latter offsets the former with respect to the impact of immigration on the demand for low-skill native workers, and hence on the wages and employment of these workers. If wage and employment declines among these workers are observed, the net shock to labor demand must be negative. Given the more direct relationship of the substitution scenario to natives' situations, as well as anticipating the empirical findings, we will assume that the net impact of immigration on low-skill native workers is negative. In other words, the dominant effect of immigration is to allow employers to substitute away from low-skill native workers.

The adverse shock to native labor demand causes a corresponding decline in native labor supply as the incentives for low-skill native workers to participate in the labor market decline. However, the labor supply adjustment is temporary. Labor markets eventually revert to their long-run equilibrium states as some of these workers migrate to other areas with greater opportunities (some of those who remain may also eventually return to the labor market if they augment their skills or lower their reservation wage). When they do, they not only return to the labor force themselves, but they also cease being counted as "not in the labor force" in the areas they left behind. Consequently, the participation rates of immigration-impacted areas eventually rise back to their previous levels.

This structure implies that local effects will be most pronounced in the short-term before a migration-induced return to a longer-run equilibrium. The local adjustment mechanism to general demand shocks is evaluated by Blanchard and Katz (1992) and Bartik (1993), who found that it takes wages up to a decade to fully adjust to the initial shock, while unemployment and labor force participation rates adjust completely after five to seven years. Much other evidence suggests that the longer-term labor supply responses indeed involve native out-migration from the local market (e.g. Filer, 1992; Frey, 1994; Mariel Boatlift in Card, 1990). These external leakages effectively muffle immigration's effects on internal local market variables such as wages and unemployment.

To fully understand the local impact of immigration on natives, the effects of immigrant inflows must be examined prior to the completion of labor market adjustments. Most research has failed to account for this shorter-term adjustment process, thus understating immigration's impact on the wages and employment of low-skill native workers. The participation adjustment should be especially pronounced for that portion of the low-skill labor force which is in most direct competition with immigrants. Since the immigrant population is skewed toward very low-skill workers, the native workers in most direct competition with them are also very low-skill. When these workers drop out of the labor force, the measured average skill and wages of the workers who remain in the labor force increases. The negative impact of immigration on wages is thereby likely to be understated.

This is akin to the argument made a quarter-century ago by James Heckman and Richard Butler that black wage gains from the Civil Rights Movement were exaggerated due to sample selection bias. They showed that work disincentives created by welfare payments would increase measured average black wages even if the wages of black workers still in the labor force stayed constant: "by removing the lowest wage blacks from the labor force, social transfer programs can manufacture wage growth by simply subtracting the least productive blacks from the population base used to measure wages and earnings" (Butler & Heckman, 1977, p. 236). Similarly, immigration can artificially manufacture wage growth by driving the least skilled native workers out of the labor market. This offsets the measured negative impact of immigration on wages.

The negative impacts of immigration also have been understated in previous literature as a result of the long-term framework most of it has employed. Some of this literature utilizes decennial Censuses statistics in static models to imply particular response patterns by native workers (Borjas, 1994). These analyses are inherently incapable of identifying dynamic responses by native workers to immigration changes. Those studies on labor market dynamics that do exist rely upon decades-long changes between Censuses to identify immigration's impacts (e.g. Altonji & Card, 1991). But since most adjustments to such labor demand shocks take place within a decade, such studies are likely to miss the short-term effects of immigration on native workers. Although these effects tend to dissipate over time (for regions if not for individuals), they nonetheless can represent substantial utility losses for impacted native workers.

Labor force participation is also an important variable in its own right. Workers who exit the labor force in response to immigrant competition have clearly suffered utility losses since they would not otherwise have chosen to change their pattern of labor supply. But this utility loss may not be captured in the measurements of wage and employment decline, particularly if those measurements suffer from understatement bias. Labor force participation adjustments derive from the negative impact of immigration on the wages and employment of low-skill native workers, but they can also absorb the shock of immigration, reducing the response of wages and employment to it. The failure of previous studies to incorporate the dynamics of participation can explain why they have found the wage and employment consequences of immigration to be surprisingly low and inconsistent (Johannsson & Weiler, 2000).

The remainder of this paper describes a set of empirical tests of the impact of immigration on the labor supply of low-skill native workers. We also examine the impact of immigration on their wages and employment. Since the impact of immigration can be absorbed by participation adjustments, and since participation adjustments can mask the wage and employment impacts, strong results on the participation variable can be consistent with weaker results on the wage and employment variables. Strong results on any of these variables implies that the net effect of immigration on the demand for low-skill native labor is negative (i.e. that substitution effects dominate growth effects).

The participation response of low-skill native workers to immigration is not expected to be constant or uniform. Labor markets characterized by high immigrant densities are likely to display stronger participation responses by low-skill native workers. This prediction is based on an analogy to the phenomenon of "tipping": when the minority share of white neighborhoods passes a certain point, white flight can occur, causing neighborhoods to suddenly become mostly minority. The residential response of whites depends upon the concentration of minorities in the local neighborhood.

Similarly, the work response of natives depends upon the concentration of immigrants in the local labor force. As concentrations increase, employers have too many opportunities to substitute immigrants for native workers, weakening the bargaining power of the latter. There may also be "network effects" as high concentrations of immigrants eases the hiring of new immigrants and their integration into the workplace. Native workers start to give up on the local labor market, which they perceive to be flooded by immigrants, and in which they feel threatened by the ability of employers to replace them with immigrants. As a result, there is "native flight" from the local labor force which adds to its immigrant density. The interactive combination of immigrants coming into the labor force and native workers exiting from the labor force can turn immigrant-density into a self-perpetuating process (like residential segregation) when it passes a certain point. For this reason we also test the hypothesis that areas with high immigrant densities will display a stronger participation response by low-skill native workers than areas with low immigrant densities.

In order to test these hypotheses, it is necessary to control for the potential endogeneity of immigrants' locational choices. Causality can be particularly hard to distinguish in the labor market adjustments we describe. In particular, immigrants may choose to settle in areas with low participation rates if they believe that less competition from low-skill native workers will improve their job opportunities. The direction of causality must be established in order for the correlations between immigrant density and native participation to speak to the hypotheses. A combination of static, reverse causation, and dynamic analyses are utilized to shed light on these issues.

3. THE EMPIRICAL MODELS AND STATIC FINDINGS

The empirical model is constructed to evaluate the impact of arriving low-skill immigrants on low-skill natives. Given the short-term focus, which limits the number of years that can be usefully incorporated, the cross-sectional depth of a pooled cross-section time-series data set is ideal. While the core regression equation employed in this study does not differ from previous studies in terms of its structure and specification, using pooled cross-section time-series data enhances the efficiency of the estimators by increasing the number of degrees of freedom.

A fixed-effects model, with individual constants for each city,[1] offers further advantages. City constants account for any structural differences between cities by incorporating them into the intercepts. Omitted variable bias is minimized, as any variable that is systematically related to cities, such as particular types of local industry mix, are effectively represented by the fixed effects constants. Although this study focuses on a relatively short time span, 1995–1999, time dummies are included to account for any structural changes across cities at particular points in time. The shortness of the time period in fact adds to the reliability of the results insofar as any bias introduced by out-migration of workers (or in-migration of firms, as in Hanson & Slaughter, 1999) is reduced. By capturing the short-term nature of the labor market and allowing for structural differences across labor markets (as well as across cities over time), the present analysis provides important new insights into the existing immigration debate.

Three sets of data are tested based on the hypothesized distinctions between immigrant-sparse and immigrant-dense cities. First, a broad sample of 68 immigrant cities produces representative benchmark results. This sample is then split into those 28 cities with the highest (i.e. greater than 25%) levels of immigrant concentrations, and the 40 with lesser densities of immigrants. The split was determined by the relatively large jump in immigrant concentration between the Top 28 and Bottom 40 cities; however, results are not substantively affected by marginal sample changes. Table 1 identifies the sample cities, detailing their immigrant concentrations and triage into the two sub-samples.

For each of the three ensuing sets of regressions, a Chow test is applied to determine whether the estimated relationships between the Top 28 and Bottom 40

Table 1. Top 68 Cities and Census City Codes Ranked by Immigrant Density (IMFR).

IMFR	City	IMFR	City
0.580	Miami, FL	0.215	Tampa-St. Petersburg-Clearwater, FL
0.559	Los Angeles-Long Beach, CA	0.210	Middlesex-Somerset-Hunterdon, NJ
0.494	Jersey City, NJ	0.208	Austin-San Marcos, TX
0.467	San Francisco, CA	0.206	Albuquerque, NM
0.447	New York, NY (White Plains Central City decoded to balance of PMSA)	0.204	Boston, MA-NH (NH portion not identified)
0.432	Brownsville-Harlingen-San Benito, TX	0.196	
0.417	San Jose, CA	0.192	Washington, DC-MD-VA-WV (West Virginia portion not identified)
0.409	San Diego, CA	0.184	Seattle-Bellevue-Everett, WA
0.409	McAllen-Edinburg-Mission, TX	0.183	Minneapolis-St. Paul, MN-WI (St. Croix County, WI not identified)
0.392	Bergen-Passaic, NJ	0.170	Denver, CO
0.371	Fresno, CA	0.166	Fort Smith, AR-OK
0.362	El Paso, TX	0.148	Tucson, AZ
0.348	Houston, TX (Chambers County not in sample)	0.146	Anchorage, AK
0.344	Stockton-Lodi, CA	0.138	Wilmington-Newark, DE-MD (Maryland portion suppressed)

Table 1. (*Continued*)

IMFR	City	IMFR	City
0.343	Las Vegas, NV-AZ (Nye County, NV and Mohave County, AZ not in sample)	0.135	Fort Worth-Arlington, TX
0.339	Fort Lauderdale, FL	0.135	Corpus Christi, TX
0.339	West Palm Beach-Boca Raton, FL	0.133	Oklahoma City, OK
0.332	Phoenix-Mesa, AZ	0.130	Milwaukee-Waukesha, WI
0.325	Bakersfield, CA	0.122	Salt Lake City – Ogden, UT
0.315	Springfield, MA	0.111	Raleigh-Durham-Chapel Hill, NC
0.304	Reno, NV	0.110	Detroit, MI
0.304	Honolulu, HI	0.109	Monmouth-Ocean, NJ
0.293	Chicago, IL (Dekalb County not in sample)	0.097	Philadelphia, PA-NJ
0.285	Riverside-San Bernadino, CA	0.095	Hickory-Morgantown, NC (Caldwell County no in sample)
0.276	Dallas, TX	0.093	Allentown-Bethlehem-Easton, PA
0.271	Portland-Vancouver, OR-WA	0.091	Kansas City, MO-KS
0.263	Newark, NJ	0.090	Rochester, NY
0.262	Boise City, ID	0.079	Atlanta, GA
0.241	Providence-Fall River-Warwick, RI-MA (Newport county, RI portion suppressed)	0.069	Charlotte-Gastonia-Rock Hill, NC-SC
0.240	Naussau-Suffolk, NY	0.057	Buffalo-Niagra Falls, NY
0.231	Orlando, FL	0.057	Cleveland-Lorain-Elyria, OH
0.227	Lakeland-Winter Have, FL	0.049	Omaha, NE-IA (Iowa portion not identified)
0.224	Sacramento, CA		
0.218	Modesto, CA		
0.216	Hartford, CT		
0.216	Oakland, CA		

samples are significantly different. Given N_1 and N_2 observations and k parameters, we first compute the pooled sum-of-squares (S_1) for each regression, with df $= n_1 + n_2 - k$. We then run each of the restricted samples separately (S_2 and S_3), adding their sum-of-squares (S_4) with df $= n_1 + n_2 - 2k$. Subtracting this sum (S_4) from the pooled sum (S_1) yields S_5. We can then compare

$$F = \frac{S_5/k}{S_4/n_1 + n_2 - 2k}$$

to the critical F at $(k, n_1 + n_2 - 2k)$. If the computed F exceeds the critical F, we can reject the null hypothesis that the regressions are describing the same relationship.

3.1. Statistical Model and Data

The core regression equation used throughout this paper follows the typical specification observed in the literature (e.g. Borjas, Freeman & Katz, 1996), i.e.

$$Y_{it} = \beta_0 + \beta_1 \text{Ethnicity}_i + \beta_2 \text{Gender}_i + \beta_3 \text{Age}_i + \beta_4 \text{Agesq}_i$$
$$+ \beta_5 \text{IMFR}_i + \beta_6 \text{Time} + \mu_{it} \quad (1)$$

where Y_{it} represents the three dependent variables for low-skilled natives, annual wages (in natural logs), unemployment rates (in levels to preserve zero values), and labor force participation rate (in natural logs). The subscript i represents the various cities in this study, $i = 1, 2, \ldots, 68$, while t represents the time frame of the study, $t = 95-99$. The error term is assumed rho be an independently, identically distributed random variable with mean zero and variance σ_μ^2. Time variable dummies are included for 1996, 1997, 1998, and 1999; 1995 is omitted. Time dummies are included to allow structural shocks across cities in particular years. Ethnicity variables are included for local percentages of Blacks, American Indians or Eskimos, and Asians or Pacific Islanders; Whites are omitted. The Gender variable represents the fraction of females in the local labor force, and the Age variables represent the average age of the native workforce. The latter variables help control for the concave age/earnings relationship.

The focal variable of interest is the fraction of immigrants in a given city, denoted as IMFR, which measures the local proportion of immigrants in the workforce. The data set focuses on low-skill workers, both natives and immigrants, with less than a high school education as the two groups are assumed to be substitutes in a given local market. The March CPS-based data set includes the 68 metropolitan areas that had non-zero counts of low-skilled immigrants in the data during all four years of the study. Descriptive statistics are reported in Table 2.

The fixed-effects regression equation was first estimated using the standard Ordinary Least Square (OLS) estimation technique. The presence of serial correlation across cities within the estimated model was tested using

$$e_{it} = \rho e_{it-1} + z_{it} \quad (2)$$

The postulated rho was significant in all cases. To account for the apparent presence of a first-order autoregressive process, the model was estimated using

Table 2. Descriptive Statistics, City Averages.

Selected Variables	Description of Selected Variables	Range
Average Age	The average age of low-skilled individuals in the sample.	35.79 (32–38.3)
Fraction of Whites	The fraction of low-skilled native whites in the sample.	81.6% (17.8–99.4%)
Average Real Wage	The average real annual wage for a low-skilled natives.	$7,159.13 (4,785.9–10,137.7)
Unemployment	The number of low-skilled natives in the civilian labor force that reported being unemployed.	3.48 (0.4–18.4)
Labor Force Participation Rates[a]	The fraction of low-skilled natives in the natives? civilian labor force.	54.2% (41.9–64.9%)
Fraction of Males	The fraction of low-skilled native males in the labor force.	49.9% (42.4–60.8%)
Fraction of Immigrants	The fraction of low-skilled immigrants in the low-skilled population (immigrants/natives + immigrants, where an immigrant is considered a person arriving to the U.S. since 1970).	22.3% (4.7–53.9%)

Note: The calculations of averages are based on the 13,908 individuals in the 68 cities during 1995–1999.

[a] These reported participation rates are in line with the rates reported in the overall March CPS sample. The overall participation rates for the five years is about 47%, for low-skilled it is about 17% while about 72% for high-skilled individuals. Furthermore, the reported immigrants' participation rates are higher than that of natives which is in line with the conclusions of other studies.

Generalized Least Squares (GLS). The general form of the fixed-effects model to be estimated is thus as follows:

$$y_{it} = \alpha + X_{it}\beta + v_i + \varepsilon_{it} \qquad (3)$$

where $i = 1, 2, \ldots, n$ and $t = 1, 2, \ldots, T$. v_i is the city-specific effect; it differs between cities, but for any particular city its value is constant. Thus the model applies GLS to

$$(y_{it} - \bar{y}_i + \bar{\bar{y}}) = \alpha + (x_{it} - \bar{x}_i + \bar{\bar{x}})\beta + (\varepsilon_{it} - \bar{\varepsilon}_i + \bar{v}) + \bar{\bar{\varepsilon}} \qquad (4)$$

where $\bar{y}_i = \sum_{i=1}^{T} y_{it}/T_i$, and similarly, and $\bar{\bar{y}} = \sum_i \sum_t y_{it}/nT$. Weighting observations by population size yielded substantively identical results in all cases, which is unsurprising given that such weighting techniques often add little to estimation precision (Dickens, 1990).

Table 3. Regression Results, Static Model.

	All 68 Cities	Top 28 Cities	Bottom 40 Cities
Dependent Variable: ln Real Wage[a]			
Coefficient	−0.0297	0.083	0.15
Standard Error	0.1404	0.3182	0.2879
Elasticity	−0.007	0.028	0.022
Dependent Variable: Unemployment Rate[b]			
Coefficient	0.064*	0.0245	0.0061
Standard Error	0.0289	0.0694	0.0464
Elasticity	0.25	0.123	0.02
Dependent Variable: ln Labor Force Participation Rate[c]			
Coefficient	−0.753*	−1.1*	−0.327
Standard Error	0.1127	0.3008	0.1786
Elasticity	−0.168	−0.37	−0.046

Note: Overall sample size 340 (68 cities over 5 years). There are 140 and 200 observations in the Top 28 and Bottom 40 cities respectively.
[a] Chow Test: $F = 0.143 < F(12, 316) = 1.75$, so therefore accept H_0.
[b] Chow Test: $F = 2.54 > F(12, 316) = 1.75$, so therefore reject H_0.
[c] Chow Test: $F = 2.78 > F(12, 316) = 1.75$, so therefore reject H_0.
* Statistically significant.

3.2. Static Results

The results of these initial static inquiries are described in Table 3. Findings are reported as elasticities for ease of comparison; lagged explanatory variables provided no additional significant insights on key results. The Chow tests can help distinguish whether the immigrant-sparse and immigrant-dense regressions are describing significantly different relationships. The critical value for the $F(12, 316)$ test at the 0.05 level is 1.75. The F-value for the wage equation is 0.41, unemployment's is 2.54, and labor force participation's is 2.78. Therefore, we can reject at the 5% level the H_0 that the participation and unemployment rate relationships are the same for the two types of cities.

In the broad 68 city sample, immigrants have adverse impact on natives' labor market performances, significantly in the case of participation and unemployment. As expected, greater concentrations of immigrants are related to lower wages, higher unemployment, and lower labor force participation of natives. However, wage effects are generally insignificant, and the Chow tests indicate that the Top 28 wage regression is not distinct from that of the Bottom 40. The puzzlingly weak immigration/wage relationship is consistent with the findings of previous static studies (e.g. Card, 1990).

Immigration's relationship to native unemployment is clearer than that of wage. In the overall sample, higher unemployment rates among low-skill native workers are significantly related to higher immigrant fractions. A 10% higher immigrant fraction creates a corresponding 2.5% increase in native unemployment, ceteris paribus. While neither the Top 28 nor Bottom 40 city results are statistically significant, the Chow test indicates that there is indeed a significant difference between the two regressions. As expected, cities with higher immigrant fractions tend to have higher native unemployment rates.

The participation findings are the most distinctive, already highlighting this often overlooked conduit for labor market adjustment. Higher densities of immigrants are significantly related to lower participation in the overall sample as well as in the Top 28 cities, with only a weak and insignificant relationship in the Bottom 40 places. The negative relation between immigrant fraction and participation is considerably stronger in the Top 28 cities, where a 10% higher immigrant fraction is related to a significant 3.7% lower native participation versus an insignificant 0.5% decrease in the immigrant-sparse areas.

These participation results suggest that a focus on wages and employment may overlook a crucial feature of native labor market behavior in response to immigrants. Labor income and unemployment imply participation in the labor force. Yet if much of the immigration relationship to local native labor market characteristics is absorbed by participation outflows, there may be few remaining adjustment pressures on the "participatory" variables of wage and unemployment. Such strong participation findings thus may explain why previous studies of immigration impacts on wages and unemployment have yielded surprisingly weak results, as were also found here.

4. LOCAL NATIVE ATTRIBUTES

The static analyses reported above do not offer direct evidence of the labor market adjustment process, which is inherently dynamic. These results simply represent a pooled cross-sectional "snapshot" of different labor markets at different points in time. Furthermore, the static patterns may in fact simply reflect endogenous destination decisions by in-migrants. This endogeneity could in fact reverse the causation between more immigrants and reduced native labor outcomes. In this section, we test the potential importance of this reverse causation by considering the impact of local native attributes on immigrant concentrations.

In the above static analysis as in other similar studies, the locational choice of immigrants is generally considered to be exogenous (see, for example, Borjas, 1994). In fact, the choice of destination by immigrants is likely to be influenced by labor market characteristics. Most basically, the migratory "beaten-path" effect has been shown to lead to increasing concentrations of immigrants in cities which have previously been the focus of such migrants. This path-dependence will tend to reinforce the concentration and character of immigrant cities.

Reversing the question of immigration impacts on low-skill natives, we seek to understand whether areas with particular native labor attributes tend to have systematically different concentrations of immigrants. To address this question, the immigrant fraction variable is introduced as the dependent variable to illuminate the relationship between immigrant concentration and local native characteristics. The simplest test is a means-on-means (i.e. "between") panel approach, regressing the mean of the dependent variable for each city over the time period on the means of the native characteristic variables along with the standard control measures for race, age, and gender. The results here are substantively the same as a more

Table 4. Regression Results, Means on Means.

	ln Real Wage	Unemployment Rate	ln LFPR
Sample: All 68 Cities (Dependent Variable: Immigrant Fraction)			
Regression 1	Coeff.: = −0.5 (0.645)		
	Elasticity = −0.22		
Regression 2		Coeff.: = 0.89* (0.408)	
		Elasticity = 0.232	
Regression 3			Coeff.: = −0.39* (0.072)
			Elasticity = −1.73
Sample: Top 28 Cities (Dependent Variable: Immigrant Fraction)			
Regression 1	Coeff.: = 0.012 (0.0815)		
	Elasticity = 0.035		
Regression 2		Coeff.: = 0.61 (0.4762)	
		Elasticity = 0.12	
Regression 3			Coeff.: = −0.26* (0.089)
			Elasticity = −0.76
Sample: Bottom 40 Cities (Dependent Variable: Immigrant Fraction)			
Regression 1	Coeff.: = 0.022 (0.0554)		
	Elasticity = 0.16		
Regression 2		Coeff.: = −0.35 (0.4071)	
		Elasticity = −0.13	
Regression 3			Coeff.: = −0.12 (0.087)
			Elasticity = −0.835

Chow Test: critical $F(8, 52) = 2.18$, the H_0 is rejected in all instances as the calculated F is 10.1, 9.85 and 7.57 for ln wage, unemployment rate, and log participation respectively.
*Statistically significant.

complex two-stage procedure, extracting fixed effects from a panel regression then regressing those fixed effects on the means of the relevant variables (e.g. Murphy & Topel, 1990; Weiler, 2000, 2001).

The results are shown in Table 4, which add an additional dimension to the static results. Contrasted with the critical $F(8, 52)$ of 2.18, all three relationships differ in the high- and low-immigrant cities. Most importantly, significant concentrations of immigrants occur in cities with low native labor participation rates (Regression 3) in both the overall sample and the Top 28 cities, directly reflecting the static panel results above. Symmetrically, cities with high unemployment rates also have higher concentrations of immigrants in the overall sample. The relationship of immigrant fraction to remaining unemployment and wage measures is considerably murkier, with insignificant effects in all cases.

In contrast, areas with higher immigrant fractions clearly feature low native participation rates. In the immigrant-dense sample, higher immigrant fractions are particularly closely associated with low native participation. Therefore, concentrations of immigrants occur in areas with low native participation rates, with that relationship strengthening in the Top 28 cities. The noted static results may thus simply be reflecting this compositional effect, with immigrants clustering in cities with already low native participation rates. The general assumption that immigrants cause reduced native labor outcomes is thus placed into doubt. Dynamic inquiries can clarify this causation conundrum.

5. DYNAMIC RESPONSE TO IMMIGRANT INFLOWS

The combination of the static and attribute results leads to clear dynamic questions. Do immigrant target areas with low native participation rates or in fact cause such reductions? Do immigrants arriving in already immigrant-dense cities affect natives more or less than those in immigrant-sparse areas? If immigrants simply target areas with already-low native labor force participation rates, then surges would not have further substantial effects on the dependent variables. However, if immigrants effectively substitute for existing local low-skilled natives, such surges would have clear impacts on natives' labor market outcomes. Furthermore, those impacts may vary systematically by the relative concentration of immigrants.

First-differences provide a simple yet effective means of assessing the impact of changes of immigrant concentrations on natives' labor market situations. The first-difference technique involves subtracting the preceding period's variable value from that of the current period, resulting in the straightforward change of the variable's value in the intervening time period. Time and demographic controls remain in levels; results are substantively identical with first-differenced controls. In sum, the model to be estimated is

$$Y_{it} - Y_{it-1} = \beta_0 + \beta_1 \text{Ethnicity}_i + \beta_2 \text{Gender}_i + \beta_3 \text{Age}_i + \beta_4 \text{Agesq}_i$$
$$+ \beta_5(\text{IMFR}_{it} - \text{IMFR}_{it-1}) + \beta_6 \text{Time}_i + \mu_{it} \qquad (5)$$

where the impact of first-differences of the key explanatory variable, immigrant fraction, is measured against consequent changes in the dependent variables. While past work (Altonji & Card, 1991) has similarly used first-differences to isolate immigration's impacts, all have focused on the decade-long gap between Censuses. As noted above, these longer-term comparisons are likely to miss the adjustments by internal indicators (e.g. wage, unemployment, participation) over the short-run before external adjustments (e.g. migration) finalize the equilibration process. Longer-term dynamic inquiries are thus likely to result in only limited perceived local market effects, which has been the standard puzzling result.

Results are shown in Table 5. As in the static results, lagged independent variables added no further substantive explanatory power. Again, the primacy of labor force participation responses to immigrant concentration is underscored, with the dynamic analyses now providing direct evidence of the adjustment process. As

Table 5. Regression Results, Dynamic Model.

	All 68 Cities	Top 28 Cities	Bottom 40 Cities
Dependent Variable: ln Real Wage[a]			
Coefficient	0.249	0.989	−0.087
Standard Error	0.215	0.522	0.345
Elasticity	0.055	0.34	−0.0124
Dependent Variable: Unemployment Rate[b]			
Coefficient	−0.15*	−0.104	−0.086
Standard Error	0.0473	0.113	0.067
Elasticity	−0.57	−0.52	−0.24
Dependent Variable: ln Labor Force Participation[c]			
Coefficient	−0.467*	−0.807*	−0.188
Standard Error	0.171	0.381	0.246
Elasticity	−0.104	−0.274	−0.03

Overall sample size 340 (68 cities over 5 years). There are 140 and 200 observations in the Top 28 and Bottom 40 cities respectively.
[a] Chow Test: $F = 0.454 < F(11, 318) = 1.79$, so therefore accept H_0.
[b] Chow Test: $F = 0.968 < F(11, 318) = 1.79$, so therefore accept H_0.
[c] Chow Test: $F = 1.91 > F(11, 318) = 1.79$, so therefore reject H_0.
*Statistically significant.

in the static and attribute cases above, we can apply the Chow test to determine the statistical distinction between the two samples, with the critical $F(11, 318)$ value at 1.79. The wage and unemployment regressions for immigrant-dense and immigrant-sparse cities are statistically similar, with respective F-values of 0.45 and 0.97 indicating that the two subsamples are describing the same overall relationship. In contrast, the F-value for participation is 1.91, thus clearly rejecting the null hypothesis that the immigrant-dense and immigrant-sparse results are describing the same relationship through the participation equation.

Surges in immigrants significantly decrease unemployment with insignificant wage impacts across the full sample; the Chow tests indicate that the distinctions between the immigrant-dense and immigrant-sparse areas in these cases are superficial. As noted at the outset, such hazy wage and unemployment results have become the norm in many such analyses. In fact, the unemployment result seems astonishing: do inflows of immigrants actually reduce competing native joblessness? The insignificant results on the wage variable speak against this conclusion. Instead it appears to be the case that the participation adjustments are distorting the measured impact of immigration on unemployment.

Increases in immigrant fraction clearly and significantly reduce the labor force participation rates of low-skilled native workers, with such effects being considerably stronger in immigrant-dense areas. Natives flowing out of the labor force appear to be accounting for so much of the adjustment to immigration that unemployment among remaining natives actually decreases. Given the strong negative participation effects, natives evidently leave the local labor force when immigration surges occur. This outflow reduces the number of potentially unemployed natives, leaving remaining native unemployment actually lower than before the surge. In other words, the participation reduction is due to a decline in employment opportunities, but that decline is masked as the least-employable native workers are subtracted out of measured unemployment. Based on the Chow tests' distinctions between the two subsamples, the greater unemployment reduction in the Top 28 cities ($\varepsilon_U = -0.52$ vs. -0.24 for Bottom 40) is consistent with this explanation, given the simultaneous higher labor absorption through participation exits in those cities ($\varepsilon_P = -0.27$ vs. -0.03 for Bottom 40).

In general, natives in immigrant-dense areas are more strongly affected by additional inflows than those in immigrant-sparse cities. A 10% increase in immigrant fraction decreases native labor force participation by a significant 2.7% in the Top 28 cities in comparison with an insignificant decrease of 0.3% in the Bottom 40. These dynamic results show that native participation in immigrant-dense cities is more affected by additional immigrant arrivals, suggesting the natives remaining in these already immigrant-dense areas are those most vulnerable to such surges.

6. CONCLUSIONS

Immigration's adverse impacts on native workers in parallel local labor markets has been widely assumed, but surprisingly little consistent evidence has yet been produced. We have shown that this evidence exists in the form of short-term adjustments in the labor supply of low-skill native workers. These adjustments represent a real utility loss for low-skill native workers. Furthermore, they tend to mask the negative impact of immigration on the wages and employment of these workers. Reductions in labor participation are in fact an important short-term absorption mechanism for labor market shocks, which tend to reduce the impact on the traditional internal indicators of wages and unemployment.

We also test the hypothesis that immigration causes low-skill natives to respond differently in immigrant-dense cities than in immigrant-sparse cities. The evidence clearly shows that participation adjustments are stronger in immigrant-dense cities. The approach was incremental, beginning with the clearly distinct participation findings in the static sample. While these heretofore neglected participation effects indicate that previous studies may have missed much of immigration's impact, these results are only incomplete assessments of the impact of immigrants on competing native workers. Static results do not offer direct evidence of the inherently dynamic adjustment process by natives. Furthermore, causation can not be disentangled easily. The native attributes of labor markets in fact suggest that immigrants concentrate in cities with low participation rates. These concentrations could have been targeted by the immigrants rather than caused by their arrival, potentially reversing the traditionally assumed direction of causation.

The concluding dynamic results indicate that immigrant inflows do in fact reduce native participation, with natives in immigrant-dense cities being considerably more affected by new arrivals than natives in immigrant-sparse areas. These strong results are especially sobering when one considers that labor markets during the period of study were among the tightest in recent history. If immigrant-induced effects are already pronounced under these labor-favorable conditions, the prospects for low-skill native workers during slack market conditions may be considerably worse.

NOTE

1. The analysis were performed at the MSA level but for convenience we refer to them as cities throughout this chapter.

REFERENCES

Altonji, J. G., & Card, D. (1991). The effects of immigration on the labor market outcomes of less-skilled natives. In: J. M. Abowd & R. B. Freeman (Eds), *Immigration, Trade and the Labor Market* (pp. 201–234). Chicago: University of Chicago Press.

Bartik, T. J. (1993). Who benefits from local job growth: Migrants or the original residents? *Regional Studies, 27*(4), 297–311.

Blanchard, O. J., & Katz, L. F. (1992). Regional evolutions. *Brookings Papers on Economic Activity, 1*, 1–61.

Borjas, G. J. (1994). The economics of immigration. *Journal of Economic Literature, XXXII*(December), 1667–1715.

Borjas, G. J., Freeman, R. B., & Katz, L. F. (1996). Searching for the effects of immigration on the labor market. *AEA Papers and Proceedings, 86*(2), 246–251.

Butler, R., & Heckman, J. (1977). The government's impact on the labor market status of Black Americans: A critical review. In: L. Hausman et al. (Eds), *Equal Rights and Industrial Relations*. Madison WI: Industrial Relations Research Association.

Card, D. (1990). The impact of the Mariel boatlift on the Miami labor market. *Industrial Labor Relations Review, 43*(2), 245–257.

Dickens, W. T. (1990). Error components in grouped data: Is it ever worth weighting? *Review of Economics and Statistics, 72*(2), 328–333.

Filer, R. K. (1992). The effect of immigrant arrivals on migratory patterns of native workers. In: G. J. Borjas & R. B. Freeman (Eds), *Immigration and the Work Force* (pp. 245–269). Chicago: University of Chicago Press.

Frey, W. H. (1994). The new white flight. *American Demographics, 16*(4), 40–48.

Hanson, G. H., & Slaughter, M. (1999). The Rybczynski theorem, factor-price equalization, and immigration: Evidence from U.S. States. NBER Working Paper No. W7074 Issued in April.

Johannsson, H., & Weiler, S. (2000). Local labor market adjustments to immigration. Working Paper.

Murphy, K. M., & Topel, R. H. (1990). Efficiency wages reconsidered: Theory and evidence. In: Y. Weiss & G. Fishelson (Eds), *Advances in the Theory and Measurement of Unemployment*. London: Macmillan.

Weiler, S. (2000). Industrial structure and unemployment in regional labor markets. *Industrial Relations, 39*(2), 336–359.

Weiler, S. (2001). Unemployment in regional labor markets: Using structural theories to understand local jobless rates in West Virginia. *Industrial and Labor Relations Review, 54*(3), 573–592.

CHILDREN, NON-DISCRIMINATORY PROVISION OF FRINGE BENEFITS, AND HOUSEHOLD LABOR MARKET DECISIONS

Mark C. Berger, Dan A. Black, Amitabh Chandra and Frank A. Scott

ABSTRACT

In the spirit of Polachek (1975) and the later work of Becker (1985) on the role of specialization within the family, we examine the relationship between fringe benefits and the division of labor within a married household. The provision of fringe benefits is complicated by their non-additive nature within the household, as well as IRS regulations that stipulate that they be offered in a non-discriminatory manner in order to maintain their tax-exempt status. We model family decisions within a framework in which one spouse specializes in childcare and as a result experiences a reduction in market productive capacity. Our model predicts that the forces toward specialization become stronger as the number of children increase, so that the spouse specializing in'childcare will have some combination of lower wages, hours worked, and fringe benefits. We demonstrate that to the extent that labor markets are incomplete, the family is less likely to obtain health insurance from the employer of the spouse that specializes in childcare. Using data from the April 1993 CPS we find evidence consistent with our model.

1. INTRODUCTION

Economists have long recognized that decisions about division of labor within the home have important implications for observable market outcomes of the family members. Becker (1965) provides a framework for understanding how families combine time and goods to maximize utility. Polachek (1975) builds a similar framework to analyze the life-cycle division of labor within the family. He argues that males are more likely to specialize in market work at the beginning of marriage due to greater stock of initial human capital, greater market wages, and/or lower household productivity. These forces toward specialization are reinforced by the presence of children by increasing the household productivity of the wife more than that of the husband. In more recent years, while there has been some convergence in the market and household activities of men and women, the pattern of men providing more market work and women providing more housework and childcare is still observed across a number of countries, including the U.S.[1]

This pattern of specialization has obvious implications for observed differences in labor force participation rates and hours of work between husbands and wives. But other observable market outcomes may be affected as well. This pattern of specialization is what lies behind the research of Mincer and Polachek (1974) and Polachek (1975) explaining gender wage differences. In this work, gaps in the labor force participation of women for the purposes of childbearing, childcare, or other household production play a key role in explaining the lower wages of women relative to men. In fact, O'Neill and Polachek (1993) show that the reductions in these gaps and the resulting increases in labor force experience are a major contributor to the narrowing of the gender wage gap over time in the U.S.

Building on this earlier work, Becker (1985) provides another explanation for the existence of female-male earnings differences tied to the household division of labor. Women, bearing a disproportionate share of childcare and household responsibilities, have less energy to devote to the labor market, and thus earn less than men do. Indeed, using Panel Survey of Income Dynamics (PSID) data, Hersch and Stratton (1997) provide substantial evidence that increases in household activities significantly reduce the wages of married women. Of course, wages are not the only form of compensation in the labor market. A significant fraction of compensation is provided in the form of fringe benefits, of which an important component is employer-provided health insurance.

Buchmueller (1996/1997) examines gender differences in health insurance outcomes using the April 1993 supplement to the Current Population Survey (CPS). He finds that the gap in health insurance coverage between men and women is for the most part due to the fact that many married women turn down health insurance coverage in order to be covered by their husband's plan.

Thus, it does not appear that employers are discriminating against women in the provision of health insurance. In fact, he finds that women are nearly as likely to be eligible for coverage as men (78.9% vs. 81.3%), and single women are more likely to be eligible than single men (78.1% vs. 72.4%). Buchmueller's results for health insurance are provocative because they contrast sharply with the results for differences in wages. Women earn lower wages than men. However, it is not the case that they are offered equivalent wages to men and then turn them down. For health insurance, wives are almost as likely to work in firms that offer health insurance, but are more likely to turn it down, and obtain coverage from their husband's plan.

What would a model of household optimization predict about female-male differences in the provision of fringe benefits? For two reasons, predictions are not as straightforward as for wages because of the complicated nature of fringe benefit provision. First, family considerations immediately come into play because workers can typically cover other family members on their employer-provided health insurance policy. The benefits of certain fringes such as health insurance coverage are not additive. Thus, it may not make sense for family members to be covered by multiple employer-provided health insurance policies. The forces leading to specialization in the family may be greater for health insurance than for wages due to this Leontief nature of health insurance benefits. Second, the family's choice of health insurance coverage is complicated by an additional factor on the demand side of the labor market. In order to maintain the tax-exempt status of fringe benefits, the IRS requires that they be provided in a non-discriminatory fashion to all eligible employees (Carrington, McCue & Brooks, 2002; Scott, Berger & Black, 1989; Scott, Berger & Garen, 1995).[2] Therefore, health insurance is provided based on the preferences of the median worker in the firm, and families may find it difficult to obtain the mix of health insurance that they desire. Taking these factors together, it is not immediately clear without a model of family optimization whether we should observe lower employer health insurance coverage and eligibility rates for women than men.

In this paper, we construct a model of household optimization in the spirit of Polachek (1975) and Becker (1985) that incorporates some of the unique features of fringe benefit provision, such as non-duplication of health insurance benefits and the rules for non-discriminatory provision across employees. The model yields testable predictions about the division of labor between spouses, health insurance choices within the family, as well as earnings, hours worked, and other fringe benefits. We are able to test directly the predictions of the model using a matched sample of husbands and wives from the April 1993 CPS. We use these data to examine how family health insurance and other labor market outcomes are influenced by household responsibilities. Our results suggest that as household responsibilities increase, measured by the number of own children, wives are less likely to be eligible for health insurance coverage and are more likely to choose coverage under their spouse's plan if eligible for coverage under both their own and their spouse's plan. Husbands are more likely to be eligible for health insurance as the number of children increase. We also find that wives with more children have lower wages, work fewer hours, and are less likely to be eligible for pensions, sick leave, and disability benefits. In contrast, among husbands additional children do not significantly affect wages, hours worked, and eligibility for pensions, sick leave, and disability benefits. These empirical findings are consistent with the hypothesis that families with more children have more incentive to engage in specialization. This specialization in childcare and other household activities by the wife in turn leads to greater inequality in labor market outcomes between husbands and wives as the number of children increase. Our findings reinforce the results of the Polachek (1975) and Becker (1985) models of the household division of labor, and complement the previous empirical work of Polachek (1975) on the effect of children on earnings and of Hersch and Stratton (1997) on the effect of housework on wages.

Other research has examined differences in labor market outcomes of husbands and wives without modeling the choice of health insurance and other fringe benefits in a family context. Waldfogel (1998) examines the "family gap" in earnings, i.e. the role of children in explaining male-female earnings differences using National Longitudinal Survey of Youth (NLSY) and British data. Waldfogel emphasizes the effect of institutional factors such as maternity leave. She concludes that maternity leave mitigates some of the gender wage difference.[3] Wellington and Cobb-Clark (1997) use 1993 March CPS data to estimate hours of work equations for a matched sample of husbands and wives. However, they do not model family health insurance choices and instead assume spouse health insurance coverage to be exogenously determined. Similarly, Buchmueller and Valletta (1999) estimate hours of work equations for married women that depend in part on exogenously determined health insurance availability and coverage of the husband. Lundberg and Rose (1999) use matched samples of husbands and wives from the PSID to examine the hours of work, wages, and earnings before and after the birth of the first child. While these studies examine earnings and hours outcomes of husbands and wives, they do not help us understand health insurance and other fringe benefit choices in a family context and their relationship to the division of labor within the household.

Olson (1998, 2000) uses the March 1990–1993 CPS to examine how health insurance benefits of the husband affect wives' health insurance coverage, and how wives' wages and hours of work are affected by their own and their husbands' employer-provided health insurance coverage. The coverage, hours of work, and wages of the wife depend on the coverage of the husband, but the reverse is not true.

While not specifying a formal model, he argues that his results are consistent with a household model of risk sharing. Wives are more likely to be working full-time and to be working on a job with coverage when the husband does not have coverage or the wife is not covered by the husband's plan. Because Olson uses March CPS data, he is unable to distinguish between coverage and eligibility. In addition, he is ultimately concerned with the relationship between married women's hours worked and health insurance and the wage-health insurance tradeoff for married women, rather than formally modeling and testing a model of household specialization.

Currie (1997) examines gender differences in fringe benefit coverage using May 1988 CPS data. She estimates linear probability models of the receipt of various benefits. These models control for demographics such as gender, marital status, and number of children, in addition to firm size, industry, and region effects. However, benefit choices are not modeled within a family context, for example by jointly estimating the benefit decisions of husbands and wives. Therefore, it is not possible to determine whether the effects of children are different on married women and married men. Currie does argue that household specialization is not at work in fringe benefit provision. She bases that conclusion on the fact that young, single, childless women are twice as likely to have sick leave as women in general, a group that includes women with children who might want sick leave to help them specialize in household production. However, it is difficult to rule out specialization on the basis of one fringe benefit such as sick leave.

Buchmueller (1996/1997) does empirically model the wife's eligibility for health insurance as a function of husband's eligibility, but his specification does not come from a model of household optimization and it assumes that the husband's job choice is exogenous to the wife's job choice. He does describe auxiliary regressions in which husband's eligibility is instrumented with husband's characteristics in a section investigating the robustness of his results. However, these results are not reported. Finally, Monheit, Schone and Taylor (1999) use the 1987 National Medical Expenditure Survey to examine the decision of households to obtain double health insurance coverage. Empirically they do examine pieces of the coverage decision, but eligibility for coverage is assumed to be exogenous to the model. In contrast, eligibility for coverage is endogenously determined in our framework and is a key factor in the labor market choices made by households.

An important contribution of our paper is to estimate a model of household decision making, in which decisions concerning spousal responsibility for childcare and labor market outcomes such as wages, hours, and the eligibility for fringe benefits are made simultaneously. Our emphasis will be on health insurance because it constitutes the largest tax-expenditure in the U.S., but we will also consider other fringes that are required to be provided in a non-discriminatory manner such as pensions and sick leave. We relax an assumption in the existing literature that husbands and wives make these decisions independently, or that one spouse's coverage or eligibility may be assumed to be exogenous to the other's. In other words, a household's choice of fringe benefit eligibility will be made a dependent variable as opposed to treating it as an exogenous regressor. As such, our paper also offers a unifying economic framework to better interpret the results of previous research. In the next section, we specify a model of household decision making that incorporates the choice of fringe benefits such as health insurance. We first consider the case of complete markets, and then turn to the case in which markets are incomplete and workers are therefore unable to perfectly sort themselves into jobs with regard to their tastes for fringe benefits. In Section 3, we describe our data and demonstrate why it is uniquely suited to test our theoretical model. Section 4 develops the econometric framework used to operationalize our model and discusses the testable predictions that it generates. Section 5 presents our empirical results, and Section 6 concludes.

2. A SIMPLE MODEL OF HOUSEHOLD CHOICE

2.1. Household Decisions with Complete Markets

Consider a married household that makes collective decisions concerning consumption and the provision of health insurance. In order to examine differences in labor market outcomes for husbands and wives, we focus on households in which both parents work. The utility function of the household is:

$$U = f(X, \max(H_f, H_m), K) \tag{1}$$

where X is a vector of consumption goods, H_f and H_m are the health insurance plans that the female's and the male's employers provide, and K is the number of children in the household. For the sake of simplicity, we consider the case in which the decision on the number of children has already been made and so K is exogenous.[4]

For purposes of the model, we assume that all health insurance plans are family plans and require no cost sharing by the worker. Because health insurance is a public good within the household, the household cares only about the most generous of the plans. These are of course simplifications, however, they do capture important aspects of employer health insurance provision. Almost all employer-provided plans provide for eligibility for family members.[5] Most employers pay at least part of the cost of plans, but many workers do pay part of the cost of their health insurance plans.[6] What is important for our purposes is that there are no systematic gender differences in costs of the plans to the workers.[7] We also rule out both spouses being covered by their own plan in this model. While holding two plans may provide some additional benefits, it is certainly true that there is a large degree of duplication and hassle that results from holding two plans. Thus, the assumption that health insurance is a public good within the household is useful. As we show below, there is no reason for duplicative plans in the case of complete markets. In the case of incomplete markets, having cases in which both spouses are offered a plan is not only possible but also quite likely. Even in this case, however, it is more likely that spouses choose one plan or another rather than be covered by both plans.[8]

Each member of the household is endowed with a productive capacity: let F_f and F_m denote the productive capacities of the female and male, respectively. Assortative mating in the marriage market will result in a positive covariance between F_f and F_m, but this is not necessary for our model. Following Becker (1985), we assume that caring for children reduces this productive capacity. Let α be the fraction of childcare provided by the male. The labor market compensation of the female and male are simply

$$F_f - (1-\alpha)C_f(K) = Y_f + H_f \qquad F_m - \alpha C_m(K) = Y_m + H_m \qquad (2)$$

where $C_i(K)$ for $i = m, f$ represents the cost of caring for children, and Y_i for $i = m, f$ represents labor market earnings. We assume that the number of children increases the cost of childcare, or $C'_i(K) > 0$ for $i = m, f$. Childcare costs are linear in the fraction of childcare services, but any fixed costs associated with the provision of childcare would reinforce the household's desire to specialize. Equation (2) simply states that the productivity of each worker, net of the reduction in productive capacity from providing childcare services, is equal to earnings plus the value of health insurance.

Following U.S. tax law, workers' earnings are taxed, but their consumption of employer-provided health insurance is not. Therefore, we may write the household budget constraint as

$$F_f + F_h - (1-\alpha)C_f(K) - \alpha C_m(K) = pX + H_f + H_m + T(Y_f + Y_m) \qquad (3)$$

where $T(Y_f + Y_m)$ is the household tax bill and p is a vector of prices for X. The problem facing the household is to maximize Eq. (1) subject to equations; (2) and (3). The household must pick a consumption bundle, X, health insurance coverages, H_f and H_m, and a division of childcare responsibilities, α.

Equations (2) and (3) implicitly assume that all markets are complete in the sense that all possible combinations of health insurance coverage are available in the market. Below, we argue that this is likely not the case. The case of complete markets, however, is informative. Three features of the solution to the household problem warrant mention:

Proposition 1. If markets are complete, then the solution to the household problem satisfies:

(1) The partner with the lower costs of providing the childcare specializes in the provision of childcare; that is,

$$\alpha = 1 \quad \text{if} \quad C_m(K) < C_f(K) \quad \text{or} \quad \alpha = 0 \quad \text{if} \quad C_m(K) > C_f(K);$$

(2) For a given set of endowments of productive capacities (F_f and F_m) household income is declining in the number of children, and this reduction is achieved through the reduction in compensation of the low-cost childcare provider;
(3) Only one partner provides health insurance, but there is no reason for one gender to be more likely to provide the insurance.

The first part is simply the insight that the partner with the lower costs of production should provide childcare services. Of course, the provision of these childcare services is not free, and the second part simply reflects that the costs of having children increases as the number of children increases. To establish part three, notice that there is no benefit from duplication of health benefits. While increases in family income will increase marginal tax rates (under progressive taxation) and hence there is a lower after-tax price of health insurance, tax rates are determined by family income, not the individual worker's income. As a result, either worker may provide the health insurance at the same price. The family simply picks their optimal level of health coverage and one spouse or the other provides it.

2.2. Incomplete Markets

While informative, the assumption of complete markets is not realistic. Empirical attempts to find a wage-fringe tradeoff have been largely unsuccessful, in part because of the existence of incomplete markets for fringe benefits.[9] In our view, the tax rules are the likely reason we observe incomplete markets. As Scott, Berger and Black (1989), and Scott, Berger and Garen (1995) emphasize, IRS rules require that fringe benefits be provided in non-discriminatory fashion. The intent of the IRS rules is to prevent firms from tailoring compensation packages of top executives to minimize their tax bills. As a result of these rules, however, firms may not tailor compensation to their lower paid workers either, and workers must be offered access to similar health plans regardless of their compensation.

Given the need to offer a common health insurance plan, firms must balance the demands for health insurance of all of their workers. These workers are likely to be a mix of single workers, single parents, one-worker, two-parent households, and two-worker, no-children households as well as two-worker, two-parent households. Faced with the need to satisfy these diverse demands, firms must offer health benefits that are compromises across the set of diverse workers. The health insurance plan that the firm offers, therefore, is necessarily a compromise among the demands of its employees. Scott, Berger and Black (1989) show that the firm offers fringe benefits such as health insurance that reflect the preferences of the median worker. Because the after-tax price falls with increases in wages (Long & Scott, 1982; Woodbury, 1983; Woodbury & Wei-Jang, 1991), firms with disproportionate numbers of high-wage workers should offer health insurance, and conditional on offering health insurance, firms with more high-wage workers should offer superior health insurance.

With incomplete markets, the household decision process is characterized by:

Proposition 2. If markets are incomplete, then the solution to the household problem satisfies:

(1) As before,

$$\alpha = 1 \quad \text{if} \quad C_m(K) < C_f(K) \quad \text{or} \quad \alpha = 0 \quad \text{if} \quad C_m(K) > C_f(K),$$

that is, the partner with the lower costs of providing childcare should do so;
(2) As before, for a given set of endowments of productive capacities (F_f and F_m) household income is declining in the number of children and this reduction occurs through the reduction in earnings of the low-cost childcare provider;
(3) The worker not providing childcare services is more likely to provide health insurance. Some families will have coverage from both partners, but the likelihood of dual coverage declines in the number of children.

The likelihood that a worker provides health insurance in a world with incomplete markets will depend on the chances that the worker is in a firm with high-wage workers. This in turn will depend on the worker's endowment of productive capacities F_i and whether the worker is responsible for providing childcare services within the household. Thus, part three reflects the fact that workers who do not produce childcare services for the household services are more likely to have greater market productivity of the two partners and more likely to be working in a firm in which the employees have a high demand for health insurance. As a result, this worker is more likely to provide the household with health insurance and the childcare specialist is likely to have a portion of their total compensation devoted to health insurance that the family does not need or want. This reduces the attractiveness of market work at the margin and may cause some childcare specialists to reduce hours. Thus, the IRS rules on non-discriminatory fringe benefit provision, which lead to incomplete markets, serve to reinforce the original specialization choices within families.[10]

To this point, we have not specified which partner is more likely to provide the childcare services. Polachek (1975) and Becker (1985) both argue that it is likely to be the wife. The very nature of childbirth requires wives to have some interruptions in their labor market participation. While this may be a relatively modest reduction in time at work, it does afford women a comparative advantage in the production of childcare services. Moreover, because of nursing, women tend to have a comparative advantage in the care of infants. In fact, Polachek (1975) argues that children are likely to reinforce earlier family decisions about market and household specialization that are made due to initial stocks of human capital, market wages, and/or household productivity. As we explain below, our model gives ample opportunity to test whether it is the husband or the wife who is the prime provider of childcare services.

3. DATA

The primary data set used in this paper comes from the April 1993 CPS. The CPS is a monthly survey of almost 60,000 households in almost 700 different geographic areas, and is the official source of the United States government's unemployment statistics. In April of 1993, the Survey of Employee Benefits was conducted as a supplement to that month's CPS. Half of those in the April sample were potential respondents, resulting in a sample size of approximately 27,000. From the regular monthly survey, comprehensive data are available on the employment status, occupation, and industry of persons 16 years and older. Personal characteristics such as age, sex, race, marital status, veteran status, and education are included. The Employee Benefits Supplement includes a series of questions on pension and health insurance eligibility and coverage through employer or union-sponsored plans. For the respondents to the April Supplement, income and earnings data from the March 1993 CPS were merged to produce an April–March match for 1993.[11] Most importantly, the April 1993 Employee Benefits Supplement is uniquely suited to test our model, as it remains the major source of data that contains both information on a worker's *eligibility* for employer-provided health insurance and an extensive amount of labor market information.[12]

There were 27,268 valid responses to the April Supplement, of which 16,832 workers were married.[13] To abstract from the labor force participation decision, we focus our analysis on families where both spouses work ($n = 12{,}674$). We do this for at least two reasons. We seek to explain differences in observed labor market outcomes (earnings, health insurance, etc.) among those who have already chosen to work. Second, if we did include nonparticipants, the results regarding family specialization would be even stronger. Families in which only one spouse works have already specialized to a large degree. We seek to determine whether the observed patterns are consistent with specialization in families in which both spouses work. Thus, by including only workers we make the empirical task of estimating the effects of household specialization more difficult. But if we find evidence consistent with our model we can be more certain that the effects of specialization are at work.

After matching workers to their spouses, we include only those families where both the worker and spouse completed the April Supplement. We then exclude everyone who is not in a primary family ($n = 178$), and those families where both husband and wife are not between 18 and 64 years of age ($n = 246$). We also exclude those families in which either spouse is a full-time student ($n = 74$). The resulting sample is a symmetric data set with 12,176 observations, coprised of 6,088 husbands and 6,088 wives. In 1993, 63% of all March CPS respondents aged 18 and 64 classified themselves as meeting this definition of marriage, 22% were never married, and 10% were divorced. A weighted analysis suggests that our sample corresponds to 53 million workers in the economy.

4. EMPIRICAL MODEL

4.1. Measurement

We use the April CPS to estimate models that are derived directly from the theoretical model. Families in our model choose X, the vector of consumption goods, and health insurance given by $\max(H_f, H_m)$. Children (K) are assumed to be exogenous for now, but we return to this issue later in this section. Families also choose α, the division of childcare responsibilities. By Propositions 1 and 2, for a given number of children K, α is either zero or one, depending on which spouse has the lower cost of providing childcare. Given Eqs (1)–(3), reduced form equations of the family's choice of consumption goods and health insurance can be rewritten as:

$$Y_f + Y_m = g(F_f, F_m, K, T, \boldsymbol{p}) \qquad \max(H_f, H_m) = h(F_f, F_m, K, T, \boldsymbol{p}) \qquad (4)$$

where given T, the average income tax rate, and $\boldsymbol{p}$, the vector of prices of consumption goods, $Y_f + Y_m$ determine the amount of consumption goods X.[14] In the empirical work, we estimate separate earnings equations for the husband

and wife because it allows us to draw inferences about the lower cost childcare provider. Therefore, we estimate:

$$Y_f = g_1(F_f, F_m, K, T, p) \qquad Y_m = g_2(F_f, F_m, K, T, p). \qquad (5)$$

We measure the exogenous variables in Eqs (4) and (5) using observable characteristics of families in the April CPS. For K we use the number of children in the household less than age 18. We do not observe T and p directly. In order to proxy for regional differences in T and p, we include dummies for Census regions and residence in an MSA. We use two specifications of F_f and F_m, the productive characteristics of husbands and wives. One (Specification A) includes demographic characteristics of the husband and wife: a quartic in age, race (black, other), education level dummies (less than high school, some college, associate degree, bachelor's degree, and schooling past a B.A. degree), and veteran status. We also construct an expanded specification of F_f and F_m (Specification B), which includes demographic characteristics, industry and firm size dummies, and a quartic in tenure. This expanded specification may control for differences in productive capacity coming from differences in firm and industry characteristics, for differences in the types of health plans offered across firms, and length of time on the job. We include tenure in our regressions to control for the fact that fertility and tenure are correlated for women, and that many health plans require a mandatory probationary period before employees are eligible for health benefits.

The dependent variables in our analysis are eligibility for health insurance on the job, health insurance coverage, wages, hours worked, and other forms of compensation. Our theoretical model includes only the market earnings outcomes of husbands and wives. Market earnings change either through a change in hourly wages or through a change in hours worked. One can imagine families adjusting either wages or hours worked in response to specialization and childcare costs. The spouse that specializes in childcare could find productive capacity reduced either through a reduction in his or her hourly earnings, a reduction in his or her hours worked, or a combination of both. Therefore, we also empirically examine both wages and hours outcomes of husbands and wives as functions of number of children.[15] Wages are measured using average hourly earnings in 1992. Hours of work are measured using average hours of work during 1992.[16] We specify our earnings equations in the usual semi-logarithmic form, implying that the earnings reduced form equation in Eq. (3) can be written in the form $Y_f + Y_m = \exp(Z\beta)$, where Z is the set of exogenous variables. Thus, we can decompose $\beta = \beta_f + \beta_m$ and estimate separate husband and wife earnings equations. Since total earnings is the product of hourly earnings and hours worked, we further decompose the estimated earnings equations into semi-logarithmic hourly earnings equations and semi-logarithmic hours worked equations.

4.2. Hourly Earnings and Hours Worked Equations

What predictions for the hourly earnings and hours worked equations come from our theoretical model? In the case of both complete and incomplete markets, additional children reduce household income, and the reduction is achieved by a reduction in the earnings capacity of the lower cost childcare provider. This generates the following predictions for hourly earnings and hours worked. If $\alpha = 0$, i.e. the wife specializes in the production of childcare, then we should see that additional children lower the hourly earnings and hours worked of wives and have no effect on the hourly earnings and hours worked of husbands. On the other hand, if $\alpha = 1$, then the results should be reversed. Thus, from the wage and hours equations estimates, we have testable predictions on the signs of the number of children coefficients in the hours and hourly earnings equations, and depending on the estimated effects we can potentially determine whether the husband or the wife is the lower cost childcare provider. For example, if increases in the number of children lower wages and hours worked of wives but have no effect on the wages and hours worked of husbands, then the wife is the childcare specialist. The reverse would be observed if the husband were the childcare specialist. Any other combination of estimated effects would be inconsistent with the model specified in the paper. This would imply that increases in number of children do not lead to increased specialization or that the specialization that occurs is more complicated than is specified in the model.[17]

4.3. Pension, Sick Leave, and Disability Benefits Equations

The April 1993 CPS also has information on other fringe benefits that can be used to test our model of household specialization. Specifically, each respondent in the April 1993 CPS is asked whether he or she is eligible for a pension, sick leave, and disability benefits. These benefits are unlike health insurance in that they typically do not include coverage of other family members, so there is not the added complication of duplication of benefits as in the health insurance case. These fringes can be considered additional forms of compensation and thus enter the model much like earnings except that they are excluded from taxation. The utility function in this case becomes

$$U = f(X, \max(H_f, H_m), P_m, P_f, S_m, S_f, D_m, D_f, K) \qquad (6)$$

where P refers to pension benefits, S refers to sick leave benefits, and D represents disability leave benefits. The market compensation and family budget constraint equations would include P, S, and D on the right-hand side.[18] The family would then choose these benefits in addition to earnings and health insurance coverage. Utility maximization subject to the market earnings and family budget constraints would yield reduced form equations for husband's and wife's P, S, and D as functions of the same set of exogenous variables as the earnings and health insurance equations. The effect of additional children on the provision of these benefits should work in the same way as earnings. The productive capacity of the childcare specialist is reduced by additional children. This can show up as a reduction in wages or hours, or in the eligibility for various fringes such as pensions, sick leave, and disability insurance. Thus, according to our model, if $\alpha = 0$, i.e. the wife specializes in the production of childcare, then additional children should lower the probability of receiving these benefits and have no effect on the probability of the husband receiving these benefits. On the other hand, if $\alpha = 1$, then additional children should have no effect on the probability of the wife receiving these benefits, and should reduce the probability of the husband receiving these benefits.[19] Similar to wages and hours worked, any other combination of estimated effects would be inconsistent with the model presented in the paper, suggesting either the additional children do not lead to greater specialization or that the specialization is more complicated than given by our model.

4.4. Health Insurance Eligibility Equations

The specification of the health insurance choice equation is not as straightforward as the other equations due to the duplicative nature of health insurance benefits. Equation (4) tells us that the maximum of the health insurance benefits of the husband and the wife is a function of the exogenous variables in the model. We typically do not observe the dollar value of the health insurance benefits of workers. Instead, in the April 1993 CPS we observe whether or not the individual is eligible for employer-provided health insurance and whether or not the individual is covered by employer-provided health insurance. Using eligibility for health insurance, there are four possible qualitative outcomes for the family: both spouses could be eligible for health insurance ($H_m = 1$, $H_f = 1$), the wife could be eligible for health insurance and the husband ineligible ($H_m = 0$, $H_f = 1$), the husband could be eligible and the wife ineligible ($H_m = 1$, $H_f = 0$), and finally neither may be eligible for employer-provided health insurance ($H_m = 0$, $H_f = 0$). While the case of having at least one spouse eligible is preferred to having neither spouse eligible, it is not clear that there is any particular ordering to the three cases in which at least one spouse is eligible for coverage.

Given this lack of ordering, the health insurance equation is amenable to estimation using multinomial logit estimation. In this model, the probability that a household with characteristics Z chooses outcome i, one of the four health insurance eligibility combinations which we can denote $i \in \{1, 2, 3, 4\}$, may be expressed as:

$$\Pr(\text{Outcome } i) = \frac{e^{Z\beta^i}}{e^{Z\beta^1} + e^{Z\beta^2} + e^{Z\beta^3} + e^{Z\beta^4}}. \qquad (7)$$

For estimation purposes, we make the normalization that $\beta^1 = 0$. Thus the probability of choosing categories 2–4 can be written as:

$$\Pr(\text{Outcome } i) = \frac{e^{Z\beta^i}}{1 + e^{Z\beta^2} + e^{Z\beta^3} + e^{Z\beta^4}}, \quad i \in \{2, 3, 4\} \qquad (8)$$

and the probability of outcome 1 is just

$$\Pr(\text{Outcome } 1) = \frac{1}{1 + e^{Z\beta^2} + e^{Z\beta^3} + e^{Z\beta^4}}. \qquad (9)$$

These expressions can be used to compute the marginal effect on the probability of each outcome given a change in Z, i.e. $\partial \Pr(\text{Outcome } i)/\partial Z$. These marginal effects of a change in Z sum to zero ($\Sigma \partial \Pr(\text{Outcome } i)/\partial Z = 0$). For example, below we will calculate the marginal effect of an additional child on each of the probabilities, starting from the sample mean set of Zs and the sample mean predicted probabilities.

What does our theoretical model predict about the marginal effects of additional children on the probabilities of each of the health insurance outcomes? Consider the case of complete markets. First of all, additional children may increase or decrease the overall household demand for health insurance. The reduction in the productive capacity within the household may reduce the demand for health insurance because of a pure income effect. On the other hand, the potential wealth loss due to poor health probably increases as the number of family members increases, which would tend to raise the demand for health insurance. If additional children increase the demand for health insurance, we would see an increase in the probability that one or the other of the spouses is eligible for health insurance

$$\frac{\partial \Pr(H_m = 1, H_f = 0)}{\partial K} > 0 \quad \text{or} \quad \frac{\partial \Pr(H_m = 0, H_f = 1)}{\partial K} > 0.$$

As Proposition 1 states, the model is silent on which spouse purchases health insurance. At the same time the probability that neither spouse is eligible for health insurance would decrease ($\partial \Pr(H_m = 0, H_f = 0)/\partial K < 0$). If additional children reduce the demand for health insurance, the opposite pattern would be observed. We would see an increase in the probability that neither spouse is eligible for health insurance and decreases in at least one of the probabilities that one of the spouses is eligible ($\partial \Pr(H_m = 1, H_f = 0)/\partial K < 0$ or $\partial \Pr(H_m = 0, H_f = 1)/\partial K < 0$; $\partial \Pr(H_m = 0, H_f = 0)/\partial K > 0$). There is no reason for both spouses to be eligible so the probability that both are eligible should remain at zero no matter how many children a couple has or whether additional children increase or decrease the family demand for health insurance ($\partial \Pr(H_m = 1, H_f = 1)/\partial K = 0$). In fact, large numbers of families with both spouses eligible for coverage would constitute evidence that markets are not complete and the incomplete markets model is more relevant.

In the case of incomplete markets, individual spouses may find it difficult to obtain the exact mix of fringe benefits and wages that they desire because fringe benefit packages in each firm are designed to satisfy the preferences of the median worker in each firm. As Proposition two states, health insurance will more likely be provided by the spouse who does not specialize in childcare, and while both spouses may be eligible for health insurance coverage due to incomplete markets, the likelihood of this occurring falls as the number of children increases. Why does this occur in the case of incomplete markets? The demand for health insurance is likely to decrease as the income of the median worker in the firm decreases. Thus, it becomes less likely that the spouse providing childcare will be working in a firm in which the median worker demands health insurance because that spouse's productive capacity falls with each additional child. In fact, the non-eligibility of the childcare specialist may result from working in a firm with lower average wages, or from the fact that the childcare specialist may choose to work part-time, and part-time workers are typically not eligible for coverage under the employer's health insurance plan. Thus, the likelihood that only the childcare specialist is eligible for health insurance or that both spouses are eligible should fall with additional children. In addition, as the number of children increases and productive capacity falls, the family has increased incentive to avoid using up part of the compensation of the childcare-providing spouse on health insurance benefits that the family does not need. Thus, the childcare specialist is likely to search for a job with more wages and less fringes, in order to allow the family to purchase as many other goods and services (X) as possible. At the same time, the probability that only the non-childcare specialist is eligible for health insurance is likely to increase with the number of children, as the childcare specialist adjusts hours or switches to a job without the unneeded health insurance coverage.

If the wife is the childcare specialist, i.e. if $\alpha = 0$, then additional children should lower the probability that we observe both spouses eligible for health insurance ($\partial \Pr(H_m = 1, H_f = 1)/\partial K < 0$), and lower the probability that we observe only the wife eligible for health insurance ($\partial \Pr(H_m = 0, H_f = 1)/\partial K < 0$). The probability that only the husband is eligible should increase due to increased forces toward specialization in the family ($\partial \Pr(H_m = 1, H_f = 0)/\partial K > 0$). If the husband is the childcare specialist ($\alpha = 1$), additional children still lower the probability that both spouses are eligible for health insurance ($\partial \Pr(H_m = 1, H_f = 1)/\partial K < 0$), but the predictions for eligibility of one spouse or the other are reversed ($\partial \Pr(H_m = 0, H_f = 1)/\partial K > 0$, $\partial \Pr(H_m = 1, H_f = 0)/\partial K < 0$). The probability of neither spouse being covered will increase or decrease depending on the effect of additional children on the family's overall demand for health insurance. This probability should decrease if the demand for health insurance increases with additional children ($\partial \Pr(H_m = 0, H_f = 0)/\partial K < 0$) and increase if more children reduce the total productive capacity of the family enough that the family substitutes out of health insurance and into other goods and services ($\partial \Pr(H_m = 0, H_f = 0)/\partial K > 0$).

The existence of incomplete markets is consistent with the findings of Carrington and Troske (1995). While they find that there is substantial gender segregation across firms, this segregation is by no means complete. However, the lack of complete segregation means that some women may find it difficult to obtain the mix of fringe benefits that they desire. In addition, even if there were perfect gender segregation, incomplete markets for fringes may arise because of differences in tastes by marital status. Single women, especially those with children, are more likely to have a higher demand for fringes like health insurance than married women. If the median worker is a single woman, married women may find themselves eligible for benefits that they would not purchase in a world where markets were complete.

4.5. Health Insurance Coverage Equations when both Spouses are Eligible for Coverage

The dependent variables in our analyses of fringe benefits thus far have been eligibility for health insurance through the employer and eligibility for other fringe benefits through the employer. We use eligibility for health insurance and other fringe benefits rather than coverage in our analysis. This is in fact one of the strengths of the April 1993 CPS data set. The firm offers a fringe benefit package based on the preferences of the median worker and adjusts wages accordingly. Thus, from the firm's point of view it is eligibility and not coverage that matters. However, in the case where only one spouse is eligible, the distinction between eligibility and coverage is not that important from the family's point of view. They are likely to choose to be covered by the plan of the eligible spouse.

The family's problem becomes more complicated when both spouses are eligible for employer-provided health insurance. This is by its very nature a case of incomplete markets. First, our model predicts that families will choose one plan or the other and not both. In the April CPS, some husbands and wives do choose to be covered by their own plans. However, the majority are cases in which both husband

and wife are covered by one plan or the other. Only a trivial number of families are not covered by any plan. As number of children increases, the productive capacity of the childcare specialist decreases. At the same time it becomes likely that the health care plan offered by the employer of the childcare specialist becomes less attractive than the health care plan of the other spouse. This occurs because the childcare specialist is increasingly likely to be working in a firm in which the median worker has a lower demand for health insurance. The more attractive of the two plans is obviously more likely to be chosen.[20] Let $\Pr(\text{Cov}_w = 1, \text{Cov}_h = 0)$ denote the probability that the family obtains coverage from the wife's plan, $\Pr(\text{Cov}_w = 0, \text{Cov}_h = 1)$ denote the probability that the family obtains coverage from the husband's plan, and $\Pr(\text{Cov}_w = 1, \text{Cov}_h = 1)$ denote the probability that the family obtains coverage under both plans. Thus, if the wife is the childcare specialist, as number of children increase, we are less likely to observe coverage from the wife ($\partial \Pr(\text{Cov}_w = 1, \text{Cov}_h = 0)/\partial K < 0$), less likely to observe coverage from both spouses ($\partial \Pr(\text{Cov}_w = 1, \text{Cov}_h = 1)/\partial K < 0$), and more likely to observe coverage from the husband ($\partial \Pr(\text{Cov}_w = 0, \text{Cov}_h = 1)/\partial K > 0$). If the husband is the childcare specialist, as number of children increase, we are still less likely to observe coverage from both spouses ($\partial \Pr(\text{Cov}_w = 1, \text{Cov}_h = 1)/\partial K < 0$), but now we expect an increase in the probability of coverage from the wife ($\partial \Pr(\text{Cov}_w = 1, \text{Cov}_h = 0)/\partial K > 0$), and a decrease in the probability of coverage from the husband ($\partial \Pr(\text{Cov}_w = 0, \text{Cov}_h = 1)/\partial K < 0$). This provides yet another test of household specialization in the context of incomplete markets and helps us understand why one spouse or the other may refuse health insurance benefits.

4.6. Potential Lendogeneity of Children

One important potential estimation problem is that number of children may be endogenous. Consider the case of hourly earnings. Women with unobservably low hourly earnings may decide to have more children, thus inducing a simultaneity bias. The typical approach taken to address this problem is to instrument for the number of children. However, this is a difficult task with CPS-type data. We first attempt to instrument the number of children by following Angrist and Evans (1998). Angrist and Evans exploit the observed parental preference for mixed sibling-sex composition, and therefore propose using three dummy variable instruments measuring the gender of the first child, whether the first two children are both boys, or whether they are both girls. These variables are likely to be correlated with fertility, but unlikely to be correlated with the outcome measures of interest to health and labor economists. We also used state level data on ancestry and religion as instruments. Because the CPS does not ask questions on a respondent's religion and ancestry, we used state-level data on the proportion of the population in twenty-two ethnic and religious groups from the 1990 decennial census and church membership data (Bradley, 1992) as instruments. These variables could serve as potential instruments because they may affect fertility but may not be correlated with the labor market outcomes under study.

5. RESULTS

5.1. Summary Statistics

We start our analysis of the results by looking at the responses of married male and female workers to employer-provided health insurance questions that are contained in Table 1.[21] Panel A reports results for all workers in our sample, and Panel B restricts the sample to full-time workers only.[22] There is very little difference between the percentage of husbands and wives that work in firms that offer health insurance. In the full sample, husbands are slightly more likely to work in firms that offer health insurance (73.54% vs. 71.32%), but among full-time workers, women are actually more likely to work in firms that offer health insurance (80.30% vs. 78.01%). Wives are less likely to be eligible for health insurance than husbands in

Table 1. Employer-Provided Health Benefits for Married Workers.

	Husband	Wife
Panel A: All households (husband and wife may, or may not be, full-time workers)		
Worker is employed at firm that offers health insurance	73.54%	71.32%
Worker is eligible for employer-provided health insurance	70.04	62.43
Worker is covered by own employer-provided health insurance	63.83	47.45
Worker is covered by spouse's health insurance	23.19	45.11
Worker is covered by some form of health insurance	86.99	87.16
N	6,088	6,088
Panel B: Full-time households (both husband and wife are full-time workers)		
Worker is employed at firm that offers health insurance	78.01%	80.30%
Worker is eligible for employer-provided health insurance	75.14	75.65
Worker is covered by own employer-provided health insurance	66.73	59.76
Worker is covered by spouse's health insurance	29.72	43.59
Worker is covered by some form of health insurance	92.68	93.01
N	3,934	3,934

Source: April 1993 CPS, Employee Benefit Supplement. The sample is all married workers aged 18–64, who are not full-time students. The percentages in these tables will not sum to 100%, since the categories are not mutually exclusive.

Table 2. Family Health Insurance Eligibility Decisions.

	Frequency	Percentage of Total
Panel A: Household outcomes for health insurance eligibility, full sample		
Outcome 1: A family where neither worker is eligible for employer-provided health insurance.	786	12.91
Outcome 2: A family where only the husband is eligible for employer-provided health insurance.	1,501	24.66
Outcome 3: A family where only the wife is eligible for employer-provided health insurance.	1,016	16.69
Outcome 4: A family where both workers are eligible for employer-provided health insurance.	2,785	45.75
Total	6,088	100.00
Panel B: Household outcomes for health insurance eligibility, full-time sample		
Outcome 1: A family where neither worker is eligible for employer-provided health insurance.	315	8.01
Outcome 2: A family where only the husband is eligible for employer-provided health insurance.	643	16.34
Outcome 3: A family where only the wife is eligible for employer-provided health insurance.	663	16.85
Outcome 4: A family where both workers are eligible for employer-provided health insurance.	2,313	58.80
Total	3,934	100.00

Source: April 1993 CPS, Employee Benefit Supplement. The sample is all married workers aged 18–64, who are not full-time students. The sample size for Panel B falls because we condition coverage on both spouses being full-time workers.

the full sample (62.43% vs. 70.04%). This is because women are more likely to be working part-time and thus be ineligible for health insurance benefits. In panel B, where the sample is restricted to full-time workers, the eligibility rates of husbands and wives are virtually identical (75.14% vs. 75.65%).[23] Wives are less likely to be covered by their own employer-provided health insurance than husbands and more likely to be covered by their spouse's plan. In the end, wives are slightly more likely to be covered by some form of health insurance than husbands. Thus, it is not the case that wives are less likely to work in firms offering health insurance than husbands or if they are working full-time are less likely to be eligible than husbands. However, they are far more likely to refuse coverage.

In Table 2, we show the health insurance eligibility choices made within the household. In the vast majority of cases, at least one spouse is eligible for health insurance. However, in 45.75% of the full sample, both spouses are eligible for health insurance. In households in which both spouses work full-time, the

Table 3. Family Health Insurance Coverage Decisions.

	Frequency	Percentage of Total
Panel A: Household choices for health insurance coverage, full sample		
Outcome 1: A family where both husband and wife are covered by their own employer-provided health insurance.	804	29.92
Outcome 2: A family where the husband is covered by his employer-provided health insurance, and his wife is covered by his plan.	1,143	42.54
Outcome 3: A family where the wife is covered by her employer-provided health insurance, and her husband is covered by her plan.	740	27.54
Total	2,687	100.00
Panel B: Household outcomes for health insurance coverage, full-time sample		
Outcome 1: A family where both husband and wife are covered by their own employer-provided health insurance.	703	31.57
Outcome 2: A family where the husband is covered by his employer-provided health insurance, and his wife is covered by his plan.	865	38.84
Outcome 3: A family where the wife is covered by her employer-provided health insurance, and her husband is covered by her plan.	659	29.59
Total	2,227	100.00

Source: April 1993 CPS, Employee Benefit Supplement. The sample is all married workers aged 18–64, who are not full-time students. Both spouses must be eligible for employer-provided health insurance. In the full sample there were 44 families where neither spouse was covered by their employer-provided health insurance, even though both were eligible. In the estimation of the multinomial logit we omit these families because of insufficient degrees of freedom.

percentage is even greater (58.80%). This suggests that markets are in fact incomplete when it comes to provision of fringe benefits such as health insurance. In a world of complete markets, households would not choose jobs such that both spouses were eligible for health insurance benefits. The four outcomes in Table 2 form the basis for the multinomial logit analysis of health insurance choice.

In Table 3, we focus on the choice of health insurance in the family given incomplete markets. In particular, we consider the universe of families in which both the husband and the wife are eligible for employer-provided health insurance. In this case, approximately 70% of the families purchase insurance from either the husband's or the wife's plan. They are somewhat more likely to purchase coverage from the husband's plan. In approximately 30% of the families, the husband is covered by his employer-provided plan and the wife is covered by her employer-provided plan.[24] The three outcomes in the table are the basis for a multinomial analysis of coverage choices among dually eligible families. A small number of families have coverage from neither plan and are omitted from the table and further analysis.

5.2. Model Estimates

Table 4 shows the results of the multinomial logit analysis of eligibility for employer-provided health insurance (Eq. (4)). We show the marginal effect of additional children on each of the four health insurance eligibility outcomes. The model is estimated for the full sample and the sample of families in which both the husband and wife are full-time workers. The full-time sample has the advantage of abstracting from eligibility issues that arise from part-time work that may be particularly important for females. Specification A includes only the demographic characteristics of the husband and wife as measures of the

Table 4. Marginal Effect of Children on Employer-Provided Health Insurance Eligibility, Multinomial Logit Estimates.

	All Workers		Full-Time Workers	
	Specification A	Specification B	Specification A	Specification B
Neither spouse is eligible for employer-provided health insurance	0.0119 (2.778)	0.0095 (2.645)	0.0066 (1.584)	0.0049 (2.178)
Only the husband is eligible for employer-provided health insurance	0.0442 (7.597)	0.0448 (6.285)	0.0254 (4.157)	0.0213 (3.647)
Only the wife is eligible for employer-provided health insurance	−0.0150 (2.858)	−0.0091 (2.016)	−0.0059 (0.908)	0.0001 (0.028)
Both workers are eligible for employer-provided health insurance	−0.0410 (5.831)	−0.0453 (5.282)	−0.0261 (3.058)	−0.0267 (3.229)
Log-likelihood	−7438.87	−4761.04	−4235.02	−2733.29
N	6,088	6,088	3,934	3,934

Dependent variable: Eligibility for employer-provided health insurance.
Source: April 1993 CPS, Employee Benefit Supplement. The sample is families where both spouses are aged 18–64, and are not full-time students. The full-time worker sample is restricted to families where both spouses are full-time workers. Absolute value of t-statistics for the marginal-effects is computed using the delta method. The multinomial logits reported in Specification A include variables measuring the characteristics of both the husband and the wife: a quartic in age, race (black, other), education level dummies (less than high school, some college, associate degree, bachelor's degree, and schooling past a B.A. degree), and veteran status; and characteristics of the household: number of children, MSA residency, and region. In Specification B we add industry controls, a quartic in tenure, and firm size for both spouses.

productive capacity of each. Specification B includes a broader array of control variables such as industry, tenure, and firm size. The marginal effects on the probability of each outcome given in the columns of Table 4 sum to zero. In other words, adding another child at the mean set of characteristics increases the probability of some outcomes and decreases the probability of others, such that the changes sum to zero and the new set of probabilities sum to one.[25]

The estimated marginal effects of children are consistent with predictions of our theoretical model of household specialization in a world of incomplete markets. The results also suggest that wives are typically the childcare specialists in the family. In the full sample, additional children lower the probability that both workers are eligible for employer-provided health insurance by 0.041–0.045, and also lower the probability that only the wife is eligible by 0.009–0.015. As the number of children increases, the productive capacity of the wife falls if she specializes in providing childcare. Thus, she is less likely to be in a job that provides health insurance benefits. On the other hand, the probability that only the husband is eligible for health insurance increases by approximately 0.044 with additional children, again consistent with incomplete markets with the wife as the childcare specialist. The probability that neither is eligible increases by about 0.010 with additional children. This is consistent with a reduction in productive capacity that causes families to substitute out of health insurance and into other goods and services. The incomplete market may reinforce this result. It may not be possible to reduce health insurance coverage linearly with income. Instead, health insurance coverage may be lumpy and below some level it is not possible to obtain. In this case, the family goes without and substitutes into other goods and services. The results for the full-time sample are similar but smaller in magnitude. This makes sense in that for full-time workers there is no eligibility effect simply through adjusting the hours of work of the husband or the wife. The other notable difference is that the probability that only the wife is eligible is insignificantly related to the number of children.

Table 5 contains the multinomial logit results for the coverage decision among families in which both the husband and wife are eligible for employer provided health insurance. The results are very similar for the full sample and the full-time sample, and for the two specifications. Specifically, the probability that both are covered falls by about 0.08 with additional children, consistent with the lack of need for duplicative coverage, especially if there is cost sharing involved in own employee coverage. The probability of coverage through the husband or through the wife increases with additional children, but the probability of coverage through the husband increases by a larger amount (about 0.06 vs. about 0.02). This may reflect the fact that the husband's plan is more likely to be the better plan as number of children increases, because he is increasingly more likely to be working at a

Table 5. Marginal Effect of Children on Employer-Provided Health Insurance Coverage, Multinomial Logit Estimates.

	All Workers		Full-Time Workers	
	Specification A	Specification B	Specification A	Specification B
Husband and wife are covered by their own employer-provided health insurance	−0.0810 (7.565)	−0.0843 (7.246)	−0.0839 (6.838)	−0.0856 (6.413)
Husband and wife are covered by the husband's employer-provided health insurance	0.0623 (5.633)	0.0593 (4.001)	0.0506 (4.146)	0.0469 (4.001)
Husband and wife are covered by the wife's employer-provided health insurance	0.0187 (1.909)	0.0257 (2.343)	0.0333 (2.958)	0.0382 (3.122)
Log-likelihood	−2791.00	−2449.26	−2337.11	−2054.24
N	2,687	2,687	2,227	2,227

Dependent variable: Coverage from employer-provided health insurance.
Source: April 1993 CPS, Employee Benefit Supplement. The sample is families where both spouses are aged 18–64, and are not full-time students. The full-time worker sample is restricted to families where both spouses are full-time workers. Absolute value of *t*-statistics for the marginal-effects is computed using the delta method. The multinomial logits reported in Specification A include variables measuring the characteristics of both the husband and the wife: a quartic in age, race (black, other), education level dummies (less than high school, some college, associate degree, bachelor's degree, and schooling past a B.A. degree), and veteran status; and characteristics of the household: number of children, MSA residency, and region. In Specification B we add industry controls, a quartic in tenure, and firm size for both spouses. Coverage from employer-provided health insurance is defined only if both spouses are eligible for employer-provided health insurance.

firm with a higher demand for health insurance benefits. Thus, the results are again consistent with the family specialization model in which the wife specializes in the provision of childcare.[26]

Table 6 shows the results for hours worked and hourly earnings for both the entire sample and the sample of full-time worker families, using both the basic and expanded specifications (see note 26). These equations are estimated using least squares rather than seemingly unrelated regressions because both models have the same set of explanatory variables. Consider the results of the full sample. There are small estimated effects of additional children on the husband's wages and hours worked and the effect on wages is insignificant. On the other hand, the wife's hourly earnings and hours worked are both significantly negatively affected by additional children. The magnitudes of the estimated effects are somewhat smaller in the full-time sample, reflecting less adjustment among those who have chosen to work full-time.[27] Thus, our results for wages and hours worked are consistent with the theoretical model for the case in which the wife specializes in

Table 6. Least-Squares Estimates of the Effect of Children on Hourly Earnings and Hours Worked.

	Hourly Earnings				Hours Worked			
	Specification A		Specification B		Specification A		Specification B	
	Husbands	Wives	Husbands	Wives	Husbands	Wives	Husbands	Wives
Panel A: All households (husband and wife may, or may not, be full-time workers)								
Number of Children	−0.0022	−0.0573	−0.0034	−0.0409	0.0096	−0.0734	0.0065	−0.0638
	(0.284)	(6.879)	(0.476)	(5.254)	(2.896)	(11.84)	(2.00)	(10.57)
N	5,880	5,786	5,880	5,786	5,880	5,786	5,880	5,786
R^2	0.1516	0.1602	0.2834	0.2872	0.0315	0.0572	0.0759	0.1201
Panel B: Full-time households (both husband and wife are full-time workers)								
Number of Children	−0.0152	−0.0478	−0.0160	−0.0355	0.0051	−0.0243	0.0022	−0.0226
	(1.507)	(4.843)	(1.775)	(3.939)	(1.348)	(5.220)	(0.611)	(4.890)
N	3,831	3,811	3,831	3,811	3,831	3,811	3,831	3,811
R^2	0.1383	0.1779	0.2828	0.3328	0.0294	0.0382	0.0976	0.0686

Source: April 1993 CPS, Employee Benefit Supplement. The sample is families where both spouses are aged 18–64, and are not full-time students. Absolute value of *t*-statistics computed from robust standard-errors are reported in parentheses. The estimates reported in Specification A include variables measuring the characteristics of both the husband and the wife: a quartic in age, race (black, other), education level dummies (less than high school, some college, associate degree, bachelor's degree, and schooling past a B.A. degree), and veteran status; and characteristics of the household: number of children, MSA residency, and region. In Specification B we add industry controls, a quartic in tenure, and firm size for both husbands and wives. Hourly earnings (last year) and hours (last year) are measured in natural logs.

the household provision of childcare. If the husband were the childcare specialist, children would significantly lower his wages and hours worked and have little or no effect on the wife's wages and hours worked. If children consistently lowered both spouses' wages and hours worked or had no effect, then the results would suggest either no specialization or a more complicated pattern of specialization. However, the results clearly suggest a pattern of childcare specialization by the wife.

The results in Table 6 are also consistent with the relative earnings regressions reported by Polachek (1975). In our models, the effect of children on the relative wages of wives to husbands can be obtained by simply subtracting the coefficient in the husband equation from the corresponding coefficient in the wife equation. For Specification A for the full sample, the effect is $-0.0573 - (-0.0022) = -0.0551$, and for Specification B, it is $-0.0409 - (-0.0034) = -0.0375$. The best comparison is probably with Polachek's (1975) results for hourly wages in 1970 in column (7) of Table 3b. The effect of increases in children <6 years old on the relative wages of wives to husbands is -0.0722, and for increases in children ages 6–18 is -0.0223. Thus, our results are very similar to those obtained by Polachek (1975).

Table 7 shows the results of logit models of the probability of eligibility for other fringe benefits that are identified in the April 1993 CPS. We estimate logit models explaining eligibility for a pension plan, eligibility for sick leave, and eligibility for disability benefits. We again use the entire sample and the full-time sample, and the basic and expanded specifications. We report the marginal effect of additional children on the probability of being eligible for each of these benefits. In each case, additional children do not significantly affect the probability of receipt of these benefits for husbands, again consistent with a model in which he is not specializing in the provision of childcare.[28] On the other hand, in the full sample, in every case additional children reduce the probability of eligibility for these benefits among wives. In the full-time sample, the effects of additional children are always negative for wives, but they are often statistically insignificant. Once wives have made the decision to work full-time, additional children have a weaker effect on the receipt of these fringe benefits. These results are also consistent with childcare specialization by the wife and inconsistent with childcare specialization by the husband.

How robust are our results? We have investigated several different issues in considering the question of stability and robustness. First of all, there is the issue of the functional form of the effect of additional children. We have also estimated models in which we include quadratic effects of number of children. In almost every case the squared term is statistically insignificant, suggesting that the linear specification is appropriate. We have also used a series of dummy

Table 7. Marginal Effect of Children on Pension Eligibility, Sick Leave Eligibility and Disability Benefits Eligibility, Logit Estimates.

	Pension Eligibility				Sick Leave Eligibility				Disability Benefits			
	Specification A		Specification B		Specification A		Specification B		Specification A		Specification B	
	Husbands	Wives	Husbands	Wives	Husbands	Wives	Husbands	Wives	Husbands	Wives	Husbands	Wives
Panel A: All households (husband and wife may, or may not be, full-time workers)												
Number of children	0.0084	−0.04088	0.0091	−0.0315	−0.0055	−0.04220	−0.0085	−0.03677	0.0127	−0.0326	0.0118	−0.0175
	(1.213)	(5.760)	(0.960)	(3.436)	(0.797)	(6.047)	(0.997)	(4.333)	(1.847)	(5.002)	(1.527)	(2.627)
N	6,088	6,088	6,088	6,088	6,088	6,088	6,088	6,088	6,088	6,088	6,088	6,088
Log-likelihood	−4055.90	−4029.88	−2416.51	−2691.92	−3958.08	−3964.93	−2833.43	−2928.46	−4064.63	−3739.44	−3334.91	−3135.48
Panel B: Full-time households (both husband and wife are full-time workers)												
Number of children	0.0093	−0.0169	0.0069	−0.0114	−0.0086	−0.0114	−0.0035	−0.0157	0.0158	−0.0148	0.0139	−0.0058
	(1.073)	(1.942)	(0.603)	(1.020)	(0.847)	(1.362)	(0.409)	(1.974)	(1.801)	(1.714)	(1.412)	(0.608)
N	3,934	3,934	3,934	3,934	3,934	3,934	3,934	3,934	3,934	3,934	3,934	3,934
Log-likelihood	−2587.95	−2564.06	−1620.87	−1735.05	−1841.51	−1705.96	−2493.94	−2284.52	−2654.28	−2605.81	−2244.76	−2240.71

Source: April 1993 CPS, Employee Benefit Supplement. The sample is families where both spouses are aged 18–64, and are not full-time students. Absolute value of *t*-statistics computed from robust standard-errors are reported in parentheses. The estimates reported in Specification A include variables measuring the characteristics of both the husband and the wife: a quartic in age, race (black, other), education level dummies (less than high school, some college, associate degree, bachelor's degree, and schooling past a B.A. degree), and veteran status; and characteristics of the household: number of children, MSA residency, and region. In Specification B we add industry controls, a quartic in tenure, and firm size for both husbands and wives.

variables indicating number of children. We cannot reject the simpler linear specification. These results provide empirical evidence for our assumption of a linear specification of the cost of childcare functions in Eqs (2) and (3) and the result that follows from that assumption that either the wife ($\alpha = 0$) or husband ($\alpha = 1$) will specialize in the provision of childcare services.

Using the April CPS, it is also possible to construct a dummy variable indicating the presence of children under six years old in the household. This is a rough control for the age composition of children in the household. If younger children require more or less childcare effort, then this variable should be significantly related to hourly earnings, hours worked, and fringe benefit eligibility of the wife. This does not appear to be the case, again indicating a linear relationship between number of children and family labor market outcomes. This could also occur because we hold age constant in the analysis and there are very few young women with many older children. Therefore there is not much variation with which to test the hypothesis.

5.3. Accounting for the Endogeneity of Children

We address the potential problem of the endogeneity of children by constructing instruments for the number of children. We use the Angrist and Evans (1998) instruments that are based on the observed parental preference for mixed sibling-sex composition, and another set of instruments based on state level data on ancestry and religion. These results are reported in Tables 8–11. In each table we report estimates using the Angrist and Evans instruments and a separate set of estimates based on the ethnic and religious group estimates. Both sets of estimates use the full sample of part-time and full-time working spouses.

It should be noted that the Angrist–Evans instrument is only defined for families with two or more children. Thus, we restricted our sample to families with two or more children in which both spouses were less than 45 years old.[29] Even though our overall R^2 on the first stage equations were similar to those obtained by Angrist and Evans (0.074 vs. 0.078 obtained by Angrist and Evans), the marginal F-statistics for the inclusion of the three identifying instruments were extremely small, suggesting that we had a weak set of instruments. For the first-stage equation, which included the Specification A covariates, the marginal F-statistic was 1.34, and when Specification B covariates were included, it fell to 0.89. The higher marginal F-statistics reported by Angrist and Evans appear to be a consequence of their significantly larger sample sizes (approximately 440,000 individuals compared to our sample size of 1,789). In the case of the ethnic and religious group instruments we were able to use the full sample of 6,088 working couples. The marginal F-statistics from the first stage equations again suggested that we had

Table 8. Marginal Effect of Children on Employer-Provided Health Insurance Eligibility, Multinomial Logit Estimates with Children Instrumented.

	All Workers			
	Angrist–Evans Instruments		Ethnic and Religious Group Instruments	
	Specification A	Specification B	Specification A	Specification B
Neither spouse is eligible for employer-provided health insurance	0.0331 (0.142)	−0.1266 (0.550)	0.0713 (1.53)	0.1224 (3.02)
Only the husband is eligible for employer-provided health insurance	0.2986 (0.841)	0.6075 (1.03)	0.0517 (0.779)	0.1222 (1.49)
Only the wife is eligible for employer-provided health insurance	0.0720 (0.281)	0.0191 (0.275)	−0.0003 (0.005)	0.0740 (1.56)
Both workers are eligible for employer-provided health insurance	−0.4036 (1.07)	−0.5000 (0.815)	−0.1227 (1.60)	−0.3187 (3.33)
Log-likelihood	−2174.89	−1356.79	−7474.12	−4778.39
N	1,789	1,789	6,088	6,088

Dependent variable: Eligibility for employer-provided health insurance.

Source: April 1993 CPS, Employee Benefit Supplement. Absolute value of *t*-statistics for the marginal effects is computed using the delta method. The multinomial logits reported in Specification A include variables measuring the characteristics of both the husband and the wife: a quartic in age, race (black, other), education level dummies (less than high school, some college, associate degree, bachelor's degree, and schooling past a B.A. degree), and veteran status; and characteristics of the household: number of children, MSA residency, and region. In Specification B we add industry controls, a quartic in tenure, and firm size for both spouses. The predicted values of children are obtained from regressions including the variables in Specification A or B and either the Angrist–Evans instruments or percentages of the population in the state of residence that are in various religious or ethnic groups. The sample used in the Angrist–Evans estimation is families in which both spouses are aged 18–45 with 2 or more children. The sample used in the ethnic and religious group estimation is families where both spouses are aged 18–64, and are not full-time students.

weak instruments; the marginal *F*-statistics on the set of twenty-two instruments ranged from 2.25 in Specification A to 2.21 in Specification B.

Table 8 shows the instrumental variables estimates of the health insurance eligibility equation. None of the estimated marginal effects for the instrumented number of children are statistically significant except in two cases in Specification B for the ethnic and religious group instruments. While these two estimates have the same sign as comparable estimates in Table 4, they are dramatically larger in size and appear unreasonable. A similar situation occurs in the health insurance coverage equation estimates shown in Table 9. While a few of the estimated marginal effects are statistically significant, they are again several orders of magnitude larger than the comparable estimates in Table 5.

The instrumental variables estimates for hourly earnings, hours worked, pensions, sick leave, and disability benefits are no more encouraging. Table 10 provides the estimates for hourly earnings and hours worked. The estimates are again extraordinarily large and lie far outside the usual effects of children on wages and hours worked found in the literature. In addition, the estimates appear very sensitive

Table 9. Marginal Effect of Children on Employer-Provided Health Insurance Coverage, Multinomial Logit Estimates with Children Instrumented.

	All Workers			
	Angrist–Evans Instruments		Ethnic and Religious Group Instruments	
	Specification A	Specification B	Specification A	Specification B
Husband and wife are covered by their own employer-provided health insurance	−0.2080 (0.445)	−0.4845 (0.789)	−0.0963 (0.876)	−0.0859 (0.702)
Husband and wife are covered by the husband's employer-provided health insurance	1.004 (1.64)	2.240 (2.53)	0.3796 (3.09)	0.3980 (2.90)
Husband and wife are covered by the wife's employer-provided health insurance	−0.7960 (1.45)	−1.760 (0.010)	−0.2833 (2.54)	−0.3169 (2.60)
Log-likelihood	−704.16	−590.59	−2816.28	−2471.62
N	723	723	2687	2687

Dependent variable: Coverage from employer-provided health insurance.

Source: April 1993 CPS, Employee Benefit Supplement. Absolute value of t-statistics for the marginal effects is computed using the delta method. The multinomial logits reported in Specification A include variables measuring the characteristics of both the husband and the wife: a quartic in age, race (black, other), education level dummies (less than high school, some college, associate degree, bachelor's degree, and schooling past a B.A. degree), and veteran status; and characteristics of the household: number of children, MSA residency, and region. In Specification B we add industry controls, a quartic in tenure, and firm size for both spouses. Coverage from employer provided health insurance is defined only if both spouses are eligible for employer-provided health insurance. The predicted values of children are obtained from regressions including the variables in Specification A or B and either the Angrist–Evans instruments or percentages of the population in the state of residence that are in various religious or ethnic groups. The sample used in the Angrist–Evans estimation is families in which both spouses are aged 18–45 with 2 or more children. The sample used in the ethnic and religious group estimation is families where both spouses are aged 18–64 and are not full-time students.

to the choice of sets of instruments. The estimated effects of additional children on log hourly earnings are larger than those reported in Table 6, but several orders of magnitude larger using the ethnic and religious group instruments. The reverse is true for the hours worked equations. Again, both sets of instruments produce larger estimates than those in Table 6, but the Angrist–Evans instruments now produce effects on hours worked that are several multiples larger than the estimates using the ethnic and religious group estimates. In addition to being large, the estimates for males are qualitatively different than those in Table 6: additional children lower male hourly earnings in Panel B, and lower hours worked in both Panels A and B.

The estimated marginal effects of children on eligibility for pensions, sick leave and disability benefits using the instrumented number of children are given

Table 10. Instrumental Variables Estimates of the Effect of Children on Hourly Earnings and Hours Worked.

	Hourly Earnings				Hours Worked			
	Specification A		Specification B		Specification A		Specification B	
	Husbands	Wives	Husbands	Wives	Husbands	Wives	Husbands	Wives
Panel A: All households – Angrist–Evans instruments								
Number of children	0.1433	−0.1007	0.3831	0.0555	−0.2568	−0.6655	−0.3994	−0.8700
	(0.373)	(0.221)	(0.923)	(0.111)	(1.50)	(1.94)	(2.02)	(2.15)
N	1,768	1,718	1,768	1,718	1,768	1,718	1,768	1,718
R^2	0.1650	0.1232	0.3575	0.2805	0.0459	0.0498	0.1463	0.1335
Panel B: All households – ethnic and religious group instruments								
Number of children	−0.2088	−0.4151	−0.2025	−0.3927	−0.0383	−0.1303	−0.0423	−0.1256
	(2.44)	(4.87)	(2.39)	(4.90)	(1.00)	(2.03)	(1.11)	(1.99)
N	5,880	5,786	5,880	5,786	5,880	5,786	5,880	5,786
R^2	0.1524	0.1558	0.2842	0.2862	0.0302	0.0286	0.0755	0.0990

Source: April 1993 CPS, Employee Benefit Supplement. Absolute value of t-statistics computed from robust standard-errors are reported in parentheses. The estimates reported in Specification A include variables measuring the characteristics of both the husband and the wife: a quartic in age, race (black, other), education level dummies (less than high school, some college, associate degree, bachelor's degree, and schooling past a B.A. degree), and veteran status; and characteristics of the household: number of children, MSA residency, and region. In Specification B we add industry controls, a quartic in tenure, and firm size for both husbands and wives. Hourly earnings (last year), and hours (last year) are measured in natural logs. The predicted values of children are obtained from regressions including the variables in Specification A or B and either the Angrist–Evans instruments or percentages of the population in the state of residence that are in various religious or ethnic groups. The sample used for the Angrist–Evans estimation is families in which both spouses are aged 18–45 with 2 or more children. The sample used in the ethnic and religious group estimation is families where both spouses are aged 18–64, and are not full-time students.

in Table 11. These estimated effects are also too large to be reasonable and are statistically significant only in a few isolated cases. Overall, the estimates in Tables 8–11 appear to be unreliable and sensitive to the choice of instruments. In light of these results and the recent literature on weak instruments (Bound, Jaeger & Baker, 1995) Staiger and Stock (1997), Wang and Zivot (1998) we are reluctant to rely on the sibling-sex composition variables or the ethnic and religious group variables as instruments for the number of children.

Given the unreliable estimates that result from the use of weak instruments, perhaps the better way to deal with the potential endogeneity is to include more variables in the model and thus directly account for the correlation between number of children and factors omitted from the model. One could argue that we have already taken this approach. First, simultaneity bias is less likely to be a problem in full-time worker families. Those who choose to work full-time probably have fewer negative unobservable wage influences, thus there is less likely to be correlation

Table 11. Marginal Effect of Children on Pension Eligibility, Sick Leave Eligibility and Disability Benefits Eligibility, Logit Estimates with Children Instrumented.

	Pension Eligibility				Sick Leave Eligibility				Disability Benefits			
	Specification A		Specification B		Specification A		Specification B		Specification A		Specification B	
	Husbands	Wives	Husbands	Wives	Husbands	Wives	Husbands	Wives	Husbands	Wives	Husbands	Wives
Panel A: All households – Angrist–Evans instruments												
Number of children	0.2989	0.0421	0.6739	0.3193	0.0982	−0.4700	0.3862	−0.2727	0.0663	−1.051	0.1556	−1.284
	(0.789)	(0.112)	(1.03)	(0.567)	(0.256)	(1.23)	(0.674)	(0.474)	(0.174)	(3.13)	(0.292)	(3.18)
N	1,789	1,789	1,789	1,789	1,789	1,789	1,789	1,789	1,789	1,789	1,789	1,789
Log-likelihood	−1175.65	−1179.49	−678.39	−775.63	−1136.14	−1186.75	−821.38	−876.68	−1191.16	−1069.92	−981.81	−869.09
Panel B: All households – ethnic and religious group instruments												
Number of children	0.1010	−0.0315	0.0077	−0.1262	0.1364	−0.0850	0.0733	−0.1961	0.1422	0.0783	0.0704	0.0596
	(1.31)	(0.405)	(0.072)	(1.24)	(1.76)	(1.11)	(0.757)	(2.04)	(1.86)	(1.11)	(0.814)	(0.829)
N	6,088	6,088	6,088	6,088	6,088	6,088	6,088	6,088	6,088	6,088	6,088	6,088
Log-likelihood	−4,055.79	−4,046.60	−2,416.96	−2,697.11	−3,956.84	−3,982.76	−2,833.64	−2,935.86	−4,064.62	−3,751.51	−3,335.75	−3,138.62

Source: April 1993 CPS, Employee Benefit Supplement. Absolute value of *t*-statistics computed from robust standard errors are reported in parentheses. The estimates reported in Specification A include variables measuring the characteristics of both the husband and the wife: a quartic in age, race (black, other), education level dummies (less than high school, some college, associate degree, bachelor's degree, and schooling past a B.A. degree), and veteran status; and characteristics of the household: number of children, MSA residency, and region. In Specification B we add industry controls, a quartic in tenure, and firm size for both husbands and wives. The predicted values of children are obtained from regressions including the variables in Specification A or B and either the Angrist–Evans instruments or percentages of the population in the state of residence that are in various religious or ethnic groups. The sample used in for the Angrist–Evans estimation is families in which both spouses are aged 18–45 with 2 or more children. The sample used in the ethnic and religious group estimation is families where both spouses are aged 18–64, and not full-time students.

between number of children and unobservables in this subsample. Our results are nearly identical for the overall sample and the full-time sample.

Second, unlike what is typically done in the literature, our models include husband's characteristics in the wife's wage, hours, and fringe benefit equations. These characteristics control for sorting that has taken place in the marriage market and are likely to be correlated with unobservables that affect labor market outcomes such as wages and hours worked. In addition, our Specification B includes an expanded set of covariates such as 1-digit industry dummies, firm size dummies, and quartics in tenure for both spouses. The inclusion of these controls helps absorb any residual covariance between the number of children and other unobservables in Specification A.

As one final exercise, we estimated models in which we included state dummies, MSA dummies, and one-digit occupation dummies for each spouse in addition to the controls in Specification B. The marginal impact of an additional child is robust to the inclusion of these additional controls.[30] This finding suggests that if the endogeneity of fertility is a problem, then the correlation between the number of children and the unobservables in Specification A must operate along dimensions that are nearly orthogonal to these additional observables that we include in the model. While this is possible, it does not seem likely to be the case.

6. CONCLUSIONS

We examine the role of family specialization in the choice of health insurance coverage and other labor market outcomes such as hourly earnings, hours worked, pensions, sick leave, and disability insurance. Overall, our results are strongly consistent with the Polachek (1975) and Becker (1985) household specialization argument. The observed patterns are consistent with specialization by the wife in the provision of childcare in the household.[31] The results suggest that additional children do not significantly affect hourly earnings, hours worked, or eligibility for pensions, sick leave, or disability insurance for husbands, but have negative impacts for wives, consistent with specialization in childcare by wives. The outcome for health insurance is somewhat more complicated because double coverage is typically not of value to the household. In families with more children, we observe a lower probability of dual eligibility for health insurance by the husband and the wife, and also lower probability of eligibility for the wife only. In families with more children, we also observe a higher probability of eligibility for health insurance by the husband only. These findings are consistent with our model in the presence of incomplete markets for health insurance coverage and again with specialization in childcare by the wife. We obtain similar results whether we rely on the estimates for all workers or just full-time workers, or whether we use a limited number of controls or a broader set of controls. Because of the lack of powerful instruments for number of children in CPS-type data, and the resulting sensitivity of instrumental variables estimates, we choose to rely on the estimates obtained in our original models of hourly earnings, hours worked, and health insurance, pension, sick leave, and disability insurance eligibility.[32]

Our results and interpretation differ from those of Currie (1997), who also examined fringe benefit provision. Our conclusion is that there appears to be ample evidence that household specialization is taking place. Families with more children do not have a higher probability that the wife has sick leave benefits, as Currie argues would be consistent with the household specialization story. However, our household model shows that the more direct effect may be a reduction in productive capacity of the wife and a reduction in all types of benefits among families with more children, including sick leave. So it is not necessarily the case that we should observe women who specialize in childcare more likely to have sick leave benefits. In fact, all of our estimates appear consistent with household specialization.

In our model, it is the spouse with the lower market productive capacity that specializes in the provision of childcare. This is very much in the spirit of the original Polachek (1975) and Becker (1985) papers. It may very well be that discrimination against women in the labor market is in part responsible for families choosing women to be the childcare specialist in the family. However, given the differences in productive capacities, there is ample evidence that is consistent with the model of specialization within the family. If the observed pattern of fringe benefit outcomes were simply due to labor market discrimination, it would likely be the case that employers would pay both lower wages and provide less fringes to women with more children. But discrimination in the provision of fringe benefits is unlikely, given that they must be provided in a non-discriminatory fashion to maintain tax deductability. In the case of health insurance, wives are eligible for coverage through their employer at similar rates as husbands. However, wives are more likely to decline coverage. The household specialization argument provides a much more plausible explanation for this observed pattern of fringe benefit choices within families than a story of labor market discrimination.

In addition to providing an explanation based on intra-household specialization for the observed pattern of fringe benefit provision, our evidence is also consistent with the hypothesis that the non-discriminatory provision of (non-additive) fringe benefits intensifies the pressure to specialize within the household. Our results imply that it is the wife who typically chooses to specialize in the provision of childcare and thus the husband is more likely to be the provider of fringe benefits. Furthermore, to the extent that markets are incomplete, wives will not be able to realize the mix of wages and fringes that they desire and many wives' compensation will include fringes that are of little value to them. For these wives, the value of their total compensation is worth less to them than the value of their marginal products to their firms. As such, the quality of job matches for married women is likely to be lower than that for married men. This fact may result in excess turnover in the labor market and lower tenure in jobs as married women seek alternative compensation packages with higher wages and fewer fringe benefits. While the purpose of the IRS legislation concerning the nondiscriminatory provision of fringes is not controversial, we believe that we have uncovered another set of potentially important unintended consequences of these policies.

NOTES

1. See, for example, Juster and Stafford (1985, 1991), Hill and Stafford (1980), and Hersch and Stratton (1997). Gronau (1986) provides an extensive review of the literature on home production.

2. In 1999, the tax-expenditures on employer contributions to health insurance are estimated to be 76.2 billion dollars, on employer-provided pension plans 72.4 billion dollars, and on the deductibility of mortgage interest 53.7 billion (U.S. Bureau of the Census, 1998). For a given employer, the magnitude of these savings can be substantial: assuming that an employee is in the 28% marginal tax bracket, is under the social-security cap of $57,600 and faces a 6% state income tax, Black (2000) demonstrates that an employer who offers a health insurance policy whose value is $131 a month would have to pay over $250 a month to increase an employees' after tax monthly salary by $131. The literature on the tax-treatment of fringe benefits is reviewed thoroughly by Long and Scott (1982), Woodbury (1983), Scott, Berger and Black (1989), Scott, Berger and Garen (1995), and Carrington, McCue and Pierce (2002).

3. In our analysis we use data from the April 1993 Current Population Survey (CPS) that was collected prior to the Family Medical Leave Act, which took effect from August 1993 to February 1994.

4. Our model is similar to a one period version of the Polachek (1975) life-cycle model in which decisions about human capital investment, number of children, and labor force participation have already been made.

5. Of those eligible for employer provided health insurance in the April 1993 CPS, only 11% report that the plan would not cover family members.

6. In the April–March 1993 CPS matched file, of workers covered by their employer, only 4% of employers pay none of the cost of the plan, 66% pay part of the cost of the plan, and 30% pay all of the cost of the plan.

7. The difference in the distribution of employers that pay for all or part of the cost of the plan is not significantly different for men and women in the 1993 April–March CPS matched file. There is no direct evidence on the quality or generosity of health plans in the CPS data. However, in our framework, it is likely that workers in higher wage firms demand more generous health plans, and if men are disproportionately represented in higher wage firms, then there is a gender difference in the generosity of plans. As we will see, families eligible for both types of plans would be more likely to choose the more generous plan.

8. Monheit, Schone and Taylor (1999) point out that some insurers now include non-duplication of benefit provisions in their health plans, which may free the secondary payer from responsibility for payments. As we will see below, in the 1993 April CPS, among families that are eligible for coverage from both the husband's and the wife's job, 70% choose coverage under one plan or the other rather than under both plans. Similarly, Monheit, Schone and Taylor (1999) report that 36% of two-worker couples choose full coverage under both spouses' plans.

9. Smith and Ehrenberg (1983) discuss the data problems inherent in identifying the tradeoff. Currie and Madrian (1999) review the literature for the wage-health insurance tradeoff, and Gruber (1994) is an example of the necessary data to successfully identify the tradeoff.

10. One could amend the model to consider, for example, two types of childcare or childcare provided on the weekdays and weekends, with different cost functions for each type of care for each spouse. While this could weaken the specialization hypothesis if one spouse were the specialist in one type and the other spouse were the specialist in the other type, it would not eliminate it entirely unless the costs of providing the two types were exactly identical – an unlikely case except by accident. In a world with two types of childcare where each spouse specialized in one type and the two types did not have identical costs of provision (i.e. reductions in market productivity), the following results would be obtained. In Proposition 1, each spouse would specialize in a type (point 1), and both spouses' productivity and thus household income would decline with number of children (point 2), and point 3 remains unchanged. Points 1 and 2 of Proposition 2 would be altered in the same way that they were for Proposition 1. Point 3 of Proposition 2 would be amended to say that the spouse who experiences the smaller reduction in market productivity from providing the type of childcare he or she specializes in is more likely to provide health insurance because he or she is more likely to be the higher market productivity worker in the household. Thus, this complication of the model produces essentially the same results as before except in the accidental case in which the costs of providing the two activities are equal and each spouse specializes in one activity. We are grateful to Sol Polachek for suggesting this potential line of inquiry.

11. These data were also used by Black (2000) in examining the relationship between family health benefits and labor market turnover. Black restricts his sample to full-time and full-year (worked at least 47 weeks) workers. Buchmueller (1996/1997) and Buchmueller and Valletta (1999) also use the April Supplement and retain a similar sample.

12. The Health and Retirement Study also reports eligibility for employer-provided health insurance, but the sample is restricted to older workers and retirees born between 1931 and 1941. Similarly, the 1987 National Medical Expenditure Survey contains health insurance eligibility information but only a limited amount of labor market information. Other datasets that have been used by labor economists to study models of family decision making include the Survey of Income and Program Participation (SIPP), the National Longitudinal Survey of Youth (NLSY), and the Panel Study of Income Dynamics (PSID). However, none of these datasets gathers information on the respondent's *eligibility* for health insurance.

13. We define 'married' to be "Married-spouse (civilian or armed forces) present." Therefore, there are married workers with absent spouses who were excluded from our sample.

14. From the utility function (1), the household chooses X, max (H_f, H_m), and K. K is assumed to be exogenous in the estimation for now. Expenditures on consumption goods (X) can be written as $pX = (1 - T)(Y_f + Y_m)$ or $X = [(1 - T)(Y_f + Y_m)]/p$. The reduced form function for X would contain K, F_f and F_m. Similarly, a reduced form equation for $Y_f + Y_m$ can be written that contains these variables along with p and T. We estimate linear or semi-log approximations of the reduced form equations.

15. We also address this issue by estimating our models for samples of husbands and wives in which both are working full-time, thus reducing the importance of any variation in hours.

16. Similar results are obtained if survey week hours are used instead of average hours in 1992.

17. For example, the cost functions in Eqs (2) and (3) could be nonlinear functions of the number of children, thus potentially leading to cases in which the childcare duties are shared in the household. In this case, increases in the number of children would reduce the earnings of both the husband and the wife. In the empirical work, we experiment with nonlinear specification of the effect of additional children.

18. Pensions, sick leave, and disability benefits enter the utility function individually because unlike health insurance they are not public goods within the household in that they cover only the husband or the wife and not both spouses.

19. Currie (1997) argues that those specializing in childcare may have a higher demand for sick leave benefits. If this is the case, it would moderate the predicted relationship resulting from the decline in the productive capacity of the childcare specialist. While it would be difficult to make a similar argument about pensions, there are other benefits that might be more in demand by the childcare specialist such as onsite childcare. Similarly, childcare specialists might want benefits in their health plan that are more beneficial to children. Unfortunately, we do not observe the presence of onsite childcare in the April CPS, nor can we observe variation in the type of health care plan.

20. The childcare specialist may actually refuse coverage from his or her own plan rather than retain duplicative coverage if the employer does not pay the entire premium or because of increased costs and hassles of dealing with two different insurance plans to obtain benefits. The recent advent of plans that cover the employee, employee plus spouse, employee plus children, or employee, spouse, and children has made the market more complete and reduced the necessity for the family to maintain duplicative coverage. Cafeteria plans also allow markets to be more complete. However, there is not a high prevalence of cafeteria plans in the 1993 April CPS data. Only 6.2% of the overall sample report some kind of cafeteria arrangement with their employer.

21. To control for the fact that the CPS over-samples certain demographic groups, we also examined tables that were weighted with the April Supplement weights. We were concerned that the over-sampling of males without health insurance would affect an unweighted table of means. However, the weighted tables are virtually identical to those presented.

22. In our sample, 91.31% of males were full-time workers and 70.29% of females worked full-time. Therefore, most of the reduction in sample size from (Table 1) Panel A to Panel B was caused by conditioning on the full-time status of the wife. Of all full-time workers, 56.51% were male and 43.49% were female.

23. The similar health insurance eligibility rates for husbands and wives occur at the same time average hourly earnings of husbands are substantially higher than those of wives. In the full-time sample, the average hourly earnings of husbands is $16.29 while they are $12.00

for wives. In the overall sample, the average hourly earnings for husbands is $16.24 for husbands and $11.59 for wives.

24. While this is ruled out in the theoretical model, it is a possible outcome in an incomplete markets situation if the employer pays only part of the premium for coverage. In this case it may be advantageous for each spouse to be covered under his or her own plan, especially if the couple has no children or if the employer has an employee plus children option for coverage.

25. The mean number of children in the full sample ($n = 6,088$) is 1.07 and in the sample of full-time workers ($n = 3,934$) is 0.97. Thus, the marginal effects show the changes in the probabilities of the various outcomes in moving from roughly one to two children.

26. Monheit, Schone and Taylor (1999), using the earlier 1987 National Medical Expenditure Survey, find insignificant effects of increases in family size on the probability of double coverage and on the probability that the wife is the policyholder when the family has no double coverage. However, their results are not directly comparable to ours. They do not jointly model the set of health coverage options facing the family but rather estimate models explaining subsets of options. In addition, their framework assumes eligibility is exogenously determined.

27. Some individuals who were working in April 1993 did not work in the previous year. Thus, the sample size for the wage and hours analyses drops from 6,088 to 5,880 (husbands) or 5,786 (wives) for the overall sample and from 3,934 to 3,831 (husbands) or 3,736 (wives) for the full-time sample.

28. It is possible that we have understated the effect of children on wages: Korenman and Neumark (1992) demonstrate that least-squares specifications that include controls for tenure and experience may understate the direct effect of children on wages because the lower tenure and experience associated with higher fertility may in fact be an endogenous response to lower wages.

29. It is worth noting that the effects of children on the difference in the probability that wives and husbands are eligible for pensions, sick leave and disability benefits can be obtained by subtracting the marginal effect of children for husbands from the marginal effect for wives. This produces a "relative" effect similar to the one Polachek (1975) estimated for earnings.

30. Angrist and Evans (1998) restrict their sample to women less than 35 years old but indicate that their results are robust to the inclusion of women up to age 45. In order to increase the number of observations remaining in our sample, we include women up to age 45, resulting in a full sample of 1,789 families.

31. In the wife's wage equation for the full sample, the estimated effect of number of children moves from -0.0409 in Specification A to -0.0573 in Specification B to -0.0344 in the specification with state, MSA, and occupation dummies. In the hours equations, the corresponding estimates are -0.0818, -0.0719, and -0.0618. All are highly statistically significant.

32. Of course, childcare is not the only form of housework. Unfortunately, unlike Hersch and Stratton (1997), who use the PSID, we do not have direct measures of the amount of housework. But as they discuss (p. 290), their measure may underreport childcare related activities (it includes cooking, cleaning and other work). In any event, number of children is closely related to the total amount of reported housework. In their regressions explaining hours of housework done by women (Appendix B), the linear effect of number of children is most precisely estimated (has the largest t-statistic) of any of the variables included in

the equation, including education, experience, tenure, union status, region, disability status, urban status, non-labor income, and spouse's characteristics.

ACKNOWLEDGMENTS

This research was supported by the Agency for Healthcare Research and Quality (AHRQ) grant R01 HS08188. The views expressed are those of the authors and not necessarily those of AHRQ. We are grateful to Sol Polachek, Julie Hotchkiss, Donna Gilleskie, Steve Woodbury and participants at the 1997 Winter Meetings of the Econometric Society and the 1999 Annual Meetings of the Southern Economic Association for helpful comments and discussions.

REFERENCES

Angrist, J. D., & Evans, W. N. (1998). Children and parents labor supply: Evidence from exogenous variation in family size. *American Economic Review, 88*, 450–477.

Becker, G. S. (1965). A theory of the allocation of time. *Economic Journal, 75*, 493–517.

Becker, G. S. (1985). Human capital, effort, and the sexual division of labor. *Journal of Labor Economics, 3*, S33–S57.

Black, D. A. (2000). Family health benefits and worker turnover. In: T. William & A. S. Woodbury (Eds), *Employee Benefits, Labor Costs, and Labor Markets in Canada and the United States* (pp. 265–294). Kalamazoo, MI: W. E. Upjohn Institute for Employment Research.

Bradley, M. B. (1992). *Churches and church membership in the United States, 1990*. Atlanta, GA: Glenmary Research Center.

Bound, J., Jaeger, D. A., & Baker, R. M. (1995). Problems with instrumental variables estimation when the correlation between the instruments and the endogenous explanatory variable is weak. *Journal of the American Statistical Association, 90*, 445–450.

Buchmueller, T. C., & Valletta, R. G. (1999). The effect of health insurance on married female labor supply. *Journal of Human Resources, 34*, 42–71.

Buchmueller, T. C. (1996/1997). Marital status, spousal coverage, and the gender gap in employer-sponsored health insurance. *Inquiry, 33*, 308–316.

Carrington, W. J., McCue, K., & Brooks, P. (2002). Non-discrimination rules and the distribution of fringe benefits. *Journal of Labor Economics, 20*(2), S5–S33.

Carrington, W. J., & Troske, K. R. (1995). Gender segregation in small firms. *Journal of Human Resources, 30*, 503–534.

Currie, J. (1997). Gender gaps in benefits coverage. In: D. Lewin, D. Mitchell & M. Zaidi (Eds), *The Handbook of Human Resource Management*. New York: JAI Press.

Currie, J., & Madrian, B. C. (1999). Health, health insurance, and the labor market. In: O. C. Ashenfelter & D. Card (Eds), *Handbook of Labor Economics* (Vol. 3C, pp. 3309–3334) Amsterdam: North-Holland.

Gronau, R. (1986). Home production – a survey. In: O. Ashenfelter & R. Layard (Eds), *The Handbook of Labor Economics* (Vol. 1, pp. 273–304). Amsterdam: North-Holland.

Gruber, J. (1994). The incidence of mandated maternity benefits. *American Economic Review, 84*, 622–641.
Hersch, J., & Stratton, L. S. (1997). Housework, fixed effects, and the wages of married workers. *Journal of Human Resources, 32*, 285–308.
Hill, R. C., & Stafford, F. P. (1980). Parental care of children: Time diary estimates of quantity, predictability, and variety. *Journal of Human Resources, 15*, 219–239.
Juster, F. T., & Stafford, F. P. (1985). *Time, goods, and well-being.* Ann Arbor: Institute for Social Research, University of Michigan.
Juster, F. T., & Stafford, F. P. (1991). The allocation of time: Empirical findings, behavioral models, and problems of measurement. *Journal of Economic Literature, 29*, 471–522.
Korenman, S., & Neumark, D. (1992). Marriage, motherhood and wages. *Journal of Human Resources, 27*, 233–255.
Lundberg, S., & Rose, E. (1999). The determinants of specialization within marriage. Working paper. Seattle, WA: Department of Economics, University of Washington.
Long, J. E., & Scott, F. A. (1982). The income tax and non-wage compensation. *Review of Economics and Statistics, 64*, 211–219.
Mincer, J., & Polachek, S. (1974). Family investments in human capital: Earnings of women. *Journal of Political Economy, 82*, S76–S108.
Monheit, A. C., Schone, B. S., & Taylor, A. K. (1999). Health insurance choices in two-worker households: Determinants of double coverage. *Inquiry, 36*, 12–29.
Olson, C. A. (1998). Comparison of parametric and semiparametric estimates of the effect of spousal health insurance coverage on weekly hours worked by wives. *Journal of Applied Econometrics, 13*, 543–565.
Olson, C. A. (2000). Health insurance coverage, labor supply and the wages of employed wives. In: T. William & A. S. Woodbury (Eds), *Employee Benefits, Labor Costs, and Labor Markets in Canada and the United States* (pp. 295–324). Kalamazoo, MI: W. E. Upjohn Institute for Employment Research.
O'Neill, J., & Polachek, S. (1993). Why the gender gap in wages narrowed in the 1980s. *Journal of Labor Economics, 11*, 205–228.
Polachek, S. W. (1975). Potential biases in measuring male-female discrimination. *Journal of Human Resources, 10*, 205–229.
Scott, F. A., Berger, M. C., & Black, D. A. (1989). Effects of tax treatment of fringe benefits on labor market segmentation. *Industrial and Labor Relations Review, 42*, 216–240.
Scott, F. A., Berger, M. C., & Garen, J. E. (1995). Do health insurance and pension costs reduce the job opportunities of older workers? *Industrial and Labor Relations Review, 48*, 775–791.
Smith, R. S., & Ehrenberg, R. G. (1983). Estimating wage-fringe trade-offs: Some data problems. In: Jack E. Triplett (Ed.), *The Measurement of Labor Cost.* Chicago: University of Chicago Press.
Staiger, D., & Stock, J. H. (1997). Instrumental variables with weak instruments. *Econometrica, 65*, 557–586.
U.S. Bureau of the Census (1998). *Statistical Abstract of the United States* (118th ed.). Washington, DC: Government Printing Office.
Waldfogel, J. (1998). The family gap for young women in the United States and Britain: Can maternity leave make a difference? *Journal of Labor Economics, 16*, 505–545.
Wang, J., & Zivot, E. (1998). Inference in structural parameters in instrumental variables with weak instruments. *Econometrica, 66*, 1389–1404.

Wellington, A. J., & Cobb-Clark, D. A. (1997). The labor supply effects of universal health coverage: What can we learn from individuals with coverage through their spouses? Working paper, Monterey, CA: U.S. Naval Postgraduate School.

Woodbury, S. A. (1983). Substitution between wage and nonwage benefits. *American Economic Review*, *73*, 166–182.

Woodbury, S. A., & Wei-Jang, H. (1991). *The tax treatment of fringe benefits*. Kalamazoo, MI: W. E. Upjohn Institute for Employment Research.

WAGE GAINS FROM BETTER HEALTH AND EMPLOYMENT-BASED HEALTH INSURANCE

Paul Fronstin, Alphonse G. Holtmann and Kerry Anne McGeary

ABSTRACT

The ultimate goal of this paper is to determine the differential effects of health insurance and health status on earnings. We believe that employment-based health insurance serves two purposes. First, health insurance provides protection against catastrophic financial losses associated with illness. Second, health insurance encourages consumption of health care services, which may ultimately improve a person's health and productivity. To determine how health insurance and health status affect earnings, we estimate an empirical model that specifically examines the relationship between health insurance, health status, and earnings. We find the following. Earnings positively affect the likelihood of having health insurance. Having health insurance improved health status for women, but not for men. Higher earnings resulted in lower health status for women, but had no effect on the health status of men, and better health status and having health insurance increased earnings for both women and men. Our analysis implies that there are some returns to employment-based health insurance that go beyond the basic purpose of insurance.

INTRODUCTION

Insurance is a common means of pooling risk, with many Americans purchasing homeowner's insurance, auto insurance, and life insurance to protect themselves from the substantial financial losses associated with largely random events. Although health insurance provides this same protection against financial loss, it also changes the insured individual's purchases of health care: insured individuals purchase more medical services than the uninsured.[1]

Many employers offer health insurance as an employee benefit. Nearly all employers with 200 or more employees offer health benefits, while 65% of employers with 3–199 employees offer it (Gabel et al., 2001). Employers offer health insurance as an employee benefit for a number of reasons. Besides providing financial security to workers and their families, employers offer health benefits as a form of compensation to recruit and retain workers. Some employers also report that they offer health benefits to promote health and to increase worker productivity (Fronstin & Helman, 2000). Hence, health insurance can be thought of as an investment in human capital (Grossman, 1972).

Some economists argue that employers provide health benefits because of its favorably tax treatment.[2] The cost of providing health benefits is deductible as a business expense to the employer and is excludable from taxable income for the employee. It should be recognized, however, that access to health care services through employment-based health benefits predates the tax advantages. For example, as early as the 1870s, railroad, mining, and other industries in the United States began providing company doctors to employees and funded it with deductions from workers' wages (Institute of Medicine, 1993). These companies had a practical interest because workers often worked in remote geographic areas without access to health care services. As another example, Montgomery Ward entered into one of the earliest group insurance contracts for workers in 1910.

Employers are more likely to offer health insurance as an employee benefit than other types of insurance products. This may be because health care services have attributes that differ from those of other services that individuals purchase, and employers may want to provide a means to increase the purchase of health care services among employees. Specifically, the purchase of health care services can increase current and future productivity. For example, flu shots are likely to reduce the number of lost workdays due to illness or to reduce the flu symptoms enough for partial productive activity. Likewise, health checkups are likely to diagnose illnesses at an early stage. Uninsured individuals are more likely to delay seeking care (Burstin et al., 1992; Fronstin, 2000; Weissman et al., 1991). Delay in receiving a mammogram would be a case in point. Uninsured women are less likely than insured women to receive mammograms (Centers for Disease Control, 1998;

Fronstin, 2000; Himmelstein & Woolhandler, 1995). Such delays may lead to higher health costs to treat advanced disease and to higher mortality rates. Prevention, early detection, and treatment activities may increase productivity in the long run.

We believe that employment-based health insurance serves two purposes. First, health insurance provides protection against catastrophic financial losses associated with illness. Second, health insurance encourages consumption of health care services, which may ultimately improve a person's health and productivity. The first aspect of employment-based health insurance is well understood, being part of non-wage benefits. However, the role of health insurance as an investment in human capital has been given much less attention by researchers.

In this paper, we focus on the investment aspects of health insurance. We estimate an empirical model to examine the relationship between health insurance, health status, and earnings. The ultimate goal of this paper is to determine the differential effects of health insurance and health status on earnings. Therefore, we need to control for both health status and health insurance separately in the earnings equation. This is complicated by simultaneity. The simultaneity issue arises because: (1) earnings affect health insurance coverage and health status; (2) health insurance affects health status and earnings; and (3) both health insurance and health status affect earnings. Therefore, a simultaneous equation system must be estimated to get unbiased estimates of the influence of health insurance and health status on earnings. In the next section of the paper we outline our empirical model. In the following section of the paper we discuss data. The section following contains the presentation of our results. The final section includes our conclusions.

ECONOMETRIC SPECIFICATION

In order to set up the empirical model, we made a number of assumptions about the relationship between our dependent variables: health insurance coverage, health status, and earnings. First, we assume that health status is not a determinant of health insurance coverage. The Health Insurance Portability and Accountability Act of 1996 (HIPAA) contains provisions that make it easier for small employers with employees who have health problems to obtain health insurance. Insurers providing coverage in the small group market must accept every small employer, and every individual able to enroll under the plan that applies for health insurance. As mentioned above, 65% of small employers offer coverage. Those that do offer coverage usually not only have to offer it to all employees, but also usually required to meet a minimum level of participation, all because of insurer imposed minimum participation requirements. In order to meet the minimum participation requirements, small employers will not usually ask employees to contribute anything in the form of payroll deduction towards the cost of coverage. As a result, (presumably healthy) employees may have health benefits whether they want them or not.

HIPAA also prohibits large employers from using discriminatory rules that affect eligibility, premiums and contributions based on health status. Employers cannot take into account health status, medical conditions, claims history or utilization, medical history or genetic information or disability. Furthermore, pre-existing condition exclusion periods may not be imposed against persons who had health insurance previous to the job change.[3] While employers could theoretically screen employees to determine health risks, denying jobs to less healthy, high-risk employees, there is little evidence that employers and insurers practice screening. Many companies provide domestic partner benefits, and insurance companies often pay for treatments that are considered experimental. Such behavior seems inconsistent with a screen for high-risk employees.

It is impossible to say whether large employers with generally less healthy work forces are less likely than other employers to offer health benefits to employees as virtually all large employers offer health benefits. While not all workers have to accept coverage, only 3% of workers offered coverage are uninsured. While large employers often exclude certain classes of workers from coverage, such as part-time employees, they do need to be careful as to who they do not offer benefits to because of non-discrimination rules under Internal Revenue Code (IRC) Section 105(h). The policy behind the non-discrimination rules suggests that highly compensated employees, who typically have significant authority and control to structure their compensation packages, do not provide themselves with tax-favored benefits that are not otherwise available to other employees. Again, because of non-discrimination rules, employees may have health benefits whether they want them or not.

To a lesser extent, health insurance is exogenous to earnings at least as far as employers offering health benefits to employees. In a small firm that offers health benefits, all workers are usually offered health benefits because of state-allowed minimum participation requirements. And as mentioned above, large firms with self-insured plans need to be concerned about non-discrimination rules in the IRC. This does not mean that earnings have no impact on health insurance. Even though only 3% of employees offered health insurance are uninsured, those that turn down coverage usually do so because of the cost of insurance relative to their income. Furthermore, employers are allowed to exclude workers from insurance coverage by class. For example, many employers do not allow part-time employees to participate in their health plan.

Our empirical analysis is based on the hypothesis that health insurance increases health care consumption, which in turn increases health status and earnings. However, as mentioned before, this estimation is complicated by the simultaneous relationship between health insurance, health status and earnings. As was described in the previous paragraphs, we believe that health insurance is a determinant of health status, health status and health insurance are determinants of earnings, and earnings is a determinant of both health status and health insurance. This functional relationship can be stated symbolically as follows:

$$I = I(E, x)$$
$$H = H(I, E, g)$$

and

$$E = E(H, I, m),$$

where I is insurance, E is the worker's annual earnings, x contains characteristics that affect the worker's insurance status, H is the worker's health status, g is a number of characteristics that influence the worker's health status, and m is a number of characteristics that influence the worker's earnings. Functionally, to find the change in earnings due to an increase in insurance coverage can be written as $\partial E/\partial I$, since this effect allows for the feedback effect of earnings in the insurance equation. In addition, to find the influence of health status on earnings this can be written as $\partial E/\partial H$, however, this effect will have to allow for the feedback effects of earnings in the insurance and health status equations, as well.

To estimate these effects, we develop a system of equations as follows:

$$I_i = \alpha_0 + \alpha_1 E_i + \alpha_2 X_i + \eta_i$$
$$H_i = \beta_0 + \beta_1 I_i + \beta_2 E_i + \beta_3 Y_i + \varepsilon_i$$
$$E_i = \gamma_0 + \gamma_1 I_i + \gamma_2 H_i + \gamma_2 Z_i + \mu_i$$

where I, H and E remain as previously defined. X, Y and Z are the individual and state level determinants of insurance (X), health status (Y) and earnings (Z). The remaining elements of the system, η, ε, and μ represent the error terms. The vectors X, Y, and Z may have some elements in common. Any correlation between unobserved individual traits, such as risk aversion and healthy behaviors, will cause correlation among the error terms, η_i, ε_i, and μ_i.

If there is no correlation among the error terms, a simple OLS regression of the earnings equation would generate the unbiased and consistent estimates of insurance and health status on earnings we are seeking. However, since we model the health insurance, health status and earnings functions simultaneously, to correctly estimate the influence of insurance on earnings separately from health status, we must estimate this entire system.

To complete the estimation we employ three stage least squares. This instrumental variables technique uses predicted values of earnings, insurance and health status in the insurance, health status and earnings equations. These predicted values are purged of their correlation with the error terms because each of the predictions are based on the use of instrumental variables that are uncorrelated with the error terms of the other equations. The resulting signs on the predicted values indicate direction of influence of the true underlying variables and the effects, $\partial E/\partial I$ and $\partial E/\partial H$.

DATA

Data for this study come from the March 2001 supplement to the Current Population Survey (CPS). The CPS is the primary source of data on labor force characteristics for the U.S. civilian non-institutionalized population. It is also the official source of data on unemployment rates, poverty, and income in the United States. Approximately 50,000 households, representing over 130,000 individuals, are interviewed each month.

This empirical analysis is based on a sample of 38,497 full-time, full-year wage and salary workers between the ages of 18 and 64. Besides providing detailed information on a large number of demographic and job characteristics, the CPS collects data on sources of health insurance coverage and it also includes a self-reported indicator of a worker's health status. The CPS data is supplemented with state-level data measuring lifestyle, access to health care, the cost of health insurance, and the prevalence of disease. These variables, to be discussed in more detail below, were included to allow us to identify our equations.

A number of observations were dropped from the original sample because of data limitations. In addition, persons residing in the District of Columbia were dropped from the sample because of missing state-level data.

Outcomes Analyzed

The three outcome variables in our equations are health insurance status, health status, and earnings. Persons interviewed in March 2001 were asked about their health insurance status during calendar year 2000, so health insurance is measured as having coverage at any time, regardless for how long, during 2000. Health insurance coverage is measured as a dummy variable equal to one if a person had it, and equal to zero if they were uninsured.

Because we are interested in the impact of health insurance provided in the workplace as opposed to not having any insurance coverage at all, individuals in our sample are coded as having health insurance coverage as long as they are covered by either their own employer or if they are covered as a dependent under someone else's employer's plan. A small number of workers reporting coverage from the public sector were dropped as well as a small number who purchased health insurance directly from an insurer.

The health status measure is self-reported by the individuals in our sample.[4] Persons are asked to report whether they are in excellent, very good, good, fair, or poor health. Overall, 34% of the sample reported excellent health, 37% very good health, 24% good health, 4% fair health, and 1% poor health. The overall distribution of health status reflects the distribution of health status for the insured sample but not the uninsured sample. The uninsured sample was less likely to report being in excellent or very good health, and were more likely to report being in good or fair health. Our dependent variable for health status is a count variable from 1 to 5 with 1 representing poor health and 5 representing excellent health.

Those with extremely poor health are not likely to be in the labor force, so it is not surprising that our sample of workers contains a large proportion of healthy individuals. Such selectivity in the sample has the effect of downwardly biasing the estimate of the effect of insurance on health status.[5] That is, the positive influence of insurance on health status is likely to be underestimated. So we are estimating a conservative test of our hypothesis that health insurance has a productivity effect which affects health status and earnings.

Earnings are measured as the log of earnings. Like health insurance, data on earnings were collected for the entire calendar year prior to the survey. We limit our sample to wage and salary workers who were employed full-time during all 52 weeks in calendar year 2000 to avoid having to calculate a wage rate based on reported annual earnings. The self-employed were excluded from the sample. Because of the way the self-employed are allowed to report earnings, many often report negative earnings, which may be more a function of how they voluntarily decided to take earnings from their business than a function of true earnings.

Explanatory Variables

Summary statistics for the explanatory variables are given in Table 1. Table 2 contains a summary of the variables included in health insurance, health status, and earnings equations. The explanatory variables are of three types: demographics, job related, and state level variables.

Table 1. Summary Statistics for Dependent and Explanatory Variables.

Variable	Females ($N = 16{,}621$)		Males ($N = 21{,}876$)	
	Mean	Std. Dev.	Mean	Std. Dev.
Dependent variables				
Health insurance ($=1$ if yes, $=0$ otherwise)	0.87	0.33	0.85	0.36
Health status ($1 =$ poor health, $5 =$ excellent health)	3.95	0.91	4.02	0.89
Log annual earnings	10.20	0.61	10.52	0.68
Explanatory variables				
Age	40.36	10.99	40.00	10.91
Age-squared	1749.36	899.35	1719.08	893.42
Marital status				
$=1$ if widowed	0.02	0.15	0.01	0.07
$=1$ if divorced	0.16	0.37	0.08	0.28
$=1$ if separate	0.03	0.17	0.02	0.12
$=1$ if never married	0.22	0.42	0.22	0.41
Years of education (educ.)	13.31	2.65	13.04	3.00
Experience (age-educ.-6)	21.05	11.30	20.96	10.98
Experience-squared	570.94	507.34	559.70	502.46
Race/ethnicity				
$=1$ if white	0.68	0.46	0.69	0.46
$=1$ if black	0.11	0.32	0.07	0.26
$=1$ if Hispanic	0.15	0.36	0.19	0.39
$=1$ if other race	0.05	0.22	0.05	0.21
Industry				
$=1$ if manufacturing	0.19	0.39	0.34	0.47
$=1$ if trade industry	0.31	0.46	0.30	0.46
$=1$ if service sector	0.42	0.49	0.16	0.37
$=1$ if public administration	0.06	0.24	0.06	0.24
Occupation				
$=1$ if service collar	0.16	0.36	0.32	0.47
$=1$ if blue collar	0.08	0.27	0.20	0.40
Firm size				
$=1$ if 10–24 employees	0.08	0.27	0.10	0.29
$=1$ if 25–99 employees	0.13	0.33	0.15	0.36
$=1$ if 100–499 employees	0.16	0.36	0.16	0.37
$=1$ if 500–999 employees	0.07	0.25	0.06	0.23
$=1$ if 1,000 or more employees	0.48	0.50	0.43	0.50
Spouse working	0.64	0.48	0.63	0.48
Number of children under 18	0.69	1.00	0.84	1.14
State-level variables (defined in Table 3)				
Prevalence of smoking	0.22	0.03	0.22	0.03
Motor vehicle deaths	0.02	0.00	0.02	0.00
Violent crime	498.29	193.64	499.37	190.79
Risk for heart disease	1.10	7.80	0.80	7.85
Support for public health	1.44	0.31	1.44	0.31
Cost of insurance per year	415.97	66.87	415.32	67.11

Table 2. Regression Structure.

	Health Insurance	Health Status	Earnings
Endogenous variables			
Health insurance		✓	✓
Health status			✓
Earnings	✓	✓	
Demographic variables			
Education	✓	✓	✓
Race/ethnicity	✓	✓	✓
Age	✓	✓	
Marital status	✓	✓	
Number of own children	✓		
Job related variables			
Experience			✓
Industry	✓	✓	
Occupation		✓	✓
Firm size	✓		✓
Spouse working	✓		
State level variables			
Prevalence of smoking		✓	
Motor vehicle deaths		✓	
Violent crime		✓	
Risk for heart disease		✓	
Support for public health care	✓	✓	
Cost of insurance	✓		

The demographic variables consist of education, race/ethnicity, age, marital status, and number of children. We assume that all of these variables affect the likelihood that a worker has health insurance. We also assume that all of these variables, except number of children, affect the health status of a worker. For earnings we assume that only education and race/ethnicity are important determinants.

The job-related variables include experience (age-education-6), industry of employment, occupation, firm size, and whether or not the worker also has an employed spouse. We assume that health insurance is affected by the industry of employment, the size of the firm and whether or not the worker has a working spouse. Health status is assumed to be affected by only industry of employment and occupation. Experience, occupation, and firm size are assumed to affect earnings.

The state level variables include the cost of insurance, and measures to pick up the effects of lifestyle variables and variables to measure access to health care. The

Table 3. Detailed Definitions of State Level Variables Used in Model.

Name	Description
Prevalence of smoking (Smoke)	Measures the percent of population over age 18 that smoked tobacco products regularly in 2000.
Motor vehicle deaths (Mvdeaths)	Measures the annual number of deaths per 100,000,000 miles driven and is complied by the National Safety Council.
Violent crime (Crime)	Measures the annual number of murders, rapes, robberies and aggravated assaults per 100,000 population. Indicator of health risk and death. Measures the effect of criminal behavior on the population's health.
Risk for heart disease (Heart)	This variable is a measure of three equal criteria: overweight, hypertension and sedentary lifestyle.
Support for public health care (Puhea)	Support for public health. State and local expenditures for public welfare, health and hospitals are divided by the total general expenditures of state and local units to calculate a percentage. This percentage is then divided by the percentage of the state's population with an annual household income below $15,000.
Cost of insurance (Cost1)	Average cost to employee of insurance for employees at private-sector establishments that offer health insurance, 1999.

lifestyle variables include the prevalence of smoking, motor vehicle deaths, violent crime, and risk for heart disease. The access to health care variable includes support for public health care programs and the average annual cost to the employee for buying employment-based health insurance. More information on these variables can be found in Table 3. We used the state level variables as exogenous variables to help us identify the model. We assume that the support for public health care and the cost of insurance affect the likelihood that a worker has health insurance. The cost of health insurance will affect whether or not an employer offers health insurance and whether a worker takes it when offered. Support for public health care is used to measure the state's commitment to providing health care services to the state population. We assume that the greater the state's commitment the more likely resources will be available for the population and the less likely will persons demand insurance, though this variable may not have an impact on our estimates because we are only examining a sample of workers, who may not qualify for any state program.

A number of state level variables are expected to influence health status, specifically the prevalence of smoking, motor vehicle deaths, violent crime, the risk for heart disease, and support for public health care. Motor vehicle deaths are a measure of risk in the population in that it provides us with a sense of risky behavior (bad driving) that is likely to have an impact on health status if persons are in unnecessary automobile accidents. Similarly violent crime is also a measure of risk in the population that may impact health status. The risk of heart disease is an index variable composed of obesity, hypertension and sedentary lifestyle, all known to contribute to heart disease and other illnesses. Finally, support for public health care may impact the health status of the population through state programs.

We assume that most of these variables affect earnings indirectly through their affect on health insurance or health status.

FINDINGS

Table 4 shows the estimated coefficients of the health insurance equation. For both women and men, earnings have a positive affect on the probability of having group health insurance. This is consistent with a common finding that higher paid wage and salary workers are more likely to have health insurance.[6] The other variables we have included in the health insurance equation generally have the expected outcome.

Table 5 contains the estimated coefficients for our health status equation. It can be seen that women with insurance report higher health status than their uninsured counter-parts. The result of the female regression is consistent with the hypothesis that health insurance improves the health status of workers. However, the influence of health insurance on health status among males is less clear, we find an insignificant (and negative) influence of health insurance on health status. This may result because health care utilization among men is lower on average (with or without health insurance) than females and, perhaps, the lower health care utilization translates into an insignificant effect for males.

We also find that earnings have a negative and significant impact on the health status of women, but a positive and significant impact on the health status of men. We would have expected earnings to have a positive impact on health status for both men and women because of the opportunity cost of poor health on earnings. Our results show that individuals with more education report a significantly higher health status than those with less education. This suggests that persons with higher education are better able to understand the opportunity cost of not being in good health and are willing to make investments to stay in good health. While earnings is a function of education, we include both variables in the model because we believe that while the effect of education may work indirectly through earnings, both

Table 4. Regression Coefficients on Health Insurance Coverage Full-Time, Full-Year Wage and Salary Workers.

	Females		Males	
	Coefficient	Std. Error	Coefficient	Std. Error
Intercept	−2.229***	0.162	−1.192***	0.136
Log annual earnings	0.308***	0.021	0.136***	0.017
Age	−0.007***	0.002	0.010***	0.002
Age-squared	0.0001***	0.00002	−0.0001***	0.00002
Widowed	−0.015	0.018	0.008	0.030
Divorced	−0.040***	0.009	−0.015	0.009
Separated	−0.109***	0.016	−0.045***	0.018
Never married	−0.055***	0.009	−0.039***	0.008
Education (in years)	−0.011***	0.002	0.007***	0.002
White	0.102***	0.008	0.156***	0.007
Black	0.079***	0.010	0.129***	0.010
Other race	0.036***	0.013	0.086***	0.011
Manufacturing	0.050***	0.019	0.082***	0.007
Trade	0.037**	0.018	0.033***	0.007
Service sector	0.060***	0.018	0.075***	0.009
Public administration	0.067***	0.021	0.084***	0.011
10–24 employees	0.052***	0.012	0.074***	0.010
25–99 employees	0.102***	0.011	0.164***	0.009
100–499 employees	0.135***	0.011	0.201***	0.009
500–999 employees	0.131***	0.013	0.196***	0.012
1,000 or more employees	0.125***	0.010	0.201***	0.009
Spouse worked	0.027***	0.007	0.041***	0.005
Number of children	0.005*	0.003	−0.007***	0.002
Support for public health	−0.012	0.009	0.016**	0.007
Cost of insurance	0.00005	0.00004	−0.0001*	0.00003

*Significant at the 10% level.
**Significant at the 5% level.
***Significant at the 1% level.

earnings and education may have direct effects on health status that are independent of each other. The effect of earnings on health status for women does not support the hypothesis that higher earnings will lead to better health because of the opportunity cost of being unhealthy. The high degree of correlation between earnings and education may be affecting the results on earnings.

Turning to the other variables in this health status model, age was found to have a significant negative influence on reported health status, as expected, for men, but no impact on the health status of women. It appears that marriage contributes to better health for women and some men. This difference may be due to the fact that

Table 5. Regression Coefficients on Health Status Full-Time, Full-Year Wage and Salary Workers.

	Females		Males	
	Coefficient	Std. Error	Coefficient	Std. Error
Intercept	6.959***	1.356	1.941**	0.818
Health insurance	0.398*	0.225	−0.107	0.100
Log annual earnings	−0.386**	0.174	0.225**	0.095
Age	−0.004	0.009	−0.013**	0.006
Age-squared	−0.0001	0.0001	−0.0001	0.0001
Widowed	−0.108**	0.049	−0.031	0.081
Divorced	−0.060**	0.025	−0.100***	0.024
Separated	−0.140***	0.050	−0.053	0.048
Never married	−0.084***	0.025	−0.056**	0.024
Education (in years)	0.074***	0.012	0.027***	0.006
White	0.149***	0.026	0.107***	0.022
Black	−0.060*	0.032	−0.022	0.030
Other race	0.015	0.038	−0.122***	0.032
Manufacturing	−0.014	0.054	0.013	0.023
Trade	−0.102*	0.056	0.024	0.024
Service sector	−0.097*	0.059	0.058*	0.033
Public administration	−0.086	0.061	0.081**	0.033
Service collar	−0.129***	0.036	−0.062**	0.025
Blue collar	−0.236***	0.048	−0.093***	0.034
Prevalence of smoking	−0.226	0.318	0.166	0.245
Motor vehicle deaths	−6.790**	2.867	−0.535	2.032
Violent crime rate	0.0002***	0.0001	0.0001	0.00004
Risk of heart disease	−0.005***	0.001	−0.003***	0.001
Support for public health	0.047*	0.027	0.012	0.022

*Significant at the 10% level.
**Significant at the 5% level.
***Significant at the 1% level.

women generally make health care decisions for their families; they are more likely to go to the doctor than men and might have an influence on their spouse's behavior, although other reasons may exist as well (Sandman et al., 2000). Finally, the health status equation suggests that white workers are in better health than workers of other races/ethnicities. This result is consistent with a number of previous studies, which have found that the better access to health care services for whites leads to better health (Braveman et al., 1989; Lieu et al., 1993; Pappas et al., 1997; Weissman et al., 1991).

With respect to the state level variables included in our equations that we expected to affect health status, we find mixed results. The smoking variable, which measures the amount of smoking in the state, had no effect on health status for either women or men. This may be because the variable does not directly measure whether or not a person smokes. The risk of death from a motor vehicle accident had a negative impact on health status for women, as expected, but no impact on men. The crime rate, which is also a measure of risk, had a counter-intuitive positive impact on health status for both men and women. Risk of heart disease had a negative impact on the health status of both women and men, as expected. Finally, public spending on health care services for the low-income population had a positive impact on the health status of women and no impact on the health status of men. The effect for men is not surprising as many public programs often only serve low-income women.

Table 6 shows the estimated coefficients of the earnings equation. As described earlier we allow both health insurance and health status to have an affect on earnings, in addition to the effect our system allows earnings to have on both health insurance and health status. We find that for both women and men, reported health status and health insurance has a positive and significant affect on earnings. In

Table 6. Regression Coefficients on Log Annual Earnings Full-Time, Full-Year Wage and Salary Workers.

	Females		Males	
	Coefficient	Std. Error	Coefficient	Std. Error
Intercept	6.124***	0.393	5.037***	0.427
Health status	0.623***	0.116	0.949***	0.111
Health insurance	0.290*	0.174	0.918***	0.116
Education (in years)	0.061***	0.004	0.034***	0.004
Experience	0.035***	0.003	0.037***	0.003
Experience-squared	−0.0004***	0.00004	−0.0003***	0.0001
White	−0.040*	0.022	−0.122***	0.027
Black	0.015	0.029	−0.100***	0.034
Other race	0.080***	0.031	0.077*	0.040
Service collar	−0.189***	0.024	−0.068***	0.020
Blue collar	−0.090***	0.025	−0.086***	0.026
10–24 employees	0.032	0.029	0.007	0.031
25–99 employees	0.057*	0.032	−0.028	0.035
100–499 employees	0.107***	0.039	−0.066*	0.038
500–999 employees	0.178***	0.046	−0.034	0.044
1,000 or more employees	0.186***	0.040	−0.029	0.037

*Significant at the 10% level.
** Significant at the 5% level.
***Significant at the 1% level.

addition, for both women and men the affect from reporting better health status is stronger than having health insurance. These findings do suggest that workers enjoy a return from better health in the form of higher earnings.

The relationship between earnings and the other variables included in the equation are mostly what we would expect to find. Education has a positive impact on earnings. Experience is positively associated with earnings up until middle age, and then earnings decline as experience increases. White-collar workers have higher earnings than service collar or blue-collar earnings, and earnings increase as firm size increases, at least for men. The findings on race were not as expected. We found that after controlling for all other variables, white-collar workers earned less than other workers. It should be noted that the only variables to be included in all three equations were race/ethnicity and education, which may be influencing our results.

SUMMARY

In the paper, we have estimated a three-stage least squares model to examine the determinants of health insurance, health status, and earnings, and to better understand the relationship between all three. We found the following. Earnings positively affect the likelihood of having health insurance. Having health insurance improved health status for women, but not for men. Higher earnings resulted in lower health status for women, but had no effect on the health status of men, and better health status and having health insurance increased earnings for both women and men. Our analysis implies that there are some returns to employment-based health insurance that go beyond the basic purpose of insurance. The economic benefits of health insurance accrue because third-party payment of health care services can be thought of as investments in workers, improving productivity and ultimately increasing earnings.

Some economists have taken a different approach towards estimating the returns to spending on health care services, rather than focusing on the returns to health insurance, as we have done. Cutler and McClellan (2001), for example, analyzed technological innovation for five health conditions to examine whether the costs or the benefits were greater. They found that the estimated benefit of technological innovation is much greater than the cost for four of the conditions – heart attacks, low-birthweight babies, depression, and cataracts – but for breast cancer, the costs and benefits were about equal in magnitude. They conclude that spending on health care services as a whole is worth the increased cost of care.

Other researchers have shown that advances in medical technology that have improved life expectancy have had a substantial impact on the economy.

Murphy and Topel (2000) found that improvements in life expectancy due to technological innovations in medical care added roughly $57 trillion to national wealth between 1970 and 1990, or $2.8 trillion per year (in 1992 dollars). After factoring out the cost of providing those medical services, the net benefit to the economy was $2.4 trillion per year. They conclude that the potential gains from future reductions in mortality are extremely large.

When it comes to health insurance in the workplace, employers tend to focus only on the cost of providing insurance, and do not usually consider how providing insurance will improve the bottom line. Quantifying the magnitude of the benefit to a specific employer, as opposed to the benefit more generally to the economy, is a much more difficult task. Even though employers should be sharing the benefit of economy wide growth due to spending on health care services, until they are shown how health benefits improve their bottom line, most employers will view health benefits as a cost of doing business rather than an investment in their business, though there are always exceptions. We think that the results in this paper are a first step towards showing a link between health insurance and productivity, and hope that it will stimulate other research in this area.

NOTES

1. A number of researchers have reviewed the literature on insurance coverage and utilization of health care. The scope of these studies includes both the effect of the financial incentives associated with insurance on the utilization of health care and the effect of being uninsured on utilization of health care. See Brown et al. (1998), Holtmann and Olsen (1978), and Newhouse (1993).

2. See Pauly (1986) for a review of this literature.

3. HIPAA requires insurers and employers to reduce the duration of pre-existing condition exclusion periods by one month for every month of prior creditable coverage, so long as the individual did not have a break in coverage exceeding 63 days.

4. Idler and Kasl (1995) find that self-reported health status is a powerful predictor of future changes in functioning and mortality, and provide a summary of the literature.

5. Because we do not observe wages and other job characteristic variables for non-workers, we are unable to correct our estimates for selectivity.

6. According to standard economic theory, employers are willing to arrange health benefits for workers because workers are willing to "buy" that health insurance through reduced wages. Rather than receiving additional cash compensation and finding and purchasing health insurance on their own, most workers prefer to receive health benefits from their employers. If true, we would expect to observe a negative relationship between earnings and insurance coverage. While most economists would argue that employees pay the entire cost for health benefits in the form of reduced wages or wage growth, Pauly (1997) provides numerous examples for why we would not observe the trade-off in practice.

ACKNOWLEDGMENTS

We would like to thank Bruce McCullough, Solomon W. Polachek, Steven A. Woodbury, and an anonymous reviewer for very helpful comments on an earlier version of this paper.

REFERENCES

Braveman, P., Oliva, G., Miller, M. G., Reiter, R., & Egerter, S. (1989). Adverse outcomes and lack of health insurance among newborns in an eight-county area of California, 1982 to 1986. *New England Journal of Medicine, 321*(8), 508–513.

Brown, M. E., Bindman, A. B., & Lurie, N. (1998). Monitoring the consequences of uninsurance: A review of methodologies. *Medical Care Research and Review, 55*(2), 177–210.

Burstin, H. R., Lipsitz, S. R., & Brennan, T. A. (1992). Socioeconomic status and risk for substandard medical care. *Journal of the American Medical Association, 268*(17), 2383–2387.

Centers for Disease Control (1998). Self-reported use of mammography and insurance status among women aged greater than or equal to 40 years – United States, 1991–1992 and 1996–1997. *MMWR Weekly* (October 9), 825–830.

Cutler, D. M., & McClellan, M. (2001). Is technological change in medicine worth it? *Health Affairs, 20*(5), 11–29.

Fronstin, P. (2000). Workers and access to health care: Consequences of being uninsured. In: P. Fronstin (Ed.), *The Economic Costs of the Uninsured: Implications for Business and Government*. Washington, DC: Employee Benefit Research Institute.

Fronstin, P., & Helman, R. (2000). Small employers and health benefits: Findings from the 2000 small employer health benefits survey. *EBRI Issue Brief*, No. 226. Washington, DC: Employee Benefit Research Institute.

Gabel, J., Levitt, L., Pickreign, J., Whitmore, H., Holve, E., Rowland, D., Dhont, K., & Hawkins, S. (2001). Job-based health insurance in 2001: Inflation hits double digits, managed care retreats. *Health Affairs, 20*(3), 180–186.

Grossman, M. (1972). On the conception of health capital and the demand for health. *Journal of Political Economy, 80*(2), 223–255.

Himmelstein, D. U., & Woolhandler, S. (1995). Care denied: U.S. residents who are unable to obtain needed medical services. *American Journal of Public Health, 85*(3), 341–344.

Holtmann, A. G., & Olsen, E. O., Jr. (1978). *The economics of the private demand for outpatient health care*. DHEW Publication No. (NIH) 78–1262. John E. Fogarty International Center for Advance Studies in Health Science.

Idler, E. L., & Kasl, S. V. (1995). Self-ratings of health: Do they also predict change in functional ability? *Journal of Gerontology: Social Sciences, 50*(6), S344–S353.

Institute of Medicine (1993). *Employment and health benefits: A connection at risk*. M. J. Field & H. T. Shapiro (Eds). Washington, DC: National Academy Press.

Lieu, T. A., Newacheck, P. W., & McManus, M. A. (1993). Race, ethnicity, and access to ambulatory care among U.S. adolescents. *American Journal of Public Health, 83*(7), 960–965.

Murphy, K. M., & Topel, R. (2000). Medical research: What's it worth? *Milken Institute Review* (First Quarter), 23–30.

Newhouse, J. P., & The Insurance Experiment Group (1993). *Free for all? Lessons from the RAND health insurance experiment*. Cambridge, MA: Harvard University Press.

Pappas, G., Hadden, W. C., Kozak, L. J., & Fisher, G. F. (1997). Potentially avoidable hospitalizations: Inequalities in rates between U.S. socioeconomic groups. *American Journal of Public Health, 87*(5), 811–816.

Pauly, M. V. (1986). Taxation, health insurance, and market failure in the medical economy. *Journal of Economic Literature, 24*(2), 629–675.

Pauly, M. V. (1997). *Health benefits at work: An economic and political analysis of employment-based health insurance*. Ann Arbor: University of Michigan Press.

Sandman, D., Simantov, E., & An, C. (March, 2000). *Out of touch: American men and the health care system*. New York, NY: The Commonwealth Fund.

Weissman, J. S., Stern, R., Fielding, S. L., & Epstein, A. M. (1991). Delayed access to health care: Risk factors, reasons, and consequences. *Annals of Internal Medicine, 114*(4), 325–331.

THE FAMILY GAP IN PAY: EVIDENCE FROM SEVEN INDUSTRIALIZED COUNTRIES

Susan Harkness and Jane Waldfogel

ABSTRACT

In this paper, we use microdata on employment and earnings from a variety of industrialized countries to investigate the family gap in pay – the differential in hourly wages between women with children and women without children. We present results from seven countries: Australia, Canada, the United Kingdom, the United States, Germany, Finland, and Sweden. We find that there is a good deal of variation across our sample countries in the effects of children on women's employment and in the effects of children on women's hourly wages even after controlling for differences between women with and without children in characteristics such as age and education. We also find that the variation in the family gap in pay across countries is not primarily due to differential selection into employment or to differences in wage structure across countries. We suggest that future research should examine the impact of family policies such as maternity leave and child care on the family gap in pay.

INTRODUCTION

Despite a good deal of progress in recent years, women still tend to have lower employment rates than men and to earn lower hourly wages when they do work.

There is a large literature that examines the gender gap in pay within countries and a growing literature that examines the gender gap in pay across countries (see, for instance, Blau & Kahn, 1992, 1995, 1996, 1998; Callan, Adams, Dex, Gustafsson, Schupp & Smith, 1996). It is taken as given in these literatures that much of the differential in hourly earnings between women and men is due to the fact that women bear children and also tend to have primary responsibility for their care. Studies within countries provide evidence of a persistent "family gap" in pay between women with children and women without children (see, Joshi, Paci & Waldfogel, 1999 for the U.K.; for instance, Waldfogel, 1998a for the U.S.). However, evidence comparing the family gap in pay across countries has been lacking. Thus, we do not know whether countries have similar family pay gaps, or whether countries that have larger family gaps in pay also have larger gender gaps in pay. We also do not know much about the relationship between the effects of children on employment and their effects on wages. In countries where children have a large negative effect on women's employment, do they also have a large negative effect on women's wages, or is the opposite true? Put another way, do women in some countries accommodate their family responsibilities by reducing their employment while women in other countries instead remain in employment but at lower wages?

In this paper, we use microdata on employment and earnings from seven industrialized countries to examine these questions. We find that there are large differences across countries in the family gap in pay, with the United Kingdom displaying the largest wage penalties to children among the seven countries we study here. We also find that there appears to be a relationship between gender and family pay gaps, and between gender and family employment gaps, across countries. Countries where there is a large negative effect of children on women's pay tend to have a large gender gap in pay as well, and countries where mothers have lower employment rates have lower employment rates of women overall. We also find that in countries where children have a large negative effect on employment, they tend to have a large negative effect on pay as well.

BACKGROUND

The Gender Gap in Pay

Human capital theory (see for instance Becker, 1985; Mincer & Polachek, 1974) is the most widely accepted explanation put forward by economists to account for both the existence of the gender gap in pay, and for its narrowing in recent years.[1] According to human capital theory, the fact that historically women have had lower levels of wage-enhancing human capital such as education and work experience than otherwise comparable men explains why women receive lower wages in the labor market. In recent years, as women have obtained more education and have taken shorter periods of time out of the labor market for marriage and childbearing, their wages relative to men's have improved (although note also that as older women re-enter the labor market with lower than average levels of work experience, average wages of women are held down, see O'Neill & Polachek, 1993).

In spite of women's recent progress in closing the gender gap in pay, to the extent that women still retain primary responsibility for children, there are at least four reasons to expect their wages to continue to lag behind otherwise comparable men's (see Becker, 1985; Mincer & Polachek, 1974). First, if taking care of children involves a great deal of effort, women who are involved in taking care of children may have less effort to bring to the labor market and/or may select jobs that require less effort and therefore would be lower paid. Second, if women take some time out of the labor market after having children, they would accumulate less human capital over their lifetime than otherwise comparable men. Third, if women change jobs after having children, they would have lower levels of tenure when they return to work than otherwise comparable men. Fourth, if women at the start of their careers anticipate having children and working less intensively over their lifetime, they may invest less in education and/or may choose less competitive careers, resulting in lower lifetime earnings.

The Family Gap in Pay

As was apparent in the above discussion, a key factor in explaining the gender gap in pay is the fact that women have more responsibility for children than do men. This suggests that the gender gap in pay should be largest for women who have responsibility for children and smallest for women who do not. Put another way, there should be a "family gap in pay" – a differential in hourly wages between women who have children and women who do not.

A growing body of research has investigated the family gap in pay in the United States and has found that women with children do have lower wages than women without children. One of the earliest to document this phenomenon was Polachek (1975b), who noticed in studying pay differences associated with marriage that there were differences associated with motherhood too. More recent studies in the U.S. have found that as the gender gap in pay between women and men has narrowed, pay differences between women with and without children have persisted. For instance, Waldfogel (1998a) reports that even after controlling for age, work experience, education, marital status, race, and ethnicity, having children lowers a woman's pay by about 10% (see also Budig & England, 2001; Fuchs, 1988; Hill, 1979; Korenman & Neumark, 1992; Neumark & Korenman, 1994; Waldfogel, 1997a, b, 1998b; Waldfogel & Mayer, 2000). Pay penalties to children have also been found in the United Kingdom (see, for instance, Joshi, 1991; Joshi, Paci & Waldfogel, 1999; Waldfogel, 1995). However, as discussed in the next section, there appears to be quite a bit of variation in the magnitude of the family gap in pay across countries.

Cross-Country Differences in the Gender Gap and Family Gap in Pay

Welfare state analysts such as Gosta Esping-Anderson (1990) typically divide industrialized countries into three regime types: Anglo-American or Anglo-Saxon; Continental European; and Nordic or Scandinavian.[2] These regime types reflect differences in the countries' political, institutional, and other structures. The Anglo-American group, which includes Britain and its former colonies, has welfare states that are characterized by a fairly high reliance on means-tested public assistance programs, in contrast with the Continental European or Nordic models, which rely to a larger extent on universal social insurance programs. A further point of difference is that that Nordic and Continental European countries tend to have more fully developed family leave and child care policies than the Anglo-American countries (Waldfogel, 1998a, 2001).

As we can see in Fig. 1, the ratio of female to male earnings has risen in countries from all three regime types in recent years.[3] The figure also shows that the gender pay gap tends to be smaller in the Nordic countries and higher in the Anglo-American countries, with the continental European countries displaying a mixed pattern.

Some analysts have linked these patterns to the pattern of family policies and equal opportunity policies on offer in these countries, arguing for instance that the Scandinavian countries' strong female–male earnings ratios reflect at least in part their strong family and equal opportunity policies while the weak performance of the Anglo-American countries reflects their weak policies (Joshi, Paci & Waldfogel, 1998; Waldfogel, 1998).[4]

Implicit in these analyses is the notion that lower wages for women with children in countries without well-developed family policies can go a long way toward explaining the higher gender pay gaps in those countries. However, direct evidence on this point has been lacking. Although there have been many analyses of the pay effects of children in recent years in the United States (see for instance Korenman & Neumark, 1992; Neumark & Korenman, 1994; Waldfogel, 1997b) and the United

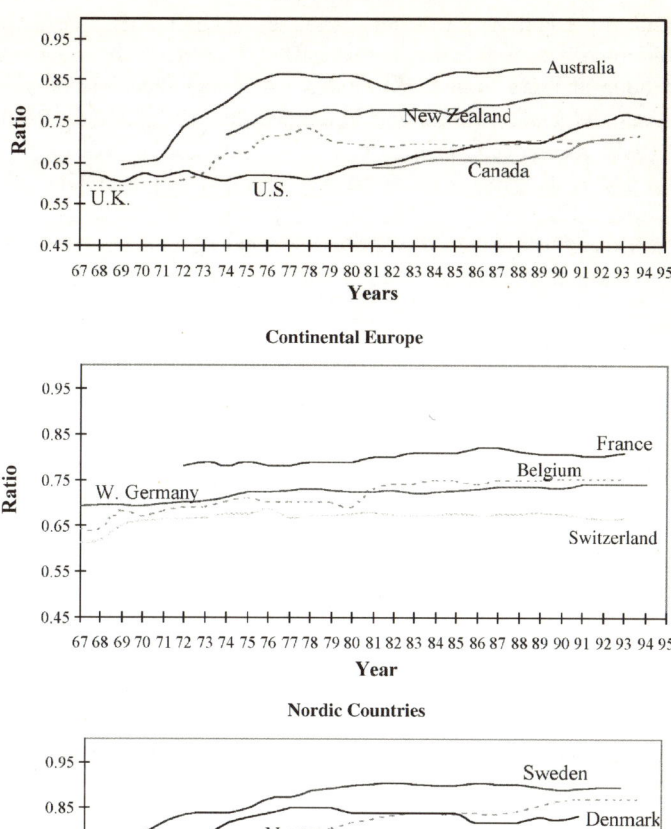

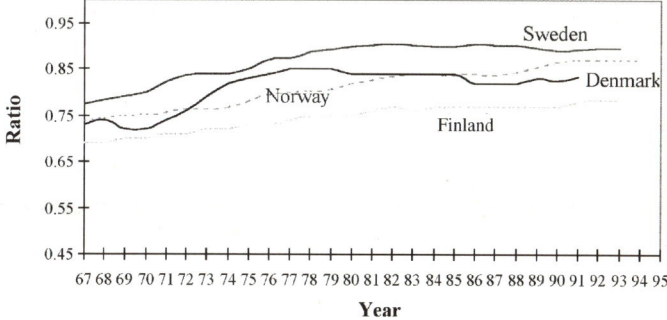

Fig. 1. Female–Male Hourly Earnings Ratios, 1967–1995.

Kingdom (see for instance Joshi, 1991), and at least one in Australia (Baxter, 1992), studies of the pay effects of children in Scandinavian and continental European countries have been much rarer.[5] Moreover, even where individual country studies exist, it can be difficult to compare results across studies given differences in samples, methodology, model specification, and so on. In this study, we overcome that difficulty by conducting our own estimates of the family gap in pay using comparable microdata from seven industrialized countries, drawing primarily on the Luxembourg Income Study (LIS) database. Although several studies have used LIS data to study gender differentials in employment and pay (see, for instance, Gornick, 1999; Jacobs & Gornick, 2001; Sorensen, 2001), none of these prior studies has had as its primary focus the pay effects of children. Ours is the first study to investigate the family gap in pay using data from more than a few countries.

In the sections that follow, we describe the data and methods and then present results. We conclude with suggestions for further research.

DATA AND METHODS

Our data come primarily from the Luxembourg Income Study (LIS), a project in Walferdange, Luxembourg that brings together in one accessible location comparable microdata from a range of industrialized countries. LIS does not release the data to researchers; rather, LIS mounts the datasets on a central computer, where analyses can be run (via remote access) by registered LIS users. In operation since 1983, LIS places particular emphasis on harmonizing the data, so researchers can estimate models using comparably defined variables. However, since LIS does not gather the data itself, there are some differences across datasets in what variables are available, and sample sizes vary widely. Further information on LIS is available at the LIS website (http://www.lis.ceps.lu; see also Smeeding, 2001 for a helpful overview).

We included in our sample every Western industrialized country in the LIS database for which gross hourly wages could be computed, in each case using the most recent year of data that was available. Because the Swedish dataset in LIS did not include earnings data, we instead used data from the most recent year (1991) of the Swedish Level of Living Survey (LNU), a nationally representative household dataset that is frequently used in studies of labor supply and earnings.[6]

Our final set of countries includes at least one representative of each regime type. Our sample countries (and original data source and year) are: Australia (Australian Income and Housing Survey, 1994), Canada (Survey of Consumer Finances, 1994), United Kingdom (Family Expenditure Survey, 1995), and United States (March Current Population Survey, 1994) from the Anglo-American group; Germany (German Social Economic Panel Study, 1994) from the Continental European group; and Finland (Income Distribution Survey, 1991) and Sweden (Level of Living Survey, 1991) from the Nordic group.[7]

For each of our sample countries, we use a sample of prime-age women and men, those between the ages of 24 and 44. We exclude individuals younger than 24 in order to avoid estimating wage equations for young people who are still in school. We exclude individuals older than 44 because women in that age range who have no children are very likely to have had children in the past; thus, including women older than 44 would confound our comparison of women with children and women without children.

Our key outcome variables are: employment, defined as having a job during the survey week; full-time employment, defined as having a job during the survey week and working 30 or more hours per week;[8] gross hourly wages, defined as gross annual earnings divided by annual hours worked (which is the product of weeks worked and hours worked per week); and the log of hourly wages. Individuals who describe themselves as self-employed are excluded from our sample, but all other workers are included.[9] We particularly wanted to include part-time workers because of the importance of part-time work among women with children. However, as detailed below, we conduct some analyses separately for full-time workers due to concerns about measurement error and part-time wages.

The datasets held by LIS, and the LNU data for Sweden, contain detailed demographic and human capital information that we use to construct independent variables for our employment and wage models (see Table A1). A description of these variables, and means for the key family status variables in our samples, are shown in the Appendices 1 and 2.

It is important to note the limitations of the data we use. Because these data are mainly cross-sectional, we are not able to trace out women's earnings or employment histories over time, as they marry and have children. Thus, we are not able to control for pre-existing differences among women that may be correlated with both having children and with having lower wages or lower levels of employment. Moreover, the data do not contain measures of actual work experience. Thus, we are not able to control for time out of the labor force associated with childbearing, which as we saw is an important factor in accounting for the gap in hourly pay between women who have had children and those who have not. As such, the analyses we present here should be considered primarily descriptive and as pointing to the overall general magnitude of the family gaps in pay that exist in various countries and the extent to which these gaps vary across countries. More precise estimates of the causes of those family gaps and the shares due to heterogeneity, work experience, and so on would require more detailed analysis of longitudinal data within countries (data that for the most part are not available through LIS or any other cross-national database).

RAW GENDER AND FAMILY GAPS IN EMPLOYMENT AND FULL-TIME EMPLOYMENT

Table 1 provides an overview of the raw gender and family gaps in employment and full-time employment in our sample countries. Comparing all women in a country to all men in the same country, we find that the raw gender gap in employment ranges widely: it is largest in Australia, where women's mean employment rate is 24 percentage points lower than men's, and smallest in Sweden, where women's employment is 4 points higher than men's.

Women with children are generally much less likely to be employed. In all but one of our sample countries, when we compare women with children to women without children, we find a substantial family gap in employment, ranging from a high of 29 percentage points in the U.K. to a low of 11 in Finland (the one exception is Sweden, where the employment rate of women with children is less than 1 percentage point lower than that of women without children). Turning to full-time employment in panel B of Table 1, we find larger gender gaps in employment but again a large range, with a high of 41 percentage points in Australia and a low of 0 in Finland, and even larger family gaps in employment, ranging from a high of 51 percentage points in the U.K. to a low of 13 in Sweden.

Figure 2 shows how these mean employment rates vary by the age of the youngest child. Across all but one of our sample countries (Sweden again is the exception), employment rises as the age of the youngest child rises, but there are some differences in timing. In Australia and Germany, for instance, there is a sharp increase in employment when the youngest child turns one and another large increase as the youngest child moves from age five to age six or seven (which may reflect women returning to work when their children start school). In Canada and the U.S., employment is somewhat flatter in the early years and then increases from age five to six (when children start school), while in the U.K., employment is low (relative to Canada and the U.S.) throughout the pre-school years but then rises to Canadian and U.S. levels by age six. In Finland, employment rates rise as children age from one and two to four, but from a fairly high base, while in Sweden, employment rates hover at around 80% until children reach age seven at which point they rise to 85 or 90%. Interestingly, employment rates become very similar across our sample countries by the time children reach age 11 which probably reflects the fact that this is when children leave primary school and start middle or secondary school.

Table 1 and Fig. 2 indicate that, across our sample countries, women, and especially women with children, have lower levels of employment, with particularly large differences in mean levels of full-time employment. Figure 2 indicates that these differences are most pronounced for women with young children in most of our sample countries.

Table 1. Employment Rates of Men and Women Age 24–44 in the Sample Countries.

	AU 1995 (N = 4,980)	CN 1994 (N = 30,227)	UK 1995 (N = 4,403)	US 1994 (N = 42,919)	GE 1994 (N = 5,113)	FI 1991 (N = 9,804)	SW 1991 (N = 2,184)
A. Share employed							
All men	0.863	0.792	0.806	0.871	0.861	0.787	0.793
All women	0.624	0.697	0.645	0.688	0.707	0.798	0.836
Women without children	0.823	0.788	0.842	0.799	0.829	0.870	0.842
Women with children	0.520	0.648	0.550	0.634	0.634	0.760	0.833
Gender gap (line 2 – line 1)	−0.239	−0.095	−0.161	−0.183	−0.154	0.011	0.043
Family gap (line 4 – line 3)	−0.303	−0.140	−0.292	−0.165	−0.195	−0.110	−0.009
B. Share employed FT							
All men	0.830	0.762	0.790	0.844	0.830	0.777	0.771
All women	0.421	0.542	0.421	0.573	0.490	0.758	0.653
Women without children	0.731	0.677	0.763	0.731	0.722	0.851	0.745
Women with children	0.258	0.469	0.256	0.495	0.352	0.710	0.611
Gender gap (line 1 – line 2)	−0.409	−0.220	−0.369	−0.271	−0.340	0.019	−0.118
Family gap (line 3 – line 4)	−0.473	−0.208	−0.507	−0.236	−0.370	−0.141	−0.134

Notes: Authors' estimates from LIS data. Employment is defined as the share who have a job during the survey week. Full-time employment is defined as the share who have a job during the survey week and who work 30 or more hours per week.

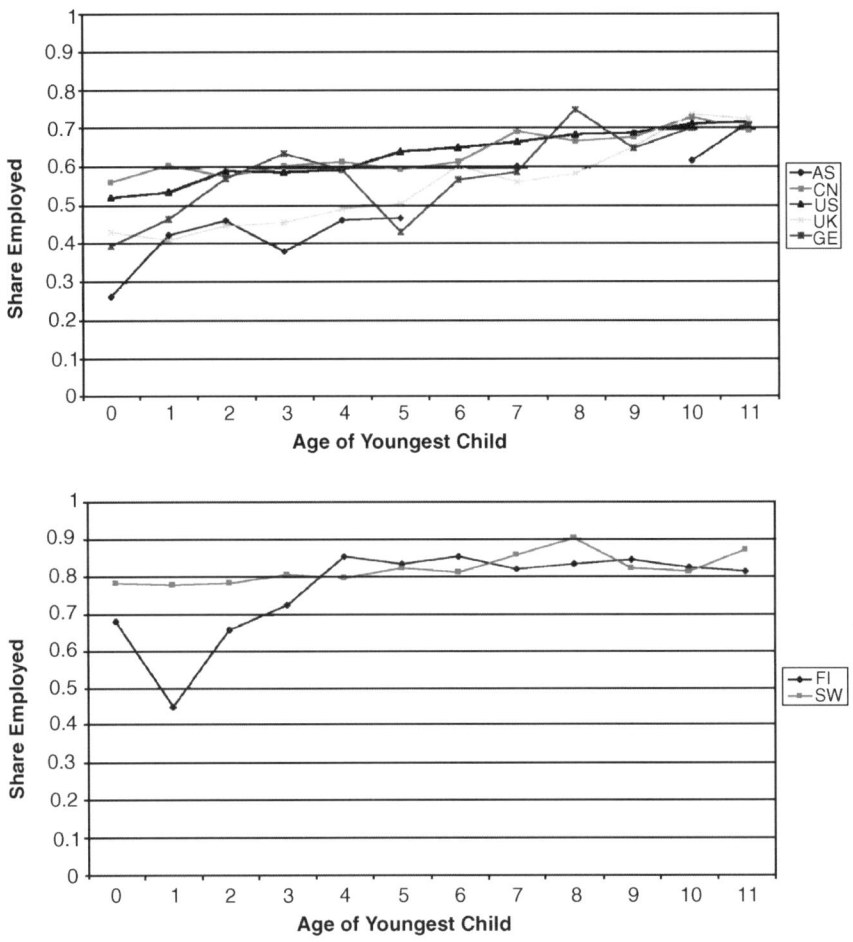

Fig. 2. Share Employed, by Age of the Youngest Child.

Marital status also affects the probability of mothers being employed. The top panels of Table 2 report the employment rate and the share employed full time for women who are married and single, with and without children. Again, there are marked differences in employment patterns across countries, with these differences being greatest for those with children. Looking first at married mothers, we find that employment rates range from 54% in Australia and 60% in the U.K., to 70% in Finland and 82% in Sweden. Contrasting employment rates of married and single

Table 2. Employment Rates and Full-Time Employment Rates by Family Type and Age Group.

	Family Type				Age Group				
	Married		Single						Difference (Age 25–29 to 40–44)
	With Children	No Children	With Children	No Children	25–29	30–34	35–39	40–44	
Employment rates									
AU 1994	0.53	0.82	0.44	0.82	0.66	0.55	0.60	0.69	+0.03
CN 1994	0.66	0.81	0.53	0.76	0.67	0.69	0.70	0.73	+0.07
UK 1995	0.60	0.87	0.37	0.80	0.63	0.61	0.62	0.74	+0.12
US 1994	0.64	0.80	0.62	0.80	0.67	0.68	0.70	0.70	+0.03
GE 1994	0.62	0.83	0.70	0.83	0.76	0.72	0.68	0.67	−0.09
FI 1991	0.74	0.83	0.85	0.89	0.81	0.78	0.79	0.81	0.00
SW 1991	0.82	0.82	0.60	0.75	0.78	0.85	0.88	0.84	+0.06
FT employment									
AU 1994	0.26	0.71	0.26	0.76	0.55	0.34	0.35	0.42	−0.13
CN 1994	0.47	0.70	0.43	0.65	0.55	0.53	0.52	0.57	+0.02
UK 1995	0.27	0.79	0.19	0.73	0.49	0.38	0.35	0.45	−0.04
US 1994	0.48	0.73	0.54	0.74	0.58	0.57	0.56	0.57	0.00
GE 1994	0.32	0.67	0.49	0.76	0.63	0.49	0.41	0.41	−0.10
FI 1991	0.69	0.81	0.84	0.87	0.78	0.74	0.75	0.77	−0.01
SW 1991	0.81	0.78	0.50	0.71	0.74	0.63	0.67	0.64	−0.10

mothers, it is notable that while in Germany and Finland single mothers are more likely to work than married mothers, in most countries the reverse is true. The difference in employment between married and single mothers is largest in the U.K., where single mothers are 23 percentage points less likely to work than those without children, and Sweden, where this gap is 22 percentage points. Similar differences are observed in the second panel of Table 2, which reports full-time employment rates.

The lower two panels of Table 2 show how employment rates vary with age across countries. Marked differences across countries emerge, particularly in full-time employment rates. Full-time employment rates vary even more widely than total employment rates, from 25% in Australia and 27% in the U.K. to 64% in Finland and 81% in Sweden. For single mothers employment ranges from just 37% in the U.K. and 43% in Australia, to 68% in Germany and 78% in Finland. We might expect employment to decline during the years when women have responsibilities for young children and therefore employment in the 30–34 age group to be lower than among those aged 25–29. However, what we find is that full-time employment rates remain relatively constant over the 25–44 age range in Canada, the U.S. and Finland. In Australia, U.K., Germany and Sweden, however, full-time employment rates dip for women in their 30s and then show some increase when women reach their 40s.

RAW GENDER AND FAMILY GAPS IN HOURLY EARNINGS

Table 3 shows the ratio of women's mean hourly wages to men's mean hourly wages for all women, and then women by family status, in our sample countries. The raw gender gap in pay varies a good deal by country, ranging from a high of 23% in the U.K. to a low of 11% in Australia. The raw family gap in pay varies as well: in five of our sample countries (Australia, Canada, Germany, Finland, and Sweden), women with children are paid about the same as or even more than women without children, while in the other two there is a family gap in pay, 8% in the U.S. and 13% in the U.K.

When only full-time workers are considered, the wages of women without children exceed the wages of women with children in each of our sample countries. This difference in results between all workers and full-time workers is due to the fact that women who work part-time are observed to have higher hourly wages than full-time workers in the raw data in several of our sample countries. This raises the possibility that some of the part-time wages are measured with error; it is also possible that part-time workers in other countries do not face

Table 3. Mean Hourly Wages of Women Relative to Mean Hourly Wages of Men in the Sample Countries.

	AU 1994 (N = 3,473)	CN 1994 (N = 21,053)	UK 1995 (N = 3,166)	US 1994 (N = 32,806)	GE 1994 (N = 3,607)	FI 1991 (N = 7,064)	SW 1991 (N = 1,755)
A. Women's wage/all men's wage							
All women	88.9%	82.8%	75.6%	78.5%	85.7%	84.0%	83.9%
Women without children	85.7%	82.4%	83.0%	83.5%	84.8%	84.0%	85.0%
Women with children	91.7%	83.1%	70.3%	75.5%	86.4%	83.9%	83.4%
Gender gap (line 1–100%)	–11.1%	–17.2%	–23.4%	–21.5%	–14.3%	–16.0%	–16.1%
Family gap (line 3–line 2)	+6.0%	+0.7%	–12.7%	–8.0%	–1.6%	–0.1%	–1.6%
	AU 1994 (N = 2,909)	CN 1994 (N = 18,337)	UK 1995 (N = 2,573)	US 1994 (N = 27,400)	GE 1994 (N = 3,135)	FI 1991 (N = 6,813)	SW 1991 (N = 1,541)
B. FT women's wage/FT men's wage							
All FT	84.6%	77.4%	81.9%	79.2%	82.6%	80.7%	82.7%
FT without children	85.9%	80.5%	83.9%	84.1%	85.2%	83.1%	85.6%
FT with children	82.4%	75.0%	79.0%	75.6%	78.8%	79.2%	81.0%
Gender gap (line 1–100%)	–15.4%	–22.6%	–18.1%	–20.8%	–17.4%	–19.32%	–17.3%
Family gap (line 3–line 2)	–3.5%	–5.5%	–4.9%	–8.5%	–7.4%	–3.9%	–4.6%

Note: Wages are defined as gross annual earnings divided by annual hours worked (the product of weeks worked and hours per week).

Table 4. Mean Hourly Wages of Women Relative to Men's Wages, by Family Type and by Age Group.

Family Type	Married		Single		
	With Children	No Children	With Children	No Children	
A. Female wage/male wage by family type					
Wage/male wage					
AU 1994	0.935	0.861	0.784	0.853	
CN 1994	0.830	0.824	0.854	0.823	
UK 1995	0.713	0.824	0.643	0.837	
US 1994	0.798	0.841	0.655	0.831	
GE 1994	0.857	0.803	0.895	0.880	
FI 1991	0.856	0.840	0.752	0.840	
SW 1991	0.838	0.971	0.809	0.901	
Age Group	25–29	30–34	35–39	40–44	Difference (Age 25–29 to 40–44)
B. Female wage/male wage by age group					
Female/male wage ratio					
AU 1994	0.949	0.906	0.859	0.859	−0.090
CN 1994	0.879	0.832	0.849	0.750	−0.129
UK 1995	0.882	0.799	0.669	0.695	−0.187
US 1994	0.878	0.841	0.740	0.700	−0.178
GE 1994	0.902	0.872	0.879	0.797	−0.105
FI 1991	0.963	0.842	0.823	0.757	−0.206
SW 1991	0.916	0.876	0.812	0.752	−0.164

the wage penalties that part-timers face in the U.S. and U.K. (see, for instance, Ferber & Waldfogel, 1998 for the U.S.; Harkness, 1996 for the U.K.).

Table 4 shows hourly earnings by marital status and by age. The top panel reports average wages of women in different family types as a ratio of the average male wage, and this shows that earnings of single mothers are lower than those of married mothers in all countries except Canada and Finland. The bottom panel shows the ratio of the average female wage to the average male wage in each age group. Women in the 25–29 age group earn close to 90% of the average wage of men aged 25–29 in all countries. However, in all countries this wage ratio falls with age and at age 40–44 the wage ratio varies from 69% in the U.K. and 70% in the U.S. to 83% in Germany and 86% in Australia.

The raw wage data indicate that there are substantial differences between the earnings of women with children and women without children in several of our sample countries, and in all our countries when only full-timers are considered.

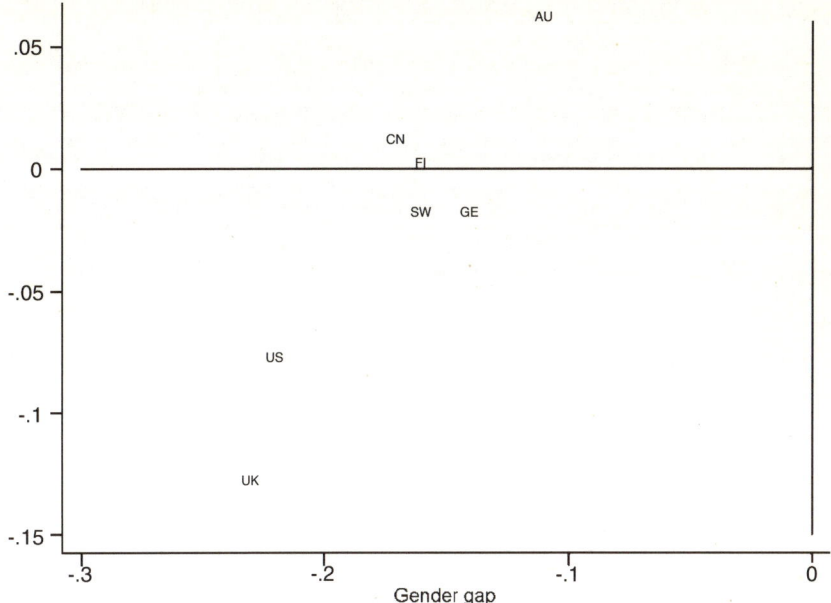

Fig. 3. The Family Gap in Pay and the Gender Gap in Pay.

The raw wage data also suggest that there is some relationship between a country's gender gap in pay and its family gap in pay. When we plot a country's gender gap in pay and its family gap in pay (see Fig. 3), we find that countries with higher family gaps in pay do tend to have higher gender gaps in pay. Interestingly, we also find that countries with higher gender employment gaps tend to have higher family employment gaps (see Fig. 4).

The raw data can also tell us something about the relationship of the employment and wage effects of children. Is it the case that countries where the employment rate of mothers is lower than that of other women are also countries where the wages of mothers are lower than those of non-mothers? Or, is there a trade-off, such that women with children either reduce their employment, or work at lower wages? Figure 5, which plots a country's employment gap between mothers and non-mothers against its wage gap between mothers and non-mothers, suggests that there is no simple relationship between a country's family gap in pay and its family gap in employment, but for the most part the relationship appears to be positive.

The raw data can not tell us to what extent the employment and wage gaps between mothers and other women simply reflect differences in human capital or demographic characteristics between the two groups. It may be that women who have children are less-educated or are from disadvantaged racial or ethnic groups

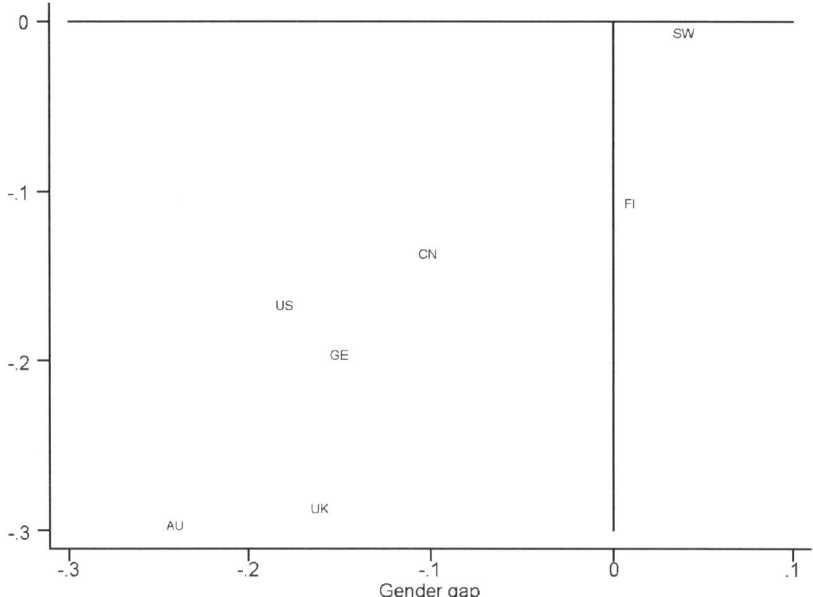

Fig. 4. The Family Gap in Employment and the Gender Gap in Employment.

in some of our countries but not others. If so, these differences in characteristics might account for some of the observed employment or pay differences between mothers and other women. Therefore, in the next sections, we estimate the effects of children on women's employment and wages, controlling for some measures of these other characteristics. Although as noted earlier, we lack measures for some important characteristics, most notably work experience (but also differences in attitudes towards work and family and towards career), nevertheless controlling for other human capital and demographic characteristics will allow us to determine the extent to which the gender gaps and family gaps we see in the raw data are due to differences in those characteristics and the extent to which they persist even after controlling for those characteristics.

THE EFFECT OF CHILDREN ON WOMEN'S EMPLOYMENT

We model a woman's employment decision as a function of the following human capital and demographic variables: age and its square, a set of dummy variables for level of education, a set of dummy variables for ethnicity, the amount of

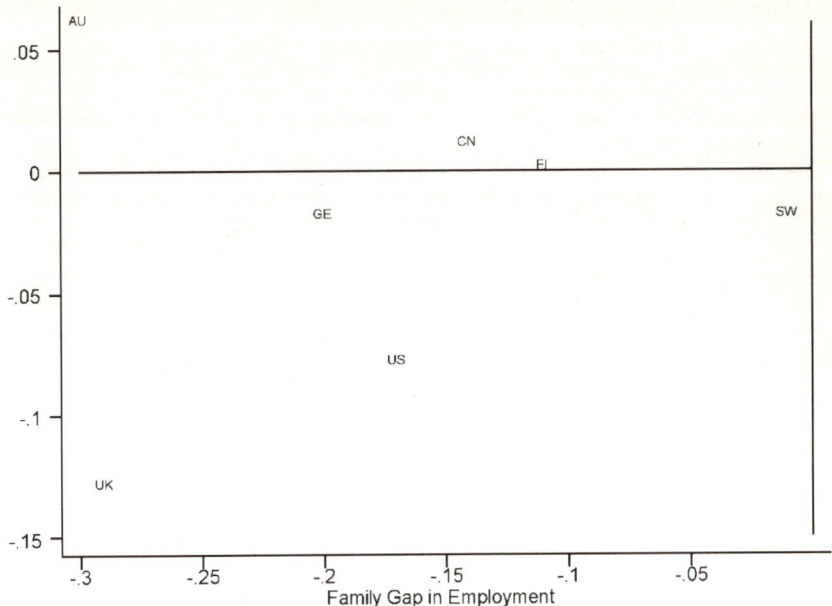

Fig. 5. The Family Gap in Pay and the Family Gap in Employment.

other family members' earnings, the amount of other family income, and a set of dummy variables for region and whether the woman resides in an urban area. In addition, we include a set of controls for her responsibility for children, which we measure with a set of dummy variables for the age of her youngest child, using the three categories youngest child under age one (infant), youngest child age one to five (pre-schooler), or youngest child age six to seventeen (school-age child).[10] Because the presence of a husband may affect a woman's employment decision, we also control for marital status by including a dummy variable for being married.[11] We estimate similar models for full-time employment (defined as working 30 or more hours per week), since as we saw in the raw data in many instances the largest impact of children is not on the employment decision but rather on the decision to work full-time. We estimate both the employment and full-time employment models using probit (because the outcome variables are categorical), and report marginal effects (and their standard errors).

The marginal effects of children (and their standard errors) on employment and full-time employment from the probit models estimated for our seven sample countries are shown in Table 5 (complete results are shown in Table A2). In all four Anglo-American countries and in Germany, there is a strong relationship

Table 5. Effects of Marriage and Age of Youngest Child on Women's Employment, Marginal Effects from Probit Models.

	AU 1994	CN 1994	UK 1995	US 1994	GE 1994	FI 1991	SW 1991
A. Employment							
Married	−0.203**	−0.019	−0.080*	−0.071**	−0.002	0.001	−0.082
	(0.037)	(0.013)	(0.038)	(0.013)	(0.044)	(0.017)	(0.041)
Child age <1	−0.597**	−0.277**	−0.479**	−0.273**	−0.297	−0.056*	−0.156*
	(0.024)	(0.018)	(0.038)	(0.016)	(0.249)	(0.028)	(0.094)
Child age 1–5	−0.424**	−0.219**	−0.402**	−0.197**	−0.347**	−0.078**	−0.103**
	(0.028)	(0.011)	(0.030)	(0.009)	(0.032)	(0.020)	(0.036)
Child age 6–17	−0.190**	−0.095**	−0.142**	−0.068**	−0.127**	0.041*	0.001
	(0.030)	(0.011)	(0.032)	(0.009)	(0.028)	(0.016)	(0.034)
Pseudo R^2	0.205	0.121	0.256	0.094	0.126	0.180	0.109
No. observations	2654	16077	2438	22091	2372	4870	1060
B. Full-time employment							
Married	−0.219**	−0.019	−0.066	−0.052**	0.006	−0.030	−0.155*
	(0.049)	(0.015)	(0.048)	(0.015)	(0.052)	(0.018)	(0.067)
Child age <1	−0.431**	−0.249**	−0.387**	−0.290**	−0.453	−0.025	−0.056
	(0.014)	(0.016)	(0.019)	(0.014)	(0.067)	(0.029)	(0.099)
Child age 1–5	−0.465**	−0.273**	−0.502**	−0.272**	−0.474**	−0.095**	−0.166**
	(0.019)	(0.011)	(0.020)	(0.009)	(0.022)	(0.022)	(0.046)
Child age 6–17	−0.311**	−0.149**	−0.358**	−0.131**	−0.280**	0.035	−0.114*
	(0.024)	(0.011)	(0.024)	(0.010)	(0.028)	(0.018)	(0.048)
Pseudo R^2	0.231	0.089	0.278	0.0911	0.216	0.167	0.077
No. observations	2654	16077	2438	21682	2372	4870	1059

Notes: Employment and full-time employment models also include controls for age, age squared, education, race or ethnicity (except in Sweden), presence of a working husband/partner, other family members' earnings, other family income, region, and urban residence (except in Germany). See Appendix for variable definitions and Table A2 for complete results.

*Statistically significant at $p < 0.05$.
**Statistically significant at $p < 0.01$.

between the age of the youngest child and women's employment. As suggested by the raw data in Fig. 2, employment of women in these countries rises steadily as the youngest child ages. Marriage, in contrast, seems to be less important, with no significant effect on employment in Finland and Germany, and a small negative impact on employment in the U.S. and U.K. Only in Australia marriage is an important factor in explaining women's employment. The results for the Nordic countries are different, as we might have expected given the pattern of the raw data in Fig. 2. In both Finland and Sweden, women with infants and pre-school age children, but not school-age children, are significantly less likely to be employed, but the effects are small compared to the Anglo-American countries and

Germany.[12] Marriage is associated with lower women's employment in Sweden, but not in Finland. With regard to the other coefficients (shown in Table A2), as expected, women are less likely to work when other family income is higher (although holding income constant, women with working partners are more likely to work). Also as expected, women with higher levels of education (and thus higher expected earnings) are more likely to work than those with lower levels of education.

The results for full-time employment are similar. We find very large negative effects of children, generally declining by the age of the child, in the Anglo-American countries and Germany. In contrast, we find much smaller effects of children in Finland and Sweden. Being married again has a negative effect in Sweden; we also see a negative effect of being married on full-time employment in Australia and the U.S. Across all our sample countries, women are less likely to work full-time when other family income is higher, and are more likely to work full-time if they have higher versus lower levels of education themselves.

Although the pattern of results is similar for the four Anglo-American countries and Germany, it is worth noting that the magnitude of the effects varies a good deal across these countries. Children reduce women's employment much more in Australia, Germany, and the U.K. than they do in Canada and the U.S. And, in turn, children have a much larger effect on women's employment in these countries than they do in our two Nordic countries. These differences across countries raise the question of the extent to which institutional or policy differences might account for these differences in outcomes. With data from just one point in time, we can not answer this question in this paper, but the variation in results across countries suggests that it is worth considering in future research.[13]

Before leaving the discussion of the effects of children on employment, it is important to note that the decision to have children may be endogenous; i.e. women who are less likely to be employed may have more children, rather than vice versa, and the strength of this reverse causality may vary across countries.[14] In order to deal with this endogeneity bias, we need an instrument such as a woman's attitudes toward family size that would affect a woman's number of children but not her employment decision. However, we lack such an instrument in our datasets. Therefore, we use as instruments two of the variables available in our datasets – the woman's age and region of residence – although arguably these might affect a woman's employment decision as well as her childbearing decisions. When we use these as instruments, the results as shown in Table A3 provide little evidence of endogeneity bias. While instrumenting for children with age and region does in several instances reduce the estimated impact of children on women's employment, the Hausman test statistics show that in only one case (the model for all workers in Finland) are the results significantly different. Thus, we cannot reject the exogeneity of children in the employment decision. However, as noted above, our datasets do not provide ideal instruments for this purpose.

THE EFFECTS OF CHILDREN ON WOMEN'S WAGES

We estimate human capital earnings functions with the natural logarithm of hourly wages as our dependent variable and a set of family status and other variables (detailed below) as our independent variables. To control for a woman's responsibility for children, we include controls for the number of children, with dummy variables for one child, two children, or three or more children. Our wage model also includes controls for: marriage; age and its square; a set of dummy variables for level of education; a set of dummy variables for ethnicity; and a set of dummy variables for region and whether the woman lives in an urban area. Because as noted earlier, we are concerned about the possibility of measurement error in the part-time wages, we estimated this model for all workers and for full-time workers only.[15]

There are many reasons why children might affect women's wages (see Becker, 1985; Mincer & Polachek, 1974). Children may affect women's wages directly, by for instance lowering a woman's effort on the job, or indirectly, by lowering the amount of work experience and job tenure a woman accumulates over time. The lower wages of women with children may also reflect other pre-existing differences among women, such as differences in their attitudes or commitment to a career. Or, the lower wages of women with children may reflect employer preferences or discrimination. Since we cannot control for effort, experience, tenure, employee attitudes or commitment, or employer preferences or discrimination in our datasets, we cannot place a causal interpretation on the wage effects of children. We can only determine whether such "child penalties" exist in our sample countries and how much they vary across countries once we control for other characteristics that can be measured in our datasets.

The effects of children from the wage models (coefficients and standard errors) are shown in Table 6 (full results are shown in Table A4). In our results for all workers, shown in panel 1, we find sizeable negative effects of children on women's wages in all four Anglo-American countries. Because our dependent variable is the log of hourly wages, the coefficients can be interpreted as percentage effects. Thus, looking at the Anglo-American countries, we find a pay penalty for one child that ranges from a low of 3% in the U.S. and 4% in Canada to a high of 7% in the U.K., a pay penalty for two children that ranges from 5% in Canada to 23% in the U.K., and a pay penalty for three or more children that ranges from 5% in Australia to 31% in the U.K. It is worth noting that in each instance, the pay penalty

Table 6. Effects of Marriage and Children on Women's Log of Hourly Wages, Coefficients (and Standard Errors) from OLS Regressions.

	AU 1994	CN 1994	UK 1995	US 1994	GE 1994	FI 1991	SW 1991
All workers							
Married	0.035	−0.005	0.037	0.060**	−0.058	0.034*	0.033*
	(0.038)	(0.015)	(0.027)	(0.009)	(0.032)	(0.014)	(0.018)
One child	−0.078	−0.036*	−0.071*	−0.027*	−0.018	−0.026	−0.008
	(0.045)	(0.017)	(0.030)	(0.011)	(0.036)	(0.016)	(0.021)
Two children	−0.106*	−0.050**	−0.232**	−0.067**	−0.175**	−0.012	−0.014
	(0.044)	(0.017)	(0.029)	(0.011)	(0.041)	(0.017)	(0.021)
Three or more children	−0.053	−0.209**	−0.309**	−0.088**	0.068	−0.064**	−0.025
	(0.062)	(0.027)	(0.045)	(0.016)	(0.072)	(0.025)	(0.025)
N	1547	10219	1564	15307	1515	3592	874
Adj R^2	0.065	0.097	0.295	0.234	0.119	0.198	0.1787
Full-time workers							
Married	0.035	−0.005	0.016	0.059**	0.013	0.020	0.037**
	(0.036)	(0.015)	(0.029)	(0.010)	(0.031)	(0.013)	(0.018)
One child	−0.110*	−0.036*	0.010	−0.014	−0.041	−0.037*	−0.031
	(0.046)	(0.017)	(0.036)	(0.011)	(0.037)	(0.015)	(0.021)
Two children	−0.168**	−0.050**	−0.169**	−0.040**	−0.108*	−0.022	−0.056**
	(0.049)	(0.017)	(0.037)	(0.012)	(0.046)	(0.016)	(0.021)
Three or more children	−0.193*	−0.209**	−0.279**	−0.062**	−0.079	−0.075**	−0.102**
	(0.082)	(0.027)	(0.059)	(0.018)	(0.091)	(0.023)	(0.027)
N	1046	7885	999	11588	1107	3385	685
Adj R^2	0.090	0.137	0.308	0.275	0.122	0.241	0.1996

Notes: Log wage models include controls for age, age squared, education, race or ethnicity (except for Sweden), region, and urban residence (except for Germany). Model 1 is estimated for all workers; Model 2 is estimated only for full-time workers (those who work 30 or more hours per week). See Appendix 1 for variable definitions and Table A4 for complete regression results.
*Statistically significant at $p < 0.05$.
**Statistically significant at $p < 0.01$.

to children is higher in the U.K. than in the other Anglo-American countries. The results for Germany are less conclusive, with an 18% penalty for two children but no significant penalties for one child or for three or more children. In Finland, in contrast, we find no significant penalty to one or two children, and a small pay penalty (6%) to three or more children, while in Sweden, we find no significant child penalties at all. The results for other variables in the model (see full results in Table A4) confirm that human capital variables such as age and education are important contributors to wages; however, as noted earlier, we lack data on actual work experience and thus are not able to estimate its effect.

When we restrict our sample to full-time workers (see panel 2 of Table 6 and of Table A4), we find generally larger negative effects of children in five of our countries (Australia, Canada, Germany, Finland, and Sweden) and smaller effects in the other two countries (the U.K. and U.S.). Nevertheless, the overall pattern of results is similar to that found for all workers, with the largest pay effects of children found in the U.K. and the smallest in the Nordic countries. Interestingly, the U.S. has relatively low child penalties when we restrict the sample to full-time workers (because the penalties become somewhat smaller in the U.S. while becoming somewhat larger in Finland and Sweden).

Taken together, these wage models provide evidence of negative pay effects of children across our sample countries. Even more interestingly, they also provide evidence that these effects vary a great deal by country. As noted above, we can not definitively explain these negative pay effects of children – they may reflect individual factors such as effort or commitment, work experience, or tenure, or employer factors such as preferences or discrimination that we do not observe in our datasets[16] – but it is worth speculating as to why they vary so much across countries. We consider several alternative explanations below.

Endogeneity Bias

One potential problem with the results from the OLS log wage regressions is that the decision to have children may be endogenous. That is, women who earn lower wages may have more children, rather than vice versa, and the strength of this relationship may vary across countries. If so, this endogeneity might bias our estimates of the pay effects of children and the extent to which they vary across countries. In order to deal with this potential endogeneity bias, ideally we would want an instrument that affects a woman's number of children (but not her wage). Lacking data on background variables that might affect a woman's preferences regarding number of children, we use her age and region as instruments. Specifically, we have run OLS regressions including a linear variable for the number of children. We have then instrumented the number of children in the log wage equation with the mean number of children by region and age. The results from OLS and instrumental variable estimation are reported in Table A5. For all workers (panel 1) the Hausman test statistic is insignificant in all countries, which indicates that either the instruments too are endogenous (as indeed the decision about where to live may be), or that the number of children a women has is exogenous to wages. For full-time workers (panel 2), the Hausman test statistic is again insignificant in all countries except Canada and Sweden. In Canada, instrumentation suggests a greater penalty to having children, suggesting that in Canada women with higher wages are more likely to be working full-time and have children. However, in Sweden instrumentation actually reduces the wage penalty. The reduced wage penalty found in Sweden could capture the effect of lower wages on the probability of having children.

Selection Bias

Another possibility is that the difference in the negative pay effects of children across countries reflects the differential selection of women into employment across our sample countries. If women with children and low earnings potential are more likely to work in the Anglo-American countries, for instance, then the pool of working mothers might include more women with lower wages and thus we would estimate a larger negative effect of children on women's pay. However, as we saw in Fig. 5 earlier, the employment and wage effects of children tend to be correlated. In countries such as the Anglo-American group where children have a large negative effect on wages, they also tend to have a large negative effect on employment. This evidence does not support the hypothesis that differential selection into employment plays an important role in explaining the differences in the pay effects of children across countries.

To test this hypothesis more formally, we estimated Heckman (1979) sample selection correction models, using the age structure of the children in the household, the amount of other family members' earnings, and the amount of other family income as our identifying variables. Specifically, we included in our wage models the same variables as before (age, age squared, controls for level of education, race/ethnicity, married, dummy variables for one child, two children, or three or more, region, and urban residence), while including in our employment probit models age, age squared, controls for level of education, race/ethnicity, married, number of children under age 1, number age 1 to 4, and number age 5 to 17, other family members' earnings, other family income, region, and urban residence.[17] The results, shown in Table A6, suggest that the estimated effects of children on women's pay are not affected a great deal by sample selection bias. The sample selection correction term, lambda, is not statistically significant in any of our countries except the U.S., where it is strongly positive. And, the relative ranking of the countries in terms of the magnitude of their family penalties is much the same as it was in the uncorrected wage models, shown in Panel 1 of Table 6: the U.K. has the largest pay penalties to children, followed by the other three Anglo-American countries, then Germany, and then the two Nordic countries. This evidence does not favor selection as a primary reason for the differences in the family gap in wages across countries.

Wage Structure

Another possibility is that the differences in the wage effects of children across countries reflect differences in wage structure. A series of studies by Blau and Kahn (1992, 1995, 1996, 1998) have found that to a large extent, the difference in the gender earnings gap across countries can be explained by the difference in the extent of earnings inequality across countries. Blau (1992) illustrates this by first ranking countries by their gender earnings ratios and then ranking countries by their mean female percentile in the male wage distribution. She finds that Sweden has a high gender earnings ratio (77% in her data) in spite of having a relatively low female percentile (28) in the male wage distribution, while the U.S. has a lower gender earnings ratio (67%) in spite of having a higher female percentile (33) in the male wage distribution. The reason for this discrepancy between the two measures is that the penalty for one's position in the wage distribution varies widely across countries, depending on the dispersion of earnings in a country; in the above example, the penalty for a low percentile position is greater in the U.S. than in Sweden, because the U.S. has a more unequal wage structure. Thus, if one wants to understand the difference in the gender gap in pay between two countries such as the U.S. and Sweden, taking wage structure into account is important.[18]

This explanation, however, may not fit as well when it comes to explaining differences in the *family gap* in pay across countries. Consider Table 4, panel A, which shows that among all workers the wages of women with and without children are nearly identical in Finland and Sweden. In this case, wage structure would not explain the smaller family gap in these two Nordic countries; the main reason for the smaller family gap is that there is little or no difference in pay between women with and without children, rather than that the difference is penalized less than it is in other countries.

To illustrate this more clearly, we calculated the position of women in each country in the male earnings distribution in their country, and then calculated the average percentile ranking of women in each country. The results are shown in Table 7. Looking first at the results for all workers, we can see that in four countries there is at most a 1 or 2 point family gap as measured by the difference between the mean percentile rankings of women with children and women without children: in Australia, both women with children and women without children have wages that are on average at about the 40th percentile of the male wage distribution; in Canada, women without children are at the 40th percentile while women with children are just two points behind; in Finland, women with children are at the 36th percentile while women with children are 2 points behind; and in Sweden, women with children are at the 32nd percentile while women with children are 1 point behind. The results for the other three countries are quite different: in the U.S. and Germany, there is about a 6 point family gap, with women without children at the 43rd (U.S.) or 45th (Germany) percentile and women with children at the 37th percentile and 39th percentiles, respectively; and in the U.K., the family gap is over 11 points, with women without children at the 40th percentile as compared to women with children at the 29th percentile.[19] Overall, these results are quite consistent with the pattern of results we obtain when we use the gender earnings

Table 7. Mean percentile Ranking of Women in the Male Wage Distribution.

	AU 1994	CN 1994	UK 1995	US 1994	GE 1994	FI 1991	SW 1991
1. All women	40.59	38.65	33.78	39.14	41.71	34.29	30.95
2. All workers							
a. Women without children	41.09	40.09	40.34	42.82	44.77	35.80	31.68
b. Women with children	40.15	37.70	28.95	36.91	39.06	33.39	30.62
c. Family gap for all workers	0.94	2.39	11.39	5.91	5.71	2.41	1.06
3. Full-time workers only							
a. Women without children	40.63	39.23	41.26	44.30	45.03	35.38	32.87
b. Women with children	37.10	35.61	36.05	38.62	38.12	32.28	28.53
c. Family gap for FT workers	3.53	3.62	5.21	5.68	6.91	3.10	4.34

Notes: Percentile ranking in the male wage distribution is calculated for each woman, and then the mean for all women in the group is calculated. The family gap for all workers is the mean percentile ranking of women workers with children minus the mean percentile ranking of women workers without children; the family gap for FT workers is the mean percentile ranking of full-time women workers with children minus the mean percentile ranking of full-time women workers without children.

ratio as our measure, as we can see in Fig. 6. On both measures, we find the largest family gaps in pay in the U.S., Germany, and the U.K.

So, how important is wage structure in accounting for the differences in the family gap in pay across countries? Following Blau (1992), it is informative to compare the rankings of countries using the percentile position of women with their rankings using the gender pay ratio, as this will tell us how important a role wage structure plays in the differences across countries. Given our interest in the position of women with children as compared to women without children, we compare these groups separately, as shown in Fig. 7. Looking first at the non-mothers, we find that using the mean percentile ranking as opposed to the mean gender pay ratio changes the ranking of our countries a good deal, with all of our seven countries changing position. We also find that, while there is relatively little spread in the pay ratio between countries, with the pay ratio of non-mothers relative to men ranging from 82 to 86%, there is much more variation in the mean percentile ranking. The mean percentile ranking of non-mothers in the male wage distribution ranges from 32 in Sweden to 45 in Germany. When we turn to mothers, we find a much larger spread in the pay ratio of mothers relative to non-mothers, ranging from a low of 70% in the U.K. to a high of 92% in Australia. In contrast to our results for non-mothers (and to Blau's (1992) results for women overall), measuring mothers' pay by their mean percentile ranking in the male distribution does not for the most part alter the ranking of the countries. Four countries change position: Sweden and Finland are now further down the ranking while the U.S. and Canada move up. Thus, wage structure seems to be important in understanding why mothers are lower paid relative to men in the U.S. or Canada than they are in Finland or Sweden.

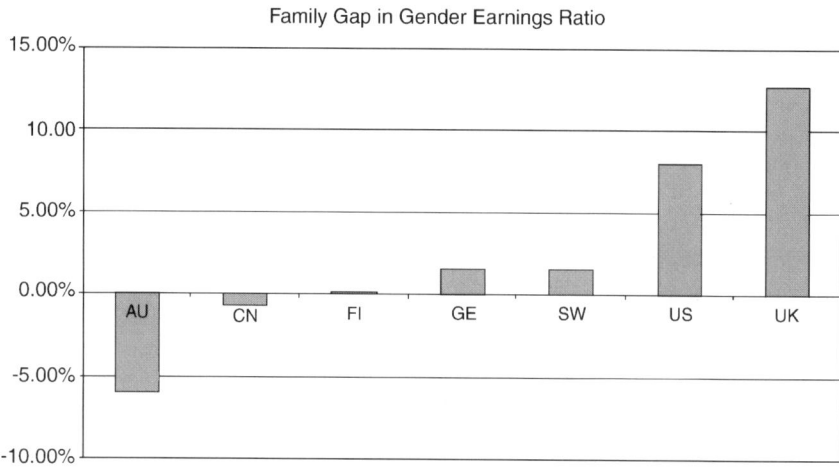

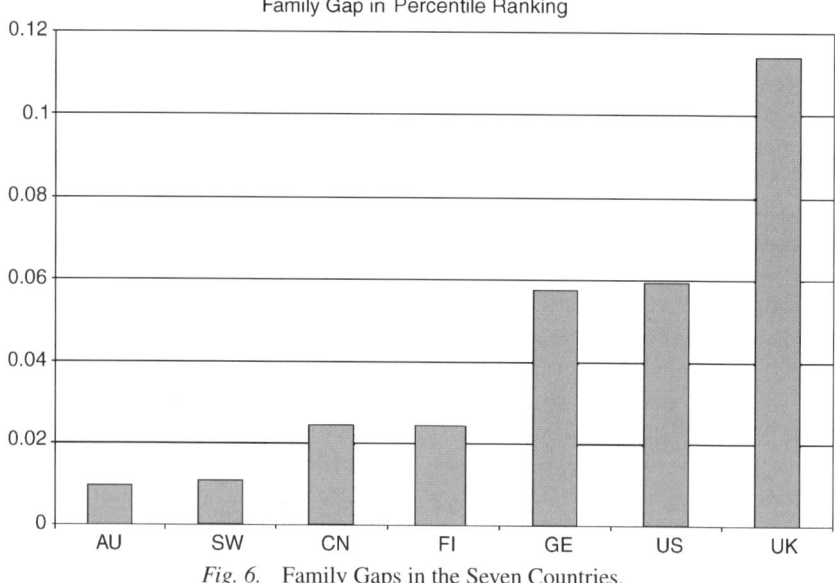

Fig. 6. Family Gaps in the Seven Countries.

However, wage structure does not fully explain why mothers are lower paid relative to non-mothers. If a country such as the U.K. adopted Sweden's pay structure, this would reduce the penalty that mothers face in the labor market for being at a lower percentile in the male wage distribution, but it would not change the fact that they are at a lower position. Thus, changing the pay structure alone would not close the family gap in pay between mothers and non-mothers in the U.K. or U.S. or Germany, since mothers in those countries are at a much lower percentile ranking than non-mothers to start with.

Differences in Family Policies
Another possibility is that the differences we observe in the pay effects of children across countries reflect differences in family policies across countries. However,

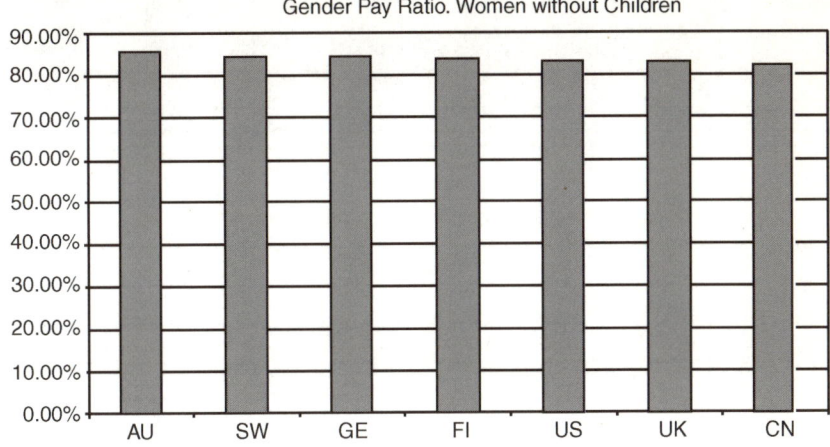

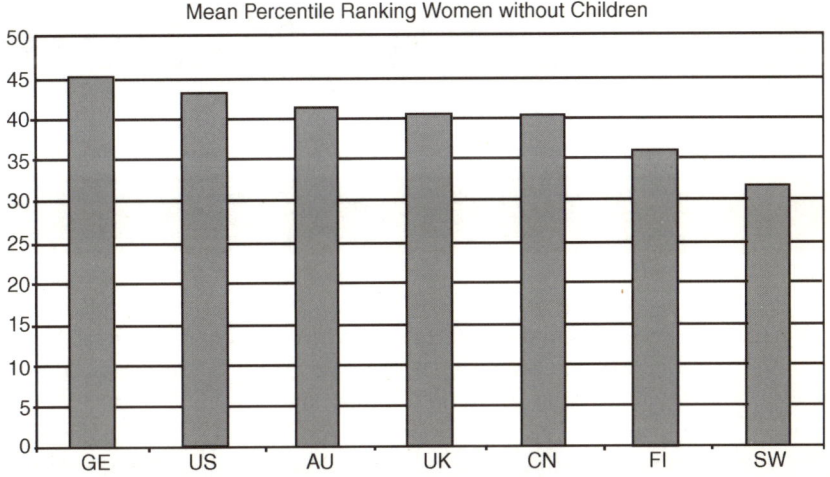

Fig. 7. Rankings of the Seven Countries.

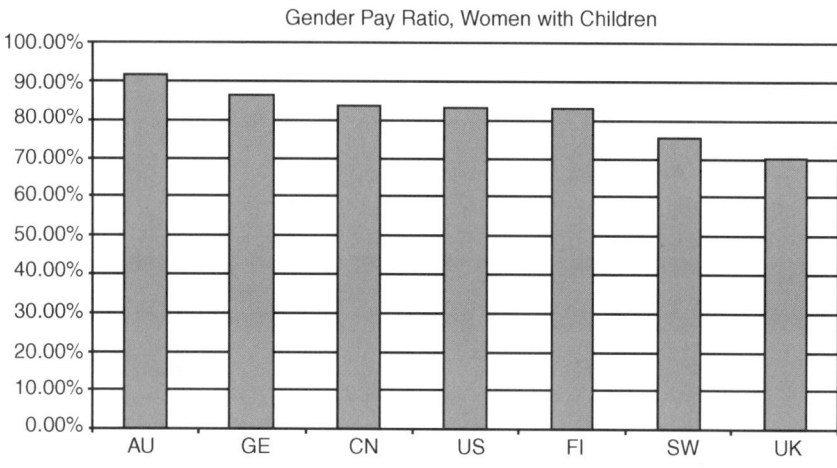

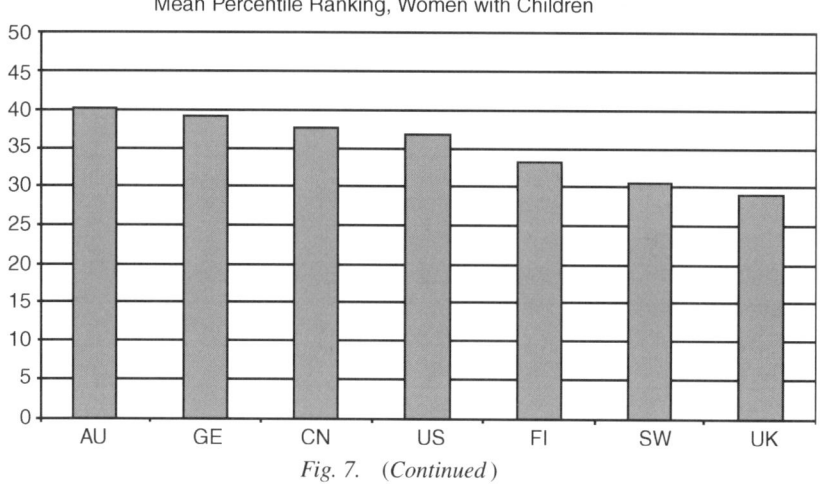

Fig. 7. (*Continued*)

whether adopting changes in family policy such as maternity leave or child care improves the pay position of mothers is an open question. It is possible that the wage parity achieved by Nordic mothers relative to non-mothers comes about as a result of their extensive family policies, which support the labor force attachment of women with children and thus are likely to raise women's levels of work experience and job tenure (Joshi, Paci & Waldfogel, 1998; Waldfogel, 1998a). But this parity may come at the price of lower wages for women overall, if employers shift the costs associated with such policies to those perceived to be most likely to benefit from them, namely, women. The low position of all Swedish women in the male wage distribution, and the under-representation of Swedish women at the top of the distribution (see Albrecht, Bjorklund & Vroman, 2001; Sorensen, 2001) may reflect the price women pay for Sweden's extensive family policy supports, or it may reflect other factors entirely. We are not able to estimate the effect of family policies here, but clearly, more research on this question, and on the impact of family policies more generally on the employment and pay of mothers, and non-mothers, is warranted.

CONCLUSIONS

This paper adds to the growing literature on the "family gap in pay" by tackling the question of whether the family gap in pay that has been documented for some Anglo-American countries is unique to those countries or whether a comparable gap is found in other Western industrialized countries. The results for the seven countries examined here indicate that, controlling for differences in earnings-related characteristics, the effect of children on women's pay is largest in the United Kingdom, followed by the other Anglo-American countries and Germany, and smallest in the Nordic countries.

We also sought to learn whether there is a link between the family gap in pay and the gender gap in pay across countries, such that countries with higher family pay gaps tend to have larger gender pay gaps as well. This was in fact the case in our data, as we saw in Fig. 3, with the U.K. displaying both the largest gender gap in pay and the largest family gap in pay. We also examined the relationship between the employment gap between mothers and other women, and the wage gap between mothers and other women, and found that they were positively correlated. Thus, we found no evidence that women with children make a choice between lower employment or lower wages; the two seem to go together. This suggests that the high pay penalty to children in the U.K., for instance, is not simply due to the fact that women with children are more likely to work in that country. We found little evidence to support the hypothesis that endogeneity or differential selection into employment account for the differences in the family gap across countries. Nor did we find much evidence that wage structure, which has been found to be so important in explaining the gender gap in pay, explains much of the cross-country differences in the family gap in pay.

Why does the family gap in pay vary so much across countries? What role do family policies such as maternity leave and child care play in closing the pay gap between mothers and other women? And what impact do such policies have on the pay of women overall? This study, using data from one point in time, could not answer these questions, but our results suggest that they are worth investigating in future. Studies that track the wages of mothers, and other women, over time within countries as family policies change would be particularly useful. So too would multi-country studies that use data from multiple points in time.

NOTES

1. Attention to issues of human capital has a long history in economics. For an excellent historical overview, see Polachek (1995a), who credits Ben-Porath (1967) with being the first to apply human capital theory to individuals' decisions about how to invest over their lifetime. Studies that have applied human capital theory to the study of the gender gap in pay include Mincer and Polachek (1974), Becker (1981), Polachek (1975a, b), Weiss and Gronau (1981), Mincer and Ofek (1982), Goldin and Polachek (1987). See also Goldin's (1990) excellent book on the gender gap in the United States. Other theories that have been proposed to account for the gender gap in pay include occupational segregation and discrimination (see, for instance, Bergmann, 1974; see also Blau, Ferber & Winkler, 1998 for a useful overview of both human capital and other theories and Polachek, 1995b for a discussion of human capital and feminist perspectives).

2. See also Sainsbury (1994) whose typology takes gender more explicitly into account.

3. The data used to produce Fig. 1 were originally collected by Francine Blau and Lawrence Kahn, updated by Heather Joshi, and then updated again by Wen-Jui Han. We are grateful to all these individuals for sharing these data with us, and to Wen-Jui Han for producing Fig. 1 for us.

4. See also the work of Gornick, Meyers and Ross (1998) who examined women's employment across a range of industrialized countries and Gustafsson, Wetzels, Vlasblom and Dex (1996) who examined women's labor force transitions in connection with childbirth in Germany, Sweden, and Great Britain.

5. An important exception is a recent study by Albrecht, Edin, Sundstrom and Vroman (1998) which found that in Sweden, children tended to have a positive or not significant effect on women's wages. See also Rosholm and Smith (1996) who find no significant effects of children on women's wages in Denmark. More recent studies include Gupta and Smith (2001), Sullivan and Todd (2001) and Todd (1999).

6. The Level of Living Survey is used by permission of the Swedish Institute for Social Research in Stockholm, Sweden. For further information on this dataset, see Fritzell and Lundberg (1994).

7. Each of these datasets comes from a large nationally representative survey (although as noted earlier sample sizes vary a good deal across countries). We use the weights provided in each dataset in all our estimates to correct for sampling variation.

8. The definition of full-time is not consistent across countries. For instance, in the U.S., usually 35 or more hours per week is considered full-time, whereas in the U.K., a cut-off of 30 hours per week is used. We use 30 hours per week here because it represented the best compromise among the definitions used by the various countries in this study.

9. For the most part, the data held by LIS have been cleaned and do not contain extreme values. However, this was not the case for the wage data for the United States.

Therefore, for the U.S. sample, we had to exclude extreme wage values (wages less than $2.00/hour or greater than $200/hour); this affected only 1.3% of the observations in the U.S. sample.

10. There is some ambiguity in the coding for Germany, where we find very few (7) women with a child age 0 in the data.

11. As noted in the Appendix, the category of married includes those living as married in all of our sample countries except the U.S. and Germany. Although we also control for other family members' earnings (including those of the husband or partner), to the extent that these are measured with error, the dummy variable for being married may also pick up some effects of income.

12. The smaller effects of pre-school age children on women's employment in Finland and Sweden probably reflect the fact that many women in those countries take advantage of the generous maternity leave provisions but then return to work while their children are still pre-schoolers, taking advantage of the extensive child care on offer, in contrast to a country such as Germany which has generous maternity leave provisions but much less extensive child care coverage.

13. We hope to be able to address this type of question in future work, by using multiple waves of data from LIS in conjunction with data on policies and institutions in the various countries.

14. A more general problem is that decisions regarding employment and childbearing may be made simultaneously and may be affected by differences in attitudes and norms across countries. See, for instance, Kiernan (1992) and Hobcraft and Kiernan (1995) for discussions of the factors that influence a woman's decision to become a parent and how those may vary across countries.

15. We also estimated models in which we added a control for whether the woman works part-time (less than thirty hours per week) since working part-time may account for some of the lower wages of women with children. The results of these models (not shown) suggest that although working part-time does have a significant negative effect on women's hourly wages in two of our countries (the U.S. and U.K.), significant negative effects of children in those countries remain even after controlling for part-time working status.

16. Another possibility is that at least some portion of these pay penalties may be due to differences in the occupations of women with children and women without children. We plan to control for occupation in future research (details on occupational coding are not currently available from LIS).

17. We also estimated similar models for selection into full-time employment. The results of these models are available upon request.

18. In a similar vein, Edin and Richardson (2001) find that changes in solidarity wage policy have been an important factor in narrowing the gender earnings gap within a country (Sweden) over time.

19. When we restrict the analysis to full-time workers only, the percentile ranking of U.K. women with children improves dramatically, which makes sense given the links in that country between motherhood, part-time work, and low pay, whereas we find the opposite result for Sweden, where as we saw earlier the wages of mothers who work full-time tend to be somewhat lower than those of mothers who work part-time. One might wonder whether these results are driven by the fact that most women in the age group considered here are mothers. However, in each of our sample countries, at least one third of women in the sample do not have children.

ACKNOWLEDGMENTS

We are grateful to Tim Smeeding and Koen Vleminckx for their help with the Luxembourg Income Study data and to Anders Bjorklund and Johan Fritzell for their help with the Swedish Level of Living Survey data. We received helpful comments from Solomon Polachek and two anonymous referees on an earlier version of this paper. Jane Waldfogel also gratefully acknowledges funding from the William T. Grant Foundation and National Institute for Child Health and Development.

REFERENCES

Albrecht, J., Bjorklund, A., & Vroman, S. (2001). Is there a glass ceiling in Sweden? Working Paper, Georgetown and Stockholm Universities.

Albrecht, J., Edin, P.-A., Sundstrom, M., & Vroman, S. (1998). Career interruptions and subsequent earnings: A re-examination using Swedish data. Working Paper, Georgetown, Uppsala, and Stockholm Universities.

Baxter, D. (1992). Domestic labor and income inequality. *Work, Employment, and Society, 6*(2), 229–249.

Becker, G. (1981). *Treatise on the family*. Cambridge, MA: Harvard University Press.

Becker, G. (1985). Human capital, effort, and the sexual division of labor. *Journal of Labor Economics, 3*, 33–38.

Ben-Porath, Y. (1967). The production of human capital over the life cycle. *Journal of Political Economy, 75*, 352–365.

Bergmann, B. (1974). Occupational segregation, wages, and profits when employers discriminate by race and sex. *Eastern Economic Journal, 1*, 103–110.

Blau, F. (1992). Gender and economic outcomes: The role of wage structure. Keynote Speech, Fourth European Association of Labor Economists Annual Conference, Warwick, England.

Blau, F., & Kahn, L. (1992). The gender earnings gap: Learning from international comparisons. *American Economic Review, 82*(May), 533–538.

Blau, F., & Kahn, L. (1995). The gender earnings gap: Some international evidence. In: R. B. Freeman & L. Katz (Eds), *Changes and Differences in Wage Structures* (pp. 105–143). Chicago: University of Chicago Press.

Blau, F., & Kahn, L. (1996). Wage structure and gender earnings differentials: An international comparison. *Economica, 63*(Supplement), S29–S62.

Blau, F., & Kahn, L. (1998). The effect of wage inequality and female labor supply on the gender pay gap: A cross-country analysis, 1985 to 1994. Working Paper, Cornell University, Ithaca.

Budig, M., & England, P. (2001). The wage penalty for motherhood. *American Sociological Review*.

Callan, T., Adams, S., Dex, S., Gustafsson, S., Schupp, J., & Smith, N. (1996). Gender wage differentials: New cross-country evidence. Working Paper No. 134, Luxembourg Income Study, Walferdange, Luxembourg.

Edin, P.-A., & Richardson, K. (2001). Swimming with the tide: Solidarity wage policy and the gender earnings gap. Forthcoming in: *Scandinavian Journal of Economics*.

Esping-Anderson, G. (1990). *Three worlds of welfare capitalism*. Princeton: Princeton University Press.

Ferber, M., & Waldfogel, J. (1998). The long-term consequences of non-standard work. *Monthly Labor Review, 121*(5), 3–12.

Fritzell, J., & Lundberg, O. (Eds) (1994). *Vardagens villkor. Levnadsförhållanden I Sverige under tre decennier (Everyday life. Living conditions in Sweden during three decades)*. Stockholm: Brombergs.

Fuchs, V. (1988). *Women's quest for economic equality.* Cambridge: Harvard University Press.

Goldin, C. (1990). *Understanding the gender gap: An economic history of American women.* New York: Oxford University Press.

Goldin, C., & Polachek, S. (1987). Residual differences by sex: Perspectives on the gender gap in earnings. *American Economic Review, 77*(May), 143–151.

Gornick, J. (1999). Gender equality in the labor market. In: D. Sainsbury (Ed.), *Gender Policy Regimes and Welfare States* (pp. 210–242). Oxford, U.K.: Oxford University Press.

Gornick, J., Meyers, M., & Ross, K. (1998). Public policies and the employment of mothers. *Social Science Quarterly, 79*(1), 35–54.

Gupta, N. D., & Smith, N. (2001). Children and career interruptions: The family gap in Denmark. Mimeo, Aarhus School of Business.

Gustafsson, S., Wetzels, C., Vlasblom, J. D., & Dex, S. (1996). Women labor force transitions in connection with childbirth: A panel data comparison between Germany, Sweden, and Great Britain. *Journal of Population Economics, 9*, 223–246.

Harkness, S. (1996).The gender earnings gap: Evidence from the U.K. *Fiscal Studies, 17*(2), 1–36.

Heckman, J. (1979). Sample selection bias as a specification error. *Econometrica, 47*, 153–161.

Hill, M. (1979). The wage effects of marital status and children. *Journal of Human Resources, 24*(4), 579–594.

Hobcraft, J., & Kiernan, K. (1995). Becoming a parent in Europe. Welfare State Programme Discussion Paper No. 116, Suntory and Toyota International Centres for Economics and Related Disciplines.

Jacobs, J., & Gornick, J. (2001). Hours of paid work in dual earner couples: The U.S. in cross-national perspective. Luxembourg Income Study Working Paper No. 253.

Joshi, H. (1991). Sex and motherhood as handicaps in the labor market. In: D. Groves & M. Maclean (Eds), *Women's Issues in Social Policy*. London: Routledge.

Joshi, H., Paci, P., & Waldfogel, J. (1998). What do we know about unequal pay? In: H. Joshi & P. Paci with G. Makepeace & J. Waldfogel (Eds), *Unequal Pay*. Cambridge: MIT Press.

Joshi, H., Paci, P., & Waldfogel, J. (1999). The wages of motherhood: Better or worse? *Cambridge Journal of Economics, 23*(5), 543–564.

Kiernan, K. (1992). The respective roles of men and women in tomorrow's Europe. *Human Resources at the Dawn of the 21st Century*. Luxembourg: Eurostat.

Korenman, S., & Neumark, D. (1992). Marriage, motherhood, and wages. *Journal of Human Resources, 27*(2), 233–255.

Mincer, J., & Ofek, H. (1982). Interrupted work careers: Depreciation and restoration of human capital. *Journal of Human Resources, 17*, 3–24.

Mincer, J., & Polachek, S. (1974). Family investments in human capital: Earnings of women. *Journal of Political Economy, 82*, 576–608.

Neumark, D., & Korenman, S. (1994). Sources of bias in women's wage equations: Results using sibling data. *Journal of Human Resources, 29*, 379–405.

O'Neill, J., & Polachek, S. (1993). Why the gender gap in wages narrowed in the 1980s. *Journal of Labor Economics, 11*(1), 205–228.

Polachek, S. (1975a). Differences in expected post-school investment as a determinant of market wage differentials. *International Economic Review, 16*, 451–470.

Polachek, S. (1975b). Potential biases in measuring discrimination. *Journal of Human Resources, 6*, 205–229.

Polachek, S. (1995a). Earnings over the lifecycle: What do human capital models explain? *Scottish Journal of Political Economy, 42*(3), 267–289.

Polachek, S. (1995b). Human capital and the gender earnings gap: A response to feminist critiques. In: E. Kuiper & J. Sap, with S. Feiner, N. Ott & Z. Tzannatos (Eds), *Out of the Margin: Feminist Perspectives on Economics* (pp. 61–79). London: Routledge.

Rosholm, M., & Smith, N. (1996). The Danish gender wage gap in the 1980s: A panel data study. *Oxford Economic Papers, 48*, 254–279.

Sainsbury, D. (1994). *Gendering welfare states*. Thousand Oaks: Sage Publications.

Smeeding, T. (2001). Procuring microdata files for the LIS project databank: Progress and promise. Luxembourg Income Study Working Paper No. 250.

Sorensen, A. (2001). Gender equality in earnings at work and at home. Luxembourg Income Study Working Paper No. 251.

Sullivan, D., & Todd, E. (2001). The effects of children on household income packages: A cross-national analysis. Paper presented at the Midwest Economics Association Meetings (March).

Todd, E. (1999). Educational attainment and family gaps in women's wages: Evidence from five industrialized countries. LIS Working Paper No. ????.

Waldfogel, J. (1995). The price of motherhood: Family status and women's pay in a young British cohort. *Oxford Economic Papers, 47*(4), 584–610.

Waldfogel, J. (1997a). Working mothers then and now: A cross-cohort analysis of the effects of maternity leave on women's pay. In: F. Blau & R. Ehrenberg (Eds), *Gender and Family Issues in the Workplace*. New York: Russell Sage.

Waldfogel, J. (1997b). The wage effects of children. *American Sociological Review, 62*(April), 209–217.

Waldfogel, J. (1998a). Understanding the 'family gap' in pay for women with children. *Journal of Economic Perspectives, 12*(1), 137–156.

Waldfogel, J. (1998b). The family gap for young women in the United States and Britain: Can maternity leave make a difference? *Journal of Labor Economics, 16*(3), 505–545.

Waldfogel, J., & Mayer, S. (2000). Gender differences in the low-wage labor market. In: D. Card & R. Blank (Eds), *Finding Jobs: Work and Welfare Reform*. New York: Russell Sage Foundation.

Weiss, Y., & Gronau, R. (1981). Expected interruptions in labor force participation and sex related differences in earnings growth. *Review of Economic Studies, 48*, 607–621.

APPENDIX

Variable Definitions

Employed Dummy variable for whether employed during survey week.
Log wage Log of gross hourly wage (annual wage and salary income divided by weeks worked & hours worked).
Age Age in years.
Age squared Age in years squared.
Married Dummy variable for whether married. Includes those cohabiting or living together as married except in U.S. and GE.
Child<1 Dummy variable for whether youngest child is under age 1.

Child 1–5 Dummy variable for whether youngest child is age 1 to 5.
Child 6–17 Dummy variable for whether youngest child is age 6 to 17.
1 Child Dummy variable for having one child.
2 Children Dummy variable for having two children.
3+ Children Dummy variable for having three or more children.
Partner work Dummy variable for whether husband/partner works.
Other earn Other family members' earnings.
Other income Other family income (total family income minus own earnings and other earnings).

Education Dummy variables defined by country:

AU 8 categories (no qualifications, basic vocational, skilled vocational, associated diploma, undergraduate diploma, bachelor degree, postgraduate diploma, higher degree)

CN 7 categories (grade 8 or lower, grade 9–10, grade 11–13 not h.s. grad, grade11–13 h.s. grad, post-secondary no degree, post sec. certificate or diploma, university degree)

UK 13 categories (dummy variables for left school at age 0–13,14,15,16, 17,18,19,20,21,22,23,24 and age 24 and over)

US 8 categories (elementary, some high school, high school, some college, associate degree, bachelor degree, masters, doctorate)

GE 7 categories (no degree, other degree, secondary, tech school degree, high school degree, technical college, university)

FI 7 categories (no years of schooling, 10–11, 12, 13–14, 15, 16, post-grad education)

SW 8 categories (unspecified, primary 1, primary 2, secondary 1, secondary 2, university 1, university 2, research)

Race or Ethnicity/Nat'l Origin. Dummy variables defined by country:

AU 4 categories (Oceania, Antarctica, Europe or USSR, Africa or Middle East, Asia, Americas)

CN 3 categories (English, French, other)

UK Not available

US 6 categories (white, black, asian/pacific islander, eskimo/aleut/indian, other race, hispanic)

GE 4 categories (W. German, Foreign, E. German, immigrant)

FI 2 categories (Finnish-speaking, Swedish-speaking)

SW Not available.

Region Dummy variable defined by country:

AU 7 categories (New South Wales, Victoria, Queensland, Southern Australia, Western Australia, Tasmania, A.C.T and N.T.)
CN 10 categories (Newfoundland, Prince Edward Island, Nova Scotia, New Brunswick, Quebec, Ontario, Manitoba, Saskatchewan, Alberta, British Columbia)
UK 11 categories (North, Yorkshire and Humberside North West, East Midlands, West Midlands, East Anglia, Greater London, South East, South West, Wales, Scotland, Northern Ireland)
US 9 categories (New England, Middle Atlantic, East North Central, North Central, South Atlantic, East South Central, West South Central, Mountain, Pacific)
GE 16 categories (West Berlin, Schleswig Holstein, Hamburg, Lower Saxony, Bremen, North Rhine Westfalia, Hesse, Rhineland, Badenwurttemburg, Bavaria, East Berlin, Mecklenburg, Brandenburg, Sachsen, Thueringen, Saxony)
FI 11 categories (Uusimaa, Turku/Pori, Home, Kymi, North Karelia, Kuopio, Central Finland, Vaasa, Oulu, Lapland, other)
SW 7 categories (Stockholm, bigger cities, south, north, north sparsely populated, Gothenburg, Malmo)

Urban Dummy variables defined by country:

AU 2 categories (state capital, rest of country)
CN 6 categories (urban 500,000+, urban 100,000 to 499,999, urban, 30,000–99,999, urban 2,500–29,999, urban <2,500, rural)
UK 5 categories (Greater London, Metropolitan districts and central Clyde, non metropolitan, 3.2+ persons, non-metropolitan 0.9–3.2 persons, non metropolitan under 0.9 persons)
US 9 categories (city<1,000,000, city 1–2.5 million, city 2.5–5 million, city >5 million, suburb <1,000,000, suburb 1–2.5 million, suburb 2.5–5 million, suburb >5 million, non-metropolitan)
GE Not available.
FI 2 categories (urban, non-urban)
SW 6 categories

Table A1. Means of Family Status Variables Used in Employment and Wage Models.

	AU 1994	CN 1994	UK 1995	US 1994	GE 1994	FI 1991	SW 1991
A. Employment models							
Married	0.736	0.724	0.726	0.619	0.666	0.677	0.763
Child <1	0.075	0.065	0.077	0.064	0.002	0.077	0.030
Child 1–5	0.264	0.248	0.291	0.288	0.224	0.266	0.323
Child 6–17	0.315	0.312	0.308	0.323	0.400	0.342	0.305
B. Wage models							
Married	0.708	0.730	0.755	0.593	0.634	0.644	0.763
One child	0.187	0.218	0.218	0.244	0.270	0.262	0.207
Two children	0.251	0.258	0.267	0.252	0.219	0.265	0.327
Three or more children	0.109	0.078	0.076	0.094	0.041	0.084	0.154
C. FT wage models							
Married	0.630	0.709	0.711	0.566	0.535	0.633	0.736
One child	0.177	0.221	0.178	0.247	0.236	0.262	0.223
Two children	0.161	0.232	0.167	0.227	0.150	0.259	0.295
Three or more children	0.046	0.063	0.056	0.078	0.025	0.081	0.130

Table A2. Marginal Effects from Employment Models.

	AU 1994	CN 1994	UK 1995	US 1994	GE 1994	FI 1991	SW 1991
A. All employed							
Married	−0.203**	−0.019	−0.080*	−0.071**	−0.002	0.001	−0.082
	(0.037)	(0.013)	(0.038)	(0.013)	(0.044)	(0.017)	(0.041)
Child under 1	−0.597**	−0.277**	−0.479**	−0.273**	−0.297	−0.056*	−0.156*
	(0.024)	(0.018)	(0.038)	(0.016)	(0.249)	(0.028)	(0.094)
Child 1–5	−0.424**	−0.219**	−0.402**	−0.197**	−0.347**	−0.078**	−0.103**
	(0.028)	(0.011)	(0.030)	(0.009)	(0.032)	(0.020)	(0.036)
Child 6–17	−0.190**	−0.095**	−0.142**	−0.068**	−0.127**	0.041*	0.001
	(0.030)	(0.013)	(0.032)	(0.009)	(0.028)	(0.016)	(0.034)
Ethnicity 1	−0.012	0.018	–	0.061**	0.173**	0.029	–
	(0.029)	(0.015)		(0.012)	(0.047)	(0.026)	
Ethnicity 2	−0.255**	−0.061**	–	0.013	0.048		–
	(0.070)	(0.012)		(0.014)	(0.049)		
Ethnicity 3	−0.195**	–	–	−0.015	0.136		–
	(0.043)			(0.045)	(0.065)		
Ethnicity 4	–	–	–	−0.015	–		–
				(0.021)			
Ethnicity 5	–	–	–	−0.000	–		–
				(0.056)			
Partner works	0.308**	0.110**	0.199**	0.071**	−0.034	–	0.020
	(0.040)	(0.012)	(0.044)	(0.013)	(0.040)		(0.052)
Other income/1000	−0.006**	−0.007**	−0.037**	−0.005**	−0.005**	−0.003**	0.004
	(0.001)	(0.000)	(0.003)	(0.000)	(0.001)	(0.000)	(0.187)
Other earning/1000	0.001	−0.004**	−0.001	−0.001**	0.001**	−0.001**	0.533**
	(0.000)	(0.000)	(0.001)	(0.000)	(0.000)	(0.000)	(0.158)
Age	−0.030	0.025**	−0.043	0.015*	0.012	−0.010	0.067**
	(0.025)	(0.008)	(0.024)	(0.007)	(0.022)	(0.016)	(0.025)
Age squared/100	0.041	−0.033**	0.068	−0.022*	−0.020	0.014	−0.095**
	(0.036)	(0.012)	(0.036)	(0.010)	(0.032)	(0.022)	(0.036)
Education 2	−0.103	0.015	0.242	0.029	−0.128*	0.067**	0.138**
	(0.167)	(0.021)	(0.073)	(0.018)	(0.066)	(0.013)	(0.023)
Education 3	−0.131	0.080**	0.241**	0.175**	−0.078	0.107**	0.134
	(0.153)	(0.020)	(0.056)	(0.015)	(0.057)	(0.013)	(0.023)
Education 4	−0.039	0.181**	0.330**	0.197**	−0.205**	0.131**	0.178**
	(0.153)	(0.015)	(0.070)	(0.013)	(0.038)	(0.011)	(0.027)
Education 5	−0.311*	0.170**	0.331**	0.246**	−0.009	0.127**	0.308**
	(0.148)	(0.014)	(0.035)	(0.010)	(0.033)	(0.014)	(0.063)
Education 6	−0.296*	0.264**	0.355**	0.247**	0.073	0.162**	0.169**
	(0.147)	(0.015)	(0.030)	(0.011)	(0.068)	(0.008)	(0.018)
Education 7	−0.275	0.268**	0.311**	0.238**	−0.084	0.153**	0.171**
	(0.150)	(0.011)	(0.021)	(0.010)	(0.049)	(0.014)	(0.031)
Education 8	−0.364**	–	0.305**	0.259**			0.164**
	(0.118)		(0.023)	(0.010)			(0.019)
Education 9	–	–	0.319**	–			–
			(0.025)				

Table A2. (Continued)

	AU 1994	CN 1994	UK 1995	US 1994	GE 1994	FI 1991	SW 1991
Education 10	–	–	0.335**	–			–
			(0.016)				
Education 11	–	–	0.314**				–
			(0.018)				
Education 12	–	–	0.305**	–			–
			(0.024)				
Education 13	–	–	0.308**	–			–
			(0.021)				
Pseudo R^2	0.205	0.121	0.256	0.094	0.126	0.180	0.109
No obs	2654	16077	2438	22091	2372	4870	1060
B. Full-time employment							
Married	−0.219**	−0.019	−0.066	−0.052**	0.006	−0.030	−0.155*
	(0.049)	(0.015)	(0.048)	(0.015)	(0.052)	(0.018)	(0.067)
Child under 1	−0.431**	−0.249**	−0.387**	−0.290**	−0.453	−0.025	−0.056
	(0.014)	(0.016)	(0.019)	(0.014)	(0.067)	(0.029)	(0.099)
Child 1–5	−0.465**	−0.273**	−0.502**	−0.272**	−0.474**	−0.095**	−0.166**
	(0.019)	(0.011)	(0.020)	(0.009)	(0.022)	(0.022)	(0.046)
Child 6–17	−0.311**	−0.149**	−0.358**	−0.131**	−0.280**	0.035	−0.114*
	(0.024)	(0.011)	(0.024)	(0.010)	(0.028)	(0.018)	(0.048)
Ethnicity 1	0.048	0.050**	–	0.013	0.090	−0.011	–
	(0.030)	(0.017)		(0.013)	(0.051)	(0.032)	
Ethnicity 2	−0.150*	−0.003	–	0.006	0.117		–
	(0.065)	(0.012)		(0.016)	(0.064)		
Ethnicity 3	−0.079	–		−0.061	0.203*		–
	(0.040)			(0.051)	(0.087)		
Ethnicity 4	–		–	0.002			
				(0.023)			
Ethnicity 5	–		–	0.031			
				(0.061)			
Partner works	0.234**	0.058**	0.090	0.019	−0.118*	–	0.084
	(0.042)	(0.058)	(0.048)	(0.015)	(0.050)		(0.075)
Other income	−0.005**	−0.008**	−0.003**	−0.001**	−0.006**	−0.003**	−0.510*
	(0.001)	(0.000)	(0.003)	(0.000)	(0.001)	(0.000)	(0.256)
Other earning	−0.001	−0.001**	−0.001	−0.002**	−0.001	−0.001**	0.158
	(0.000)	(0.000)	(0.001)	(0.000)	(0.000)	(0.000)	(0.185)
Age	−0.038	0.024**	−0.017	0.030**	0.018	−0.018	0.047
	(0.026)	(0.009)	(0.026)	(0.007)	(0.026)	(0.017)	(0.034)
Age squared/100	0.046	−0.032*	0.022	−0.045**	−0.035	0.027	−0.063
	(0.038)	(0.013)	(0.037)	(0.011)	(0.038)	(0.024)	(0.050)
Education 2	0.185	0.030	0.165	0.033	−0.157*	0.075**	0.213
	(0.127)	(0.026)	(0.231)	(0.022)	(0.065)	(0.015)	(0.090)
Education 3	0.043	0.097**	0.381**	0.206**	−0.035	0.116**	0.256*
	(0.114)	(0.027)	(0.111)	(0.019)	(0.062)	(0.015)	(0.073)

Table A2. (*Continued*)

	AU 1994	CN 1994	UK 1995	US 1994	GE 1994	FI 1991	SW 1991
Education 4	0.058	0.191**	0.417**	0.221**	−0.148**	0.145**	0.274*
	(0.119)	(0.021)	(0.111)	(0.018)	(0.039)	(0.016)	(0.083)
Education 5	−0.033	0.178**	0.516**	0.278**	0.015	0.147**	0.370**
	(0.115)	(0.022)	(0.083)	(0.016)	(0.038)	(0.018)	(0.107)
Education 6	−0.089	0.265**	0.574**	0.285**	0.164	0.196**	0.306**
	(0.105)	(0.020)	(0.068)	(0.016)	(0.081)	(0.010)	(0.059)
Education 7	−0.129**	0.299**	0.536**	0.279**	−0.130**	0.191**	0.279
	(0.101)	(0.019)	(0.058)	(0.017)	(0.048)	(0.019)	(0.085)
Education 8	−0.172	–	0.556**	0.328			0.337**
	(0.107)		(0.054)	(0.017)			(0.048)
Education 9			0.563**				
			(0.050)				
Education 10			0.560**				
			(0.050)				
Education 11			0.584**				
			(0.031)				
Education 12			0.494**				
			(0.081)				
Education 13			0.522**				
			(0.068)				
Pseudo R^2	0.231	0.089	0.278	0.091	0.216	0.167	0.077
No obs	2654	16077	2438	21682	2372	4870	1059

Note: Regional and urban dummies are also included.
*Significant at 5%.
**Significant at 1%.

Table A3. OLS and Instrumental Variable Estimates of the Impact of Children on Employment.

	AU 1994		CN 1994		UK 1995		US 1994		GE 1994		FI 1991		SW 1991	
	OLS	IV	OLS	IV	OLS	IV	OLS	IV	OLS	IV	OLS	IV	OLS	IV
All workers														
Married	-0.222**	-0.252**	-0.037**	-0.045**	-0.077*	-0.082*	-0.077**	-0.077**	-0.018	-0.038	0.008	-0.088	-0.093	-0.094
	(0.035)	(0.055)	(0.012)	(0.014)	(0.032)	(0.034)	(0.013)	(0.007)	(0.041)	(0.046)	(0.014)	(0.048)	(0.057)	(0.018)
Number of children	-0.119**	-0.086*	-0.064**	-0.047**	-0.089**	-0.081**	-0.059**	-0.060**	-0.119**	-0.088**	-0.011*	0.100	-0.038**	-0.035*
	(0.008)	(0.055)	(0.003)	(0.014)	(0.008)	(0.020)	(0.003)	(0.007)	(0.009)	(0.035)	(0.006)	(0.053)	(0.011)	(0.018)
Adj R^2	0.198	0.19384	0.138	0.137	0.253	0.253	0.109	0.109	0.146	0.142	0.159	0.092	0.061	0.061
Hausman test	0.70		1.20		0.46		-0.020		0.93		2.18*		0.19	
Number obs	2654		16077		2438		22091		2372		4870		1060	
FT workers														
Married	-0.177**	-0.196**	-0.025	-0.031*	-0.039	-0.040	-0.055**	-0.050**	-0.047	-0.078	-0.017	-0.104	-0.138	-0.144
	(0.035)	(0.047)	(0.013)	(0.015)	(0.033)	(0.035)	(0.014)	(0.014)	(0.042)	(0.048)	(0.015)	(0.051)	(0.073)	(0.074)
Number of children	-0.159**	-0.138**	-0.094**	-0.083**	-0.138**	-0.137**	-0.086**	-0.096**	-0.160**	-0.111**	-0.021**	0.079	-0.070**	-0.061**
	(0.008)	(0.046)	(0.004)	(0.016)	(0.008)	(0.021)	(0.003)	(0.008)	(0.010)	(0.037)	(0.006)	(0.056)	(0.015)	(0.023)
Adj R^2	0.251	0.242	0.116	0.115	0.253	0.253	0.119	0.119	0.243	0.234	0.159	0.110	0.103	0.066
Hausman test	0.47		0.70		0.08		-1.34		1.42		1.85		0.50	
Number obs	2654		16077		2438		21682		2372		4870		1059	

Note: Number of children is instrumented by the average number of children of women by age and region.
*Significant at 5%.
**Significant at 1%.

Table A4. Wage Equations – Full Results.

	AU 1994	CN 1994	UK 1995	US 1994	GE 1994	FI 1991	SW 1991
A. All employees							
Married	0.035	−0.005	0.037	0.060**	−0.058	0.034*	0.033
	(0.038)	(0.015)	(0.027)	(0.009)	(0.032)	(0.014)	(0.018)
One child	−0.078	−0.036*	−0.071*	−0.027*	−0.018	−0.026	−0.008
	(0.045)	(0.017)	(0.030)	(0.011)	(0.036)	(0.016)	(0.021)
Two children	−0.106*	−0.050**	−0.232**	−0.067**	−0.175**	−0.012	−0.014
	(0.044)	(0.017)	(0.029)	(0.011)	(0.041)	(0.017)	(0.021)
Three + children	−0.053	−0.209**	−0.309**	−0.088**	0.068	−0.064**	−0.025
	(0.062)	(0.027)	(0.045)	(0.016)	(0.072)	(0.025)	(0.025)
Ethnicity 1	0.013	0.002	–	0.112**	0.096	−0.035	–
	(0.045)	(0.027)		(0.017)	(0.070)	(0.030)	
Ethnicity 2	−0.202	−0.096**	–	0.022	0.066	–	–
	(0.133)	(0.020)		(0.020)	(0.087)		
Ethnicity 3	−0.139	–	–	−0.031	−0.022	–	–
	(0.072)			(0.062)	(0.110)		
Ethnicity 4	–	–	–	−0.013	–	–	–
				(0.030)			
Ethnicity 5	–	–	–	0.082	–	–	–
				(0.079)			
Age	0.069	0.098**	0.107**	0.097**	0.074*	0.022	0.013
	(0.038)	(0.014)	(0.024)	(0.009)	(0.030)	(0.017)	(0.016)
Age squared/100	−0.088	−0.117**	−0.135**	−0.123**	−0.087*	−0.019	−0.009
	(0.056)	(0.020)	(0.035)	(0.013)	(0.044)	(0.019)	(0.023)
Education 2	0.064	0.115	−0.182	0.064	−0.350**	0.051**	−0.114
	(0.169)	(0.052)	(0.225)	(0.034)	(0.084)	(0.017)	(0.098)
Education 3	−0.044	0.176**	−0.045	0.288**	−0.388**	0.175**	−0.063
	(0.155)	(0.054)	(0.154)	(0.030)	(0.084)	(0.018)	(0.098)
Education 4	−0.054	0.317**	0.068	0.399**	−0.389**	0.336**	−0.047
	(0.160)	(0.046)	(0.152)	(0.031)	(0.047)	(0.026)	(0.094)
Education 5	−0.210	0.315**	0.203	0.523**	−0.128**	0.410**	0.018
	(0.167)	(0.048)	(0.153)	(0.032)	(0.043)	(0.031)	(0.093)
Education 6	−0.281	0.425**	0.425**	0.718**	−0.045	0.533**	0.082
	(0.156)	(0.045)	(0.153)	(0.031)	(0.093)	(0.028)	(0.096)
Education 7	−0.253	0.671**	0.472**	0.890**	−0.066	0.755	0.116
	(0.159)	(0.046)	(0.162)	(0.037)	(0.058)	(0.084)	(0.095)
Education 8	−0.346**	–	0.430**	1.030**	–	–	0.230*
	(0.151)		(0.166)	(0.046)			(0.096)
Education 9	–	–	0.644**	–	–	–	–
			(0.156)				
Education 10	–	–	0.646**	–	–	–	–
			(0.158)				
Education 11	–	–	0.742**	–	–	–	–
			(0.169)				
Education 12	–	–	0.520**	–	–	–	–
			(0.171)				
Education 13	–	–	0.550**	–	–	–	–
			(0.183)				
Adj R^2	0.065	0.137	0.295	0.234	0.119	0.198	0.179
No obs	1547	7885	1564	15307	1515	3592	874

Table A4. (Continued)

	AU 1994	CN 1994	UK 1995	US 1994	GE 1994	FI 1991	SW 1991
B. Full-time employees							
Married	0.035	−0.005	0.016	0.059**	0.013	0.020	0.033
	(0.036)	(0.015)	(0.029)	(0.010)	(0.031)	(0.013)	(0.018)
One child	−0.110*	−0.036*	0.010	−0.014	−0.041	−0.037*	−0.008
	(0.046)	(0.017)	(0.036)	(0.011)	(0.037)	(0.015)	(0.021)
Two children	−0.168**	−0.050**	−0.169**	−0.040**	−0.108*	−0.022	−0.014
	(0.049)	(0.017)	(0.037)	(0.012)	(0.046)	(0.016)	(0.021)
Three + children	−0.193*	−0.209**	−0.279**	−0.062**	−0.079	−0.075**	−0.025
	(0.082)	(0.027)	(0.059)	(0.018)	(0.091)	(0.023)	(0.025)
Ethnicity 1	0.008	0.003	–	0.113**	0.068	−0.041	–
	(0.045)	(0.027)		(0.018)	(0.069)	(0.029)	
Ethnicity 2	−0.202	−0.096**	–	0.028	−0.026	–	–
	(0.130)	(0.020)		(0.021)	(0.086)		
Ethnicity 3	−0.044	–	–	−0.020	−0.012	–	–
	(0.069)			(0.068)	(0.102)		
Ethnicity 4	–	–	–	−0.006	–	–	–
				(0.031)			
Ethnicity 5	–	–	–	0.109	–	–	–
				(0.081)			
Age	0.079*	0.098**	0.107**	0.099**	0.058	0.014	−0.009
	(0.038)	(0.014)	(0.027)	(0.010)	(0.030)	(0.016)	(0.024)
Age squared/100	−0.100	−0.117**	−0.131**	−0.123**	−0.070	−0.005	−0.009
	(0.055)	(0.020)	(0.040)	(0.014)	(0.044)	(0.023)	(0.023)
Education 2	0.070	0.115*	−0.031	0.082	−0.127	0.056**	−0.114
	(0.170)	(0.052)	(0.374)	(0.037)	(0.094)	(0.016)	(0.098)
Education 3	−0.037	0.176**	0.390	0.338**	−0.290**	0.173**	−0.063
	(0.155)	(0.054)	(0.232)	(0.033)	(0.083)	(0.017)	(0.098)
Education 4	−0.036	0.317**	0.557*	0.457**	−0.284**	0.351**	−0.047
	(0.163)	(0.046)	(0.230)	(0.034)	(0.050)	(0.026)	(0.094)
Education 5	−0.210	0.315**	0.667**	0.564**	−0.062	0.434**	0.018
	(0.167)	(0.048)	(0.232)	(0.035)	(0.043)	(0.029)	(0.093)
Education 6	−0.274	0.425**	0.860**	0.764**	−0.057	0.551**	0.082
	(0.157)	(0.045)	(0.231)	(0.034)	(0.091)	(0.026)	(0.096)
Education 7	−0.247	0.671**	0.841**	0.972**	−0.040	0.707**	0.116
	(0.159)	(0.046)	(0.238)	(0.039)	(0.060)	(0.077)	(0.095)
Education 8	−0.345	–	0.912	1.077**	–	–	0.230
	(0.151)		(0.240)	(0.048)			(0.096)
Education 9	–	–	10.60**	0.890**	–	–	–
			(0.233)	(0.037)			
Education 10	–	–	1.071**	1.030**	–	–	–
			(0.235)	(0.046)			
Education 11	–	–	1.146**	–	–	–	–
			(0.242)				
Education 12	–	–	0.827**	–	–	–	–
			(0.244)				
Education 13	–	–	0.980**	–	–	–	–
			(0.254)				
Adj R^2	0.090	0.137	0.308	0.275	0.122	0.241	0.179
No obs	1046	7885	999	11588	1107	3385	874

*Significant at 5%.
**Significant at 1%.

Table A5. OLS and Instrumental Variable Estimates of the Impact of Children on Wages.

	AU 1994		CN 1994		UK 1995		US 1994		GE 1994		FI 1991		SW 1991	
	OLS	IV	OLS	IV	OLS	IV	OLS	IV	OLS	IV	OLS	IV	OLS	IV
All workers														
Married	0.025	0.015	−0.004	0.027	0.045	0.056	0.065**	0.065**	−0.074	−0.073	0.039**	−0.040	0.034	0.024
	(0.038)	(0.075)	(0.016)	(0.026)	(0.027)	(0.030)	(0.009)	(0.011)	(0.032)	(0.051)	(0.014)	(0.071)	(0.018)	(0.019)
Number of children	−0.039*	−0.024	−0.038**	−0.090**	−0.107**	−0.129**	−0.036**	−0.037**	−0.030	−0.033	−0.017*	0.069	−0.009	0.004
	(0.016)	(0.095)	(0.006)	(0.034)	(0.011)	(0.032)	(0.004)	(0.011)	(0.017)	(0.068)	(0.006)	(0.075)	(0.007)	(0.010)
Adj R^2	0.063	0.062	0.095	0.090	0.296	0.294	0.236	0.236	0.124	0.107	0.198	0.159	0.218	0.215
Hausman test	0.158		−1.58		−0.77		−0.06		−0.05		1.17		1.901	
Number obs	1547		10219		1564		15307		1515		3592		874	
FT workers														
Married	0.025	−0.038	0.003	0.046	0.027	0.042	0.066**	0.073**	0.014	−0.025	0.026*	−0.022	0.037	0.025
	(0.038)	(0.076)	(0.015)	(0.025)	(0.029)	(0.033)	(0.009)	(0.011)	(0.031)	(0.040)	(0.013)	(0.065)	(0.018)	(0.019)
Number of children	−0.039*	0.026**	−0.051**	−0.130**	−0.087**	−0.121**	−0.031**	−0.044**	−0.047*	0.063	−0.022**	0.030	−0.030**	−0.013
	(0.016)	(0.123)	(0.007)	(0.037)	(0.014)	(0.039)	(0.004)	(0.013)	(0.020)	(0.075)	(0.006)	(0.070)	(0.018)	(0.011)
Adj R^2	0.095	0.064	0.137	0.141	0.308	0.304	0.277	0.277	0.124	0.099	0.241	0.224	0.202	0.196
Hausman test	0.916		−2.18*		−0.77		−1.03		1.54		1.17		2.227**	
Number obs	1046		7885		999		11588		1107		3385		685	

Note: Number of children is instrumented by the mean number of children by age and region.
*Significant at 5%.
**Significant at 1%.

Table A6. Effects of Marriage and Children on Women's Log of Hourly Wages, Coefficients (and Standard Errors) from OLS Regressions, Corrected for Sample Selection Bias.

	AU 1994	CN 1994	UK 1995	US 1994	GE 1994	FI 1991	SW 1991
Married	0.037	−0.009	0.048*	0.059**	−0.031	0.034**	0.033**
	(0.038)	(0.017)	(0.027)	(0.010)	(0.031)	(0.017)	(0.018)
One child	−0.086**	−0.035**	−0.093**	−0.067**	−0.019	−0.044**	−0.006
	(0.049)	(0.019)	(0.033)	(0.013)	(0.037)	(0.018)	(0.021)
Two children	−0.120**	−0.050**	−0.255**	−0.105**	−0.107**	−0.027	−0.013
	(0.048)	(0.019)	(0.032)	(0.013)	(0.042)	(0.019)	(0.020)
Three or more children	−0.113**	−0.123**	−0.321**	−0.152**	0.003	−0.063**	−0.026
	(0.061)	(0.026)	(0.044)	(0.016)	(0.064)	(0.024)	(0.025)
Lambda	0.030	−0.011	0.031	0.162**	0.019	0.028	−0.028
	(0.049)	(0.033)	(0.034)	(0.031)	(0.055)	(0.024)	(0.043)
N	1,046	16,077	2,438	22,091	1,107	4,870	685

Notes: Log wage models include controls for age, age squared, education, race or ethnicity (except for Sweden), region, and urban residence. Model is estimated for all women in the sample using the standard sample selection correction technique as described in the text. See Appendix for variable definitions. Complete regression results available from the authors on request.

*Significant at 5%.
**Significant at 1%.

WHY CHOOSE WOMEN'S WORK IF IT PAYS LESS? A STRUCTURAL MODEL OF OCCUPATIONAL CHOICE

M. Melinda Pitts

1. INTRODUCTION

It is well-known that the majority of women work in a limited number of occupations characterized by a proportionately high number of female workers. Moreover, workers in these female-dominated (FD) occupations earn less, on average, than workers in traditionally male or integrated occupations (McPherson & Hirsch, 1995). This occupational wage differential is widely accepted as a partial explanation for the pervasive gender wage-differential. However, it is unclear why an individual would enter into a FD occupation if the wages are lower than in nonfemale-dominated (NFD) occupations. It is also unclear if women who choose FD occupations could earn more in occupations that are NFD. Therefore, attributing a portion of the gender wage differential to occupational differences may be incorrect. Indeed, differences in the occupational choices of men and women will only explain the wage differential between genders if females in FD occupations could expect to earn higher wages elsewhere.

Occupational segregation by gender and the gender wage differential have been the focus of much empirical research, with the majority of work using data from the 1970s and early 1980s. The consensus is that a negative relationship exists between the percentage female in an occupation and the wage. Many of these studies, however, are plagued by problems associated with selection bias arising from the endogeneity of occupational choice and the work decisions to one's wage. If the error terms of the occupational choice and work decision equations are correlated with the error term in the wage equation, this could lead to biased coefficient estimates. Furthermore, while many studies have shown that workers in FD occupations earn less than workers in other occupations, there is little evidence concerning whether workers in these FD occupations would be better or worse off in other occupations.

This study controls for the selection bias on wages associated with occupational choice and the work decision by estimating a bivariate probit with selection as the first stage and the wage estimation as the second. This is accomplished using data from the May 1979 and April 1993 supplements of the *Current Population Survey*. In order to capture any penalty for working in a typically female occupation, a wage differential between FD and NFD occupations is estimated using the predicted wage for each individual in each occupation. Contrary to earlier research, the results indicate that women are not choosing the occupation that pays less when they enter a FD occupation. In fact, for the most part, women who choose to work in FD occupations receive a wage premium for doing so. This result, in effect, indicates that there is efficient matching between occupations and skills for the women in the labor force. Furthermore, it refutes the explanation that occupational segregation or crowding explains part of the gender gap in wages, as the gender gap would be larger if more women worked in NFD occupations.

As the results in this research differ from much of the earlier research, I also estimate a model which is similar to previously reported models that do not control for selection bias. The results of this estimation indicate a penalty for entering a FD occupation for all workers, which is consistent with earlier findings. This outcome supports the argument that self-selection matters and indicates that the selection model results are not merely a product of the data.

Finally, the estimated wage differential from the selection model is included in a structural model of occupational choice. The results indicate that the wage penalty is a dominating factor in the occupational choice decision, thus mitigating support for occupational crowding due to discriminatory hiring practices as an explanation for the different choices in occupation.

A review of previous literature is in Section 2, followed by the theoretical and empirical models in Sections 3 and 4, respectively. A description of the data is included in Section 5, followed by the estimation procedures in Section 6, the results in Section 7, and the conclusion in Section 8.

2. PREVIOUS RESEARCH

Two key economic theories have commonly been used to explain occupational segregation and the resulting wage differential: gender differences in human capital and occupational crowding. Polachek and Siebert (1993) narrow human capital theory to focus specifically on the impact of intermittent labor force participation. They propose that women anticipating periods of absence may invest less in human capital and that acquired skills will depreciate during these spells of absence from the labor force. The implication is that because women have more intermittent participation than men, women choose occupations that have a lower atrophy rate of skills and flatter earnings profiles. While this earnings profile minimizes the penalty for absence from the labor force and maximizes the woman's lifetime earnings, it results in lower relative wages when compared to men.

Blau, Ferber and Winkler (1998) suggest that women may also limit their pursuit of human capital because of social influences that lead them to make choices that may adversely affect their labor market outcomes.[1] In addition, the authors note that direct labor market discrimination lowers the return to human capital and thus lowers the incentive to invest. Polachek (1995) indicates that societal discrimination, in the form of division of labor in the home, also further reduces the incentive for women to invest in human capital.

Bergmann (1974) hypothesizes that discriminatory hiring practices which prevent women from entering a large number of available occupations have resulted in women being crowded into a small number of occupations. This occupational crowding leads to an excess supply in these occupations, and hence, lower market wages. In general, past research (Blau & Beller, 1988; Chiswick et al., 1975; Johnson & Solon, 1986; Sorenson, 1990; among others) has found occupational segregation to explain a portion of the wage differential between genders.

Chiswick et al. (1975), using data from the 1970 Census, found that if white women had the same occupational distribution as white men, the earnings of white women would increase by 15%. However, for single women who have never been married there is no benefit to changing the occupational distribution. This implies that the wage differential for this group is not attributed to occupational segregation.

Blau and Beller (1988), using data from the 1981 Current Population Survey, estimate a log annual earnings equation for white individuals. In addition to controlling for education, potential work experience, geographic characteristics, marital status, and part-time work status, they include two dummy variables to control for the percent female in the individual's chosen occupation. The first dummy variable is equal to one if the occupation is at least 70% male (a male-dominated occupation), and the second is equal to one if the occupation is between 40% and 70% male (an integrated occupation). Their results indicate that women in male-dominated occupations have 16% higher earnings and women in integrated occupations have 9% higher earnings compared to women in FD occupations. Blau and Beller (1988) also estimate the same equation separately for men and find that men in FD occupations earn 27% and 16% less than men in male-dominated and integrated occupations, respectively.

Sorenson (1990) uses the 1984 Panel Study of Income Dynamics and the May/June 1983 Current Population Survey to examine the affect the proportion of female workers in an individual's chosen occupation has on hourly earnings. Sorenson (1990) finds that between 20% and 23% of the wage gap is attributed to the percentage of workers in the occupation that are female, after controlling for differences in human capital and industry. In a similar analysis, Johnson and Solon (1986), using data from the May 1978 Current Population Survey, find that the percent female in an occupation explains 14% of the earnings gap.

McPherson and Hirsch (1995) explain part of the negative relationship between wages and working in a female-dominated occupation using data from the Current Population Survey Outgoing Rotation Group from January 1983 to December 1993. They determine that differences in worker and occupational characteristics explain two-thirds of the gender composition effect for women and four-fifths for men. Therefore, they conclude that the key issue is the wage differential between genders and not the occupational wage gap.

A major shortcoming of these studies is that treating the gender composition of one's chosen occupation as an exogenous variable in the wage equation means there is no control for the self-selection of individuals into different occupations. In addition, the selection bias associated with the decision to enter the labor force is largely ignored as well. Sorenson (1989) controlled for this potential self-selection by estimating a bivariate probit for the decision to work and the decision to enter the labor force as the first stage and the wage equations for FD occupations and other occupations as the second stage, using data on women from the 1984 Panel Study of Income Dynamics. Sorenson (1989) finds a positive sign on the occupational selection bias variable in the wage equations, indicating that workers enter the occupation to which they are best suited. When Sorenson (1989) breaks down the average wage differential, calculated at the sample means, she finds that females in FD occupations would expect to earn between 6% and 15% more in male-dominated occupations, dependant upon the specification of the wage equation. However, there are a few shortcomings to this paper that lend doubt to these results. First, the reduced form estimate of the occupational choice decision does not include all job related information that is included in the wage equations, such as industry, union status, geographical location, self-employment status, and job tenure. Therefore, the reduced form model does not fully control for the expected wage differential between the two occupational groups. In addition, the data does not include information on non-pecuniary benefits such as pension, health insurance, and disability benefits.

3. THEORETICAL MODEL

The theoretical model builds upon the foundation of Atrostic (1982) and Killingsworth and Heckman (1986). Atrostic (1982) examines the joint demand for leisure and non-pecuniary job characteristics and theorizes that an individual's total compensation from work (assumed to be constant across firms) is the sum of the money wage compensation and the compensation from job characteristics. While the total compensation is constant, the mix of money wages and job characteristics varies across firms. Therefore, when choosing a job, an individual chooses the utility maximizing combination of wages and job characteristics. Atrostic modifies the standard utility maximization model to account for this wage-job characteristic tradeoff. This is done by allowing an individual's utility to be a function of not only leisure time and consumption of market goods, but job characteristics as well. The individual then chooses a combination of hours of work, consumption goods, and job characteristics that maximizes total utility. In their review of Atrostic's work, Killingsworth and Heckman (1986) build upon this model by treating job characteristics the same as consumption goods. They assume that the individual buys desirable job characteristics at a cost of lower wages or accepts undesirable job characteristics in order to receive higher wages.

This model extends the work of Killingsworth and Heckman (1986).[2] The individual is assumed to simultaneously choose the utility maximizing levels of leisure time, L, the composite market consumption good X_1, and a set of additional consumption goods that are job characteristics consumed per hour of work, X_2:

$$U = U(L, X_1, X_2) \qquad (1)$$

subject to a time constraint of

$$T = L + H \qquad (2)$$

and a budget constraint of

$$P_1 X_1 = H W_M + Y. \qquad (3)$$

The vector of purchased goods and services, X_1, are purchased at price P_1. Time is allocated between non-market activities and market work, where L is the number of hours per period spent on leisure or non-market work, H is the number of hours per period spent on market work, and T is the total number of hours available per period. The hourly money wage rate is given by W_M and Y is exogenous money income.

In addition to choosing the utility maximizing level of consumption goods and leisure, an individual may also choose non-pecuniary job characteristics. The levels of non-pecuniary job characteristics, X_2, are utility increasing.[3] There is an inverse relationship between these job characteristics and the money wage an individual receives. Thus if the individual purchases a job characteristic, the price paid is reduced money wages and the gain is increased utility. The resulting hourly wage rate is defined as:

$$W_m = W(Z) - P_2 X_2. \qquad (4)$$

The neutral wage, $W(Z)$, is the hourly wage an individual would receive if X_2 were equal to zero. The neutral wage is solely a function of the individual's human capital, Z. The individual decreases the value of his or her monetary wage when he or she buys X_2 at a price of P_2 per hour of work or HP_2.[4] Therefore, if men and women, on average, have different preferences for job characteristics then one would expect men and women to purchase different types of job characteristics and select into different occupations. If the job characteristics women purchase are, on average, more costly than those purchased by men, then it would also be expected that average wages for women would be lower.

4. EMPIRICAL MODEL

The theoretical model suggests that the choice of job characteristics are both endogenous to the labor force participation decision and directly related to the money wage an individual receives. However, there are a limited number of job characteristics typically reported in the data and the ones that are available are objective, such as the availability of a pension plan or employer-sponsored health insurance. There is generally no subjective information readily available to quantify an individual's tastes and preferences concerning issues such as the type of workplace, coworkers, or duties performed.

Nevertheless, one can assume that the occupation an individual chooses reflects the utility-maximizing tradeoff between wages and job characteristics. As the focus of this research is gender differences in the labor force, the gender distribution of an individual's occupation is used as a proxy for the bundle of job characteristics that makes the job attractive to that individual. For example, an individual who prefers characteristics associated with a typically female occupation will be more likely to enter a FD occupation than someone who prefers characteristics associated with a typically male occupation, ceteris paribus. Previous empirical evidence indicates that women and men do, on average, choose different types of occupations which suggests that women and men have different utility-maximizing choices of occupation.

Killingsworth and Heckman (1986) point out that the occupational choice decision, in a world with heterogeneous jobs, is endogenous to the participation

A Structural Model of Occupational Choice

decision because occupation is chosen along with participation. This endogeneity implies that individuals have complete information regarding their opportunities in the labor force and take into account occupational characteristics when deciding whether to enter the labor force. Furthermore, when examining heterogeneous labor supply of men, Killingsworth (1985) found a significant relationship between labor supply and discrete job choices. However, when Sorenson (1989) estimated the pay disparity for women between typically female occupations and other occupations, she found the correlation coefficient to be insignificant. As there is no consensus in the literature, and since the theoretical model indicates that there is a relationship, the work decision and occupational choice will be estimated together.

The individual has two questions to consider: (1) what occupation will provide he or she the most utility; and (2) are the gains from working in that occupation greater than the costs? In other words, the individual must choose whether the market wage they would earn in their chosen occupation, W_{mi}, is greater than the reservation wage, W_{ri} (Heckman, 1974). The work decision is expressed as a simple probit:

$$Y^*_{1i} = (W_{mi} - W_{ri}) = \alpha_0 + \alpha_1 \mathbf{Z}_{1i} + v_{1i}, \qquad (5)$$

where Y^*_{1i} is an unobserved latent variable and $v_{1i} \sim N(0, \sigma^2_{v1})$. $\mathbf{Z}_{1i}$ contains exogenous socioeconomic and personal characteristics assumed to influence the relative values of W_{mi} and W_{ri}: age, gender, marital status, having children under the age of 18, race, education, non-labor and other household income, and controls for region of the country and Standard Metropolitan Statistical Areas (SMSA). The socioeconomic and human capital variables are interacted with gender to capture any potential gender differences. For example, it is expected that married men and men with children would be more likely to participate in the work force as these variables are indicators of fiscal responsibility. For women these same characteristics have traditionally been viewed as an indicator of an increased value of nonmarket time and thus negatively related to the work decision (Bowen & Finnegan, 1969).

It is expected that individuals with greater amounts of human capital will be more likely to participate in the labor force. Higher education, in general, leads to a higher reward for market work and, therefore, a higher cost for non-market activities (Rees, 1973). Interacting education with gender allows for the determination of whether these returns differ between women and men.

In addition to participation, the individual must also consider which occupation will be utility-maximizing. The worker may enter either a FD occupation or a NFD occupation, which is dependent not only on the choice of the individual but also on the hiring choices of employers.[5] If the characteristics of NFD occupations are not appealing then the individual may be willing to give up money wages in order to enter into a FD occupation. Likewise, if characteristics of the individual are not appealing to employers of NFD occupations, the choices of the individual may be limited.

It is assumed that an individual will only enter a FD occupation if there is a net gain from doing so. If the wage an individual could expect to earn is lower in FD occupations relative to NFD occupations, then the individual would only enter a FD occupation if the wage penalty for doing so is less than the value of the non-wage characteristics of the FD occupation, ρ_i.[6] Thus, an individual who expects to earn lower wages in a FD occupation, is assumed to enter a FD occupation if:

$$\left| \frac{W_{FDi} - W_{NFDi}}{W_{NFDi}} \right| < \rho_i, \qquad (6)$$

where W_{NFDi} and W_{FDi} are the NFD and FD wages for the individual i.

More specifically, the individual's willingness to enter a FD occupation is expressed as:

$$\rho_i = \beta_0 \, Z_{2i} + \beta_1 \, C_{2i} + \varepsilon_{1i} \qquad (7)$$

The vector of individual characteristics is Z_{2i} and C_{2i} is a vector representing the non-pecuniary benefits of entering a FD occupation, many of which are not observable. Therefore, C_{2i} is modeled using an unobservable variables approach, which assumes that the benefits of entering a FD occupation for the individual i is a function of the observable individual characteristics plus an unobservable residual.

$$C_{2i} = \gamma_0 + \gamma_1 \, Z_{2i} + \varepsilon_{2i}. \qquad (8)$$

Substituting Eqs (7) and (8) into Eq. (6) indicates that the individual will enter into a FD occupation if:

$$\left| \frac{W_{FDi} - W_{NFDi}}{W_{NFDi}} \right| < (B_0 + B_i \, \gamma_i) Z_{2i} + B_1 \, \gamma_0 + B_1 \, \varepsilon_{2i} + \varepsilon_{1i}. \qquad (9)$$

Equation (9) indicates that there need not be a zero cost of choosing a FD occupation, just that the net benefit be greater than zero. This may be written in the form of a probit:

$$Y_{2i}^* = \delta_0 + \delta_1 \left(\frac{W_{FDi} - W_{NFDi}}{W_{NFDi}} \right) + \delta_2 \, Z_{2i} + v_{2i}. \qquad (10)$$

The vector Z_{2i} contains observable exogenous socioeconomic and personal characteristics related to occupational choice: age, gender, marital status, race, education, other family labor income, and other forms of unearned income.[7] In addition, the expected wage penalty for working in a FD occupation is included.

A Structural Model of Occupational Choice

Equation (9) predicts that individuals will enter FD occupations only if the value of the nonpecuniary benefits of working in a FD occupation are greater then the wage penalty for doing so. This implies that a decrease in the wage penalty, or an increase in the return to working in FD occupations relative to NFD occupations, will lower the cost of FD job characteristics and increase the likelihood that an individual will enter a FD occupation. Therefore, it is expected that the sign on the wage penalty will be positive. However, if there is no significant effect of the wage penalty on the occupational decision this implies the individual would enter a FD occupation regardless of the monetary cost. Assuming the job characteristics associated with typically female occupations are a normal good, this would violate rational economic behavior. Therefore, an insignificant result would lend support for the theory of discriminatory hiring practices by employers as an explanation for occupational segregation.

The human capital and socioeconomic variables are once again interacted with gender to determine if there are gender differences in both the labor demand and labor supply sides of the hiring market. For obvious reasons, it is expected that women will be more likely to enter FD occupations. If Polachek's (1981) theory holds, thus implying that FD occupations require less investment in human capital or requires skills that have a lower atrophy rate, then workers with high levels of education would be less likely to enter FD occupations. If job characteristics associated with the FD occupation are normal goods, then as income increases, there would be an increase in demand for these characteristics, resulting in a positive relationship between unearned and other household income and the decision to enter a FD occupation.

As shown in Eq. (11), there are separate wage equations for workers in FD occupations and workers in NFD occupations, which allows for the full interaction between the gender distribution of an occupation and the independent variables in the wage equation. The vector Z_{3i} contains the socioeconomic and demographic characteristics age, gender, marital status, race, and level of education. The vector X_{2i} contains the characteristics of the job: current job tenure, part-time status, being a government worker, being represented by a labor union, non-pecuniary compensation such as a pension, employer-sponsored group health insurance, and disability benefits, and controls for industry, SMSA, and regional differences.

$$\log W_{\text{FD}i} = \phi_0 + \phi_1 Z_{3i} + \phi_2 X_{2i} + v_{3i};$$
$$\log W_{\text{NFD}i} = \omega_0 + \omega_1 Z_{3i} + \omega_2 X_{2i} + v_{4i}. \qquad (11)$$

The dependant variable of interest in the wage equations is the natural log of the wage. This allows for a simplification in the equation for the occupational choice of $(\log W_{\text{FD}i} - \log W_{\text{NFD}i})$, which is approximately equal to $(W_{\text{FD}i} - W_{\text{NFD}i})/W_{\text{NFD}i}$ (Lee, 1979).

5. DATA

The data are taken from the May 1979 and the April 1993 supplements to the *Current Population Surveys* (CPS), a nationally representative survey that includes information on an individual's demographic and human capital characteristics as well as information on the worker's employee benefits in the previous year.

The 1980 and 1990 *Public Use Microdata Samples* (PUMS) are used to estimate the gender distribution of the detailed occupational categories in the U.S. Labor Force for the years 1980 and 1990 as the cell size in the CPS is not large enough within the detailed 3-digit occupations to allow for statistical analysis.[8] The occupational categories determined by the 1980 PUMS are then merged with the 1979 CPS and the categories determined by the 1990 PUMS are merged with the 1993 CPS.[9]

The detailed occupational categories are labeled female-dominated (FD) or non-female-dominated (NFD), depending upon the percentage of females in the occupation. The methods previously used to define the gender classification of an occupation are varied. Beller (1982), when estimating the probability of entering a male occupation, calculates the female share of the labor force and adds five percentage points to reach the minimum percentage of females for a female-dominated occupation and subtracts five percentage points to reach the maximum percentage of females in a male-dominated occupation. Sorenson (1989, 1990) and Blau and Beller (1988) use a threshold of greater than 60% female to be considered a female-dominated occupation.

These methods may be problematic because the criteria for determining the type of the occupation is arbitrary. This research employs an inference test to determine if the distribution of the occupation is statistically different from the distribution of the labor force. If all occupations are perfectly integrated by gender, then all occupations would be distributed the same as the labor force.[10] If the percent female in a 3-digit occupation is statistically higher than the percent female in the labor force then the occupation is labeled female-dominated (FD). If the percent female is statistically lower than the percent female in the labor force or there was no statistical difference, the occupation is labeled nonfemale-dominated (NFD).[11]

The distributions of occupations, as shown in Table 1, indicates that 32.3% of the occupations are classified as FD in 1980 and 35% in 1990. The distribution of males and females by occupation is presented in Table 2. Approximately 78% of women entered FD occupations in 1980 and 76% did so in 1990, indicating a slight decrease.

The full sample means and the means for workers taken from the CPS are presented in Table 3. There is information on 31,497 individuals in the 1979 sample and 36,440 individuals in the 1993 sample. Of these, 51% in 1979 and

Table 1. Distributions of Occupations by Year.

Occupation	1980	1990
Non-female-Dominated	67.7%	65.0%
Female-Dominated	32.3%	35.0%

53% in 1993 are working. The percentage of the full sample that is married decreased from 67% in 1979 to 57% in 1993. The 1993 sample has a higher educational attainment as the percentage of the sample with some college is nine percentage points higher in 1993 and the percentage with less than a high school education is ten percentage points lower. In addition, the percentage of the sample that is of Hispanic origin is two and one-half percentage points greater in 1993.

For the workers, the biggest difference is the percentage of the labor force that is female. In 1979 females constituted 43% of the work force. This percentage increased to 51% in the 1993 sample. Again, the 1993 sample has a higher level of educational attainment, fewer married individuals, and a larger percentage of individuals of Hispanic origin. Fewer workers are represented by a union, a greater number work part-time, and fewer have pension plans.

Table 4 contains sample means stratified by occupation. The percentage female in FD occupations declined from 76% in 1979 to 72% in 1993. The real hourly wage in NFD occupations is $3.67 per hour higher than the wage in FD occupations in 1979 and $1.86 higher in 1993, thus indicating a decline in the wage differential over this period.

One interesting differential between occupational groups arises with respect to education. More workers in FD occupations have some college education and a smaller portion have less than a high school diploma when compared to workers in NFD occupations. There are more part-time and more government workers in FD occupations than in NFD occupations. However, workers in NFD occupations are more likely to be represented by a union and to have non-pecuniary benefits such as pension, disability, and health insurance.

Table 2. Distributions of Workers by Occupation.

Year	Occupation	All	Males	Females
1980	Non-female-Dominated	55.06	81.99	21.87
	Female-Dominated	44.94	18.01	78.13
1990	Non-female-Dominated	52.91	78.63	23.60
	Female-Dominated	47.09	21.37	76.40

Table 3. Sample Means (Standard Deviation).

Variable	Full Sample		Workers	
	1979	1993	1979	1993
Individual Characteristics				
Age	45.6533	46.1395	39.4993	37.9649
	(19.0585)	(19.7448)	(13.3672)	(12.4145)
Married	0.6684	0.5674	0.7267	0.6044
	(0.4708)	(0.4954)	(0.4457)	(0.4890)
Female	0.5756	0.5781	0.4266	0.5102
	(0.4943)	(0.4939)	(0.4946)	(0.4999)
Black	0.0990	0.0924	0.0895	0.0819
	(0.2987)	(0.2896)	(0.2855)	(0.2743)
Hispanic Origin	0.0435	0.0668	0.0416	0.0662
	(0.2039)	(0.2496)	(0.1997)	(0.2487)
No High School Diploma	0.3596	0.2559	0.2094	0.1296
	(0.4799)	(0.4364)	(0.4069)	(0.3359)
High School Diploma	0.3293	0.3392	0.3808	0.3484
	(0.4700)	(0.4734)	(0.4856)	(0.4765)
Some College Education	0.3111	0.4049	0.4098	0.5220
	(0.4630)	(0.4909)	(0.4918)	(0.4995)
Work	0.5105	0.5342		
	(0.4999)	(0.4988)		
Job Characteristics				
Female-Dominated Occupation			0.3978	0.5791
			(0.4895)	(0.4945)
Hourly Wage (1993 $)			14.1718	11.5895
			(7.7994)	(8.0538)
Current Job Tenure			8.6808	7.0964
			(8.3318)	(7.7773)
Government Employee			0.2212	0.1827
			(0.4150)	(0.3864)
Part-time Employee			0.1298	0.2024
			(0.3361)	(0.4018)
Represented by a Union			0.3366	0.1870
			(0.4726)	(0.3899)
Employer-Sponsored Pension Plan			0.6044	0.4772
			(0.4890)	(0.4995)
Employer-Sponsored Disability Benefits			0.3981	0.3937
			(0.4895)	(0.4886)
Employer-Sponsored Health Insurance			0.7475	0.7881
			(0.4345)	(0.4087)
Household Characteristics				
Children Under the Age of 18	0.4334	0.3488	0.4908	0.4381
	(0.4956)	(0.4766)	(0.4999)	(0.4962)

Table 3. (*Continued*)

Variable	Full Sample		Workers	
	1979	1993	1979	1993
Other Household Income ($10,000) (1993 $)	2.0580	2.4590	1.8327	2.2657
	(2.2856)	(2.7057)	(14.1718)	(2.4975)
Northeast Region	0.2329	0.2381	0.2303	0.2278
	(0.4227)	(0.4259)	(0.4210)	(0.4195)
Midwest Region	0.2612	0.2509	0.2720	0.2611
	(0.4393)	(0.4335)	(0.4450)	(0.4393)
West Region	0.2986	0.3020	0.2873	0.2966
	(0.4576)	(0.4591)	(0.4525)	(0.4568)
Southern Region	0.2073	0.2091	0.2105	0.2144
	(0.4054)	(0.4066)	(0.4076)	(0.4104)
SMSA	0.5933	0.5473	0.6098	0.5480
	(0.4912)	(0.4978)	(0.4878)	(0.4977)
n	31497	36440	16079	19465

Table 4. Sample Means by Occupation (Standard Deviation).

Variable	1979		1993	
	NFD	FD	NFD	FD
Individual Characteristics				
Age	39.7225	39.1615	38.0411	37.9084
	(13.2268)	(13.5711)	(11.8526)	(12.8157)
Married	0.7637	0.6706	0.6440	0.5749
	(0.4248)	(0.4700)	(0.4788)	(0.4944)
Female	0.2036	0.7642	0.2280	0.7196
	(0.4027)	(0.4245)	(0.4196)	(0.4492)
Black	0.0872	0.0930	0.0752	0.0870
	(0.2821)	(0.2905)	(0.2637)	(0.2818)
Hispanic Origin	0.0485	0.0311	0.0706	0.0630
	(0.2149)	(0.1736)	(0.2561)	(0.2430)
No High School Diploma	0.2544	0.1413	0.1560	0.1101
	(0.4355)	(0.3484)	(0.3628)	(0.3130)
High School Diploma	0.3774	0.3860	0.3918	0.3162
	(0.4848)	(0.4869)	(0.4882)	(0.4650)
Some College Education	0.3683	0.4726	0.4522	0.5737
	(0.4824)	(0.4993)	(0.4977)	(0.4946)
Job Characteristics				
Hourly Wage (1993 $)	15.6348	11.9568	12.6594	10.7959
	(8.2783)	(6.4059)	(9.0761)	(7.0994)

Table 4. (*Continued*)

Variable	1979		1993	
	NFD	FD	NFD	FD
Current Job Tenure	9.3997	7.5926	7.7818	6.5879
	(8.7955)	(7.4458)	(8.2712)	(7.3488)
Government Employee	0.1689	0.3003	0.1228	0.2271
	(0.3746)	(0.4584)	(0.3282)	(0.4190)
Part-time Employee	0.0761	0.2111	0.1086	0.2719
	(0.2652)	(0.4081)	(0.3111)	(0.4450)
Represented by a Union	0.3758	0.2772	0.2136	0.1672
	(0.4844)	(0.4477)	(0.4099)	(0.3732)
Employer-Sponsored Pension Plan	0.6418	0.5477	0.5099	0.4529
	(0.4795)	(0.4978)	(0.4999)	(0.4978)
Employer-Sponsored Disability Benefits	0.4490	0.3210	0.4392	0.3600
	(0.4974)	(0.4669)	(0.4963)	(0.4800)
Employer-Sponsored Health Insurance	0.8017	0.6654	0.8084	0.7730
	(0.3987)	(0.4719)	(0.3935)	(0.4189)
Household Characteristics				
Other Household Income ($10,000) (1993 $)	1.5316	2.2886	1.9418	2.5060
	(1.9623)	(2.3888)	(2.2946)	(2.6122)
Children Under the Age of 18	0.5100	0.4619	0.4435	0.4340
	(0.4999)	(0.4986)	(0.4968)	(0.4956)
Northeast Region	0.2243	0.2394	0.2142	0.2379
	(0.4171)	(0.4267)	(0.4103)	(0.4258)
Midwest Region	0.2753	0.2669	0.2688	0.2555
	(0.4467)	(0.4424)	(0.4433)	(0.4362)
West Region	0.2853	0.2902	0.3054	0.2901
	(0.4516)	(0.4539)	(0.4606)	(0.4538)
Southern Region	0.2150	0.2036	0.2116	0.2165
	(0.4109)	(0.4027)	(0.4085)	(0.4119)
SMSA	0.6016	0.6223	0.5276	0.5630
	(0.4896)	(0.4849)	(0.4993)	(0.4960)
n	9683	6396	8290	11175

6. ESTIMATION

The theoretical model gives rise to a system of equations that can be solved given a functional form for the utility function. However, the statistical model has to accommodate the conditional outcomes of observable data. In this case, the conditional outcome is that the individual's wage in an occupation is observed only if the individual chooses to participate in the labor force in that occupation. Therefore, the statistical model has to account for three situations: (1) the endogeneity of the occupational choice to the work decision; (2) the selection bias associated with observing only the wages of individuals who work; and (3) the selection bias associated with observing an individual's wage in an occupation only if the individual chooses to work in that occupation.[12]

The first stage of estimation is a bivariate probit with qualitative dependant variables of Work and FD, which controls for only observing the occupational choice of those who work. These results are the first stage in the sample selection model that is used to estimate the log wage regression for each of the occupational categories. The occupation decision is a reduced form estimation in which the wage equations are substituted for the wage penalty variable in the FD equation. This results in a typical bivariate probit model with sample selection:

$$Y_{1i}^* = \alpha_0 + \alpha_1 Z_{1i} + v_{1i};$$
$$Y_{2i}^* = \delta_0 + \Omega_1 X_{2i} + \delta_2 Z_{2i} + v_{2i}; \qquad (12)$$
$$[v_{1i}, v_{2i}] \sim BVN[0, 0, 1, 1, \rho];$$

where Z_i includes all characteristics of the individual; X_{2i} includes the observed characteristics of the job; Ω is a vector of δ, ϕ, and ω' and Y_{1i}^* and Y_{2i}^* are unobserved latent variables. Observed in the data is the outcome of the work and the occupational choice decisions, with the latter being a function of the relationship described in Eq. (9).

As shown in Eq. (13), if Y_1^* is less than zero, there is a net loss to working and the individual will not work. However, if Y_1^* is greater than or equal to 0 there is a net benefit to working and the individual will work. Likewise, if Y_2^* is less than zero, there is a net loss to working and the individual will not work. If Y_2^* is greater than or equal to 0 there is a net benefit to working and the individual will work. The caveat arises in that while Work$_i$ is always observed, FD$_i$ is observed if, and only if, Work$_i$ is equal to one. Therefore, if the individual decides not to work we do not observe the occupation they would have chosen.

$$\text{Work}_i = 1 \quad \text{if } Y_{1i}^* \geq 0; \qquad \text{Work}_i = 0 \quad \text{if } Y_{1i}^* < 0;$$
if $Y_{1i}^* \geq 0$ then: $\qquad\qquad\qquad\qquad\qquad\qquad\qquad\qquad (13)$
$$\text{FD}_i = 1 \quad \text{if } Y_{2i}^* \geq 0; \qquad \text{FD}_i = 0 \quad \text{if } Y_{2i}^* < 0;$$

There is a separate wage estimation performed for individuals in FD occupations and individuals in NFD occupations, with sample selection used to control for the biases of observing the wage only in the chosen occupation of individuals who have chosen to work.

$$\log W_{\text{FD}i} = \phi_0 + \phi_1 Z_{3i} + \phi_2 X_{2i} + d_1 \lambda_{1i} + d_2 \lambda_{2i} + v_{3i};$$
$$\log W_{\text{NFD}i} = \omega_0 + \omega_1 Z_{3i} + \omega_2 X_{2i} + d_3 \lambda_{3i} + d_4 \lambda_{4i} + v_{4i}; \qquad (14)$$

The selection terms associated with the occupational decision are λ_{1i} and λ_{3i} while the selection terms associated with the decision to work are λ_{2i} and λ_{4i}. It is expected that individuals will enter the occupation for which there will be greater returns and that individuals with greater labor market potential will enter the labor force. Therefore, the expected signs on the selection coefficients are positive for d_2, d_4, and d_1 and negative for d_3. Once the wage penalty has been estimated, it is substituted into the FD equation and the bivariate probit is re-estimated with a structural model for FD.

7. RESULTS

7.1. Wage Equations

The first stage results, presented in Table 5, indicate that women are penalized relative to the men in their occupation no matter which occupation they choose. However, they are penalized to a lesser degree in the FD occupations.[13] Although the coefficient on female is positive across all four wage estimations, and significant in the FD estimation for both years, the total effect of being female, evaluated at the sample means and considering the interaction terms, is negative.

Age, education, marital status and job tenure all interact with female to determine if there are gender differentials in the return to human capital and/or socioeconomic characteristics explaining the overall gender wage differential. The most consistent difference arises from the return to age. In general, it is expected that earnings will increase at a decreasing rate with age. However, there is a negative and significant coefficient on the interaction terms between female and both age and age-squared. There is still an overall positive return to another year of age for a female but it is much smaller than for men and the peak is reached at an earlier age. In fact, at the sample means, females are experiencing a negative return for an additional year of age while men are receiving a positive return. As there is no measure of general work experience available in the data set, the variable may be picking up some of the return to market experience, which is, in general, expected to be higher for men than women because of the previously discussed intermittent participation and non-market commitments.

There is a positive return to being married for both men and women, albeit a much smaller one for women, in both occupations in 1993 and in FD occupations in 1979. Married women in NFD occupations in 1979 face a marriage penalty while the men face a premium. Although there is no statistical difference in the return to a high school education between men and women in 1993, women in NFD occupations receive a greater return than men for some college education

Table 5.

Variable	1979		1993	
	FD	NFD	FD	NFD
Constant	0.9359***	1.1717***	0.3793***	0.6167***
	(0.1592)	(0.0795)	(0.1136)	(0.1278)
Individual Characteristics				
Age	0.0466***	0.0473***	0.0512***	0.0515***
	(0.0059)	(0.0040)	(0.0054)	(0.0057)
Age Squared	−0.0005***	−0.0005***	−0.0006***	−0.0006***
	(0.0001)	(0.0001)	(0.0001)	(0.0001)
Female	0.4120***	0.0522	0.3950***	0.0437
	(0.1407)	(0.1245)	(0.0900)	(0.1589)
Married	0.0918***	0.0986***	0.1141***	0.0905***
	(0.0252)	(0.0137)	(0.0195)	(0.0161)
Black	−0.0732***	−0.1221***	−0.1292***	−0.1872***
	(0.0176)	(0.0146)	(0.0151)	(0.0189)
Hispanic Origin	−0.0909***	−0.1389***	−0.0879***	−0.1612***
	(0.0271)	(0.0184)	(0.0164)	(0.0192)
No High School Diploma	−0.2224***	−0.1341***	−0.1226***	−0.1097***
	(0.0383)	(0.0147)	(0.0279)	(0.0195)
Some College Education	0.1442***	0.1599***	0.3094***	0.1695***
	(0.0318)	(0.0118)	(0.0263)	(0.0175)
Job Characteristics				
Current Job Tenure	0.0118***	0.0057***	0.0183***	0.0140***
	(0.0035)	(0.0017)	(0.0028)	(0.0019)
Current Job Tenure Squared	−0.0002***	0.0000	−0.0002***	−0.0003***
	(0.0001)	(0.0000)	(0.0001)	(0.0001)
Part-time Employee	−0.0458***	−0.1058***	−0.0630***	−0.1191***
	(0.0139)	(0.0169)	(0.0107)	(0.0190)
Represented by a Union	0.0449***	0.0193**	0.0845***	0.0527***
	(0.0124)	(0.0090)	(0.0120)	(0.0124)
Government Employee	0.0313*	−0.1276***	0.0171	−0.1018***
	(0.0190)	(0.0186)	(0.0157)	(0.0208)
Employer-Sponsored Pension Plan	0.0549***	0.0812***	0.1191***	0.1771***
	(0.0137)	(0.0120)	(0.0102)	(0.0118)
Employer-Sponsored Disability Benefits	0.0448***	0.0875***	0.0960***	0.0919***
	(0.0130)	(0.0106)	(0.0091)	(0.0104)
Employer-Sponsored Health Insurance	0.0802***	0.1261***	0.0700***	0.1320***
	(0.0123)	(0.0117)	(0.0110)	(0.0143)
Female Interaction Terms				
Age × Female	−0.0260***	−0.0198***	−0.0158***	−0.0137***
	(0.0059)	(0.0051)	(0.0041)	(0.0067)
Age Squared × Female	0.0003***	0.0002***	0.0001***	0.0001
	(0.0001)	(0.0001)	(0.0000)	(0.0001)

Table 5. (*Continued*)

Variable	1979		1993	
	FD	NFD	FD	NFD
Married × Female	−0.0489	−0.1329***	−0.1061***	−0.0500*
	(0.0306)	(0.0282)	(0.0251)	(0.0307)
No High School	0.0895**	0.0503*	−0.0447	−0.0404
Diploma × Female	(0.0381)	(0.0291)	(0.0318)	(0.0374)
Some College	0.0276	0.0747***	−0.0609**	0.1317***
Education × Female	(0.0343)	(0.0233)	(0.0284)	(0.0261)
Current Job	0.0038	0.0179***	0.0005	−0.0024
Tenure × Female	(0.0041)	(0.0038)	(0.0032)	(0.0043)
Current Job Tenure	0.0001	−0.0005***	0.0000	0.0001
Squared × Female	(0.0001)	(0.0001)	(0.0001)	(0.0002)
Household Characteristics				
Northeast Region	0.0299**	−0.0320***	0.1020***	0.0940***
	(0.0130)	(0.0108)	(0.0110)	(0.0135)
West Region	−0.0137	−0.0540***	0.0088	0.0113
	(0.0129)	(0.0105)	(0.0103)	(0.0122)
Southern Region	0.0683***	0.0837***	0.0786***	0.1111***
	(0.0141)	(0.0115)	(0.0113)	(0.0137)
SMSA	0.1110***	0.0989***	0.1435***	0.1322***
	(0.0100)	(0.0083)	(0.0080)	(0.0097)
Selection Variables				
λ_1	0.1623**		0.2037***	
	(0.0717)		(0.0701)	
λ_2	0.0143		0.1439***	
	(0.0308)		(0.0379)	
λ_3		−0.1277*		−0.1034
		(0.0668)		(0.0783)
λ_4		0.0768**		0.1125**
		(0.0321)		(0.0509)
R^2	0.4435	0.4650	0.5043	0.4701

Notes: 22 industry dummy variables are included in the estimation. These results are available from the author upon request.
*Significant at the 10% level.
**Significant at the 5% level.
***Significant at the 1% level.

and men in FD occupations in 1993 receive a great return than women to some college education. There is no statistical gender difference in the return to tenure at current job, except in the NFD occupations in 1979 where women see a greater return than men for an extra year of tenure.

For the base case of a single female with a high school education working in a FD occupation, evaluated at the female sample means for age and years of job tenure, the expected wage is 11% lower than a male would expect in 1979 and 6% lower in 1993. For the NFD occupations, the differences are much larger: 32% less in 1979 and 35% less in 1993. As mentioned earlier, a large part of this negative effect is attributed to age. At an age of 25, females are estimated to earn only 2 percentage points less than males in the 1979 FD occupations. In 1993 there is a positive return to being female for this age group, with females expecting 7% higher wages than the males in FD occupations. However by age 33, any positive affect for being female had disappeared.

There is also a negative effect for being female in NFD occupations, regardless of age or survey year, with the differential increasing with age. This relative advantage for the younger cohorts of women could be due to relatively better opportunities for younger cohorts of women and/or less variation in entry level jobs in general.

The receipt of employer-sponsored pension plans, disability, and health insurance benefits are associated with higher wages for all categories. This is not unexpected as the value of these benefits are greater for the high wage worker (Rosen, 2002).[14] However, the effect is much higher in NFD occupations than in FD occupations. One possible explanation for the different magnitudes could be that workers in FD occupations are willing to give up more wages to receive these benefits than workers in NFD occupations.

The other results are as expected, with blacks and individuals of Hispanic origin facing a wage penalty. However, it is interesting to note that the wage penalty is larger in FD than in NFD occupations, and the magnitude of the coefficient on black increases over the time period. This does not support Cain's (1986) theory that the unexplained wage differentials are "vintage effects" from the pre-civil rights discrimination and should diminish over time. In addition, the effect of working part-time is negative, as expected, due to lower level of attachment to the labor force (Hotchkiss, 1991).

7.2. Wage Penalty

The second stage wage equations are used to estimate the FD wage penalty, $\log W_{FDi} - \log W_{NFDi}$, each worker would receive for working in a FD occupation compared to a NFD occupation. This is the expected wage penalty variable that is included in the structural model. These wage penalties are summarized in Tables 6 and 7. The results differ greatly by survey year, by gender, and by chosen occupation. Contrary to expectations, there is not a FD wage penalty for all individuals in the sample, rather some individuals earned a FD wage premium. On average,

Table 6. FD Wage Premium ($\log W_{\text{FD}i} - \log W_{\text{NFD}i}$) (Percentage).

Gender	Occupation	All		Level of Education					
				No HS Diploma		HS Diploma		Some College	
		1979	1993	1979	1993	1979	1993	1979	1993
Female	FD	11.24	0.28	9.97	5.40	10.04	2.54	12.90	−2.13
	NFD	2.50	−3.88	3.77	1.35	4.46	−1.84	−1.62	−6.92
Male	FD	−14.76	−15.30	−26.81	−20.74	−21.54	−23.68	−9.99	−11.21
	NFD	−27.06	−24.23	−29.90	−29.49	25.71	−30.73	−26.52	−16.52

female workers in 1979 would expect to earn 9% higher wages for entering a FD occupation relative to a NFD occupation. For the females who choose to work in FD occupations, the average benefit to working in a FD occupation is 11%. However, as expected, there is an average FD wage penalty for all males in 1979, although the penalty is lower for the males who choose to work in FD occupations.

In 1993 there is an overall average FD wage penalty of half of a percentage point for females, although there is a benefit, albeit very small, for working in FD occupations for the women who choose to do so. As expected, there is a FD wage penalty for males working in a FD occupation, but, once again, the penalty is lower for the males who choose to enter FD occupations.

There is a significant difference in the wage penalty between the two survey years. While the women who choose to work in FD occupations in 1993 still face a slight FD wage premium, the value decreased by approximately 11%. This could indicate that these workers are investing more in human capital characteristics that are more appealing to employers in NFD occupations or that the characteristics associated with workers in typically female occupations are becoming more valuable in NFD occupations.[15]

Table 7. FD Wage Premium ($\log W_{\text{FD}i} - \log W_{\text{NFD}i}$) (Percentage).

Gender	Occupation	Race					
		White		Black		Hispanic Origin	
		1979	1993	1979	1993	1979	1993
Females	FD	10.41	−0.49	18.86	8.13	9.05	1.05
	NFD	1.38	−4.21	9.69	0.56	3.29	−5.47
Males	FD	−15.26	−15.67	−7.55	−10.44	−16.03	−22.46
	NFD	−27.65	−24.72	−20.24	−18.74	−26.78	−25.62

A Structural Model of Occupational Choice

As shown in Fig. 1, age plays a large role in determining the wage penalty and it differs greatly between the two survey years. For female workers in FD occupations in 1979 there is a clear increase in the FD wage premium with age, which appears to be driven by a relative decrease in value in NFD occupations rather than an increasing value in FD occupations. No age group has an average FD wage penalty, thus indicating that the characteristics of these workers are not as valuable in NFD occupations. By 1993, the distribution for the female workers in FD occupations had changed dramatically. Younger and older women face a FD wage premium, but women in their thirties and forties face a very slight FD wage penalty. Once again, the increase in the FD wage premium for older workers appears to be driven by a relative decrease in the expected wage in NFD occupations rather than an increase in expected wage in the FD occupations.

Overall, the wage premium for working in FD occupations in both years is not just attributable to lower expected wages than their counterparts in the NFD occupations but also to relatively higher expected wages in FD occupations. For example, women working in FD occupations in 1979 have a 20 cent higher expected hourly wage in FD occupations than the women working in NFD occupations but a 20 cent lower expected wage in the NFD occupations. This indicates that there exists sorting that is resulting in a relatively better return on skills in FD occupations for the workers that choose FD occupations.

These results mitigate the ability of occupational crowding to explain the wage differential. While it is true that workers in FD occupations earn, on average, less than workers in NFD occupations, the wage differential would not decrease by significant amounts, and could actually increase in some circumstances, if the workers in FD occupations switched to NFD occupations.

7.3. Work and Occupational Choice

The estimation results for the structural occupational choice and labor supply model are reported in Table 8. The dominant explanatory variable in both years is the wage differential, $\log W_{\mathrm{FD}i} - \log W_{\mathrm{NFD}i}$, or the wage penalty for working in a FD occupation. The sign on this variable is positive, indicating that, ceteris paribus, a positive benefit for working in a FD occupation results in a higher probability of entering a FD occupation. This suggests that individuals enter the occupation that provides the greatest monetary reward and does not support the theory that there are discriminatory hiring practices preventing women from entering certain occupations in this time period.

Workers with some college education are more likely to enter FD occupations than workers with a high school diploma or less, with no statistical difference

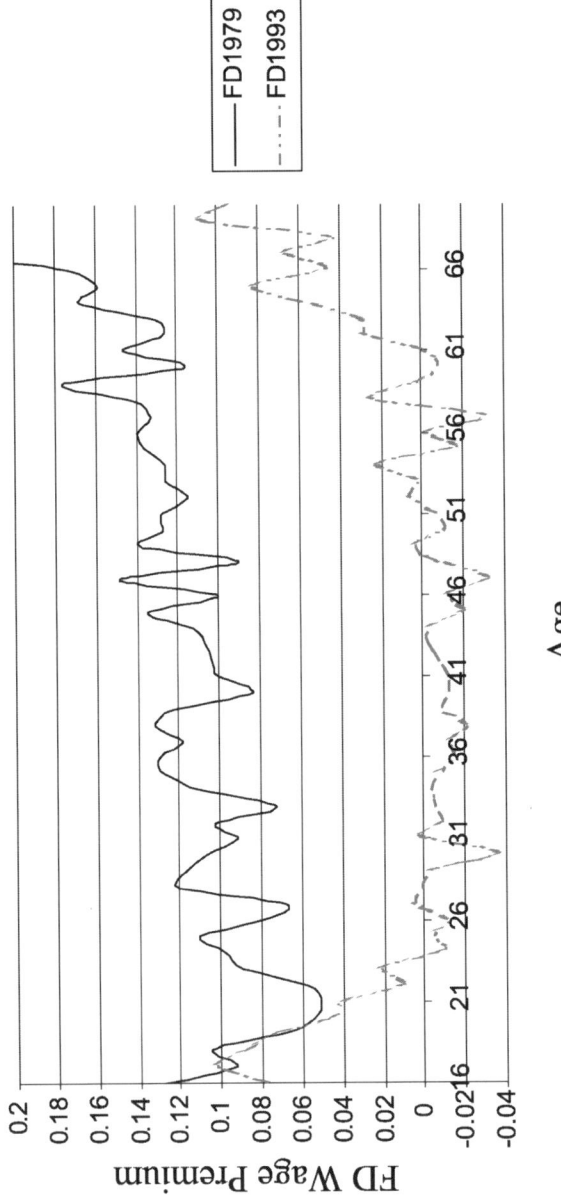

Fig. 1. Females in FD Occupations (FD Wage Premium by Age).

Table 8. Bivariate Probit Structural Model (Standard Errors).

Variable	1979		1993	
	FD	Work	FD	Work
Constant	−0.8008***	−2.5850***	0.5221**	−1.9179***
	(0.2277)	(0.1157)	(0.2547)	(0.0966)
NFD Wage Premium	2.4419***		2.3686***	
(log W_{FDi} − log W_{NFDi})	(0.0800)		(0.0792)	
Individual Characteristics				
Age	0.0134	21.5769***	−0.0272**	0.1767***
	(1.1455)	(0.5470)	(0.0129)	(0.0043)
Age Squared	−0.0002	−0.0003***	0.0002*	−0.0024***
	(0.0001)	(0.0001)	(0.0002)	(0.0000)
Female	1.3354***	0.9390**	1.0622***	0.4035***
	(0.2184)	(0.1394)	(0.1948)	(0.1218)
Married	−0.0455	0.7161	−0.2200***	0.5754***
	(0.0470)	(0.0418)	(0.0388)	(0.0350)
Black	−0.2843***	−0.0630	−0.1033***	−0.3094***
	(0.0429)	(0.0285)	(0.0417)	(0.0282)
Hispanic Origin	−0.2756***	−0.0787***	−0.0755*	−0.1250***
	(0.0625)	(0.0428)	(0.0429)	(0.0321)
No High School Diploma	−0.0983*	−0.6247***	0.0187	−0.5232***
	(0.0541)	(0.0384)	(0.0556)	(0.0352)
Some College Education	0.3913***	−0.0739*	0.2253***	0.1035***
	(0.0387)	(0.0425)	(0.0334)	(0.0330)
Female Interaction Terms				
Age × Female	−0.0129	−0.0648***	−0.0237***	−0.0308***
	(0.0113)	(0.0068)	(0.0099)	(0.0057)
Age Squared × Female	0.0001	0.0008***	0.0003***	0.0004***
	(0.0001)	(0.0001)	(0.0001)	(0.0001)
Married × Female	−0.1591**	−1.1714*	0.3706***	−0.8150***
	(0.0705)	(0.0494)	(0.0597)	(0.0422)
Children Under the Age		−0.5271***		−0.2780***
of 18 × Female		(0.0452)		(0.0422)
No High School	−0.2627***	0.1304***	−0.2504***	−0.0446
Diploma × Female	(0.0671)	(0.0464)	(0.0700)	(0.0450)
Some College	−0.1819***	0.2211***	0.0180	0.1853***
Education × Female	(0.0555)	(0.0497)	(0.0494)	(0.0404)
Household Characteristics				
Children Under the		−0.0466		0.0006
Age of 18		(0.0376)		(0.0346)
Other Household Income	0.0129**	−0.2842***	0.0012***	−0.0041***
($10,000) (1993 $)	(0.0562)	(0.0366)	(0.0004)	(0.0003)

Table 8. (*Continued*)

Variable	1979		1993	
	FD	Work	FD	Work
Northeast Region	−0.0936***	−0.0828***	0.0585**	−0.1214***
	(0.0340)	(0.0250)	(0.0295)	(0.0234)
West Region	−0.0183	−0.1090***	0.0347	−0.0477**
	(0.0326)	(0.0237)	(0.0279)	(0.0225)
Southern Region	−0.0389	−0.1600***	0.1193***	−0.1338***
	(0.0353)	(0.0260)	(0.0305)	(0.0244)
SMSA	0.0542**	−0.0030	0.0390*	−0.0305*
	(0.0249)	(0.0183)	(0.0210)	(0.0169)
Correlation Coefficient	0.1240		0.0755	
	(0.0814)		(0.1107)	

*Significant at the 10% level.
**Significant at the 5% level.
***Significant at the 1% level.

between genders. Married women also have a higher probability of entering a FD occupation. An increase in other household income increases the probability of choosing a FD occupation as does living in an SMSA. Blacks and workers of Hispanic origin are less likely to be working in a FD occupation.

For the work decision, the results are as expected. The probability of working increases at a decreasing rate with age, although the interaction of female with age has a negative coefficient. Women are more likely to work than men although this probability decreases for married women and women with kids. Finally, more education increases the probability of working while increasing the level of other income lowers the probability.

The correlation coefficient between the occupation and the work decisions is not significant in the structural model in either year but is significant in the reduced form model in 1979. Therefore, the results seem to indicate that unbiased estimates of occupational choice could be estimated independently of the work decision, especially with more recent data. This implies that workers do not have a higher probability of entering one occupation or the other when compared to non-workers (Sorenson, 1990).

7.4. Selection Bias

The selection coefficient for occupational choice in the FD wage equation, d_1, is positive and significant for the FD wage equation for both years, indicating that

A Structural Model of Occupational Choice

workers in FD occupations expect to earn a higher wage in that occupation than workers in NFD occupations. The occupational selection coefficient in the NFD wage equation, d_3, is negative although only significant in 1979. This indicates that the workers in NFD occupations would expect to earn higher wages in NFD occupations than workers who choose FD occupations. The selection coefficients for the work decision, d_2 and d_4, are positive, and significant for all categories except FD in 1979, indicating that those who choose to work have a higher earnings potential than those who do not.

In order to better understand the impact of the selection biases accounted for in the previous estimation, a wage equation is estimated for workers in each occupation that did not control for any selection bias. These equations are used to compute wage differentials that are comparable to earlier research. However, the outcomes are drastically different than in the selection models.

Under this methodology there is a penalty for entering a FD occupation, which is the opposite of what is found in the selection model. The penalty for working in FD occupations is higher for females than males and is higher for workers in FD occupations than workers in NFD occupations. Thus, the non-corrected results overstate the occupational wage differential facing women but understate the occupational wage differential facing men. Treating the endogenous work and occupational choice decisions as exogenous would predict that workers in FD occupations would earn higher wages in NFD occupations, thus erroneously indicating that occupational segregation is at least partially responsible for the wage differentials between genders, as has been found the earlier literature.

8. CONCLUSION

The primary question addressed in this article is why workers would enter an occupation where the expected wage is less. For women working in FD occupations, the answer is that they can expect wages that are similar or even greater in FD occupations as compared to NFD occupations. In other words, there is a wage premium for women associated with choosing to work in FD occupations. Thus, occupational segregation theory is not likely to be the explanation for the wage differential between genders. If occupational segregation is the primary cause of the gender wage differential, then the women working in FD occupations should be able to earn higher wages in NFD occupations – something which is not supported by this research. The results presented here differ from the earlier literature because the selection bias inherent in the decision to work and the decision of what occupation to work in are explicitly incorporated into the analysis. When models are estimated ignoring these effects, the results are similar to those in the past which supported occupational segregation as the cause of the gender wage differential. However, the selection model results support McPherson and Hirsch (1995), who suggest policies designed to alter women's occupational choices will not impact the gender wage differential, since a large percentage of women are as well, or better off, in FD occupations as compared to NFD occupations.

An additional result of this research is that the occupational wage differential reduces the probability that women will enter a FD occupation. In other words, while women who do choose to work in FD occupations do so because they are better off than in NFD, if the wage differential between FD and NFD occupations increases, fewer women will continue to choose FD occupations. Because the wage-differential between these occupations (the "cost" of choosing a FD occupation) is an important predictor of occupational choice, I again suggest there is little support for the occupational crowding model. Had the wage-differential been found not significant, it would indicate workers are not taking into account the relative costs of their occupational choice and would have lent support for discriminatory hiring practices causing workers to not enter occupations with the highest return. However, as the magnitude is quite large, these results seem to support that there are gender differences in human capital, tastes, and/or preferences that result in the self-selection of individuals into different occupations. This research leaves unanswered why the characteristics of workers in FD occupations appear to be less valuable in the labor force relative to the characteristics of workers in NFD occupations – discrimination may be a possible explanation.

Lastly, while this research suggests that FD occupations are preferable market outcomes for many women, there is still a persistent unexplained wage-differential associated with being female regardless of whether the occupational choice is FD or NFD. In FD occupations, women are estimated to earn 11% less than men in 1979 and 6% less in 1993. For NFD occupations, the differences are much larger and persistent over time: women earned 32% less than men in 1979 and 35% less in 1993. Once again, discrimination cannot be ruled out as a possible explanation.

NOTES

1. The authors refer to these limitations as "societal discrimination."
2. For a full explanation of the theoretical model, see Pitts and McDermed (1994).
3. Examples of non-pecuniary job characteristics include levels of explicit fringe benefits such as pensions and health insurance and inexplicit benefits such as levels of safety, degree of time flexibility, and status. This analysis holds constant the quality of the matching of the individual's abilities and human capital with the skill requirements of the job.

4. For simplicity, the price of a job characteristic is assumed to be independent of hours of work.

5. This empirical model follows the framework developed by Lee (1978) to examine the decision to enter a labor union.

6. ρ_i can take on a positive or a negative value.

7. The variable indicating the presence of children under the age of 18 is used to identify the work equation. In previous estimations, the coefficient on this variable in the occupational choice estimation was insignificant and removing the variable from the model did not affect the results.

8. The PUMS is a stratified sample consisting of a subsample of the housing units that received the 1980 or 1990 Census of Public Housing "long form" questionnaire and consists of approximately 16% of all housing units. The 1% and 5% samples are combined to provide a nationally representative sample with detailed information on 6% of the U.S. population.

9. There were changes in the classification system of the detailed occupations used by the Census between 1979 and 1993. A transformation of this system was necessary to make comparisons between the two years available. The U.S. Bureau of the Census Technical Paper 59 was used in this process.

10. The female share of the workforce in the PUMS sample increased from 43.18% to 47.29% over this time period.

11. A 60% cutoff would result in 59 occupations that have statistically more females than in the labor force not classified as FD in 1980 and 109 in 1990. Adding 5 percentage points to the percentage of females in the labor force would result in three occupations that have statistically more females than in the labor force not classified as FD in 1979 and 52 in 1990. In addition, in 1980 there would have been three occupations with statistically the same number of females as in the labor force classified as FD and in 1990 there would have been one.

12. A full derivation of the statistical model is available from the author.

13. The results from the reduced form estimation of the occupational choice and labor force participation decision are available in the Appendix.

14. One would expect to observe a trade off between benefits and wages. However, only the offered wage is observed. As high wage workers value the tax benefit of non-pecuniary income at a higher level, these workers will be more likely to make the wage/benefits tradeoff.

15. There is more evidence for the latter explanation as the FD wage premium becomes a small FD penalty when the coefficients from the 1993 wage equations are combined with the 1979 data to estimate a predicted wage differential.

ACKNOWLEDGMENTS

Thanks to Brian Armour, Robert Clark, Julie Hotchkiss, Ann McDermed, Bob Moore, Paula Stephan and Laura Taylor for helpful suggestions in this research. Any errors are, of course, my own. The views expressed here are those of the author and do not necessarily represent the views of the Federal Reserve Bank of Atlanta or the Federal Reserve System.

REFERENCES

Atrostic, B. K. (1982). The demand for leisure and non-pecuniary job characteristics. *American Economic Review, 72*(3), 428–440.
Beller, A. H. (1982). Occupational segregation by sex: Determinants and changes. *Journal of Human Resources, XVII*(3), 371–392.
Bergmann, B. (1974). Occupational segregation, wages, and profits when employers discriminate by race or sex. *Eastern Economic Journal, 1*(2), 103–110.
Blau, F. D., & Beller, A. H. (1988). Trends in earnings differentials by gender, 1971–1981. *Industrial and Labor Relations Review, 41*(4), 513–529.
Blau, F. D., Ferber, M., & Winkler, A. E. (1998). *The economics of women, men, and work*. Upper Saddle River, NJ: Prentice-Hall.
Bowen, W. G., & Finnegan, T. A. (1969). *The economics of labor force participation*. Princeton, NJ: Princeton University Press.
Cain, G. G. (1986). The economic analysis of labor market discrimination: A survey. In: O. Ashenfelter & R. Layard (Eds), *The Handbook of Labor Economics* (pp. 693–785). The Netherlands: North-Holland.
Chiswick, B., Facklar, J., O'Neill, J., & Polachek, S. (1975). The effect of occupation on race and sex differences in hourly earnings. *Review of Public Data Use, 3*(2), 2–9.
Heckman, J. (1974). Shadow prices, market wages, and labor supply. *Econometrica, 42*(4), 679–694.
Hotchkiss, J. (1991). The definition of part-time employment: A switching regression model with unknown sample selection. *International Economics Review, 32*(4), 899–917.
Johnson, G., & Solon, G. (1986). Estimate of the direct effects of comparable worth policy. *American Economic Review, 76*(5), 1117–1125.
Killingsworth, M. R., & Heckman, J. J. (1986). Female labor supply: A survey. In: O. Ashenfelter & R. Layard (Eds), *The Handbook of Labor Economics* (pp. 103–204). The Netherlands: North-Holland.
Lee, L.-F. (1978). Unionism and wage rates: A simultaneous equations model with qualitative and limited dependent variables. *International Economic Review, 19*(2), 415–432.
McPherson, D. A., & Hirsch, B. T. (1995). Wages and gender composition: Why do women's jobs pay less? *Journal of Labor Economics, 13*(3), 426–471.
Pitts, M. M., & McDermed, A. A. (1994). Is there such a thing as women's work? Unpublished manuscript.
Polachek, S. W. (1981). Occupational self-selection: A human capital approach to sex differences in occupational structure. *Review of Economics and Statistics, 63*, 60–69.
Polachek, S. W. (1995). Human capital and the gender earnings gap: A response to feminist critiques. In: E. Kuiper & J. Sap with S. Feiner, N. Ott & Z. Tzannatos (Eds), *Out of the Margin: Feminist Perspectives on Economics* (pp. 61–79). London: Routledge.
Polachek, S. W., & Siebert, W. S. (1993). *The economics of earnings*. Cambridge University Press.
Rees, A. (1973). *The economics of work and pay*. New York: Harper and Row.
Rosen, S. (2002). *Markets and diversity*. The American Economic Association Presidential Address. Presented by Edward Lazear.
Sorenson, E. (1989). Measuring the pay disparity between the typically female occupations and other jobs: A bivariate selectivity approach. *Industrial and Labor Relations Review, 42*(4), 624–639.
Sorenson, E. (1990). The crowding hypothesis and comparable worth. *The Journal of Human Resources, XXV*(1), 155–189.

U.S. Bureau of the Census (1989). Technical paper 59. *The relationship between the 1970 and 1980 industry and occupation classification systems.* Washington, DC: U.S. Government Printing Office.

APPENDIX

Bivariate Probit Reduced Form (Standard Error).

Variable	1979		1993	
	FD	NFD	FD	NFD
Constant	−1.2000***	−2.5850***	0.0209	−1.9142***
	(0.2369)	(0.1159)	(0.2818)	(0.0965)
Individual Characteristics				
Age	0.0178	0.0216***	−0.0172	0.1766***
	(0.0123)	(0.0055)	(0.0144)	(0.0043)
Age Squared	−0.0002	−0.0028***	0.0002	−0.0024***
	(0.0001)	(0.0001)	(0.0002)	(0.0000)
Female	2.1280***	0.9389***	1.8939***	0.4001***
	(0.2338)	(0.1396)	(0.2098)	(0.1218)
Married	−0.0445	0.7164***	−0.1517***	0.5753***
	(0.0482)	(0.0419)	(0.0411)	(0.0350)
Black	−0.1473***	−0.0619**	0.0528	−0.3092***
	(0.0447)	(0.0285)	(0.0449)	(0.0282)
Hispanic Origin	−0.0942	−0.0788*	0.1008**	−0.1256***
	(0.0653)	(0.0428)	(0.0459)	(0.0321)
No High School Diploma	−0.3010***	−0.6246***	0.0296	0.5231***
	(0.0555)	(0.0384)	(0.0623)	(0.0352)
Some College Education	0.2691***	−0.0740*	0.3979***	0.1028***
	(0.0402)	(0.0425)	(0.0344)	(0.0330)
No High School Diploma × Female	−0.1961***	0.1302***	−0.2369***	−0.0449
	(0.0697)	(0.0465)	(0.0783)	(0.0450)
Some College Education × Female	−0.2480***	0.2209***	−0.3957***	0.1861***
	(0.0566)	(0.0497)	(0.0493)	(0.0404)
Job Characteristics				
Current Job Tenure	0.2011		−0.0048	
	(0.0063)		(0.0055)	
Current Job Tenure Squared	0.4601		0.0001	
	(0.0002)		(0.0016)	

Appendix (*Continued*)

Variable	1979		1993	
	FD	NFD	FD	NFD
Part-time Employee	0.1186***		0.1795***	
	(0.0406)		(0.0325)	
Represented by a	−0.0689**		−0.0646**	
Union	(0.0298)		(0.0334)	
Government Employee	0.2097***		0.0326	
	(0.0509)		(0.0460)	
Employer-Sponsored	−0.0021		0.0156	
Pension Plan	(0.0370)		(0.0282)	
Employer-Sponsored	−0.0752**		−0.0237	
Disability Benefits	(0.0339)		(0.0252)	
Employer-Sponsored	−0.0104		−0.0957***	
Health Insurance	(0.0337)		(0.0325)	
Female Interaction Terms				
Age × Female	−3.5130***	−0.0648***	−0.0360***	−0.0307***
	(0.0125)	(0.0068)	(0.01107)	(0.0057)
Age	0.0004***	0.0008***	0.0004***	0.0004***
Squared × Female	(0.0001)	(0.0001)	(0.0001)	(0.0001)
Married × Female	0.0349	−1.1716***	0.2089***	−0.8155***
	(0.0719)	(0.0495)	(0.0625)	(0.0422)
Children Under the Age		−0.5273***		−0.2767***
of 18 × Female		(0.0452)		(0.0422)
Current Job Tenure ×	0.005111		0.0045	
Female	(0.9388)		(0.0082)	
Current Job Tenure	−0.0008		0.0000	
Squared × Female	(0.0000)		(0.0003)	
Household Characteristics				
Other Household	0.0091	0.0284***	0.0005	−0.0041***
Income ($10000)	(0.0058)	(0.0037)	(0.0004)	(0.0003)
Children Under the		−0.0468		0.0015
Age of 18		(0.0375)		(0.0346)
Northeast Region	0.0383	−0.0831***	0.0648**	−0.1219***
	(0.0344)	(0.0250)	(0.0310)	(0.0234)
West Region	0.0429	−0.1091***	−0.0023	−0.0479**
	(0.0338)	(0.0237)	(0.0293)	(0.0225)

Appendix (*Continued*)

Variable	1979		1993	
	FD	NFD	FD	NFD
Southern Region	−0.0665*	−0.1601***	0.0207	−0.1337***
	(0.0361)	(0.0260)	(0.0322)	(0.0245)
SMSA	0.0655***	−0.0031	0.0605***	−0.0303*
	(0.0258)	(0.0183)	(0.0223)	(0.0169)
Correlation Coefficient	0.1635**		−1.5780	
	(0.0845)		(0.1359)	

*Significant at the 10% level.
**Significant at the 5% level.
***Significant at the 1% level.

NEW EVIDENCE ON CULTURE AND THE GENDER WAGE GAP: A COMPARISON ACROSS ETHNIC ORIGIN GROUPS

Heather Antecol

ABSTRACT

Antecol (2001) finds that cultural factors play a role in explaining inter-ethnic variation in the gender wage gap across immigrant groups in the United States. This paper presents new evidence on the importance of cultural factors by exploring the relative importance of culture across specific immigrant sub-groups. More specifically, I begin with the entire immigrant sample and then progressively restrict the sample to married immigrants and then to married immigrants whose spouse is from the same country of origin. I find a positive correlation between the gender wage gaps for all immigrant groups in the United States with the same gaps in those groups' countries of origin, however the effect is larger for married immigrants. While these results suggest the importance of cultural factors, this positive correlation is overstated when controls for differences in female labor force participation rates (LFPR) across ethnic groups are excluded, particularly for married immigrants whose spouse if from the same country of origin. Nevertheless, I also find a negative correlation between the variation in the gender wage gap of immigrants in the United States and the variation in female LFPR of immigrants in the United States, which is more consistent with unobserved cultural factors than selection of the usual type.

1. INTRODUCTION

There exists substantial variation in the gender wage gap across countries. For example, column 1 of Table 1 illustrates that the gender wage gap ranges from 9.59 log points for the Philippines, to 30.83 log points for Germany, to 68.63 log points for Japan.[1] Economists have become increasingly interested in explaining this cross-country variation in the gender wage gap. While cross-country studies (Blau & Kahn, 1996; Gregory & Daly, 1991; Gregory, Daly & Ho, 1986; Kidd & Shannon, 1996) have traditionally focused on two factors – human capital and wage setting institutions, a recent within-country study (Antecol, 2001) examines the role of an additional factor – culture.

In particular, Antecol (2001) compared the gender wage gaps of first generation and second-and-higher generation immigrants in the United States with the same gaps in those groups' countries of origin. In the earlier paper, I found that for first generation immigrants, even after controlling for all observable characteristics in the United States, there is a strong positive correlation between the home country gender wage gap and the gender wage gap across ethnic origin groups in the United States. Antecol (2001) argues that the observed relationship between home and host country gender wage gaps is evidence that cultural factors explain part of the difference in gender wage gaps across immigrant groups. This relationship is not particularly surprising, as one would expect cultural attitudes towards family and work to follow immigrants to their chosen destination country.

Antecol (2001) was a first step in documenting the role of cultural factors in explaining inter-ethnic variation in the gender wage gap for first generation immigrants in the United States. However, many questions remain unanswered. For example, can the results for first generation immigrants (henceforth referred to as immigrants) be generalized to all immigrants, or is a particular sub-set of the immigrant sample driving the result? Casual empiricism suggests that cultural factors, such as preferences regarding family structure and women's roles in market versus home work, may be more evident among married immigrants whose spouse is from the same country of origin.[2]

This paper attempts to shed new light on the role cultural factors play in explaining inter-ethnic variation in the gender wage gap by examining sub-samples of the immigrant population. More specifically, I begin with the entire immigrant sample and then progressively restrict the sample to married immigrants (henceforth

Table 1. Gender Wage Gaps and Weighted Standard Deviation (WSD) Measures.

Place of Birth (POB)	Home Country	Total		Married		Married to Immigrant of Same POB	
	Unadjusted	Unadjusted	Adjusted	Unadjusted	Adjusted	Unadjusted	Adjusted
	(1)	(2)	(3)	(4)	(5)	(6)	(7)
Argentina	26.00	36.62	38.93	42.76	45.23	48.34	49.12
Brazil	33.69	26.41	33.99	33.97	40.31	34.97	38.67
Canada	31.99	42.38	41.91	53.81	52.98	75.70	77.29
China	19.12	25.43	22.28	28.15	25.45	27.49	24.22
Colombia	24.00	27.18	30.56	32.48	34.34	36.01	36.03
Czechoslovakia	34.85	43.98	39.65	51.24	46.13	46.31	43.74
Egypt	17.44	24.63	27.69	35.66	36.75	46.93	45.14
El Salvador	9.68	22.30	29.43	26.15	32.52	34.33	36.24
Germany	30.83	53.81	47.72	65.81	58.26	80.21	82.60
Greece	24.49	34.80	33.50	40.61	38.76	42.35	40.40
Hong Kong	31.84	19.12	24.17	31.49	33.99	35.30	35.96
Hungary	21.32	42.24	35.94	44.84	38.56	55.19	51.42
Ireland	36.62	43.45	46.73	54.60	56.94	64.02	63.58
Italy	32.49	46.76	45.88	53.22	51.62	52.34	51.49
Japan	68.63	70.49	78.39	83.24	92.13	84.78	92.70
Korea	64.11	32.34	32.29	39.53	39.70	35.55	35.77
Mexico	24.92	22.24	26.64	24.40	28.20	32.54	33.28
Philippines	9.59	12.42	10.32	18.34	15.62	11.44	9.22
Portugal	36.23	41.99	45.03	44.76	49.04	47.01	53.40
Thailand	44.82	30.18	27.15	38.76	34.91	15.56	12.84
UK	34.99	59.87	60.88	74.15	74.67	93.21	93.70
WSD		13.75	13.27	15.77	15.33	20.68	20.70

Note: Sampling weights used. The number of observations are 181875, 134813, and 64928 for the total, married, and married to immigrant of same place of birth samples, respectively. For a breakdown of sample size by gender and place of birth see Table A1 in Appendix. The predicted unadjusted gender wage gap is based on a regression of (natural) log hourly wages on a constant, an indicator variable for gender, and gender crossed with ethnic origin. The adjusted gender wage gap also includes a vector of personal characterisitcs (both in levels and interactions with gender). See Table 2 for the personal characteristic coefficient estimates underlying the adjusted predicted gaps. For a discussion of the interpretation of the WSD measures see Section 4 in the text.

referred to as the unrestricted married sample) and then to married immigrants whose spouse is from the same country of origin (henceforth referred to as the restricted married sample). This estimation strategy allows one to explore the relative importance of cultural factors for immigrants with different family characteristics, especially with respect to spousal nativity.

I begin my analysis by replicating earlier results: there exists substantial variation in the unadjusted gender wage gap across immigrant groups in the United States for the total and the (unrestricted and restricted) married samples. Furthermore, the variation in the gender wage gap is larger among the restricted married sample than the total and the unrestricted married samples. I show that controlling for human capital factors does not eliminate inter-ethnic variation in the gender wage gap for all the immigrant samples. I further illustrate that after controlling for human capital factors, the gender wage gap of immigrants in the United States is positively correlated with the gender wage gaps in those groups' countries of origin, however the effect is larger for married immigrants. This suggests that there exists an unobservable portable cultural factor, which is not captured by observable human capital measures, that affects outcomes.

Moreover, I show that the gender wage gap of immigrants in the United States is negatively correlated with female labor force participation rates (LFPR) of immigrants in the United States, and that this negative correlation is more pronounced among the restricted married sample. This suggests the presence of unobservable differences across ethnic origin groups such that certain ethnic origin groups have a high fraction of women participating in the labor market and high female relative wages (that is, small gender wage gaps). I argue that such a pattern is more consistent with unobserved cultural factors than with the typical selection problem that researchers are usually concerned about, that is, that only the most "able" women participate in the labor market.

Finally, I show that the home country effect is substantially reduced when controls for the fraction of women participating in the labor market are included in the analysis, and that this reduction is more pronounced among the restricted married sample. In fact, the home country gender wage gap is no longer statistically significant at conventional levels for the restricted married sample. This result suggests that in the absence of these controls, home country factors appear to absorb some of the systematic differences in female LFPR across ethnic origin groups, which are themselves influenced by culture, that we observe.

The remainder of the paper is as follows. Section 2 describes the data. Section 3 discusses the differences in the unadjusted gender wage gap across immigrant groups to the United States for the total and the (unrestricted and restricted) married samples. Sections 4 and 5 present the two-stage estimation approach and results, respectively. Section 6 concludes.

2. DATA

The data set used for the host country analysis is the 1990 United States Census 5% Public Use Microdata sample. The data contains indicators of ethnic origin (ancestry, race, and place of birth), a rich set of labor market variables (employment status, hours worked in the previous year, weeks worked in the previous year, wages and salary in the previous year, industry, and occupation), personal characteristics (age, year of arrival, education, marital status, fertility, English fluency, and region), and spousal information (for the household head and the spouse of the household head).

I restrict the sample to immigrants between the ages of twenty-five and fifty-four who earned positive wages in 1989. Individuals earning less than one dollar per hour or greater than one hundred dollars per hour are excluded from the sample. Further, individuals who earned self-employment income in 1989, and those attending school at the time of the survey are excluded from the sample.[3] Additionally, immigrants whose parents were born in the United States are excluded from the sample.

Because the objective is to compare outcomes of immigrants in the United States with the same outcomes in those groups' countries of origin, I use place of birth to determine ethnic origin. Similarly, place of birth is utilized to determine the ethnic origin of a respondent's spouse.

Based on the above criteria, I restrict the sample to twenty-one ethnic origin groups as these are the most detailed groups that I can make comparable across the total immigrant sample, the married immigrant sample, the sample of married immigrants whose spouse is from the same country of origin, and across home countries, and have large enough sample sizes (see Table 1 for a list of these countries).[4,5]

The sample restrictions leave a total sample size of 181,875 immigrants of whom 74% are married, that is, the unrestricted married sample includes 134,813 individuals. The unrestricted married sample includes all immigrants in the census who report being married. In order to obtain information on the respondent's spouse I only focus on the household head and the spouse of the household head.[6] By restricting to the household head and the spouse of the household head, the unrestricted married sample is reduced by 9% to 122,498 individuals. Of the 122,498 individuals, approximately 13% of them do not have any spousal information and/or spousal information on place of birth, leaving a sample of 107,007 individuals. Finally, restricting the sample to married immigrants whose spouse is from the same country of origin leaves a sample of 64,928 individuals, which represents a further reduction of 39%.[7] For a breakdown of the sample size by gender and place of birth see Table A1 in Appendix.

Home country wage data are from various issues of ILO's *Yearbook of Labour Statistics* for Czechoslovakia, Germany, Greece, Hungary, Ireland, Japan, Philippines, Portugal, and the United Kingdom; from ILO's *LABORSTA* for Brazil, Egypt, El Salvador, Hong Kong, Korea, and Thailand; from Htun (1998) for Argentina and Colombia; from the Survey of Consumer Finances (SCF) for Canada; from Meng (2001) for China; from Blau and Kahn (1996) for Italy; and from STPS/INEGI, Encuesta Nacional de Empleo (ENE) for Mexico.[8] In an attempt to make the home country data as comparable as possible with the host country data (that is, the 1990 U.S. Census), the home country wage data (if available) are based on 1989 hourly wages in the non-agricultural sector.[9]

There is probably substantial measurement error in the home country wage data because the data are from a number of different sources. The variation in sources causes the home country wage data to be based on different industries, different time units, and different years. For example, countries where the wage data are based on monthly wages implicitly assumes that men and women would have to work the same number of hours per month for the gender wage gap to be the same as it would have been if hourly wage data had been observed.

3. INTER-ETHNIC VARIATION IN THE UNADJUSTED GENDER WAGE GAP AMONG IMMIGRANTS IN THE UNITED STATES

Figure 1 presents the unadjusted gender wage gap among immigrants in the United States from the total sample, and the unrestricted married sample, and the restricted married sample. The unadjusted gender wage gap within each ethnic origin group is measured as the difference in the mean (natural) log hourly wages of men and the mean (natural) log hourly wages of women.

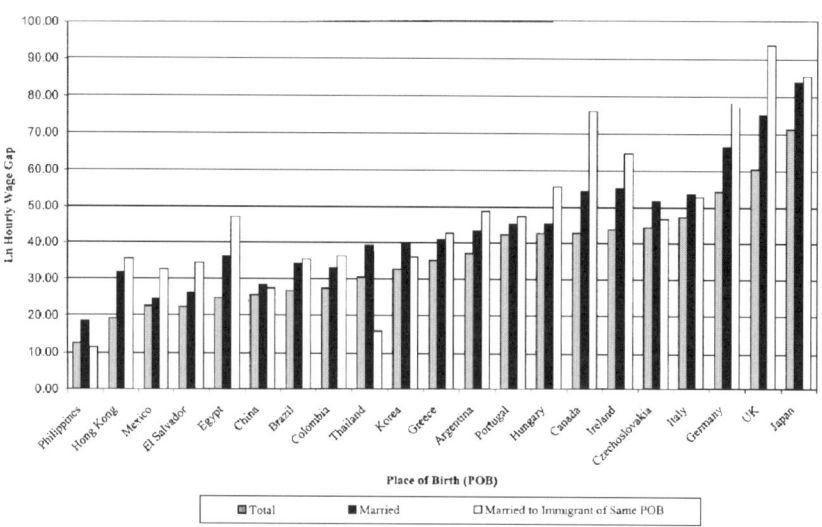

Fig. 1. Unadjusted Gender Wage Gaps of Immigrants in the United States.

It is clear that there is substantial variation in the gender wage gap across ethnic origin groups for the total sample: the gender wage gap ranges from 12.42 log points for the Philippines, to 34.80 log points for Greece, to 70.49 log points for Japan (see column 2 of Table 1). Furthermore, for all ethnic origin groups the gender wage gap is larger among the unrestricted married sample relative to the total sample. Finally, the gender wage gaps are even larger among the restricted married sample, that is, those married to immigrants from the same country of origin, relative to the unrestricted married sample.[10] This may reflect the fact that immigrants who marry outside of their ethnic origin group are systematically different than immigrants who marry within their ethnic origin group. In particular, cultural influences, such as preferences regarding family structure and women's roles in market versus homework, may be more prevalent among the restricted married sample.

4. ESTIMATION APPROACH

A two-stage estimation approach is used to determine the role of two factors, human capital and culture, in explaining differences in the gender wage gap across immigrant groups in the United States.[11] I estimate the following first-stage regression:

$$w_i = \beta_0 + \beta_1 M_i + \beta_2 X_i + \beta_3 X_i M_i + \sum_{j=1}^{J-1} \beta_{4j} E_{ij} + \sum_{j=1}^{J-1} \beta_{5j} E_{ij} M_i + e_i \quad (1)$$

where i and j index the individual and the ethnic origin group, respectively, w is the (natural) log hourly wage, M is a male dummy variable, X are observable personal characteristics, and E are ethnic origin dummy variables.

The model includes two types of observable personal characteristics: characteristics that influence wages but seem unlikely to be correlated with cultural factors (a quadratic in age, nine regional dummy variables, a dummy variable for metropolitan status, and eight year of arrival dummy variables) and characteristics that influence wages, but could also depend on cultural factors (years of education, English fluency, marital status (for the total sample), and number of children).[12,13]

I predict an adjusted gender wage gap for each ethnic origin group from Eq. (1). For comparative reasons and for the calculation of the weighted standard deviation measure discussed below, I re-estimate Eq. (1) without the observable personal characteristics (both in levels and interactions) and predict an unadjusted gender wage gap.

In order to have a summary statistic of the inter-ethnic variation in the gender wage gaps in the United States, I calculate weighted standard deviation (WSD) measures for the unadjusted and the adjusted gaps.[14] While inter-ethnic variation in the gender wage gap can be attributed to observable personal characteristics if the WSD for the adjusted gap is substantially smaller than the WSD for the unadjusted gap, most of the inter-ethnic variation in the gender wage gap remains unexplained if the WSDs remain similar in magnitude.

In the second stage, I estimate an equation of the following form:

$$\hat{\beta}_{5j}^* = \gamma_1 h_j + \varepsilon_j \tag{2}$$

where $\hat{\beta}_{5j}^*$ is the deviation from the mean in the $\hat{\beta}_{5j}$ from Eq. (1) and h is deviations from the mean in the home country gender wage gaps. I estimate Eq. (2) by generalized least squares (GLS) to take into account the fact that the dependent variable is estimated.[15]

The parameter of interest is γ_1. If $\gamma_1 > 0$, evidence of an additional determinant of gender wage gaps exists. This factor is transmitted between countries with different wage setting institutions, as one would expect to be the case for cultural attitudes to family and work.[16]

5. RESULTS

Before presenting the predicted (unadjusted and adjusted) gender wage gaps (see Table 1), a brief discussion of the coefficient estimates underlying the adjusted gaps is warranted. Table 2 presents the coefficient estimates for the observable personal characteristics from the first stage regression for the total, the unrestricted married, and the restricted married sample. For ease of interpretation, coefficient estimates for females ($\hat{\beta}_2$) are presented in the first column, coefficient estimates for males ($\hat{\beta}_2 + \hat{\beta}_3$) are presented in the second column, and the coefficient estimates for the difference between males and females ($\hat{\beta}_3$) are presented in the third column for each sub-sample of immigrants.

In general, the results are as expected. First, for both men and women earnings increase with age, education, and English fluency and more recently arrived immigrant cohorts earn less than immigrants who arrived prior to 1950. Second, children and marriage have a negative effect on earnings for immigrant women, while marriage has a positive effect on earnings for immigrant men. Third, the returns to age, English fluency, and marital status are higher for immigrant men than immigrant women. Finally, the returns to education are higher for immigrant women than immigrant men in the total and unrestricted married samples while the reverse is true for the restricted married sample.

Table 2. Ln Hourly Wage Regressions: Observable Characteristic Coefficients.

	Total			Married			Married to Immigrant of Same POB		
	Female	Male	Male–Female	Female	Male	Male–Female	Female	Male	Male–Female
Age	0.039***	0.042***	0.003	0.037***	0.050***	0.012***	0.025***	0.043***	0.018***
	(0.003)	(0.002)	(0.004)	(0.003)	(0.003)	(0.004)	(0.005)	(0.004)	(0.007)
Age Squared/10	−0.005***	−0.004***	0.000	−0.004***	−0.005***	−0.001	−0.003***	−0.005***	−0.002*
	(0.000)	(0.000)	(0.000)	(0.000)	(0.000)	(0.001)	(0.001)	(0.001)	(0.001)
Years of Education	0.044***	0.038***	−0.006***	0.045***	0.040***	−0.005***	0.034***	0.037***	0.003*
	(0.001)	(0.001)	(0.001)	(0.001)	(0.001)	(0.001)	(0.001)	(0.001)	(0.002)
English Fluency	0.090***	0.160***	0.070***	0.079***	0.170***	0.092***	0.094***	0.166***	0.072***
	(0.007)	(0.005)	(0.008)	(0.008)	(0.006)	(0.010)	(0.010)	(0.008)	(0.013)
Married	−0.016**	0.156***	0.172***						
	(0.007)	(0.006)	(0.009)						
Sep/Div/Wid	−0.007	0.035***	0.042***						
	(0.008)	(0.009)	(0.013)						
Number of Children	−0.019***			−0.019***			−0.015***		
	(0.002)			(0.002)			(0.003)		
Immigrant 1950–1959	−0.044**	−0.022	0.022	−0.027	−0.019	0.007	−0.064	0.097**	0.161*
	(0.018)	(0.018)	(0.026)	(0.022)	(0.019)	(0.029)	(0.073)	(0.044)	(0.085)
Immigrant 1960–1964	−0.044**	−0.032*	0.012	−0.028	−0.020	0.008	−0.048	0.114***	0.162*
	(0.018)	(0.018)	(0.026)	(0.022)	(0.019)	(0.029)	(0.072)	(0.043)	(0.084)
Immigrant 1965–1969	−0.057***	−0.013	0.044*	−0.050**	−0.003	0.047*	−0.053	0.119***	0.172**
	(0.018)	(0.018)	(0.025)	(0.022)	(0.018)	(0.028)	(0.071)	(0.042)	(0.082)
Immigrant 1970–1974	−0.067***	−0.045**	0.022	−0.056***	−0.038**	0.018	−0.065	0.065	0.130
	(0.018)	(0.018)	(0.025)	(0.022)	(0.018)	(0.029)	(0.071)	(0.042)	(0.082)
Immigrant 1975–1979	−0.113***	−0.082***	0.030	−0.094***	−0.082***	0.011	−0.118*	0.004	0.121
	(0.018)	(0.018)	(0.026)	(0.022)	(0.018)	(0.029)	(0.071)	(0.042)	(0.082)
Immigrant 1980–1984	−0.185***	−0.157***	0.028	−0.174***	−0.166***	0.008	−0.198***	−0.090**	0.109
	(0.018)	(0.018)	(0.026)	(0.022)	(0.019)	(0.029)	(0.071)	(0.042)	(0.083)
Immigrant 1985–1990	−0.285***	−0.253***	0.033	−0.276***	−0.274***	0.002	−0.296***	−0.176***	0.120
	(0.019)	(0.018)	(0.026)	(0.023)	(0.019)	(0.029)	(0.072)	(0.042)	(0.083)
Sample Size	181875			134813			64928		

Note: Sampling weights used. Regressions also include controls (in levels and interactions) for 8 regional dummy variables, a metropolitan status dummy variable, 20 ethnic origin dummy variables, and an intercept. Omitted categories are single, immigrant pre-1950, pacific, and the United Kingdom. Robust standard errors in parentheses.

* Significant at the 10% level.
** Significant at the 5% level.
*** Significant at the 1% level.

Table 1 presents the predicted unadjusted and adjusted gender wage gaps based on the first stage regression for the total, the unrestricted married, and the restricted married samples. Differences in the gender wage gap across ethnic origin groups are largest for the restricted married sample (married immigrants whose spouse is from the same country of origin), followed by the unrestricted married sample, and then the total sample. For example, the adjusted WSD measures are 13.3, 15.3, and 20.7 log points for the total, the unrestricted married, and the restricted married samples, respectively (see the bottom row of Table 1). Furthermore, despite controls for personal characteristics, there continue to exist large differences in the estimated gender wage gap across ethnic origin groups in the United States. In particular, the adjusted WSDs remain similar in magnitude to the unadjusted WSDs.[17]

The first stage results illustrate that, despite controls for personal characteristics, there continues to exist inter-ethnic variation in the gender wage gap. What can explain this variation? Panel 1 of Table 3 presents the second stage regression results, which examines the role of cultural factors in explaining differences in the adjusted gender wage gap across immigrant groups in the United States, for the total and the (unrestricted and restricted) married samples.

There are several key points to note. First, the coefficient estimates on the home country gender wage gaps are positive and significant for all samples. Second, the magnitude of the home country coefficient is larger for the (unrestricted and restricted) married samples relative to the total sample. For example, a 1 log point increase in the home country gender wage gap is associated with a 0.63 log point increase in the adjusted host country gender wage gap for the unrestricted married sample while a 1 log point increase in the home country gender wage gap is associated with a 0.51 log point increase in the adjusted host country gender wage gap for the total sample. These results suggest that portable cultural factors seem to play a role in explaining inter-ethnic variation in the gender wage gap, with unobservable portable cultural factors being most important.

Finally, for the total and the (unrestricted and restricted) married samples there remains an unexplained component of the inter-ethnic variation in the gender wage gap, as indicated by the R-squared, which range from 0.13 to 0.33. Portable cultural factors explain as little as 13% and as much as 33% of the variation in the gender wage gap across ethnic origin groups.

A concern with these results is sample selection bias: of necessity my wage regressions only include individuals who earn positive wages. This is not so much a problem for men because their probability of employment is similar across ethnic origin groups, but it might be problematic for women. An examination of Table 4 reveals that there is substantial inter-ethnic variation in female labor force participation rates (LFPR).[18] For example, for the total sample in female

Table 3. Second Stage Regression Results.

	Total	Married	Married to Immigrant of Same POB
Panel 1: Without Selection			
Home Country Gender Wage Gap	0.5082***	0.6280***	0.5410*
	(0.1727)	(0.1934)	(0.2991)
R-Squared	0.2888	0.3300	0.1327
Panel 2: With Selection (Inverse Mills Ratio)			
Home Country Gender Wage Gap	0.3585*	0.4478**	−0.0279
	(0.1850)	(0.2024)	(0.2840)
Selection	−0.3482*	−0.3795*	−0.5860***
	(0.2079)	(0.2010)	(0.1640)
R-Squared	0.3755	0.4295	0.4587
Panel 3: With Selection (Log Functional Form)			
Home Country Gender Wage Gap	0.3566*	0.4418**	−0.0250
	(0.1869)	(0.2044)	(0.3009)
Selection	−0.3315*	−0.3481*	−0.4326***
	(0.2024)	(0.1859)	(0.1345)
R-Squared	0.3720	0.4280	0.4157

Note: The dependent variable is the estimated coefficients of the mean differences in the gender wage gap across ethnic origin groups from the first stage regression. The independent variables are the mean differences in the gender wage gap and the fraction of women participating in the labor market (for the models including selection). A constant term is included in the selection models. The coefficient on the selection term for the inverse mills ratio is multiplied by minus one in order for it to have the same interpretation as the log functional form, that is, an increasing function in the fraction of women participating in the labor market. Sample size in the second stage regression is 21. Standard errors in parentheses.
* Significant at the 10% level.
** Significant at the 5% level.
*** Significant at the 1% level.

LFPR range from 46.7% for Japan, to 69% for the United Kingdom, to 85.7% for the Philippines. Moreover, LFPR are lower among female immigrants in the unrestricted married sample compared to the total sample. In particular, for the unrestricted married sample female LFPR range from 40.5% for Japan, to 62.3% for the United Kingdom, to 84.3% for the Philippines. Finally, LFPR are, in general, the same or even lower among female immigrants in the restricted married sample relative to the unrestricted married sample.[19]

To control for the sample selection bias I re-estimate Eq. (2) for the total and (unrestricted and restricted) married samples adding controls for the fraction of women participating in the labor market across ethnic origin groups within their respective sample.[20] In other words, the selection correction variable for the total

Table 4. Female Labor Force Participation Rates.

Place of Birth (POB)	Total	Married	Married to Immigrant of Same POB
	(1)	(2)	(3)
Argentina	64.29	57.81	52.16
Brazil	64.64	55.69	53.57
Canada	69.92	64.41	52.39
China	72.69	71.22	71.30
Colombia	69.28	62.81	61.05
Czechoslovakia	74.19	71.08	75.57
Egypt	62.17	58.64	57.88
El Salvador	71.48	66.29	66.46
Germany	69.44	64.06	51.03
Greece	57.37	52.92	48.23
Hong Kong	79.64	75.08	72.42
Hungary	67.01	62.38	61.00
Ireland	67.18	60.72	54.25
Italy	60.21	55.82	51.68
Japan	46.65	40.48	16.69
Korea	60.11	56.43	55.22
Mexico	54.43	49.19	48.25
Philippines	85.70	84.26	90.41
Portugal	74.15	72.97	74.43
Thailand	73.37	70.44	73.10
UK	68.94	62.26	49.94
Sample Size	122627	93356	44723

Note: Sampling weights used.

sample is based on column 1 of Table 4, while the selection correction variable for the unrestricted (restricted) married sample is based on column 2 (3) of Table 4. I use two functional forms for this new regressor: the inverse mills ratio and a log functional form.[21] If the sample selection correction coefficient is positive and significant, then a sample selection problem of the usual type exists: in ethnic origin with low participation rates, only the most able women participate. If on the other hand, the sample selection correction coefficient is negative and significant, this suggests the presence of unobservable differences across ethnic origin groups such that certain ethnic origin groups have a high fraction of women participating in the labor market and high female relative wages (that is, small gender wage gaps). Such a pattern is more consistent with unobserved cultural factors than the usual selection problem.

Panels 2 and 3 of Table 3 add controls for selection for each immigrant sub-sample using the inverse mills ratio and a log functional form, respectively.[22] The selection correction coefficient, which is not sensitive to functional form, is negative for all samples. Further, the selection correction term is significant at the 1% level for the restricted married sample but is only significant at the 10% level for the total and unrestricted married samples. As stated previously, the estimated negative coefficients are more consistent with unobserved cultural factors than with selection of the usual type.

Not surprisingly, the addition of the selection correction term reduces the unexplained component of the inter-ethnic variation in the gender wage gap for all immigrant groups in the United States.[23] For example, the R-squared for the total sample increases from 0.29 to 0.38 when controls for selection are added. Of note, however, is the large reduction in the unexplained component for the restricted married sample when controls for selection are added; the R-squared increases from 0.13 to 0.46. This reflects the fact that female differences in LFPR explain a substantial amount of the variation in host adjusted gender wage gaps for married immigrant women whose spouse is from the same country of origin.

Finally, controlling for sample selection reduces the magnitude of the home country gender wage gap coefficient for the total and the (unrestricted and restricted) married samples, although the reduction is bigger for the restricted married sample. In fact, for the restricted married sample the coefficient on the home country gender wage gap is no longer statistically significant.

The lack of correspondence between the home and host country gender wage gaps once controls for selection are added for the restricted married sample seems counterintuitive. However, the result on the selection correction coefficient suggests that most of the differences for the restricted married sample are manifested in female labor force participation decisions and these decisions are themselves influenced by cultural factors.

6. CONCLUSIONS

Using the 1990 United States Census, I find substantial variation in the gender wage gap across immigrant groups for the total immigrant sample, the married immigrant sample, and the sample of married immigrants whose spouse is from the same country of origin. Controlling for human capital factors does not eliminate inter-ethnic variation in the gender wage gap for all samples. Moreover, while I find that the variation in the gender wage gap of immigrants in the United States is positively correlated with the gender wage gaps in those groups' countries of origin, the effect is larger for married immigrants. These results suggest that there exists an unobservable portable cultural factor, which is not captured by observable human capital measures, that affects outcomes.

The second important finding in this paper is that the gender wage gap of immigrant groups in the United States is negatively correlated with female labor force participation rates (LFPR) of immigrant groups in the United States, and that this negative correlation is more pronounced among the restricted married sample. I argue that a negative correlation is more consistent with unobserved cultural factors than with selection of the usual type, that is, that only the most "able" women participate in the labor market.

Finally, I find a reduced role of home country factors once differences in female LFPR across ethnic origin groups are included, particularly for the restricted married sample. This result suggests that in the absence of these controls, home country factors appear to absorb some of the systematic differences in female LFPR across ethnic origin groups, which are themselves influenced by culture, that we observe.

The importance of cultural factors in explaining differences in the gender wage gap across immigrant groups in the United States may have important policy implications. As with Polachek (1995), my results suggest an increased role for supply-side factors in explaining gender wage gaps (e.g. cultural factors cause a division of labor in the home, in turn causing differential lifetime labor supply and differential human capital investment, thereby causing gender wage differentials). At the very least, there is more to this than just demand-side factors (whereby firm discrimination causes differential labor demand, in turn causing occupational segregation and giving rise to gender wage differentials). Polachek (1995) argues that as long as there exist differences in human capital incentives caused by differences in lifetime labor supply, government policies that focus on outcome measures (like equal opportunity laws) will not be able to eliminate gender differences in labor market outcomes.

NOTES

1. In general, the home country gender wage gap is measured as natural log (average male wages) minus natural log (average female wages).
2. This is consistent with a number of economic models. For example, a model of assortative mating suggests that immigrants with strong cultural ties to the same country of origin marry each other. While an alternative model suggests that cultural factors get reinforced in the household when two people from the same country of origin happen to marry, and where marriage is more likely to occur between these people simply because social contact is more likely.

3. Approximately 6500, 5160, and 2260 self-employed immigrants are excluded from the total sample, the unrestricted married sample, and the restricted married sample, respectively, which is less than four percent of each sub-sample.

4. Each gender/place of birth cell must have at least one hundred observations.

5. Ideally, singles would also be included in the analysis; however, I am only able to identify sixteen ethnic origin groups of large enough sample sizes for singles. See footnote 22 for a further discussion of singles.

6. By focusing only on the household head and the spouse of the household head, married immigrants who are related to the household head (that is, the (step) son/daughter, the brother/sister, the father/mother, the grandchild, and/or other relative) and married immigrants who are not related to the household head (that is, a roomer/boarder/foster child, a housemate/roommate, an unmarried partner, and/or other non-relative) are excluded from the sample.

7. The thirty-nine percent reduction is made up of 33,748 immigrants married to natives (U.S. born) and 8,331 immigrants married to immigrants from a different country of origin.

8. Home country data are not exclusively drawn from the ILO because ILO wage data by gender are not available for all countries.

9. There are a number of exceptions: data for Brazil, China, Czechoslovakia, Hungary, Japan, Korea, the Philippines, and Thailand are based on monthly wages; data for Egypt and Mexico are based on weekly earnings; data for Hong Kong are based on daily earnings; data for Italy is based on annual wages adjusted for hours worked; data for El Salvador, Greece, and Ireland are based on the manufacturing industry; data for Mexico and the U.K. include agricultural workers; data for Colombia are based on the formal sector; data for the Philippines are based on 1993 earnings; data for Hungary are based on 1992 earnings; data for Mexico and Thailand are based on 1991 earnings; data for Colombia are based on 1990 wages; data for Italy are based on 1987 wages; and data for China are based on 1988 wages.

10. There are two obvious exceptions, the Philippines and Thailand.

11. The two-stage estimation approach for the linear random effects model was proposed by Amemiya (1978), and was adapted by Borjas and Sueyoshi (1994) for probit models with structural group effects.

12. Number of children is only included as a direct term because it is only observable for women.

13. Ideally, controls for actual labor market experience would be included in the list of personal characteristics that influence wages, but could also depend on cultural factors. Census data, however, does not allow one to control for actual labor market experience, that is, one can only proxy for actual labor market experience with age and education (potential experience). Unfortunately, at this time, no data set exists that allows investigation of the effect of actual labor market experience on inter-ethnic variation in the gender wage gap for immigrants.

14. The WSD is the standard deviation of the gender wage gap across ethnic origin groups, which corrects for least squares sampling errors. For a detailed discussion of how the WSD is calculated see Krueger and Summers (1988) and Haisken-DeNew and Schmidt (1997).

15. For a detailed discussion of how the weighting matrix for the GLS estimation is calculated see Borjas and Sueyoshi (1994).

16. Alternatively, it can be argued that the above correlation reflects unobserved differences in human capital factors across ethnic origin groups. Even so, cultural factors

could underlie the differences in unobserved human capital factors across ethnic origin groups. It should also be noted that unobserved human capital factors must differ for men and women, further strengthening the cultural argument.

17. The variables, which cause these changes in the WSD measures, are highly jointly significant (that is, a p-value of 0.000) for all samples.

18. Reimers (1985) and Antecol (2000) also find substantial inter-ethnic variation in female LFPR.

19. The main exceptions are Czechoslovakia, the Philippines, Portugal, and Thailand.

20. For a detailed description of the group selection model see Card and Payne (1997).

21. The inverse mills ratio is calculated as $\phi(\Phi^{-1}(\pi))/\pi$ where π is the fraction of women participating in the labor market. The inverse mills ratio in this case is a decreasing function in π. Thus, the selection correction coefficient reported for the inverse mills ratio functional form is multiplied by minus 1 in order for it to have the same interpretation as the log functional form, that is, an increasing function in π.

22. The results in this section do not appear to be driven by the countries included in the estimation. In particular, for a total sample based on an additional 14 ethnic origin groups I find a positive correlation between the host and home country gender wage gaps, and the magnitude and significance level of this correlation is substantially reduced once controls for selection are included. Furthermore, home country factors nor selection play a role in explaining inter-ethnic variation in the gender wage gap for the single sample based on 16 ethnic origin groups. Both sets of results are available from the author upon request.

23. Some of the remaining unexplained component may be attributable to labor market discrimination, that is, equally qualified individuals are being paid differently based solely on ethnic background. It should be noted however, that, as for unobserved human capital factors, in order for labor market discrimination to explain some of the remaining inter-ethnic variation in the gender wage gap, discrimination would have to affect men and women of a given ethnic origin group differently.

ACKNOWLEDGMENTS

I thank Kelly Bedard, Francine Blau, Solomon Polachek, Jennifer Ward-Batts, Seminar participants at the 2002 American Economic Association Meetings, and two anonymous referees for helpful comments.

REFERENCES

Amemiya, T. (1978). A note on a random coefficients model. *International Economic Review*, 19(3), 793–796.

Antecol, H. (2000). An examination of cross-country differences in the gender gap in labor force participation rates. *Labour Economics: An International Journal*, 7(4), 409–426.

Antecol, H. (2001). Why is there interethnic variation in the gender wage gap? The role of cultural factors. *Journal of Human Resources*, 36(1), 119–143.

Blau, F., & Kahn, L. (1996). Wage structure and gender earnings differentials: An international comparison. *Economica*, 63(250), S29–S62.

Borjas, G., & Sueyoshi, G. (1994). A two-stage estimator for probit models with structural group effects. *Journal of Econometrics, 64*(1–2), 165–182.

Card, D., & Payne, A. A. (1997). School finance reform, the distribution of school spending, and the distribution of SAT scores. Working paper No. 387, Industrial Relations Section, Princeton University.

Gregory, R., & Daly, A. (1991). Can economic theory explain why Australian women are so well paid relative to their United States counterparts? *International Review of Comparative Public Policy, 3*, 81–125.

Gregory, R., Daly, A., & Ho, V. (1986). A tale of two countries: Equal pay for women in Australia and Britain. Discussion paper No. 147, Centre for Economic Policy Research, Australian National University.

Haisken-DeNew, J., & Schmidt, C. (1997). Interindustry and interregion differentials: Mechanics and interpretation. *The Review of Economics and Statistics, 79*(3), 516–521.

Htun, M. N. (1998). Women's rights and opportunities in Latin America: Problems and prospects. Presented at the Women's Leadership Conference of the Americas.

ILO. *LABORSTA*. http://laborsta.ilo.org/

ILO. Various years. *Yearbook of Labour Statistics*. Geneva.

Kidd, M., & Shannon, M. (1996). The gender wage gap: A comparison of Australia and Canada. *Industrial and Labor Relations Review, 49*(4), 729–746.

Krueger, A., & Summers, L. (1988). Efficiency wages and the inter-industry wage structure. *Econometrica, 56*(2), 259–293.

Meng, X. (2001). Institutions and culture: Women's economic position in mainland China and Taiwan. Australian National University, mimeo.

Polachek, S. W. (1995). Human capital and the gender earnings gap: A response to feminist critiques. In: E. Kuiper & J. Sap (Eds), *Out of the Margin: Feminist Perspectives on Economics* (pp. 61–79). New York: Routledge.

Reimers, C. W. (1985). Cultural differences in labor force participation among married women. *American Economic Association Papers and Proceedings, 75*(2), 251–255.

STPS/INEGI, Encuesta Nacional de Empleo (ENE).

APPENDIX

Table A1. Sample Size by Gender and Place of Birth.

Place of Birth (POB)	Total		Married		Married to Immigrant of Same POB	
	Male	Female	Male	Female	Male	Female
Argentina	964	651	726	456	304	182
Brazil	778	654	512	388	216	124
Canada	4655	5152	3361	3616	702	497
China	4368	3909	3818	3339	2178	1843
Colombia	2800	2656	1872	1562	995	647
Czechoslovakia	411	389	306	271	127	117
Egypt	964	413	723	330	320	199
El Salvador	4501	3444	2876	1907	1428	1039
Germany	4374	6338	3234	4452	516	318
Greece	1645	1019	1317	799	617	386
Hong Kong	1481	1423	975	1025	332	276
Hungary	730	505	560	359	145	111
Ireland	1165	1095	850	741	354	227
Italy	4078	2722	3428	2165	1404	917
Japan	2374	1846	1861	1402	1279	272
Korea	3524	4606	2939	3677	2417	1825
Mexico	46996	23740	35591	16432	18549	10445
Philippines	8263	11727	6461	8808	4589	4588
Portugal	2195	1737	1893	1506	1290	1083
Thailand	678	1069	495	815	297	264
UK	4748	5092	3480	3484	950	561
Total	101689	80186	77278	57535	39008	25920

Note: Sampling weights used.

GENDER DIFFERENCES IN REASONS FOR JOB MOBILITY INTENTIONS IN HIGHER EDUCATION

Jennifer VanGilder, John Robst and Solomon Polachek

ABSTRACT

The purpose of this paper is twofold. First, it assesses motives for intended mobility among academics in institutions of higher education. Second, it investigates gender differences. Women have twice the intention to leave their institution than men during their first few years, but this difference narrows with seniority. Women report monetary reasons such as salary and promotion opportunities, as well as non-monetary reasons such as spousal employment to motivate their intended mobility. Gender differences across the reasons are minor once one controls for tenure status.

INTRODUCTION

Standard cost-benefit analysis suggests that individuals change jobs upon receiving an offer whose present value minus the cost of switching is greater than their current job's present value. Using this type of framework, men and women would change jobs with the same frequency if they had similar characteristics and face similar offer rates. However, migration frequencies differ by gender.

A number of studies examine why job mobility varies between men and women. Articles include Barnes and Jones (1974), Viscusi (1980), Blau and

Kahn (1981a, b), Bartel and Borjas (1981), Mincer (1986). Flinn (1986), Ruhm (1987) and Sicherman (1996), all of which consider various factors responsible for gender differences. These reasons include family responsibility, tastes for populated areas, discrimination, as well as many other considerations. Most analyses are sector neutral, referring to jobholders in all industries. However, some studies examine gender mobility in particular economic arenas. For example, Althauser and Kallegerg (1981), Rosenfeld and Jones (1986), and Chronister, Baldwin and Conley (1998) concentrate on turnover in the academic labor market.

Higher education provides an interesting backdrop for mobility research. Because academic faculty represents an occupation with relatively large amounts of human capital, one would think both male and female academics act efficiently to protect their investments. Further, high levels of human capital investment lead to increased lifetime female labor force participation, thus differentiating academic women from other women job incumbents.

When contemplating mobility, these labor market differences could lead faculty women to consider alternative factors compared to most women. These differences allow for some interesting comparisons. For example, in looking at an insurance company, Sicherman (1996) finds that women are more likely to cite non-market reasons for departure. In his analysis, he reports on eleven occupational categories that consist of a large proportion of "female jobs" such as secretary, typist, clerk, and other administrative jobs. Such occupations require low human capital investments (Sicherman, 1991) and often attract women with low labor force attachment (Polachek, 1981). In such jobs, non-market reasons for mobility might be more prevalent. On the other hand, post-secondary education faculty is predominantly male. It requires substantial human capital investment. Thus, female faculty may change jobs for different, more market-oriented reasons than women in the insurance industry. For this reason, it is important to widen the vista of industries studied.

By the same token, recruiting highly educated manpower raises the turnover costs of any institution (Oi, 1962). Highly trained workers are hard to find and come from further distances. In addition, university faculty often require large startup packages. Failing to fill vacant positions may mean that important classes go untaught while the position remains unfilled. At least for planning purposes, these relatively high turnover costs make it important for academic institutions to assess mobility probabilities. As such, focusing on intended mobility provides institutions with information that mitigates future costs. For this reason this paper's purpose is to analyze the reasons for intended job mobility among higher education faculty, with an emphasis on gender differences in such reasons.

LITERATURE REVIEW – GENDER DIFFERENCES IN THE REASONS FOR MOBILITY

Much research focuses on differences in male and female job mobility, but conclusions drawn from this research are mixed. For instance, Mincer (1978) finds women exhibit less mobility compared to their male colleagues, Light and Ureta (1992) find women have a four times greater probability of moving than men, while Royalty (1998) finds highly educated men and women portray similar turnover behavior.

Employee versus Employer Initiated Turnover

Of course, there are many reasons why men and women change jobs, and the reasons differ by gender. Blau and Kahn (1981a, b) distinguish between employee initiated (quits) and employer initiated (layoffs) turnover. Loprest (1992) finds women are seven times more likely than men to cite an employee initiated termination. He concludes that most of the mobility difference in returns relates to how jobs were terminated. Keith and McWilliams (1997) use four categories (layoff, fired, quit for family reasons, and quit for other reasons) related to who initiates the termination. They find that females more often report employee initiated terminations than males, and conclude that men and women have similar returns to mobility when controlling for employer or employee initiated departures.

Employee Initiated Turnover – Job Related versus Non-job Related Reasons

To differentiate job related and non-job related reasons for turnover, a number of studies concentrate on employee initiated turnover. Felmlee (1984) suggests that men's and women's work-lives follow sufficiently different patterns so that quit rates vary by gender. Barnes and Jones (1974) come to a similar conclusion in their assessment of male and female mobility behavior. Their research suggests that turnover is a function of several factors not equally shared between men and women. For instance, family responsibilities such as child-care contribute more to female than male quit rates. Thus, not accounting for the reasons for mobility leads to an inaccurate view of male-female differences in mobility behavior.

Similarly, Viscusi (1980) argues the stereotype that females have larger turnover is only suggestive because it does not distinguish between sex-specific differences in mobility from other factors such as job characteristics and wages. Viscusi states that higher female turnover might be attributable to reasons exogenous to the labor market. Some of these reasons include leaving to have children, transfer of husband's job, or categorization as a secondary worker only temporarily in the labor force. In addition, one half of the difference in mobility is explained by differences in jobs and regional economic conditions faced by men and women.

To partly account for such issues, Bartel and Borjas (1981) separate their sample into two groups based on job related and non-job related motivations for quitting. Job related departures stem from some type of dissatisfaction with the current job such as salary, working conditions, or hours. Non-job related quits result from individual and family changes, including a spouse being transferred, family member illness, or pregnancy. They conclude that the reason for departure plays a key role in the monetary returns from the move.

Several studies examine specific occupations or industries and find men and women differ in time preferences between market and non-market activities. Using Southeastern Psychological Association data, Kimmel (1974) reports that men are more likely to cite professional advancement or an unsatisfactory job as a reason for changing jobs, while women are more likely to give spouse-related or personal reasons.

In the most rigorous analysis of gender differences in the reasons for job mobility, Sicherman (1996) examines eighteen distinct reasons for departure from a large insurance company. A larger proportion of women report that quits are due to non-market reasons such as household duties or illness in the family, while men report that quits are due to market reasons such as better opportunities and more interesting work.

Gender Differences in Academic Turnover

The academic setting provides an interesting framework for the study of gender differences in job mobility and the reasons for departure. As a group, professors have been categorized as mobile (Brown, 1967) where the ability to change schools can be crucial for career advancement, but where too much or ill-timed mobility might actually disrupt one's career. Althauser and Kallegerg (1981) refer to the pursuit of the academic career as the occupational internal labor market since people in academia typically identify with their disciplines rather than their institution. As such, they build their careers between as well as within schools (Rosenfeld & Jones, 1986).

Mobility also varies by type of position (Chronister, Baldwin & Conley, 1998). For example, those at high ranks change jobs less often than faculty at low ranks.

Assistant professors are more likely to have poor job matches than associate or full professors. Associate professors, especially those with tenure, often remain where they are until they become full professors. Full professors might move to seek new colleagues, but may choose to stay at their present institution because of their long involvement with the school and community.

Several studies look at gender differences in mobility in an academic setting. For example, Ahern (1981) and Rosenfeld and Jones (1986) find that women change institutions faster than men and gain less from their mobility, but variables predicting mobility vary little by gender. Neither study has information on the worker's reasons for leaving the institution.

DATA

The 1993 National Study of Postsecondary Faculty (NSOPF) provides a unique profile of the nation's faculty, what they do, and why many aspects of the profession are changing.[1] The NSOPF was designed to provide data about faculty to postsecondary education researchers, planners, and policy makers, and represents the most comprehensive study of faculty in postsecondary educational institutions ever undertaken.

While the majority of past mobility research focuses on actual job changes, the NSOPF contains information on mobility intentions. Each respondent was asked: During the next three years are you very likely to seek or accept a (different) full-time job? The possible answers are very likely, somewhat likely, or not likely. We assume individuals who respond they are very likely to seek or accept a different full-time job intend to change jobs.

Several studies look at mobility intentions. For example, Smart (1990) uses the 1984 Carnegie Foundation for the Advancement of Teaching National Survey of Faculty to formulate a causal model of faculty turnover intentions. Several studies also suggest that mobility intentions are a reasonable measure of actual mobility. Steel and Orvalle (1984) find turnover intentions are better predictors of turnover than satisfaction measures alone, while Sager, Futrell and Varadarajan (1989) show turnover intentions to be the immediate attitudinal predecessor to actual turnover.

In addition, there are a number of reasons to study desired mobility in higher education. First, mobility intentions during the early 1990s may be particularly important in the academic labor market, since the period marked a time of budget cutbacks and limited hiring at colleges and universities. As a result, some individuals who desired job changes were unable to obtain new positions and observed mobility may understate mobility intentions. Second, higher education institutions are interested in retaining quality faculty. An individual's desired mobility is defined as "a sleeping giant, inconspicuously swallowing a significant portion of a worker's productivity" (Futrell & Parasuraman, 1984, p. 35). This mobility, if realized, can lead to many monetary and non-monetary costs, including recruiting, relocation, and the opportunity cost of the classes that go untaught while the position remains unfilled. While not all intended mobility is due to being dissatisfaction at the current institution, such intended mobility not realized can lower morale, reduce collaboration between faculty, and lower effort in the classroom. Thus, focusing on intended mobility will provide institutions with information that could mitigate future costs.

The NSOPF contains fourteen questions that provide information on the reasons important to the mobility decision. Each faculty member was asked "How important would each of the following reasons be in your decision of accepting another job at either another academic institution or outside academia." Faculty members could respond in one of three ways: very important, somewhat important, or not important. Factors potentially important to accepting a job include salary level, tenured position, job security, opportunity for advancement, benefits, no publishing pressure, research facilities, instructional facilities, geographic location, teaching opportunity, research opportunity, administrative opportunity, schools for children, and job for spouse.[2] While most of these reasons are job related, the importance of location, schools, and spousal employment provides information on non-job related reasons. A reason is considered important to the mobility decision if the faculty member is very likely to move in the next three years and responds that the individual reason is very important to the departure decision. Workers must express an intention to change jobs since the interpretation of an affirmative response to a reason is unclear when the person is unlikely to change jobs.

Two points are worth noting. First, the reasons are derived from questions that ask about the decision to accept another job, while prior studies focus on the reasons for leaving the current employer. By examining the factors important to the decision to accept another job, we provide a different perspective on the mobility decision. Second, Sicherman's (1996) data only allow respondents to provide the most important reason for departing the firm. The NSOPF data allow individuals to respond to each potential reason. This is beneficial since multiple factors may be important to the mobility decision. For example, a wife probably considers both salary and spousal employment important when deciding whether to accept employment in a different geographic area. However, on the downside, there is no information on the relative importance of each reason. Simply because an individual responds that several reasons are very important to accepting a new job does not indicate equal importance.

The sample is restricted to faculty ages 25–65 that have been with an institution for twenty-five years or less. These restrictions are imposed to include faculty members that show greater mobility patterns. Faculty members over the age of 65 or with an institution greater than twenty-five years are likely to exhibit a low probability of moving. The sample is also restricted to full time faculty of the rank full, associate, or assistant professor employed at a research, doctoral, comprehensive, or liberal arts institution. With these restrictions, the sample consists of 9,124 faculty members (6,096 males and 3,028 females).

THE REASONS FOR ACCEPTING A NEW POSITION

Most faculty members do not intend to change jobs within the next three years. However, consistent with prior research, women more often report mobility intentions than men with 11.5% of men and 15.2% of women reporting they are very likely to change jobs. In addition, there are important differences between men and women in the reported reasons for accepting a new position. Table 1 details the responses to each reason for accepting a new job for those who intend to change jobs. The reasons for departure are divided into three categories: monetary, non-monetary, and opportunity differences.

Female faculty are more likely than male faculty to respond that monetary reasons are important to the mobility decision. Women are more likely to report that a tenured position, job security, opportunity for advancement, and benefits are factors in the decision to accept a new position. Two reasons, job security and opportunity for advancement, are reported by over 70% of women and approximately 65% of men in the sample. Salary is the least reported monetary reason among women (61%), whereas salary is fourth out of five among men. Brown (1967) suggests that faculty base the mobility decision on "what he will be doing at his new job. How much he will be paid is noticeably less important" (p. 149). Such a result suggests the true gains to mobility are difficult to measure simply using salaries as is typical in research.

Non-monetary considerations are important, as well. While women are more likely to report that instructional facilities, a lack of publishing pressure, and a job for spouse are important, men are more likely to report that geographic location and schools for children are factors in the decision to accept a new job. Overall, the decision to accept another job depends on monetary reasons more than non-monetary reasons with non-monetary reasons reported less often than monetary reasons. Also, noteworthy, while women report a lack of publishing pressure as important more often than men, less than one-quarter of faculty who intend to change jobs rate this factor as important.

Table 1. Percentage Responding that the Reason is Important to the Decision to Accept Another Position.

Reason for Departure	Men					Women				
	Total	Married	Single	Children	No Children	Total	Married	Single	Children	No Children
Monetary										
Salary level	61.5	60.6	65.2	65.2	49.4	60.8	63.3	58.2	66.5	55.7
Tenured position	58.9	57.2	65.9	60.7	53.0	65.2	65.6	64.8	65.1	65.3
Job security	65.7	64.6	70.4	67.1	61.4	72.5	70.8	74.2	73.1	71.9
Opportunity for advancement	64.3	63.7	67.0	66.6	56.9	73.8	75.3	72.3	73.4	74.1
Benefits	65.2	64.8	67.0	67.6	57.8	68.4	67.2	69.7	70.9	66.3
Non-monetary										
No publishing pressure	19.6	20.1	17.2	20.1	17.7	24.1	24.2	24.0	26.0	22.4
Research facilities	54.7	53.5	59.6	54.7	54.5	56.6	53.1	60.1	53.3	59.4
Instructional facilities	57.6	57.2	59.2	59.2	52.4	63.8	63.8	63.7	62.9	64.5
Geographic location	64.2	63.8	66.3	63.6	66.2	61.0	64.1	58.0	56.8	64.8
Schools for children	56.9	62.4	33.3	63.4	36.2	45.2	55.5	35.0	61.2	31.0
Job for spouse	47.8	50.7	35.6	49.9	41.3	50.8	69.0	32.6	54.3	47.8
Difference in opportunity										
Teaching opportunity	27.0	27.4	25.1	27.2	26.3	26.6	25.3	27.9	28.0	25.4
Research opportunity	43.8	41.9	51.7	43.1	45.8	46.0	42.2	49.9	40.4	51.0
Administrative opportunity	12.5	13.0	10.5	13.6	9.0	14.0	13.5	14.4	13.3	14.5
Number of observations	703	558	145	527	176	459	228	231	217	242

Note: Number of observations includes only faculty members who responded in the affirmative to very likely to leave in the next three years and reported the reason as very important reason in the decision to accept a new position.

Thus, higher education faculty do not look to avoid publishing pressure when changing jobs.

There is little difference between men and women in reporting teaching, research, or administrative opportunities important to the mobility decision. Less than half the faculty report such departure reasons affect the decision to accept another position, and only 12.5% of women and 14.0% of men report administrative opportunities.

What does seem apparent is that female respondents are more likely to accept a new position for monetary reasons compared to men. Although this finding may appear a bit surprising, the Department of Education finds that full-time female faculty average lower salaries than male faculty (Nettles et al., 2000). Using 1993 NSOPF data, 66% of women earn base salaries of less than $40,000 compared with 37% of men. In contrast, while 5% of female faculty report salaries of $60,000 or more, 19% of men do so. Indeed, if women face wage and promotion discrimination at colleges and universities, mobility due to monetary factors may be greater for women than men. While men may advance within institutions, women may change institutions to rise in rank and salary.

Reported Reasons by Marital Status

Marriage has important effects on men's and women's job mobility. Married women are often considered tied-stayers that consider potential jobs for their spouse when deciding to accept another job. Single women may report reasons similar to men for job mobility. As reported in Table 1, no clear difference exists between married and single women in the importance of monetary factors. Married women more often report salary and opportunities for advancement, but single women more often report job security and job benefits are important. Although the magnitude of the difference is small (69.7 vs. 67.2%), job benefits may be more crucial to single women since married women often purchase health insurance through their husband's employment.

Single males consistently report monetary reasons for mobility are important more often than married males. For example, 65.2% of single men report salary is a factor compared to 60.6% of married men. Seventy-one percent of single men report job security affects the decision to accept a new job, the highest of the non-monetary reasons. Married men report job security and benefits almost equally often, with 64.6 and 64.8% of reporting these factors important.

Among the non-monetary departure reasons, 69% of married female faculty respond that a job for spouse affects the decision to leave the current institution compared to 50% of married males. Thus, a job for their spouse is more important for married women than married men. Interestingly, 35% of single men and 32.6% of single women report that job for spouse is important in the mobility decision. This could indicate long term relationships, future expectations of marriage, or erroneous reporting on the part of these faculty members. Comparing single and married women, single women more often report that research facilities are important (60 vs. 54%), while married women more frequently report geographic location and schools for children. Geographic location is the most reported non-monetary reason for both single and married women with 66.3% of single women and 63.8% of married women indicating location is important. When comparing single and married men, married men more often report no publishing pressure and schools for children, while single men more frequently report research facilities, instructional facilities, and geographic location.

Consistent with the importance of research facilities reported above, single men consider research opportunities more often than married men do. Fifty percent of single men report that research facilities affect the mobility decision compared to 42% of married men. Similar results are found for women.

The Impact of Children on Reported Reasons

Married men and women face different mobility decisions than single men and women. Similarly, the presence of children in the household can have implications for job mobility, and the factors important to the mobility decision. Many parents are hesitant to move children between schools and away from friends, and those parents that do intend to change jobs will consider the quality and availability of schools for children.

Table 1 contains the reported reasons for men and women with the samples divided based on whether or not the respondent has children. Among the monetary reasons for departure, women with children more often report that salary and benefits are important. Men with children report each of the monetary reasons more often than men without children. For example, 65% of men with children report salary as a significant issue compared to 49% of men without children.

Several interesting differences emerge when looking at the non-monetary reasons. Women with children are more likely to desire jobs that have no publishing pressure, while women without children report that research facilities and geographic location affect the mobility decision. Such results suggest that women with children desire positions that have fewer research expectations, and are likely to require fewer work hours. As expected, schools for children are a factor for over 60% of males and females with children in the home. Again similar to the case of single individuals reporting that a job for their spouse is important, approximately 30% of individuals without children report that schools are an issue. Such a finding may result from the expectation of having children, erroneous reporting, or may suggest schools for children proxy for other quality-of-life issues in areas. Locations with high quality schools are likely to have better housing, parks, and other amenities. Among all male and female faculty, schools for children are reported by eleven percent more men than women, suggesting that men might consider schools to be more important than women. However, the differential between men and women with children is only two percent (63 vs. 61%), suggesting the overall differential between men and women results from more male faculty having children than female faculty.

Once again, women without children desire research positions. Fifty-one percent of women without children declare research opportunities to be important compared to only 40% of women with children.

THEORETICAL MODEL

We adopt survival analysis techniques to examine how gender affects reasons for intended job mobility in higher education. Survival analysis is defined as a collection of statistical procedures to analyze data in which the outcome variable is the time-duration until an event occurs (Kleinbaum, 1996). By event, we mean intended job mobility. The time-duration variable is usually referred to as survival time, while the event is referred to as failure. Most survival analyses consider a key data problem called censoring that occurs when limited information about the individual survival time is known. Most data is right-censored meaning that the true survival time interval has been cut off (i.e. censored). Thus, using survival analysis we can draw implications about the true survival time.

To begin, define the time when mobility occurs as the time to failure. One can represent the sample of failure times as $\{(y_i, \delta_i) : i = 1, \ldots n\}$ where y_i is the minimum of the failure time and δ_i is the censoring time. Assuming that the failure and censoring times are independent, we depict Kaplan-Meier estimates of the survivor function $S_{KM}(t)$.

Assume that there are exactly k distinct "mobility" events out of the n observations. Thus $\{t_{(j)} : j = 1, \ldots, k\}$, and that there are d_i intended movements at mobility time $t_{(i)}$. Assume that the $t_{(i)}$'s are ordered from smallest to largest. Now we define the "risk" set corresponding to the ith mobility time, that is the collection of individuals who have no intentions of leaving their current position prior to time $t_{(i)}$ as R_i. Also assume the number of individuals in the risk set, R_i, is n_i. Much of the information in the actual data is contained in $\{(d_i, R_i, n_i) : i = 1, \ldots, k\}$

except the actual times of censoring for the censored observations. However, the information that is available provides an acceptable nonparametric estimate of S.

Let $t = t_{(i)}$ for the moment, and consider $S(t)$ for this choice of t. Note that $S(t) = pr(T > t) = pr(T > t, T > t_{(i-1)})$ since $\{T > t_{(i)}\} \Rightarrow \{T > t_{(i-1)}\}$ where T is the random variable for a person's survival time and t is any specific value of interest for the variable T. More specifically the previous relationship denotes that since the first event implies the other the probability of the intersection must be the probability of the smaller event. Then using the definition of conditional probability, we obtain $S(t) = pr(T > t) = pr(T > t | T > t_{(i-1)}) pr(T > t_{(i-1)})$.

Let $q_j = pr(T > t_{(j)} | T > t_{(j-1)})$. The same argument as above can be applied to obtain $pr(T > t_{(i-1)}) = pr(T > t_{(i-1)} | T > t_{(i-2)}) pr(T > t_{(j-1)})$. Then with $q_1 = pr(T > t_{(t)})$ and applying this same argument repeatedly, we obtain $S(t) = \prod_{j=1}^{i} q_j$.

The next step is to estimate q_i, the probability of surviving or having no mobility intentions within the time period. Thus, $1 - q_i$ would be the probability of mobility intentions within the interval $(t_{(j-1)}, t_{(j)})$. Note that $(1 - q_j) = pr(t_{(j-1)} < T \leq t_{(j)} | T > t_{(j)})$. The number of individuals known to have mobility intentions in this interval is denoted by d_j. If the width of this interval were narrow, then the approximate number of individuals available to have mobility intentions would be about n_j. So under this assumption, the natural estimate is $(1 - \hat{q}_j) = d_j/n_j$. Another way to think about this is that the proportion of individuals in the sample possessing mobility intentions is a small neighborhood just before and including $t_{(i)}$ is d_j/n_j. The proportion showing mobility intentions after $t_{(j-1)}$ and before this small neighborhood is zero.

Now that the estimate $\hat{q}_j = 1 - d_j/n_j$ is known, the Kaplan-Meier (KM) estimate of the survivor function for $t = t_{(i)}$ is $\hat{S}_{KM}(t) = \prod_{j=1}^{i} \hat{q}_j = \prod_{j=1}^{i} 1 - d_j/n_j$. The general KM estimator is defined to be the same as this definition at the failure, such that it does not decrease between adjacent failure times, and will not decrease after the last failure if there are censored observations after it. Thus the curve only jumps at failure times, is constant in-between, and will drop to zero at the last failure time if there is no censoring after it, and will not if there are censored observations after it. This estimate is called the product-limit estimator where the limit is determined by the value t that is considered.

Using this information the nonparametric estimation of the cumulative hazard and hazard function can be performed. The natural estimate of the cumulative hazard function is $\hat{H}_{KM}(t) = -\ln(\hat{S}_{KM}(t)) = \sum_{i:t(i) \leq t} -\ln(1 - d_i/n_i)$, using our derived formula for the KM estimator above. Using a Taylor approximation, $-\ln(1 - d_i/n_i) d_i/n_i$ can be obtained. Integrating this function from zero to t provides a function that is calculated as the number of individuals who have mobility intentions in the given interval divided by the approximate number of persons available to have mobility intentions during that interval, and is typically referred to as an incidence density.

THE HAZARD OF LEAVING AN INSTITUTION

The Kaplan-Meier estimates provide hazard rates used to construct hazard curves. Using these curves it is easy to note which group demonstrates higher hazards of leaving for each reason for departure.

Figure 1 illustrates the empirical hazards of departure as a function of years at an institution (a faculty member's job seniority). The likelihood of departure for both men and women declines as seniority increases. Women are more likely to leave the institution than men are, with women twice as likely to leave the institution during the first five years. The difference narrows as seniority increases until approximately twenty years with the institution when male hazards begin to rise and become slightly higher than female hazards. This finding is consistent with Viscusi (1980) and Sicherman (1996) who find that women have a higher quit rate initially, but the difference between men and women narrows with seniority.

While these results are interesting, the following sections examine whether these gender differences exist across the reasons for mobility, and remain when controlling for variables commonly found to influence mobility decisions.

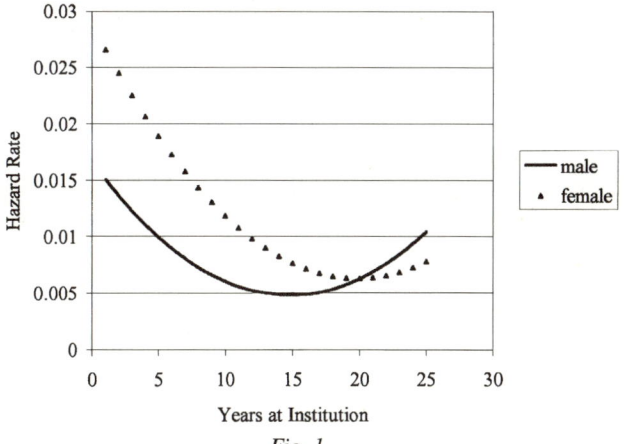

Fig. 1.

FACTORS ASSOCIATED WITH INTENDED MOBILITY

An important question in this paper is whether worker and job characteristics affect the likelihood of accepting a new position differently depending on the reason for mobility. Below we discuss the variables and their expected influence on mobility intentions.

The categorical variable "*if have children*" indicates the presence of children in the household.[3] The presence of dependents increases the total cost of the move, thereby decreasing the probability of mobility over most reasons. Many studies find workers with more children, especially of school age, exhibit lower turnover (e.g. Polachek & Horvath, 1977; Taki & Tachibanki, 1995). Sicherman (1996) finds that children reduce the hazard of quitting across all reasons, with the marginal effect of children on departure greater (in magnitude) for men than women. Among the fourteen reasons for mobility, a faculty member with children is likely to consider the availability and quality of schools for their children when contemplating their mobility decision. Thus, while the presence of children is expected to reduce mobility in most cases, children have a positive effect on mobility when schools for children are important to the mobility decision.

"*Married*" individuals are expected to have a lower probability of mobility across most reasons. For example, Jacobsen and Levin (1997) conclude that married individuals display less mobility reflecting their status of tied-stayers. This finding can be partially attributed to the household costs to mobility that must be included in the decision-making process (Freedman & Kern, 1997). The one exception is likely to be intended mobility with a job for spouse being an important reason. While thirty-percent of single individuals who intend to change jobs report a job for spouse affects the decision to accept a new job, we anticipate married individuals exhibit greater mobility intentions when job for spouse is reported as important.

The "*age of the faculty member*" influences intended mobility with younger faculty expected to exhibit greater mobility. Many studies look at the influence of age on mobility patterns. For instance, Mathieu and Zajac (1990) find that organizational commitment increases with a worker's age, which in turn decreases turnover. The authors note the limited alternative opportunities and greater sunk costs as reasons for lower turnover. Smart (1990) reports similar results when looking at intentions to leave. Weiler (1991) finds older faculty are less likely to search for a new job or move as a result of search. We expect the effect of age to vary across the reasons for departure. Younger individuals are more likely to change jobs due to monetary reasons, particularly in order to gain tenured positions. Older individuals are expected to consider non-monetary reasons such as geographic location important to accepting a new job.

Seniority represents the number of months the faculty member has been with his or her current institution. Standard human capital theory predicts that a stronger attachment between the worker and firm results from a greater investment in firm specific human capital. Time with the firm, holding time in the labor market constant, is an indirect measure of investment in firm specific human capital, therefore a negative correlation between tenure and the hazard of departure is expected. Most studies find the hazard of quitting decreases with seniority (Blau & Kahn, 1981a; Sicherman, 1996; Viscusi, 1980). Meitzen (1986) provides an exception by finding the probability of women quitting increases with seniority among recently hired, low-skilled workers.

White is a categorical variable that indicates the faculty member's race is white. This variable is included to capture racial differences in mobility possibly due to discrimination at the current institution. If minorities have greater difficulty becoming tenured at the institution, they may change jobs in order to gain advancement. Sicherman (1996) finds that white men have a lower hazard of departure from a firm across the majority of reasons, while the results are mixed for women. For example, non-white women are more likely to depart due to poor health (both personal and family), dismissal, or to return to school. White women are more likely to depart for higher earnings, to work nearer home, in a more interesting job, or due to household duties.

Faculty rank is measured by two categorical variables denoting the *ranks of full* and *associate professor*. These variables capture the different amenities (e.g. tenure, benefits, research opportunities), available to faculty members of different rank. It is expected that if a faculty member does not possess, but desires a particular amenity, the probability of mobility due to that reason is higher. For example, Brown and Woodbury (1995) find higher female separation rates are explained by differences in male and female ranks, with female faculty having higher turnover rates because a greater percentage hold low rank positions. Among our reasons for mobility, assistant professors are expected to change jobs relative to full professors to achieve tenure, job security, improve their opportunities for advancement and reduce the pressure to publish.

Carnegie classification categorical variables capture differences in the research and teaching emphasis across institutions. Institutions with Carnegie classifications of research or doctoral are considered research-oriented institutions, while comprehensive and liberal arts schools are considered teaching oriented. Ehrenberg, Kasper and Rees (1991) find higher turnover rates among assistant professors at research schools compared to two-year and four-year undergraduate institutions. This finding is associated with the difficulties lower rank faculty have obtaining tenure at research institutions relative to teaching institutions. Retention rates are also lower for females than for males at comprehensive, four-year, and two-year institutions but not doctoral institutions. A priori predictions are difficult to make for these variables. Research facilities and opportunities may be very important for faculty at research institutions when considering a new position. On the other hand, faculty at research institutions may plan to seek a position with less publishing pressure.

RESULTS

Variable Means

Table 2 contains means for the fourteen departure reasons and the independent variables. Women report greater intentions to leave the institution within the next three years. Since we only examine the departure reasons for those who report intended mobility, a greater proportion of women than men report each reason as being important to the mobility decision.

Female faculty are less likely to have children in the household or be married than male faculty. Seventy-seven percent of male faculty have children compared to 49% of women. Eighty-four percent of male faculty are married, while 58% of female faculty are married. Women have been with their respective institutions for shorter periods of time (13.5 years vs. 9.7 years) and hold lower ranks than their male colleagues. Forty-eight percent of men are full professors, compared to only 22% of women. Such differences partly reflect the large increase in the proportion of female faculty in recent decades. Women are also less likely to be employed at research institutions with 53% of men at Research or Doctoral institutions compared to 39% of women.

Cox Proportional Hazard Results

The Cox Proportional Hazard model is used to examine how the variables affect the likelihood of changing jobs with the specific reason reported as important to the decision. The Cox Proportional Hazard Model is a popular mechanism for this type of analysis since the model results are analyzed in a manner similar to a linear regression.

Separate estimations are performed for each departure reason using the Cox Proportional Hazard model. Failure occurs if the individual intends to change jobs and lists the reason as important to the decision. The hazard model examines the risk of failure relative to individuals not reporting mobility intentions or not

Table 2. Variable Means.

	Total	Male	Female
Reasons for intention to leave			
Salary level	0.074	0.068	0.090
Tenure position	0.074	0.065	0.096
Job security	0.083	0.073	0.107
Opportunity for advancement	0.082	0.071	0.109
Benefits	0.080	0.072	0.101
No publication pressure	0.026	0.022	0.036
Research facilities	0.067	0.060	0.083
Teaching facilities	0.072	0.064	0.094
Job for spouse	0.059	0.053	0.075
Geographic location	0.076	0.071	0.090
School for children	0.064	0.063	0.067
Teaching opportunity	0.033	0.030	0.039
Research opportunity	0.054	0.048	0.068
Administrative opportunity	0.016	0.014	0.021
Intention to leave in next 3 years	0.120	0.110	0.150
Independent variables			
If have children	0.690	0.770	0.490
Male	0.710	–	–
Married	0.760	0.840	0.580
Age	36.579	36.277	37.319
Seniority	148.940	162.510	115.790
White	0.850	0.860	0.850
Rank of full professor	0.407	0.483	0.220
Rank of associate professor	0.312	0.301	0.339
Research institution	0.299	0.331	0.221
Doctoral institution	0.187	0.193	0.173
Liberal arts institution	0.406	0.382	0.466
Number of observations	9124	6096	3028

Notes: White is a dummy variable equaling one if the faculty member is white. Rank of assistant professor and comprehensive institution are the omitted dummy variables. Seniority is measured as months at the institution. Reasons are coded one if the faculty member answered affirmatively to very likely to move and very important reason in mobility decision.

reporting the reason as important to the decision. Table 3 provides the results for each departure reason segmenting the sample by gender.

Male faculty are more likely to change jobs when children are in the household while female faculty are less likely to change jobs. The one exception for women is when schools for children are important to the departure decision with the presence

Table 3. The Hazard Departure from an Institution. Cox Regression Results.

	Male Sample		Female Sample		Male Sample		Female Sample	
	B	Std. Error	B	Std. Error	B	Std. Error	B	Std. Error
	Reason: Salary Level		Reason: Salary Level		Reason: Tenure Position		Reason: Tenure Position	
If have children	0.4977	0.102*	0.1047	0.100	0.3353	0.101*	−0.0577	0.098
Married	−0.3986	0.100*	−0.2891	0.101*	−0.3680	0.101*	−0.3039	0.098*
Age	0.5203	0.357	−0.5984	0.241*	0.9332	0.418*	−1.1301	0.233*
Age squared	−0.0770	0.044**	0.0620	0.026*	−0.1576	0.054*	0.1034	0.026*
Seniority	−0.5565	0.058*	−0.5993	0.135*	−0.6845	0.102*	−0.5559	0.119*
Seniority squared	0.0004	0.0002*	0.0004	0.071	0.0005	0.003*	0.0003	0.010
White	−0.4209	0.081*	−0.5727	0.107*	−0.5105	0.081*	−0.4161	0.107*
Rank of full professor	−0.7536	0.114*	−0.6781	0.197*	−0.5509	0.119*	−0.6346	0.192*
Rank of associate professor	−0.4806	0.096*	0.1274	0.114	−0.4321	0.099*	−0.1201	0.117
Research institution	−0.2520	0.121*	0.2258	0.173	−0.1629	0.123	0.5752	0.174*
Doctoral institution	−0.1752	0.129	0.3548	0.174*	−0.2291	0.134**	0.5575	0.179*
Liberal arts institution	−0.1791	0.119	0.2236	0.157	−0.1858	0.122	0.3900	0.165*
N	6096		3028		6096		3028	
Log-likelihood	−10613.0		−5238.2		−10117.3		−5632.0	
Number of events	415		273		396		291	
	Reason: Job Security		Reason: Job Security		Reason: Opp. Advancement		Reason: Opp. Advancement	
If have children	0.2561	0.094*	−0.0155	0.092	0.3188	0.097*	−0.0709	0.092
Married	−0.2612	0.097*	−0.3769	0.093*	−0.2449	0.098*	−0.2811	0.092*
Age	0.0986	0.345	−0.9074	0.228*	−0.1923	0.334	−0.7625	0.270*
Age squared	−0.0395	0.043	0.0811	0.026*	−0.0078	0.042	0.0602	0.032**
Seniority	−0.6786	0.091*	−0.5670	0.118*	−0.6666	0.087*	−0.7161	0.156*
Seniority squared	0.00003	0.00001*	0.00003	0.00009	0.00002	0.00000*	0.00000	0.00004
White	−0.4595	0.077*	−0.4955	0.100*	−0.5109	0.077*	−0.5391	0.098*
Rank of full professor	−0.6565	0.112*	−0.6976	0.183*	−0.6425	0.115*	−0.9908	0.197*
Rank of associate professor	−0.4044	0.093*	−0.1367	0.109	−0.3090	0.093*	−0.3181	0.111*
Research institution	−0.2583	0.115*	0.2508	0.154	0.0182	0.124	0.2075	0.147
Doctoral institution	−0.2876	0.125*	0.2733	0.158**	−0.1552	0.136	0.1298	0.154
Liberal arts institution	−0.2246	0.113*	0.1740	0.143	0.0198	0.123	0.0675	0.137
N	6096		3028		6096		3028	
Log-likelihood	−1413.6		−6252.2		−1145.3		−6382.5	
Number of events	445		324		433		330	

Gender Differences in Reasons for Job Mobility Intentions

	Reason: Benefits	Reason: Benefits	Reason: No Pub Pressure	Reason: No Pub Pressure
If have children	0.2993	0.095*	0.1973	0.170
Married	-0.2612	0.098*	-0.0079	0.187
Age	0.4631	0.337	0.0375	0.546
Age squared	-0.0642	0.042	0.0182	0.066
Seniority	-0.6873	0.095*	-0.5425	0.161*
Seniority squared	0.0005	*	0.0003	
White	-0.4902	0.077*	-0.3347	0.146*
Rank of full professor	-0.7762	0.110*	-1.3310	0.202*
Rank of associate professor	-0.4736	0.093*	-0.3403	0.161*
Research institution	-0.1643	0.117	-0.4673	0.213*
Doctoral institution	-0.2792	0.129*	-0.4625	0.233*
Liberal arts institution	-0.1692	0.115	-0.1311	0.199
N	6096		6096	
Log-likelihood	-11292.84		-4850.032	
Number of events	439		134	

	Reason: Research Facilities	Reason: Research Facilities	Reason: Teaching Facilities	Reason: Teaching Facilities
If have children	0.1418	0.102	0.2387	0.100*
Married	-0.2210	0.106*	-0.2388	0.104*
Age	-0.3787	0.345	-0.5325	0.310**
Age squared	-0.0018	0.044	0.0507	0.038
Seniority	-0.6908	0.102*	-0.5955	0.068*
Seniority squared	0.0005	*	0.0005	*
White	-0.5000	0.084*	-0.4678	0.083*
Rank of full professor	-0.4585	0.124*	-0.6312	0.116*
Rank of associate professor	-0.04926	0.106*	-0.4345	0.101*
Research institution	0.0621	0.138	-0.3262	0.122*
Doctoral institution	0.1000	0.146	-0.3631	0.134*
Liberal arts institution	-0.0254	0.138	-0.1992	0.118**
N	6096		6096	
Log-likelihood	-9429.749		-9931.208	
Number of events	366		390	

	Reason: Benefits	Reason: Benefits	Reason: No Pub Pressure	Reason: No Pub Pressure
If have children	0.0361	0.094	0.0765	0.159
Married	-0.3896	0.095*	-0.3173	0.159*
Age	-0.5419	0.247*	-0.3726	0.391
Age squared	0.0549	0.027*	0.0390	0.044
Seniority	-0.6257	0.103*	-0.6779	0.213*
Seniority squared	0.0005	*	0.0006	*
White	-0.4923	0.102*	-0.8399	0.163*
Rank of full professor	-0.7357	0.178*	-1.4738	0.311*
Rank of associate professor	-0.2094	0.111**	-0.6696	0.192*
Research institution	0.2120	0.162	-0.3753	0.254
Doctoral institution	0.2873	0.164**	-0.3524	0.263
Liberal arts institution	0.2548	0.146**	-0.1850	0.214
N	3028		3028	
Log-likelihood	-5912.332		-1987.76	
Number of events	309		109	

	Reason: Research Facilities	Reason: Research Facilities	Reason: Teaching Facilities	Reason: Teaching Facilities
If have children	-0.1367	0.105	-0.0989	0.098
Married	-0.4164	0.105*	-0.2722	0.099*
Age	-0.8902	0.244*	-0.8476	0.227*
Age squared	0.0842	0.027	0.0819	0.025*
Seniority	-0.5958	0.138*	-0.6238	0.111*
Seniority squared	0.0004		0.0005	*
White	-0.6450	0.109*	-0.5276	0.106*
Rank of full professor	-0.8153	0.211*	-0.9283	0.194*
Rank of associate professor	-0.2369	0.127**	-0.3685	0.120*
Research institution	0.7227	0.194*	0.1311	0.173
Doctoral institution	0.6830	0.198*	0.3577	0.172*
Liberal arts institution	0.4151	0.186*	0.2893	0.155**
N	3028		3028	
Log-likelihood	-4855.501		-5457.938	
Number of events	251		285	

Table 3. (Continued)

	Male Sample		Female Sample		Male Sample		Female Sample	
	B	Std. Error	B	Std. Error	B	Std. Error	B	Std. Error
	Reason: Job for Spouse		Reason: Job for Spouse		Reason: Geo. Location		Reason: Geo. Location	
If have children	0.1088	0.1094	−0.2186	0.109*	0.0313	0.091	−0.2665	0.101*
Married	0.2833	0.1260*	0.4903	0.118*	−0.1515	0.098	−0.1320	0.101
Age	−0.4208	0.3458	−1.2598	0.330*	−0.1722	0.302	−0.8684	0.244*
Age squared	0.0227	0.0433	0.1042	0.039*	0.0100	0.037	0.0814	0.028*
Seniority	−0.6868	0.1064*	−0.7204	0.192*	−0.7103	0.095*	−0.6335	0.116*
Seniority squared	0.0006	0.0001*	0.0006	*	0.0006	*	0.0005	*
White	−0.6731	0.0868*	−0.4083	0.121*	−0.3982	0.080*	−0.5065	0.110*
Rank of full professor	−0.6644	0.1335*	−0.6978	0.220*	−0.4413	0.110*	−0.7857	0.193*
Rank of associate professor	−0.2446	0.1070*	−0.3503	0.138*	−0.2979	0.096*	−0.2518	0.120*
Research institution	−0.1474	0.1344	0.2818	0.179	−0.0347	0.129	0.0187	0.163
Doctoral institution	−0.4022	0.1514*	0.2356	0.189	0.1140	0.135	0.0924	0.167
Liberal arts institution	−0.2092	0.1338	0.0932	0.171	0.0642	0.126	0.0556	0.147
N	6096		3028		6096		3028	
Log-likelihood	−8274.626		−4380.172		−11168.84		−5230.007	
Number of events	323		227		433		273	
	Reason: School for Kids		Reason: School for Kids		Reason: Teaching Opportunity		Reason: Teaching Opportunity	
If have children	0.4858	0.113*	0.5460	0.122*	0.0660	0.140	0.0373	0.151
Married	0.3591	0.128*	−0.0757	0.121	0.0004	0.154	−0.3928	0.153*
Age	−0.8426	0.325*	−1.6892	0.316*	0.2357	0.461	−0.2328	0.377
Age squared	0.0647	0.041*	0.1364	0.037*	−0.0083	0.056	0.0129	0.046
Seniority	−0.6068	0.080*	−0.7304	0.207*	−0.6559	0.114*	−0.5473	0.137*
Seniority squared	0.0005		0.0006	*	0.0005	*	0.0004	*
White	−0.4606	0.082*	−0.5627	0.123*	−0.6885	0.116*	−0.7653	0.157*
Rank of full professor	−0.9055	0.124*	−0.4669	0.223*	−1.1614	0.168*	−1.2054	0.287*
Rank of associate professor	−0.5784	0.101*	−0.3244	0.148*	−0.5156	0.142*	−0.6980	0.186*
Research institution	−0.1995	0.126	0.3063	0.207	−0.5144	0.179*	−0.3250	0.312
Doctoral institution	−0.1548	0.134	0.3459	0.212	−0.4112	0.192*	0.4946	0.277**
Liberal arts institution	−0.1836	0.124	0.4529	0.190*	−0.2284	0.168	0.5543	0.249*
N	6096		3028		6096		3028	
Log-likelihood	−9779.632		−3808.002		−588.228		−2176.353	
Number of events	384		203		183		118	

	Reason: Research Opportunity	Reason: Research Opportunity	Reason: Admin. Opportunity	Reason: Admin. Opportunit
If have children	0.0559 0.111	−0.2590 0.117*	0.3490 0.225	−0.1169 0.208
Married	−0.2976 0.114*	−0.3959 0.117*	−0.0858 0.230	−0.3483 0.207**
Age	0.7842 0.450**	−0.9047 0.297*	0.7299 0.726	0.8084 0.697
Age squared	−0.1451 0.058*	0.0823 0.033*	−0.0612 0.085	−0.0641 0.078
Seniority	−0.6089 0.076*	−0.4976 0.129*	−0.7171 0.209*	−0.7355 0.0362*
Seniority squared	0.0005 0.0001*	0.0000 0.0006	0.0006 0.0002*	0.0007 0.0003*
White	−0.7857 0.089*	−0.4232 0.127*	−0.9435 0.162*	−0.6361 0.223*
Rank of full professor	−0.2918 0.136*	−0.6599 0.230*	0.3347 0.262	−0.2679 0.339
Rank of associate professor	−0.5328 0.121*	−0.2238 0.141	0.8961 0.230*	0.0063 0.233
Research institution	0.0696 0.163	0.3204 0.203	0.3717 0.413	−0.2432 0.327
Doctoral institution	0.2158 0.170	0.4753 0.203*	1.0015 0.411*	−0.5420 0.367
Liberal arts institution	0.1691 0.160	0.2962 0.186	1.0640 0.394*	−0.1301
N	6096	3028	6096	3028
Log-likelihood	−7483.181	−4008.117	−2068.375	−1196.922
Number of events	293	206	85	64

Notes: If have children, married, white, rank of full and associate professor, and research, doctoral, and liberal arts institutions are dummy variables equalling one if the respective category can be answered in the affirmative. Senioriyt is the number of months at the institution. Age is measured in (age/10) units.

*Significant at 5% level.
**Significant at 10% level.

of children increasing the likelihood of a job change. This result provides some evidence that people may "vote with their feet" by changing jobs for local amenities such as schools.

Married individuals have a lower hazard of mobility for monetary reasons, (salary, tenure, job security, opportunity for advancement, and benefits), but a greater hazard of leaving for non-monetary reasons (job for spouse and school for kids). Such results suggest that family considerations are important to the mobility decision. The negative relationship for monetary reasons indicates that faculty members are tied-stayers, while the positive relationship for non-monetary reasons indicates the spouse and children are important to the mobility decision. When spousal employment is important to the mobility decision, the marginal effect of being married is considerably larger for women than men, once again implying that the husband finding a job is more important to a woman than a wife's employment is to a man.

Seniority reduces the likelihood of mobility across all reasons. One gender cannot be pinpointed as to which has the stronger negative effect since the marginal effects are similar across all reasons for mobility. White faculty have a lower hazard of leaving their current institution for each departure reason. Such a result suggests that minorities feel it is necessary to change institutions in order to gain promotions, higher salary, and a desired balance between teaching and research.

Full and associate professors are less likely than assistant professors to intend to change jobs. Several differences across departure reasons are worth noting. Full professors are much less likely to change jobs for teaching opportunities or a lack of publishing pressure. Among women, full professors are much less likely to move for teaching facilities. Of course, an alternative interpretation is that assistant professors are more likely than full professors to accept a new job because of teaching opportunities and facilities, and a lack of publishing pressure.

Finally, men have a lower likelihood of leaving research institutions than teaching oriented Comprehensive institutions. In contrast, women have a greater likelihood of departure from research institutions. The one exception is administrative opportunity for men where the coefficient is positive and significant for Doctoral and Liberal Arts institutions. Men at research institutions are less likely to change jobs for teaching facilities and opportunities, or a lack of publishing pressure. Women at research institutions are more likely to change jobs due to research facilities. Overall, individuals at teaching institutions consider teaching related issues to be important in accepting a new job, while individuals at research institutions consider research issues to be important in accepting a new job.

Kaplan-Meier Results

Three figures examine gender differences by reason for departure using the results from Table 3. Figure 2 includes male and female hazard rates for the monetary

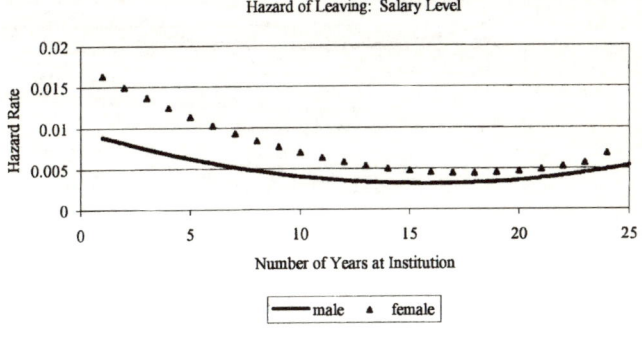

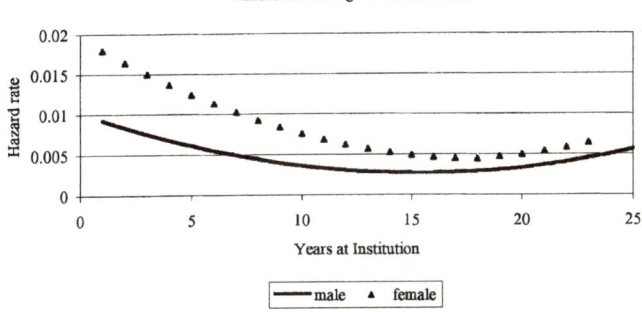

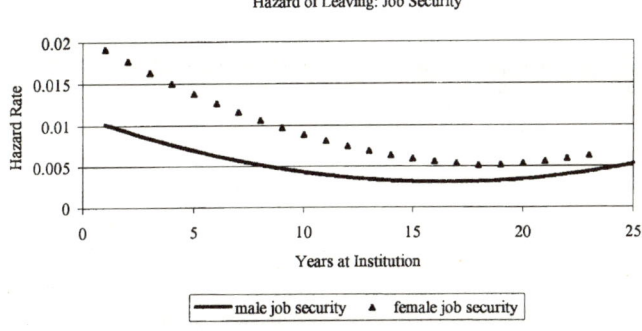

Fig. 2.

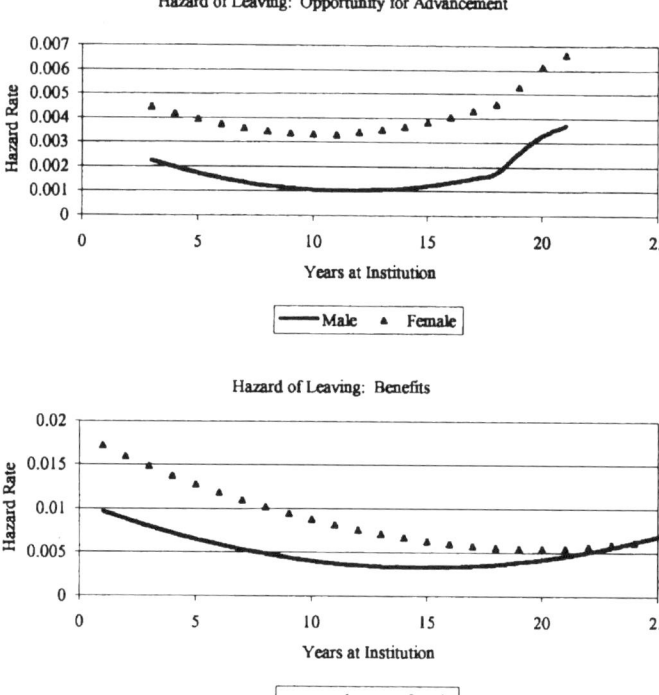

Fig. 2. (*Continued*)

reasons for departure. Similarities exist in shapes and magnitudes among all reasons with the likelihood of departure relatively high at a low level of seniority and declining as seniority increases. Female hazard rates are higher than males at low seniority levels, but converge with seniority. One exception is opportunity for advancement where intended departure is much lower compared to the other reasons, and increases after the fifteenth year at the institution with little noticeable convergence.

Figure 3 contains the hazard rates for non-monetary departure reasons. Once again female hazard rates are greater than males. The hazard of departure due to three of the reasons, research and instructional facilities, and job for spouse, is higher at low seniority and declines as seniority increases. Once again female mobility intentions decline more rapidly than males, with the likelihood of departure converging with seniority. Geographic location, school for kids, and no publishing pressure show less variability throughout a faculty member's seniority except at the extreme beginning and end of the faculty's employment. The hazard rates for geographic location and school for kids are small in magnitude

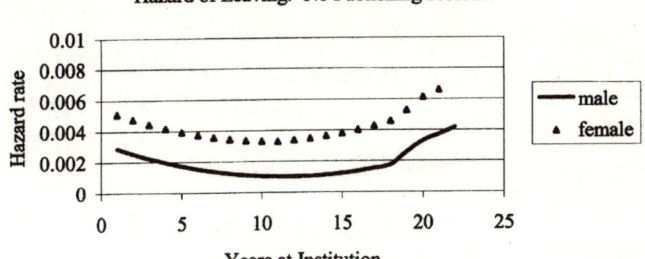

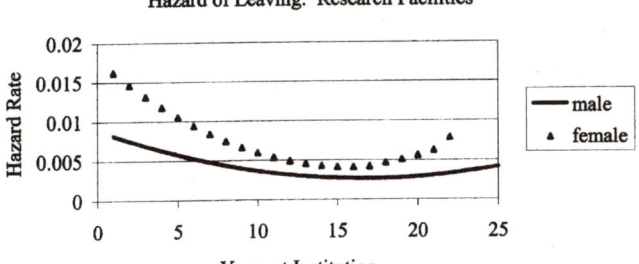

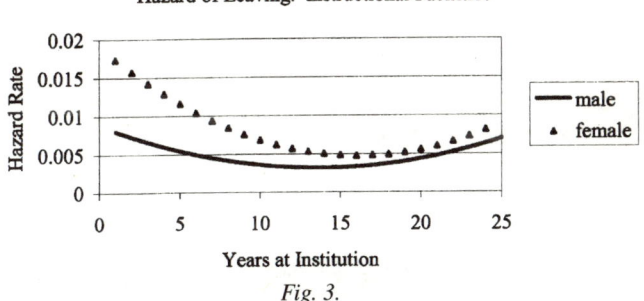

Fig. 3.

regardless of time at the institution. No publishing pressure begins with a small hazard rate, but increases to a magnitude similar to departure due to research and instructional facilities during a faculty member's later years with an institution. These hazards do not converge nor continuously decrease, with the female likelihood of departure remaining larger than males.

Figure 4 illustrates the hazard rates for research, teaching, and administrative opportunities. Departure for a research opportunity is more frequent at low levels of seniority and decreases with seniority. Most institutions have lower research

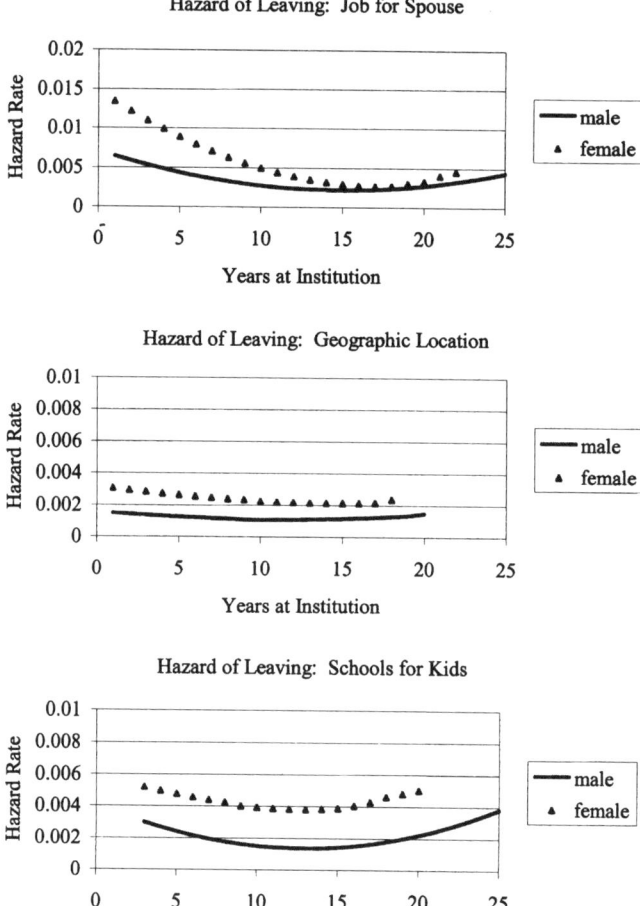

Fig. 3. (Continued)

expectations for tenured faculty, reducing the need to seek out positions with research opportunities. The likelihood of leaving for a teaching opportunity is highest for males and females in the early and later years at the institution with females showing higher turnover over all years. The hazard of leaving for a research opportunity is greater than teaching or administrative opportunities until approximately ten years seniority (i.e. once almost all faculty are tenured) when the magnitudes become similar. Finally, intended mobility for an administrative

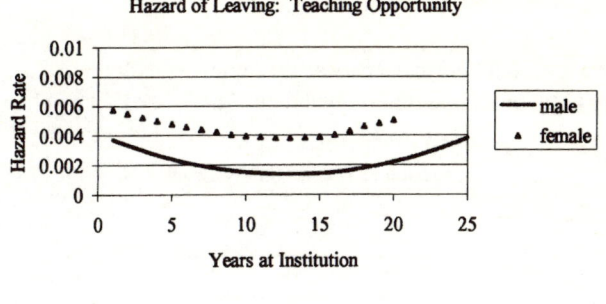

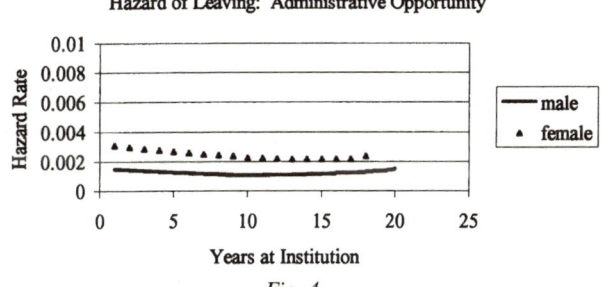

Fig. 4.

opportunity has the lowest magnitude than any of the fourteen reasons. Departure for an administrative opportunity shows less variation over time at the institution, but the female hazard rate remains higher across all years.

Gender differences in departure reasons vary based on factors such as whether faculty are tenured versus tenure track, married versus single, in research versus teaching institutions, or between those with and without children. Below we consider two of these factors in more detail: marital status and tenure status. See VanGilder (1999) for comparisons between teaching and research institutions.

Marital Status

Male faculty are more likely to be married than female faculty, and one might expect married men to be more market oriented than single men, but single women to be

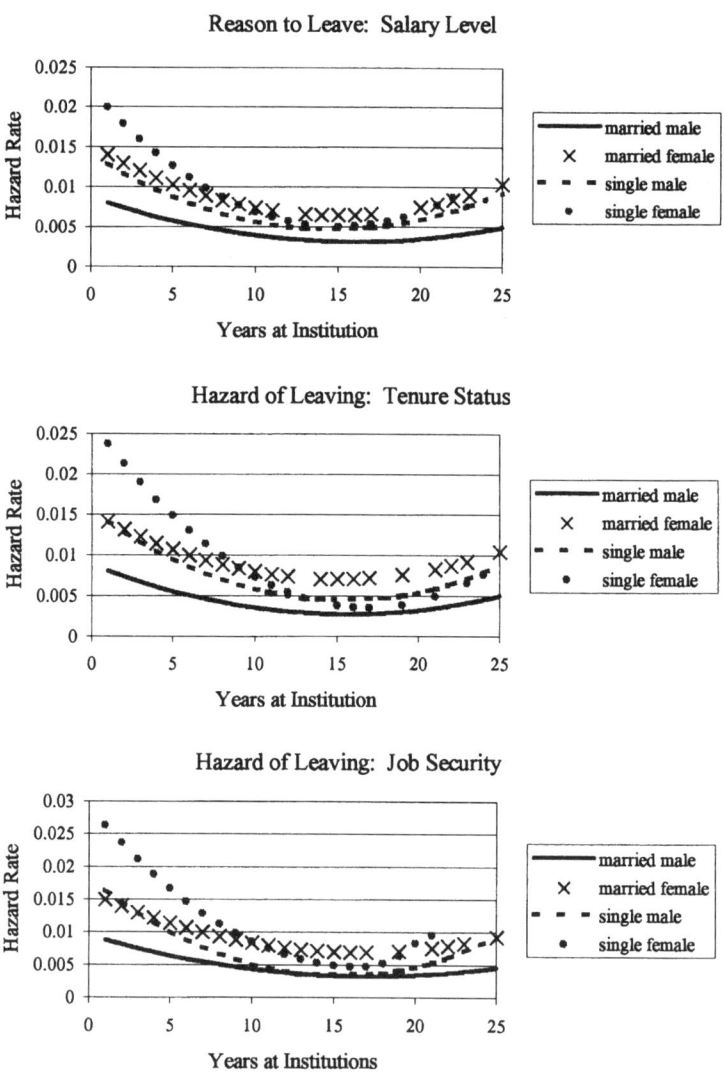

Fig. 5.

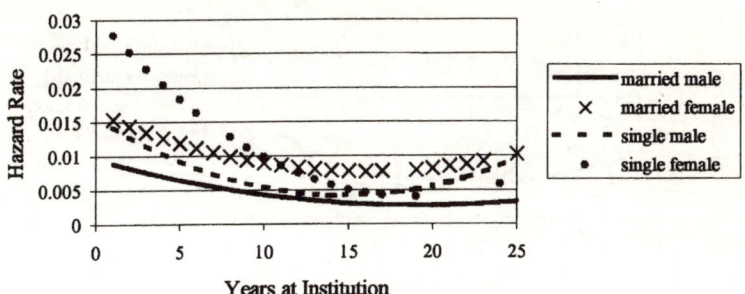

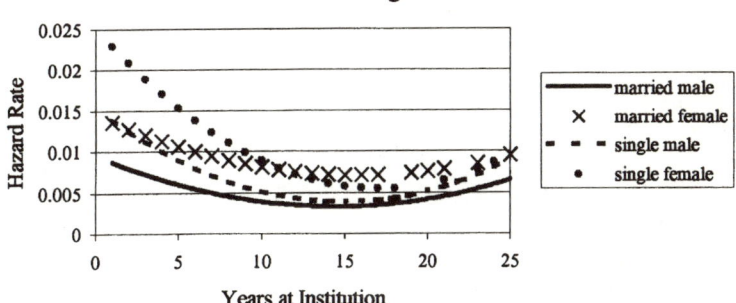

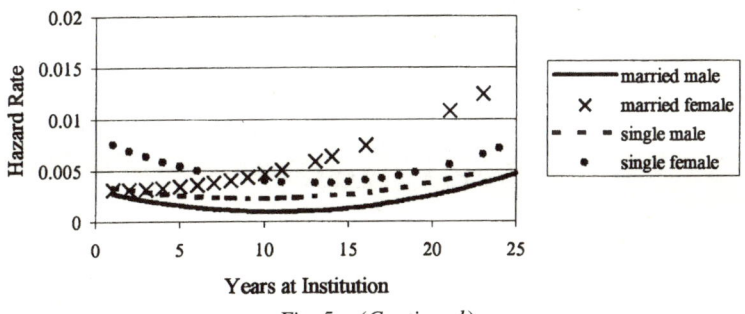

Fig. 5. (*Continued*)

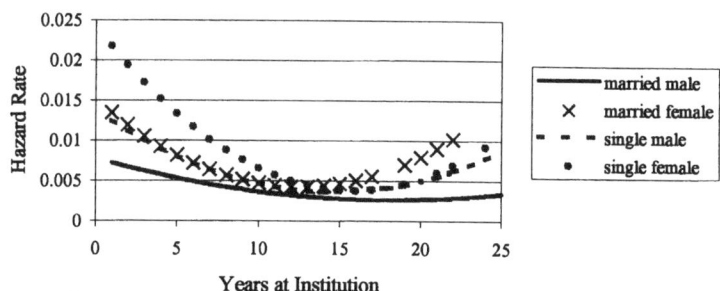

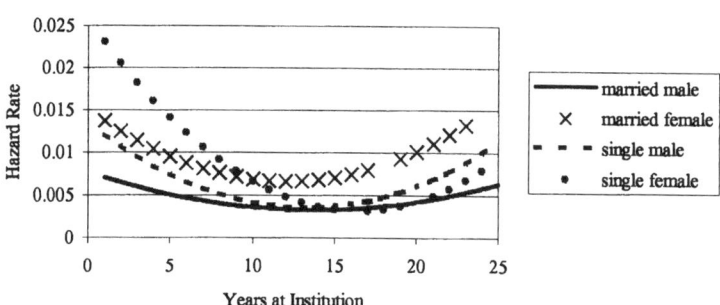

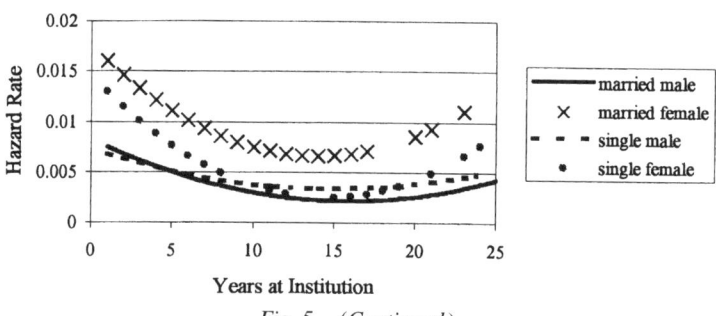

Fig. 5. (*Continued*)

more market oriented than married women. Hazard rates are provided in Fig. 5 for married and single male and female faculty.

Several findings are of interest. First, among the monetary reasons for mobility, single female faculty have the highest hazard rate for approximately the first eight years at the institution. Single women typically have greater mobility than married

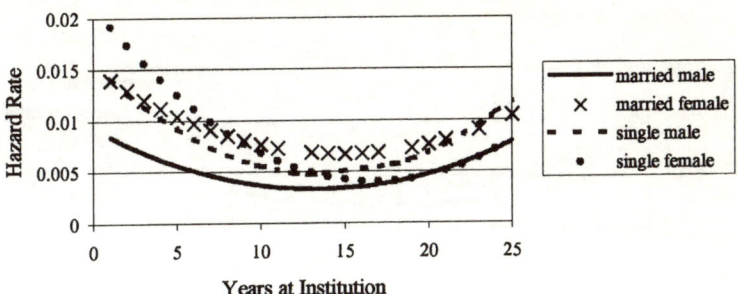

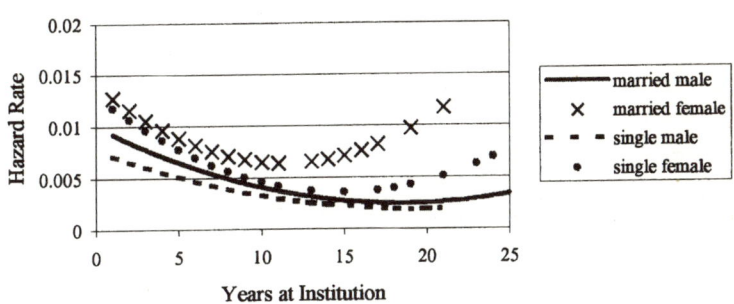

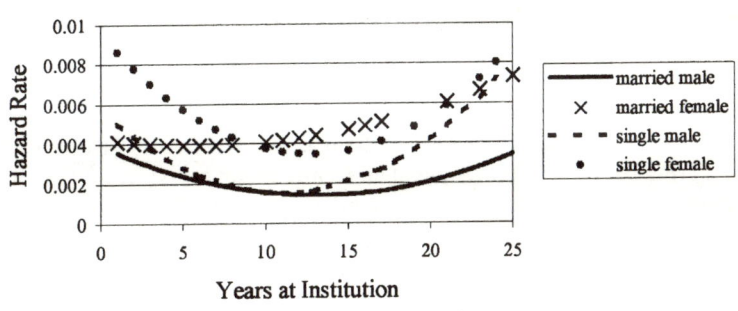

Fig. 5. (Continued)

women across most occupations due to the lower mobility costs incurred by single women. As discussed earlier, single women may have greater mobility than single men if female assistant professors have more difficulty becoming tenured or if women face other forms of discrimination within higher education institutions (Kahn, 1998). Second, married female faculty have the highest hazard rates for

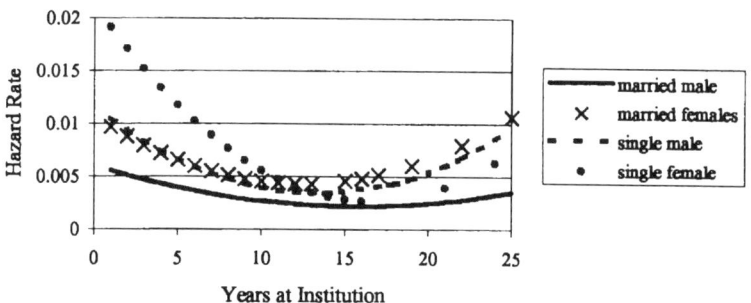
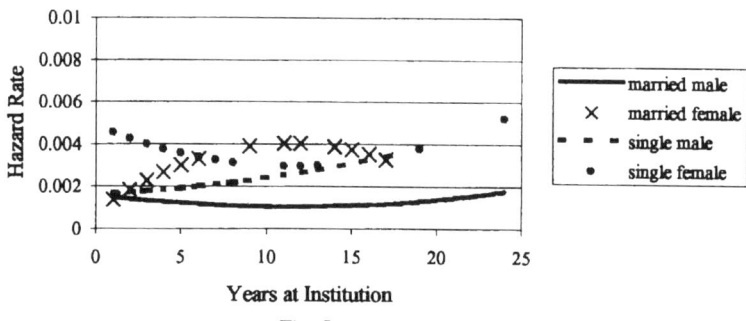

Fig. 5. (*Continued*)

non-monetary reasons such as job for spouse and school for kids. Thus, despite examining a female sample that considers monetary reasons to be important to the mobility decision, married women still consider family considerations to a greater degree than married males. Third, although single female faculty have the highest hazard rates during the early years and married female faculty have the highest during the later years, single male faculty members typically have hazard rates above married male faculty throughout all years at the institution. This result could be due to married males displaying actions of tied workers and therefore exhibiting lower rates of mobility with respect to single male faculty.

Tenure Status

The previous results include faculty rank in the specification, controlling to a large degree for whether the individual is tenured or tenure track. Consistent

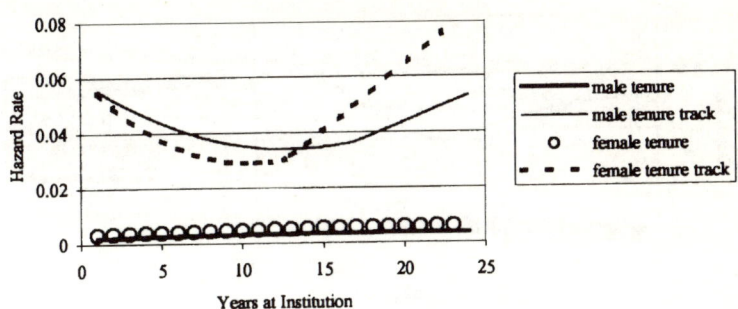
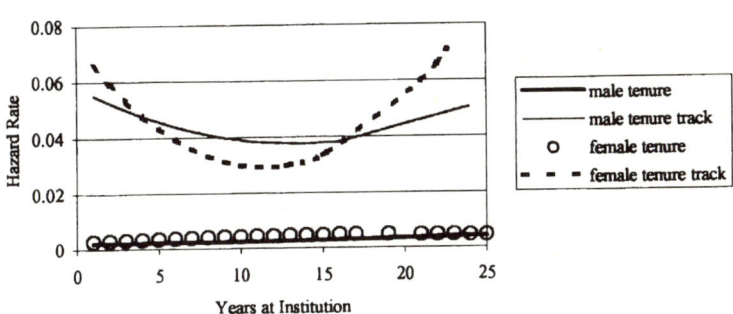
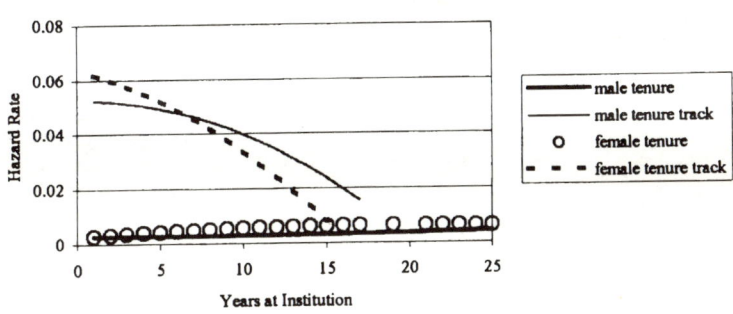

Fig. 6.

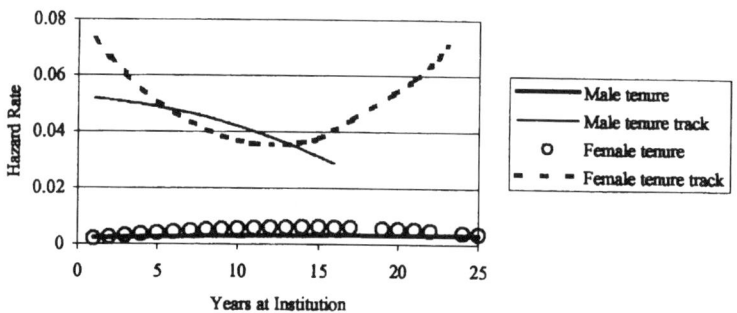
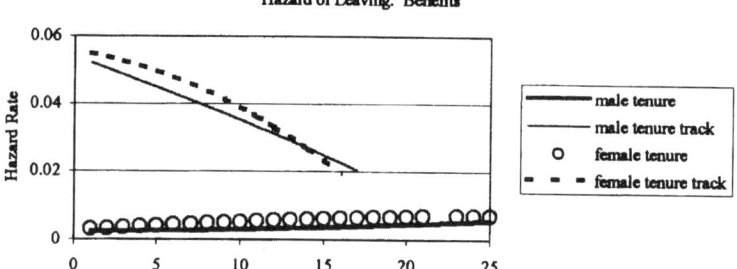
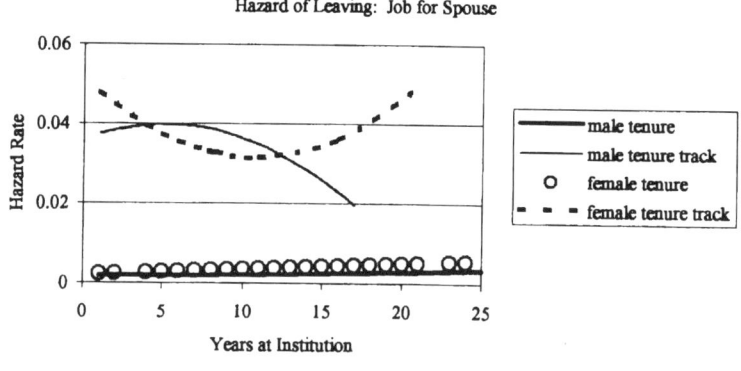

Fig. 6. (*Continued*)

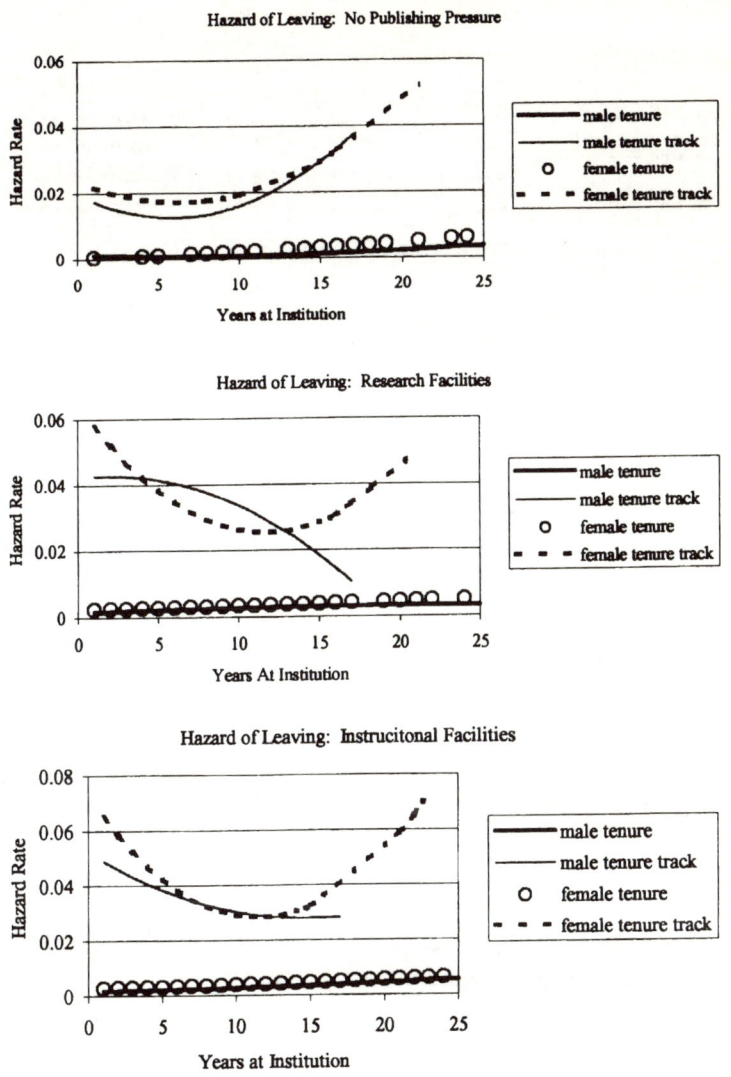

Fig. 6. (Continued)

with expectations, we find that full and associate professors are less mobile than assistant professors across the reasons for departure. Below we consider differences between tenured and tenure track faculty in more detail.

Figure 6 plots the hazard rates for tenured and tenured track faculty as a function of seniority. We focus the discussion of tenure track faculty on the early

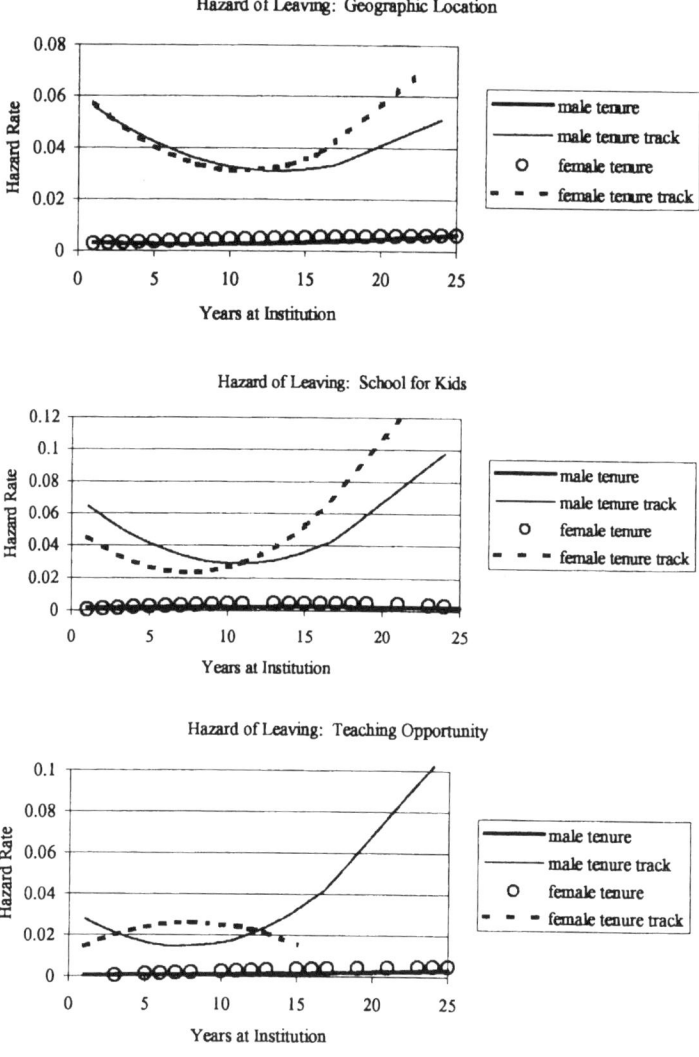

Fig. 6. (*Continued*)

years with an institution since there are relatively few untenured faculty with an institution for 10 or 15 years. Similarly, we focus the discussion of tenured faculty on the later years, since many tenured faculty have been with the institution for many years (although some tenured faculty do change jobs). The most interesting point from these graphs is the similarities between male and female hazard rates

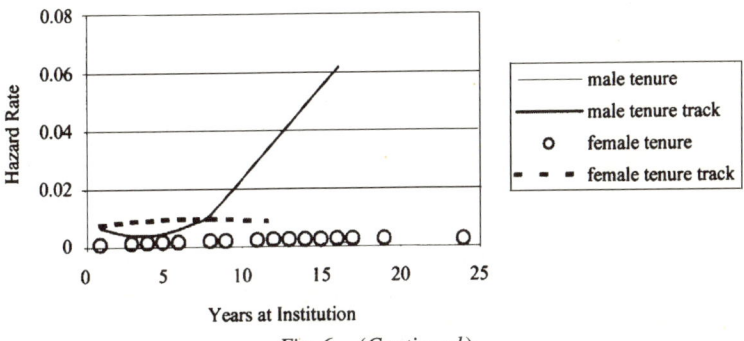

Fig. 6. (Continued)

within tenure groups. For example, across all reasons for departure, male and female tenured faculty report almost identical hazard rates, while male and female tenure track faculty report a much higher hazard of leaving the institution. Focusing on tenured track faculty members it can be seen that for most monetary reasons, on average, females report a slightly higher hazard of leaving at lower levels of job seniority. Hazard rates for non-monetary reasons are similar for male and female tenure track faculty. For example, estimated departure due to the reasons no publishing pressure and geographic location is very similar for men and women.

CONCLUSION

The purpose of this paper was twofold. First, to enumerate motives (reasons) for intended mobility and assess each motive's importance. Second, to investigate gender differences in the frequency and reasons for this intended mobility. Past studies concentrate on who initiates turnover (employer or employee) and on detailed reasons for mobility within specific occupations. This study's innovation is to use the NSOPF data, which provide a wide array of reasons for mobility *intentions* within the academic labor market. These data allow us to examine a different industry and occupation than most prior research.

We find that faculty intentions of leaving an academic post decrease with seniority. Women are twice as likely to move as men during the first few years at the institution, but the differential narrows with seniority. The magnitude of the gender difference varies somewhat depending on the reason for mobility. These results have important policy implications for institutions. Barbezat and Hughes (2001) find women hold more academic jobs than men supporting the finding in this paper that women have greater intended mobility. Colleges and universities wishing to retain female faculty should review policies to ensure there is gender equity in salary and promotion potential. However, institutions are unlikely to eliminate gender differences given that women also are more likely to change jobs due to non-monetary reasons such as spousal employment.

Single female faculty display the highest hazard of leaving over all monetary reasons for departure, while married female faculty display the highest hazard rates over many non-monetary reasons for departure. Single male faculty hazard rates are consistently higher than married male hazard rates, with married male faculty displaying the lowest hazard of leaving over all reasons. Tenure plays an important role in mobility intentions as untenured faculty members have a higher hazard of leaving compared to tenured faculty members. Gender differences across the reasons for mobility are minor once controlling for tenure status.

Future research may further investigate differences in departure between research and teaching institutions. Many research institutions are historically difficult to achieve tenure at, and investigating intended mobility that may be due to being denied tenure would be useful. Clearly faculty may intend mobility because they do not anticipate being granted tenure, and such mobility may result in different factors being important to the decision to accept another job.

NOTES

1. This is a restricted use data set that we cannot share with other researchers. Please contact the NCES for information on data accessibility.
2. Although some questions can be raised about the validity of self-reported data, Bound (1991) finds that self-reported measurements of a worker's health play a much stronger role than the objective measure in the determination of retirement. Bound states that

self-reported data can have several problems. First, these values may not be comparable across respondents, thus underestimating the variable's impact. Secondly, the values may not be independent of the labor market outcomes that are trying to be explained, thus overestimating the variable's impact. Finally, some researchers feel that people respond in a way to rationalize their behavior. Therefore the response is dependent on the economic environment. Bound finds the first and second bias to be the most important. Additionally he notes that the biases are opposite directions, and therefore tend to cancel each other out. Bound concludes that in some cases self-reported data may be superior to an objective measure that may be biased in only one direction.

3. Although it would be preferable to have both number of children and their ages, this information is not available from NSOPF-93.

ACKNOWLEDGMENTS

We thank Stan Masters, Tom Cowing, and Kathy Bratton for helpful discussions. The opinions in this paper are the authors' and do not represent those of the Centers for Medicare & Medicaid Services.

REFERENCES

Ahern, N. (1981). *Career outcomes in a matched sample of men and women Ph.D.'s*. Washington, DC: National Academy Press.

Althauser, R., & Kallegerg, A. (1981). Firms, occupations, and the structure of labor markets: A conceptual analysis. In: I. Berg (Ed.), *Sociological Perspectives on Labor Markets* (pp. 119–149). New York: Academic Press.

Barbezat, D. A., & Hughes, J. W. (2001). The effect of job mobility on academic salaries. *Contemporary Economic Policy*, *19*(4), 409–423.

Barnes, W., & Jones, E. (1974). Differences in male and female quitting. *Journal of Human Resources*, *9*, 439–451.

Bartel, A., & Borjas, G. (1981). Wage growth and job turnover: An empirical analysis. In: S. Rosen (Ed.), *Studies in Labor Markets*. Chicago: University of Chicago Press.

Blau, F., & Kahn, L. (1981a). Race and sex differences in quits by young workers. *Industrial and Labor Relations Review*, *34*(4), 563–577.

Blau, F., & Kahn, L. (1981b). Causes and consequences of layoff. *Economic Inquiry*, *19*(2), 270–295.

Bound, J. (1991). Self-reported versus objective measures of health in retirement models. *Journal of Human Resources*, *26*(1), 106–138.

Brown, D. (1967). *The mobile professors*. Washington, DC: American Council on Education.

Brown, B. W., & Woodbury, S. A. (1995). Gender differences in faculty turnover. Upjohn Institute Staff Working Paper 95-34, 1–10.

Chronister, J. L., Baldwin, R. G., & Conley, V. M. (1998). *Retirement and other departure plans of instructional faculty and staff in higher education institutions*. NCES Statistical Analysis Report 98-254.

Ehrenberg, R., Kasper, H., & Rees, D. (1991). Faculty turnover at American colleges and universities: Analyses of AAUP data. *Economics of Education Review, 10*(2), 99–110.
Felmlee, D. (1984). The dynamics of women's job mobility. *Work and Occupations, 11*, 259–281.
Flinn, C. (1986). Wages and job mobility of young workers. *Journal of Political Economy, Part 2* (June), S88–S110.
Freedman, O., & Kern, C. R. (1997). A model of workplace and residence choice in two-worker households. *Regional Science and Urban Economics, 27*(3), 241–260.
Futrell, C., & Parasuraman, A. (1984). The relationship of satisfaction and performance to salesforce turnover. *Journal of Marketing, 48*(4), 33–48.
Jacobsen, J. P., & Levin, L. M. (1997). Marriage and migration: Comparing gains and losses from migration for couples and singles. *Social Science Quarterly, 78*(3), 688–709.
Kahn, S. (1998). Gender and the Ph.D. economist: An analysis of differences in promotion, salaries, first jobs, publications and mobility. Working paper, Boston University.
Keith, K., & McWilliams, A. (1997). Job mobility and gender based wage growth differentials. *Economic Inquiry, 35*, 320–333.
Kimmel, E. (1974). Women as job changers. *American Psychologist, 29*, 536–539.
Kleinbaum, D. (1996). *Survival analysis A self learning text.* New York: Springer.
Light, A., & Ureta, M. (1992). Panel estimation of male and female job turnover behavior: Can female non-quitters be identified? *Journal of Labor Economics, 10*(2), 156–181.
Loprest, P. (1992). Gender differences in wage growth and job mobility. *American Economic Review, 82*, 527–532.
Mathieu, J., & Zajac, D. (1990). A review and meta-analysis of the antecedents, correlates, and consequences of organizational commitment. *Psychological Bulletin, 108*, 107–194.
Meitzen, M. (1986). Differences in male and female job-quitting behavior. *Journal of Labor Economics, 4*(2), 151–167.
Mincer, J. (1978). Family migrations decisions. *Journal of Political Economy, 86*, 749–773.
Mincer, J. (1986). Wage changes and job changes. In: R. Ehrenberg (Ed.), *Research in Labor Economics.* Greenwich, CT: JAI Press.
Nettles, M., Perna, L., Bradburn, E., & Zimbler, L. (2000). *Salary, promotion, and tenure status of minority and women faculty in U.S. colleges and universities.* NCES Statistical Analysis Report 2000-173.
Oi, W. (1962). Labor as a quasi-fixed factor. *Journal of Political Economy, 70*(6), 538–555.
Polachek, S. (1981). Occupational self-selection: A human capital approach to sex differences in occupational structure. *Review of Economics and Statistics, 63*, 60–69.
Polachek, S., & Horvath, F. (1977). A life cycle approach to migration: Analysis of the perspicacious peregrinator. In: R. Ehrenberg (Ed.), *Research in Labor Economics* (pp. 103–149). Greenwich, CT: JAI Press.
Rosenfeld, R., & Jones, J. (1986). Institutional mobility among academics: The case of psychologists. *Sociology of Education, 59*, 212–226.
Royalty, A. (1998). Job to job and job to nonemployment turnover by gender and education level. *Journal of Labor Economics, 16*(2), 391–443.
Ruhm, C. (1987). The economic consequences of labor mobility. *Industrial and Labor Relations Review* (October), 30–49.
Sager, J., Futrell, C., & Varadarajan, R. (1989). Exploring salesperson turnover: A causal model. *Journal of Business Research, 18*(4), 303–326.
Sicherman, N. (1991). Overeducation in the labor market. *Journal of Labor Economics, 9*(2), 101–122.

Sicherman, N. (1996). Gender differences in departures from a large firm. *Industrial and Labor Relations Review, 49*(3), 484–505.

Smart, J. (1990). A causal model of faculty turnover intentions. *Research in Higher Education, 31*(5), 405–424.

Steel, R., & Orvalle, N. (1984). A review and meta-analysis of research on the relationship between behavioral intentions and employee turnover. *Journal of Applied Psychology, 69,* 679–686.

Taki, A., & Tachibanki, T. (1995). In: M. Okabe (Ed.), *The Structure of the Japanese Economy* (pp. 81–108). New York, NY: St. Martins Press.

VanGilder, J. A. (1999). *Faculty mobility intentions: Implications of environmental and institutional components on turnover in higher education.* Unpublished dissertation, SUNY – Binghamton.

Viscusi, W. (1980). Sex differences in worker quitting. *Review of Economics and Statistics, 62*(August), 388–398.

Weiler, W. (1991). Job changing decisions of faculty members: A case study of a model with multiple selection. *Applied Economics, 23,* 591–598.